The Story of God Bible Commentary Series Endorsements

"Getting a story is about more than merely enjoying it. It means hearing it, understanding it, and above all, being impacted by it. This commentary series hopes that its readers not only hear and understand the story, but are impacted by it to live in as Christian a way as possible. The editors and contributors set that table very well and open up the biblical story in ways that move us to act with sensitivity and understanding. That makes hearing the story as these authors tell it well worth the time. Well done."
Darrell L. Bock
Dallas Theological Seminary

"The Story of God Bible Commentary series invites readers to probe how the message of the text relates to our situations today. Engagingly readable, it not only explores the biblical text but offers a range of applications and interesting illustrations."
Craig S. Keener
Asbury Theological Seminary

"I love The Story of God Bible Commentary series. It makes the text sing, and helps us hear the story afresh."
John Ortberg
Senior Pastor of Menlo Park Presbyterian Church

"In this promising new series of commentaries, believing biblical scholars bring not only their expertise but their own commitment to Jesus and insights into today's culture to the Scriptures. The result is a commentary series that is anchored in the text but lives and breathes in the world of today's church with its variegated pattern of socioeconomic, ethnic, and national diversity. Pastors, Bible study leaders, and Christians of all types who are looking for a substantive and practical guide through the Scriptures will find these volumes helpful."
Frank Thielman
Beeson Divinity School

"The Story of God Bible Commentary series is unique in its approach to exploring the Bible. Its easy-to-use format and practical guidance bring God's grand story to modern-day life so anyone can understand how it applies today."
Andy Stanley
North Point Ministries

"I'm a storyteller. Through writing and speaking I talk and teach about understanding the Story of God throughout Scripture and about letting God reveal more of his story as I live it out. Thus I am thrilled to have a commentary series based on the Story of God—a commentary that helps me to Listen to the Story, that Explains the Story, and then encourages me to probe how to Live the Story. A perfect tool for helping every follower of Jesus to walk in the story that God is writing for them."

Judy Douglass
Director of Women's Resources, Cru

"The Bible is the story of God and his dealings with humanity from creation to new creation. The Bible is made up more of stories than of any other literary genre. Even the psalms, proverbs, prophecies, letters, and the Apocalypse make complete sense only when set in the context of the grand narrative of the entire Bible. This commentary series breaks new ground by taking all these observations seriously. It asks commentators to listen to the text, to explain the text, and to live the text. Some of the material in these sections overlaps with introduction, detailed textual analysis, and application, respectively, but only some. The most riveting and valuable part of the commentaries are the stories that can appear in any of these sections, from any part of the globe and any part of church history, illustrating the text in any of these areas. Ideal for preaching and teaching."

Craig L. Blomberg
Denver Seminary

"Pastors and lay people will welcome this new series, which seeks to make the message of the Scriptures clear and to guide readers in appropriating biblical texts for life today."

Daniel I. Block
Wheaton College and Graduate School

"An extremely valuable and long overdue series that includes comment on the cultural context of the text, careful exegesis, and guidance on reading the whole Bible as a unity that testifies to Christ as our Savior and Lord."

Graeme Goldsworthy
author of *According to Plan*

ACTS

Editorial Board
of
The Story of God Bible Commentary

Old Testament general editor
Tremper Longman III

Old Testament associate editors
George Athas
Mark J. Boda
Myrto Theocharous

New Testament general editor
Scot McKnight

New Testament associate editors
Lynn H. Cohick
Michael F. Bird
Joel L. Willitts

Zondervan editors

Senior acquisitions editor
Katya Covrett

Senior production editor, Old Testament
Nancy L. Erickson

Senior production editor, New Testament
Christopher A. Beetham

The Story of God Bible Commentary

ACTS

Dean Pinter

Tremper Longman III & Scot McKnight
General Editors

ZONDERVAN

Acts
Copyright © 2019 by Dean Pinter

ISBN 978-0-310-32717-2 (hardcover)

ISBN 978-0-310-59905-0 (ebook)

Requests for information should be addressed to:
Zondervan, *3900 Sparks Dr. SE, Grand Rapids, Michigan 49546*

"The Apologist's Evening Prayer" by C. S. Lewis © copyright CS Lewis Pte Ltd.

Excerpt from the poem "Love and Fear" in *When I Talk to You: A Cartoonist Talks to God* (Sydney: HarperCollins) by Michael Leunig, © 2006. Used by permission.

Excerpt from the poem "Repentance" in *Barefoot Prayers: A Meditation a Day for Lent and Easter* (London: SPCK) by Stephen Cherry, © 2013. Used by permission.

All Scripture quotations, unless otherwise indicated, are taken from The Holy Bible, New International Version®, NIV®. Copyright © 1973, 1978, 1984, 2011 by Biblica, Inc.® Used by permission of Zondervan. All rights reserved worldwide. www.Zondervan.com. The "NIV" and "New International Version" are trademarks registered in the United States Patent and Trademark Office by Biblica, Inc.®

Scripture quotations marked ESV are taken from the ESV® Bible (The Holy Bible, English Standard Version®). Copyright © 2001 by Crossway, a publishing ministry of Good News Publishers. Used by permission. All rights reserved.

Scripture quotations marked KJV are taken from the King James Version. Public domain.

Scripture quotations marked NASB are taken from the New American Standard Bible®. Copyright © 1960, 1962, 1963, 1968, 1971, 1972, 1973, 1975, 1977, 1995 by The Lockman Foundation. Used by permission. (www.Lockman.org).

The Scripture quotations marked NRSV are taken from the New Revised Standard Version Bible. Copyright © 1989, Division of Christian Education of the National Council of the Churches of Christ in the United States of America. Used by permission. All rights reserved.

Any internet addresses (websites, blogs, etc.) and telephone numbers in this book are offered as a resource. They are not intended in any way to be or imply an endorsement by Zondervan, nor does Zondervan vouch for the content of these sites and numbers for the life of this book.

No part of this publication may be reproduced, stored in a retrieval system, or transmitted in any form or by any means—electronic, mechanical, photocopy, recording, or any other—except for brief quotations in printed reviews, without the prior permission of the publisher.

Cover design: Ron Huizinga
Cover image: iStockphoto ®
Interior composition: Kait Lamphere

Printed in the United States of America

For

Gordon Fee & Eugene Peterson—
the spiritual fathers I needed

and

Mikael Tellbe & John Barclay—
the older brothers I hoped for

Old Testament series

1. Genesis—*Tremper Longman III*
2. Exodus—*Christopher J. H. Wright*
3. Leviticus—*Jerry E. Shepherd*
4. Numbers—*Jay A. Sklar*
5. Deuteronomy—*Myrto Theocharous*
6. Joshua—*Lissa M. Wray Beal*
7. Judges—*Athena E. Gorospe*
8. Ruth/Esther—*Marion Taylor*
9. 1–2 Samuel—*Paul S. Evans*
10. 1–2 Kings—*David T. Lamb*
11. 1–2 Chronicles—*Carol M. Kaminski*
12. Ezra/Nehemiah—*Douglas J. Green*
13. Job—*Martin A. Shields*
14. Psalms—*Elizabeth R. Hayes*
15. Proverbs—*Ryan P. O'Dowd*
16. Ecclesiastes/Song of Songs—*George Athas*
17. Isaiah—*Mark J. Boda*
18. Jeremiah/Lamentations—*Andrew G. Shead*
19. Ezekiel—*D. Nathan Phinney*
20. Daniel—*Wendy L. Widder*
21. Minor Prophets I—*Beth M. Stovell*
22. Minor Prophets II—*Beth M. Stovell*

New Testament series

1. Matthew—*Rodney Reeves*
2. Mark—*Timothy G. Gombis*
3. Luke—*Kindalee Pfremmer DeLong*
4. John—*Nicholas Perrin*
5. Acts—*Dean Pinter*
6. Romans—*Michael F. Bird*
7. 1 Corinthians—*Justin K. Hardin*
8. 2 Corinthians—*Judith A. Diehl*
9. Galatians—*Nijay K. Gupta*
10. Ephesians—*Mark D. Roberts*
11. Philippians—*Lynn H. Cohick*
12. Colossians/Philemon—*Todd Wilson*
13. 1, 2 Thessalonians—*John Byron*
14. 1, 2 Timothy, Titus—*Marius Nel*
15. Hebrews—*Radu Gheorghita*
16. James—*Mariam J. Kamell*
17. 1 Peter—*Dennis R. Edwards*
18. 2 Peter, Jude—*C. Rosalee Velloso Ewell*
19. 1, 2 & 3 John—*Constantine R. Campbell*
20. Revelation—*Jonathan A. Moo*
21. Sermon on the Mount—*Scot McKnight*

Contents

Author's Preface 13
The Story of God Bible Commentary Series 16
Abbreviations 19
Introduction 21
Resources for Teaching and Preaching 31

PANEL 1: Acts 1:1–6:7 33

1. Acts 1:1–11 35
2. Acts 1:12–26 50
3. Acts 2:1–41 60
4. Acts 2:42–47 81
5. Acts 3:1–10 94
6. Acts 3:11–26 100
7. Acts 4:1–22 109
8. Acts 4:23–31 118
9. Acts 4:32–37 126
10. Acts 5:1–11 131
11. Acts 5:12–16 138
12. Acts 5:17–42 143
13. Acts 6:1–7 155

PANEL 2: Acts 6:8–9:31 167

14. Acts 6:8–15 169
15. Acts 7:1–53 175
16. Acts 7:54–8:3 190
17. Acts 8:4–25 197

18. Acts 8:26–40 210
19. Acts 9:1–19a 218
20. Acts 9:19b–31 231

PANEL 3: Acts 9:32–12:24 237

21. Acts 9:32–43 239
22. Acts 10:1–48 247
23. Acts 11:1–18 266
24. Acts 11:19–30 274
25. Acts 12:1–24 284

PANEL 4: Acts 12:25–16:5 295

26. Acts 12:25–13:12 297
27. Acts 13:13–52 307
28. Acts 14:1–7 320
29. Acts 14:8–20 325
30. Acts 14:21–28 334
31. Acts 15:1–21 339
32. Acts 15:22–35 354
33. Acts 15:36–41 360
34. Acts 16:1–5 365

PANEL 5: Acts 16:6–19:20 369

35. Acts 16:6–10 371
36. Acts 16:11–15 376
37. Acts 16:16–40 381
38. Acts 17:1–9 391
39. Acts 17:10–15 400
40. Acts 17:16–34 404
41. Acts 18:1–17 417

42. Acts 18:18–28 426
43. Acts 19:1–20 433

PANEL 6: Acts 19:21–28:31 445
44. Acts 19:21–41 447
45. Acts 20:1–16 458
46. Acts 20:17–38 467
47. Acts 21:1–17 476
48. Acts 21:18–26 486
49. Acts 21:27–36 493
50. Acts 21:37–22:21 499
51. Acts 22:22–29 509
52. Acts 22:30–23:11 514
53. Acts 23:12–35 522
54. Acts 24:1–27 532
55. Acts 25:1–27 544
56. Acts 26:1–32 557
57. Acts 27:1–44 574
58. Acts 28:1–16 589
59. Acts 28:17–31 599
Scripture Index 609
Subject Index 641
Author Index 653

Author's Preface

The offer to participate in The Story of God Bible Commentary Series came as a gentle invitation from a friend, Cherith Fee Nordling. At a Society of Biblical Literature meeting years ago, Cherith invited me to come and meet Scot McKnight. Scot was keen to have Cherith participate in this series, but Cherith asked if she could bring me into the project on Acts with her. From that moment, Cherith and I began collaborating on the commentary, and we soon taught a course on Acts together that helped get the work off the ground. Although she eventually had to drop out of the project, our conversations on Acts over the years are woven into the fabric of this commentary.

As the initial conversations with Cherith illustrate, any commentary is a dependent work. At minimum it is dependent on one's context and one's conversation partners. I wrote this commentary in the context of being a working priest in a small, vibrant parish located on the Canadian prairies. This means that God incarnates the reality of the story of Acts in the place where I live and the people I live with. As such, I recognize that the everyday miracle of breathing in and out is the context in which the Spirit whispers and grants insight. I am grateful for the support and rootedness of my parish, St. Aidan Anglican Church, Moose Jaw. For over five years, this parish released me every Friday to listen to and write about Acts. In the last year, the vestry graciously provided an additional three months of leave so that I could complete the manuscript. This meant that the other three members of our "clergy quartet"—Frs. Cal Macfarlane and Dustin Resch and Deacon Arleen Champion—kindly carried an extra load in the parish so I could be free to write. To the clergy, vestry, and parish of St. Aidan I owe a deep debt of gratitude.

My conversation partners in the writing of this commentary are many and varied. Some of them are ancient, like John Chrysostom and the Venerable Bede. Some of them are contemporary and with whom I have had the pleasure of personal connections. In particular, I am grateful for the work on Acts by professors Loveday Alexander (who listened to my first postgraduate paper during a joint Durham-Sheffield colloquium), James (Jimmy) Dunn (who, among many kindnesses, played Sudoku with my young son, Carl, on a difficult day during Carl's cancer treatment), C. K. Barrett (to whom I occasionally gave rides home after the Durham NT Seminar), and N. T. Wright (who was my bishop in Durham). Although I do not know them personally, I have also benefitted greatly from reading and reflecting on the work of Rev. Timothy Keller, professors Jack Levison, Richard N. Longenecker, David G. Peterson, C. Kavin Rowe, and, especially, Beverly Roberts Gaventa. All of them are great theologians and gifts to the church.

My conversation partners extended further to personal friends who talked me through passages, listened to me explain what I thought Luke was trying to say, or read (parts of) the manuscript. In this regard, I am grateful for the listening ears and critical eyes of Dr. David Miller, Doug Reichel, Dr. Richard Briggs, Dr. Wes Olmstead, and Dr. Eric Ortlund. I am grateful to Bishop Todd Atkinson and the Via Church (Lethbridge, Alberta), who let me share gleanings on Acts during several Canon Conferences. One dear friend in particular merits special mention: Jordan Duncan. Jordan, a former student and now youth pastor, read the entire manuscript. His thoughtful comments, probing questions, and encouragement throughout the process were invaluable.

I am grateful for the critical and yet kind support of my editors, Scot McKnight and Joel Willitts. They encouraged me through times of what Scot referred to as "acute normalcy" (i.e., when I felt acutely inadequate for the task at hand!). Christopher Beetham, senior production editor with Zondervan, also provided superb analysis of my manuscript and saved me from more errors than I care to admit. Editors like these do hero's work.

Of course, I owe much more than I could ever say to my family. My parents, Alex and Dolores Pinter, and my mother-in-law, Ellen Israelson, have always been kind and generous in their support. Our three children, Evan, Emily, and Carl—all gone off to university now—made space (and quiet) in our home for many years so that I could write. My wife, Darlene, from her lifetime of sensitive engagement with the biblical text, willingly and frequently engaged with me in reflective conversation as I wrestled through many sections of "Live the Story." Her sensitivity to the Spirit and skills as a writer contributed in many ways to this manuscript, but her love, friendship, and encouragement throughout this project mean the world to me.

Finally, I wish to express my deep gratitude to four individuals. For many years, John Barclay and Mikael Tellbe have been the older brothers I always hoped for and faithful companions along "the Way." They are both great scholars in their own right, but they are even better people. For over twenty-five years, Eugene Peterson and Gordon Fee have been the spiritual fathers I always needed and wise guides along "the Way." Eugene has taught me to listen to God with congruence to who I am as a person and as a priest. He never lets me forget that the Story of God is always lived in the context of people and parish, of worship and work, of prayer and play. Gordon has taught me to read the Story of God thoughtfully and carefully since my first days as his student and teaching assistant at Regent College. He kindly read and interacted with more than half of this manuscript. His incisive and critical comments, often with small, hand-written, red-pen notes, reminded me of joyful days of discovery when he first did this as my supervisor for my ThM thesis. Gordon has treated me as one of his children—and I am grateful to Mark, Cherith, Brian, and Craig for sharing him with me. While I am responsible for the shortcomings that are undoubtedly associated with this work, I could never have written this commentary without the support of John, Mikael, Eugene, and Gordon. It is a joy and a privilege to dedicate this book to them all.

Pentecost 2018

The Story of God Bible Commentary Series

The word of God may not change, but culture does. Think of what we have seen in the last twenty years: we now communicate predominantly through the Internet and email; we read our news on iPads and computers; we can talk on the phone to our friends while we are driving, while we are playing golf, while we are taking long walks; and we can get in touch with others from the middle of nowhere. We carry in our hands small devices that connect us to the world and to a myriad of sources of information. Churches have changed; the "Nones" are rising in numbers and volume, and atheists are bold to assert their views in public forums. The days of home Bible studies are waning; there is a marked rise in activist missional groups in churches, and pastors are more and more preaching topical sermons, some of which are not directly connected to the Bible. Divorce rates are not going down, marriages are more stressed, rearing children is more demanding, and civil unions and same-sex marriages are knocking at the door of the church.

Progress can be found in many directions. While church attendance numbers are waning in Europe and North America, churches are growing in the South and the East. More and more women are finding a voice in churches; the plea of the former generation of leaders that Christians be concerned not just with evangelism but with justice is being answered today in new and vigorous ways. Resources for studying the Bible are more available today than ever before, and preachers and pastors are meeting the challenge of speaking a sure word of God into shifting cultures.

Readers of the Bible change too. These cultural shifts, our own personal developments, the progress in intellectual questions, as well as growth in biblical studies and theology and discoveries of new texts and new paradigms for understanding the contexts of the Bible—each of these elements works on an interpreter so that the person who reads the Bible today asks different questions from different angles.

Culture shifts, but the word of God remains. That is why we as editors of The Story of God Bible Commentary series, a commentary based on the New International Version 2011 (NIV 2011), are excited to participate in this new series of commentaries on the Bible. This series is designed to address this generation with the same word of God. We are asking the authors to explain what the Bible says to the sorts of readers who pick up commentaries so they can understand not only what Scripture says but what it means for today. The Bible does not change, but relating it to our culture changes constantly and in differing ways in different contexts.

When we, the New Testament editors, sat down in prayer and discussion to choose authors for this series, we realized we had found fertile ground. Our list of potential authors was staggering in length and quality. We wanted the authors to be exceptional scholars, faithful Christians, committed evangelicals, and theologically diverse, and we wanted this series to represent the changing face of both American and world evangelicalism, with both ethnic and gender diversity. I believe this series has a wider diversity of authors than any commentary series in evangelical history.

The title of this series, emphasizing as it does the "Story" of the Bible, reveals the intent of the series. We want to explain each passage of the Bible in light of the Bible's grand Story. The Bible's grand Story, of course, connects this series to the classic expression *regula fidei*, the "rule of faith," which was the Bible's story coming to fulfillment in Jesus as the Messiah, Lord, and Savior of all. In brief, we see the narrative built around the following biblical themes: creation and fall, covenant and redemption, law and prophets, and especially God's charge to humans as his image-bearers to rule under God. The theme of God as King and God's kingdom guides us to see the importance of Israel's kings as they come to fulfillment in Jesus, Lord and King over all, and the direction of history toward the new heavens and new earth, where God will be all in all. With these guiding themes, each passage is examined from three angles.

Listen to the Story. We believe that if the Bible is God speaking, then the most important posture of the Christian before the Bible is to listen. So our first section cites the text of Scripture and lists a selection of important biblical and sometimes noncanonical parallels; then each author introduces that passage. The introductions to the passages sometimes open up discussion to the theme of the passage, while other times they tie this passage to its context in the specific book. But since the focus of this series is the Story of God in the Bible, the introduction leads the reader into reading this text in light of the Bible's Story.

Explain the Story. The authors follow up listening to the text by explaining each passage in light of the Bible's grand Story. This is not an academic series, so the footnotes are limited to the kinds of texts typical Bible readers and preachers readily will have on hand. Authors are given the freedom to explain the text as they read it, though you should not be surprised to find occasional listings of other options for reading the text. Authors explore biblical backgrounds, historical context, cultural codes, and theological interpretations. Authors engage in word studies and interpret unique phrases and clauses as they attempt to build a sound and living reading of the text in light of the Story of God in the Bible.

Authors will not shy away from problems in the texts. Whether one is examining the meaning of "perfect" in Matthew 5:48, the problems with Christology in the hymn of Philippians 2:6–11, the challenge of understanding Paul in light of the swirling debates about the old, new, and post-new perspectives, the endless debates about eschatology, or the vagaries of atonement theories, the authors will dive in, discuss evidence, and do their best to sort out a reasonable and living reading of those issues for the church today.

Live the Story. Reading the Bible is not just about discovering what it meant back then; the intent of The Story of God Bible Commentary series is to probe how this text might be lived out today as that story continues to march on in the life of the church. At times our authors will tell stories about what this looks like; at other times they may offer some suggestions for living it out; but always you will discover the struggle involved as we seek to live out the Bible's grand Story in our world.

We are not offering suggestions for "application" so much as digging deeper; we are concerned in this section with seeking out how this text, in light of the Story of God in the Bible, compels us to live in our world so that our own story lines up with the Bible's Story.

      Scot McKnight, general editor New Testament
      Lynn Cohick, Joel Willitts, and Michael Bird, editors

Abbreviations

AB	Anchor Bible
ABD	*Anchor Bible Dictionary*. Edited by David Noel Freedman. 6 vols. New York: Doubleday, 1992
ACCA	Francis Martin, ed. *Ancient Christian Commentary on Scripture—New Testament*. Volume 5: Acts. Downers Grove, IL: InterVarsity Press, 2006
Ag. Ap.	Josephus, *Against Apion*
ANF	*Ante-Nicene Fathers*
ANRW	*Aufstieg und Niedergang der römischen Welt: Geschichte und Kultur Roms im Spiegel der neuren Forschung*. Part 2, *Principat*. Edited by Hildegard Temporini and Wolfgang Haase. Berlin: de Gruyter, 1972–
Ant.	Josephus, *Jewish Antiquities* (translated by William Whiston)
BDAG	Danker, Frederick W., Walter Bauer, William F. Arndt, and F. Wilbur Gingrich. *Greek-English Lexicon of the New Testament and Other Early Christian Literature*. 3rd ed. Chicago: University of Chicago Press, 2000
DJG	*Dictionary of Jesus and the Gospels*. Edited by Joel B. Green, Scot McKnight, and I. Howard Marshall. Downers Grove, IL: InterVarsity Press, 1992
DLNT	*Dictionary of the Later New Testament and Its Developments*. Edited by Ralph P. Martin and Peter H. Davids. Downers Grove, IL: InterVarsity Press, 1997
DNTB	*Dictionary of New Testament Background*. Edited by Craig A. Evans and Stanley E. Porter. Downers Grove, IL: InterVarsity Press, 2000
DPL	*Dictionary of Paul and His Letters*. Edited by Gerald F. Hawthorne and Ralph P. Martin. Downers Grove, IL: InterVarsity Press, 1993
ESV	English Standard Version
ICC	International Critical Commentary
JBL	*Journal of Biblical Literature*
JSNT	*Journal for the Study of the New Testament*
J.W.	Josephus, *Jewish War*

KJV	King James Version
LCL	Loeb Classical Library
Life	Josephus, *The Life*
LSJ	Liddell, Henry George, Robert Scott, Henry Stuart Jones. *A Greek-English Lexicon*. 9th ed. with revised supplement. Oxford: Clarendon, 1996
LXX	Septuagint (Greek Old Testament)
m.	Mishnah
NASB	New American Standard Bible
NDT	*New Dictionary of Theology*. Edited by Sinclair B. Ferguson and David F. Wright. Downers Grove, IL: InterVarsity Press, 1988
NICNT	New International Commentary on the New Testament
NIV	New International Version
NRSV	New Revised Standard Version
NT	New Testament
NTS	*New Testament Studies*
OCD	*The Oxford Classical Dictionary*. 3rd ed. Edited by Simon Hornblower and Anthony Spawforth. Oxford: Oxford University Press, 1996
OT	Old Testament
SBLMS	Society for Biblical Literature Monograph Series
SNTSMS	Society for New Testament Studies Monograph Series
TNTC	Tyndale New Testament Commentaries
WUNT	Wissenschaftliche Untersuchungen zum Neuen Testament
ZECNT	Zondervan Exegetical Commentary on the New Testament

Introduction

On "the Way" with Acts

One of Luke's favorite images for discipleship is "the Way." This is helpful to keep in mind as one reads Acts because it is a traveling story; it is a story on the move. The author invites us to take a journey as the gospel moves from Jerusalem to Rome. As important as it is to know this, it is also vital, when beginning a journey, to know where you are starting. Luke alerts his readers to the starting point in his first phrase: "In my *former book* . . ." (Acts 1:1). That is, Acts is the second part of one larger story about Jesus; it is a continuation of a journey that has already begun. In fact, the reason why this one story is told in two parts of almost equal length is pragmatic. Each "book" contains what would fit on a standard papyrus scroll (approximately thirty-five feet).[1]

Although separated in the New Testament (NT) canon, these two documents are *thematically* and *geographically* connected. For example, thematically, they both begin with Spirit conceptions (the descent of the Spirit upon Mary in the Gospel; the descent of the Spirit upon the church in Acts) and the "fulfillment" of the promises God made in Scripture (Luke 1:1, 35–38, 54–55, 70; 2:29–32, 38; 24:49; Acts 1:4; 2:33, 39). As for geographic correspondence, Luke shapes his Gospel account in such a way that (apart from the birth narrative) the movement progresses from Galilee to Jerusalem; in Acts, the movement progresses from Jerusalem and radiates outward to Judea, Samaria, Asia Minor, Macedonia and Achaia (i.e., Greece), and finally to Rome. In both books, the movement is stylized in such a way that the gospel reaches every person on the social strata, whether they were rich or poor, men or women, sophisticated or simple, elite or outcast (i.e., the Gospel of Luke), and every person regardless of their ethnicity, whether they were Jew or gentile, Samaritan or Ethiopian, Greek or Roman (i.e., Acts of the Apostles).

Wisdom in Reading the Story of Acts

Most of the same interpretative strategies and prayerful focus that one would bring to reading any other part of the Bible are required when reading the

---

1. Joel B. Green, "Acts of the Apostles," *DLNT* 12.

story of Acts. There are several suggestions, however, that one might note, given some of Acts's unique features.

First, despite the canonical arrangement that divides the Gospel of Luke and Acts, it is important to read Acts mindful that it is the second part of one larger story written by Luke. Any reading of Acts should have an eye to the Gospel of Luke in terms of overlapping or complementary themes and parallel features (e.g., introductions, trial scenes, stylized geographic movements).

Second, it is vital to read Acts as one would a story. That is, the reader ought to think in terms of larger chunks of narrative rather than isolated verses or individual chapters. This will help the reader to notice how the parts of the narrative are connected to the whole. Here, reading from an English Bible that does not have chapter and verse notations can be of great benefit (after all, these were added by scribes centuries after Luke wrote Acts). *The Books of the Bible, NIV* (Grand Rapids: Zondervan, 2012) is one such helpful resource.

Third, since Acts is a narrative, full of drama and even humor, spanning a long period of time, readers should give particular consideration to places where the story slows down. For example, Luke describes the *months* of Paul's return travels through Macedonia and Greece in a few sentences (Acts 20:1–6), but then devotes a great deal of space to describe Paul's first few *days* back in Jerusalem (21:17–23:35). When Luke slows down the pace of his narrative, he is signaling his readers to pay attention. In those places the reader will often discover Luke's primary theological concerns.

Finally, again because of the story-like account of Acts, one should notice how Luke foreshadows characters (e.g., Barnabas, Saul/Paul, John Mark) and events (e.g., Paul's arrest; Paul's testimony before Caesar) in the narrative. As one recognizes this, one will see how Luke highlights tension and/or significant elements in the story.

Who Wrote the Story?

While there is broad scholarly agreement that the same author wrote both Luke and Acts, there is no consensus on who wrote them. The reason is simple: the author is anonymous. Yet, the author was *not* anonymous to the original recipients, and the author indicates that he intends his readers to regard him as a reliable source (see Luke 1:1–4). Whoever wrote these two documents wrote with excellent, cultured Greek. This suggests that the author was writing for an educated audience in Theophilus (1:3)—and whomever Theophilus would share Luke-Acts with. Yet there is also a sense that this story is not just meant for an educated elite. It is a story that speaks to simple

Bethlehem shepherds and Galilean fishermen just as much as to Jerusalem widows and Philippian slave girls.

The earliest witnesses addressing the authorship of Luke-Acts come from the end of the second century. The Muratorian Canon (ca. AD 170–200) notes that "Luke, the well-known physician, after the ascension of Christ, when Paul had taken him with him . . . composed [the Gospel] in his own name . . . . Moreover, the acts of all the apostles were written in one book. For 'most excellent Theophilus' Luke compiled the individual events that took place in his presence" (lines 2–6 and 35–36).[2] The second-century apologist Irenaeus writes about "the testimony of Luke regarding the apostles."[3] Clement of Alexandria (ca. AD 190) reports how "Luke also in the Acts of the Apostles relates that Paul said, 'Men of Athens, I perceive that in all things . . .'"[4] What this evidence suggests is that from about AD 170 onward, it is the unanimous opinion of early church writers, in various locations around the empire, to refer to Acts as written by "Luke the beloved physician" (Col 4:14 ESV; cf. Phlm 24; 2 Tim 4:11). The "we passages" in Acts (i.e., 16:10–17; 20:5–15; 21:1–18; 27:1–28:16) seem to corroborate this. This evidence, however, is not persuasive to all scholars. Some suggest that a later author inserted notes from a travel diary from one of Paul's companions;[5] others suggest that an author created these passages to lend authenticity to the narrative—a need, it is argued, because the author seems to diverge from some details that Paul conveys in his own letters (e.g., apostleship, visits to Jerusalem). Still, despite these issues the simplest solution is to follow the traditional conclusion that Luke, an occasional traveling companion of Paul, is the author of Acts. This seems to best account for the level of "eyewitness" detail of the "we passages" and for the unanimous agreement of the early-church tradition. While we can never be certain about this, this commentary will refer to the author of Acts as "Luke."[6]

If Luke were the author of Luke-Acts, this would date Acts sometime in the period between the mid-sixties to the early eighties in the first century. Again, there is no certainty beyond this range if one thinks Luke is the author.

---

2. Bruce Metzger, *The Canon of the New Testament: Its Origin, Development, and Significance* (Oxford: Clarendon, 1987), 305–6.

3. Irenaeus, *Against Heresies* 3.13.3 (as found in the *The Ante-Nicene Fathers*, ed. A. Roberts and J. Donaldson, 10 vols. [1885–87; repr., Peabody, MA: Hendrickson, 1994], 1:437 [hereafter *ANF*]). See http://www.ccel.org/ccel/schaff/anf01.ix.iv.xiv.html.

4. Clement of Alexandria, *Strom.* 5.12.83 (*ANF* 2:463).

5. A weakness of this suggestion is that there is complete uniformity in language and style between the "we passages" and the rest of Acts.

6. For a recent, detailed review of the question of authorship, see Craig S. Keener, *Acts: An Exegetical Commentary*, 4 vols. (Grand Rapids: Baker Academic, 2012), 1:402–16.

Some may be inclined to lean toward a date in the sixties because Acts does not provide an account of Paul's death (which took place in the mid-sixties). Others might lean toward a date in the seventies or eighties because Luke uses the Gospel of Mark (probably written in the mid-sixties) as a primary source for his Gospel. Important for whatever one concludes is the fact that Acts is not a biography of Paul (or any other apostle); Acts is a story about the good news of Jesus and how this news spread from Jerusalem to Rome. We do not know when, exactly, Acts was written. What we *can* determine with more accuracy is the shape of Luke's story.

How the Story of Acts Unfolds

The Ghent Altarpiece in Belgium is a large and complex fifteenth-century altarpiece in St. Bravo's Cathedral. It is an artistic and theological masterpiece and treasured the world over. It visually tells the story of Christ the King through its multiple panels. The panels are hinged and are painted on both sides so that, depending on what panel is open, they communicate a different part of the story.

The book of Acts is also a large and complex work of art that tells the story of Christ the King. Because it is a long and intricate document, there have been numerous attempts to describe how the story unfolds. Acts can be viewed from the perspective of its two major apostles, Peter (chs. 1–12) and Paul (chs. 13–28). It can also be viewed taking Jesus's final command to be his witnesses (1:8) as providing an outline for the narrative. From this viewpoint, Acts unfolds with the witness in Jerusalem (1:1–5:42), then the witness in Judea and Samaria (6:1–11:18), and, finally, the witness to the ends of the earth (11:19–28:31).[7]

As illuminating as these different approaches are, this commentary will follow a pattern that attends to six different "panels" in Acts. The clue to this shape is suggested by five summary "hinges" or markers that Luke has inserted into the narrative (6:7; 9:31; 12:24; 16:5; and 19:20).[8] Each panel is separated by one of these summary hinges. At each hinge, there is a brief pause where Luke refers to one, or more, of the following elements: (1) a geographic note; (2) an indication about numerical increase; and (3) the word of God increasing. After the hinge marker, the next panel opens up to a new direction in the

---

7. See I. H. Marshall, *The Acts of the Apostles* (Sheffield: Sheffield Academic Press, 1992), 28–30.
8. R. N. Longenecker, "The Acts of the Apostles," in *The Expositor's Bible Commentary*, ed. F. E. Gaebelein, vol. 9 (Grand Rapids: Zondervan, 1981), 233–34; see also D. Gooding, *True to the Faith* (London: Hodder & Stoughton, 1990); and Gordon D. Fee and Douglas Stuart, *How to Read the Bible for All Its Worth* (Grand Rapids: Zondervan, 2003), 111.

narrative. Each of the six panels in Acts unfolds to a new and expanding vision of the gospel and serves to give the overall story a continually forward movement with the Holy Spirit orchestrating the onward progression. With this in mind, the story of Acts unfolds as follows:

Panel 1 (1:1–6:7): The ascent of Jesus, the descent of the Spirit, and the early church in Jerusalem
Panel 2 (6:8–9:31): The gospel goes to Judea and Samaria
Panel 3 (9:32–12:24): The gospel goes to the gentiles
Panel 4 (12:25–16:5): The gospel goes to Asia Minor
Panel 5 (16:6–19:20): The gospel goes to Macedonia and Achaia
Panel 6 (19:21–28:30): The gospel goes to Rome

The Purpose of Acts

Why was Acts written? This short question addresses the complex issue of the *purpose* of Acts and is linked with the kind of literature one views this document to be. That is, if Acts is regarded as a form of an ancient novel, then its primary purpose would be to entertain.[9] Or, if Acts is viewed as a form of biography, the purpose would be to detail the life and affairs of an individual or individuals.[10] The problem is, much like other distinctive types of literature reflected in the NT,[11] Acts appears to be a unique combination—a hybrid—of literary types. Loveday Alexander has persuasively argued that the form of Acts most closely resembles that of an "ancient scientific treatise."[12] Still, even if the *form* of Acts resembles this kind of literature, the *content* of Acts reflects that of ancient histories (e.g., with its formal introductions,[13] the use of historical "markers,"[14] speeches, eyewitness accounts) from both the Greco-Roman and Jewish historical traditions. In particular, Luke—in both parts of his two-volume account—intends his account to be a reliable

---

9. See R. I. Pervo, *Profit with Delight: The Literary Genre of the Acts of the Apostles* (Philadelphia: Fortress, 1987).

10. See C. H. Talbert, *Literary Patterns, Theological Themes and the Genre of Luke-Acts*, SBLMS 20 (Missoula, MT: Scholars Press, 1974).

11. The canonical Gospels are a unique literary form; the Revelation of John is a hybrid epistle, prophecy, and apocalypse; and even Paul's letters, apart from Philemon, are unique types of epistles due to their unusual length, argumentation, and theological content.

12. Loveday C. A. Alexander, *The Preface to Luke's Gospel: Literary Convention and Social Context in Luke 1:1–4 and Acts 1:1*, SNTSMS 78 (Cambridge: Cambridge University Press, 1993).

13. Luke 1:1–4; Acts 1:1–5.

14. E.g., in the Gospel, Luke makes reference to specific historical markers that can be dated by way of the reign of individuals (see Luke 1:5; 2:1–2) or, in Acts, a unique historical occurrence (see Acts 11:28) or the decree of an emperor (18:2).

source of history (see Luke 1:3). It is important, however, that Luke not be judged as a "historian" against modern categories of historiography. Nonetheless, a number of recent studies have demonstrated that even in this regard, Luke can be viewed as a reliable historian.[15] This position may not convince some modern readers who have decided beforehand that accounts of signs and wonders, angelic visitations, and resurrection are not proper history. Even in the first century, there were loyal and devout Jews who doubted the veracity of such things (e.g., the Sadducees).

Decades ago, A. C. Winn published an essay on the purpose of Acts, which he dubbed the "elusive mystery."[16] Circumstances have not changed much in over fifty years, and there is little consensus on the purpose of Acts. Acts is an intricate, interesting, and vibrant narrative, and we should not be surprised that this has generated numerous suggestions. Mark Alan Powell groups the most significant proposals regarding the purpose of Acts into six groups: irenic, polemical, apologetic, evangelistic, pastoral, and theological.[17]

The irenic approach originated in the nineteenth century when F. C. Baur proposed that Acts was written to provide a *peaceful* solution for the emerging "catholic" (i.e., "universal") church as it sought to overcome the tension that existed between Peter and Paul. This theory has been mostly rejected or revised, not least of all because the tension in Acts, if there is one, is not between Peter and Paul as much as it is between James (the brother of Jesus) and Paul.

The polemical perspective, advocated by the likes of Charles Talbert, views Acts not as a peaceful mediation but as a *confrontational attack* by Luke against heretical Christians (e.g., gnostics). This might be one of Luke's intentions, but most scholars are doubtful that this is the *primary* purpose of Acts.

The apologetic angle reads Acts as a *defensive brief* either for Paul or, more broadly, for the church against the misunderstandings of the Roman Empire. In this "defense," Luke is supposedly trying to demonstrate that Christians are not a threat to the political stability of the empire. If this were the case, however, one wonders if any Roman official could wade through all the theological and biblical dynamics in order to get to this point. In the end, procurator Festus may speak for many confused Roman officials when he concludes, "I [am] at a loss how to investigate such matters" (Acts 25:20).

---

15. See M. Hengel, *Acts and the History of Earliest Christianity* (London: SCM; Philadelphia: Fortress, 1979); and C. J. Hemer, *The Book of Acts in the Setting of Hellenistic History*, ed. C. H. Gempf (Winona Lake, IN: Eisenbrauns, 1990).

16. A. C. Winn, "Elusive Mystery: The Purpose of Acts," *Interpretation* 13 (1959): 144–56.

17. Mark Allan Powell, *What Are They Saying about Acts?* (New York: Paulist, 1991), 13–19.

The *evangelistic* theory is one that sees Luke's purpose focused on the non-Christian world. In this view, Acts is to be read as an evangelistic tool to persuade non-Christians about the truth of the gospel. Here, one would have to regard the intended audience as pagan rather than Christian. Theophilus would be a representative pagan who has been "taught" (Luke 1:4) about the gospel, but not yet converted.

The *pastoral* approach assumes that Luke's audience is not primarily pagan but Christian. If this is the case, the story of Acts is meant to offer pastoral strength and encouragement. For example, it would reassure a primarily gentile church that they are in continuity with God's long-term plans for his people.

Finally, the *theological* perspective suggests that Acts was written to address theological issues facing the early church. For example, Hans Conzelmann argues that Acts is an attempt to answer the "problem" of the delayed return of Christ. This approach assumes that Luke has abandoned the hope of the imminent return of Christ.[18] Another theological angle, with substantially more evidence in Acts to support it, is the one advocated by I. H. Marshall. Marshall suggests that Acts functions "to give the original readers confidence that *the Christian message* which they have heard and accepted *is valid and true*—both as a record of what has happened and in its theological significance as the gospel of divine salvation."[19]

Marshall's approach has much to commend it. It accounts for many of the theological details (e.g., fulfillment of promises, repentance/forgiveness, witness, the reception/empowerment of the Spirit, preaching about the kingdom of God, teaching about Jesus, progress of the gospel) in Luke's own statements at the beginning and ending of his narratives (Luke 1:1–4; 24:47–49; Acts 1:1, 8; 28:31). We could also add to this the summary "hinge" markers—with their mention of the word of God multiplying and the church increasing—alongside the multiple notices of hindrances to the progress of the gospel that are overcome (e.g., controversies in Jerusalem, 6:1–6; persecution, 9:1–31; Jewish opposition, 12:23–24 and 13:13–52; internal divisions, 15:1–41; the Roman state, 16:16–17:9; shipwrecks and snakes, 27:1–28:6). At the very end of Acts, Luke's overriding conclusion is that nothing can hinder gospel proclamation (28:31).

In the end, no one purpose may be able to account for all the rich complexity that exists in Acts. It is better, I think, to regard Acts as containing complementary and layered purposes.

---

18. As cited by Powell, *What Are They Saying*, 18; see Hans Conzelmann, *The Theology of St. Luke*, 2nd ed. (Philadelphia: Fortress, 1982; German original, 1957).

19. Marshall, *Acts*, 45 (emphases his).

Key Theological Themes in the Story of Acts

Since Acts is such a rich and intricate document, it should not be surprising that it also has a wide array of themes. A helpful way into this rich forest of themes may be to attend to focal points in Luke's introduction (Acts 1:1–11), his recurring, summary "hinge" points (see above), and his conclusion (28:17–31). Writers often use literary locations like these to express their main emphases and key themes, and it appears that Luke has done just that. In particular, these locations highlight the story about *King Jesus* (i.e., who he is and what he has done) and the *kingdom of God*, and how this story spreads throughout the world through the *witness* of Jesus's followers.

First, in emphasizing who King Jesus is and what he has done, Luke immediately alerts us to the fact that Jesus is not alone in his work. Jesus cannot be understood apart from his Father and the Holy Spirit. This Trinitarian theme is theologically related to what is reflected by other NT authors, including Matthew (Matt 3:16; 28:19); Paul (1 Cor 12:4–6; 2 Cor 13:14; Eph 4:4–6); Peter (1 Pet 1:2); and John (John 14:26; Rev 1:4b–5). Of course, Luke does not use a word like *Trinity*, but what is important for him is that Jesus—who he is and what he does—is not viewed in isolation. Luke writes about "all that Jesus began to do and to teach" (Acts 1:1), but this story is intimately linked to what Jesus's "Father promised" (v. 4)—that is, "the Holy Spirit" (v. 5). This connection between God the Father, his Son Jesus, and the Holy Spirit will recur at key junctures in the narrative, including Peter's speech on the Day of Pentecost (2:32–33); when believers gather together to pray (4:24–25); just before Stephen, the church's first martyr, is stoned (7:55); when the gospel is first declared to gentiles and goes into the gentile world (10:38; 11:15–17, 23–24); at the first council in Jerusalem (15:8–11); during Paul's farewell speech to the Ephesian elders (20:22–24); and in the final speech in Acts (28:23–28). It is God the Father who has all authority (1:7), and therefore God is the one who "accredits" Jesus (2:22), "appoints" Jesus (3:20), "anoints" Jesus (10:38), "raises" Jesus (2:24, 32; 3:15, 26; 4:10; 5:30; 10:40; 13:37; 17:31; 25:8), "exalts" Jesus (2:33; 5:31), and who has "made this Jesus . . . both Lord and Messiah" (2:36). The Spirit affirms the testimony of the Father (5:32) and Jesus's own teaching (1:2), often through Israel's Scriptures (1:16; 4:25; 28:25), and directs the witness of Jesus's followers (5:32; 8:29; 11:12; 13:2; 15:28; 16:6–7; 20:22–23; etc.).

Second, the kingdom of God is an important theme in the narrative. The phrase "kingdom of God" does not occur as often in Acts as it does in the Gospel of Luke (and Matthew and Mark). It does, however, occur in the first and last sentences of Acts (1:3; 28:31) and at key moments in between (in the mission to Samaria, 8:12; in the mission to Asia, 14:22; in the mission to Ephesus, 19:8; and in Paul's closing words to the Ephesian elders, 20:25). Further, the kingdom of God is expressed more than just through the word *kingdom*. The content of the kingdom of God is linked to the *reign* of the King. This accounts for Luke's emphasis on how people are persuaded about this king in regal language that would resonate with different ethnic groups, that is, the language of "Lord and Messiah" (2:36). For many Jews, kingship was closely associated with the title "Messiah" (see 2:31; 3:18, 20; 5:42; 8:5; 9:22; 17:3; 18:5); for gentiles, notions of rule and authority were closely connected to the title "Lord" (see especially 10:36; 13:48; 15:17). Even further, the kingdom message is more than just about specific words or titles; it also involves action. The King *does* things. King Jesus brings about change for the good, liberates his people from bondage, and restores them. In light of this "good news," various subthemes connect to this kingdom proclamation, including salvation, repentance, forgiveness, baptism, healing, deliverance from spiritual oppression, light/dark, etc. In all of this, the key evidence that this kingdom of God is inaugurated and "the last days" have already begun is the vital thematic emphasis on the gift of the Holy Spirit (2:17–18). The Spirit fills (2:4; 8:17–19; 9:17; 10:44; 13:9, 52; 19:6), speaks to (8:29; 10:19; 11:12, 28; 13:2; 21:11), directs (15:28; 16:6–7), and empowers (1:8; 6:10) God's people for witness in the world.

Third, Luke highlights for his readers that witness is a primary emphasis for those who have been overtaken by the kingdom of God and follow the Lord and Messiah, Jesus. This theme occurs at the beginning of Acts with Jesus's final command to the disciples before his ascension (1:8). It is then highlighted as Luke summarizes the progress of this witness (6:7; 9:31; 12:24; 16:5; 19:20; 28:31) as the word of God spreads and grows, not only geographically to the ends of the earth but also to all peoples of the world (1:8; 13:46–47; cf. Isa 49:6). The theme of witness to the gospel of King Jesus also accounts for other related themes, including the witness *both* to Jews *and* to gentiles (Acts 2:8–11; 3:25; 10:35; 11:18, 20; 15:1–35; 20:21; 22:21; 26:23; 28:28), the joyful response to the gospel (2:46–47; 3:8; 4:21; 8:8; 10:46; 11:18; 13:52; 15:31; 16:25, 34; 21:20), and the opposition the witness receives from satanic powers (5:3; 8:9–24; 13:6–11; 16:16–18; 26:18), Jews (4:1–22; 5:17–20, 27; 6:9–8:3; 13:45, 50), gentiles (14:5, 19–20; 16:19–21; 17:5–9; 19:23–41), and the state (12:1–4; 16:19–21; 24:27). In the end, nothing can hinder the progress of witness to the gospel: not Jewish or gentile rulers, not persecution or reluctant disciples, and not storms or snakes. The proclamation of the kingdom and the teaching of Jesus, the Lord and Messiah, progresses "with all boldness and without hindrance" (28:31).

A thread connecting many of these theological themes is the providence of God. *Providence* is an old, but not worn out, theological word. It refers to the "gracious outworking of the divine purpose in Christ within the created order of human history."[20] In Acts, providence expresses itself, from start to finish, in the repeated ways Luke roots the story of Jesus and the gift of the Spirit in the promise of God (1:4) and the hope of Israel (28:20). Acts tells the story of Jesus working through his people as one that emits from the word of God in Israel's Scriptures. The prophet Joel spoke about the outpouring of the Spirit in "the last days" (Acts 2:16–21; cf. Joel 2:28–32). The prophet Moses attested to the great prophet, Jesus, to whom the people of God must listen and follow (Acts 7:37; cf. Deut 18:15, 18). The inclusion of the gentiles in the people of God—as full and equal family members alongside the Jews—was promised to Abraham (Acts 3:25; cf. Gen 12:3; 22:18), foreseen by Isaiah (Acts 13:46–47; cf. Isa 49:6), testified by apostles (Acts 10:39–43), confirmed by the Spirit (10:44; 11:15–17), and all this was graciously orchestrated by God (10:34–39). What Luke is telling us by threading this theme of providence throughout his narrative is that this story is true and has meaning. The things that happen to people in it are not random, but there is a purpose to it all—the story is going somewhere. Further, there is purpose and meaning not only for those people acting *in* the story but also for those people *hearing* or *reading* the story.

God is the primary actor in the story of Acts. This means that Acts is rooted in and radiates out from the much larger Story of God. This is why all the primary witnesses of Jesus in Acts—Peter, Stephen, Paul—repeatedly look downstream to God's providence in Israel's story as they travel upstream proclaiming Jesus as Messiah and Lord to all people, whether they are in Jerusalem, Judea, Samaria, or the ends of the earth. At every turn the spread of the good news about King Jesus is initiated by God and led by the Spirit. As such, Paul speaks for every witness to this good news when he confesses, "God has helped me to this very day; so I stand here and testify to small and great alike. I am saying nothing beyond what the prophets and Moses said would happen—that the Messiah would suffer and, as the first to rise from the dead, would bring the message of light to his own people and to the Gentiles" (26:22–23).

---

[20]. Stanley J. Grenz, David Guretzki, and Cherith Fee Nordling, *Pocket Dictionary of Theological Terms* (Downers Grove, IL: InterVarsity Press, 1999), 97.

Resources for Teaching and Preaching

As any preacher or teacher will tell you, when it comes to reading the Bible well, we need the wisdom of others. Here are some of the first resources that I turn to when I prepare to preach and teach on Acts.

Brief Overviews

Fee, Gordon D. *How to Read the Bible Book by Book: A Guided Tour.* Grand Rapids: Zondervan, 2014.

Green, Joel B. "Acts of the Apostles." Pages 7–24 in *Dictionary of the Later New Testament and Its Developments.* Edited by Ralph P. Martin and Peter H. Davids. Downers Grove, IL: InterVarsity Press, 1997.

Help with Geographical and Historical Contexts

Bietzel, Barry J. *The Zondervan Atlas of the Bible.* Grand Rapids: Zondervan, 2010.

Winter, Bruce, and Andrew Clark, eds. *The Book of Acts in Its First-Century Setting.* 5 vols. Grand Rapids: Eerdmans, 1993–96.

Go-To Commentaries for Sermon Preparation

Alexander, Loveday. *Acts: The People's Bible Commentary.* Oxford: The Bible Reading Fellowship, 2006.

Dunn, James D. G. *The Acts of the Apostles.* Grand Rapids: Eerdmans, 2016.

Gaventa, Beverly Roberts. *The Acts of the Apostles.* Nashville: Abingdon, 2003.

Wright, N. T. *Acts for Everyone.* 2 vols. Louisville: Westminster John Knox, 2008.

Critical Commentaries for Digging Deep

Barrett, C. K. *Acts*. 2 vols. ICC. London: T&T Clark, 1994, 1998.

Keener, Craig S. *Acts: An Exegetical Commentary*. 4 vols. Grand Rapids: Baker, 2012–15.

Peterson, David G. *The Acts of the Apostles*. Pillar New Testament Commentary. Grand Rapids: Eerdmans, 2009.

Insightful and Rich Monographs

Levison, Jack. *Inspired: The Holy Spirit and the Mind of Faith*. Grand Rapids: Eerdmans, 2013.

Rowe, C. Kavin. *World Upside Down: Reading Acts in the Graeco-Roman Age*. Oxford: Oxford University Press, 2010.

PANEL 1
Acts 1:1–6:7

In the opening panel in Acts, Luke describes a dynamic new community that has emerged *within* Judaism, who continue to live *under* the authority of its leaders (see 3:1; 6:9). But this new community also understands itself as having entered "the last days" by the work of the Spirit. These "last days" are actually the firstfruits of "new creation," and this time of new creation is marked by fresh practices and unforeseen challenges. Structurally the first panel begins with the introduction to the whole narrative (1:1–5) and a brief description of Jesus's final instructions to his apostles before his ascension (1:6–11). The panel concludes with two distinct groups: Greek-speaking and Aramaic-speaking believers (6:1–7). In between, there are foundational moments (i.e., Pentecost in 2:1–12) and dramatic "firsts." For example, Peter's *first* sermon in 2:14–40; a *first* description of the new community's common life in 2:42–47; the *first* healing by the apostles in 3:1–10; the *first* sign of opposition in 4:1–7; and the *first* judgment within the community in 5:1–11. There is no word from Luke about the length of *time* or *geography* in this opening stage about the early followers of Jesus. How this new community extends itself from a Jerusalem-based, Jewish-led sect of Judaism to become a worldwide movement including gentiles is what the next panel is all about—and why the first panel probably ends with mention of the Hellenist (i.e., Greek-speaking) Jews. It is Hellenist Jews like Stephen and Philip who will lead this break from the apostles, even though the apostles recognize and release them.

CHAPTER 1

Acts 1:1-11

 LISTEN to the Story

¹In my former book, Theophilus, I wrote about all that Jesus began to do and to teach ²until the day he was taken up to heaven, after giving instructions through the Holy Spirit to the apostles he had chosen. ³After his suffering, he presented himself to them and gave many convincing proofs that he was alive. He appeared to them over a period of forty days and spoke about the kingdom of God. ⁴On one occasion, while he was eating with them, he gave them this command: "Do not leave Jerusalem, but wait for the gift my Father promised, which you have heard me speak about. ⁵For John baptized with water, but in a few days you will be baptized with the Holy Spirit."

⁶Then they gathered around him and asked him, "Lord, are you at this time going to restore the kingdom to Israel?"

⁷He said to them: "It is not for you to know the times or dates the Father has set by his own authority. ⁸But you will receive power when the Holy Spirit comes on you; and you will be my witnesses in Jerusalem, and in all Judea and Samaria, and to the ends of the earth."

⁹After he said this, he was taken up before their very eyes, and a cloud hid him from their sight.

¹⁰They were looking intently up into the sky as he was going, when suddenly two men dressed in white stood beside them. ¹¹"Men of Galilee," they said, "why do you stand here looking into the sky? This same Jesus, who has been taken from you into heaven, will come back in the same way you have seen him go into heaven."

Listening to the Text in the Story: Isaiah 32:15; 44:3–5; Ezekiel 11:19–20; 36:25–27; 1 Corinthians 15:1–8.

EXPLAIN the Story

The Story continues. In one respect it is unfortunate that the Gospel of John separates Luke's two volumes—the Gospel of Luke and the book of Acts—in the canonical arrangement of the NT.[1] John's Gospel *is* magnificent, to be sure, but it blocks the clear links Luke makes between part I and part II of the Jesus story. For that is what Acts is. It is a continuation of the story about the work and teaching of Jesus now in the lives of his followers. It is important to keep in mind that the opening of Acts serves a similar function to the opening of Luke. The Holy Spirit is active in bringing about the birth of Jesus in Luke 1–2, and the Spirit is now active in bringing about the birth of the church in Acts 1–2. Furthermore, as the Spirit propels Jesus's ministry (see Luke 3:22; 4:1, 14, 18) into the world, so also the Spirit will propel his followers into the world, beginning "in Jerusalem, and in all Judea and Samaria, and to the ends of the earth" (Acts 1:8).

The opening eleven verses of Acts are compact and full of important details. Luke makes the connection between "all that Jesus began to *do* and to *teach*" in his former book with the agenda that is set for his followers to *do* and *teach*. In Luke, Jesus's actions and instructions proclaimed that he was the Lord of the new kingdom around whom God was restoring and reconstituting Israel. Now his apostles are to be "witnesses," heralding that good news throughout the world. In the opening section (Acts 1:1–5), Luke offers a short summary of Jesus's teaching from the previous volume before clarifying the new direction that will be taken by his followers (1:6–8). The key that connects the work and words of Jesus and the work and words of his followers is the person of the Holy Spirit. In these opening few lines, the Holy Spirit is mentioned three times (vv. 2, 5, 8). The same Spirit who empowered Jesus will empower his people. But in order for the Spirit to empower God's people, Jesus must ascend into heaven, and so Luke closes his introduction with a description of this (1:9–11).

Introduction and Summary of Jesus's Teaching (1:1–5)

The first five verses of Acts are one long sentence in the Greek text. Introductions to ancient documents are important, and this introduction sets the

---

1. The canonical history of the NT accounts for this grouping. The earliest records we have listing the contents of the NT (e.g., the Muratorian Canon list, Origen's list, and Eusebius's list) grouped the four Gospels together, followed by Acts and then the Epistles. By the second century it appears the order for the Gospels was set, beginning with Matthew, followed by Mark and Luke, with John rounding them out. This ordering accounts for the disconnection of Luke with Acts. There are no ancient manuscripts that group Luke and Acts next to each other. For an excellent account of the history of the NT canon, see Metzger, *Canon of the New Testament*. See Graham N. Stanton on the early separation of Luke and Acts in "The Fourfold Gospel," *NTS* 43 (1997): 334–35; cf. C. Kavin Rowe, "History, Hermeneutics, and the Unity of Luke-Acts," *JSNT* 28 (2005): 131–57.

theme, shape, and tone for the whole of the narrative. As he did in the opening to the Gospel (Luke 1:1–4), Luke follows the introductory conventions of other historical narratives (e.g., Josephus, *Ag. Ap.* 1.1–5), by addressing his recipient, Theophilus, and providing a summary of what he has already written and what he will write next (see also *Ag. Ap.* 2.1; Eusebius, *Hist. eccl.* 2.1). The order in which Luke alerts Theophilus to what Jesus "began to do and to teach" until his ascension is interesting (Acts 1:1). Luke places what Jesus did first by describing his "doings" (vv. 3–4). While there is much that Jesus did in his lifetime, according to Luke his most significant "doing"—in his order—is the combined action of his ascension (v. 2), his suffering (v. 3a), and proof of life (v. 3b). In mentioning that Jesus gave many "convincing proofs" that he was alive (v. 3), Luke outlines what these proofs are: Jesus *appeared* to his disciples, *spoke* to his disciples, and *ate* with his disciples—all of which remind the reader of actions depicted at the end of the Gospel (see Luke 24:36–49).

Beyond what he did, Jesus also taught his disciples. After his resurrection he continued to teach about the "kingdom of God" (Acts 1:3) and offered a final command not to leave Jerusalem but to wait for the gift the Father promised and Jesus spoke about: the Holy Spirit (vv. 4–5). Jesus's teaching on the kingdom of God is his most important teaching. It is mentioned no less than thirty-nine times in the Gospel and at crucial junctures in Jesus's career (e.g., at the beginning of his ministry [Luke 4:43]; in his sending out of the Twelve [9:2]; in his teaching about prayer [11:2–4]; in his disputes with Pharisees [17:20–21]; and at the last supper [22:16, 18, 29–30]). Although the language of the kingdom of God appears only eight times in Acts, it does emerge at the beginning (Acts 1:3) and at the end of the narrative (28:31). Clearly the kingdom of God remains an important theme for Luke. The teaching on the Spirit, so fundamental in the Gospel of Luke, will continue to be important in the book of Acts as well. Further, the promise of the Father that concluded the Gospel (see Luke 24:49) sets the stage in Acts (Acts 1:4). The language of "the promise[d]" Holy Spirit not only evokes themes from the Gospel of Luke, it also echoes numerous OT passages from prophets like Isaiah (see 32:15; 44:3–5) and Ezekiel (11:19–20; 36:25–27). Importantly, then, the two teachings on the kingdom and the Spirit are linked for Jesus since he viewed the beginning of God's reign and the rescue of sinners as coinciding with the return of the Spirit's presence in his mission (see Luke 4:16–19). As John baptized people in water at the Jordan River as a signal of their readiness to follow the coming Messiah, Jesus in Acts 1:5 echoes the words of John (Luke 3:16) that "in a few days" the disciples will be baptized with the Holy Spirit as the fulfillment of God's promise to return the Spirit to his people in the last days.

In this one long and important sentence Luke provides almost a mini-catechism, similar to Paul's own gospel summary (1 Cor 15:1–8), of what he received and passed on to others. Luke describes the most significant actions Jesus *did*: he suffered (and died, Acts 1:3); he rose from the dead (v. 3, "he was alive"); and, after a period of forty days, he ascended to heaven (v. 3; cf. v. 9). Luke then encapsulates the most significant things Jesus *taught*: the kingdom of God and the promise of the Holy Spirit. Even though he does not speak in the language of later Trinitarian formulations, it should not be overlooked that in Luke's introductory sentences he mentions Jesus, "my Father," and the Holy Spirit.

A New Way for the Disciples (1:6–8)

The next three sentences (1:6–8) serve as the climactic section of Jesus's post-resurrection instruction to the apostles, especially as they relate to the key teaching already mentioned: the kingdom of God and the Holy Spirit. In order to clarify the apostles' role in the continued work of Jesus on earth, Luke follows his opening sentence with a joint question from those gathered around Jesus. Their initial inquiry is, "Lord, are you at this time going to restore the kingdom to Israel?" (1:6). Many times it seems that Jesus's apostles are portrayed as simply misunderstanding what Jesus taught. At this point, it appears they have done it again. After misunderstanding that Jesus would be enthroned as king through suffering and death, they now think that the resurrection of Jesus puts back on track their hopes for the national restoration of Israel. This is signaled in their address to him as "the Lord." It was the "Lord," the God of Israel, who would restore the fortunes of his people (see Deut 30:3; Isa 49:8; Jer 30:18).

It is important to note that "Lord" (*kyrios*), which was the Greek substitute for the Hebrew tetragrammaton in the Greek translation of the OT, is used almost exclusively for Jesus Christ in Acts. Whatever else they may have misunderstood, the disciples were convinced that Jesus was the "Lord"—an unequivocally high view of the person of Jesus. In this hope of Jesus as the Lord, and in full continuity with the prophets, they believed Israel would shake off the chains of foreign domination, a king like David would be reinstated, and that God would establish Israel as the leading nation of the world. Oddly enough, Jesus does not deny their hope, but he does qualify and correct it. It is a question that arises naturally from Jesus's teaching about the kingdom of God in 1:3. Jesus corrects their speculation about the "time" of restoration of the kingdom by qualifying their role as "witnesses" to the king in the concluding sentences (vv. 7–8). Strictly speaking, they were not simply to reiterate Jesus's teaching about the kingdom of God. The risen and soon-to-be ascended King

Jesus instructs them to "be my witnesses"—with their own lives if necessary. They were to begin their work in Jerusalem, the cultural and theological center of Israel, but continue to bear testimony of the risen king to their kin in Judea, to their neighbors (the Samaritans), and ultimately to all people. The narrative of Acts may end in Rome, but the goal is not Rome; it is the *people* of the whole earth. Luke's story may have a westerly direction because that is the story he knows and has participated in personally, but the church's movement in all directions exists beyond the boundaries of this narrative. The command of Jesus is not primarily about geography but about salvation for Jews and gentiles (see Acts 13:47; cf. Isa 49:6).

Important in Jesus's commission to the apostles is the repetition of the promise of the Holy Spirit (Acts 1:8; cf. 1:4–5 and Luke 24:49). While the Father has "the authority" (Acts 1:7) to set history and shape important events, the followers of Jesus receive "power" to announce his rule. The power is the personal presence of the Holy Spirit in their lives. It is strategically in Jerusalem, the geographic center to so much of Israel's history and hopes, where they are to wait for this "gift." The gift of the Spirit and what this means is pivotal to what Acts 2 is all about, but for now they are promised that the same Spirit who empowered their Lord Jesus in his own life and work of proclaiming the kingdom would also empower them to be his witnesses to the ends of the earth. For Luke, the church is empowered for its mission with the same Spirit who empowered the mission of Jesus.

Jesus's Ascension (1:9–11)

With these final words of Jesus still ringing in their ears, Luke describes Jesus's ascension in his next four sentences (1:9–11), which is one of the important elements that he had noted in the beginning (1:2); this again is reminiscent of the end of his Gospel (Luke 24:50–53). Although the resurrection and ascension of Jesus are distinct events in terms of their meaning and significance, Luke is the only writer who describes them as separated by a forty-day period. With these four sentences the focus shifts from Jesus to the apostles. This shift prepares the audience for the next phase of the narrative where the followers of Jesus are the ones called into action. Even with this shift, the phrase "after he said this" in Acts 1:9 links Jesus's missional directives with his ascension and the instructions from the two men in white. Richard Longenecker offers a useful insight on this: "Luke's point is that the missionary activity of the early church rested not only on Jesus's mandate but also on his living presence in heaven and the sure promise of his return."[2]

---

2. Longenecker, *Acts*, 258.

For the curious reader, a number of questions are easily generated from these concluding sentences: What kind of body does Jesus have? Where is heaven? How long before Jesus returns? Of course, the last question is easily answered from what Jesus said earlier: "It is not for you to know the times or dates the Father has set" (v. 7). As for the other questions, Luke does not feel compelled to answer them. Instead, he keeps our intent gaze linked with the apostles and his answers are "hid . . . from [our] sight" (v. 9).

The narrative does, however, make several key points. First, Jesus keeps his resurrection body in the other reality known as "heaven." Jesus does not generate his own ascension, but is passively "taken up" (v. 9), and the men in white—presumably angels—instruct the onlookers that "this *same* Jesus" (v. 11) will come back. For forty days Jesus has intermittently appeared to them as the risen Lord. His ascension confirms what has been on display "before their very eyes" (v. 9) all along: Jesus is the king of glory. David Peterson helpfully reminds us that "the ascension was not the beginning of the heavenly exaltation. It was the ultimate confirmation of the status that had been his from the moment of his resurrection."[3] Second, in a manner similar to the transfer of prophetic power from Moses to Joshua and from Elijah to Elisha, Jesus must ascend so that the promised and empowering Holy Spirit may descend upon these disciples.[4] Finally, and related to the previous point, after Jesus is taken from them with a "cloud" hiding him from their sight (v. 9), as tempting as it is for the "men of Galilee" to stand looking into "the sky" (v. 10, literally, "into heaven"),[5] there is a job for them to do between Jesus's ascension and his return. Luke's audience would already know from the Gospel that Jesus's second coming would be different from his little-known departure (only the apostles saw him leave). His return will be powerful and obvious to everyone (Luke 17:24–26), and it will be personal and glorious (21:27). In the face of possible doubts and disappointments on the part of his disciples, the ascension of Jesus is also a promise that he will return again. For now, a portion of earth has been joined to heaven in the resurrection body of Jesus. Until the Lord's Prayer is fulfilled when heaven is finally and comprehensively joined with earth, his servants are to be occupied in the mission agenda provided by their master.

---

3. David G. Peterson, *The Acts of the Apostles*, The Pillar New Testament Commentary (Grand Rapids: Eerdmans, 2009), 115.

4. See James D. G. Dunn, *The Acts of the Apostles* (Grand Rapids: Eerdmans, 2016), 14.

5. The language of Jesus's "ascent" in the clouds likely picks up on the imaginative resources of Jewish apocalyptic literature. For example, in Daniel 7:13 the appearance of one like "a son of man" is described as "coming with the clouds of heaven." Jesus also envisions his second coming as the Son of Man in final power and glory with similar language (see Luke 21:27). It is unsurprising that Luke reports the "ascent" of Jesus with imagery resembling the "descent" of his second coming.

LIVE the Story

When the Christian story is truly understood and lived, it is an expansive and enlivening power. But for many Christians, especially those living in the West, this is not their lived story. A significant reason why they may not be living this story is that the original teaching of Christianity is not always clearly understood and woven into the fabric of their lives. In fact, many people, including many Christians, are vague on the central aspects of the Christian faith and simply have no sense of what story they are trying to live. Try asking a neighbor or a fellow parishioner a question like, "What is the core teaching of the Christian faith?"[6] I have. It is amazing that most people answer with vague responses like: love, joy, peace, tolerance, etc. This is *not* what Luke impresses upon his audience.

So, what is the essential teaching of the Christian faith according to Luke? What are the primary themes to incorporate into the story of our lives? Luke provides us with them in the introductory verses of Acts: "*All that Jesus began to do and to teach* until the day he was *taken up to heaven*. . . . After *his suffering*, he presented himself to them and gave many convincing *proofs that he was alive*. . . . and spoke about the *kingdom of God*." (1:1b–3). The core of the Christian faith has to do with something that Jesus has already done, which Luke described in his first book. This is crucial. Christianity is about what Jesus *has done* and what he *continues to do* through his disciples.[7] But what has Jesus done? Luke alerts us to four "doings" of Jesus in his introductory words to Acts. First, he has suffered (1:3); second, he offered many convincing proofs he was alive (1:3); third, he taught about the kingdom of God (1:3); and fourth, he ascended to heaven (1:2, 9–11).

Jesus Suffered

Why did Jesus suffer? Christian thinkers over the centuries have pondered this question at length. While there are many reasons that could be offered, theologians regularly appeal to at least two. First, Jesus's suffering is necessary because we *do* wrong. I grew up working on our family farm, and the general rule of thumb was that if you lent machinery or tools to a neighbor (which you do without question), don't be surprised if they come back broken. When this happens, a "debt" must be paid. Either my neighbor pays the debt, or else I forgive him and pay for the damages. Either way, someone pays the cost of

---

6. You may consider listening to Timothy Keller as he articulates his response to this question in his superb sermon on this text entitled "Truth and Power" (preached at Redeemer Presbyterian Church on Sept. 10, 1995, https://gospelinlife.com/downloads/truth-and-power-6406).
7. Keller, "Truth and Power."

damage. This is what happens on an economic level, but it also occurs on a much deeper level if we wrong someone emotionally or physically or we are violated in some way. Again, we can make someone else pay the cost of the wrong, and we often seek this in the judicial system. We can also choose to forgive people who have hurt us, whether or not we seek redress in the courts as well. Now that kind of forgiveness still "costs"—it costs us considerably to forgive someone who has hurt us. When we refrain from seeking retribution, it is often agony to forgive. As Brené Brown suggests, genuine forgiveness requires that there be "blood on the floor."[8] Why? Because something has to die: there has to be a death for forgiveness to happen. It might be the death of our expectations, our bitterness, our anger, etc. The point is that forgiveness on a human level entails suffering—either for the perpetrator or the forgiver. If we know at a human level that forgiveness always entails suffering for the forgiver, then we also know that any hope of reconciliation and justice and righting of wrongs only occurs through paying the cost of suffering. If we know all this on a human level, we should not be surprised that the way God forgives the sin of the entire human race is only through the suffering of his Son. I "*must* suffer," says Jesus (Mark 8:31). Either we must pay the penalty for wrongdoings, or Jesus must. Either we have justice inflicted on us, or God, through his Son, takes on the task himself to "forgive us our debts" (cf. Matt 6:12).

Jesus not only suffered to pay the debt of forgiveness because we *do* wrong but because we *are* wrong. The story of Scripture tells us that death has power over us. Death is the certain end for all. The Scriptures offer a theological reason for this physical reality. The wrong that exists within us, our sin, leaves an indelible mark of separation between God and us; it is simply not good enough for us to be "good." Both the OT and NT agree on this point. Fundamentally each one of us experiences the grip of "principalities and powers," and the most fundamental power that holds all of us in its grip is death. In this world, we all know that the worst thing corrupt powers can do is kill us. Corrupt powers try to control and coerce people by threatening them with death. The Czech priest and theologian Tomás Halík comments on this well:

> [Christianity] does not censor the reality that violence is part and parcel of our world and our Lord was not spared from it. But it also says that *violence does not have and must not have the last word*, that Jesus preferred to allow himself to be killed through violence, rather than use or condone violence. Christian belief states that after Christ took violence upon himself, violence no longer existed as a harrowing absurdity, but

---

8. Brené Brown, "Jesus Wept," http://www.theworkofthepeople.com/jesus-wept.

underwent an inner transformation, by the meaning that Christ gave his suffering and death. The cross is not a "demonstration" of violence, suffering, and death; on the contrary, it is a message about a love that is "stronger than death." It preaches the strength of hope that relativizes and mocks death itself: "Where, O death, is your victory? Where, O death is your sting?"[9]

All this means that death is not an ultimate threat if you truly know and follow Jesus. The threat of death is serious and menacing, but for a Christian who truly understands and lives their faith, death is not the last thing, it is the next-to-last thing. Resurrection is the last thing, and death is the doorway to resurrection. When death loses its sting, when death loses its power over you because of what Jesus did on the cross, then nothing has power over you. Luke reminds us in his Gospel account, which he refers to as his "former book" (Acts 1:1), that Jesus stands between us and death and declares that he will not let death have his brothers and sisters. The result is that all the malice and destruction of death falls upon him. Jesus pays for us, the barrier is gone, and all because of "his suffering" (1:3).

While we can be assured that Jesus suffers *with us* as a part of our union with him, it is not always easy to understand why Jesus *must* suffer *for us*. Personally, I find that it is almost impossible to live and lean into this truth apart from prayer. The Scottish minister P. T. Forsyth sums up the meaning of Jesus's suffering and the place of prayer this way:

> Our atonement with God is the pregnant be-all and end-all of Christian peace and life; and what is that atonement but the head and front of the Saviour's perpetual intercession, of the outpouring of His sin-laden soul unto death? Unto death! That is to say, it is its outpouring utterly. So that His entire self-emptying and His perfect and prevailing prayer are one. In this intercession our best prayer, broken, soiled, and feeble as it is, is caught up and made prayer and indeed power with God. This intercession prays for our very prayer, and atones for the sin in it. This is praying in the Holy Ghost, which is not necessarily a matter either of intensity or elation. This is praying "for Christ's sake." If it be true that the whole Trinity is in the gospel of our salvation, it is also true that all theology lies hidden in the prayer which is our chief answer to the gospel. And the bane of so much theology, old and new, is that it has been denuded of prayer and prepared in a vacuum.[10]

---

9. Tomás Halík, *Night of the Confessor* (New York: Image, 2012), 160.
10. P. T. Forsyth, *The Soul of Prayer* (London: Independent, 1949; repr., Vancouver: Regent College, 1995), 38.

Proofs That He Was Alive

Secondly, Luke says that Jesus showed himself alive: "He presented himself to them and gave many convincing *proofs that he was alive*" (1:3). There is sometimes a condescending attitude possessed by modern people who think that first-century Christian peasants and fishermen were gullible, superstitious, and primitive people who would believe anything. But what do Luke and Matthew say was the response of the first disciples when the women returning from the tomb tell them that it is empty? Some thought it was nonsense (Luke 24:11); some doubted (Matt 28:17). The truth is that first-century Jews like them were far less likely to believe in the resurrection of Jesus than most moderns. Most of the Jews of that time were strict monotheists who believed in a transcendent God who would never become human, let alone be cursed and hung on a cross. Even the Jews who did believe in the resurrection[11] were anticipating a general resurrection of all people at the end of time; no one looked for one person who would be resurrected in the middle of time.[12] In this regard, Jesus may have had a far harder audience to persuade than we do now, yet he does convince them. And those early disciples, once convinced of his incarnation and resurrection, were transformed men and women. They carried the wonder and message of resurrection into a pluralistic, multicultured world and, to a person, never changed their story that they had witnessed the living and resurrected Jesus. As for proof, they did what any ancient person would do: they pointed to eyewitnesses who could attest to their claims (see 1 Cor 15:5–8). From what we know regarding the early-church record, none of these eyewitnesses ever changed their story about the resurrection. Many of them even went to their deaths without ever denying what they saw and affirmed.

When the late Chuck Colson reflected on the fact of the resurrection in the light of his own role in the Watergate cover-up, he was convinced that the earliest disciples could not have perpetuated a hoax:

> Watergate involved a conspiracy to cover up, perpetuated by the closest aides to the President of the United States—the most powerful men in America, who were intensely loyal to their president. But one of them, John Dean, turned state's evidence, that is, testified against Nixon, as he put it, "to save his own skin"—and he did so only two weeks after informing the president about what was really going on—two weeks! The real cover-up, the lie, could only be held together for two weeks, and then

---

11. It is important to remember that some Jews, like the Sadducees, did not believe in resurrection.
12. This is a point I've learned from N. T. Wright; he makes this observation often in many of his books, but a good place to reflect on this is in *Surprised by Hope: Rethinking Heaven, the Resurrection, and the Mission of the Church* (San Francisco: HarperOne: 2008).

everybody else jumped ship in order to save themselves. Now, the fact is that all that those around the President were facing was embarrassment, maybe prison. Nobody's life was at stake. But what about the disciples? Twelve powerless men, peasants really, were facing not just embarrassment or political disgrace, but beatings, stonings, execution. Every single one of the disciples insisted, to their dying breaths, that they had physically seen Jesus bodily raised from the dead.[13]

Colson understood, better than many of us, how difficult it is to live, let alone die, for a lie. This is why Colson was so struck by the resolve of the early church. Hundreds of eyewitnesses experienced intense pressure to recant. Yet they went on for years, often at great personal expense, consistently telling the same story—"Jesus was raised on the third day"—and none of them changed their story. The "many convincing proofs that [Jesus] was alive" (Acts 1:3) sustained the early church, and these proofs convinced Nixon's hardened political hatchet man, Charles Colson, too.

The Kingdom of God

My friend and mentor Gordon Fee was once asked what he would focus on if he were a pastor of a congregation and not a professor in a college. His reply was vintage Gordon: "I would spend my first year preaching and teaching on nothing else besides the kingdom of God. Well . . . maybe I would spend more than a year on that!" The reason Gordon holds this conviction is that he knows from decades of teaching students, many of whom were raised in evangelical Christian homes, that when he asked them to state in five words or less what Jesus's primary teaching was, Christians rarely answered, "The kingdom of God."[14] More often than not Christians assume that Jesus's primary teaching was some combination of love, peace, and hope—some even think "justification by faith" was Jesus's primary teaching! I'm not exactly sure why many Christians miss this, but after sitting under Gordon's teaching, I know that I will never miss this again.[15]

---

13. Chuck Colson, "An Unholy Hoax?: The Authenticity of Christ," http://www.breakpoint.org/2002/03/an-unholy-hoax.

14. It should be noted that the phrase "the kingdom of God" is synonymous with the phrase "the kingdom of heaven." The Gospel of Matthew follows the common Jewish practice of substituting "heaven" for "God."

15. What follows is a broad summary of Gordon's lectures I heard during my graduate studies. His lectures on the kingdom of God are available through his "New Testament Survey" and "Life and Teaching of Jesus" courses. Both courses are available for mp3 download from the Regent College bookstore: http://www.regentaudio.com/collections/gordon-fee. A well-known scholar who takes a similar view to the kingdom of God as Fee is George Eldon Ladd, *The Gospel of the Kingdom: Scriptural Studies in the Kingdom of God* (Grand Rapids: Eerdmans, 1990); see also several chapters in Ladd's *A Theology of the New Testament*, rev. ed. (Grand Rapids: Eerdmans, 1993). For a fresh and

The Gospels agree that Jesus's primary teaching prior to his resurrection was the kingdom of God. We should not be surprised, then, that his focus in the forty days after his resurrection remained the same and he "*continued speaking*"[16] about the kingdom of God (Acts 1:3). Whenever the Gospel writers summarize Jesus's teaching, they express it in terms of the kingdom. For example, Mark writes, "After John was put in prison, Jesus went into Galilee, proclaiming the good news of God. 'The time has come,' he said. 'The kingdom of God has come near. Repent and believe the good news!'" (Mark 1:14–15; cf. Matt 4:17; 9:35; Luke 9:1–2). Whenever Jesus sent out his disciples, he instructed them to proclaim the kingdom of God. He instructed the Twelve, "As you go, proclaim this message: 'The kingdom of God is near'" (Matt 10:7), and to the seventy-two disciples he instructed, "Heal the sick who are there and tell them, 'The kingdom of God has come near to you'" (Luke 10:9). If we are ever going to understand Jesus, we must begin by understanding the kingdom of God.

So, what is the kingdom of God about? To answer that, we must first remind ourselves that prior to Jesus's teaching, other Jewish teachers also talked about the kingdom of the messiah and the rule of God in contrast to what they saw about them.[17] That is, earlier than Jesus, many Jews believed that they lived during a corrupt time when evil ruled and that the evidence for this was all around: wicked rulers reigned supreme, injustice abounded, and humankind itself was living in rebellion to God. Many Jews gave up any hope for change within history and instead looked for God to bring this present age, with all its evil and oppression, to an end. In place of the present age would be "the coming age"—a time at the end of history when the future would be ushered in by divine intervention. Usually, they thought a powerful messiah would accompany this end, one who would come in triumph to set the world right, restore Israel to its former glory, bring back the Spirit of God, and deliver the oppressed. They came to refer to this time of God's rule as "the kingdom of God."

Before we go further, it is important to remember that the kingdom is not primarily a *place* (either in "heaven" or in one's "heart") but a *time*—the time when God will reign supremely. This does not mean that the kingdom is disconnected from place and land but that in the Gospels the primary question asked of Jesus about the kingdom was not "where?" but "when?" While many

---

provocative approach, see Scot McKnight, *Kingdom Conspiracy: Returning to the Radical Mission of the Local Church* (Grand Rapids: Brazos, 2014).

16. Here the grammar is important. The Greek participle translated as "spoke" by the NIV is a *present* participle and the tense here emphasizes a *continuing* and *ongoing* activity by Jesus.

17. C. C. Caragounis, "Kingdom of God/Heaven," *DJG*, 419, notes that "although the term 'kingdom of God' is rare in Judaism, the idea is almost ubiquitous, either explicitly as the kingdom of the Messiah or implicitly in descriptions of the messianic age."

in Jesus's day would certainly have agreed with him when he taught that the kingdom would come as a future event (e.g., see Matt 8:11–12; Mark 10:31), the startling aspect to Jesus's teaching concerning the kingdom was that it was a *present* reality in his own words and deeds. To the synagogue in Nazareth he proclaimed that the great messianic prophecy of Isaiah 61:1–3 was *already* being fulfilled: already the great reversal is taking place, already the blind see, already the oppressed are being released, and the time of God's favor has already come (Luke 4:16–21). He sees his various actions, from sitting at table with outcasts (14:8–24) to casting out demons (11:20), as evidence that the kingdom and saving reign of God had come with him, "the Anointed One," the King. For King Jesus,[18] the ushering in of his kingdom comes in stages. That is, his mission and message initiates the *beginning* of the end, the *inauguration* of the coming age. But that which has begun is also going to be concluded, and the inaugurated coming age is going to be *consummated* when he returns again in glory.

Thus, in Jesus's first advent—expressed in the humility of the incarnation—the seed has been planted (Luke 13:18–19), the yeast has been put in the dough (13:20–21), the future has been set in motion, and the life of the coming age and its values are already at work in the present. Already we know its goodness; already we experience its gifts; already salvation has come; already we sit at the King's table; already we are the children of God who have been overtaken by the kingdom. But there is still a future when what is already present will be brought to its final conclusion. That which God has set in motion is going to be fully realized. To put it in Paul's words, "He who *began* a good work in you will carry it on to *completion* until the day of Christ Jesus" (Phil 1:6). There is inevitability to the growth of the mustard seed and to the yeast's influence on the dough. Thus, the kingdom of God is both *already* and *not yet*.

This understanding of time and the kingdom of God not only serves as the basic structure for understanding Jesus's mission and message but also for the entire NT. The future has begun, and it is guaranteed by its beginnings in Jesus. In his life and teaching, in his death, burial, resurrection, and ascension, the NT writers understood that Jesus grappled with the enemy and dealt him the decisive blow. He triumphed on our behalf and overcame sin and death with his forgiveness and resurrection. The resurrection of all believers still belongs to the future, but *the* resurrection—the resurrection of Jesus—has already happened, and this guarantees our own resurrection and the renewal of all things when the ascended King returns at his second advent.

---

18. I appreciate this phrase "King Jesus" when referring to "Christ Jesus," as it helps remind us of the royal dimensions of the title "Christ" (i.e., Messiah). I think that I picked this up after reading Scot McKnight's superb book *The King Jesus Gospel: The Original Good News Revisited* (Grand Rapids: Zondervan, 2011).

Jesus Ascended to Heaven

The fourth aspect of the core of Christianity as Luke enumerates it in the beginning of Acts is that Jesus ascended to heaven. The founders of every other religion in the world no longer personally do or teach anything after they die. Jesus, however, not only rose from the dead but also ascended to heaven. As the risen and ascended Lord, Jesus, according to Luke, only "*began* to do and to teach." Jesus did not ascend to heaven because he wanted to get away from us, he did so in order to continue to live and work among us as the risen and reigning King. How so? The ascension does not mean that Jesus is no longer here among us but that Jesus is accessible *everywhere* through the Holy Spirit enlivening his followers. Jesus is still present to everyone who calls on his name. The Victorian evangelist Henry Drummond offers this summary of the ascent of Jesus and the descent of the Spirit: "The Holy Spirit is just what Christ would have been had He been here. He ministers comfort just as Christ would have done—only without the inconveniences of circumstance, without the restriction of space, without the limitations of time."[19] The Holy Spirit does this work through ordinary people—like you and me—who respond to Jesus's call to follow him and be his witnesses in the world.

Luke tells the story of Jesus's ascension both in the final words of his Gospel (Luke 24:50–52) and in the opening words of Acts (1:9–11). Further, reference to the ascended Lord or ascension themes punctuate Acts at critical moments in almost every one of the first eleven chapters.[20] The ascension is important for Luke and is vital to the health and work of Jesus's church. Old Testament scholar Bruce Waltke offered the address at my graduation from Regent College. That day also happened to be close to Ascension Day in 1994. Bruce described this day as one of the most overlooked events in the church calendar.[21] It occurs on a Thursday—the fortieth day of Easter—and it normally passes without notice by many Christians. Yet without the ascension, there can be no Pentecost. Without Jesus's enthronement to the right hand of God the Father, there can be no empowerment through the Spirit for God's people. The remembrance and celebration of Ascension Day in the gathered worship of the church deserves rehabilitation.

Ascension Day, or "Holy Thursday" as it has been called in some quarters of the church, provides the liturgical counterpoint to Ash Wednesday.

---

19. Henry Drummond, *The Ideal Life: Listening for God's Voice, Discerning His Leading* (New Kensington, PA: Whitaker, 2014), Kindle edition.

20. After chapter 1 notice the references to Jesus's status at the "right hand of God," manifestations from Jesus's place in heaven on earth, or "the Lord" speaking from heaven to earth (Acts 2:2, 33; 3:21; 4:12; 5:31; 7:56; 9:3–6; 10:11–15; 11:4–10).

21. See Bruce K. Waltke, "He Ascended and Sitteth: Reflections on the Sixth Article of the Apostles Creed," *Crux* 30.2 (June 1994): 2–8.

Once, in one of England's grand cathedrals, I attended an Ascension Day service. In this great Norman cathedral there is also a chorister school, and the children from it were attending that service as well. The presiding minister asked the children to come forward to receive a mark of the cross on their foreheads, as they had on Ash Wednesday forty days prior to Easter.[22] But on this occasion, now forty days after Easter, they did not receive a smudge of ash on their foreheads, reminding them of their mortality and need for a Savior. Rather, this time the children received a glitter cross on their foreheads. With this symbol they were to recall the glory of the risen Christ who, because of his ascension, now marks all his people with the glory of his personal presence in their lives through the Holy Spirit. This glory empowers us, puts wings on our feet, and gets us moving from heavenly gazing and static standing to earthly worship and energetic witness.

---

22. That is, forty days prior to Easter excluding Sundays.

CHAPTER 2

Acts 1:12-26

 LISTEN to the Story

¹²Then the apostles returned to Jerusalem from the hill called the Mount of Olives, a Sabbath day's walk from the city. ¹³When they arrived, they went upstairs to the room where they were staying. Those present were Peter, John, James and Andrew; Philip and Thomas, Bartholomew and Matthew; James son of Alphaeus and Simon the Zealot, and Judas son of James. ¹⁴They all joined together constantly in prayer, along with the women and Mary the mother of Jesus, and with his brothers.

¹⁵In those days Peter stood up among the believers (a group numbering about a hundred and twenty) ¹⁶and said, "Brothers and sisters, the Scripture had to be fulfilled in which the Holy Spirit spoke long ago through David concerning Judas, who served as guide for those who arrested Jesus. ¹⁷He was one of our number and shared in our ministry."

¹⁸(With the payment he received for his wickedness, Judas bought a field; there he fell headlong, his body burst open and all his intestines spilled out. ¹⁹Everyone in Jerusalem heard about this, so they called that field in their language Akeldama, that is, Field of Blood.)

²⁰"For," said Peter, "it is written in the Book of Psalms:

"'May his place be deserted; let there be no one to dwell in it,'[1]

and,

"'May another take his place of leadership.'[2]

²¹Therefore it is necessary to choose one of the men who have been with us the whole time the Lord Jesus was living among us, ²²beginning from John's baptism to the time when Jesus was taken up from us. For one of these must become a witness with us of his resurrection."

²³So they nominated two men: Joseph called Barsabbas (also known

---

1. Psalm 69:25.
2. Psalm 109:8.

as Justus) and Matthias. ²⁴Then they prayed, "Lord, you know everyone's heart. Show us which of these two you have chosen ²⁵to take over this apostolic ministry, which Judas left to go where he belongs." ²⁶Then they cast lots, and the lot fell to Matthias; so he was added to the eleven apostles.

Listening to the Text in the Story: 2 Samuel 17:23; Psalm 41:10; Proverbs 16:33.

EXPLAIN the Story

In-between periods can be awkward. Just a few lines of narrative (Acts 1:12–26) are the only details Luke chose to include to describe the ten days of uncomfortable time between the absence of Jesus's earthly presence (ascension) and the empowerment of the Spirit's presence (Pentecost). It is a period straddling two ages: the present age and the age to come. In this interim the apostles obediently return to wait and pray in Jerusalem. While they wait, they choose Matthias to replace Judas among the Twelve. The passage is simple enough to outline and falls into three parts: the setting of their prayer vigil (1:12–14); Peter's speech to the gathered believers (1:15–22); and the election of Matthias (1:23–26).

The Prayer Vigil (1:12–14)

It is not apparent from the earlier narrative where the ascension took place, but the mention of returning from "the Mount of Olives" (v. 12) locates the ascension in the vicinity of Bethany—a "Sabbath day's walk" (i.e., about one kilometer)—as described in the closure to the Gospel (cf. Luke 24:50). Luke desires to show that the apostles obediently followed Jesus's instruction not to leave Jerusalem (Acts 1:4). As James Dunn notes, it is important that the descent of the Spirit is seen in "continuity with Israel's past and the previous phases of God's purposes which Jerusalem symbolized."³

The list of the eleven apostles described as having gathered in "the upper room" (v. 13) follows very closely the earlier list in Luke (6:14–16), except for a few name reversals.⁴ The implication is that their lodging must have been large enough to accommodate the named apostles during the difficult

---

3. Dunn, *Acts*, 15.
4. For example, in Acts 1:13 Andrew is placed after James rather than Peter, and Thomas occurs before Bartholomew and Matthew.

period between their time with Jesus and the establishment of the church in Jerusalem. The first phrase—"they all joined together constantly in prayer" (Acts 1:14)—draws together a number of themes that are important to Luke throughout the narrative. The word translated as "together"[5]—or "in one accord" as some of the older translations have it—highlights the *unity* of believers (cf. 2:46; 4:24; 5:12) and emphasizes the importance of *faithfulness* often cited in Acts (cf. 2:42, 46; 6:4). The third item is *prayer*, a theme that is significant in both of Luke's two volumes.[6]

It is of interest to note that Luke mentions that women,[7] including Jesus's mother Mary, and his brothers are also present with the apostles (1:14). A number of women played prominent roles in Jesus's earlier mission (Luke 8:1–3; 23:49, 55–56; 24:1–10, 22), and they obviously continued to do so—a fact that will become clearer later on (e.g., Acts 2:17; 5:14; 8:3, 12; 9:2; 22:4). The mention of Mary is not entirely surprising since her perspective is highlighted in Luke's birth narrative and her presence here indicates that she likely continued to play an important role among the early church in Jerusalem. Despite appearing ambiguously in Gospel accounts (e.g., Mark 3:20–21, 31–35; Luke 8:19–21), the mention of Jesus's "brothers" prepares the reader for the significant role that James, the brother of Jesus, will play in the Jerusalem church later in Acts (see 12:17; 15:13–21; 21:18–25).

Peter's Speech to the Believers (1:15–22)

The next movement in this portion of the narrative is Peter's speech. After Jesus's parting words before the ascension (vv. 4–8), this is the first of many speeches in Acts. It should be noted that intermittent speeches are an important component of ancient historiography. Instead of simply narrating events, Luke follows the conventions of other ancient historians, like Josephus, by including set speeches. Presumably, these speeches heightened the interest of the audience since the earliest recipients of these historical documents were primarily *hearers* and not *readers*. We have no reason to doubt that the demise of Judas and the need to fill his place were items spoken about by Peter. We must remember, however, that in its present form the speech is aimed at

---

5. The Greek word is *homothymadon* and occurs ten times in Acts (Acts 1:14; 2:46; 4:24; 5:12; 7:57; 8:6; 12:20; 15:25; 18:12; and 19:29). The word occurs only one other time in the NT in Rom 15:6. Cf. Dunn, *Acts*, 16.

6. Dunn, *Acts*, 16, points us to the following passages: Luke 1:10; 3:21; 5:16; 6:12, 28; 9:18, 28–29; 11:1–2; 18:1, 10–11; 19:46; 20:47; 22:40–41, 44, 46; Acts 1:24–25; 2:42; 3:1; 4:24–30; 6:4, 6; 8:15; 9:11; 10:2, 4, 9, 30–31; 11:5; 12:5, 12; 13:3; 14:23; 16:13, 16, 25; 20:36; 21:5; 22:17; 28:8.

7. The Greek word, *gynaixin*, translated as "women," can also be translated as "wives," but "women" is appropriate given that the women who witnessed the resurrection may not have been married.

Luke's own hearers/readers. The parenthetical material (1:18–19) indicates this along with the fact that Peter would deliver his speech in Aramaic and likely quote the Hebrew text; Peter's words in Acts are in Greek, and the biblical texts quoted here, and in other speeches in Acts, are consistently from the LXX, the Greek translation of Scripture used by the Hellenistic church.[8] All of this is to say that the priority of Acts is the mission of *communicating Jesus* "to the ends of the earth," not a verbatim record of historical speeches in the early church.

The speech of Peter makes two clear points: (1) it was *necessary* for the Scriptures to be fulfilled about the downfall of Judas (v. 16), and (2) it was *necessary* for the church to fill his place of leadership (v. 21). Both of these counts demonstrate the continuity of divine purpose in the story of the early church. Further, both are connected with the interchange between the "lot" of ministry Judas carried among the Twelve (v. 17) and the "lot" that is cast in favor of Matthias (v. 26).[9] But before continuing with the speech, the narrative takes an aside in 1:18–19 (indicated by parentheses in many English translations; e.g., NIV, NRSV, ESV, NASB) to describe the death of Judas.

There are three versions of the death of Judas in early Christian tradition. Besides the account here in Acts, there is one in Matthew (27:3–10) and one attributed to Papias of Hierapolis, a second-century disciple of the apostle John. According to Papias, Judas did not die from hanging but from a disease of severe swelling.[10] While this account may be dismissed, the two biblical accounts diverge significantly and raise a number of questions: How did Judas die, by accident or suicide? Who bought the field? Why is it called "field of blood"? According to Matthew, Judas hanged himself in a fit of remorse over his betrayal of Jesus, then the chief priests bought a field (possibly in Judas's name) with the thirty silver pieces Judas returned, and the burial ground was called "field of blood" because it was bought with "blood" money—Jesus's blood. According to Acts, Judas died by accident in a fall after having bought a field with his "reward" money, and the ground where his intestines burst out was called "field of blood"—Judas's blood. In the end, the two biblical accounts cannot be easily harmonized. It is best to view this as "the divergent purposes of the Evangelists which have determined how such information as

---

8. While the LXX is the basis of the quotations in Acts, the quotations in Acts do not always precisely match the LXX.

9. The same Greek word, *klēros*, is translated by the NIV as "share" (v. 17) and "lot" (v. 26).

10. See Papias of Hierapolis, fragment 18, in Michael W. Holmes, *The Apostolic Fathers in Translation* (Grand Rapids: Baker, 2006), 316: "Judas was a terrible, walking example of ungodliness in this world, his flesh so bloated that he was not able to pass through a place where a wagon passes easily.... After much agony and punishment, they say, he finally died in his own place, and because of the stench the area is deserted and uninhabitable even now."

was available to them was used."[11] For Matthew, Judas's death was another example of the fulfillment of prophecy (see Jer 32:6–9; Zech 11:12–13); for Luke, Judas's death is the just demise of a wicked person (see 2 Sam 17:23; Wis 4:18–19; 2 Macc 9:7–18).[12]

After the aside, the speech of Peter resumes (Acts 1:20) with two citations from the Psalms. The first quotation is from Psalm 69:25. This Davidic psalm is frequently cited in the NT (e.g., John 2:17; Rom 11:9–10; 15:3). It may have become a "messianic psalm" in the early church because of its Davidic roots and its content that calls for judgment against enemies who have caused him to suffer (see Ps 69:21 and Luke 23:36). For Luke (Acts 1:18–20), Judas's demise is viewed as a fulfillment of Psalm 69:25: "Let there be no one to dwell in it." The second quotation from Psalm 109 carries a similar theme to that of Psalm 69 with a call for David's enemies to be cursed. Psalm 109:8 is used in Acts as prophetic confirmation that Judas's place of leadership should be filled by someone else.

The criteria for Judas's replacement are outlined (Acts 1:21–22) and indicate Luke's view of what an "apostle" is. Any potential candidate must meet several requirements. First, they must have accompanied the earthly Jesus at all the crucial points of his ministry since John's baptism. Second, and most important, they must have seen the risen Jesus so that they might be a witness to his resurrection. These are the fundamental requirements for apostleship. Even though Luke is often closely linked with Paul, it should be noted that this view in Acts is different from Paul's. For Paul, "apostleship" appears to be more of a functional term. Paul knows of the references to "the Twelve" that appear in the Gospel traditions and Acts (see 1 Cor 15:5; cf. Luke 8:1; 9:1, 12; 18:31; 22:3, 47; Acts 6:2 etc.). "The Twelve" carry through the historical continuity between the twelve tribes of Israel and the Israel that is being reconstituted around Jesus as indicated by the apostles' question in Acts 1:6 (see also Luke 22:30). For Paul, however, the notion of "apostleship" certainly included "the Twelve," but it also included himself, and others.[13] What designates an "apostle" for Paul relates primarily to those who had been commissioned for missionary work (1 Cor 9:1; 15:5), who enacted mighty deeds (2 Cor 12:12), and, most importantly, engaged in mission (1 Cor 9:1–2; 15:8–11). In this sense Paul's view overlaps with the requirements listed in Acts, but his view is more functional. Luke knows of "apostles" beyond "the Twelve" (see Acts 14:14), but his emphasis in Acts 1 is on the role of "the Twelve" as the

---

11. Dunn, *Acts*, 19.
12. Dunn, *Acts*, 19; Keener, *Acts*, 1.761–65.
13. For example, Junia and Andronicus (Rom 16:7); James (Gal 1:19); Barnabas (1 Cor 9:5–6); and even those Paul considers false apostles (see 2 Cor 11:5).

official guarantors of the origins of the faith. This fluid sense of "apostleship" in Luke may explain why "the Twelve" fall out of view in the latter half of Acts where the role of the apostle as a missionary is the focus.[14]

The Election of Matthias (1:23–26)

After Peter's speech is finished, the only thing left to do is make the selection for Judas's replacement (1:23–26). Two men are put forward: Joseph Barsabbas (also known as "Justus") and Matthias.[15] The recording of their names is clearly rooted in authentic early Christian tradition since nothing more is heard of these two even after much is made of the necessity to replace Judas.[16] It is unclear whether it is the remaining eleven apostles who put forward the two men to the community or whether the community puts forward the two to the apostles. Nonetheless, in a remarkable expression of their high view of Christ, they pray to the exalted "Lord" Jesus to assist them in making the selection since, after all, it is Jesus who "chose" the original twelve in the first place (Luke 6:13; cf. Acts 1:2). After praying, they follow guidelines set out in the Scriptures and cast lots for the two candidates as a means of determining God's will (cf. Lev 16:7–10; Num 26:55; 1 Sam 10:20–21; Prov 16:33; Jonah 1:7–8). The "lot" falls on Matthias. He is numbered with the eleven and then quietly disappears from the narrative altogether. Interestingly, casting lots as a means of discerning God's direction according to the framework of the old era will never be used again in Acts. In a few days, a new era will open and with it a new means of discerning God's will by the empowering and personal presence of the Holy Spirit.

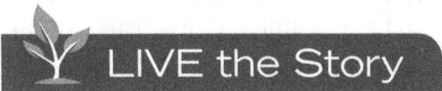

LIVE the Story

Suicide and the Struggle to Will to Live[17]

Very few sermons or church classes discuss the suicide of Judas. If they do, it is usually to use him as a negative example of what not to do with remorse or shame. Suicide is a difficult topic to discuss, and often the simplest course

---

14. Dunn, *Acts*, 20.

15. Eckhard J. Schnabel, *Acts*, ZECNT (Grand Rapids: Zondervan, 2012), 101, reminds us not to overlook the courage these men possessed in letting themselves be put forward as the "Twelfth Man." That is, it was still a dangerous situation (Jesus was crucified only days earlier), and their vocation as witnesses to the world was, frankly, unprecedented.

16. Dr. David Miller, professor at Briercrest College and Seminary, pointed out that there is also an interesting parallel in choosing Zechariah by lot in Luke 1:8–9.

17. For the shape of the following discussion on suicide, I am indebted to the Ven. Norbert Haukenfrers, rector of St. David's Anglican Church in Prince Albert, who led our diocesan clergy through an excellent course for suicide prevention.

of action is to avoid it altogether. This is not helpful. Suicide is a reality that must not be ignored. In my home country of Canada, the demographic most at risk for suicide are First Nations youth; white middle-aged men are the second most at risk group.[18] For every "successful" suicide, there are approximately 20–25 attempted suicides. I live in Saskatchewan where there is a large First Nations population. Unfortunately, in our province the indigenous suicide-attempt rate is *five times* the national average. This means that in many First Nations communities, 50–75 percent of young people under the age of twenty-five *attempt* suicide. The factors that place individuals at risk are complex, but they most often include depression, mental illness, alcohol and drug dependency, hopelessness, low self-esteem, sexual abuse, violence, parental loss, and homelessness. For those who serve on the front lines in dealing with suicide and suicide prevention (e.g., social workers, first responders, ministers), what can we learn from the biblical tradition about suicide?

Suicide is not recorded often in Scripture. In fact, the suicide of Judas is the only one documented in the NT, and there are no recorded incidents of those who considered or attempted suicide in the NT. In the OT, however, the record of suicides and the formation of thoughts[19] about suicide are more common. There are six recorded suicides in the OT: Abimelek (Judg 9:54); Samson (Judg 16:25–31); Saul and his armor-bearer (1 Sam 31:1–5); Ahithophel (2 Sam 17:23); and Zimri (1 Kgs 16:18). Interestingly, in most of these cases, where their bodies could be recovered they were then buried, usually with their ancestors. What is more remarkable is the number of ideations of suicide in the OT. It is a veritable who's who of the faith: Rebekah (Gen 27:46); Moses (Num 11:12–15); Elijah (1 Kgs 19:3–4); Job (Job 3:1–26); David (2 Sam 18:33; Ps 13:2–4); Jonah (Jonah 1:12; 4:3); and Jeremiah (Jer 15:10; 20:14–18).

This biblical evidence suggests at least several points for reflection and action. First, suicide, however tragic for the victim and devastating for their family and friends, is never regarded as an unpardonable sin. This is indicated by the respectful burials granted to those who took their own lives (i.e., Samson, Saul, Ahithophel). Suicide is clearly not part of God's creation intent for human flourishing and wholeness, but there is no suggestion that those who take their own lives are beyond the pale of God's grace or human grief.

---

18. According to the Centre for Suicide Prevention and Health Canada, the suicide rate for First Nations male youth (ages 15–24) is 126/100,000 people compared to 24/100,000 non-Aboriginal male youth. For First Nations females, the suicide rate is 35/100,000 compared to 5/100,000 for non-Aboriginal females. White men (ages 45–54) in Canada have a suicide rate of 28/100,000.

19. Clinicians refer to these thoughts and formation of ideas about suicide as "ideations."

Second, as the numerous ideations of suicide among our greatest patriarchs and prophets suggest, deep faith and commitment to God often go hand in hand with the struggle to will to live. Third, we do have resources to meet the risk of suicide. Prayer, the promises in Scripture, the sacraments, the fellowship of the community, and the empowering presence of the Spirit are all important for maintaining health and hopefulness in our individual lives, our families, and our churches. Yet even with all these resources, we may need additional professional medical and mental help. We must not shame those we know who need this help, and when necessary we must love ourselves enough to seek it. For those of us who minister to and respond to those in need, it is vital that we equip ourselves with the tools necessary to help us identify and assist those at risk of taking their own lives.[20]

Could Judas have been prevented from taking his own life? We will never know. We do know the shame and remorse he experienced were great enough to cause him to despair (see Matt 27:3–4). Yet we should also remember that *both* Judas *and* Peter betrayed Jesus. Unfortunately, Judas did not live long enough to know the end of the story—the story that Jesus's resurrection and love are greater than any betrayal of him. Judas did not have the same opportunity as Peter did to hear words of forgiveness and receive the offer of reconciliation. The difference between Judas and Peter was only a couple of days. In Judas's world there was just cause for despair, but he did not have anyone come alongside of him to help him see the broader picture. What might his life have been, next to his fellow apostle Peter, had he been able to endure just a few more days?

Suicide is a genuine peril even for the church, and it has been seen so since its earliest days. It is vital that we acknowledge that thoughts of suicide are *not* signs of insufficient faith or lack of devotion to God. Each life is precious—whether they be a Judas or a Peter—and any person's death diminishes us all. As the priest and poet John Donne so eloquently put it:

> No man is an island, entire of itself; every man is a piece of the continent, a part of the main. If a clod be washed away by the sea, Europe is the less, as well as if a promontory were, as well as if a manor of thy friend's or of thine own were: any man's death diminishes me, because I am involved in mankind, and therefore never send to know for whom the bells tolls; it tolls for thee.[21]

---

20. Clergy, in particular, have no excuse for ignoring the many excellent suicide-prevention courses available online or in our communities.

21. John Donne, "Meditation XVII," *The Literature Network*, http://www.online-literature.com/donne/409.

The Uncertainty of "In-Between"

Uncertainty, awkwardness, and powerlessness seem to mark the episode between Jesus's ascension (Acts 1:1–11) and the descent of the Spirit (Acts 2:1–11). The disciples, apparently still no better off than Israel of old, must resort to the ancient method of casting lots to choose a replacement for Judas. Furthermore, with the reminder of Judas's wicked betrayal of Jesus, dark undertones are intermingled with the joyful anticipation of the disciples in ways that are similar to the opening two chapters of Luke's Gospel. For example, Simeon's first oracle proclaiming salvation as "a light for revelation to the Gentiles, and the glory of your people Israel" is followed by a second oracle announcing that "this child is destined to cause the falling and rising of many in Israel. . . . And a sword will pierce your own soul too" (Luke 2:32, 34–35).

What follower of Jesus, either ancient or modern, has not faced ambiguities like this in their lives and in their service? I often thought as a young Christian that my mature years of discipleship would be characterized by confidence, gracefulness, and empowerment. Along a similar vein, Anne Lamott described matters this way: "It's funny: I always imagined when I was a kid that adults had some kind of inner toolbox, full of shiny tools: the saw of discernment, the hammer of wisdom, the sandpaper of patience. But when I grew up I found that life handed you these rusty bent old tools—friendship, prayer, conscience, honesty—and said, 'Do the best you can with these, they will have to do.' And mostly, against all odds, they're enough."[22]

In a similar way, the disciples relied on the "old tools" of Scripture and prayer as they faithfully waited together for the fulfillment of Jesus's promise on Pentecost. They could have despaired amid their situation. Jesus was gone, they still misunderstood his primary teaching about the kingdom and the future (see Acts 1:6–8), one of their own number had committed suicide, and—let's be honest—in the first hours and days after Jesus's arrest and crucifixion, the rest of "the Twelve" did not conduct themselves with bravery or boldness. So, they prayed together. They listened to Scripture together. They discerned the will of God together, using the rusty old tool of casting lots.

Casting a lot was very much like flipping a coin.[23] But even in the midst of their ambiguous and awkward situation, they would have remembered the promise in Proverbs: "The lot is cast into the lap, but its every decision is from the LORD" (16:33). Even the smallest things are fixed by God's plan. None of us know how to hold the categories of free choice and God's providence

---

22. Anne Lamott, *Traveling Mercies: Some Thoughts on Faith* (New York: Pantheon, 1999), 103.
23. Lots are always "thrown," "shaken," or "cast" in the Bible and were presumably specially marked objects such as pebbles, pottery pieces, or sticks.

together. Scripture, though, is not ambiguous. In the Bible we are told that we are absolutely free and absolutely determined at the same time. Just prior to the proverb on casting lots are these other two proverbs:

> Commit to the LORD whatever you do,
> and he will establish your plans. (Prov 16:3)

> In their hearts humans plan their course,
> but the LORD establishes their steps. (Prov 16:9)

The earliest disciples would have been familiar with these texts, and as they cast the lot for their twelfth apostle, they embraced both realities. On the one hand, our plans are our own. Our choices belong to us, and God does not force us one way or another. Whether we do something wicked or selfish or stupid, it means there will be bad consequences for which we will be held accountable. God will hold us accountable, both for what we do (v. 3) and what we plan (v. 9). But as for what happens as a result of those deeds and plans in history, the Scriptures tell us that those are absolutely fixed by God: the Lord "establishes" them. Nothing happens which is not according to God's plan. Our plans do indeed belong to us, but God establishes what actually happens. Both of these realities are true under the sovereignty of God.

The history of those trying to figure this out is one that bounces back and forth between these two positions: there are those who think *either* everything is determined by God *or* everything is determined by our own free choice. Intellectually, it is difficult to hold together the reality of free will and God's providence. But if we honestly live only in either one of these camps, we are in trouble. If you honestly believe that everything you do is determined and set, it will lead to boredom, cynicism, and passivity. If you honestly believe that your future is completely set by your own choices, you may not even get up in the morning because, from experience, we know that many of our choices are flawed, corrupt, or simply wrong. Many of the things we think we need, if we really got them, would likely distort or damage us. In contrast, the biblical perspective, which seems so odd and intellectually difficult, is very wise. The Bible does not say your choices have no connection to your destiny or that your choices alone determine your future. Scripture affirms that God, in his sovereignty, relates your choices partially to your destiny, but it is God who *establishes* your future. From this position, despite their awkward position between the ascension and Pentecost, the disciples could, in unity and in faith, listen to Scripture, commit their ways to God in prayer, and cast their lot. They relaxed, chose their candidates based on their own criteria (Acts 1:21–22), turned to an old method of decision making, and trusted God to establish their plans and steps.

CHAPTER 3

Acts 2:1-41

 LISTEN to the Story

¹When the day of Pentecost came, they were all together in one place. ²Suddenly a sound like the blowing of a violent wind came from heaven and filled the whole house where they were sitting. ³They saw what seemed to be tongues of fire that separated and came to rest on each of them. ⁴All of them were filled with the Holy Spirit and began to speak in other tongues as the Spirit enabled them.

⁵Now there were staying in Jerusalem God-fearing Jews from every nation under heaven. ⁶When they heard this sound, a crowd came together in bewilderment, because each one heard their own language being spoken. ⁷Utterly amazed, they asked: "Aren't all these who are speaking Galileans? ⁸Then how is it that each of us hears them in our native language? ⁹Parthians, Medes and Elamites; residents of Mesopotamia, Judea and Cappadocia, Pontus and Asia, ¹⁰Phrygia and Pamphylia, Egypt and the parts of Libya near Cyrene; visitors from Rome ¹¹(both Jews and converts to Judaism); Cretans and Arabs—we hear them declaring the wonders of God in our own tongues!" ¹²Amazed and perplexed, they asked one another, "What does this mean?"

¹³Some, however, made fun of them and said, "They have had too much wine."

¹⁴Then Peter stood up with the Eleven, raised his voice and addressed the crowd: "Fellow Jews and all of you who live in Jerusalem, let me explain this to you; listen carefully to what I say. ¹⁵These people are not drunk, as you suppose. It's only nine in the morning! ¹⁶No, this is what was spoken by the prophet Joel:

¹⁷"'In the last days, God says,
  I will pour out my Spirit on all people.
Your sons and daughters will prophesy,
  your young men will see visions,
  your old men will dream dreams.

>   ¹⁸Even on my servants, both men and women,
>   I will pour out my Spirit in those days,
>   and they will prophesy.
>   ¹⁹I will show wonders in the heavens above
>   and signs on the earth below,
>   blood and fire and billows of smoke.
>   ²⁰The sun will be turned to darkness
>   and the moon to blood
>   before the coming of the great and glorious day of the Lord.
>   ²¹And everyone who calls
>   on the name of the Lord will be saved.'[1]

²²"Fellow Israelites, listen to this: Jesus of Nazareth was a man accredited by God to you by miracles, wonders and signs, which God did among you through him, as you yourselves know. ²³This man was handed over to you by God's deliberate plan and foreknowledge; and you, with the help of wicked men, put him to death by nailing him to the cross. ²⁴But God raised him from the dead, freeing him from the agony of death, because it was impossible for death to keep its hold on him. ²⁵David said about him:

>   "'I saw the Lord always before me.
>   Because he is at my right hand,
>   I will not be shaken.
>   ²⁶Therefore my heart is glad and my tongue rejoices;
>   my body also will rest in hope,
>   ²⁷because you will not abandon me to the realm of the dead,
>   you will not let your holy one see decay.
>   ²⁸You have made known to me the paths of life;
>   you will fill me with joy in your presence.'[2]

²⁹"Fellow Israelites, I can tell you confidently that the patriarch David died and was buried, and his tomb is here to this day. ³⁰But he was a prophet and knew that God had promised him on oath that he would place one of his descendants on his throne. ³¹Seeing what was to come, he spoke of the resurrection of the Messiah, that he was not abandoned to the realm of the dead, nor did his body see decay. ³²God has raised this Jesus to life, and we are all witnesses of it. ³³Exalted to the right hand of God, he has received from the Father the promised Holy Spirit and has

---

1. Joel 2:28–32.
2. Ps 16:8–11 (see Septuagint).

poured out what you now see and hear. ³⁴For David did not ascend to heaven, and yet he said,

> "'The Lord said to my Lord:
> "Sit at my right hand
> ³⁵until I make your enemies
> a footstool for your feet."'³

³⁶"Therefore let all Israel be assured of this: God has made this Jesus, whom you crucified, both Lord and Messiah."

³⁷When the people heard this, they were cut to the heart and said to Peter and the other apostles, "Brothers, what shall we do?"

³⁸Peter replied, "Repent and be baptized, every one of you, in the name of Jesus Christ for the forgiveness of your sins. And you will receive the gift of the Holy Spirit. ³⁹The promise is for you and your children and for all who are far off—for all whom the Lord our God will call."

⁴⁰With many other words he warned them; and he pleaded with them, "Save yourselves from this corrupt generation." ⁴¹Those who accepted his message were baptized, and about three thousand were added to their number that day.

Listening to the Text in the Story: Exodus 20:5; 34:7; Leviticus 23:15–21; Isaiah 44:3; 56:3–8; 57:19; 65:23; Joel 2:28–32; Psalms 16:8–11; 110:1.

EXPLAIN the Story

The second chapters in Luke's two narratives parallel each other. In Luke 2 there is a Spirit conception and a Bethlehem birth. In Acts 2 there is a Spirit conception and a Jerusalem birth.⁴ While this is more obvious, a variety of other questions frequently interest modern readers when they approach Acts 2: What does it teach about the baptism in the Holy Spirit? Or what is the meaning and purpose of speaking in tongues? As important as these questions are, the first and fundamental question is: What does the Pentecost narrative mean for Luke and his understanding of the birth of the church? In this light, the questions of when and how an individual is saved or when one receives the Holy Spirit

---

3. Ps 110:1.
4. See Eugene H. Peterson, *Practice Resurrection: A Conversation on Growing Up in Christ* (Grand Rapids: Eerdmans, 2010), 24–25.

fade from view. For Luke, his primary interest rests with the coming of the Spirit and how this fulfills the "promise of the Father" (see Luke 24:49; Acts 1:4; 2:33, 39) at the dawn of the new age and the birth of the church. Without this fulfillment of Spirit baptism there is no power, no witness, no church.

The Pentecost narrative has four basic movements: the first describes the outpouring of the Holy Spirit upon the followers of Jesus (2:1–4); the second records the initial reaction of the crowds as surprise or scorn (vv. 5–13); the third recounts Peter's speech, which explains the behavior and invokes a response (vv. 14–36); and the fourth relates the second reaction of the crowds as repentance and reception (vv. 37–41). Embedded in each movement is a theological contribution.[5] In the first movement, the occasion of the outpouring of the Spirit is linked with the day of Pentecost, the feast of "firstfruits," which echoes Paul's understanding of the Spirit (Rom 8:23). In the second movement, the reversal of Babel (when "the LORD confused the language of the whole world" [Gen 11:9]) may be indicated by "every nation under heaven" hearing "their own language being spoken" (Acts 2:5–6). In the third movement, Peter explains the strange behavior in terms of the promise/fulfillment of Joel 2:28–32 and ties this to the death, resurrection, and exaltation of the Davidic Messiah, the Lord Jesus. In the fourth movement, the reaction of the crowd to Peter's sermon models the proper response to the gospel and prepares the foundation for the church's life together.

The Outpouring of the Spirit (2:1–4)

The opening movement (2:1–4) describes the outpouring of the Holy Spirit on the day of Pentecost. Pentecost, also known as the Festival (or Feast) of Weeks (see Lev 23:15–21; cf. Exod 34:22; Num 28:26–31; Deut 16:9–12), was the second of the three major pilgrim feasts, held fifty days after Passover. It was a feast to mark the firstfruits of the harvest. Both ancient Jewish sources[6] and early Christian writers[7] suggest that Pentecost points to a renewal of the covenant after the original Passover and deliverance of Israel from Egypt. Luke does not draw this connection explicitly, but his language does emphasize "fulfillment" even in verse 1. Literally, the opening clause states: "When the day of Pentecost was being *fulfilled.*" This identical language is also used one other time in Luke: "When the days were *fulfilled* for Jesus to be taken up to heaven" (Luke 9:51, my translation). With this use of language in both the Gospel and Acts, Luke indicates a new phase of ministry. In the case of the Gospel, after Luke 9:51 Jesus sets his face resolutely toward Jerusalem and his

---

5. As Dunn, *Acts*, 22, thoughtfully points out.
6. E.g., Jub. 6:17–19.
7. E.g., Augustine, *The Spirit and the Letter* 17.29.

approaching death, resurrection, and ascension to heaven; in the case of Acts, after 2:1 the early church embarks on a transformed ministry because of the empowerment of the Spirit.

Luke begins with "they were all together in one place" (2:1). It is difficult to know whom Luke intends by his word "all." Was it the 120 mentioned earlier (1:15) or merely just the Twelve as indicated later (2:14)? Most likely, Luke is referring to all 120 with the Twelve standing out from the rest later in the narrative. Another question arises from the reference "in one place." Is it the upper room or the temple? The word "house" (see 2:2) was a term that could mean the temple, but Luke does not use the word that way in his narratives. Nonetheless, a large space is implied in the descriptions provided in 2:14 and 41 where Peter addresses a "crowd" of at least three thousand people. Despite the ambiguity of the text, "all" of the believers find themselves outdoors and exposed to a large pilgrim crowd (2:5). Beverly Roberts Gaventa expresses the point of the narrative well by writing, "In some unexplained way, the walls of the house dissolve and the community finds itself outdoors and in the presence of Jews 'from every nation under heaven living in Jerusalem.'"[8] This may also suggest that the newly empowered mission of the church means dissolving doors—that is, it means going public with a courage and conviction previously unknown to the believers.

The empowering source of the believers for mission is the same empowering source of Jesus for mission: the Holy Spirit. Luke's second sentence describes the first phenomenon of the Spirit as audible: "A *sound* like the blowing of a violent wind" (v. 2). The mention of "wind" (*pnoē*) prepares the way for the mention of "Spirit" (*pneuma*) in the concluding sentence of this section (v. 4). After the initial audible phenomenon the next one is visible: "They *saw* what seemed to be tongues of fire" (v. 3). Both the audible sound of wind and the visible sight of fire alert us to the reality of the divine presence of God (see also Exod 3:2; 13:21–22; 19:18; 1 Kgs 19:11–12; Ps 104:4; Isa 66:15). But what is important is not simply *that* God is present in their midst, it is *where* the presence originates. The wind/Spirit and fire "came from heaven" (Acts 2:2). This, again, creates an intimate connection between the ascended Jesus and the descended Spirit. The ascended Christ is the catalyst for the descended Spirit.

For many, it is difficult to come to Acts 2 without vested interests of a personal or theological nature. Whatever our interests may be in reading Acts 2, Luke's interests never directly address questions of personal and individual Christian experience (for example, how is one saved? Or when does one receive

---

8. Beverly Roberts Gaventa, *The Acts of the Apostles* (Nashville: Abingdon, 2003), 74–75.

the Spirit?). Neither is he interested in outlining a theology of "baptism in the Holy Spirit" or the purpose of speaking in tongues. What *is* clear is that "all" who were gathered (v. 1) are "all" filled with the Holy Spirit. In unity, all those who were previously empty are now filled to overflowing so that which was promised (1:5) is now fulfilled. The Spirit unites (or *should unite*) God's people on earth with the reality of heaven. The Spirit's presence leads to a miracle of speaking (literally, "uttering")—or as the Venerable Bede expressed it, "The Holy Spirit appeared in fire and in tongues because all those whom he fills he makes simultaneously to burn and to speak."[9] First, all of them utter praise to God in different languages (v. 4), and later Peter utters proclamation of the word (v. 14). Luke nowhere reflects on the "gift of tongues" and how it operates in the community (as Paul does in 1 Cor 12–14). Rather, in each instance where "tongues" appears he refers to the initiation of people into the new age of the Spirit and their birth as Christians. People may be amazed by tongues (or ridicule it), yet it is not the miracle of tongues that brings individuals to repentance but rather the preaching of the word, anointed by the Holy Spirit.

The Reaction of the Crowd (2:5–13)

The wind and fire of the Spirit's presence blows the doors of the house open and ignites wonderment in Jerusalem in the second movement of the Pentecost narrative (2:5–13). Luke seems to have two purposes here: first, to prepare the ground for Peter's sermon, and, second, to establish the Jewish pilgrims both as a symbolic regathering of scattered exilic Israel and as a kind of anticipation for the "nations" later in Acts. Luke writes that "there were staying in Jerusalem God-fearing Jews from every nation under heaven" (2:5). By the first century, both Jewish (e.g., Philo, *Embassy* 281–82; Josephus, *Ant.* 14.115) and non-Jewish (e.g., Strabo, recorded in Josephus, *Ant.* 14.118) sources tell us that Jews had spread into every major city and island around the Mediterranean basin. Each year thousands of Jews from every point of the compass would come to Jerusalem on pilgrimage for the major feasts (i.e., Passover, Pentecost, and Tabernacles), drawn by the magnetic field of the temple. Some of these dispersed Jews would eventually settle in Jerusalem permanently for business or personal reasons (e.g., Greek-speaking Jews from places like Cyrene, Alexandria, Cilicia, and Asia; see Acts 6:9). It is unclear whether the "Jews from every nation under heaven"[10] are pilgrims or diaspora returnees (2:5). Perhaps they are both (see below on 2:14). Wherever they are from, they "came together in bewilderment, because each one heard their own

---

9. Bede, *Commentary on the Acts of the Apostles*, in *ACCA*, 22.
10. This phrase appears to be a deliberate rhetorical overstatement. The intent of the phrase meant something like "from almost everywhere."

language being spoken" (2:6). On this day there was no need for simulcast translation. This time the "translators" are not sophisticated linguists but, shockingly, simple folk from the hills of Galilee. For one brief moment in time, the language barriers created at Babel (Gen 11:1–9) were overcome. As the sixth-century Christian poet and orator Arator writes: "Long after the old ark had overcome the waters of the sea, malicious people wished to extend their tower [of Babel] into heaven. In them, irreligious hearts divided the forms of their speech. . . . Now there is one [language] for many since [that language] rejoices at the appearance of the coming church . . . and the humble order gathers again what arrogant people scattered."[11]

The catalogue of nations (Acts 2:8–11) that Luke describes initially appears random. It seems roughly to circle the Roman Empire, but not quite, and it oddly includes "Judeans" in the list almost as "resident aliens." Gaventa offers an interesting explanation for this sequencing if we think like a first-century Jew whose worldview fixes Jerusalem at the center of the cosmos (see Ezek 5:5; Jub. 8:19; 1 Enoch 26:1; Josephus, *J.W.* 5.212) with four compass points around it.[12] "The first group begins east of Jerusalem (Parthians, Medes, Elamites, Mesopotamians) and then moves back to Judea; the second group moves north from Jerusalem (Cappadocia, Pontus, Asia, Phrygia, and Pamphylia) and then back in the direction of Jerusalem; the third group moves west from Jerusalem to north Africa, Rome, and then again back to Jerusalem by means of Crete; and the fourth compass point is represented by the collective 'Arabs.'"[13] This helpful observation elegantly explains the puzzling inclusion of "Judeans" in the list.

The miracle of Pentecost, however, elicits a double response by the God-fearing Jews in Jerusalem. Initially, for all of them (the NIV omits "all" in v. 12) it evokes wonder and amazement from them, but soon after it leads some to scoff and mock. The latter sneer and even suggest that the Galileans have had too much "wine" (v. 13). Much like responses to Jesus's mighty deeds, miracles alone do not induce faith, for faith requires not only hearing but also careful explanation from the word of God. This varied response points the way forward to Peter's sermon.

Peter's Speech (2:14–36)

The mixed response prompted an explanation from Peter (2:14–36). This is the second time that Peter has "stood up" to speak (see 1:15), but this is

---

11. Arator, *On the Acts of the Apostles*, in *ACCA*, 26.
12. See also James M. Scott, *Geography in Early Judaism and Christianity: The Book of Jubilees* (Cambridge: Cambridge University Press, 2002).
13. Gaventa, *Acts*, 75.

the first time he does so to an unbelieving Jewish audience—and in this case with a remarkable boldness and authority. All told, this is an amazing turnaround from the Peter who could not stand up to the questions of a servant girl (Luke 22:56–57) on the night of Jesus's trial! The early church father Chrysostom remarked that this is "an indisputable proof of the resurrection. . . . For wherever the Holy Spirit is present, people of clay are changed into people of gold."[14] After formally addressing his "fellow Jews" (festival pilgrims?) and those "who live in Jerusalem" (diaspora returnees?), he first dismisses the sarcastic accusation of drunkenness with a comic reply: Come on, it is only nine[15] in the morning! The real explanation, however, revolves around three OT quotations—Joel 2:28–32; Psalm 16:8–11; and Psalm 110:1—which focus on two concerns and two themes. The two concerns are to explain the Pentecost miracle as evidence of "the last days" outpouring of the Spirit and to explain this incident in terms of the other recent events in Jerusalem connected to Jesus of Nazareth. The two themes revolve around the dynamic action of God and God's action realized through Jesus the Messiah.

Peter begins (2:14–21) with an explanation of Pentecost by quoting from the Greek translation of Joel 2:28–32.[16] But he does not simply quote the text; he *interprets* the text by making several slight, but significant, alterations to it so as to explain Pentecost in terms of God's fulfillment of his promises. He does so first by replacing Joel's "afterward" with "in the last days" (v. 17). This change connects the outpouring of the Spirit with the promises of God, the prophetic witness of believers, and the return of Jesus. Peter does not invent this connection—these are the same interconnected links that Jesus made earlier (see Acts 1:6–11).

The next slight alteration of the text in Joel is the addition of the words "God says" (2:17). This alerts us to our key theme of God's dynamic action in Pentecost—a theme that carries through the speech eight more times, where God is explicitly named as the prime mover (see vv. 22 [twice], 23, 24, 30, 32, 33, and 36). This reinforces another addition to the Joel passage (v. 18), the word "my" before "servants, both men and women" and the phrase "and they will prophesy." It is upon the obedient servants of God that the Spirit will be poured out so that they may speak God's prophetic words. All this is evidence that the old age of the quenched Spirit is over and the new age—the "last days"—has arrived. This echoes an even older yearning of Moses: "I wish that all the Lord's people were prophets and that the Lord would put his Spirit

---

14. Chrysostom, *Homilies on the Acts of the Apostles* 4, in *ACCA*, 28.
15. Literally, "the third hour of the day."
16. It is numbered 3:1–5 in the LXX.

on them!" (Num 11:29). This "equal-opportunity" outpouring of the Spirit upon "sons and daughters"/"both men and women" is a theme featured several times in Luke's narrative (see Acts 5:14; 8:3, 12; 9:2; 22:4). Allen Black makes the insightful conclusion that Luke was likely prompted by passages in Isaiah (e.g., Isa 43:6–7; 49:22; 60:4) where Israel is promised that her "sons and daughters" will be recipients of future divine blessings. So convinced is Luke that early Christianity is the fulfillment of these hopes that he underscores the male-female duality of early Christian circles.[17] The primary point of the Joel passage, with all of the alterations, is not only the explanation of Pentecost in terms of promise/fulfillment but also that "everyone who calls on the name of the Lord will be saved" (Acts 2:21).

The invitation of salvation in the Joel passage—the restorative inclusion into the people of God by the outpoured Spirit—leads to the second part of Peter's explanation with a presentation of Jesus of Nazareth (2:22–28). A remarkable theological turn is made in Peter's presentation of Jesus. Whereas in the Joel passage "the Lord" refers to God, in the context of Peter's message "the Lord" is Jesus (see 2:36). Peter's presentation of this "Jesus of Nazareth" begins by highlighting his life, death, and resurrection (vv. 22–24). Along with a later episode (10:36–39) these are the only places in Acts where Luke tells us anything about the pre-crucifixion ministry of Jesus. Luke's concern here is to demonstrate that Peter's audience all know about Jesus, and this knowledge implicates them in his death. By pointing out that Jesus was accredited by God by "miracles, *wonders* and *signs*" (2:22), the link is made between the evidence of the "last days" in the Joel passage just cited where God shows "wonders" in heaven and "signs" on earth. But ultimately the key concern about their knowledge of Jesus and their condemnation of Jesus to crucifixion with the help of "wicked men" (v. 23), the Romans, is that this is all part of God's plan. Peter now draws on a second biblical passage (Ps 16:8–11) to bring the second part of the sermon to a head, to demonstrate that Jesus of Nazareth's death was not only part of God's primary plan but also that his resurrection marks this descendant of David as someone completely different from his well-known forefather.[18]

Peter's speech now comes to a climactic third phase (Acts 2:29–36). The form of direct address, "brothers,"[19] marks the beginning of this final phase of

---

17. Allen Black, "'Your Sons and Your Daughters Will Prophesy': Pairings of Men and Women in Luke-Acts," in *Scripture and Traditions: Essays on Early Judaism and Christianity in Honor of Carl R. Holladay*, ed. Patrick Gray and Gail R. O'Day (Leiden: Brill, 2008), 193–206.

18. It should also be noted that "the Lord" in Ps 16:8, referring to the God of Israel, is again used to refer to Jesus.

19. The NIV deliberately changed this to "fellow Israelites" since women would have been present to hear Peter's address.

his message. The primary hope for a "messiah" among first-century Jews often focused on a Davidic or royal messiah. Therefore it is unsurprising that Peter begins by comparing the anointed[20] king David and the future messiah he prophesied about (Ps 16). He notes that both David and Jesus were subject to death, but, unlike David, the power of death could not keep its hold on Jesus. The power at work in this descendant of David frees him from the realm of death and decay. Peter points out that the promise expressed in the psalm not to be abandoned "to the realm of the dead . . . [and] decay" cannot apply to David because the patriarch is dead and buried. It can and does in fact only apply to a future messiah, the one whom God has "raised"—a point that Peter makes near the beginning (Acts 2:24) of his presentation of Jesus and now again at the end (v. 32). Jesus of Nazareth is the focus of this second part of his message, but God drives all the action. It is God who "accredited" Jesus (v. 22), who planned the course of his life and death (v. 23), and who raised him from the dead (vv. 24, 32).

God does not only resurrect Jesus and confirm his messianic identity; he exalts him to the honored right-hand and royal position in heaven. Resurrection leads to exaltation, which in turn leads to the outpoured Spirit from heaven (v. 33). We are now back to the "promise" declared at the beginning (vv. 14–21), but now with an understanding of the day of Pentecost linked closely to the person and work of Jesus. In this way, Luke connects the two parts of Jesus's ministry on earth (Luke) and in heaven (Acts). The final and climactic point is exaltation, and again Peter draws on the prophet David by quoting a third OT passage, this time from Psalm 110:1. This OT text was a favorite of early Christians and was used to express the elevated and royal status of Jesus (see, e.g., Mark 12:36; 1 Cor 15:25; Heb 1:13). Among other implications, the title "Lord" indicates royalty and sovereignty—which is the whole point of sitting on the honored, right-hand throne of God. Again, Peter notes that the passage cannot apply to David, who did not ascend to heaven and receive this honor. Rather, he applies it to Jesus, who did ascend to heaven and sits in the exalted position next to the Father.

With a climactic "therefore" (v. 36), Peter invites all the house of Israel to grasp the significance and status of Jesus in that God has made him both "Lord and Messiah." Humanity's action toward Jesus is crucifixion; God's action toward Jesus is exaltation. The resurrection of Jesus is not a necessary outcome of his life as if the movement of history alone could overcome death with life. Rather, Jesus's resurrection is an act of God, and this act is the basis of Christian mission. This is significant. C. Kavin Rowe writes:

---

20. The Hebrew word "to anoint" is *mashakh*, the verb behind the noun "Messiah."

The ultimate origin of the Christian mission lies in the act of God. That is why the Christian mission is a *novum*: it does not, it cannot arise naturally out of the mundane sphere—death is the final boundary of natural human life—but comes directly from the new life given by God to Jesus on the other side of death. The location of the origin of Christian mission according to Acts, that is, is beyond death, and in this way Christian mission exceeds dramatically all human possibilities of creation and initiation."[21]

This is, then, a remarkable conclusion by Peter, and one that picks up the key themes from the quotations taken from Joel (salvation in the name of the Lord) and the two Davidic psalms (the hope for a powerful and exalted messiah from David's line).

The Response (2:37–41)

The response described in the conclusion (2:37–41) is the closing action, the denouement, of the Pentecost narrative. Whatever else, the effect of the earliest proclamation of Jesus as "Lord and Messiah" was that many people were transformed and the number of followers increased dramatically. These final sentences have in the past received a large amount of attention from commentators in their efforts to discern a "pattern" or "order" of salvation: (1) preaching calls for (2) repentance, which is marked by a (3) baptism for forgiveness, and followed by the (4) reception of the Spirit. Many of us appreciate order and precision, but it is not at all clear whether there is such an apparent sequence for Luke, especially if we keep in mind the episode of John's baptism related in the Gospel (Luke 3:3–18). John's baptism is *not* a baptism for forgiveness, but a baptism of repentance for forgiveness,[22] and Jesus reminds the disciples that they will preach repentance in his name for the forgiveness of sins (24:47). The real clincher, however, is expressed in Luke's own narratives themselves. While Luke usually describes salvation narratives beginning with (1) forgiveness/repentance, sometimes (2) the gift of the Spirit is given next as the mark of the individual believer, followed by (3) baptism as recognition of incorporation into the community.[23] On other occasions, however, the latter two events are flipped in order.[24] At other times, the gift of the Spirit is not mentioned at all.[25] In no case is either forgiveness or the Spirit tied to baptism in Acts. The point then is that Peter's response to this query (Acts 2:38–39) is no more a prescriptive

---

21. C. Kavin Rowe, *World Upside Down: Reading Acts in the Graeco-Roman Age* (Oxford: Oxford University Press, 2009), 123.
22. Further, in Luke 3:7–14 repentance seems to *follow* baptism.
23. See Acts 9:17–18; 10:44.
24. E.g., Acts 2:38; 8:12, 16–17; 19:1–7.
25. E.g., Acts 8:35–36; 16:31–33; 18:8.

sequence of salvation than any other similar text in Acts. The primary point that Luke makes here is that the presence of the Spirit is the focus, not baptism.

The entire Pentecost narrative is carefully told by Luke in Acts 2:1–41. What Luke seems to be after is a faithful narrative of the event itself, not a formal transcript (there was no court reporter transcribing Peter's sermon, after all!). More than that, Luke illustrates that the whole future—"the last days"—has been set in motion by the gift of the Holy Spirit. The gift of the Spirit is the "promise" of the Father (v. 39), a theme that has run right through the narrative from the end of the Gospel (Luke 24:49), through Jesus's postresurrection appearances (Acts 1:5), and now culminates in the day of Pentecost (see 2:30, 33). As Peter's sermon suggests, the appropriate response to hearing about the mighty deeds, death, burial, resurrection, and exaltation of Jesus is faith, forgiveness, and repentance. The climactic mark of salvation is the gift of the Spirit. Peter states in verse 39 that this gift, using language that echoes OT Scripture (Exod 20:5; 34:7; Isa 44:3; 65:23), is available both to Israelites ("you and your children") and to gentiles ("for all who are far off"; see Isa 56:3–8; 57:19). He thus further develops the words from Joel where the Spirit is available for "all people" (Acts 2:17).

The episode ends by noting that Peter continued speaking to his audience "with many other words" (v. 40) and by describing the remarkable response that day to his message. It takes only three or four minutes to read Peter's message out loud. From this phrase at the end it appears that Peter continued with his preaching and pleading for some time. Part of his communication to his Jerusalem audience also included a measure of chiding, since the language of "save yourselves from this corrupt generation" echoes the words of Deuteronomy (32:5) and a psalm (78:8) that exhort Israel for its false and faithless dealings with God. The final element in the Pentecost narrative is an accounting of the three thousand converts who respond to Peter's message. As many as two-hundred thousand people may have populated Jerusalem for a major feast like Pentecost, according to Joachim Jeremias.[26] Ancient historians[27] had a tendency to "round up" their numbers, but even so we can be confident that there was a significant influx of believers into the emerging Christian community. Further, there was ample water, especially in the pools of Siloam and Bethesda, in Jerusalem for baptisms in recognition of their receiving God's "last days" promises to his people.

---

26. J. Jeremias, *Jerusalem in the Time of Jesus: An Investigation into Economic and Social Conditions during the New Testament Period* (London: SCM, 1969), 83.

27. An example of exaggerated numbers can be observed in the work of the Jewish historian Josephus; for example, he estimates the number of Jews under siege in Jerusalem by the Romans in AD 70 to be about six hundred thousand (*J.W.* 5.569).

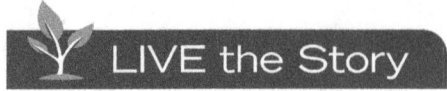
LIVE the Story

A Foretaste of the Future

The day of Pentecost, the birth of the church, flags up numerous points to reflect on and lean into. Timothy Keller helps sharpen our focus by suggesting three important realities from this pivotal narrative in the history of the world for the ongoing life of the church: a foretaste of the future, the personal presence of God, and a commission sending believers to the nations, including the Jewish people dispersed throughout the nations of the world.[28]

First, it is helpful to remember that the day of Pentecost was an important day in the Jewish calendar before it was an important day in the Christian calendar. Pentecost, as the name from the Greek word *pentēkostē* indicates, refers to the Feast of Pentecost held fifty days after the beginning of Passover to mark the firstfruits, the first taste, of the harvest. As a mark of the firstfruits, Pentecost is a foretaste of what is to come later when the harvest is complete. In Acts 2 the descent of the Spirit upon followers of the ascended Christ is a firstfruit; it is an indication of what is to come in final, future fullness. In this believers encounter the *eschaton*—the Greek word for "last," or future things. On the day of Pentecost, believers encounter this presence of the future, and the descent of the Spirit upon believers is a foretaste of that future. What God is announcing on this day is a foretaste, a guarantee of what is to come, and as such it reminds us that while everything on earth presently is subject to decay, one day everything will become glorious and liberated from the bondage of decay. Paul reflects this same kind of perspective when he writes to the Corinthians the encouraging words that God "anointed us, set his seal of ownership on us, and put his Spirit in our hearts as a deposit, guaranteeing what is to come" (2 Cor 1:21–22). The claim is that the Spirit of God fills every believer as the first installment, the deposit, of the glory of heaven. It is the promise of resurrection. It is a taste of the life, the power, and the joy of the future.

The Spirit's presence reminds us who we are and who we have in our life. The Spirit is a mark of the presence of the future, but it is so as the firstfruits. We have the firstfruit of heaven, the Spirit, who provides us with tremendous

---

28. Although I develop the details differently, I take these three key aspects in the passage from Timothy Keller's thoughtful sermon on Acts 2:1–13, "The Spirit of God," gospelinlife.com, 17 Sept. 1995, https://gospelinlife.com/?fwp_categories=sermons-talks&fwp_speaker=timothy-j-keller&fwp_bible=acts-2. I regard Keller as one of the finest "oral" commentators on living the story alongside the written commentaries by the likes of Loveday Alexander, C. K. Barrett, James Dunn, Beverly Gaventa, David Peterson, Eckhard Schnabel, and Tom Wright. Keller's sermons are available through the Redeemer Presbyterian Church website store (see http://www.gospelinlife.com).

resources for life and service in wisdom and gifts—but this is only the firstfruit. The Spirit reminds us that there is more to come, and what we currently experience is just the beginning. It is vital to remember the firstfruit dimension of all this. On the one hand, it instills a hope and power that guards against self-pity and small-mindedness; on the other hand, it imparts a humility and dependence that guards us from pride and triumphalism. The Spirit can work both ways because the Spirit gives us a foretaste of the future.

The Personal Presence of God

Second, the descent of the Spirit on the day of Pentecost points us to the personal presence of God. In Acts 2 we read of "wind" and "fire" (vv. 2–3). Wind and fire in Scripture indicate the presence of God. When God appears to Job, he speaks out of the storm wind (Job 38:1); when God appears to Abraham, he appears as a blazing torch passing between the animals (Gen 15:17); when God leads his people out of Egyptian bondage, he does so with a pillar of cloud by day and fire by night (Exod 13:21–22); when God spoke through Jeremiah, it was like a fire shut up in his bones (Jer 20:9); and when God appears on the day of Pentecost, the indicators of his presence are wind and fire. The followers of the ascended Christ receive the transcendent presence of God through the Spirit. The Spirit is God's *personal* presence; it is not divine fireworks.

But how does the Spirit come? To be filled with the Spirit of God is not to be filled with an intangible and impersonal power. Why? Because the Holy Spirit is a person, the third person of the Holy Trinity, and despite frequent use of the word "it" to refer to the Spirit, we must guard against mistakenly relating to the Spirit impersonally. Poet and priest Malcolm Guite offers insight on how we might think about and appropriate somewhat "impersonal" descriptors for the Spirit in a personal way. He notes that it is striking the way that

> Scripture expresses the presence of the Holy Spirit through the three most dynamic of the four elements, the air (a mighty rushing wind, but also the breath of the Spirit), water (the waters of baptism, the river of life, the fountain springing up to eternal life promised by Jesus) and of course fire, the tongues of flame at Pentecost. Three out of four ain't bad, but I was wondering, where is the fourth? Where is earth? And then I realised that we ourselves are earth, the "Adam" made of the red clay, and we become living beings, fully alive, when the Holy Spirit, clothed in the three other elements, comes upon us and becomes a part of who we are.[29]

---

29. Malcolm Guite, "A Pentecost Sonnet," *Malcolm Guite*, 12 June 2011, http://malcolmguite.wordpress.com/2011/06/12/a-pentecost-sonnet/.

When the Spirit is poured out upon earth, those who are formed from the dust of the earth find their tongues loosed in the personal language of love. Speech, conversation, and listening are all *personal* interactions. Yet the disciples do not dwell on personal feelings or ecstatic experiences; rather, when believers are filled with the Spirit they declare "the wonders of God" (Acts 2:11) and speak "the word of God" (4:31). The words that come from Peter's mouth in his sermon following the descent of the Spirit declare that the crucified, risen, and ascended Jesus is both Lord and Messiah (2:36). The presence of the Lord, the filling of the Spirit, points to Jesus and declares his lordship and his royalty; the personal presence of the Lord at work in our lives is not intended just to make us feel good. The Spirit brings believers into personal relationship with the King of heaven, in whom we see all the goodness of God, and then the Spirit leads people to declare the wonders of God to others.

Sent to the Nations

Third, the descent of the Spirit on the day of Pentecost sends believers to the nations because the Spirit draws people from the four points of the compass. The last time we heard about the table of the nations was at the Tower of Babel when the people of the earth decided to be their own masters and "make for ourselves a name" (Gen 11:4). The result of their pride and folly was their confusion of "tongues." God came down on the Tower of Babel to interrupt their personal relationships by confusing their language. This is a way of showing humanity that when we usurp God's authority and establish ourselves as autonomous lords, kings, and queens on earth, the result is ethnic hostility and destruction of human community. When the Spirit descends on Pentecost, the first worship service is conducted in the language of *all* nations. "Today the gospel crosses every border/All tongues are loosened by the Prince of Peace/Today the lost are found in His translation/Whose mother-tongue is Love, in every nation."[30] When God comes down by his Spirit, the effects of racial and cultural superiority are leveled and ethnic boundaries are removed. The way we know that the Spirit has filled a person and a community is not that they have a new experience but that they have a new identity that leads them to a new attitude toward others. The "other" is no longer a person who has a different language, a different nationality, a different ethnicity; the other is my brother and my sister.[31]

---

30. Malcolm Guite, "Pentecost," in *Sounding the Seasons: Seventy Sonnets for the Christian Year* (Norwich: Canterbury, 2012), 47.

31. For a fulsome treatment of what this kind of gospel-shaped living looks like in the harsh realities of embracing the "other" who has wounded us, see the challenging but important book by Miroslav Volf, *Exclusion and Embrace: A Theological Exploration of Identity, Otherness, and Reconciliation* (Nashville: Abingdon, 1996). See also Volf's more recent book, *Free of Charge: Giving and Forgiving in a Culture Stripped of Grace* (Grand Rapids: Zondervan, 2006).

Further, we know the Spirit is present when we see believers sent out into the world to engage others with whom they would never have anything to do before.

For a number of years prior to our marriage, my wife served with a Christian mission organization called Operation Mobilization (OM) in India and Pakistan. The priority of OM from its inception was to bring the gospel to the world's most unreached people groups—a work they continue to do with thoughtful verve. In particular, they work amidst some very difficult places. While many people in the West think first about political turmoil and increasing persecution in countries that end with the syllable "stan," there are signs of hope even in these hard-to-reach places. Due to the courageous and sacrificial work of Spirit-empowered Christians working in one especially difficult and dangerous Muslim majority country, OM attests that they "have reliable reports that there are now more [formerly Muslim] believers meeting in more house churches than ever before!"[32] This kind of mission is possible only because of Pentecost and because followers of Jesus are filled with the Spirit, who gives them a taste of the future so that they can live and enact it now. Because the Spirit is personally at work in their lives, these OM workers are propelled in courageous and selfless mission to the nations—whether they are across Main Street or across the Muslim world.

The day of Pentecost and Peter's dramatic Jerusalem address are powerful events. They are generative and transformative. It can be tempting to want to replicate either the experience of Pentecost or the effect of Peter's preaching (i.e., three thousand people "added to their number" in one day). While all of us should be expectant to what the Spirit might do in our lives and preachers should seek to be effective in their proclamation of the gospel, it is important that we not try to seize the initiative in these things. On the day of Pentecost, God, as always, seized the initiative by sending the Spirit; God had—and continues to have—the first and the final word. All too often, Christians, especially Christian leaders, can focus on easily definable results: How large or beautiful is the building? How robust is the budget? How many bodies are in attendance? Yet this focus on buildings, budgets, and bodies can misunderstand and misrepresent reality and take *what we are doing* as the starting point. Peter didn't do that, and neither should we. He pointed out *what God was doing* and *what God had said*. This is important. It shifts the priority from us and aims it where it should be, on God. Now the questions can become more like these: What is God doing with these people? What has the gospel of Jesus set in motion? How can we come alongside and participate with what the Spirit is already doing?

---

32. "Stories from the Silk Road," *On the Silk Road* 8 (2014–2015): 3.

Speaking in Other Tongues—a Theological and Ecclesiological Footnote

I was raised in a Pentecostal denomination in Canada that traces its roots to the early twentieth-century revivals of the Azuza Street Mission in Los Angeles, California. My memories growing up in the church are fond ones. I heard dynamic preaching that often circled back to the book of Acts. Why? Because Acts was the manual, the primary Christian text that reminded us that the Holy Spirit was not only a doctrine to be believed but an empowering presence to be encountered. The experience that was taught and sought was that followers of Jesus *needed* to live the Spiritual (capital "S"!) realities of the apostolic age, including the joyful experience of speaking in other tongues. When I became an adult, I never doubted the importance of this kind of Spiritual experience. I did, however, recognize that there was an intellectual depth and historical breadth that was lacking in my life and which I couldn't find in the tradition I was raised in. I needed theological balance. One does not need to go to graduate school to find this, but I did. It came as a surprise (to me!) that when I arrived at Regent College in 1991, two of the most thoughtful and rigorous biblical scholars I met were *both* Pentecostal. As our friendship developed over the years, I came to realize that neither of them believed that one needed to choose between loving God with the mind and loving God with the heart. One of those scholars tells a memorable story from when he was about to enter graduate school to study the New Testament. Upon hearing his intentions, a fellow Pentecostal confronted him with the potential dangers of graduate-level theological education for his faith. His fellow Pentecostal commented, "I would rather be a fool on fire than a scholar on ice." With that, he committed himself "to be a scholar on fire."[33] What a perfect answer.

As my own vocational journey progressed over the years, I was called to be an ordained priest in the Anglican Church of Canada. I was drawn to the Anglican tradition for many reasons, not least of all because in it I discovered a theological rigor to it. Many of my Pentecostal friends understood why I might be attracted to the tradition that brought us the King James Version Bible along with great ancient and modern theologians like John Donne, J. B. Lightfoot, C. S. Lewis, Rowan Williams, and N. T. Wright. Still, many of them also thought I was leaving behind the robust life of the Holy Spirit in my change to an intellectually robust tradition. Little do many of them know that the experienced life of the Holy Spirit—including speaking in tongues—was what I found in every Anglican bishop I've served under both in England and

---

33. Gordon D. Fee, "Scholar on Fire," in *I (Still) Believe: Leading Scholars Share Their Stories of Faith and Scholarship*, ed. John Byron and Joel N. Lohr (Grand Rapids: Zondervan, 2015), 74.

in Canada. In addition, some of the most fruitful "charismatic" ministries like *Alpha* and *New Wine Ministries* are rooted in the Anglican communion.

The reason for telling these personal stories is twofold. First, it illustrates a theological point that is evident in the narrative of Acts as it relates, narrowly, to the phenomena of speaking in tongues and, broadly, to the life of the Spirit. That is, the experienced life of the Spirit has *both* ecstatic *and* cogitative dimensions to it. Jack Levison has demonstrated this thoughtfully in his studies on the Holy Spirit and the mind of faith. He makes the important observation that in three key junctures in Acts—at the birth of the church (Acts 2:4), the "gentile Pentecost" (10:44–46), and the completion of John's baptism in Ephesus (19:3–6)—there is a clear connection made between speaking in tongues and intelligible speech. "Ecstasy and comprehension fuse in the fiery experience of Pentecost."[34]

In the first instance of speaking in tongues in Acts, the earliest followers of Jesus "began to speak in *other* tongues" (2:4). That is, they spoke in discernible dialects[35] that were understood by those visiting Jerusalem from around the empire. The form of their speech was ecstatic, but what they spoke was understandable. Further, their "tongues" were not only intelligible, but their words declared "the wonders of God"—the powerful acts of the Lord in Israel's history—in those different languages. Finally, the verb that Luke uses to describe the believers' speech is "enabled" (*apophthengesthai*, v. 4). This verb is used only three times in the entire NT, all in the book of Acts (see also 2:14, translated by the NIV as "addressed," and 26:25, translated as "saying"). As Levison notes, Luke uses this word when he wants to express clear, intelligible, and lucid speech.[36] When he wants to emphasize that the believers are not drunk, or that Peter is an able interpreter, or that Paul is not insane, this verb is used. The linkage between ecstasy and comprehension is also made in the other two times when Luke describes accounts where believers speak in tongues.[37] The theological point of this is not to downplay the ecstatic experience of tongues but to illustrate that vibrant, unexpected experiences of the Holy Spirit are connected to intelligible and content-laden speech.

---

34. Jack Levison, *Inspired: The Holy Spirit and the Mind of Faith* (Grand Rapids: Eerdmans, 2013), 91; cf. 91–97. See also Jack Levison, *Fresh Air: The Holy Spirit for an Inspired Life* (Brewster: Paraclete, 2012), ch. 8.

35. This is what the word "other" suggests.

36. Levison, *Inspired*, 95.

37. In the "gentile Pentecost" in Cornelius's home, new gentile believers speak in tongues, "praising God" (Acts 10:46). In the third and final instance of speaking in tongues in Acts when Paul meets up with a band of disciples who have not heard of the Holy Spirit, after Paul lays his hands on them "they spoke in tongues and prophesied" (19:6). Both praise and prophecy in Acts are understandable manners of speech.

The life of the Spirit is bonded to the life of the mind, despite the fact that some traditions in the church have tried to drive a wedge between them:

> It is a pity that interpreters tend to line up on one side of the debate or the other, according to whether they understand speaking in tongues *either* as speech in comprehensible foreign dialects *or* as incomprehensible speech. What Luke does is more subtle than to opt for *either* ecstatic tongues speech *or* comprehensible foreign languages. The power of Pentecost may lie, in Luke's estimation, not in either incomprehensibility or apprehension, but in the early believers' ability to straddle both worlds. The holy spirit combines both in the alchemy of inspiration in order to create one magnificent experience.[38]

Second, my personal story is congruent with a broader ecclesiological note that is sounded in the narrative of Acts. In the apostolic age, despite its many challenges, the church was broad enough to hold together both the empowering presence of the Holy Spirit in ecstatic experience and the Holy Spirit's inspiration for rigorous theology and teaching. Sadly, as the history of the church unfolded, the church became divided on a number of issues. With the rise of global Pentecostalism—often in response to the rigidity and aridness of traditional churches—there is often an implicit priority given to *either* fresh experiences of the Spirit *or* careful intellectual reflection on Scripture and theology. Further, like me, many people who grew up with evangelical, Pentecostal expressions of worship have begun to be drawn to more sacramental emphases in corporate worship. Why not hold all these different strands together in the spirit of my friend who wanted to be "a scholar on fire"?

Gordon Smith, in his groundbreaking book *Evangelical, Sacramental, and Pentecostal: Why the Church Should Be All Three*, argues these three dominant strands in the church today need each other.[39] By *evangelical*, Smith has in mind those churches that place a priority on Scripture. By *sacramental*, Smith refers to those churches that focus on the sacraments of baptism and the Eucharist. By *Pentecostal*, Smith is attending to those churches that desire an immediate and experienced presence of the Spirit akin to the apostolic age. In his book, he does not so much suggest that each of these strands can learn something from the other but that they need each other if the church—as the "one, holy, and apostolic" body of Christ—is going to survive and thrive in the modern world.

---

38. Levison, *Inspired*, 97.
39. Gordon T. Smith, *Evangelical, Sacramental, and Pentecostal: Why the Church Should Be All Three* (Downers Grove, IL: InterVarsity Press, 2017).

Smith surveys the territory in Luke-Acts to demonstrate that the early church expressed all three of these strands and wove them together in one unified garment.[40] As we will notice in the next section (Acts 2:42–47), the early church was a community whose life together was marked by word ("the apostles' teaching"), sacraments ("the breaking of bread"), and the Spirit ("wonders and signs"). There was not an optional "opt out" of Spirit, sacrament, or word in the early church. All three strands were essential for its common life.

In his review of Smith's book for *Christianity Today*, Michael Bird agrees with Smith's thesis—and I would also add, it is Luke's too—that it is essential for the church today to maintain our existence. Each strand, like the main arteries to the heart, is vital if we are going to stay alive and beat strong. Bird writes:

> Without the Word, we will have an atrophied mind that is easily dragged away by the latest winds of false teaching and is vulnerable to forms of faith that are superficial and shallow. Without the sacraments, we will forget the joy of new birth that baptism declares, while remaining hungry for the fellowship and nourishment that only the Lord's Table can provide. Without the Spirit, we will be left with the scraps of man-made religion and struggle to be faithful by our own meager strength.[41]

It is a mistake to think that any one strand of the church can survive without the other. The day of Pentecost reminds us that the Spirit works in tandem with God's word and sacraments. It is easy to imagine that the tradition we belong to has the corner on truth. In fact, some Christians think "tradition" is an empty vessel altogether. Yet, as we listen to the ancient voice of Luke's narrative and the contemporary reminders by writers like Smith, we may come to recognize that our three-part Christian "tradition" begun on the day of Pentecost is a living reality.

The Austrian composer Gustav Mahler is attributed with saying, "Tradition is not to preserve the ashes but to pass on the fire." Whether or not he said this, this statement resonates with the relevance of the book of Acts and the church's effort to live that story today. We are not called to repeat the past—God is infinitely more creative than to allow that—but in unified witness to a world that is increasingly fragmented, we need the genius that is the "three-part harmony" of the church:

---

40. Ibid., ch. 2.
41. Michael Bird, "The Church's Three-Part Harmony: Why Evangelical, Sacramental, and Pentecostal Christians Belong in One Body," *Christianity Today* (April 2017): 69.

The church is a community that lives with the same immediacy of the Spirit as that witnessed to in the experience of Jesus and the early church; the church is a community of the Word, devoted to the apostolic teaching; and the church is a community of the Table, the gathering of the baptized, who, when they gather, "break bread" together.[42]

---

42. Smith, *Evangelical, Sacramental, and Pentecostal*, 35.

CHAPTER 4

Acts 2:42-47

LISTEN to the Story

⁴²They devoted themselves to the apostles' teaching and to fellowship, to the breaking of bread and to prayer. ⁴³Everyone was filled with awe at the many wonders and signs performed by the apostles. ⁴⁴All the believers were together and had everything in common. ⁴⁵They sold property and possessions to give to anyone who had need. ⁴⁶Every day they continued to meet together in the temple courts. They broke bread in their homes and ate together with glad and sincere hearts, ⁴⁷praising God and enjoying the favor of all the people. And the Lord added to their number daily those who were being saved.

Listening to the Text in the Story: Luke 22:19; 24:30–31; Acts 4:32–35; 5:12–16; 2 Corinthians 13:14; Philippians 2:1.

EXPLAIN the Story

Luke regularly pauses to summarize key points of his story. This passage is the first one of these summary statements, with two similar ones (4:32–35; 5:12–16) to follow in the first panel (1:1–6:7) of Acts. This first summary provides a cameo of the early community of believers after the day of Pentecost. But these summaries, particularly this first one, are not only looking back but are preparing for what will follow in the narrative.[1] In the present case, these verses offer a bridge between the birth of the church (Acts 2) and its early days of ongoing life in Jerusalem (Acts 3–5). The opening sentence describes four broad elements, grouped in two pairs, which characterized a Christian gathering in the early church and what the early believers devoted themselves

---

1. E.g., 2:46 mentions that the early community met every day in the temple courts; this interaction in the temple is a primary concern of chs. 3–6.

to: (1) the apostles' teaching and (2) fellowship; (3) the breaking of bread and (4) prayer. The next four verses fill out these four lines of devotion (2:43–47).

The opening sentence (v. 42), which serves as something of a summary, outlines the significant features of the Christian life in the early church to which they "devoted" themselves. The word translated as "devoted," *proskarterountes*, is an important word in Acts.[2] Besides its occurrence here (v. 42), it also appears in 1:14; 2:46; 6:4; 8:13; 10:7. It means "to be devoted to," "to hold fast to," "to continue in," or "to persevere in" something. The point is that the four nouns that follow this verb are not just marginal activities but the primary signs of life in the early church.

The Apostles' Teaching (2:42a)

The first feature is "teaching," but not just any teaching; it is the teaching of the apostles. Does this refer to a body of apostolic teaching (i.e., the content of the apostles' doctrine) or to the fact of their teaching (i.e., the activity of learning from the apostles)? It is most likely the latter, and as we see in the following chapters, the teaching of the apostles is not confined to believers.[3] But apostolic "doctrine" is not incidental either. The apostles were trained and taught by Jesus, and he authorized them to convey the truth about him. As for the believers' devotion to their teaching, the great British scholar C. K. Barrett states it well: "The steady persistence in the apostles' teaching means (a) that the Christians listened to the apostles whenever they taught and (b) that they assiduously practiced what they heard."[4] Samples of this teaching[5] to fellow Jews bracket this verse in Peter's address on the day of Pentecost (2:14–36) and immediately following in the next episode (3:12–26). Further confirmations that apostolic teaching continues to be at the center of the church's life when it will later engage with gentiles are scattered throughout Acts (e.g., 11:25–26; 18:11; 19:9–10; 20:7–12, 20–21, 28–32; 28:30–31). The apostles' teaching was not only based on what Jesus communicated to them personally, but it also follows the model of Jesus's teaching that turns to the Scriptures to discover what "Moses and all the Prophets" say about Christ (see Luke 24:27).

---

2. Outside of its six occurrences in Acts, this word occurs only four times in the rest of the NT (Mark 3:9; Rom 12:12; 13:6; Col 4:2).

3. E.g., the address to the people in 3:12–26 is described as "teaching the people" (4:2), which is further elaborated there as "proclaiming in Jesus the resurrection of the dead." In 4:18 the apostles are ordered not to teach in "the name of Jesus"; in 5:20–21 an angel instructs the apostles to tell the people about this new life, and they began "to teach"; in 5:42 we are told that every day in the temple courts and from house to house they never stopped teaching and preaching.

4. C. K. Barrett, *Acts*, 2 vols., ICC (London: T&T Clark, 1994, 1998), 1:163.

5. Preaching and teaching cannot be sharply distinguished from one another in Acts. Part of the problem is that these gerunds serve as both content and activity. For example, the word "teaching" occurs in Acts 5:28, but it is clearly public proclamation (see also 13:12 and 17:19).

For later generations, the written deposit of the apostles' teaching forms what we know as the NT. Although the recognition of the documents that would constitute the NT canon occurs decades later, here we begin to see how the church's "rule of faith"—established upon the teaching of the apostles—would grow out of this. As the early church "devoted" itself to the apostles' teaching, it is not surprising that the documents that would become authoritative for the church must align and reflect their instruction.

Fellowship (2:42b)

Second, the early Christians devoted themselves "to fellowship." This is the only occurrence in Acts of one of the few Greek words that many contemporary Christians know: *koinōnia*. This "fellowship" refers to the community formed by their shared experience of the Spirit since the day of Pentecost.[6] By all counts, this fellowship was diverse and inclusive. That is, the Spirit formed communities initially from Jews of a variety of cultural, ethnic, social, and linguistic backgrounds (see 2:9–11), and this diversity would continue when the gospel was introduced into gentile contexts. From the very beginning this Spirit-based fellowship is, in the words of Paul, inclusive of all people whether they are "Jews or Gentiles, slave or free" (1 Cor 12:13). What is obviously portrayed is a fellowship of love and generosity (see v. 44 below for the manifestations of this "fellowship" in the early church).

Breaking Bread (2:42c)

Third, the early Christians devoted themselves "to the breaking of bread." Scholars are divided on whether this "breaking bread" refers simply to sharing meals together[7] or whether it refers to the Lord's Supper.[8] Most likely it refers to the Lord's Supper, which is supported by the fact that in a few sentences later (2:46) Luke seems to distinguish between breaking bread and sharing food (although they probably both happened together). Furthermore, the present sentence (2:42) seems to have two pairings: "apostles' teaching and to fellowship" followed by "breaking of bread and to prayer." In this regard, "breaking bread" belongs to the liturgical life of the community and

---

6. Paul also connects "fellowship" with the experience of the Spirit (e.g., 2 Cor 13:14 [Gk: 13:13]; Phil 2:1).

7. E.g., both Ernst Haenchen, *The Acts of the Apostles: A Commentary* (Philadelphia: Westminster, 1971), 584, and Peterson, *Acts*, 161, view this as simple meal sharing.

8. John Calvin, *Commentary upon the Acts of the Apostles*, ed. Henry Beveridge, 2 vols. (Grand Rapids, Baker, 1998); the Christian Classics Ethereal Library, http://www.ccel.org/ccel/calvin/calcom36.ix.viii.html; Joachim Jeremias, *The Eucharistic Words of Jesus*, trans. Norman Perrin (London: SCM, 1974), 120–21; Barrett, *Acts*, 1.165; Joseph A. Fitzmyer, *The Acts of the Apostles: A New Translation with Introduction and Commentary*, AB 31 (New York: Doubleday, 1998), 271; and Keener, *Acts*, 1.1003–4, all view this as referring to the Lord's Supper.

not having "everything in common" (2:44). The final thread of support in favor of this referring to the Lord's Table is the much later evidence in 20:7 where "break[ing] bread" can only refer to the Lord's Table, which at that time apparently occurred weekly and on a Sunday. In the end, if one takes seriously that Acts is Luke's second volume and is meant to be read in connection with volume one (the Gospel of Luke), it is appropriate to connect "the breaking of bread" back to the meal Jesus shared with his followers in the upper room in Luke 22:19. It is in the "breaking of bread" that the eyes of people are opened to recognize Jesus (see Luke 24:30–31). In this sense, whenever bread is broken and shared with other believers, it is always done "in remembrance of [Jesus]" (22:19) and is a significant act that actually connects people in fellowship.

The Prayers (2:42d)

Fourth, the early Christians devoted themselves "to the prayers." The NIV, as do all English versions, translates this in the singular (that is, "to prayer"), but it is plural ("to the prayers") in Greek.[9] It seems that Luke is referring to regular times of prayer. Devout Jews kept set times of prayer,[10] as did the apostles (e.g., see 3:1). In the keeping of traditional Jewish set times of prayer, we see one of many examples of how early believers retained connections to their Jewish contexts.[11] But beyond set times, prayer is an important part of communal life whenever believers gather together, whether it be in small groups meeting for meals in households (2:46), in larger gatherings (4:31), or as a feature of the apostles' leadership in the community (6:4).

Life Together (2:43–47)

The next sentence of this paragraph (v. 43) illustrates the amazement, apparently among outsiders,[12] associated with the apostles' ministry as they per-

---

9. Here is a clear place where translations are doing their best to accommodate meaning and an economy of words. In this place, if the NIV translators had given us "prayers," it would have required them to add explanatory words not in the Greek text—instead, they left this to commentators. Furthermore, to render the word as "the prayers" would confuse most ordinary readers as to whether it referred to an activity or to people.

10. Devout Jews prayed three times a day following the prescribed pattern for sacrifices in Exod 29:38–41: early in the morning, at the time of the morning sacrifice; at the ninth hour when the evening sacrifice was offered; and at sunset. See also Dan 6:10; Josephus, *Ant.* 14.65.

11. E.g., even though they knew that Jesus replaced the temple in the purpose of God (see Matt 12:6; John 2:19–22; 4:21–24), the early Jewish disciples did not disengage themselves from worship and prayer in the temple. Until the Holy Spirit explicitly directed them toward a gentile mission, they also maintained their kosher food laws too (see Acts 10). Even in terms of places of worship for the early Christian church, Louis Bouyer demonstrates how the Christian house of God comes into being in significant continuity with Jewish synagogues. See Louis Bouyer, *Liturgy and Architecture* (Notre Dame: University of Notre Dame Press, 1967).

12. Since vv. 44–47 is limited to believers only.

form "wonders and signs." Many specific wonders and signs carried out by the apostles will be depicted in Acts, including the very next scene when a crippled man is healed near the temple gate called Beautiful (3:1–10). But more than this, the signs and wonders—just as much as the apostles' teaching—are connected to Jesus. The words of Joel that Peter quotes in his first sermon declared that "in the last days" God would pour out his Spirit and attest these days with "*wonders* in the heavens above and *signs* on the earth below" (2:19). Peter then adds that "wonders and signs" confirmed Jesus's work of heralding the kingdom (2:22), and in a similar way Jesus's apostles' work is also authenticated by "wonders and signs" (2:43).

The rest of this passage (vv. 44–47) is then devoted to the believers and the activities of their life together. Twice Luke states specifically what this fellowship in 2:44, and later in 4:32, entails; he writes that the believers "had everything in common." He will elaborate on the abbreviated version of 2:44–45 of what this means in the second summary in 4:32–35. The key is that they gave "to anyone who had need" (4:35). Other Jewish groups in the first century—like the community at Qumran (see Josephus, *J.W.* 2.122)—held their possessions in common as a *requirement* of communal life.[13] In contrast, the Spirit-shaped Christian community chose *voluntarily* to sell property and possessions to meet the needs of their members. Their tangible expressions of fellowship were motivated by love and concern for one another. Not all is perfect in this regard, of course, as the Ananias and Sapphira episode illustrates (see Acts 5:1–11). But overall, this community cared for one another and, apparently, experienced joy in one another's company.

One of the sure signs of friendship in the ancient world, as well as in ours, is sharing a meal together. While the earlier use of the phrase "breaking of bread" (2:42) points to sharing the Lord's Supper together, here (v. 46), as it does elsewhere in Acts (e.g., 20:11; 27:35), it simply means eating a meal together. The early church ate together in their homes often and with glad hearts. This "open table" was a characteristic of Jesus's practices, and his disciples carried it on. In most cultures, table fellowship tends to be class defined (e.g., the upstairs and downstairs cultures of *Downton Abbey*), something the apostle Paul will condemn in Corinth (1 Cor 11:17–34). In contrast, Jesus practiced a radically inclusive and socially open table fellowship as one of his central strategies for announcing and redefining the in-breaking kingdom of God.[14]

---

13. It is notable that neither in the ancient Greek nor Roman world was caring for the poor a priority as it was for ancient Israel and early Judaism. The followers of Jesus simply carried on this well-established practice. See Bruce W. Longenecker, *Remember the Poor: Paul, Poverty, and the Greco-Roman World* (Grand Rapids: Eerdmans, 2010).

14. See S. S. Bartchy, "Table Fellowship," *DJG* 796–800.

It is not surprising that table fellowship receives special attention in Acts as it builds on the Gospel of Luke, a document that pays more attention to Jesus's table etiquette, table fellowship, and the households where they occurred than any other book in the NT.[15]

Verse 47 provides the last feature of the early community: they were a people of praise. Although the previous phrase (v. 46) already hints at this by noting that the disciples met daily in the temple—a place set aside for prayer and worship—this phrase (v. 47) describes a fundamental quality of God's people. God's people express their prayer in praise.

All together, these characteristics—apostolic teaching, fellowship, breaking bread, and prayer/praise—help to account for the winsomeness of the early Christian church. Apparently, these qualities appealed to their contemporaries, and they received favor from them. A clear indication of this favor was that others wanted to get in on the signs of life that these believers were experiencing. Echoing the words of the passage from Joel quoted by Peter (2:21), this bridge section concludes by noting that "the Lord added to their number daily those who were being saved."

All in all, this summary or bridge section performs several functions in the early portion of the narrative in Acts. First, it roots the ministry of the apostles in the ministry of Jesus. Mighty words ("teaching") and mighty deeds ("wonders and signs"; v. 22) characterized Jesus's Spirit-led ministry. In a similar way, the apostles follow Jesus with powerful teaching (v. 42) and wonders and signs (v. 43). Secondly, it provides a general description of the character of the community shaped by the Holy Spirit. The first and only mention of "fellowship" (*koinōnia*) in Acts occurs in verse 42. As Luke's traveling companion, the apostle Paul would also articulate in his letters (see 2 Cor 13:14) that one of the primary characteristics of God's newly constituted people is Spirit-shaped "fellowship" or "participation" with other believers. The experience of the Spirit does not only bring individuals into intimate and abiding relationship with God, it brings individuals into intimate and abiding relationship with the people of God. The text mentions two simple and profound expressions of this intimacy: caring for those in need (v. 45) and joyfully sharing meals together (v. 46). Finally, the summary positively highlights how this community was initially embedded within the life and structure of Judaism. This community was not a threat to the temple, the primary institution of Judaism, and in fact its adherents met together daily for "prayers" in the temple courts and were well received by the populace of Jerusalem. The language "praising God and

---

15. See Luke 5:29–39; 6:1–5; 7:36–50; 9:12–17; 10:38–40; 11:37–52; 14:1–14; 15:1–2; 19:1–10; 22:17–20; 24:13–32, 36–43. Jesus's open table was also the likely basis of Paul's advice on table fellowship in 1 Cor 8–10.

enjoying the favor of all the people" reminds us of Luke's description of the young Jesus who "grew . . . in favor with God and man" (Luke 2:52).

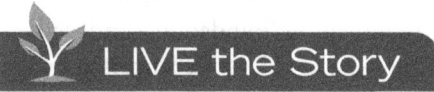
LIVE the Story

For those of us who attend to life—whether it is a garden or a gathered community of believers—there are "signs of life" we look for. In a garden we look for good soil, established roots, healthy foliage, and fruitfulness. In our churches today, we should look for the signs of life highlighted by Luke in Acts 2:42–47: learning and loving, breaking bread and prayerful praise. These are key signs of life for healthy Christian communities. They were the familiar features of life in the early church, and they have been the marks of mature Christian community ever since. None of these marks are optional signs as if someone looking at them could say, "Well, we have three out of four; that isn't bad." Rather, all these elements, together, are signs of those who are hungry for life, filled with the Spirit, and devoted to Christ.

Learning Our Faith

The first healthy sign of life in a plant or a person is nourishment. In the case of healthy church life, the "food" is derived from learning the apostles' teaching. Of course, the deposit of the apostles' teaching eventually became the NT. It is vital, however, to recognize that for the early church, their teaching came from Jesus and his reading of the Old Testament. A key principle of the early church was not simply that they listened to the Scriptures but that they were constantly alert to what "Moses and all the Prophets" said concerning Christ (see Luke 24:27). After the day of Pentecost the apostles read and taught Scripture through the lens of Christ. Believers responded to this with earnest devotion; they did not have to be prodded to learn about their new life. Why? Because they were "cut to the heart" and wanted to know *what* cut them and *who* cut them—this is *why* they became devoted to this teaching.

Although our focal text is Acts 2:42, it is linked in Greek with a simple connective word (*de*)—not translated in the NIV text—that links it to the previous verses. It is important to remember that early Christians devoted themselves to the teaching of the apostles because when they heard that Jesus, whom they had crucified, was made both Lord and Messiah by God, they were "cut to the heart" (2:36–37). What can cut to the quick? What can pierce flesh and bone? A sword can. Like the work of hardened steel and razor blade, we are "cut to the heart" when we give way to a truth that is firmer and sharper than us.¹⁶ This means we realize and yield to a transcendent truth; the reason early believers persistently sought the apostles' teaching is because it led them to the piercing truth that had become flesh, Jesus Christ. The apostles' teaching, along with the Old Testament, is foundational and leads to an encounter with Christ (see Eph 2:20). We should not be surprised by the unique power and place of God's word. Our Lord Jesus based his whole life on Scripture. When Jesus faced temptation, he devoted himself to the truth of Scripture (Luke 4:4, 8, 12). When Jesus taught—in the beginning (4:17–21), the middle (10:26–28), and at the end (24:27) of his ministry—he did so from Scripture. When Jesus faced his most severe testing on the cross, his mind turned to Scripture (Matt 27:46, crying out the words of Ps 22:1). For our Lord the living word was foundational; if we are going to know Jesus and have a relationship with him, then we too must devote ourselves to the Scriptures.

The Scriptures are not information *about* God but writings *by* God and *from* God *about* Christ. Too often it seems that contemporary Christians try to find a verse or two that will help guide them through the day. What is needed is regular and comprehensive immersion in large chunks of biblical text that allows us to be drawn into the broad biblical story. Dietrich Bonhoeffer argues for this important point:

> We become a part of what once took place for our salvation. Forgetting and losing ourselves, we, too, pass through the Red Sea, through the desert, across the Jordan into the promised land. . . . We are torn out of our own existence and set down in the midst of the holy history of God on earth. There God dealt with us, and there He still deals with us, our needs and our sins, in judgment and grace. It is not that God is the spectator and sharer of our present life, howsoever important that is; but rather that we are the reverent listeners and participants in God's action in the sacred story, the history of Christ on earth. . . . [Then] a complete reversal occurs. It is not in our life that God's help and presence must still be proved, but rather God's presence and help have been demonstrated for us in the life of Jesus Christ. It is in fact more important for us to know what God did to Israel, to His Son Jesus Christ, than to seek what God intends for us today. The fact that Jesus Christ died is more important than the fact that *I* shall die, and the fact that Jesus Christ rose from the dead is the sole ground of my hope that I, too, shall be raised on the Last Day. Our salvation is "external to ourselves." I find no salvation in my life history, but only in the history of Jesus Christ.¹⁷

---

16. Timothy J. Keller, "Cut to the Heart," sermon on Acts 2:32–41, gospelinlife.com, 24 Sept. 1995, https://gospelinlife.com/downloads/cut-to-the-heart-6408/.

17. Dietrich Bonhoeffer, *Life Together* (New York: Harper & Row, 1954), 53–54.

It is only in this light and as we listen to and live God's story of Christ that we too may beat with hearts devoted to the teaching of the apostles.

Loving Fellowship

God puts his word into the mouths of people so that it may be communicated to others. The natural consequence of learning apostolic teaching is the creation of loving Christian fellowship. The dominant theme of Luke's summary in Acts 2:42–47 is a *togetherness* shared by believers. He begins by noting (v. 42) that they were devoted to "fellowship," and this relational connection is further expressed as "all the believers were *together*" (v. 44) and "every day they continued to meet *together*" and "ate *together*" (v. 46). While there might have been aspects about one another's company that individuals within the early church in Acts 2 found appealing, the explicit diversity of this community suggests that their loving fellowship was based on something more than mutual interest. Whereas most societies—ancient or modern—tend toward establishing exclusive barriers based on ethnicity, political interests, gender, wealth, or class, the early church is notable for its inclusiveness. The earliest audience who heard and responded to the apostles' teaching may have all been Jews, but they were Jews "from every nation under heaven" (2:5), and this meant they came from varied cultural contexts, spoke different languages, and represented every social stratum. Eventually, these Christian Jews, from a people often criticized for their so-called "hatred" of other races,[18] began sharing their fellowship with outsiders: a eunuch from Ethiopia (Acts 8); a Roman centurion (Acts 10); and Macedonians (Acts 16). What accounts for this inclusiveness? Early Christianity grasped that true and loving fellowship is not an ideal they had to muster up on their own; rather, it is a reality created by God in Christ and through the Holy Spirit. As they lived into this reality, they experienced love and concern for one another, they enjoyed being together, and they attracted others. The historian Kenneth Scott Latourette once asked, "Why, from being the faith of a small, persecuted minority in competition with other religions which appeared to have better prospects of success, did Christianity eventually enroll the large majority of the population of the Roman Empire?" One of the significant contributing factors was its welcoming fellowship. Latourette concludes: "The Church was inclusive: its brotherhood included both sexes, rich and poor, intelligentsia and men and women of no intellectual attainments."[19]

---

18. See Tacitus, *Hist.* 5.5, where he describes Jewish "hatred" of the rest of the world. Roman slurs also included claims that the Jews were lazy because they kept the Sabbath. The first charge objects to their exclusivism mandated by the law of Moses, the second to Sabbath observance. Both charges reflected a lack of understanding of the Jewish people and their laws/customs by many Romans.

19. Kenneth Scott Latourette, *Christianity through the Ages* (New York: Harper & Row, 1965), 38.

One of the healthiest churches I have been a member of is Lynn Valley Church (or "Valley Church") located in ethnically diverse North Vancouver, British Columbia. A clear sign of life and vitality in Valley Church is that this community is as diverse as the community around it. At any given service of worship, one will meet Filipinos, Indians, Iranians, Eastern Europeans, South Africans, Singaporeans, and Chinese. The diversity is not simply in the congregation as a whole but also reflected in the leadership team. They serve their community with gusto, and when they gather together for fun, they eat. One will have a "taste of the world" if you are privileged to join them for a church potluck! Of course, not all of us live and work in ethnically diverse communities, but if our churches are not diverse, if they do not represent the diversity of the community around us in terms of age, gender, marital status, and social status, then our "fellowship" lacks a key sign of life.

You do not need to tell a growing baby to cry—crying is a sign of life. The early church did not need to be told to come together for the same reason—fellowship is a sign of life. The apostles could not keep believers apart because they were devoted to loving fellowship, fellowship that was diverse and deep. The unity in diversity that contemporary society most wants and most needs simply happened in the early church. Their devotion to inclusive, caring, and loving fellowship is one of the most important signs of life of the early church and one that is absolutely necessary for the contemporary church. This is possible only when believers come to know that our commonality in Christ creates fellowship that is deeper than national bonds, deeper than racial bonds, deeper than political bonds, and deeper than biological bonds.

Breaking Bread Together

Besides persisting in the teaching of the apostles and in loving fellowship, the early church frequently broke bread and regularly engaged in prayer. The traditional word used to describe this is *liturgy*. For centuries, Christians have gathered in groups both small and large to remember our Lord's suffering death on the cross for our redemption, sharing a common loaf and a common cup together. We do so as a prayerful and joyful response of thanksgiving to Jesus's command to remember his sacrifice for us until he comes again. In the early days of the church, it appears that this celebration of the Lord's Supper may have been closely associated with their common meals together. In this sense, it should not be surprising that scholars often debate whether "the breaking of bread" refers to sharing the Lord's Table or simply a common meal together. In some ways, it appears that Luke may not want us to draw too sharp a distinction between the two meals.

This was pressed home for me at one of the first services I presided over in my parish in Moose Jaw. While I have been a NT professor for a number of years, I am a rookie Anglican priest. As a priest, I make a lot of mistakes in the liturgy. I do not mean to; thankfully, I have a very experienced deacon, Arleen, who regularly rescues me. On one occasion she drove home this point of the connection between sharing the Lord's Table and our common meals together. Every Sunday my parish shares a common meal. This meal feeds not only our church congregation but many visitors too. Our church building shares a wall with a pub; it is across the street from the city's community services center and is within one block of the bus station, a homeless mission, and a casino. On any given day, and especially when we share an open meal together, we feed a wide variety of visitors. On one of my first Sundays, just before Deacon Arleen was about to dismiss our parish with the words, "Go in peace to love and serve the Lord," I whispered in her ear, "Shouldn't we pray for our following meal in the parish hall?" She furrowed her brow and shook her head at me and dismissed the congregation with the usual words. After everyone had proceeded to the hall for the meal, Arleen pulled me aside and reminded me why we do not pray over that meal separately. She told me I had already given thanks when I spoke the words of thanksgiving at the Lord's Table. It was a gentle admonishment that every meal we share together is connected to Christ and the bread he broke. As Christians, we constantly need to remember that in Christ, all that we do outside of our common liturgy is connected to our common life. As Paul would remind us, in everything that we do—whether it is worship or work, whether it is praying or playing—we "do it all in the name of the Lord Jesus, giving thanks to God the Father through him" (Col 3:17).

Prayerfulness

A vital sign of life for individual Christians and congregations alike is prayerfulness. We all know this. So why, for many of us, is our life of prayer so anemic and infrequent? The answer to that is complex. But I would like to offer one suggestion. I think many of us overlook a primary tool for prayer that God has given us in the Psalms. The book of Psalms was Israel's prayer book. This may be behind the final phrase in Acts 2:42: literally, "and to the prayers."[20] We know that first-century Jews, including the apostles and the early church, kept regular times of prayer. When they were in Jerusalem, they did so at the temple. Their prayers were rooted in the Psalms. That is, when they prayed, they did so using set prayers—even when they were in extreme circumstances. For example, Jonah prays a set prayer mirroring the Psalms from his tight quarters inside the great fish (Jonah 2). When Jesus

---

20. Note again that while the NIV translates the phrase as "and to prayer," in the Greek it is plural, "and to [the] *prayers.*"

was in breathless agony on the cross, his mind turned to Psalm 22. Early church fathers like Augustine[21] embraced the Psalms as a school of prayer; Ambrose referred to them as our "gymnasium for the soul";[22] and Athanasius viewed them as God's words that speak for us.[23] Unfortunately, many contemporary Christians seem to think that prayer must come extemporaneously "from the heart" rather than from a set prayer. While spontaneous prayer is important, maybe our feeble prayer life reflects a lack of rootedness in "the [set] prayers" of God's people for centuries, the Psalms. For me, I know that praying the Psalms is my lifeblood. Left on my own without these resources given to me by God, my prayers arc toward self-centeredness and shallowness. The Psalms—as "the prayers" of Israel, Jesus, and the early church—keep me rooted and nourished.

The more the early church engaged in learning and loving, breaking bread and praying, the more they cared for those in need (Acts 2:45), and the more they grew. Each of these signs of life combined and reinforced the others. Not one characteristic is superfluous. One final note is important. While they were learning and loving, while they were breaking bread and praying, Luke writes that they were "praising God." The engine behind their devotion was praise. Every beautiful object demands praise. We complete our joyful devotion by praise. C. S. Lewis speaks about this eloquently:

> I think we delight to praise what we enjoy because the praise not merely expresses but completes the enjoyment; it is its appointed consummation. . . . If it were possible for a created soul fully . . . to "appreciate," that is to love and delight in, the worthiest object of all, and simultaneously at every moment to give this delight perfect expression, then that soul would be in supreme beatitude. . . . To see what the doctrine really means, we must suppose ourselves to be in perfect love with God—drunk with, drowned in, dissolved by, that delight which, far from remaining pent up within ourselves as incommunicable, hence hardly tolerable, bliss, flows out from us incessantly again in effortless and perfect expression, our joy is no more separable from the praise in which it liberates and utters itself than the brightness a mirror receives is separable from the brightness it sheds. The Scotch catechism says that man's chief end is "to glorify God

---

21. Augustine's classic work *The Confessions* opens with a quotation from the Psalms, and for the rest of the work hardly a page goes by without a reference to the Psalms. For an excellent reflection on this, see the article by Rowan Williams, "Augustine and the Psalms," *Interpretation* 58.1 (Jan 2004): 17–27.

22. Ambrose, *Commentary on the Psalms*, 1.4, as quoted in Milton Walsh, *Witness of the Saints: Patristic Readings in the Liturgy of the Hours* (San Francisco: Ignatius, 2012), 197.

23. Athanasius, *Letter to Marcellinus*, 10, in *Athanasius: The Life of Antony and the Letter to Marcellinus*, trans. Robert C. Gregg (New York: Paulist, 1980).

and enjoy Him forever." But we shall then know that these are the same thing. Fully to enjoy is to glorify. In commanding us to glorify Him, God is inviting us to enjoy Him.[24]

Christians who express the signs of life praise God in every situation; we do so because we must express the joy we know in Christ. Of course, we are not perfect, and our churches have many problems, yet we are not bereft of hope and help. Our hope and help is in the Lord and in the provision of the Holy Spirit. In response to this hope and help we offer praise. As we look at Christ and praise him, we break the bonds of brokenness because we praise the One broken for us. As we look at Christ and praise him, we break the bonds of greed because we praise the One who became poor for us. As we look at Christ and praise him, we break the bonds of divisiveness because we praise the One who shared our human life together with us.

---

24. C. S. Lewis, *Reflections on the Psalms* (New York: Harcourt, Brace, Jovanovich, 1954), 95–97.

CHAPTER 5

Acts 3:1–10

 LISTEN to the Story

¹One day Peter and John were going up to the temple at the time of prayer—at three in the afternoon. ²Now a man who was lame from birth was being carried to the temple gate called Beautiful, where he was put every day to beg from those going into the temple courts. ³When he saw Peter and John about to enter, he asked them for money. ⁴Peter looked straight at him, as did John. Then Peter said, "Look at us!" ⁵So the man gave them his attention, expecting to get something from them.

⁶Then Peter said, "Silver or gold I do not have, but what I do have I give you. In the name of Jesus Christ of Nazareth, walk." ⁷Taking him by the right hand, he helped him up, and instantly the man's feet and ankles became strong. ⁸He jumped to his feet and began to walk. Then he went with them into the temple courts, walking and jumping, and praising God. ⁹When all the people saw him walking and praising God, ¹⁰they recognized him as the same man who used to sit begging at the temple gate called Beautiful, and they were filled with wonder and amazement at what had happened to him.

Listening to the Text in the Story: Isaiah 35:5–6; Luke 5:17–26.

 **EXPLAIN the Story**

There is no indication at the beginning of this next phase of the story as to how much time has transpired between the day of Pentecost and what occurs next. The NIV translates Luke's simple Greek connecting particle as "one day" (3:1).[1] Although Luke does not provide us with temporal markers, like most good storytellers he links individual episodes like this one to the

---

1. This "one day" may almost give readers the impression that the time that transpired is only "one day" from the last event.

broader narrative by a number of connecting themes. The encounters with the people and the leaders of the temple in chapters 3–4 are sparked by the first miracle enacted through the apostles followed by the two addresses by Peter. Not only does the miracle echo Jesus's healing of a lame man (see Luke 5:17–26), but also the pattern described about Jesus in the opening of Acts— "[what] Jesus began to do and to teach" (1:1)—is mirrored in the doings and teachings of his apostles. If a significant reason for the descent of the Spirit was so that Jesus's followers might carry on his ministry in the same power that Jesus did, then it is unsurprising that the first episode after Pentecost describes the apostles healing and teaching, and—much like Jesus in similar circumstances—experiencing opposition from some of the Jewish leadership (e.g., see Luke 5:21; also Mark 2:6–7; 3:6; John 11:51–53).

The present narrative offers a detailed description of the healing of a man who had been lame from birth. This short narrative has two parts. First, there is a description of the meeting between Peter and John and the lame man (3:1–5), and secondly there is an account of his healing and his reaction (3:6–10).

Peter and John Meet a Lame Man (3:1–5)

Peter and John encountered the lame man as they were entering the temple for prayer as the evening sacrifice was being carried out (see Exod 29:38–41; Num 28:4; Dan 9:21). Despite their profound reception of the Spirit that indicated that they were experiencing "the last days" (see 2:17), the disciples of Jesus carried on with the custom of temple worship until the authorities force them outside the temple. While some[2] might conclude that they had not yet come to the realization that the sacrifices were unnecessary (Heb 10:1–18), the disciples may not have disengaged from the temple yet because it was a primary place for bearing witness to Jesus's sacrifice and as a place for teaching (see Acts 3:11; 4:2).

Readers are not provided with personal details about the lame man. We do not know his name or where he comes from, but we learn about the seriousness of his condition, the place where he begs, and what he seeks. The man is lame and has been so from birth. He is immobile, and walking is what he could not do. For over forty years (see 4:22) he has lived with his debilitating and congenital condition. He was placed at the entrance to the temple courts called the Beautiful Gate (3:2). There are no ancient sources that refer to such a gate, and most scholars suggest that this may be the "Nicanor Gate," a gate to the temple that Josephus describes as an ornate gate made of Corinthian brass that "greatly

---

2. E.g., see Dunn, *Acts*, 40.

excelled those that were only covered with silver and gold" (*J. W.* 5.201).[3] This gate was located at the eastern entrance to the temple and led into the court of the women from the court of the gentiles. This gate would provide easy access to Solomon's Colonnade, the scene of the next episode (3:11), located nearby along the east side of the temple platform. The lame man chose this location at the gate not necessarily because he could not gain access to the temple because of his disability,[4] but because it provided him with a high-traffic area from which to beg for alms. As Dunn notes, "One of the most impressive features of Judaism past and present is the major emphasis it places on provision for the poor and disadvantaged. . . . Almsgiving was . . . a principal act of religious responsibility (e.g., Sir. 3.30; 29.12; Tobit 12.9; 14.11)."[5] This concern for the poor is also a characteristic of Jesus and his followers.[6]

Peter and John learned well from Jesus about their responsibility to the poor. As they approached the temple (Acts 3:3), they did not turn their attention away from the request of the lame man. After hearing his cry for money, Peter looked "straight at him" (v. 4), and no doubt the lame man looked expectantly at Peter. But the man received far more than he asked for. Peter's reply will resonate throughout the coming chapters in Acts: "Silver or gold I do not have, but what I do have I give you. In the name of Jesus Christ of Nazareth, walk" (v. 6). The apostle, in one respect, is as impoverished as the lame man, yet the real treasure in Peter's hand is bestowed upon him directly by Jesus. Whereas Jesus may have only said, "Rise and walk," the apostles' power is derivative. It is in the *name of Jesus* that power resides. There is healing in the name of Jesus (3:16; also 4:10, 30), and there is salvation in the name of Jesus (4:12). This is not mere magic, connected with money—something expressly disavowed later (see 8:9–20); rather, it is a power related to the name of Jesus, the risen and ascended Lord.

The Healing of the Lame Man (3:6–10)

The command to walk (3:6) is echoed four times in the next few verses (vv. 8 [2x], 9, and 12). Instead of repeating requests for money at the entrance to the temple, the healed man repeatedly praises God as he leaps on his way into

---

3. *The Works of Flavius Josephus: Complete and Unabridged*, trans. William Whiston (Peabody, MA: Hendrickson, 1987). See Keener, *Acts*, 2:1048–49.

4. Lev 21:16–18 restricts access to the temple only for *priests* with physical defects; the lame man's defect would not necessarily bar him from entrance to worship.

5. Dunn, *Acts*, 41. This primarily was directed toward widows, orphans, the poor, and foreigners; for example, see Deut 15:7–11; 24:14–22; Isa 58:6–10; Jer 7:6. For a helpful summary, see Keener's excursus on poverty, the disabled, and begging (*Acts*, 2:1050–62).

6. Luke frequently portrays Jesus as a champion of the poor (see Luke 10:30–37; 12:33–34; 14:12–14; 16:19–31). His followers carry on this ministry in Acts (see 9:36; 10:2; and 24:17).

the temple. The exuberant response of "walking and jumping, and praising God" on the part of the healed lame man echoes the language of Isaiah. Isaiah pointed forward to a future time of restoration when the "the eyes of the blind [will] be opened and the ears of the deaf unstopped. . . . The lame [will] leap like a deer, and the mute tongue shout for joy" (Isa 35:5–6). This healing also points to the future. For now, however, the healing leads this restored man to connection with the believing community who meet in the temple courts "praising God and enjoying the favor of all the people" (see Acts 2:46–47).

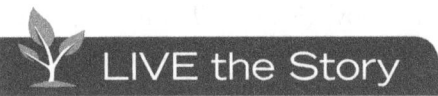

LIVE the Story

Interconnections in the Story

The Russian writer Anton Chekhov observed that in any dramatic performance, "If in Act I you have a pistol hanging on the wall, then it must fire in the last act."[7] This principle of "Chekhov's Gun," related to foreshadowing and plot interconnectivity, has been a characteristic of many good writers, including Luke. Good writers, especially those telling a memorable story, are careful to connect elements in a variety of subtle ways. Often we notice them only when we hear or read the story again. It is not surprising then that the first healing of the apostles in Acts 3 connects to broader themes both before and after in Acts. Yet it also connects with themes in Luke's Gospel and, indeed, in the broader biblical story. In particular, this miracle connects to a theme highlighted early in Acts (see 1:1–2) that Jesus's followers continue what he "began to do and to teach." They had seen Jesus do mighty deeds that were then followed by teaching and, often, opposition from Jewish religious authorities (e.g., see Luke 5:17–26). This is explicit in the words of Peter to the lame man as he speaks to him "in the name of Jesus Christ" (Acts 3:6). Henri Nouwen offers this important insight about serving in the name of Jesus:

> Ministry is acting in the Name of Jesus. When all our actions are in the Name, they will bear fruit for eternal life. To act in the Name of Jesus, however, doesn't mean to act as a representative of Jesus or his spokesperson. It means to act in an intimate communion with him. The Name is like a house, a tent, a dwelling. To act in the Name of Jesus, therefore, means to act from the place where we are united with Jesus in love. To the question "Where are you?" we should be able to answer, "I am in

---

7. Anton Chekhov, as quoted in Elizabeth Knowles, ed., *The Oxford Dictionary of Quotations*, 5th ed. (Oxford: Oxford University Press, 1999), 208.

the Name." Then, whatever we do cannot be other than ministry because it will always be Jesus himself who acts in and through us. The final question for all who minister is "Are you in the Name of Jesus?" When we can say yes to that, all of our lives will be ministry.[8]

The interconnectivity of this story does not end there, however. The healing in Acts 3 connects to a passage further back in the biblical story in Isaiah. Isaiah writes about a future time of restoration when "the eyes of the blind [will] be opened and the ears of the deaf unstopped. Then will the lame leap like a deer, and the mute tongue shout for joy" (35:5–6). The healing of the paralytic indicates that part of what Isaiah foretold was already starting to happen first through Jesus, then the ministry of Jesus's disciples. Just as the descent of the Spirit in Acts 2 was an indication of the future breaking into the present, now the healing of the lame also reflects this same reality. Suffering, lameness, and blindness are not part of the created order of God's world. Nonetheless, just walking alone does not make people whole; after all, plenty of people walk or see with both eyes and yet fail to experience the kind of restoration Isaiah describes. The issue is deeper than the physical issue of lameness; the issue is one of the heart, and the healing points inward. What this man experienced was a profound connection to Jesus: he leaped and praised, because part of the future restoration of all things had already begun in his life. He received more than he expected; he wanted money, but they gave him Jesus. The healing of the lame man led him into a wholeness that connected and oriented him to Christ and to others. The lame man finally enters the temple after years of sitting at the gate looking in; it brought him into community where his lameness had once left him isolated. Although the early Christians were open to sharing what material means they had to meet the needs of others (see Acts 2:45; 4:32–35), money was not the most important thing for them. For many of the early Christians, money was just a thing—but Jesus was everything. The life of the future that is brought into the present through the "name" of Jesus is the kind of life that brings ultimate joy and wholeness. It might even lead you to walking and jumping and praising God.

Do What You Can in the Name of Jesus

This story in Acts is a profound illustration for Christian inaction and action. In fact, the first thing Peter did when he encountered the lame man asking him for a few spare coins was to admit his inability to do something—he confessed his economic inability. He didn't have any money and admits this: "Silver or gold I do not have" (3:6). He didn't, however, let this lack of money

---

8. Henri Nouwen, *Bread for the Journey* (San Francisco: HarperOne, 2006), entry for Nov. 18.

be an excuse for inactivity: "But what I do have I give you. In the name of Jesus Christ of Nazareth, walk" (v. 6). He did what he could do in the name of Jesus. This is a helpful model for what Christian compassion can look like. It is not a matter of repeating what Peter said and did as if this is the only way that we continue to live out the unfolding story of Acts in our world. Rather, it is the willingness to respond with what we do have for those we encounter in need. God doesn't ask that we do anything other than what we can do. But he does ask that we do that. Christian mission is the willingness to respond to the needs around you with that which is distinctively you and is in your capacity to do.[9] It is not a matter of mustering up enough power or piety so that you too work "signs and wonders" like Peter and John did. Even Peter had enough sense to recognize that. He acknowledges as much just a few moments later when he asks, "Why do you stare at us *as if by our own power or godliness* we had made this man walk?" (v. 12).

A good friend, Frances Barclay, reminded me of this through her own work with urban homeless people in Edinburgh, Scotland. Many of us encounter homeless people sitting on the ground as we walk around our cities. Frances suggests a "grounded" start to meeting the needs of the homeless by sitting with them on the ground.[10] For most of us, when we notice homeless people, we rarely stop to look at them with the intense gaze that Peter offered the lame man. Frances suggests that we can learn a lot and begin the process of helping the homeless by first sitting down and listening. It isn't much, granted, but it is a start and is something most of us can do. That is one of the significant aspects of Peter's actions. He did what he could do rather than bemoan what he could not do.

---

9. See Eugene Peterson, *Conversations: The Message with Its Translator* (Colorado Springs: NavPress, 2007), 1685.

10. Frances Barclay, "Finding Common Ground: What I've Learned Sitting Down," TEDx Talks, 13 March 2013, https://www.youtube.com/watch?v=slFKNJINwxA.

CHAPTER 6

Acts 3:11-26

LISTEN to the Story

¹¹While the man held on to Peter and John, all the people were astonished and came running to them in the place called Solomon's Colonnade. ¹²When Peter saw this, he said to them: "Fellow Israelites, why does this surprise you? Why do you stare at us as if by our own power or godliness we had made this man walk? ¹³The God of Abraham, Isaac and Jacob, the God of our fathers, has glorified his servant Jesus. You handed him over to be killed, and you disowned him before Pilate, though he had decided to let him go. ¹⁴You disowned the Holy and Righteous One and asked that a murderer be released to you. ¹⁵You killed the author of life, but God raised him from the dead. We are witnesses of this. ¹⁶By faith in the name of Jesus, this man whom you see and know was made strong. It is Jesus' name and the faith that comes through him that has completely healed him, as you can all see.

¹⁷"Now, fellow Israelites, I know that you acted in ignorance, as did your leaders. ¹⁸But this is how God fulfilled what he had foretold through all the prophets, saying that his Messiah would suffer. ¹⁹Repent, then, and turn to God, so that your sins may be wiped out, that times of refreshing may come from the Lord, ²⁰and that he may send the Messiah, who has been appointed for you—even Jesus. ²¹Heaven must receive him until the time comes for God to restore everything, as he promised long ago through his holy prophets. ²²For Moses said, 'The Lord your God will raise up for you a prophet like me from among your own people; you must listen to everything he tells you. ²³Anyone who does not listen to him will be completely cut off from their people.'¹

²⁴"Indeed, beginning with Samuel, all the prophets who have spoken have foretold these days. ²⁵And you are heirs of the prophets and of the covenant God made with your fathers. He said to Abraham, 'Through

---

1. Deut 18:15, 18, 19.

your offspring all peoples on earth will be blessed.'² ²⁶When God raised up his servant, he sent him first to you to bless you by turning each of you from your wicked ways."

> *Listening to the Text in the Story*: Genesis 22:18; 26:4; Deuteronomy 18:15, 18, 19.

EXPLAIN the Story

After the remarkable healing of the lame man that opens this chapter (3:1–10), the remainder of the chapter (3:11–26) presents Peter's response to the unexpected opportunity to preach to an astonished group. The walking and jumping man draws a running crowd. The scene shifts from the Gate Beautiful to Solomon's Colonnade (v. 11), a portico a short distance away along the eastern wall of the temple precincts.³ Peter's speech is in two parts, each part opening with an address to his "fellow Israelites" (vv. 12, 17). The first part of the address (vv. 12–16) focuses on the actions of the inhabitants of Jerusalem, especially their disavowal of Jesus, "the author of life." The second part of the address (vv. 17–26) focuses on the actions of God, especially his appointment of Jesus as the Messiah.

The Actions of the People of Jerusalem (3:11–16)

Not surprisingly, there are similarities between this sermon and Peter's previous address on the day of Pentecost. For example, he opens this sermon by identifying with his audience as "fellow Israelites" (3:12, 17) as he did similarly in his first sermon (see 2:14, 22, 29). As was required on Pentecost, Peter also begins by clarifying a misconception held by the crowd (see 2:15). The same word used of Peter's focused gaze at the lame man (translated as "looked straight," 3:4), is now used to describe the amazement of the crowd as they "stare" (v. 12) at Peter and John. In this case, Peter makes clear it was not by their own power that this man was healed (v. 12), but by faith "in the name of Jesus" (v. 16). Furthermore, as Peter calls upon his audience to

---

2. Gen 22:18; 26:4.

3. Solomon's Colonnade was located along the eastern platform of the Temple, overlooking the Kidron Valley. This location became a kind of "believers" corner where the early Christian community regularly gathered for fellowship, teaching, and prayer (see Acts 5:12–13). These regular gatherings also included opportunity for evangelism (preaching, signs and wonders, etc.).

repent from their sins (v. 19), he does so in the same way he did on Pentecost (2:38). Despite these similarities with the earlier sermon (2:14–36), this second sermon is more remarkable by way of contrast. If Peter's Pentecost address presents a kind of general introductory sermon, this second one has elements that indicate it is aimed at a particular situation. In doing so, Peter draws on specifically Jewish ascriptions of God, some uncommon titles for Jesus, and unique, future-oriented terms in framing his sermon.

In these opening words, it is important not to miss the focus of Peter's sermon. In the opening section (3:12–16), Peter uses a rhetorical device, a chiasm, familiar to his audience but often missed by modern eyes and ears.[4] Derived from the Greek letter *chi* (which is shaped like a letter X), a chiasm uses parallel lines of a text/speech that correspond in an X pattern, such as A-B-C-D-D′-C′-B′-A′ (in this case, the center of the chiasm is D, and on either side line A will correspond to line A′ and so on). Normally, a chiasm is used to express progression of thought and intensification of meaning, especially at the center of the chiasm. The structure in these opening words looks like this:

  A Why do you stare at us as if by our own power or godliness we had made this man walk? (v. 12)
    B God . . . has glorified his servant Jesus (v. 13a)
      C You handed him over to be killed (v. 13b)
        D You disowned him before Pilate (v. 13b)
        D′ You disowned the Holy and Righteous One (v. 14)
      C′ You killed the author of life (v. 15a)
    B′ God raised him from the dead (v. 15b)
  A′ Faith in the name of Jesus . . . made [this man] strong (v. 16)

As this pattern indicates, the focus of Peter's opening is not a general message about the gospel but a particular concern about (1) Jesus being responsible for the healing of the lame man (A-A′) and (2) Peter's audience being responsible for Jesus's death (D-D′). At the heart of this, is the One who is the healer: "The Holy and Righteous One" (v. 14). Both of these titles are often used in reference to God in the Old Testament ("the Holy One": see 1 Sam 2:2; 2 Kgs 19:22; Job 6:10; Pss 16:10; 22:3; 71:22; Isa 1:4; 6:3; 57:15; Hos 11:9; Hab 1:12; "the Righteous One": see Ezra 9:15; Pss 11:7; 116:5; 119:137; 129:4; 145:17; Jer 12:1; Lam 1:18; Dan 9:7; Zeph 3:5; cf. Exod 9:27). Schnabel notes that Isaiah makes a strong link between the words "righteous" and "the Servant of the Lord" (cf. Isa 53:11). As such, "the combined title 'the Holy and Righteous One' has messianic connotations

---

4. I am indebted to Gordon Fee for alerting me to this chiasm.

and describes Jesus as the one who was unreservedly devoted to do God's will, being holy as only God is holy, and that he is the one set apart by God to accomplish his will as his Servant."[5] Jesus, the one disowned before Pilate, is far more than just a healer!

The Actions of God (3:17–26)

In the second half of the sermon—signaled by "now" (v. 17)—Peter ties these two realities to their present situation. Here we have the gospel of Jesus applied to a specific and fully Jewish setting. The first implication of the gospel of Jesus is repentance (vv. 17–19). Peter somewhat softens the earlier disavowal of his fellow Israelites (vv. 13–14) by acknowledging that they acted in ignorance. Despite this ignorance, the death of Jesus fulfills prophecy. The appropriate response for Peter's "fellow Israelites" is repentance for their culpability so that, just as the lame man received a foretaste of future restoration by leaping and shouting for joy (see Isa 35:6), they might also now experience times of refreshing, a foretaste of the time of restoration associated with the return of the Messiah, Jesus (Acts 3:19–21). Repentance, according to Peter, is the means by which those on earth may begin to experience "times of refreshing." Again, the ascension of the risen Christ means that what Jesus is experiencing in heaven can begin to be experienced now, on earth, in the present. But this is merely a foretaste, a beginning of the end of time when God will restore all things.

This understanding of "time" as something that is already begun but not yet completed is a vital theological framework that shaped the perspective of every NT writer and the outlook of the early church. There is a time coming in the future when God will restore all things, a promise expressed in Paul's letters (Rom 8:21; 1 Cor 15:28; Col 1:20), in Peter's letters (1 Pet 1:3–4; 2 Pet 3:13), in Hebrews (Heb 6:4–5, 17–20; 11:16), and, of course, in John's apocalypse (Rev 21:1). In the present, however, a foretaste of the future is anticipated in the "times of refreshing." The advance anticipation, Peter declares in this passage (Acts 3:19), can be received when people turn away from their wickedness and turn to the Lord in the present.

The closing words of Peter's sermon (3:22–26) draw the relationship between the present and the future by calling on the witness of the prophets. He draws on many of the key spokesmen from Israel's past. The first in line is Moses, the greatest prophet of all, who foretold the arrival of a greater prophet than himself (see Deut 18:15–20). Jesus *is* that promised messianic prophet. Indeed, Samuel and "all the prophets" (Acts 3:24) announced these *present*

---

5. Schnabel, *Acts*, 210.

days. The gentile mission declared to Abraham (Gen 12:3) is a part of this fulfillment (Acts 3:25). But it is to the Jews *first* (v. 26; cf. 13:46; Rom 1:16) that the blessing of God occurs, namely, by their turning from their wicked ways. Peter identifies his audience as "heirs [lit., "sons"] of the prophets" (Acts 3:25). After providing this litany of prophets who line up to point to Jesus, these descendants of Israel are called to respond appropriately with repentant lives. Will they? Or will they be like their forefathers who persecuted and killed the prophets? This question will take on an even more intense response later in Acts when Stephen raises the same question whether they will be like their ancestors who betrayed and murdered "the Righteous One" (7:51–52).

In the course of this remarkable address, a number of elements stand out that suggest its particular Jewish audience and an early setting within the primitive church. First, there are a number of distinctly Jewish ascriptions to God. Early on (3:13), Peter refers to the "God of Abraham, Isaac and Jacob" and "the God of our fathers." The first phrase draws on the language of the initial promises to Abraham and from the covenant when God promised Moses that he would deliver Israel from their bondage in Egypt (Exod 3:6, 15), a phrase repeated by Jesus (Luke 20:37; cf. Matt 22:32; Mark 12:26). The second phrase, "the God of our fathers," is a phrase used only in Acts (5:30; 22:14 [NIV: "ancestors"]; cf. 7:32) and is used always in Jewish contexts. By beginning (3:13) and ending (3:25) with the same covenant promises to Abraham and the patriarchs, the speech emphasizes that what has happened to Jesus is what God promised to his people from the very beginning.

Second, the speech employs some very uncommon titles for Jesus, including "servant," "Holy and Righteous One," and "author of life" (3:13–15). Gaventa makes the important observation that the language used here of Jesus is used to contrast the actions of the people against him.[6] The people "handed [Jesus] over," they "disowned" him, they "killed" him. In response, God glorified his "servant" Jesus (v. 13). This language is almost certainly a reflection of the suffering servant in Isaiah (Isa 52:13). Jesus is also the "Holy and Righteous One"—two titles that are used rarely of Jesus in the NT ("holy": see Mark 1:24; John 6:69; Rev 3:7; "righteous": see Matt 27:19 [see ESV]; Acts 7:52; 22:14; 1 John 2:1). They are probably placed together here to highlight the Mosaic-prophet theme mentioned later in the sermon (Acts 3:22). Finally, Jesus is the "author of life." The Greek word translated "author" (*archēgos*) is rare and appears once more in Acts (5:31, "Prince") and elsewhere in the NT only in Hebrews (2:10 and 12:2, "pioneer"). The irony is that the people are charged with killing the originator of life.

---

6. Gaventa, *Acts*, 87.

Third, Peter uses unique, future-oriented terms to frame his sermon. In particular, the phrases "times of refreshing"[7] and "time . . . to restore everything" are not found anywhere else in the NT. In the Greek text, Luke uses two different words that are both translated into English as "time,"[8] both in the plural ("times"). The same combination of words referring to "time" are also used earlier when Jesus reminds his disciples that "it is not for you to know the times [*chronous*] or dates [*kairous*] the Father has set by his own authority" (Acts 1:7). The important point for readers of Acts is that "Luke employs time designations in the plural for those events that lead up to some culminating event, and time designations in the singular for the event itself (e.g., Luke 17:22–31; Acts 2:17, 20)."[9] The culminating event for Peter's original audience is the revelation of Jesus as God's appointed Messiah to the people of Israel and preparation for when "heaven" will send him again. Whatever else, for Luke any discussion about the future has less to do with chronology than it does with Christ. That is, it is more important to recognize Jesus as God's Messiah than in wondering when he will come again.

LIVE the Story

My son once asked me if God changed his mind between the OT and the NT. This is one of the most common questions I've been asked both as a professor and a priest. That is, how do the OT and NT relate? One of the most fundamental Christian convictions is that God speaks his truth through Scripture. If you want to hear God's voice and know God's will, this is expressed through his prophets, including those OT prophets who communicated God's truth in writing. This does not imply that a form of divine stenography occurred when they wrote down their prophecies. God spoke through the prophets—Moses, Samuel, David, Isaiah, etc.—in a manner that reflected all their own personalities and modes of communication. The carefully crafted laws in the Pentateuch read differently in style from the narratives of Samuel, or the poetry of David, or the plaintive cries of Job, or the soaring oracles of Isaiah. Regardless of the style and vocabulary, the apostles' proclamation of the gospel was connected to the OT. The apostles' teaching—here (3:11–26) and elsewhere (cf. 2:42)—that the newly baptized were so "devoted to" was shaped by the story of the God who was at work in the lives of Abraham, Isaac, and Jacob (3:13) and, further, by "all the prophets" (3:18, 24). The apostles were not introducing

---

7. Although this phrase is contained in 3:19 in the NIV (and KJV), it is actually in 3:20 in the Greek text (and in the NRSV and ESV).
8. In v. 20 the Greek word is *kairoi*, in v. 21 the word is *chronōn*.
9. Gaventa, *Acts*, 88.

an idiosyncratic or individualistic teaching. Rather, their teaching was rooted in the story of Scripture, which for them was simply our "Old Testament," and supremely in the teaching of Jesus.

Rooted in the Old Testament

It is important for us to remember this "rootedness" to our faith; it keeps us from the historical forgetfulness that infects most of our culture. But there is more to it than simply remembering the past story in the OT and looking for hints or clues about our Christian faith today. No, it is as Peter proclaimed: God has fulfilled what the prophets foretold in Jesus (3:18–20). This is why whenever we read the OT without reading it in reference to Christ, it may make us arrogant, anxious, or even apathetic. These can be conflicting emotions for Christians who read the Old Testament. For example, there may be some who proudly proclaim in relationship to the OT law, "I can do that." Others may respond more pessimistically, "I can never do that." Even worse than either of these responses might be one like that of the second-century heretic Marcion: "Who needs the OT anyway?"[10] In each of these we miss the apostles' organic relationship to the OT. In following the footsteps of the apostles in Acts, we need not be arrogant, anxious, or apathetic, but we should be *attentive*. If the law ultimately points to Jesus, then it will show you that you can never possibly be good on your own and can never fulfill it on your own. Jesus alone fulfills the law. Now that Jesus has fulfilled the law through his gracious self-giving, we have a way of pleasing God without being anxious because the law shows us what pleases him: Jesus. If we see the whole trajectory of the biblical narrative climaxing in Jesus, the Messiah, we will not dismiss the OT as irrelevant but treasure it as the beloved revelation of our Lord.

Look for Jesus

What, then, are the OT legal passages pointing to? What is the sacrificial system about? What does the purity code signify? In short, they are God's way of getting across to people that we are never fit, pure, or clean enough to come into his presence on our own. But as we will see later in Acts 10, Peter is given a vision from God where he sees a large sheet full of unclean animals that are given to him to eat. He hears a voice from heaven say, "Kill and eat" (10:13). Of course, Peter refuses because he argues that he has never eaten

---

10. B. E. Foster, "Marcion," *NDT* 411, writes: "[Marcion] rejected the OT as a Christian book and collected the earliest known Christian canon, composed of an abbreviated version of Luke's Gospel and ten edited Pauline epistles (lacking the Pastorals). He presented his theological views in the *Antitheses*, in which he set forth contradictions between the OT and the NT. His works do not survive, so his positions must be reconstructed from the refutations made by his opponents, the fullest of which is Tertullian's five books *Against Marcion*."

anything unclean. The voice responds, "Do not call anything impure that God has made clean" (10:15). After this vision, what happens next? A trio of unwashed gentiles show up at the door who are impure, eat the wrong things, and touch unclean things. Finally, Peter realizes that in Jesus all people can be made clean and can enter into the presence of God without following the purity laws of the OT. Why? Because the purity laws point to cleanness made possible through Christ.

All of this is to say that when Peter began to speak to his own people about Jesus, the Messiah, he did so not by asking them to strike out on a new path but to follow the lead from their own story that began with their father Abraham and continued through all their prophets. Repeatedly, the book of Acts invites people to put themselves into the grand story of God. In this instance, it is the Jews themselves who are invited to hear their own prophets afresh. Later we will hear how an Ethiopian eunuch (Acts 8) might see himself in the story, even though he may have felt marginalized after his temple pilgrimage to Jerusalem. After that, it will be gentiles like the Roman centurion Cornelius (Acts 10), the proconsul Sergius Paulus on Cyprus (Acts 13), and Lydia, a dealer in purple cloth, in Philippi (Acts 16) who will each in turn be invited to put themselves into the story of God. All of them, Jew and gentile, will be invited to hear and celebrate the promise made to Abraham that through his "offspring *all peoples* on earth will be blessed" (Acts 3:25; Gen 22:18; 26:4). This message came "first" to the Jews, but its goal is the world.

The promise made to Abraham comes to us whether we are Jews or gentiles. But it is important to remember the blessings of that promise do not come because humans, Abraham or otherwise, kept their end of the deal. Jesus is the only Israelite, the only human, who ever kept the covenant promise perfectly, and so, according to Paul, God has summed up all things in Christ (Eph 1:10). It is through Christ that God "reconcile[s] to himself all things . . . by making peace through his blood, shed on the cross" (Col 1:20). And in the end, when the time comes to restore everything, he will make a "new heaven and a new earth, where righteousness dwells" (2 Pet 3:13; Rev 21:1), where the whole of creation will be "liberated from its bondage to decay" (Rom 8:21).[11]

What this means is that all the basic Jewish beliefs about the future and its blessings are reshaped and rethought around the mission and message of Jesus. This is what we see going on with the ultimate promise of Acts 3:21: Jesus fulfills all the covenant promises so that all humanity can receive the blessings. Jesus is the fulfillment and climax of all Scripture. The Law points to Jesus, the Prophets point to Jesus, the Psalms point to Jesus (Luke 24:44). When we hear

---

11. This line of reading texts comes from N. T. Wright, *Acts for Everyone*, 2 vols. (Louisville: Westminster John Knox, 2008), 1:58.

and understand what Peter declares in Acts 3, we begin to grasp that the covenant is not about Abraham but points to Jesus; the kosher laws are not about food but point to Jesus; the purity laws are not about cleanliness but point to Jesus; the Psalms are not about David but point to Jesus; the Prophets do not merely predict the future but point to Jesus. When we recognize this about the OT, as the early church leaders like Peter did, the OT becomes for us a gift and an authority and not merely a tedious introduction to the "real thing" in the NT. If we don't read the OT through Jesus, or "Christocentrically" as some theologians like to put it, Paul says we read it with a veil over our eyes and will never see its glory (2 Cor 3:7–16).

Jesus, therefore, is the ultimate prophet, or as the text describes him, he is God's "servant" (Acts 3:26). Is it true that God raised up Jesus and sent him to you and to me, we who are living in the twenty-first century? How is this possible? Whenever the gospel is preached from the OT or NT, Jesus is also present. He comes to us, blesses us, speaks to our hearts, and reaches you and me—regardless of how eloquent or effective the preacher may or may not be. Jesus is present in the proclamation of the gospel. Jesus deals with us in truth through all Scripture, all of God's story.

CHAPTER 7

Acts 4:1-22

LISTEN to the Story

¹The priests and the captain of the temple guard and the Sadducees came up to Peter and John while they were speaking to the people. ²They were greatly disturbed because the apostles were teaching the people, proclaiming in Jesus the resurrection of the dead. ³They seized Peter and John and, because it was evening, they put them in jail until the next day. ⁴But many who heard the message believed; so the number of men who believed grew to about five thousand.

⁵The next day the rulers, the elders and the teachers of the law met in Jerusalem. ⁶Annas the high priest was there, and so were Caiaphas, John, Alexander and others of the high priest's family. ⁷They had Peter and John brought before them and began to question them: "By what power or what name did you do this?"

⁸Then Peter, filled with the Holy Spirit, said to them: "Rulers and elders of the people! ⁹If we are being called to account today for an act of kindness shown to a man who was lame and are being asked how he was healed, ¹⁰then know this, you and all the people of Israel: It is by the name of Jesus Christ of Nazareth, whom you crucified but whom God raised from the dead, that this man stands before you healed. ¹¹Jesus is

> "'the stone you builders rejected,
>   which has become the cornerstone.'[1]

¹²Salvation is found in no one else, for there is no other name under heaven given to mankind by which we must be saved."

¹³When they saw the courage of Peter and John and realized that they were unschooled, ordinary men, they were astonished and they took note that these men had been with Jesus. ¹⁴But since they could see the man who had been healed standing there with them, there was nothing they could say. ¹⁵So they ordered them to withdraw from the Sanhedrin and

---

1. Ps 118:22.

then conferred together. ¹⁶"What are we going to do with these men?" they asked. "Everyone living in Jerusalem knows they have performed a notable sign, and we cannot deny it. ¹⁷But to stop this thing from spreading any further among the people, we must warn them to speak no longer to anyone in this name."

¹⁸Then they called them in again and commanded them not to speak or teach at all in the name of Jesus. ¹⁹But Peter and John replied, "Which is right in God's eyes: to listen to you, or to him? You be the judges! ²⁰As for us, we cannot help speaking about what we have seen and heard."

²¹After further threats they let them go. They could not decide how to punish them, because all the people were praising God for what had happened. ²²For the man who was miraculously healed was over forty years old.

Listening to the Text in the Story: Psalm 118:22; Daniel 3:6–18; Luke 20:17–19.

EXPLAIN the Story

There is an old adage that goes "no good deed goes unpunished." In the apostles' case this meant that the healing of the lame man (see previous section) led them into conflict with the temple authorities. Specifically, it was the teaching of the apostles after the healing itself that "greatly disturbed" (4:2) them. This narrative (4:1–22) describes the first major conflict episode in Acts, with two more soon to follow (see 5:17–42; 6:8–8:4), between the followers of Jesus and the leaders of Israel in the early stages of the church's existence. While it is a picture of truth speaking to power, it also marks a division between the leadership of Israel associated with the temple and the Israel reconstituted and restored around Jesus. As Peter declared, those who will not listen to Jesus "will be completely cut off from their people" (3:23). Peterson rightly notes, "The apostles as [Jesus's] prophetic successors, in healing and convicting proclamation, emerge as the leaders of a renewed Israel, whose ministry is profoundly threatening to the old order."[2]

The entire scene occurs over the course of one day (from evening to evening). The first paragraph (4:1–4), set in the evening, provides the stage for

---

2. Peterson, *Acts*, 186.

what follows and the narrative bridge from what preceded (3:1–26). The next short paragraph (4:5–7), set in the morning, describes the primary questions and concerns the temple leaders have for the apostles: What kind of power do you have? In whose name are you healing and teaching? These questions provide the launching pad for another short speech by Peter (4:8–12). The day ends with a reaction from the Jewish leaders and their final threats to Peter and John before their release (4:13–22). All along the way we are reminded that this clash is associated with the healing of the lame man (see vv. 7, 9, 14, 21–22), but the real issue is much deeper. It is a foundational issue that separates them, or, to put it another way, it is a "cornerstone" issue that divides them. The response of the apostles to the resistance of the chief priests and elders is simple and profound: they hold a prayer meeting (4:23–31).

The Arrest of Peter and John (4:1–4)

In the opening four verses of chapter four, we are alerted to two contrasting responses to the apostles' teaching. "The people"[3] listen, believe, and respond in number to the apostles' teaching. In contrast, "the priests and the captain of the temple guard and the Sadducees" are greatly disturbed by the teaching. Within this second group, the first two are representatives of the temple authorities and Levites; indeed, the captain of the guard was the highest-ranking priest after the high priest, with the power to arrest troublemakers in the temple area. We do not know much about the third group, the Sadducees.[4] They were likely a small but politically influential group of wealthy, aristocratic priests who were based in the temple in Jerusalem. As such, the Sadducees were keenly interested in any disruption or new teaching that was occurring in and around the temple. They may have been named after Zadok, the priest (2 Sam 8:17; 15:24; 1 Kgs 1:34), but theologically they did not believe in angels, spirits, or the resurrection of the dead and accepted only the five books of Moses as Scripture (see Acts 23:8; Josephus, *Ant.* 18.16; *J.W.* 2.164–66). Because they were centered in the temple in Jerusalem, it is not surprising that we no longer hear about them after the Romans destroyed the temple in AD 70. The key points, however, are that teaching about the resurrection of Jesus is divisive and that every messianic movement endangered the comfortable existence of the Sadducees. It threatens not just the theology of the Jewish leaders but their role as leaders in Israel itself. If the power of the resurrected Jesus indicates the restoration of everything (Acts 3:21) and

---

3. "The people" (*ton laon*; v. 1) is a specific title for Israel and is rooted in OT covenant theology (e.g., Exod 3:12; 15:13–16; Deut 27:9, 11, 12, 15–26; 28:9; 33:3, 5, 7, 29).
4. See Gary G. Porton, "Sadducees," *DNTB* 1050–51; See also Jeremias, *Jerusalem*, 222–32; Keener, *Acts*, 2:1129–31.

if miracles of healing, like the one of the lame man, are advance signs of the future (including future judgment), then it is unsurprising that this is greatly disturbing to the political elites. The two groups Peter identified earlier (the people and their leaders, 3:17) now begin to separate. The implication is that "the people" receive the promises (see 3:19) even if their leaders continue to reject Jesus and face the consequence of being "completely cut off" (3:23; see also Luke 20:17–19).

Questions to be Faced (4:5–7)

The opposition to the apostles constituted the full weight of the Jewish leadership in Jerusalem: "The rulers, the elders and the teachers of the law" (Acts 4:5). Later this group is simply referred to as "the Sanhedrin" (v. 15).[5] The Sanhedrin roots may go as far back historically to the time of Ezra and Nehemiah when a priestly nobility, who formed an aristocratic council, led the community of Jerusalem (Neh 2:16; 5:7). By the first century, the Sadducees, who often included the high priest and his family who controlled the temple and its precincts, dominated this council. The temple was far more than just a large building for worship. With its sacrificial system, large treasury, and its own police, the temple exerted significant religious, social, and political power. When a Roman governor wanted to do business with the Jews, he dealt with high priests—like Annas, Caiaphas, John, and Alexander—and the leadership of the Sanhedrin. But more than simply alerting us to the power brokers who are calling Peter and John to question, the mention of "the rulers" foreshadows the prayer meeting later in the day when the disciples remind themselves, in the words of Psalm 2, that "the rulers" band together against the Lord and his Christ (Acts 4:26). These rulers, threatened by the power and authority these simple peasants are exerting, ask them an interrelated question: "By what power or what name did you do this?" (v. 7). This question not only relates to the "power" (see 3:12) and "name" (see 3:6, 16) that the apostles called upon in healing the lame man in the previous episode, but it also echoes questions that were hurled at Jesus. Jesus is accused of performing acts of power by the name "Beelzebul" (see Luke 11:14–23), and when he came teaching in the temple he was also questioned about the source of his "authority" (20:2).

Peter's Answer (4:8–12)

If the questions aimed at the apostles are reminiscent of those confronting Jesus, then we should not be surprised that their response to the questions of

---

5. See G. H. Twelftree, "Sanhedrin," *DNTB* 1061–63; Keener, *Acts*, 2:1137–41.

the powerful also reminds us of Jesus. After his baptism and the descent of the Spirit, Jesus is driven into the desert to face difficult questions. "Full of the Holy Spirit" (Luke 4:1), Jesus answers the questions with boldness (Luke 4:8–12). Likewise, Jesus's apostle Peter, "filled with the Holy Spirit" (Acts 4:8), responds to difficult questions. This is precisely as Jesus said it would be: "When you are brought before synagogues, rulers and authorities, do not worry about how you will defend yourselves or what you will say, for the Holy Spirit will teach you at that time what you should say" (Luke 12:11–12). This alerts us to the reality that it is not by the apostles' own "power" that they have healed the lame man but by the power of the Spirit. Again, we are reminded that all that Jesus began to do and teach (see Acts 1:1) continues with his followers in the same way and by the same empowerment.

Peter then continues his short address (4:9–10) by restating and transforming the questions the rulers ask. The question about "power" and "name" are transformed into an opportunity to restate the core of the gospel that he proclaimed on the day of Pentecost (2:23–24) and on the previous day (3:13–15). The "name" in question is Jesus, the Messiah from Nazareth. He also adds a phrase that was sure not to endear himself to his audience: "Whom you crucified but whom God raised from the dead" (4:10). Not only was this phrase theologically offensive to the Sadducees, who did not believe in the resurrection, but it also implicates the leaders in an act of injustice in handing Jesus over to the Romans to be executed. This "name" of Jesus, then, is both offensive to rulers and powerful to heal.

Peter goes further in his speech (vv. 11–12) by quoting from Psalm 118 (v. 22), a well-known "temple psalm." As the apostles stand defending themselves under the shadow of the temple, they remind their inquisitors that Jesus is the "stone *you* builders rejected." Peter emends the wording of the psalm from "the stone the builders rejected" by indicting them with the pronoun "you." Again, Peter's words recall Jesus's story when the teachers of the law and the chief priests questioned him within the temple. Jesus too quoted Psalm 118, and this "stone testimonial" challenged the authorities at the heart of their power in their temple. No longer is the temple in Jerusalem the seat of power and the place of restoration; rather, Jesus is the focus of God's new temple. Stephen in Acts 7 will take up this subversive line even further. For now, however, the apostles declare the words of this wonderful psalm that celebrates God's work of salvation (Ps 118:21, 25) and life-giving power (vv. 15–20) and equate this salvation and power unequivocally with the name of Jesus (Acts 4:12). The final sentence (v. 12) makes it clear that to think of Jesus is at the same time to think of salvation, and to think of salvation is at the same time to think of Jesus. Although the NIV uses the word "healed" (v. 9) to describe what has happened for the lame man who instigated this whole discussion, the word often means "saved" (*sōzō*). Salvation is not just a "spiritual" reality but a physical reality too, just as Jesus taught (Luke 7:22–23). The healing of the lame is a powerful image that indicates the age to come is *already* an enacted truth. The ascended Lord and descended Spirit create wholeness for the broken, boldness for the church, and resistance from the old order.

The Leaders React (4:13–22)

The reaction from the Jewish leaders as they hold a closed council among themselves is first a matter of wonder followed by weakness (Acts 4:13–17). Thus, at first they are amazed at the courage of the apostles, especially because they were unschooled (not necessarily illiterate but certainly unlettered) and ordinary laymen.[6] They did, however, take note that they had been with Jesus (v. 13). What a superb compliment! That is, what made the difference for these men was Jesus—a theological point, not merely a factual one. On the heels of this wonder is a profoundly weak resolution: "There was nothing they could say" because the proof of the power in Jesus's name was standing before them in the person of the healed man (v. 14). Those who possessed so-called *real* power and who asked intimidating questions are now left dumbfounded and asking feeble questions among themselves: "What are we going to do with these men?" (v. 16). It is almost laughable. The boldness of the apostles and the power in Jesus's name is undeniable, and yet the Jewish leaders somehow imagine that a stern warning not to teach in "this name" (v. 17) will silence them!

The leaders call Peter and John back into their presence and issue their decree (vv. 18–22) by commanding them not to utter a word or to teach in the name of Jesus. This command is almost on par with trying to hold back the tide. Yet there is even a deeper irony than this. The apostles retort with a question, inviting them to judge (v. 19), as the rulers and leaders of Israel, on something they should know already: should we listen to you or to God? Many commentators[7] alert us to a parallel story when Socrates responds to the decree of Greek leaders who command him to stop his teaching. Socrates replies: "Men of Athens, I respect and love you, but I shall obey the god rather than

---

6. Longenecker, *Acts*, 300, notes that both accounts of the arrest and appearance of the apostles before the Sanhedrin in 4:1–22 and 5:17–40 "reflect a significant point in Jewish jurisprudence. . . . Jewish law . . . held that a person must be aware of the consequence of his crime before being punished for it." This meant that common people or "unschooled" men like the apostles were first given a legal warning not to speak anymore in the name of Jesus. When the apostles are arrested again (5:17–18), they are reminded of their first "warning" (5:28) before being turned over to be punished for their disobedient ways.

7. E.g., F. F. Bruce, *The Book of the Acts*, rev. ed., NICNT (Grand Rapids: Eerdmans, 1988), 96; Fitzmyer, *Acts*, 304; Schnabel, *Acts*, 246.

you" (Plato, *Apology* 29d). This Greek story may have come to mind for Luke's first audience, Theophilus; but for listeners sensitive to the wider biblical story it might also have evoked the response of the three Hebrew children in Daniel (Dan 3:16–18). Shadrach, Meshach, and Abednego did not feel the need to adhere to the decree of King Nebuchadnezzar to worship his image of gold. The God they served could deliver them from the fiery furnace and from the hand of the king. The apostles had "seen and heard" the truth of the resurrected and ascended Jesus (Acts 4:20; cf. 22:15; 1 John 1:3). Armed with this living truth, they did not fear the rulers' commands and could not hold their tongues. What could the rulers do? After further feeble threats (v. 21), they released them because they could not agree on a punishment that would not result in inciting the people who were now praising God because of the healing. Again, the contrast between the hostile leadership and hospitable people is reinforced in the narrative. Where God's power is at work enacting real change and real healing—even if it is staring them straight in the face in their own midst—there will always be real opposition and real consequences. Real discipleship has always been, and continues to be, costly.

LIVE the Story

Inviting Persecution

Those who carry salvation, healing, and wholeness to others in the name of Jesus will often invite trouble and persecution rather than thanksgiving and praise from those around them. In the days close to when I first wrote these lines, the world was appalled by images of attacks on churches in Pakistan, where eighty-five people died when two suicide bombers rushed into a worship service at All Saints Anglican Church in Peshawar, and in Kenya, where an assault on a Roman Catholic church in Wajir left one dead and two injured. As difficult as these tragedies are, they are part of a larger narrative that has largely been ignored by the Western world, including Western Christians. While Christians in the UK and North America have used words like "persecution" to describe threats to their religious freedom, the reality is that this "persecution" means that Christians might be sued; in places like Pakistan, Syria, Iraq, North Korea, and Burma, Christian persecution means that Christians might be martyred. John L. Allen described this often unnoticed "war on Christians" in an article in *The Spectator*. Allen puts this into perspective by writing the following:

> Consider three points about the landscape of anti-Christian persecution today, as shocking as they are generally unknown. According to the

International Society for Human Rights, a secular observatory based in Frankfurt, Germany, 80 percent of all acts of religious discrimination in the world today are directed at Christians. Statistically speaking, that makes Christians by far the most persecuted religious body on the planet.

According to the Pew Forum, between 2006 and 2010 Christians faced some form of discrimination, either *de jure* or *de facto*, in a staggering total of 139 nations, which is almost three-quarters of all the countries on earth. According to the Center for the Study of Global Christianity at Gordon-Conwell Theological Seminary in Massachusetts, an average of 100,000 Christians have been killed in what the centre calls a "situation of witness" each year for the past decade. That works out to 11 Christians killed somewhere in the world every hour, seven days a week and 365 days a year, for reasons related to their faith.[8]

The reality for many Christians living outside the West is that following Jesus means doing and saying the right thing, even if that doing and saying elicits opposition. My father often reminds me that leadership means "doing the right thing and doing the right thing in the right way." This is well and good, but it still can create tension and, sometimes, even bitter opposition. But if the right thing is done in the name of Jesus and the power of the Spirit, doing and speaking the truth can accomplish remarkable results even in the face of costly persecution.

Ecotones—Transitional Space

One day, my son told me about studying ecotones in biology in high school. *Ecotones* are places of transition between living areas. For example, an ecotone is a transitional space from plains to mountains or from land to water. These are places that are usually teeming with life, filled with both predators and prey. My son found this all fascinating. He described these zones to me with almost breathless excitement because these transitional zones are places of danger and death (important narrative components for a teenage boy), but they are also the places of life and power too. So it is with Jesus. The proclamation of Jesus creates an "ecotone," a transitional space, where there is both healing and opposition, life-giving power and threatening persecution.

In this place of transition, it is the *name* of Jesus that brings life. The early followers of Jesus were keenly aware that there was no other name they could rely on. It reminds me of a scene from Lewis's Narnian book *The Silver Chair*.

---

8. John L. Allen, "The War on Christians," *The Spectator*, 5 October 2013. See also his book *The Global War on Christians: Dispatches from the Front Lines of Anti-Christian Persecution* (Colorado Springs: Image, 2013).

It is Jill Poll's first visit to Narnia, and she is desperately thirsty. Unfortunately, what lies between Jill and a life-giving stream is a ferocious lion. Jill has found herself in a dangerous transitional space—an ecotone—near a river. But there is no other stream that can give her life, and there is no other way to drink from it without passing the lion. There is no other life-giving water; there is no other life-giving way.

Christians are often criticized for their singular commitment to proclaiming salvation in no other name than Jesus (Acts 4:12). But the "name" of Jesus is not some magical formula. It has power only for those who "know Jesus"—who have been with the Lord (4:13). Without a connection to the person behind the name, there is no power. Jesus, as Luke often tells us, is "the Lord" (e.g., Acts 2:36; 4:33; 9:5, 17; 10:36). When Moses inquired of God what he should do when he returns to Egypt and declares to the Israelites that he has come to redeem them from slavery, he asked:

> Suppose I go to the Israelites and say to them, "The God of your fathers has sent me to you," and they ask me, "What is his name?" Then what shall I tell them? God said to Moses, "I AM WHO I AM. This is what you are to say to the Israelites: 'I AM has sent me to you.'" God also said to Moses, "Say to the Israelites, 'The LORD, the God of your fathers—the God of Abraham, the God of Isaac and the God of Jacob—has sent me to you.'" (Exod 3:13–15)

The phrase "I AM" is verbally linked to the small-capped title "LORD" in Hebrew, the NIV's substitute for the tetragrammaton, the personal name of God. It is done out of deference for this sacred name. It is a mark of Luke's exalted view of Jesus in Acts that he regularly refers to him as the "Lord" (*kyrios* in Greek). Just as Moses worked powers of deliverance in the name of the Lord in the first exodus, so now the apostles work miracles of salvation in the name of Jesus, the one they also now call "Lord." This illustrates that the ascended Lord Jesus *in heaven* is never severed from the power that functions through his people *on earth*, especially so for those who are facing the uncertainties of persecution.

CHAPTER 8

Acts 4:23-31

LISTEN to the Story

²³On their release, Peter and John went back to their own people and reported all that the chief priests and the elders had said to them. ²⁴When they heard this, they raised their voices together in prayer to God. "Sovereign Lord," they said, "you made the heavens and the earth and the sea, and everything in them. ²⁵You spoke by the Holy Spirit through the mouth of your servant, our father David:

> "'Why do the nations rage
>   and the peoples plot in vain?
> ²⁶The kings of the earth rise up
>   and the rulers band together
> against the Lord
>   and against his anointed one'¹

²⁷Indeed Herod and Pontius Pilate met together with the Gentiles and the people of Israel in this city to conspire against your holy servant Jesus, whom you anointed. ²⁸They did what your power and will had decided beforehand should happen. ²⁹Now, Lord, consider their threats and enable your servants to speak your word with great boldness. ³⁰Stretch out your hand to heal and perform signs and wonders through the name of your holy servant Jesus."

³¹After they prayed, the place where they were meeting was shaken. And they were all filled with the Holy Spirit and spoke the word of God boldly.

Listening to the Text in the Story: Deuteronomy 6:4; Nehemiah 9:6; Job 41:11; Psalm 2:1, 2; Isaiah 37:16; Daniel 9:25; Hebrews 1:9.

---

1. Ps 2:1, 2.

EXPLAIN the Story

Good storytellers are careful to provide narrative foreshadowing along with repetition of key themes for their audience. These devices need not be obtrusive, but they are necessary tools for the good storyteller. Luke is a master storyteller. Once again, through the natural progression of describing the climax to the subnarrative begun in 3:1, he also reaches back to weave other strands of the story together. He does this in several ways, including the following: with David as a source of prophecy, Luke connects Peter's first speech (1:16) and his words on the day of Pentecost (2:25) with the believers' prayer meeting (4:25); the mentioning of the rulers gathered together (4:27–29) reminds us of the elders and teachers gathered together earlier (4:5–6); the alliance of gentiles and Jewish rulers reaches all the way back to the Gospel when Herod and Pilate first became friends in their common aversion to Jesus (Luke 23:1–25); the theme of God's providence (Acts 2:23; 3:18; 4:12) now returns (4:28); the request for "boldness" (4:29) is reminiscent of earlier episodes (2:29; 4:13); there are repeated fillings of the Spirit (2:4; 4:8; and now in 4:31); and finally, the "name" of Jesus continues to play an important role in the mouth of the apostles (4:30) as it already has in chapter 3 (vv. 6, 16) and earlier in chapter 4 (vv. 7, 10, 12, 17, 18).[2]

Besides all these verbal and thematic links, we are introduced to a new rhythm of disengagement and engagement. That is, there are occasions of temporary disengagement after rejection or persecution followed by renewed engagement with even greater power that occurs regularly throughout Acts. Sometimes these rhythms are difficult for the modern reader to discern, both for those who are reading portions of Scripture devotionally or those who are preparing to preach or teach from a passage, because we tend not to read larger texts, or whole biblical books for that matter, at one sitting. Still, these devices are important to those who are trying to tell or understand a cohesive story—and the story Luke is trying to communicate is the most important story of all, the gospel.

In Luke's grand gospel narrative, this prayer (4:23–31), set in its present context, marks the second description of how the early Christians actually prayed.[3] We are often reminded *that* they prayed, but here is an example of *what* they prayed. After resetting the scene (v. 23), the disciples are brought together in unity to pray by means of a number of biblical passages (vv. 24–26). It is instructive again that these OT passages are viewed through the lens of Jesus's passion (vv. 27–28). This biblical and Christ-centered praying then

---
2. Dunn, *Acts*, 56.
3. The first description was between the ascension and the day of Pentecost (Acts 1:24–25).

shapes their intercessions for their current situation (vv. 29–30). The prayer meeting ends with a remarkable divine "yes" to their petitions (v. 31): the prayer room is shaken, they are refilled with the Holy Spirit, and they are granted the boldness of speech they requested.

The Scene is Reset (4:23)

The narrative is reset after the release of Peter and John, who immediately return to "their own" (v. 23). As detailed as Luke will be about the substance of the ensuing prayer meeting, we simply do not know where "their own" would have been gathered. They are possibly once again at Solomon's Colonnade, which had become a kind of "believers' corner" on the edge of the temple grounds, but this is only a guess.

The Disciples Pray (4:24–30)

The prayer itself opens (v. 24) with an address to God as the sovereign Lord of creation, using language from multiple places in Scripture and elsewhere in Acts (e.g., Acts 14:15; 17:24). The words "who made the heavens and the earth and the sea, and everything in them" are almost a direct quotation from Psalm 146:6 (145:6 LXX). While it might seem unusual to begin by appealing to God as the Creator to open their prayer, it becomes clearer why the disciples did so when we recall that God's sovereignty over his creation is "the basis for confidence in God's ability to help his people when they are oppressed."[4] God, who creates all things, is declared as sovereign over all things, even over the human affairs of those who rebel against him. Beyond Psalm 146, these words also echo the words of the Jews in Nehemiah 9:6 when the law had been recovered and Judah was reestablished after its long Babylonian exile. By echoing this passage in Nehemiah, the early Christians may also be recognizing themselves as the true Israel, just as the returned Babylonian exiles did, but now as the Israel of God that has accepted and identifies with the Messiah, Jesus. While this "Israel" will certainly come to include gentiles as well—an inclusion that is in view from the beginning[5]—the Jewish and Jerusalem-based followers of Jesus are beginning to separate themselves from other claimants of "Israel," just as matters played out in Nehemiah's day. Finally, the text also echoes the prayer of Hezekiah (Isa 37:16). This text is helpful in illuminating the prayer in Acts because, like the disciples who pray to be delivered from the threats of those conspiring against them, Hezekiah also asks God, the sovereign and creator of all, to deliver God's people from the threat of the army of Sennacherib.

---

4. Peterson, *Acts*, 199.
5. See Acts 1:8; 2:39 (those "who are far off"); cf. with 3:25–26.

Shaped by Scripture's narrative arc (Ps 146:6; Neh 9:6; Isa 37:16) at the beginning (Acts 4:24), the early Christians continue to pray by quoting directly from a set prayer in Psalm 2. It may appear difficult to conceive of all the disciples initially raising "their voices *together* in prayer," yet it is possible that they could say or sing this part of the prayer in unison because they knew the book of Psalms by heart. Again, it is important to remember that the Psalter was Israel's prayer book, as it continues to be the prayer book of the people of God today. There is not only continuity in the prayers that are offered, but there is also continuity between the Spirit who spoke through David and the same Spirit who speaks through the disciples in their testimony (cf. Acts 4:8, 31). Furthermore, with David identified as "our father" (v. 25), the early church establishes another signpost to remind themselves that they are the true Israel and the inheritors of the OT patriarchal promises, connected to God's anointed Davidic family line.

The prayer of David that they choose to recite is from the opening of Psalm 2. This psalm is not a random selection. Rather, it reflects themes that bear on their present situation. Like cascading truth, they have affirmed that God is sovereign over heaven and earth. From there, they turn to Psalm 2 to affirm that the Lord who sits enthroned in heaven has established Israel's king as his "anointed one." As such, the king is not only destined to rule Israel but also the entire earth. Of course, the nations, kings, and rulers of the earth are not pleased with this, and they conspire against the Lord and his anointed one. How foolish! They somehow imagine that their plots and threats could dethrone the plan of the sovereign Lord of all creation. Indeed, God has declared the king of Israel to be his Son, and his purposes for his Son will not fail. With this psalm on their lips and its truth in their hearts, the early church envisions itself as caught up in the providential story of God. Although Herod, Pilate, the gentiles, and the people of Israel conspired against Jesus, this was done according to God's preordained power and will (Acts 4:27–28).

The psalm is then applied to their present situation by the emphatic expression "indeed" (v. 27).[6] In a sense, Luke is demonstrating how the early Christians were "living the text" in their own day. The Psalter, in words that were provided by God through "the Holy Spirit" (v. 25), is now understood in relationship to Jesus. The "nations," "kings," and "rulers" of Psalm 2 are mirrored in the gentiles,[7] King Herod, and Pontius Pilate (Acts 4:27). Whereas unnamed forces lined up against God's "anointed one" in Psalm 2, the early Christians name those who conspired against God's "holy servant Jesus, whom

---

6. This connection between Psalm 2 and Jesus is also made grammatically by the connective word "for" (*gar*) at the beginning of v. 27; this word is not reflected in the NIV translation.

7. The NIV's "nations" of v. 25 and "Gentiles" of v. 27 are both from the same Greek word, *ethnē*.

you anointed" (Acts 4:27). All their plots, however, did not catch God off guard; rather, they were all part of God's providential plan. Providence is an important theological feature for Luke and the "fore-" compound words (e.g., "foretold" in 1:16 [NASB; NIV: "spoke long ago"]; "foreknowledge" in 2:23; "foretold" in 3:18) have dotted the narrative in every chapter thus far.[8]

A bridge in the prayer ("now, Lord," v. 29) moves the prayer to the disciples' present situation. They petition God to "consider *their* threats" and act accordingly. The action they desire does not follow the narrative trajectory of Hezekiah to destroy the enemy army of Sennacherib or dash the nations to pieces like broken pottery (cf. Ps 2:9). Instead, they ask that God empower them to speak his word with "boldness" (vv. 29–30). Altogether, the prayer runs through OT passages, interprets them in light of Jesus's trial and execution, and concludes by applying the truth of these texts into their present situation. The reference to "their" threats is somewhat odd since the enemies of the early church are not the same ones that "their" grammatically relates to (v. 27); that is, Herod and Pilate. Still, the relevant point that the early Christians understood is not that the enemies of David, Hezekiah, and Jesus are identical to their own but that their situation *corresponds* to those circumstances, especially the one that Jesus faced.[9]

Once again, the situation corresponds to the words and deeds of Jesus as depicted in the Gospel accounts. It also corresponds to the opposition Jesus faced from his own people. The disciples ask for boldness, attested by signs, so that the "word" they speak will not destroy their enemies but will be heard and received by them. The "word" is qualified as "your word" (v. 29) and "the word of God" (v. 31). "To speak . . . the word" or similar phrases in Acts consistently relate to the preaching of the gospel.[10] It is not their own words that they pray to speak boldly. They ask for boldness to speak *the word*, inspired by the Holy Spirit, about God's Son and Messiah. They ask for boldness, for it is an authoritative word they wish to speak. This is not an authoritative word to manipulate or control people, but like God's authority it is a bold, true word that is designed to liberate people through judgment and mercy. This kind of "gospel authority" both judges and condemns evil and sin (Ps 2 makes plain that judgment falls on those who reject God's Son), in order to set people

---

8. These English "fore-" compound words often stem from Greek words beginning with "*pro-*." That is, "spoke long ago" is the translation for the Greek word *prolegō* (1:16); "foreknowledge" is the translation of *prognōsis* (2:23); and "foretold" is the translation of *prokatangellō* (3:18). In each of these instances God prepares for future eventualities that he will fulfill through the work of the Holy Spirit and prophecy. This theme of providence will continue to reappear throughout Acts (e.g., 7:52; 10:41; 13:24; 22:14; and 26:16).

9. Gaventa, *Acts*, 97.

10. See Acts 8:25; 11:19; 13:46; 14:25; 16:6, 32.

free to be truly human. It is in this sense that the bold word of God brings judgment upon those who reject it, and freedom (see "times of refreshing" in Acts 3:19) to those who accept this "word."

The Prayer is Answered (4:31)

The answer to the disciples' prayer at the end (v. 31) is dramatic. Their meeting place is shaken, they are filled with the Holy Spirit, and they are empowered to speak the word of God boldly. The early church writer Chrysostom is helpful in unpacking God's answer to their prayer. Chrysostom writes:

> Why did [the shaking] happen? Listen to the words of the prophet: "He looks on the earth and it trembles [Ps 104:32]." For by this he revealed that he is present to their prayers. . . . God did this both to make it more fearsome and to lead them to courage. After those threatening conditions, they gained increased boldness. Since it was the beginning of their ministry and they had prayed for a sensible sign for their persuasion (this never happens again afterwards), great was the encouragement they received. In fact, they had no means of proving that [Jesus] was risen except by miraculous signs. Thus it was not only their own assurance that they sought but also that they might not be put to shame, that they might speak with boldness. "The place was shaken," and that made them all the more unshaken.[11]

The shaking was important, but in the end it was the filling that was the source of their boldness. Besides shaking the place where they were staying, this final sentence (v. 31) states two other results of their prayer: *they were filled* with the Holy Spirit, and as a consequence of that filling *they were empowered* to speak the word of God boldly. The dynamic presence of the Spirit at work in the lives of the believers is no match for the threats of the kings and rulers banded together against them. This is no second Pentecost, but it is an assurance that the Spirit continues to work in their lives and ministry. The metaphor, "to fill," is sometimes misunderstood as if prior to this the believers were "empty" of the Spirit. This is certainly not the case (see 2:4; 4:8). We must remember the primary role of the Spirit taught elsewhere (John 14:26). The Spirit's role is to comfort the disciples in trouble and remind them of Jesus's teaching. As they face their first real opposition, the disciples are fearful. They need this ministry of the Spirit. The Spirit is to spotlight the work of Jesus and give peace, and this is what the Spirit's "filling" does for them. They are reminded of the teaching of Jesus, and they are comforted with boldness in

---

11. John Chrysostom, *Commentary on the Acts of the Apostles* 11, in *ACCA*, 54.

the midst of opposition. In a similar manner, the apostle Paul asked for a fresh "provision of the Spirit" so that he would have boldness to proclaim Christ to the opposition he faced (Phil 1:19–20). Likewise, the early Christians receive a fresh provision of the Spirit to enable them to continue their ministry of witnessing to the resurrection of the Lord Jesus (Acts 4:33).

LIVE the Story

In one sense, this episode already provides us with a vivid example of how to "live the story." The early church prayed their Scriptures carefully, understood them in the light of Jesus's life and ministry, and in their own situation leaned into that story of salvation. The goal of their prayer, however, was not trivial. They did not "claim" promises of Scripture to make themselves richer or help them find a good place to sit in the temple. The goal of their prayer was for "boldness"—a boldness to proclaim the gospel effectively, often in the face of opposition. It is a frequent experience among Christians that when they desire to make an effort to speak about Jesus, the cross, and the resurrection, they face considerable resistance. Tom Wright expresses well the effects of this battle: "Sometimes it is with actual, official authorities, as in Acts 4. Sometimes it is with the spirit of the age. . . . Sometimes the battle is internal. . . . Whatever, the battle is real."[12] This should not surprise us. The NT regularly alerts us that we struggle with unseen powers lined up against us when we seek to speak authoritative words that bring freedom, wholeness, and life to people.[13] All of us need this kind of Spirit-empowered boldness to speak words that are effective and true.

It is tempting when we read or experience the Spirit's presence in a unique and powerful way to try to repeat those experiences. In the passage from Chrysostom above, he adds an important aside related to the sign of the Spirit's "shaking" the place where the disciples were praying. He notes, "This never happens again afterwards."[14] How often are we ready with strategies to recruit the Spirit to perform in a particular way? More often than not, the Spirit's work in our lives goes unnoticed. For the most part in Acts, the Spirit nudges and leads gently and unobtrusively. The Spirit's work is not less powerful for doing so. As F. Dale Bruner and William Hordern have carefully explored, the Holy Spirit is the "shy member of the Trinity."[15] God uses us just where

---

12. Wright, *Acts*, 1:71.
13. E.g., Eph 6:12 and 1 Pet 5:8.
14. The earthquake in Philippi (Acts 16:26) may be a notable exception.
15. F. Dale Bruner and William Hordern, *The Holy Spirit: Shy Member of the Trinity* (Eugene, OR: Wipf & Stock, 2001; repr., Minneapolis: Augsburg Fortress, 1984).

we are, often unobtrusively, and yet all the same empowered by the Spirit to give witness to Jesus as we serve, heal, care, teach, and love. The Spirit breathes the creating and living salvation of God in us, body and soul, as we go to work, make meals, run errands, meet friends, and greet strangers. This anonymous, often unheralded work of the Spirit is an apt portrayal of the Spirit in most of Acts; that is, outside of Acts 2 and 4. And yet, even though the Spirit is usually quiet, it is also, as Eugene Peterson notes, a powerful, nurturing presence. "There is a kerygmatic, attention-getting, dramatic quality to the Father's work in creation and the Son's work in salvation that makes the public square an appropriate venue for consideration. When creation and salvation are embodied by the Holy Spirit in ordinary men and women and in ordinary circumstances, these ordinary men and women and circumstances don't ordinarily make headlines, but they are no less powerfully and effectively the work of God."[16]

Given what we know from Scripture and the history of the church about the Spirit's well-known tendency for anonymity, wouldn't it be wiser to pay careful attention to the ways that the Spirit is continually working around us and enter into our part in *that* work with praise? This kind of work, while unglamorous, is vital for healthy hearts, healthy homes, and healthy churches. It requires paying attention to the local and ordinary ways that God is forming the fullness of Christ in my life and the lives of those around me. In pastoral ministry I am acutely aware that many people I know in my parish and community experience the pain of hopelessness. Employment woes, sudden turns in health for us or our loved ones, and unexpected relational strains and breakdowns beset lives every day. We should not minimize these realities or try glibly to explain them away. But neither should we be ignorant to the fact that Jesus is present with us in the midst of whatever difficult circumstances we face. That is the bold interpretive move the first disciples made when they connected the plight of Jesus at the hands of the Jewish authorities and the threats made against them by those same leaders (Acts 4:29). What is needed in the face of opposition, whether it is an external, visible threat or internal, invisible threat, is the "boldness" for witness. This boldness, however, does not come from ourselves as if we could simply muster up courage on our own. The boldness that disciples of Jesus ask for comes as a gracious response by God to prayer through the giving of the Holy Spirit to meet our needs. As we receive the Spirit afresh in our lives, the result should not only be gratitude for this gift but also a declarative witness to Christ's work in our lives.

---

16. Peterson, *Practice Resurrection*, 200–201.

CHAPTER 9

Acts 4:32-37

LISTEN to the Story

³²All the believers were one in heart and mind. No one claimed that any of their possessions was their own, but they shared everything they had. ³³With great power the apostles continued to testify to the resurrection of the Lord Jesus. And God's grace was so powerfully at work in them all ³⁴that there were no needy persons among them. For from time to time those who owned land or houses sold them, brought the money from the sales ³⁵and put it at the apostles' feet, and it was distributed to anyone who had need.

³⁶Joseph, a Levite from Cyprus, whom the apostles called Barnabas (which means "son of encouragement"), ³⁷sold a field he owned and brought the money and put it at the apostles' feet.

Listening to the Text in the Story: Leviticus 25; Deuteronomy 15:4; Joshua 21; Isaiah 58:6–10.

EXPLAIN the Story

We have here another summary from life in the primitive church in Jerusalem similar to one earlier in Acts (2:42–47). Both summaries seem to introduce succeeding narratives, and only at this point do we catch a glimpse of the community's inner life. After each summary there are several vignettes that seem parallel to each other. There are two accounts of miracles (3:1–10 and 5:12–16), both of which lead to encounters with Jewish authorities (4:1–22 and 5:17–42). Additionally, there is an example of the early church's preaching (3:12–26) and praying (4:23–31), plus frequent notices of the effects on the populace, including conversions (2:41, 47; 4:4; 5:14; 6:1), wonder, fear, and glorifying God (2:43; 3:10; 4:13, 21; 5:11, 13, 26). In all of this, Luke seems to have two primary concerns: first, a feeling for the community itself in terms of its inner life and its powerful witness to the gospel; and, second, the new community's relationship to Judaism, which sometimes reflected favor with the people and at other times confrontations with the authorities. Yet for all this, we still are not provided with a sense of chronology or of an inclination on the part of the early church to move outside of Jerusalem. Along with the previous summary (2:42–47), this present summary (4:32–37) describes the apostolic witness to the resurrection (v. 33), the shared fellowship of the early believers in unity (4:32; see 2:42, 44) and goods (4:32, 34–37; see also 2:44–45), and the response of the people (5:11; see also 2:43, 47).

What is portrayed at this point of the story in the life of the early church is their shared fellowship of love and care. Although this important aspect was mentioned earlier (2:44–45), Luke now elaborates on it with an illustration. This generosity and expression of love and care, however, did not mean that everything was peace and light! The episode immediately following this summary is a painful story of deceit (5:1–11), and the episode after that describes the distribution of money to those who had need as a matter that produced friction (6:1–6). So, what was going on? Twice Luke writes that they shared everything they had (2:44; 4:32). This, then, is variously described. The key is "it was distributed to anyone who had need" (4:35), which is reinforced by "there were no needy persons among them" (v. 34). The Jerusalem Christian community fulfilled the biblical ideal, expressed throughout the Law (e.g., Lev 25; Deut 15:4) and the Prophets (e.g., Isa 1:17; 58:6–10; Mic 6:8–12), that there be no "needy" people among them. The reason there was no need among them, as was mentioned earlier (see comments on Acts 2:42–47), was *not* that they were required to sell their property on entry into the believing community. Whatever else, the following two episodes (4:32–37 and 5:1–11) make it clear that this is *not* what "they shared everything they had" means (4:32). The two stories that follow imply that both men (i.e., Barnabas and Ananias) were already members of the community who sold property as the need arose. We will see later (5:4) that Peter's question to Ananias indicates that even after he sold his property the money was still his to do with as he pleased.

One in Heart and Mind (4:32–35)

What motivated the early church to share "everything they had"? The answer is that "all the believers were one in heart and mind" (4:32) and "God's grace was so powerfully at work in them all" (v. 33). This unity and grace expressed itself in their attitude toward possessions. No one claimed that any of their possessions was their own property. As needs arose, their approach was to live as if "what's mine is yours." After they sold their property, the proceeds were given to the apostles, who then distributed them to all as they had need. This is the way, then, that "they shared everything they had."

In order to understand this kind of unity and generosity, it may be helpful to recognize some contextual dynamics existing in the first century.[1] To begin with, the Jerusalem of this time was a city of extremes. There was extravagant wealth for a few (e.g., Herod and his court; merchants; landowners; tax farmers; bankers; and the priestly aristocracy) alongside enormous poverty for the many. Jerusalem's location was a contributing factor for much of this. In many ways Jerusalem existed not because it was located on a fertile plain, at an important trading route, or alongside a major body of water; Jerusalem existed for religious reasons only. It was a terrible location for commerce, and its remoteness created high costs of living for its residents at the best of times. There were high levels of unemployment to go alongside numerous destitute beggars and widows. For those who could find employment, many of them were day laborers that existed hand to mouth. Of course, there were organized charities in the city, including a daily distribution of food at the temple, plus a whole theology of almsgiving. Jesus himself, along with his disciples, was supported by the goodwill of women of means like Joanna and Susanna (see Luke 8:3). It is no surprise that Jesus was aware of and concerned for the poor, and his disciples, following their master, did the same. What all of this suggests is that in caring for the needs of others, the early church was not experimenting with an early form of socialism; their actions were born out of necessity (see 6:1: "*their* widows") and their understanding of what the new life in Christ and discipleship meant.

Barnabas (4:36–37)

The clearest representative of an early disciple who understood that the appropriate response to great "grace" (v. 33) is great generosity is the Levite named Joseph, also known as Barnabas. Luke remarks, as an aside, that his nickname, "Barnabas," means "son of encouragement" (v. 36). Scholars have not yet been able to discover this meaning for "Barnabas" either in Hebrew or Aramaic.[2] We are not sure how Luke came to this definition for his name. Keener suggests that his original name, "Joseph," was so common that he was given a "nickname to distinguish him from others by that name."[3] While the origin of Barnabas's name is unclear, what is clear is that this quality of encouragement is a well-deserved moniker for him. Barnabas is one of the most attractive and winsome characters in the early church. He will figure prominently in later

---

1. For an excellent resource on this see Jeremias, *Jerusalem*. See also Ze'ev Safrai, *The Economy of Roman Palestine* (London: Routledge, 1994).
2. Barrett, *Acts*, 1:258–59, offers a detailed discussion of the name "Barnabas."
3. Keener, *Acts*, 2:1180–81.

chapters of Acts as a kind of relational bridge-builder, who works tirelessly in the expansion of the gospel among the gentiles along with the apostle Paul (see 13:1–2). In fact, it was Barnabas who provided Paul with a crucial endorsement after his conversion and drew him into the circle of the apostolic company. The early-church leadership was initially skeptical of Paul, given his previous role in persecuting the church. It was the support and encouragement of Barnabas that certified Paul's credentials with the Jerusalem church (9:27) and later with the leadership in Syrian Antioch (11:25–26).

At this stage, however, it is not merely Barnabas's generosity of spirit that is highlighted; it is his generosity with his possessions that is noted. Although Levites in the OT were not given allotments of land,[4] by NT times Levites like Barnabas owned property. At this point in the narrative the inclusion of his sale of a field and use of the proceeds to benefit the needs of others in the Jerusalem church not only indicates his generous response to God's grace but also marks him as a comparative foil to Ananias's actions with the sale of his property recorded immediately following this passage. Up until Acts 5, the church had been experiencing great grace and generous unity, as well as rapid growth and some external opposition. The story of Ananias will, for the first time, introduce a crisis internally within the church. In this sense, the summary that began in 4:32 really extends into the next part of the story up to 5:11.

LIVE the Story

In ways that are sometimes subtle and sometimes overt, Luke has been offering descriptive marks of authentic Christianity in the first few chapters of Acts. Those marks include knowing God, speaking about God, and following the generosity of God—all done with great "boldness" (see 4:29, 31). The connection between boldness and generosity is important. In 4:31 we read that the people experience boldness, and immediately after that they are generous in sharing what they had (v. 32). What is the connection? People certainly hold on to their money and possessions because they are greedy or materialistic. But what the story of the early church reminds us is that another fundamental reason we hold tightly to our money is because we are scared or fearful. Fear, like love, is a powerful motivator. Michael Leunig, a wonderful Australian cartoonist and writer, picks this up in his prayer:

> *There are only two feelings.*
> *Love and fear.*

---

4. See Deut 10:9; 12:12; 14:27–29; 18:1; Josh 21:1–41.

> *There are only two languages.*
> *Love and fear.*
> *There are only two activities.*
> *Love and fear.*
> *There are only two motives,*
> *two procedures, two frameworks,*
> *two results.*
> *Love and fear.*
> *Love and fear.*[5]

When we are afraid, whether it is fear that the banks will fail or our retirement savings will be insufficient or our property will not hold its value, our tendency is to clutch our money even tighter. It is not always greediness; it is fearfulness that often prevents us from being generous. When God is revealed to our hearts through the presence of the Holy Spirit, as he was to the early church, we discover that we don't look to savings and lands to give us security in the world. Only God can do this; only God can make us safe and sound. When God is secondary to us, our money often becomes primary; when God is not the spring of our security, we hold onto our money because we are afraid it will dry up. But when the love of God is made real to our hearts and minds, we are able to share our money because we are bold.[6] The result is that one of the marks of genuine Christianity is profound generosity. Mature and bold Christians are generous with their time, they are generous with their talents, and they are generous with their treasure. This generosity tends to increase as we become more rooted in God, more mature in Christ, and experience more of the Spirit in our lives. We may not often be "shaken" by the Spirit, but we have an unshakable quality that produces boldness and openhandedness with our time, our energy, our relationships, and our finances.

Genuine Christian community is presented in 4:32–37—and throughout chapters 1–4, for that matter—as involving knowledge of God and God's word, mission, and mutual support. Such community is possible only through a powerful encounter with God's grace and the empowering presence of God's Spirit. The warmth of the witness of Barnabas, described both as a "son of encouragement" (4:36) and later as "a good man, full of the Holy Spirit and faith" (11:24), is a model for discipleship. He is a person who weaves together belief in God with behavior that is expressed in mission and mutual support for other believers.

---

5. Michael Leunig, *When I Talk to You: A Cartoonist Talks to God* (Sydney: HarperCollins, 2004), n.p. Used by permission.

6. Timothy J. Keller, "Shaken: A Sermon on Acts 4:23–35," gospelinlife.com, 29 Oct. 1995 (available through Redeemer Presbyterian store: https://gospelinlife.com/downloads/shaken-6413/).

CHAPTER 10

Acts 5:1-11

 ## LISTEN to the Story

¹Now a man named Ananias, together with his wife Sapphira, also sold a piece of property. ²With his wife's full knowledge he kept back part of the money for himself, but brought the rest and put it at the apostles' feet.

³Then Peter said, "Ananias, how is it that Satan has so filled your heart that you have lied to the Holy Spirit and have kept for yourself some of the money you received for the land? ⁴Didn't it belong to you before it was sold? And after it was sold, wasn't the money at your disposal? What made you think of doing such a thing? You have not lied just to human beings but to God."

⁵When Ananias heard this, he fell down and died. And great fear seized all who heard what had happened. ⁶Then some young men came forward, wrapped up his body, and carried him out and buried him.

⁷About three hours later his wife came in, not knowing what had happened. ⁸Peter asked her, "Tell me, is this the price you and Ananias got for the land?"

"Yes," she said, "that is the price."

⁹Peter said to her, "How could you conspire to test the Spirit of the Lord? Listen! The feet of the men who buried your husband are at the door, and they will carry you out also."

¹⁰At that moment she fell down at his feet and died. Then the young men came in and, finding her dead, carried her out and buried her beside her husband. ¹¹Great fear seized the whole church and all who heard about these events.

Listening to the Text in the Story: Joshua 7:1; 2 Samuel 6:3, 6–7; 1 Chronicles 13:7, 9–10; Titus 2:10.

EXPLAIN the Story

Despite the chapter break, the stories at the end of chapter 4 and the beginning of chapter 5 are related.[1] They are related thematically and verbally. The thematic link is the sale of property for the benefit of the community; the verbal link is the repeated reference to "feet"—whether it is the "apostles' feet" (Acts 4:35, 37; 5:2; cf. 5:10) or the "feet" of the ones who carry out the bodies of Ananias and Sapphira (5:9). They are linked stories, but also contrasting stories. Barnabas represents a generous and virtuous example for the Christian community; Ananias, along with his wife Sapphira, represents those who follow the deceits of Satan and lie to the Holy Spirit and their brothers and sisters in Christ. This short, ominous passage is arranged in two movements: Ananias's deception and the repercussions of his lie (5:1–6) and Sapphira's complicity with Ananias's dishonesty (5:7–11).

Up to this passage in Acts, the budding Christian community in Jerusalem has been experiencing remarkable numeric and spiritual growth alongside emerging opposition from the Jewish religious leadership. Any problems they have faced have come from outside their community until now. Several key questions emerge from listening to this passage: What have Ananias and Sapphira actually done to deserve death? How does Peter interpret their actions? And, finally, what impact does this encounter have on the young Jerusalem church?

The first two verses set the scene of the episode (5:1–2). Like Barnabas and others able to do so (see 4:34–37), Ananias, on his own initiative and without compulsion from the Jerusalem leadership, sold a piece of property and gave the proceeds to the believing community for the needs of others.[2] We are not told the amount of money received from the property or the amount withheld in the donation. The text only tells us that Ananias "kept back" (5:2) part of the sale for himself, with the full knowledge of his wife, and proceeded to put the rest of it at the apostles' feet. The uncommon word for "kept"[3] may echo

---

1. Peterson, *Acts*, 207, observes that Luke's second summary of the life of the church in Jerusalem includes all the material from Acts 4:32–5:16. Even more interesting, he suggests that this second summary serves as an "expanded version of 2:42–47." A significant reason for the inclusion of the Ananias and Sapphira episode is to explain why "everyone was filled with awe" (2:43).

2. Although the word for "field" is different in Acts 5:1 from 4:37, both words indicate that it was landed property.

3. The Greek word is *nosphizō*. The word is used only twice in the LXX (Josh 7:1; 2 Macc 4:32), and only once more (outside of its two uses in Acts 5:2, 3) in the NT in Titus 2:10, where it is translated as "steal." Outside of its biblical usage, this verb refers to the misappropriation of funds or a skimming operation regarding the distribution of booty. See examples of this in Polybius, *Histories* 10.16.6; 2 Macc 4:32; Josephus, *Ant.* 4.274; Plutarch, *Pompey* 4.1. See BDAG, s.v. *nosphizō*, 679.

the story of Achan in Joshua 7.[4] In that story, the Israelites are fresh off their victory at Jericho after years of desert wandering, only to experience their first reversal with the deception of Achan (see Josh 7:1, 19–26). The circumstances in these two cases, of course, are vastly different. Ananias did not embezzle "devoted things" as Achan did; rather, Ananias "kept" part of the money from the sale of his property. Still, the Greek word that Luke chooses to express Ananias's deceit—translated as "kept" in the NIV (Acts 5:2, 3)—is the same uncommon word used in the Greek LXX where Achan "took" (as in "stole") some of the devoted things from the conquest of Jericho. The implication is that once items or property are devoted to the Lord they are no longer the possession of the person who gave it.[5] In this sense, Ananias's actions are similar to those of Achan. In both circumstances the result is judgment and death for the perpetrator and members of their immediate family.

The temperature begins to rise in the next sentences (vv. 3–4) with a series of four questions directed at Ananias by the apostle Peter and concluding with a final analysis of the result of Ananias's actions in the last statement (v. 4). This accusation reveals a theological interpretation for Ananias's deceit: he has "lied" not merely to human beings but to God (v. 4).[6] The nature of this deceit is indicated in Peter's first question to Ananias, "How is it that Satan has so filled your heart that you have *lied to the Holy Spirit. . .* ?" (v. 3), and later in a similar question to his wife, "How could you conspire to *test the Spirit of the Lord?*" (v. 9). The failure on the part of this couple is not that they retained part of the sale of the property for themselves. It was never compulsory in the early Christian community to sell property and give everything to the common fund. The issue is that they lied about what they did. This is where the larger theological issue enters the frame. The confrontation between Ananias and Sapphira and the apostle Peter is not merely a human-to-human conflict but is another instance of the longstanding clash between Satan and the Holy Spirit. In a similar way, Satan, the great tempter and adversary,[7] who tested Jesus in the wilderness (Luke 4:1–13) and who "entered" Judas in order to pervert the plans of God (22:3), is now at work within the early church. Ananias, with his heart "filled" with Satan (Acts 5:3),[8] has lied to God, and along with his

---

[4]. Peterson, *Acts*, 209, also highlights that the collusion of husband and wife to try to lie to God indicates a parallel with Adam and Eve in Gen 3 (cf. Keener, *Acts*, 2:1184).

[5]. Gaventa, *Acts*, 102.

[6]. Calvin, *Acts*, 1.5.1, correctly notes: "Luke condemneth no other fault in Ananias than this, that he meant to deceive God and the Church with a [false] offering."

[7]. Satan is established as the primary adversary of God in the Gospel of Luke in 10:18; 11:18; 13:16; 22:31; cf. Acts 26:18.

[8]. In contrast with being "filled" with the fruit of the Spirit (see Acts 13:52).

wife Sapphira, who conspired to "*test* the Spirit of the Lord" (v. 9),⁹ receive the consequence of their calculating and corrupt actions.

The story of Ananias and Sapphira is in many ways regrettable and, to many modern readers, harsh. The episode does, however, serve a number of purposes in the broader narrative. First, it is worth noting the sheer folly of lying to God. Second, it serves to enhance the authority of the apostles, especially Peter. The apostles are not merely the CEOs of a human corporation but are God's representatives on earth and, inspired by the Holy Spirit, speak for God. Jesus gave Peter the authority to bind things on earth, and this is a vivid example of what this kind of authority can do. More importantly, this confrontation serves to enhance the "fear" (see vv. 5 and 11) of the Lord and the person of the Holy Spirit. It is not Peter who causes the death of Ananias and Sapphira; it is God. This is reminiscent of the "awe" associated positively with God's power at work through "wonders and signs performed by the apostles" after Pentecost (2:43). From this angle, this regrettable and negative episode can be seen to serve as further evidence that God is with his church (5:11) and is keen to protect it from that which would seek to corrupt and pervert it from within.¹⁰ The episode also functions as a bridge to the next section, which summarizes the continuance of "signs and wonders" performed by the apostles (5:12) and the galvanizing of the church resulting from conflict with the Jewish leadership. It is a strength that the apostles and the church will need when they face further persecution (5:17–42), arrests (6:8–15), and even martyrdom (7:1–60).

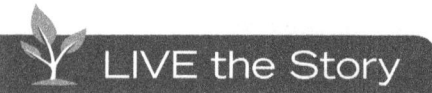

LIVE the Story

This is a strange story. There are parts difficult to figure out; there are questions hard to find answers for; moreover, there seems to be gaps in the narrative. Still, there is something about the true nature of Christian community that is revealed here. The people of God who are filled with the Holy Spirit are to

---

9. The notion of putting God to the test is a familiar theme in Israel's desert wanderings (e.g., Exod 17:2, 7; Num 14:22; Deut 6:16; 33:8; Ps 95:8–10).

10. Interestingly, this is the first instance in Acts (5:11) where the word "church" (*ekklēsia*) occurs. The Greek word *ekklēsia* is used frequently in the LXX (e.g., Deut 9:10; 18:16; 23:1–2 [23:2–3 LXX]; 31:30; Josh 8:35 [9:2 LXX]; Judg 20:2; 1 Kgs 8:14; 1 Chr 13:4; Ezra 10:12; Ps 22:22 [21:23 LXX]; Prov 5:14; Joel 2:16) to describe Israel as the assembly of people gathered by God. The word "church" (*ekklēsia*) never appears in the Gospel of Luke. Peterson, *Acts*, 213, observes that "by reserving the use of such a significant term for this climactic moment in the narrative, Luke was characterizing the group that God had been gathering to himself through the preaching of the gospel as the community saved by Jesus for entrance into his end-time kingdom. . . . God was unmistakably designating them as his own, the new Israel in the midst of the old."

live holy lives that represent Jesus's visible presence on earth. This is expressed later in Acts (9:5) where Jesus's words reveal to Paul another aspect of the same reality: "I am Jesus, whom you are persecuting" (see 22:8; 26:15). That is, what Paul was doing in persecuting those who follow Jesus and were "in Christ" was, in effect, done to Jesus himself. This should be sobering for us. Years ago, Eugene Peterson warned me and other graduates at Regent College that we should post signs around our church buildings: "Beware God! Religion is a dangerous thing, and attending to the things of God can lead us into difficulties and dangers that may cost our lives."[11] He drew on the related stories of Uzzah and David (cf. 2 Sam 6) to illustrate that we need to be protected against religion that does not fear the Spirit of the Lord.

This episode accentuates the danger of mishandling "holy things"—that which has been set apart for the Lord. Although Ananias did not have to sell his property and donate the proceeds to the early church's common fund, once he set the money apart it was recognized as holy. If we use or touch things that have been set apart to God for our own personal gain, we are in danger just as much as Ananias. We are like Uzzah, son of Abinadab (2 Sam 6:3, 6–7; 1 Chr 13:7, 9–10), who tried to manage and control God by steadying the ark of the covenant when David was bringing it to Jerusalem. The story of Ananias and Sapphira too reminds us that holy things, set-apart things, are also perilous things. Every Sunday I am conscious of this, and it is why I wash my hands and pray before beginning the communion service in my parish. I pray this prayer: "Give virtue to my hands, O Lord, that every stain may be removed; so that I may be enabled to serve thee without defilement of mind or body." I know that I am a sinner and that my hands are not holy. I wash them as a reminder that Jesus is the one who cleanses me so that as I touch holy things in his name—the bread and cup—I might not endanger myself. Verse 4 says that when Ananias told the apostles the price of the property he sold and the actual money he offered, he lied not just to humans but also to God (cf. 4:19 and 5:29). His actions and his deceitful words in relationship to this holy offering put him in a very dangerous place. As if Ananias, or any of us for that matter, could get away with lying to the living and holy God!

The story of Ananias and Sapphira reminds us that our offerings are part of our worship, and we worship a God who enters history, supremely through his incarnate Son and now by his Spirit. We are not in relationship with an idea or an abstract God—some kind of sentimental fog in the universe. We worship a God who makes and keeps covenant, who in the words of Zechariah has raised up salvation for us through Jesus "to remember his holy covenant,

---

11. Eugene Peterson, "Why Did Uzzah Die? Why Did David Dance?," the 1995 Regent College convocation address (https://www.regentaudio.com/products/why-did-uzzah-die-why-did-david-dance).

the oath he swore to our father Abraham" (Luke 1:72–73). God enters into our history, makes covenant with his people, and expects us to take seriously this covenantal relationship through our worship and our thank offerings. We worship the merciful and all-loving God who seeks the lost and comforts the brokenhearted, and because of this we must express profound gratitude to him. We also worship the holy and all-knowing God, and because of this we must express profound humility before him.

With all this in mind, we must turn to the "awe-full" question: Why did Ananias and Sapphira die? For us, this is a difficult question that arises from a difficult passage in Acts. How harshly God appears to react to this dishonest couple is not easy to reconcile with how graciously God reveals himself to us elsewhere in Acts and, for that matter, elsewhere in Scripture. The overarching story of Scripture tells us about the God who relentlessly seeks those who are far off from him. We may understand the judgment associated with disobedience, but sudden death? How did we get from a lie about some money to capital punishment within the space of what appears to be a brief conversation? This is a significant gap in the narrative. Eugene Peterson also reminded us young graduates that "when a storyteller [like Luke] leaves gaps in the story, there is an implicit invitation for us to enter into it, to participate in it. . . . We are not permitted to do anything we wish with that or imagine anything we wish. We are constrained by the context, by this revelation we have been given; but within the constraints of the revelation of God showing himself to us we are invited to participate and bring our prayerful imaginations into the text."[12]

There is a gap in what has been narrated, so how do we bridge this gap and what are we to learn from this story? It seems that we must learn that it is fatal—if not utterly foolish—to try to manipulate God. We must not think that we can tell God what he can and cannot do, and we are not responsible for God or his judgments. Somewhere along the line, Ananias had decided, for selfish reasons, that he would try to lie to the apostles and, more importantly, lie to God. Somehow Ananias had forgotten that he could not put God to his service in support of his own ego or to establish his own credibility. Luke tells us that this way of acting indicates that the ways of Satan filled the heart of even a follower of Jesus. Ananias had crossed a line with the God who had filled his people with the Holy Spirit at Pentecost and established his holy presence in their midst. This presence is not to be trifled with nor a line to be crossed any more than the line that marked out Mount Sinai when God's presence descended on that mountain to meet with Moses (Exod 24:1–18) or that marked out the ark of the covenant as David was bringing it to Jerusalem

---

12. Peterson, "Why Did Uzziah Die?"

(2 Sam 6:1–7) or that marked out the holy of holies in the tabernacle and temple itself (Exod 28:29–43; cf. 1 Kgs 8:1–11; 2 Chr 5:2–14). In this case, Ananias and Sapphira are given to us as witnesses to the reality of God at work in the world, just as the apostles and the Holy Spirit are witnesses to that reality. The fourth-century Cappadocian father Gregory of Nyssa wrote:

> Peter says to Ananias, "Why has Satan filled your heart, to lie to the Holy Spirit?" showing that the Holy Spirit was a true witness, aware of what Ananias had dared to do in secret, and by whom the secret was made known to Peter. For Ananias became a thief of his own goods, secretly, as he thought, from all people and concealing his sin. But the Holy Spirit at the same moment was in Peter, and detected his intent, dragged down as it was to avarice, and gave to Peter from himself the power of seeing the secret, while it is clear that the Spirit could not have done this had it not been able to behold hidden things.[13]

Thus, the Spirit and the apostles are witnesses, but Ananias and Sapphira uniquely are "witnesses of warning" to remind us that we cannot manage or deceive God. While some might regard this story as an example of the arbitrariness of God, we could also view it along the lines that Lewis frequently used to refer to the unpredictability of Aslan in *The Chronicles of Narnia*: he is not a *tame* lion. In this sense, we do not worship and follow a "tame" God whose ways can be predicted or controlled by the actions (including the prayers) of his people. In this knowledge, we do well to be seized with a holy awe and fear of the Lord of all.

---

13. Gregory of Nyssa, *On Not Three Gods*, in *ACCA*, 60.

CHAPTER 11

Acts 5:12–16

 LISTEN to the Story

¹²The apostles performed many signs and wonders among the people. And all the believers used to meet together in Solomon's Colonnade. ¹³No one else dared join them, even though they were highly regarded by the people. ¹⁴Nevertheless, more and more men and women believed in the Lord and were added to their number. ¹⁵As a result, people brought the sick into the streets and laid them on beds and mats so that at least Peter's shadow might fall on some of them as he passed by. ¹⁶Crowds gathered also from the towns around Jerusalem, bringing their sick and those tormented by impure spirits, and all of them were healed.

Listening to the Text in the Story: Exodus 7:3; 11:10; Deuteronomy 4:34; 26:8; 34:11; Psalm 78:43; 105:27; Jeremiah 32:20; Luke 8:43–48.

 EXPLAIN the Story

This short paragraph in Acts (5:12–16), much like two earlier ones (2:42–47 and 4:32–35), functions to introduce the material that is to follow (5:17–42)—the occasion of the apostles' second appearance before the Jewish authorities in Jerusalem—a thread that may have been lost after the Ananias and Sapphira episode (5:1–11). Luke weaves together the story line by connecting it with what has come just before and with what will soon follow. For example, the apostles evoked a sense of fear and awe from the people who saw and heard what they were doing (see 5:11, 13), and the regard the people had for the apostles gave the captain and his guard a healthy sense of "fear" when they apprehended them in the following narrative (see 5:14, 26). This summary paragraph, especially the first three sentences (vv. 12–14), reaches back further with the mention of "Solomon's Colonnade" (see 3:11) and the addition of believers (see 2:47), and the increasingly bold witness to the resurrection of Jesus recalls earlier episodes in Acts. The plot, which appears sometimes jumbled in this summary paragraph, progresses from the reverential fear of the church and people (cf. 5:5, 11) to the growing animosity from the Sadducees (5:17–33), to the final increased joy and confidence of the apostles (5:41–42).

For all that Luke does to weave this paragraph to its immediate context in Acts, the accent on the apostles "signs and wonders" connects it to God's much broader story. The phrase "signs and wonders" is a familiar phrase found often in the LXX to describe God's mighty deeds on behalf of his people, especially in delivering them from their bondage in Egypt (e.g., Exod 7:3; Deut 4:34; 26:8; 34:11; Jer 32:20; cf. Exod 11:10; Pss 78:43; 105:27). Most importantly, God expressed his supreme act of deliverance through Jesus, accredited by "wonders and signs" (Acts 2:22; see also 2:19). Here is yet another example in Acts of Jesus's followers continuing the work that their Lord commanded and empowered them to do. Peterson notes that the signs and wonders authenticate and affirm the missionary preaching of the word of God.[1] The point, however, is not to highlight "signs and wonders" carried on by followers of Jesus but to cast the spotlight on the apostles and other leaders in the early church (see also 6:8 and 15:12) as a means of expressing the life of the resurrected and risen Jesus in their midst. Or, to put it another way, the signs and wonders performed by followers of Jesus made earth begin to look like heaven.

Despite the shock that the crisis of Ananias and Sapphira created for early believers in Jerusalem, this paragraph describes a restored and even reinforced community. In the first two sentences (5:12) we return to the "signs and wonders" performed by the apostles (see 2:43), as well as to their favorite place of meeting at "Solomon's Colonnade" in the temple grounds (see 3:11). They met here because they had no building or space of their own; or perhaps they viewed the broader world as their meeting place. Dunn helpfully suggests that meeting here "implies that the leaders of the new movement saw the Temple, or at least the huge Temple platform, as the natural place for them to be in these last or interim days."[2] The reminder of their meeting place in the temple also foreshadows the conflict that will come later (ch. 7) where Stephen highlights the Christian community at odds with the temple, the primary symbol of Jewish faith.

If the "signs and wonders" of the apostles are clearly communicated by Luke to begin this paragraph, the responses by different groups of people generated by the apostles' deeds are somewhat difficult to follow. Luke refers to three groups of people who respond to the apostles' mighty deeds with a

---

1. Peterson, *Acts*, 215. See also Leo O'Reilly, *Word and Sign in the Acts of the Apostles: A Study in Lucan Theology*, Analecta Gregoriana 243 (Rome: Editrice Pontificia Università Gregoriana, 1987).
2. Dunn, *Acts*, 65.

mixture of holy fear and respect. The first group are the believers, which in the Greek text is literally "all those who gathered at Solomon's Colonnade" (v. 12b). The second group referred to is accounted for as "no one else" (v. 13a; lit., "the rest"), who did not dare to join the believers out of trepidation or reverent awe. This almost certainly refers to unbelieving Jews. The third group mentioned are "the people" (v. 13b; cf. v. 12), referring to the population at large who "highly regarded" the apostles. C. K. Barrett observes, "The Christians were (according to this verse) popular and left in peace, when not actually joined."[3] From this group of sympathetic Jews, Luke adds parenthetically that there came "more and more men and women [who] believed in the Lord" (v. 14). It is interesting to note Luke's concern for both men *and women*. The characteristic inclusion of women as disciples of Jesus in Acts[4] is something that carries through from the Gospel of Luke and is especially noteworthy for that culture.[5]

The final sentences (vv. 15–16) continue the logic that begins earlier (v. 13). Again, the "people"—not only believers—are drawn to the healing power at work through the apostles. The sense of awe at the wonders performed by the apostles is a profound answer to Peter's earlier prayer (4:29–30). As healing followed from those who simply touched the edge of Jesus's cloak (Luke 8:43–48), so also Luke describes how even the shadow of Peter casts healing virtue when it falls upon the weakened bodies lining the streets (Acts 5:15). This is the second place in Acts describing healing power flowing through Peter (see 3:1–10). Yet in this instance it is not just a single cripple being healed, it is "crowds . . . from the towns around Jerusalem" (5:16) who are being healed and receiving relief from impure, tormenting spirits. Beyond the number of those being impacted by the apostles, the scope of their work is notable too. This is the first instance in Acts where the news from Jerusalem reaches beyond the city to the surrounding area, and is thus the first hint of what Jesus promised at the beginning (1:8). Furthermore, this is also the first mention of something characteristic of Jesus's own healing ministry: exorcisms. The exorcism of evil spirits may be linked to the previous episode: as with Ananias who allowed himself to be an agent of "Satan" (5:3), so with those possessed by "impure spirits" (v. 16). The Evil One, and his minions, is no match for the discerning and delivering power of the Holy Spirit. The holiness

---

3. Barrett, *Acts*, 1:275.
4. Notice how women are included as equal recipients of the Spirit (Acts 2:18) and the gospel (8:12; 9:2; 17:12) and, as such, are also deemed worthy targets for persecution too (8:3; 22:4).
5. E.g., note the key roles of women like Elizabeth, Mary, and Anna in Luke 1–2, along with Mary Magdalene, Joanna, and Susanna in Luke 8:2–3. Again, in 24:10 Mary Magdalene and Joanna reappear, along with Mary the mother of James, as the first witnesses to the empty tomb who carried the news to the apostles.

of the community who name Jesus as Lord and live in the power of the Spirit remains a central virtue. With their numbers growing, their scope enlarging, and their power increasing, it is little wonder the jealousy of the Sadducees is inflamed (5:17).

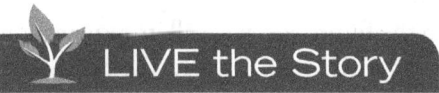
LIVE the Story

As we listen to Luke tell us about "signs and wonders" performed by the apostles, it should certainly remind us both of the signs and wonders that God performed on behalf of Israel in releasing them from bondage in Egypt as well as of Jesus's own powerful signs and miraculous wonders. Exodus from Egypt and "new exodus" in Jesus frame this episode in Acts within the larger biblical and theological map of God's power going out and doing new things as part of reversing the effects of the fall and bringing about the new creation. The significance in pointing all this out is that signs and wonders are not simply about providing critical medical care for people who need it. Nor do they offer a "gospel show" that pushes aside other religious or political spectacles. The signs and wonders are part of the demonstration that the *future* kingdom of God (see Acts 1:6–8) is *already* breaking in with new and creative power, first in the life and work of Jesus and now through the lives and work of his followers. In part, this is what it means to practice the resurrection life of Jesus in the world. For some, this resurrection life is cause for celebration and rejoicing, for seeing and believing. For others, it is also cause for concern because it not only challenges the worldviews of those who don't believe in the supernatural, but challenges political powers as well. After all, what can earthly threats of punishment have over those who see people healed?

An ongoing problem of Luke's descriptions of signs and wonders is that we may either dismiss them or try to duplicate them. Luke's point seems simply to offer a narrative account of the gospel's growth and not a prescriptive account of how God is supposed to answer our prayers or meet our needs. God is neither predictable nor democratic. Here in Jerusalem, Peter's shadow falling on the infirm brought them healing, but nowhere else in Luke's narrative does this happen with his shadow.[6] We sometimes expect God to be fair and equal everywhere; if God worked with Peter's shadow in Jerusalem, then why not the shadow here in my town or in my life? Frankly, I have no idea why God may immediately heal a crippled boy in one place and allow a suffering child to die after years of treatment in another. God does not do the same thing for everybody. For example, later in chapter five Peter and the other apostles

---

6. There is, however, a similar situation with Paul and handkerchiefs and aprons (Acts 19:11–12).

are delivered from prison, while a few chapters later James is executed by the sword (12:2); in chapter seven Stephen is stoned to death in Jerusalem, while in chapter fourteen Paul is stoned in Lystra and yet recovers from his injuries.

A good friend has a wonderful description of the prayer of those who grapple with the mystery of living between the overlap of the ages: the present age, with all its suffering and grief, and the future age, with all its resurrection life and power. Cherith describes the prayer that we make to God this way: "Lord, is this an already day or a not-yet day?" In the apostles' day no less than ours, we must accept that God can do whatever he pleases. Our place is to pray and trust in him. Sometimes God will outstrip our feeble expectations by meeting our needs in our "already" existence; other times, we accept that tragedies occur, people get sick, and all of us (even Lazarus who was resuscitated by Jesus) will die as we wait for all that is not yet healed to be restored. In the meantime—and often the overlap of the ages is extremely dangerous and cruel—we should not look for a simple burst of signs and wonders in our midst identical to those described in Acts. God is far too creative to offer any dittoes. Although he could easily do that as well, we look for the power of the living God to become a tangible and irrefutable reality in the difficult and dangerous places where we live. In northern Nigeria, it may mean the power for Christians to withstand the violent threat of Islamic extremists while reaching out with love to work for peace with Islamic moderates. In Pakistan, it might mean the courage to run a Christian hospice, caring for disabled and abandoned children with little funding from Christian brothers and sisters in the West. In North America, it might mean the empowerment that Christian social workers need to help establish a housing project for those who cannot afford soaring local rents, or to work with drug users to kick abusive and addictive habits. In this way, our expectations of God can be both tempered and expanded as we consider Christian existence between the "already" present age and the "not-yet" realities of the age to come. As the church, we may then begin to consider our task between the times more like "that of a midwife than as an epidural," as Brené Brown suggests. She describes how in her own grief she came to realize this: "I thought faith would say, I'll take away the pain and discomfort, but what it ended up saying was, I'll sit with you in it."[7] In this difficult in-between space, may we have the hope to expect more than we can ask or imagine and the patience to accept that things don't always work out the way we would like them to.

---

7. Brené Brown, "Jesus Wept," *The Work of the People*, http://www.theworkofthepeople.com/jesus-wept.

CHAPTER 12

Acts 5:17-42

 LISTEN to the Story

¹⁷Then the high priest and all his associates, who were members of the party of the Sadducees, were filled with jealousy. ¹⁸They arrested the apostles and put them in the public jail. ¹⁹But during the night an angel of the Lord opened the doors of the jail and brought them out. ²⁰"Go, stand in the temple courts," he said, "and tell the people all about this new life."

²¹At daybreak they entered the temple courts, as they had been told, and began to teach the people.

When the high priest and his associates arrived, they called together the Sanhedrin—the full assembly of the elders of Israel—and sent to the jail for the apostles. ²²But on arriving at the jail, the officers did not find them there. So they went back and reported, ²³"We found the jail securely locked, with the guards standing at the doors; but when we opened them, we found no one inside." ²⁴On hearing this report, the captain of the temple guard and the chief priests were at a loss, wondering what this might lead to.

²⁵Then someone came and said, "Look! The men you put in jail are standing in the temple courts teaching the people." ²⁶At that, the captain went with his officers and brought the apostles. They did not use force, because they feared that the people would stone them.

²⁷The apostles were brought in and made to appear before the Sanhedrin to be questioned by the high priest. ²⁸"We gave you strict orders not to teach in this name," he said. "Yet you have filled Jerusalem with your teaching and are determined to make us guilty of this man's blood."

²⁹Peter and the other apostles replied: "We must obey God rather than human beings! ³⁰The God of our ancestors raised Jesus from the dead—whom you killed by hanging him on a cross. ³¹God exalted him to his own right hand as Prince and Savior that he might bring Israel to repentance and forgive their sins. ³²We are witnesses of these things, and so is the Holy Spirit, whom God has given to those who obey him."

> ³³When they heard this, they were furious and wanted to put them to death. ³⁴But a Pharisee named Gamaliel, a teacher of the law, who was honored by all the people, stood up in the Sanhedrin and ordered that the men be put outside for a little while. ³⁵Then he addressed the Sanhedrin: "Men of Israel, consider carefully what you intend to do to these men. ³⁶Some time ago Theudas appeared, claiming to be somebody, and about four hundred men rallied to him. He was killed, all his followers were dispersed, and it all came to nothing. ³⁷After him, Judas the Galilean appeared in the days of the census and led a band of people in revolt. He too was killed, and all his followers were scattered. ³⁸Therefore, in the present case I advise you: Leave these men alone! Let them go! For if their purpose or activity is of human origin, it will fail. ³⁹But if it is from God, you will not be able to stop these men; you will only find yourselves fighting against God."
>
> ⁴⁰His speech persuaded them. They called the apostles in and had them flogged. Then they ordered them not to speak in the name of Jesus, and let them go.
>
> ⁴¹The apostles left the Sanhedrin, rejoicing because they had been counted worthy of suffering disgrace for the Name. ⁴²Day after day, in the temple courts and from house to house, they never stopped teaching and proclaiming the good news that Jesus is the Messiah.
>
> *Listening to the Text in the Story:* Deuteronomy 21:22–23; Daniel 3:16–28; 6:1–28; Hebrews 2:10; 12:2.

EXPLAIN the Story

The signs and wonders performed by the apostles elicit both fear (5:11) and honor (5:13) from the people of Jerusalem, but jealousy (5:17) and rage (5:33) from its leaders. After all the popular attention the apostles receive, they are again arrested to face the Jewish leadership council, the Sanhedrin. Luke displays his flair for storytelling in this section with a dramatic escape, a comic moment, and unexpected characters. In all this, Luke emphasizes the developing attitudes against the apostles in Jerusalem by noting the increased hostility from the high priest and Sadducees, which stands in contrast to the openness from the people and moderation from a Pharisee. In both opposition and acclaim the apostles experience increasing joy and confidence.

This section bears striking resemblance to what has preceded (4:1–31) where the apostles' healing of a cripple led to arrest, confrontation, and threats from the Jewish leaders. Yet for all the similarities with the earlier episode, in what follows (5:17–42) the drama is heightened. It is not just one healing that draws attention; rather, multitudes have gathered to receive healing. The high priest and his associates are not merely inquisitive about the power and boldness of the Galilean apostles; they are now jealous and enraged. Finally, while the main characters are reintroduced, in this episode two unexpected individuals appear—first an angel in the jail and then a moderate Pharisee, Gamaliel, in the Sanhedrin. Yet for all these new and amplified elements, this section follows a simple outline: the apostles are arrested and escape (5:17–21a); they are arrested a second time (5:21b–26); the high priest confronts the apostles, and Peter and the other apostles respond with a courageous reply (5:27–32); Gamaliel intervenes with a word of caution, which leads to the apostles' release (5:33–40); and finally, upon their release, the apostles' joy, confidence, and status are renewed and reinforced (5:41–42). The narrative intensifies as the Christian proclamation faces increasing opposition, which serves to prepare the reader for the death of Stephen and the arrival of Saul in the following two episodes (chs. 6 and 7).

Arrest and Escape (5:17–21a)

It should come as no surprise that after their initial encounter with the high priest and Sanhedrin (4:5–22), which resulted in a stern warning "not to speak or teach at all in the name of Jesus" (4:18), that they are arrested again and thrown into a public jail. After all, Jesus's followers should expect trouble from the very group who executed Jesus in the first place. When the apostles continue to speak and teach despite the warning, the high priest and his Sadducean associates are filled with "jealousy" (5:17). The reason for their zealous indignation was given concisely in the previous paragraph: the apostles continued with their proclamation of Jesus among the people with many "signs and wonders" accompanying their ministry (v. 12). The antagonism of the Sadducean, temple-based leadership operates on several levels. Theologically, the Sadducees thought the apostles' preaching of Jesus's resurrection was an egregious falsehood.[1] Socially, they rejected the untutored apostles' determination to teach the people on the temple grounds. Politically, the royal overtones of their proclamation that Jesus was the Messiah endangered the Sadducees' comfortable existence as Jewish leaders in Jerusalem, who theologically had no room or category for a messiah.

---

1. Luke makes this explicit later in Acts 23:8. Josephus discusses the antisupernatural philosophy of the Sadducean "sect" in *J.W.* 2.164–66; *Ant.* 13.173; 18.16.

Luke follows the expected arrest of the apostles with a brief account of their surprising deliverance. An angel[2] of their Lord opens the prison door, leads them outside, and instructs them to return to their position in the temple courts and resume teaching the people about this way of life. It is not only surprising that an angel delivers them but that Luke narrates this so matter-of-factly. It is easy to overlook the contrast between the jealous will of the high priest and the limited power of his officers with the generous care of the Lord and the unlimited power of his angels. John Calvin writes:

> The Lord brought the apostles out of prison, not because he would rid them quite out of the hands of their enemies, for he suffered them afterwards to be brought back again, and to be beaten with rods; but he meant to declare, by this miracle, that they were in his hand and tuition . . . [although] we must not hope always, nay, we must not always desire that God will deliver us from death; but we must be content with this one thing, that our life is defended by his hand, so far as is expedient. In that he useth the ministry of an angel, in this he doth according to his common custom; for he testifieth every where in the Scriptures, that the angels are ministers of his goodness towards us. Neither is that a vain speculation, for this is a profitable help for our infirmity, that we know that not only God doth care for us, but also that the heavenly spirits do watch for our safety.[3]

Second Arrest (5:21b–26)

The second arrest is almost comedic. The reader may smile at the description of the exalted high priest convening the full weight of the political, legal, and religious authority of the Jewish leadership to put the apostles to trial again,[4] but when their soldiers arrive at the prison to retrieve the apostles, they find the cell locked and guarded, but empty (5:23)! Of course, the chief priest and his officers were perplexed. Instead of asking what this might mean

---

2. Dunn, *Acts*, 68, suggests that we "cannot exclude the possibility that . . . 'the angel or messenger (same word) of the Lord' was actually an early sympathizer with the new movement within the prison staff." While it is correct that the same word can be translated both as "angel" or "messenger," the regular occurrence of angelic messengers along with the descriptor "of the Lord" (which elsewhere in Luke-Acts indicates an angelic being: see Luke 1:11; 2:9; Acts 8:26; 12:7, 11, 23) seems to indicate that it was not a human messenger.

3. Calvin, *Acts*, 1.5.17.

4. Because our sources are limited, it is difficult to know what constituted the Sanhedrin prior to the destruction of Jerusalem in AD 70. The Sanhedrin could either mean a meeting place, like a courtroom, or an assembled leadership body. In Acts 5:21, however, Luke uses two words to refer to the gathered assembly—*synedrion* and *gerousia*—with the intended effect to indicate the significance of the authorities arrayed against the apostles. For a more detailed description of the Sanhedrin, see G. H. Twelftree, "Sanhedrin," *DJG* 729–33.

and pondering the divine will, the chief priest responds to the news that the prisoners are back standing and teaching in the temple by stubbornly using the only force at his disposal, the captain of the temple guard and his officers, to arrest the apostles again. But it is now a chastened power, since Luke notes that the captain and his officers apprehended the apostles without using force "because they feared that the people would stone them" (5:26; see 4:21). Gaventa writes: "Instead of the apostles being afraid of the powerful, the powerful are afraid of the apostles."[5]

Peter's Courageous Reply (5:27–32)

After the apostles are brought to the Sanhedrin, the high priest opens with the charge that they are blatantly ignoring the previous command not to "teach in this name" (5:27–28; cf. 4:17–18). It is interesting that in this second accusation the high priest seems at pains not to mention the name "Jesus" itself. Furthermore, Peter and the apostles attach bloodguilt to the priestly leaders (5:28). Although this has not been mentioned in Acts since prior to their first arrest (2:23; 3:13–15), it can be assumed that this was emphasized by the apostles whenever they preached. The net result is not only have they ignored the high priest's commands, but they have redoubled their efforts so that they have "filled Jerusalem" with their teaching, including the fact that the Jewish leaders are regarded as culpable in Jesus's death.

The apostles respond in unison to the high priest's order: "We must obey God rather than human beings!" (5:29). This reiterates their previous reply, "Which is right in God's eyes: to listen to you, or to him?" (4:19). In many ways the apostles are following the footsteps of other biblical models of civil disobedience represented in the well-known stories of Daniel. Like Shadrach, Meshach, Abednego, and Daniel (Dan chs. 3 and 6), the apostles confess that the legal duty of law-abiding citizens to obey the courts is overridden by the higher duty to obey God.[6]

The short but carefully crafted response to the charges (5:29–32) is framed at the beginning and ending with the same word, "obey." Between these two poles, the relational center of obedience is highlighted by the repeated mention of the word "God." God is named four times in the space of the four verses. Not only is God named, but God is the primary subject: God raised Jesus (5:30), God exalted Jesus to his right hand (v. 31), and God has given the Holy Spirit to those who obey him (v. 32). While the response is theologically rooted in God's actions, it also strikes significant christological notes. The emphasis is

---

5. Gaventa, *Acts*, 107.
6. Another similar model, albeit a nonbiblical one, is Socrates, who replies to the charges of the Greek court, "I shall obey the god rather than you" (Plato, *Apology* 29D).

on Jesus's resurrection first and only secondly his death. Yet when the speech does mention the means of Jesus's death, it does so echoing the language of Deuteronomy (21:22–23), where anyone "hanging on a tree" for a capital offense is cursed by God.[7] There is evidence that by the first century this phrase was applied to death by crucifixion, as Paul does in Galatians 3:13.[8] It may be that the apostles' accusers used this passage in Deuteronomy to discredit the claim that a crucified man could also be the Messiah. Although the messiahship of Jesus will not be affirmed again until the end of this passage (Acts 5:42), the short speech does assert that Jesus's exalted status implies that he is both "Prince[9] and Savior."[10]

These two claims for Jesus would certainly have struck a blow to the high priest and to the integrity of the temple itself. Why? Because the high priest was considered the leader, a prince so to speak, of the people of Israel, not least on the Day of Atonement, that day when once a year the high priest went into the holy of holies in the temple to offer the sacrifice for the forgiveness of sins. Yet the apostles boldly declare that the resurrected Jesus is the true prince, their pioneering leader who leads them into new creation and is the link connecting heaven and earth. Jesus is also Savior, the one who has broken the power of death and rescues his people from other dangers too—such as political oppression, religious persecution, or imprisonment. As such, Jesus is presented as the new focal point for Israel, and he will do what Israel previously looked for in their high priest and temple. Jesus brings them God's gifts of repentance and forgiveness of sins. What a challenge! The short speech then

---

7. That is, the word translated as "cross" in the NIV at Acts 5:30 is *xylon*, which can also be translated as "tree." In Acts, whenever Luke refers to the "cross," he only uses the word *xylon* (cf. 10:39; 13:29); in the Gospel, whenever Luke refers to the "cross" he only uses the word *stauros* (cf. Luke 9:23; 14:27; 23:26).

8. Fitzmyer, *Acts*, 337, observes "in the last pre-Christian centuries 'hanging on a tree' became a way of referring to execution by crucifixion." For example, the Qumran community, commenting on Nahum 2:11–13, notes: "Its interpretation concerns the Angry Lion who filled his den with a mass of corpses, carrying out revenge against those looking for easy interpretations, who hanged living men from the tree, committing an atrocity which had not been committed in Israel since ancient times, for it is horrible for the one hanged alive from the tree" (4QpNah [or 4Q169] 3–4 II, 6–8) in *The Dead Sea Scrolls Translated: The Qumran Texts in English*, trans. Florentino Garcia Martinez (Leiden: Brill, 1994), 195. Further, "if there were to be a spy against [God's] people who betrays his people to a foreign nation or causes evil against his people, you shall hang him from a tree and he will die" (11QTemple LXIV, 7–8) in *Dead Sea Scrolls*, 178.

9. *Archēgos* is the Greek word translated as "prince" in Acts 5:31. It is not an easy word to translate. It can mean "leader, prince, ruler," or "someone who begins something," or "originator, founder, pioneer." Each of these meanings was used to refer to patrons, founders, or heroes in the Greco-Roman world. It is a rare word in the NT and is used only one other time in Acts (3:15), where it is translated in the NIV as "author." It is used only two other times in the NT, both in Hebrews (2:10; 12:2), where it is translated in the NIV as "pioneer."

10. This title is used only once more in Acts (13:23), but it does encapsulate the concept of salvation through repentance and forgiveness of sins, one of Luke's favorite themes.

ends with the double declaration that not only are the apostles witnesses to these things, but God's very own Spirit is a witness to them as well.

Gamaliel's Intervention (5:33–40)

The provocative words of the apostles' speech resulted in rage and death threats from the high priest and his council. What is surprising is that someone from within this leadership group "stood up" and offered temperate counsel. The man who stands up is Gamaliel, a Pharisee (v. 34). Notice of Gamaliel's intervention should take the reader completely off guard—even more so than that of Joseph of Arimathea after the council's action against Jesus (Luke 23:1, 50–53). Up until this point in Acts, the Pharisees have not even been mentioned alongside the aristocratic Sadducees and priestly leadership in Jerusalem. Now, Luke introduces a Pharisee in the Sanhedrin itself! We can guess that Luke has known about the Pharisees' inclusion in the council before this, but he introduces Gamaliel at this point into the story with considerable dramatic effect. Steve Mason writes, "This implies that he has a specific role for the Pharisees in his narrative, which he does not wish to confuse with the Sadducean chief priests' role."[11] Furthermore, in Acts Gamaliel is the first nonbeliever to speak at length.

Gamaliel is also known as "the Elder."[12] He is the grandson of the rabbi Hillel, known for his moderate posture on matters of the law in contrast to the other great rabbi of the day, Shammai, who always endorsed zealous keeping of the law that included, if necessary, violent enforcement of the law. Clearly, Gamaliel followed his grandfather. He was a leading and honored Pharisee, esteemed both for his personal piety and his extensive knowledge of the law. He was also, according to Acts (22:3), a teacher of the apostle Paul. Among his students, he is noted as the first rabbi to be granted the title "Rabban" ("our Master") rather than the ordinary Rabbi ("my master").[13] Although it is easy for modern ears to hear the word "Pharisee" and associate it with hypocrisy, we need to be aware that Luke did not make this association. Gamaliel is portrayed as a thoughtful and esteemed man, "a teacher of the law, who was honored by all the people." Whatever else, he is a shrewd, popular official, who is careful to weigh prevalent piety against political practicalities.

The argument of Gamaliel is relatively straightforward (5:35–39). He takes seriously Peter's claim (5:29), as his answer indicates: if the purposes of this

---

11. Steve Mason, "Chief Priests, Sadducees, Pharisees and Sanhedrin," in *The Book of Acts in Its Palestinian Setting*, ed. Richard Bauckham, vol. 4 of *The Book of Acts in Its First Century Setting*, ed. Bruce W. Winter (Grand Rapids: Eerdmans; Carlisle: Paternoster, 1995), 150.
12. P. L. Maier, "Chronology," *DLNT* 186.
13. See m. Sotah 9:15. See Maier, "Chronology," *DLNT* 186.

movement are from God, there is no stopping it, but if it is not from God it will certainly fail. Gamaliel's conclusion is drawn not only from common sense but also by the precedence of history. He provides two examples to demonstrate his point. The two rebel cases he cites were well known, and they substantiate the conclusion he makes.[14] Both Theudas and Judas the Galilean led popular revolt movements, and since they both lacked support from God, they were defeated and their followers scattered. Gamaliel's conclusion represents the climax not only of this scene but also of the story of opposition that began earlier (4:1): if these men are indeed from God, they cannot and will not be stopped or silenced.

Gamaliel's wait-and-see approach, which doesn't exclude a sound flogging of the apostles and a repetition of the old threats, proves to be persuasive to the other leaders (5:40). This may have been due to his effective oratorical skills and argument. It may also have been due to others factors related to "the people" of Jerusalem. The leaders may also have considered the threefold reality that this Pharisee was highly respected by the people (5:34), the people supported the apostles (5:13), and the leaders were afraid of the people (5:26). At this point, the story line could go one of two ways: Gamaliel's influence among the leaders may lead to increasing openness to the Christian faith in the Sanhedrin, or the Pharisees and the people might be drawn toward the opposing stance of the chief priests. The upcoming episode involving Stephen will prove to be decisive.

Renewed Joy (5:41–42)

At this point in the narrative, the apostles emerge from their ordeal with renewed joy and reinforced vigor. A couple of aspects in these two sentences are noteworthy. First, the apostles rejoiced as they "left the Sanhedrin." They had just been flogged, presumably with the forty lashes minus one (see 2 Cor 11:24). As frequent and familiar a punishment as this may have been, their

---

14. The details accord quite closely to Josephus's account in *Ant.* 18.1–10; 20.97–98; *J. W.* 2.117–18; 7.252–53, but the chronology differs significantly. According to Josephus, the Theudas episode occurs in AD 44, about ten years later than Gamaliel's speech, and the Judas episode occurred before Theudas, not after it, in AD 6 when the census was taken. We need not judge Luke's record too harshly by modern standards of historiography. Loveday Alexander points out that Luke is providing the occasion and gist of the argument even if circumstantial details are amiss; this is "in line with the normal practices of ancient historians like Thucydides" (*Acts: The People's Bible Commentary* [Oxford: The Bible Reading Fellowship, 2006], 53). Another important observation, alerted to me by Christopher Beetham (personal communication), is that if Luke is accurately narrating what Gamaliel said on this occasion then the issue is not Luke's historiography but Gamaliel's! That is, the discrepancy would be Gamaliel's account vs. Josephus's account, not Luke vs. Josephus. In the end, the important issue is that the rhetorical point of Gamaliel's speech remains the same regardless of the chronological details.

identity that has been shaped by "the Name" offset and reframed their understanding of suffering. The priority of the name of Jesus, the one who is now reaffirmed as the Messiah, provides them not only with the sum and substance of their teaching but also with the source of their strength. Their prayer for power and boldness has been answered (4:29–30).

Second, despite the threats and persecution, the apostles maintain their center of operation in the temple courts in Jerusalem (5:42). For now, Gamaliel has provided them some space to maneuver, and they take full advantage of it to never stop "teaching and proclaiming the good news that Jesus is the Messiah" (v. 42). Luke also mentions that they continued to meet "from house to house" as well. This anticipates the climactic struggle that will take place next (chs. 6–7) in the temple and the need for a secondary base of operation.

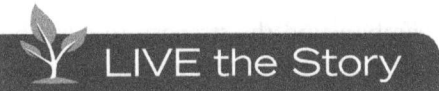

LIVE the Story

The Courage of Le Chambon

Tucked inside the southeastern corner in a remote and mountainous region of France near the Italian and Swiss borders is Le Chambon-sur-Lignon. For centuries the area has been home to dissident Protestant groups, primarily the Huguenots, and during the Nazi occupation of France the five thousand residents of Le Chambon became a very open pocket of resistance. They did not resist with guns but with goodness. The local Huguenot pastor was a man named André Trocmé.[15] On the Sunday after France fell to Germany, Trocmé preached a sermon, declaring that if the Germans required them to do anything contrary to Jesus and the gospel, then they would not obey. Trocmé reminded his listeners, "The responsibility of Christians is to resist the violence that will be brought to bear on their consciences through the weapons of the spirit."[16] When the Vichy government demanded that school children must begin their day with the fascist salute, they refused. When the teachers in Le Chambon's school were required to sign an oath of loyalty to the government, they refused to sign it.

---

15. For a thoughtful reflection on André Trocmé and the fierce and passive resistance he led against the Nazis, see Malcolm Gladwell, *David and Goliath: Underdogs, Misfits, and the Art of Battling Giants* (New York: Little, Brown, 2013), 263–75. See also Carol Rittner and Sondra Myers, *The Courage to Care: Rescuers of Jews During the Holocaust* (New York: New York University Press, 1986), 99–121; Marianne Ruel Robbins, "A Grey Site of Memory: Le Chambon-sur-Lignon and Protestant Exceptionalism on the Plateau Vivarais-Lignon," *Church History* 82.2 (2013): 317–52. For online resources, see United States Holocaust Memorial Museum, "Le Chambon-Sur-Lignon," Holocaust Encyclopedia, https://www.ushmm.org/wlc/en/article.php?ModuleId=10007518, and Yad Vashem, "André and Magda Trocmé, Daniel Trocmé," Yad Vashem.org, http://www.yadvashem.org/righteous/stories/trocme.

16. Chambon Foundation, http://www.chambon.org/weapons_colombat1_en.htm#_edn2.

Before long, Jewish individuals and families began to make their way to Le Chambon. Without question and without demands, the residents of Le Chambon took them in. Over the course of the war over five thousand Jews were fed, hidden, or transferred to safety across the borders—in clear and open defiance to the Nazi regime.[17] On one occasion when Nazi officials came to the town, a group of students met them and presented them a letter stating the reasons for their brazen defiance: "We feel obliged to tell you that there are among us a certain number of Jews," the letter stated. "But, we make no distinction between Jews and non-Jews. It is contrary to the Gospel teaching. If our comrades, whose only fault is to be born in another religion, received the order to let themselves be deported or even examined, they would disobey the order received, and we would try to hide them as best we could. We have Jews. You're not getting them."[18]

Where did the residents of Le Chambon find the strength to defy the Nazis? Trocmé declared that their heroic handling of opposition, persecution, and suffering came from "the weapons of the spirit." The Huguenots endured just such opposition before in seventeenth-and eighteenth-century France when they were ruthlessly persecuted by the state. But the model for Christian courage goes back much further to Acts when the apostles defied the Sanhedrin in Jerusalem with the words, "We must obey God rather than human beings" (5:29). This set the bar for the repeated periods of persecutions of Christians over the next three centuries, and it fueled the hearts of the residents of Le Chambon in 1941. When the apostles spoke, they knew they were looking into the eyes of people who wanted to kill them. Their heroism was virtuous and principled in the face of opposition and persecution; they consulted their consciences despite the danger and opposition.

Jesus Christ Our Hero

While many of us will never face the kind of stark challenges of a threatening Sanhedrin or an oppressive regime, we all need courage. Most of us need daily courage to tell the truth to people who might respond with anger; to face another difficult day seeking employment in a difficult job market; or to work for a supervisor who takes us for granted or belittles our work. Most of us need courage just to face the daily fears and anxieties that gnaw at the foundation of our lives. All of us need courage for life, and in the end everyone will face death and will need courage then, because despite all the great intentions to avoid death and surround ourselves with friends and

---

17. See "Le Chambon-Sur-Lignon," https://www.ushmm.org/wlc/en/article.php?ModuleId=10007518.
18. Gladwell, *David and Goliath*, 267.

family, we will ultimately do so alone. For these and countless other acts of courage, we require the character formation to live and speak with principled courage. So how do we get it?

Peter and the apostles identify the source of their courage in their defiant speech to the Sanhedrin. The source of their courage came from their "Prince" and "Savior," Jesus.[19] While many of us identify with Jesus as our Savior, the apostles use the word *archēgos* to sit alongside that title. Again, this word is used in the NT only four times, twice in Acts (3:15 and 5:31) and twice in Hebrews (2:10 and 12:2). *Archēgos* is a word that in the Greco-Roman world could also be translated as "pioneer," "author," or "hero." In the Greco-Roman world, one of the ways people developed courage in their children was by telling them stories of heroes like Achilles, Hercules, and Odysseus. On one level it appears the early Christians are inspired by their culture to tell their own story of a hero—the hero Jesus, who is both like and unlike the Greco-Roman heroes. Jesus, like other heroes, had power, but his fundamental difference is that he gave up his power: he gave up his invulnerability and immortality. He relinquished his glory to save us all. That was his courage and his heroism, and it stands in contrast to the world's view of heroism and courage. Furthermore, that kind of heroism is not subject to misuse and abuse as it constantly was by the "heroes" of the ancient world. It is this kind of heroism that the apostles needed; it is this kind of heroism that the residents of Le Chambon needed; and it is this kind of heroism we need. We need a courage that is not just for those who are innately strong but also for those of us who are all too aware of our weaknesses.

Yet how do we obtain this courage? Timothy Keller reminds us that there are only two ways.[20] The first is to turn our focus inward. For example, top athletes and leaders often meditate on important phrases or use visualization techniques to drive out fear by focusing on positive images or thoughts. Some of us may even wish to try Jedi-like techniques recommended by Obi-Wan Kenobi in *Star Wars* to "let go your conscious self and act on instinct. . . . Your eyes can deceive you; don't trust them." The problem here is that one must ignore large portions of reality in the process if we are relying only on our own inner resources. To try to banish fear this way is to be blind to the fact that bad things can and do happen. This approach requires one to be ignorant in order to be courageous. Whatever else, the residents of Le Chambon were not

---

19. Fr. Thomas Hopko, former dean emeritus of St. Vladimir's Seminary, offers superb reflections on the names of Jesus, including "Pioneer and Perfector," through his podcast series entitled "The Names of Jesus," Ancient Faith Ministries, started March 2009, http://www.ancientfaith.com/podcasts/namesofjesus.

20. Timothy J. Keller, "The Hero of Heroes: A Sermon on Acts 5:27–42," gospelinlife.com, 3 Feb. 2013, https://gospelinlife.com/downloads/the-hero-of-heroes-6211/).

uninformed about what the Nazis could do to them, and their "weapons of the spirit" refer to a power given to them inwardly—the gift of the personal presence of the Holy Spirit—to stand up to the reality of soldiers and guns and laws of the state.

The second way is to focus outward. As important as it is to discern the Spirit's leading from within, we also need to look outward, beyond ourselves to something or Someone else who can be our focal point amid our fear. While the Spirit led Jesus, he also took an outward look when courage was most required of him. Jesus acted courageously when he went to the cross. He was still fearful, he was afraid, he was human—so how did he do it? The author of Hebrews says that he looked at something that enabled him to go forward despite his fears: "For the joy set before him he endured the cross, scorning its shame" (Heb 12:2). What was that joy? What joy did Jesus not have in heaven that existed on the other side of the cross? What was he looking at? He already had the joy of loving his Father and living in unity with the Holy Spirit. I would suggest that a joy he did not have was his family, his "many brothers and sisters" (cf. Rom 8:29). As the author of Hebrews also notes, the hero of our salvation "is not ashamed to call [us] brothers and sisters" (Heb 2:11). It was the joy of sharing his relationship with his Father and loving us that focused our hero's gaze.[21] Jesus wasn't looking at himself; he was looking outward. He focused on fulfilling the will of his Father and on lovingly bringing us into his family.[22] Jesus was looking at his Father and on us, and this enabled him to be courageous despite his fears. Now if we, like the apostles and author of Hebrews, want to be brave, we must fix "our eyes on Jesus the pioneer [*archēgos*] of [our] faith" (Heb 12:2a).

---

21. See F. F. Bruce, *The Epistle to the Hebrews*, rev. ed., NICNT (Grand Rapids: Eerdmans, 1990), 339. Bruce makes the connection between the joy that the author of Hebrews speaks about and the joy that Jesus makes frequent reference to in the upper room discourses in the Gospel of John (cf. John 15:11; 16:20, 21, 22, 24).

22. N. T. Wright, *Hebrews for Everyone* (Louisville: Westminster John Knox, 2004), 150.

CHAPTER 13

Acts 6:1-7

LISTEN to the Story

¹In those days when the number of disciples was increasing, the Hellenistic Jews among them complained against the Hebraic Jews because their widows were being overlooked in the daily distribution of food. ²So the Twelve gathered all the disciples together and said, "It would not be right for us to neglect the ministry of the word of God in order to wait on tables. ³Brothers and sisters, choose seven men from among you who are known to be full of the Spirit and wisdom. We will turn this responsibility over to them ⁴and will give our attention to prayer and the ministry of the word."

⁵This proposal pleased the whole group. They chose Stephen, a man full of faith and of the Holy Spirit; also Philip, Procorus, Nicanor, Timon, Parmenas, and Nicolas from Antioch, a convert to Judaism. ⁶They presented these men to the apostles, who prayed and laid their hands on them.

⁷So the word of God spread. The number of disciples in Jerusalem increased rapidly, and a large number of priests became obedient to the faith.

Listening to the Text in the Story: Exodus 18:13–27; Numbers 11:16–30; 27:16–23; Luke 22:26–27.

EXPLAIN the Story

The claims that Luke makes in previous summaries in Acts (2:44; 4:32) that the earliest community in Jerusalem "had everything in common" begin to make more sense at the beginning of chapter 6. From their shared resources or "community of goods" the early church in Jerusalem *daily* ensured that those among them who were in need were looked after in the context of fellowship over daily meals.¹ One of the most vulnerable kinds of individuals in the ancient world was a widow, especially a widow who did not have immediate family to care for her.² Within the broader narrative of Acts, Luke takes the occasion of the dispute between "Hellenistic" and "Hebraic" Jews to draw together a number of threads from the previous panel as a whole and introduce several new elements before launching into the next panel (6:8–9:31).

This short section casts a backward glance by reminding us that the growing community of believers continues to engage in daily fellowship in Jerusalem, under the leadership of "The Twelve," the apostles. In addition to looking back, this section also introduces new elements, such as the "Hellenistic" Jewish Christians, a new group of leaders known from elsewhere as "the Seven" (21:8), and a new term in Acts—"disciples"—used to refer to early followers of Jesus. These seven verses are pivotal words in the narrative. In them we are introduced to key components as to how the church makes its break from being a Jerusalem-based, Jewish-led sect of Judaism to becoming a worldwide movement full of gentiles as well; this is what the next panel is all about and why the first panel probably ends with mention of the Hellenists. For it is Hellenist Christians, like Stephen and Philip, who lead this new initiative apart from the apostles, even though they are recognized by the apostles.

Grumbling in the Camp (6:1–4)

The Greek word translated as "complained" (6:1) by the NIV is *gongusmos*. It has a wonderful onomatopoetic quality to it—the word, as you roll it around in your mouth, has a rumbling and grumbling sound to it. It is the same word used in the LXX when the Israelites were grumbling, often about food, in their desert camp against God and his leader, Moses (see Exod 16:7–9, 12; Num 17:5, 10 [17:20, 25 LXX]). The source of the grumbling in the opening sentence of this next narrative (v. 1) relates to the daily distribution of food, especially for widows. Luke does not spend any time diagnosing who is at fault. It should not be surprising though that a community, by now numbering in the thousands, should run into logistical problems like this. There was likely a large number of widows in the community, especially from Jews born outside of Palestine, who now lived in Jerusalem. Haenchen suggests that "perhaps the number of Hellenistic widows was relatively large, for many pious Jews in the evening of their days settled in Jerusalem so as to

---

1. For an excellent discussion of the early church's gathering and use of their "community of goods," see Brian Capper, "The Palestinian Cultural Context of Earliest Christian Community of Goods," in Bauckham, *Book of Acts in Its Palestinian Setting*, 323–56.

2. The OT has much to say about the care of vulnerable widows. See, e.g., Exod 22:22–27; Deut 10:17–18; 24:17–22; Pss 68:5; 146:9; Isa 1:17. The welfare of widows seems to be of particular interest in Luke's writings: Luke 2:36–38; 4:24–26; 7:12; 18:1–8; 21:2–3; Acts 9:39, 41.

be buried near the Holy City; the widows of such men had no relatives at hand to look after them and tended to become dependent on public charity."[3] Luke describes the widows who were overlooked as being Hellenists (v. 1, *Hellēnistai*) in contrast to the Hebraists (v. 1, *Hebraioi*). Before commenting on the solution to the dispute, it is important to consider what Luke meant by "Hellenistic" and "Hebraic."

The question of the distinction between these two words is difficult. Luke is the only writer in the NT to use the Greek word translated "Hellenistic" (Acts 6:1; 9:29; 11:20 [NIV: "Greeks"]).[4] Since the word "Jew" does not appear in the original Greek text alongside either of these two nouns, the question is this: Is Luke referring to Jews and gentiles or distinguishing between two kinds of Jews? H. J. Cadbury argues on the basis of a later sentence (11:20), where Luke uses the term almost certainly to refer to gentiles over against Jews, that "Hellenists" in the present sentence refers to gentile Christians.[5] But it is important for the investigation to begin here, not with 11:20. Here, Luke likely intends a differentiation between Jewish Christians, something we can infer from a number of factors. First, just a few sentences later a certain "Nicolas"—a gentile convert to Judaism—is named among the seven Hellenists responsible for caring for their widows; describing Nicolas as a proselyte makes no sense if all seven were gentiles already. Secondly, Stephen, another of the seven Hellenists, is confronted by diaspora Hellenist Jews now gathered in Jerusalem (6:9), is tried before a Jewish council (6:12), and gives a thoroughly Jewish speech (7:2–53). Finally, for Luke there simply are no gentiles in the church before Cornelius (10:1–48). All in all, this suggests that the distinction between "Hellenistic" and "Hebraic" is likely one between two groups of Jewish Christians, probably based on differences in language and origin.

Virtually all Jews in Palestine in the NT spoke some Greek, since this was the common language spoken throughout the eastern Mediterranean ever since the days of Alexander the Great (late fourth-century BC). In the first instance, "the 'hellenists' were probably those Jews who knew *only* Greek, but no Aramaic or Hebrew."[6] As such, these Jews gathered in Greek-speaking synagogues in Jerusalem and were comprised of those who had been dispersed throughout the Roman Empire but were now living in or visiting the holy city. The gospel seemed to have had a significant impact in the Greek-speaking

---

3. Haenchen, *Acts*, 261.
4. The word is clearly connected to the word *Hellēn*, which refers to someone who is Greek or, more broadly, to any non-Jew (see Acts 14:1; 18:4; 19:10; 20:21).
5. H. J. Cadbury, "The Hellenists," in *Additional Notes to the Commentary*, ed. F. J. Foakes Jackson and Kirsopp Lake (1932; repr., Grand Rapids: Baker, 1979), 69.
6. Capper, "Palestinian Cultural Context," 353.

synagogues. We know that language shapes cultural identity,[7] and it is unsurprising that a conflict may have developed from Jewish Christians coming from the Greek-speaking community in Jerusalem who already had developed an independent identity apart from the Palestinian Jews even before they became Christians. All this helps us understand why just a few sentences later Stephen comes into conflict with non-Christian Jews in the Greek-speaking synagogues. A persecution will quickly arise against Stephen's fellow Greek-speaking, Christian Jews (6:9–8:3), but it is one that will largely ignore the apostles and the other "Hebraic" Jews in Jerusalem, who were associated with Jews who spoke their language and were more culturally in tune with them.

In order to find a solution to the dispute over the distribution of community goods, the Twelve summoned the disciples together to move matters forward (Acts 6:2–4). It is interesting to note that this is the only time in Acts where the apostles are referred to as "the Twelve," and the first time in the narrative that the word "disciples" is used to refer to the followers of Jesus.[8] Longenecker suggests "in using both these terms, Luke has gone back to the language of the earliest Christians and tried to make idiomatic use of it, though this may not have been natural for him."[9] Even more interesting is the solution to the disruption of their unity. Instead of integrating the Hellenist widows into the daily distribution of the Hebraic widows, the Twelve decide to turn over care for the Hellenists' widows to seven officers. The leadership, however, begins first by recognizing different kinds of "ministry." There is the "ministry" to basic human needs—"the daily distribution [*diakonia*]" (v. 1) and "wait[ing] [*diakoneō*] on tables" (v. 2)—and then there is "prayer and the ministry [*diakonia*] of the word" (v. 4). The apostles are certainly not above caring for the needy,[10] and the proclamation of the word is not above the work of others.[11] Rather, the apostles recognize that their primary commission from Jesus is to bear "witness" to his resurrection and proclaim the gospel (see 1:8, 22; 2:32; 3:15; 4:33; 5:32). Since the response to the proclamation of the Twelve has resulted in thousands of people, many of them needy, being added to their community, the need is simple: more workers are required. To broaden the leadership base, the solution echoes that offered to the overburdened Moses (see Exod 18:13–27; Num 11:16–30; 27:16–23).

The requirements for these ministers among the Jewish, Greek-speaking

---

7. It is noteworthy that all the names of the Seven are Greek names.
8. Prior to this, Luke uses other designations like "apostles" (Acts 1:2; 2:37; 4:33; etc.), "believers" (2:44; 4:32); "church" (5:11); "brothers and sisters" (1:16); and "Galileans" (2:7).
9. Longenecker, *Acts*, 330.
10. This is, after all, the kind of ministry that Jesus identifies with himself (see Luke 22:26–27).
11. We will see shortly that the Seven, especially Stephen and Philip, have a ministry of word as well.

community are several (Acts 6:3). First, for obvious cultural reasons they must be men—as the gender-specific *anēr* ("man") indicates. Secondly, there are to be seven of them. Why seven? There is no clear answer to this question. Gaventa suggests this may pick up on occasions in the OT where seven leaders play a specific role (e.g., Josh 6:4; Esth 1:14; Jer 52:25).[12] Thirdly, while these ministers need not be witnesses to the resurrection per se, they must be of good repute among the community.[13] Fourthly, they are to be "full of the Spirit and wisdom." Just like the apostles themselves, these men must be full of the Spirit, as well as maturity and wisdom; Stephen would need this kind of wisdom shortly when facing fierce opposition himself (Acts 6:10).

The Seven (6:5–6)

Who were the seven? While their names are all Greek, which may suggest they come from the Hellenistic, Jewish-Christian community,[14] whatever else, these men are not "deacons." This word (*diakonos*) does not occur here, even though the related word for the daily "ministry" (*diakonia*) to tables and the word may suggest this idea. Oddly enough, while these seven men will be commissioned to assist with the daily distribution of food for the Hellenist widows, in the narrative itself they never are described carrying out this function. Rather, Stephen, just as the apostles did, performs "great wonders and signs among the people" (6:8; cf. 2:43; 5:12; 8:6), and at least one of them is an evangelist, that is, "Philip the evangelist" (Acts 21:8; cf. 8:5–13). Stephen heads the list of the Seven likely because of the significant role he will play a little later in the narrative (6:8–7:60). We will also hear more about the second person in the list, Philip, who figures prominently in chapter eight and then makes another appearance much later (21:8–9), where it also mentions that he is the father of "four unmarried daughters who prophesied." As for the remaining five persons—Procorus, Nicanor, Timon, Parmenas, and Nicolas—other than their names little else is known about them. Nicolas, from Antioch, is described as a "convert to Judaism."[15] The primary point to notice in all of this is that this section is not describing the beginning of church order. Rather, the "apostles" lay hands on these chosen men for

---

12. Gaventa, *Acts*, 114.
13. The NIV does not translate the word *martyreō* in Acts 6:3. Besides meaning "to bear witness," this word, as in this verse, can also mean "be well spoken of, be approved."
14. Dunn, *Acts*, 83, concludes that this "suggests they were all Hellenists. The deduction is by no means certain: some of Jesus's own disciples also had Greek names (Andrew and Philip). But the sequel (chaps 6–8) seems to indicate that Stephen and Philip were Hellenists."
15. See also Acts 2:11. The word "convert" (*prosēlutos*) literally means "one who has come over." It refers to a gentile who has been won for the Jewish community through missionary efforts (cf. Matt 23:15) or some other means. Besides following the teachings and observances of Judaism, male converts would also submit to circumcision.

ministry (cf. 13:1–3).[16] Why were only these seven chosen, since they were already leaders among the Hellenists? In doing so, this commissioning of these men amounts to a separation in the Christian movement in Jerusalem, and it is precisely among these people that the sacred fire of the Spirit will spread. In other words, for cultural reasons they are the logical ones to initiate the spread of the gospel into the gentile world.

A Summary Note (6:7)

It was noted above that Luke has almost no interest in church order as such. Yet it is important that the apostles "lay hands" on their leaders since at every crucial forward movement of the gospel, the Jerusalem church gives its blessing. In marking out these seven leaders, they are not to be viewed as constituting a maverick movement within the church. Luke's basic concern has to do with the expansion of the gospel. The first expansion has two facets to it. First, it will mark a break with Judaism, as Stephen's upcoming speech will indicate. It is a break in the sense that the Christian believers assume their own self-identity, especially apart from the temple in Jerusalem. Secondly, the expansion is geographical, with the ultimate aim being the gentile mission. The main sections of Acts show the steady progression from Jerusalem to Rome, and when it arrives to Rome it comes to a sudden conclusion. To indicate a transition in the narrative, Luke includes five short "markers" in Acts to alert his readers (Acts 6:7; 9:31; 12:24; 16:5; 19:20). In each of these texts the narrative seems to pause to "take a breath" before plunging off on a new path.[17] We must remember that when Luke wrote Acts he did not include chapter and verse divisions. So, to indicate a change, writers (both ancient and modern) will provide appropriate narrative indicators. In Acts, these markers contain one or more of the following three elements: (1) a geographical note; (2) an indication about church growth; and/or (3) a reference to the word of God increasing. In the first marker (6:7), all three elements are present. In this way Luke informs his reader that all the disciples were in Jerusalem, which is incredible given that all of Jesus's earliest followers were Galileans.

It is difficult to know how much time has transpired in the narrative since there is absolutely *no* chronology after the day of Pentecost (2:1). What we do know is that there is a powerful new community within Judaism, whose members continue to live *within* Judaism and under the authority of its leaders

---

16. Mikeal C. Parsons and Martin M. Culy, *Acts: A Handbook on the Greek Text* (Waco, TX: Baylor University Press, 2003), 110, note that the Greek syntax is not clear whether it is only the apostles or the whole group that laid their hands on the Seven. See also Fitzmyer, *Acts*, 351; Dunn, *Acts*, 84; Keener, *Acts* 2:1288–89.

17. Fee and Stuart, *How to Read the Bible for All Its Worth*, 111; cf. Keener, *Acts*, 2:1289–90.

(cf. 3:1; 6:9). This may be why Luke includes the note that "a large number of priests became obedient to the faith" in this summary verse (6:7). This is Luke's way of indicating the continuity with Israel and its primary symbol, the temple. This assertion of the early church will be one among a number of factors that will prove to be provocative in Jerusalem. It will change the dynamic of the Christian community, its witness, and its life. As was noted earlier, the section concludes with two distinct groups, Hellenist and Hebraic disciples. How the church makes a break from a Jerusalem-based, Jewish-led sect of Judaism and becomes a worldwide movement full of gentiles is what the next panel is all about, and is why the first panel ends with mention of the Hellenist Christians.

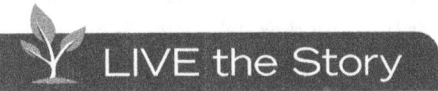

LIVE the Story

One of the challenges in reading a narrative like Acts is the temptation either to isolate authentic "biblical" practices to be put into use (if previously neglected or overlooked) in the contemporary church or to find biblical warrant for contemporary practices (i.e., proof-texting). Usually, both kinds of efforts are not done maliciously or deceptively. For the most part, the desire of contemporary Christian teachers and preachers is that they want to listen to the Bible carefully and live it out authentically today. This is difficult, however, when it comes to narrative accounts like Acts, because it is not always clear whether Luke is pointing to prescriptive practices for his readers to follow (or avoid by negative example) or whether he is simply offering descriptive accounts of what happened. For example, it might be tempting to discern a form of church order from Acts 6:1–6 to distinguish "ministers of the word" and calling them pastors/teachers, from "ministers of the table" and calling them deacons. While not denying that the church has, over the centuries, developed discreet "offices" in the church like bishops, presbyters, pastors, and deacons, there is no indication that this is what Luke is describing, let alone prescribing, in Acts 6.

Delegation Is Invitation, Not Imposition

So what can we learn from this passage and lean into today? The contemporary church could learn from the creativity and flexibility with which the early believers in Jerusalem dealt with new and significant issues. Richard Longenecker writes, "The early church seems to have been prepared to adjust its procedures, alter its organizational structure, and develop new posts of responsibility in response to existing needs and for the sake of the ongoing proclamation of the Word of God."[18] While not trying to replicate what Luke

---

18. Longenecker, *Acts*, 331.

describes, we should be open to the fact that improvisation and innovation are sometimes required when we face challenging situations. In the early church, the challenge of appropriate care for widows could easily have fractured their fellowship and stunted their effectiveness. The fact was the apostles had too many responsibilities vying for their attention. They were not above "serving tables," but they were needed to carry out their primary vocation to pray and preach in the early community. Instead of becoming defensive, they became innovative and delegated some of the load.

The godly and gifted young man who is the youth minister in our church reminded me recently about this important principle. After his second year of leading our youth ministry—a period when our youth group doubled in size—he reflected on the importance of learning that delegation is an invitation, not an imposition:

> At the start of this second year of youth ministry I invited volunteer youth leaders to join me. I wanted to venture into running small groups and needed extra support to do it. . . . [Yet] I was afraid to overburden my leaders, for fear of turning their youth-group involvement into a heavy yoke, so I told them their only responsibility would be to show up. I would produce and provide everything for them. So, throughout th[e] year I . . . prepared weekly discussion sheets for the Bible study time, group activities, compline prayer liturgies, and, for much of the year, music. I worked tirelessly each week to produce quality stuff, and to be able to hand my leaders what they needed.
>
> A job well done? Well . . . Several months into the year I started to feel the strain. It's difficult to maintain creativity when the clock is always ticking. A most wonderful youth leader mentioned to me near the end of the year that I should consider delegating portions of the work each week. She said, "Going to youth group is fun for us. We don't feel burdened at all." When I protested, saying that I'd be afraid to shove too much onto their plates, she replied, "We're offering. We all have pockets of time when we can plan things." Ah. Wise. So, this summer I am doing just that. I'm letting go of the fear of imposition, and embracing the notion that this ministry is as much theirs as it is mine.[19]

Feeding the Spirit and Feeding the Body—A Bifocal Practice

This opening paragraph should remind us that we need not be afraid of caring for the whole person in meeting both their spiritual and physical needs.

---

19. Luke Johnson, "What I've Learned after Two Years as a Youth Minister," *Luke Johnson*, 18 June 2014, https://www.lukejohnson.ca/what-ive-learned-after-two-years-as-a-youth-minister.

At the conclusion of this first panel in Acts, it is notable that by now in the narrative there is a long-standing and biblical, bifocal practice among the early church of feeding both the spirit and the body. The early church knew their Scriptures well, and they recognized how much of it reminded them to care for widows and, more broadly, the poor in Israel. Many widows in the first-century world faced extreme poverty, especially if they had no immediate family to care for them. Within the church, a principle emerged early and prevailed late that there should not be any needy person among the believers (see Acts 2:45; 4:34 [cf. Deut 15:1–11]; Jas 1:27). There was no disconnection between "ministry of the word" and "ministry of the table"—they were both, equally, ministry.

The dual focus of preaching grace and graciously providing for the poor by the early church, in time, changed the very shape of their culture. Kenneth Scott Latourette observed, "Never in so short a time has any other religious faith or, for that matter, any other set of ideas, religious, political or economic, without the aid of physical force or of social or cultural prestige, achieved so commanding a position in such an important culture."[20] The reality is that early Christianity emerged in a world that was brutal in its care for the aged, the young, and the poor—in short, it felt free to discard and displace any of those people who were unwanted. For example, the exposure of unwanted infants was a well-established practice of family limitation in the Greco-Roman world. This is expressed, somewhat briskly, in a papyrus letter found in first-century, Greek-speaking Egypt; the businessman Hilarion wrote to his wife Alis: "Above all, if you bear a child and it is male, let it be; if it is a female, cast it out."[21] Yet this brutal culture was changed within a few hundred years by the Christian gospel. Why? A spirit of generosity characterized the lifestyle of the Christians in such a profound way that it won over the people who observed them.

While there are many differences between the first-century world and the twenty-first century world, brutality on a massive scale certainly is not one of them. As I write this, the United Nations High Commissioner for Refugees (UNHCR) estimates that there are globally over fifty million refugees—the largest number of displaced persons since World War II. As an urban parish priest, I see these refugees literally on our church doorstep. Beyond them are the many displaced persons who wander our streets impoverished, often because they have mental illnesses that make it difficult for them to find or sustain employment. The numbers are staggering. Yet Acts reminds us that

---

20. K. S. Latourette, *A History of the Expansion of Christianity* (Grand Rapids: Zondervan, 1970), 112.

21. Letter of Hilarion, P.Oxy. 4.744. See http://www.papyri.info/apis/toronto.apis.17/.

the possibility of transforming our own culture through the ministry of the word and the ministry of the table is no less important and no less within our Spirit-empowered capacity today than it was two thousand years ago. The early church took care of the poor in radical and wholistic ways; so should we.

Prayer and Preaching, Not Blame and Shame

When faced with the complaint by the Greek-speaking widows, it may well have been tempting to get into a finger-pointing fight where shame and blame were doled out. The apostles did not assign shame and blame. This reflects an attitude that seeks to expend energy in ways that rights social injustices *and* attends to prayer and the proclamation of the gospel. When things go wrong in a church community, it is stunning how much effort can be expended to answer the questions, "Why did this happen?" and "Who is responsible for this mess?" Sometimes it is important to do so, but often we would be better off simply to acknowledge a problem exists and find a solution to fix it. The problem exacerbates itself in churches if its leaders, who are given the primary tasks of praying and preaching, abandon these duties—often in a pious effort either to look busy or demonstrate that they are humble. The reality is that the early church empowered their community for enhanced, wholistic ministry by inviting others to a priestly lifestyle. That is, the eighteen thousand or so priests that lived in Judea and Galilee at this time had, as one of their responsibilities, the care for the temple.[22] If the early church began to understand their own community, filled with the glory of God, as a new "temple" not made with hands but one made of people, then a primary role for them as "priests" in this new kind of temple would be to care for that temple, especially its poorer members. With the large Christian sect now caring for the poor in cooperative ways, they acted in a sense as priests caring for this new temple. This is all somewhat speculative, but it might account for the odd side note, "a large number of priests became obedient to the faith" (6:7). These priests may have been impressed not only by what they heard (that is, "the word of God") but also by the "priestly lifestyle" they witnessed. What we do know for certain is that as the church grew and expanded and eventually swept through the entire Roman Empire, a key reason for their extensive and deep impact was linked to the dynamic of their caring and "intense community."[23]

---

22. Jeremias, *Jerusalem*, 204. On the varied circumstances of first-century priests, see Keener, *Acts*, 2:1291–93.

23. Sociologist Rodney Stark, *The Rise of Christianity* (San Francisco: HarperOne, 1997), 215, concluded that the social structure of care and community in the early church contributed significantly to its broad appeal in the Roman Empire: "Christianity did not grow because of miracle working in the marketplaces (although there may have been much of that going on), or because Constantine said it should, or even because the martyrs gave it such credibility. It grew because Christians constituted

Because the whole community engaged in generous care and support of the needy among them, their leaders were able to devote themselves to prayer and the preaching of the word. It is not that serving tables was beneath them, but that prayer and preaching were how the entire church was nurtured and understood its vocation. Early in Acts (2:42), the Jerusalem church is portrayed as a model because "they devoted [*proskarterountes*] themselves" to the apostles' teaching and to prayer. Now, the apostles are portrayed as a model for those who lead and nourish such communities because they give "attention [*proskarterēsomen*] to prayer and the ministry of the word" (6:4). Sadly, the experience of many contemporary pastors and priests is that their lives and ministry are very little devoted to prayer and ministry of the word. In their place, leaders increasingly focus their energy on organizational meetings and church programming and responding to the deluge of email and text messages.

I once sat around a table with half a dozen experienced, godly, and thoughtful priests who lamented this fact. Despite making vows at their ordination to "be diligent in the reading and study of the holy scriptures," "minister the word of God and the sacraments of the new covenant," "undertake to be a faithful pastor," and "persevere in prayer, both in public and private,"[24] these focal practices increasingly get pushed to the edges of busy lives. How can this be? Eugene Peterson has reflected at length about this in many of his writings aimed at pastors. He argues that a "busy pastor" is symptomatic of betrayal, not devotion: "The adjective busy set as a modifier to pastor [or priest] should sound to our ears like adulterous to characterize a wife, or embezzling to describe a banker. It is an outrageous scandal, a blasphemous affront. Hilary of Tours diagnosed our pastoral busyness as *irreligiousa solicitudo pro Deo*, a blasphemous anxiety to do God's work for him."[25] His observations are chastening, but restorative:

> I am busy because I am vain. I want to appear important. Significant. What better way than to be busy? The incredible hours, the crowded schedule, and the heavy demands on my time are proof to myself—and to all who will notice—that I am important. . . . I live in a society in which crowded schedules and harassed conditions are evidence of importance,

---

an *intense community* [emphasis mine], able to generate the 'invincible obstinacy' that so offended [Romans] but yielded immense religious rewards. And the primary means of its growth was through the united and motivated efforts of the growing numbers of Christian believers, who invited their friends, relatives, and neighbors to share the 'good news.'"

24. These are the vows taken by all priests in the Anglican Church of Canada. See "Ordination of a Priest" in *The Book of Alternative Services of the Anglican Church of Canada* (Toronto: Anglican Book Centre, 1985), 647.

25. Eugene Peterson, "The Unbusy Pastor," in *The Contemplative Pastor* (Grand Rapids: Eerdmans, 1993), 17–18.

so I develop a crowded schedule and harassed conditions. When others notice, they acknowledge my significance and my vanity is fed.

I am busy because I am lazy. I indolently let other people decide what I will do instead of resolutely deciding myself. I let people who do not understand the work of the pastor write the agenda for my day's work because I am too slipshod to write it myself. The pastor is a shadow figure in these people's minds, a marginal person vaguely connected with matters of God and good will. Anything remotely religious or somehow well-intentioned can be properly assigned to the pastor.[26]

If busyness is not the proper mark of a Christian leader, what is? In this passage (Acts 6:4), Luke identifies two of the primary characteristics for leaders. *Leaders pray.* They are those who have developed a life of prayer that comes not from busy activity but from disciplined and deliberate time set aside to pay attention to the God who speaks. Christian leaders serve the church by leading people into a deeper relationship with God in prayer. Prayer reminds us that we are dependent on the Lord to give boldness in speaking and to protect its agents from pride. *Leaders also preach.* They speak the word of God in the natural rhythm and language of the people they serve by having first engaged the Scriptures personally, thoroughly, and intimately. This does not occur merely in the time it takes to prepare a sermon—sermon preparation can be done quite well in a few hours. Preaching for maturity and Christlikeness is a creative act. It requires reflective hours, searching the pages of Scripture, and intense struggle, discerning the meaning of Scripture for the people you live with and lead. This kind of drenching in Scripture takes time, lots of it. Prayer and preaching are two of the primary means God uses to grow his people into Christlike maturity. For leaders who don't want to be cheerleaders but shepherds, who don't want to be CEOs but teachers, devoting themselves to prayer and preaching is key. This pleases the Lord, and it would be well if "this proposal please[s] the whole group" of Christians in the world too (6:5).

---

26. Ibid., 18.

PANEL 2

Acts 6:8–9:31

The second "panel" in Acts marks the first geographic expansion of the gospel from Judea to Samaria carried out by Greek-speaking, Jewish Christians like Philip. There are also several other notable firsts in this frame. In this section we have the first Christian martyr, Stephen. The opposition that began in chapter four and resulted in the arrest of Peter and John in chapter five turns violent and culminates in the death of Stephen and the persecution of the church in Jerusalem. This is an important episode for Luke, an importance signaled by the focus on Stephen's arrest (6:8–15), his lengthy speech (7:1–53)—the longest discourse in the entire book of Acts—and his subsequent martyrdom (7:54–60). The other significant first in this section is the introduction of the apostle Paul, at this time known as a "young man named Saul" (Acts 7:58), who approved of Stephen's stoning and became the chief persecutor of the church (8:1–3). Before we hear more about Saul and his dramatic conversion along the road to Damascus in chapter nine, chapter eight describes the Samaritan mission (8:4–25) and the heart-warming story of the conversion of an Ethiopian proselyte of Judaism through the witness of Philip.

CHAPTER 14

Acts 6:8-15

LISTEN to the Story

⁸Now Stephen, a man full of God's grace and power, performed great wonders and signs among the people. ⁹Opposition arose, however, from members of the Synagogue of the Freedmen (as it was called)—Jews of Cyrene and Alexandria as well as the provinces of Cilicia and Asia—who began to argue with Stephen. ¹⁰But they could not stand up against the wisdom the Spirit gave him as he spoke.

¹¹Then they secretly persuaded some men to say, "We have heard Stephen speak blasphemous words against Moses and against God."

¹²So they stirred up the people and the elders and the teachers of the law. They seized Stephen and brought him before the Sanhedrin. ¹³They produced false witnesses, who testified, "This fellow never stops speaking against this holy place and against the law. ¹⁴For we have heard him say that this Jesus of Nazareth will destroy this place and change the customs Moses handed down to us."

¹⁵All who were sitting in the Sanhedrin looked intently at Stephen, and they saw that his face was like the face of an angel.

Listening to the Text in the Story: Exodus 20:16; Proverbs 14:5; 24:28; Matthew 26:59-66; Luke 21:5, 15; 1 Peter 2:4-5.

EXPLAIN the Story

The second panel in Acts (6:8–9:31) opens with the arrest of Stephen. Opposition to the disciples of Jesus has been building, and it boils over in the Greek-speaking synagogue in Jerusalem. Luke provides a few descriptive words in the first paragraph (vv. 8–10) that add to and complement what little we know about Stephen (cf. 6:3). He is portrayed as a faithful witness and an example of the fulfillment of Jesus's prophecy: "I will give you words and wisdom that none of your adversaries will be able to resist or contradict" (Luke 21:15). This is followed with Stephen's arrest and his adversaries' accusation (Acts 6:11–14). They accuse him of blasphemy. That is, he is accused of speaking against "this holy place" (i.e., the temple) and against Moses (i.e., the law). These are precisely the two points where the new "sect" does not fit with Judaism. What comes next is a dramatic pause as the whole counsel "looked intently" at him, anticipating how he will respond (v. 15).

This brief introduction not only picks up on the Hellenistic-Jewish note that ended the last panel (6:1–7), but it also reaches further back into the story of Jesus and reminds us of his arrest and the accusations of blasphemy brought against him as he stood before the same council in Jerusalem (see Luke 22:66; cf. Matt 26:59–66). These verses not only look back, they also point forward. For example, a number of thematic and verbal links prepare the audience for what will follow in Stephen's speech, especially ones that connect him to Moses and the law, including, "wonders and signs" (Acts 6:8 and 7:36), "wisdom" (6:10 and 7:22), and "angels" (6:15 and 7:30, 35, 38, 53).

Stephen (6:8–10)

Despite the fact that the longest speech in Acts is offered by Stephen (7:1–53), we are not given much personal information about him. Still, what we are given is significant. First, he is a person of "grace and power" (6:8). He is a gifted man, who uses those gifts effectively. He performed great "wonders and signs" (v. 8) among the people. Wonders and signs are near synonyms, known as a *doublet*, which emphasizes the miraculous nature of his deeds. More importantly, they highlight the continuity between Stephen and Moses (7:36), Jesus (2:22), the apostles (2:43; 5:12), and later, Paul and Barnabas (14:3; 15:12)—all who performed signs and wonders. Besides his deeds, he was known to be "full" of the Spirit (6:3)—along with the rest of the Seven. Stephen was also full of "wisdom" (v. 3), "faith" (v. 5), and "grace and power" (v. 8). The adjective "full" (*plērēs*) occurs only sixteen times in the NT, but four of those occurrences relate to Stephen and his "full" portion of Spirit empowerment.[1] He will need this fullness for his ordeal ahead.

The text does not explicitly state it, but we can infer that Stephen was a member of "the Synagogue of the Freedmen" in Jerusalem. This synagogue existed for Greek-speaking Jewish pilgrims from various parts of the Roman Empire, many who were former slaves, hence its name, "Freedmen."[2] This may be the same synagogue that Theodotus refers to in this inscription in Jerusalem dated prior to AD 70:

---

1. I.e., Acts 6:3, 5, 8; 7:55.
2. For more information, see Barrett, *Acts*, 1:323–24.

Theodotus, son of Vettenos, the priest and *archisynagōgos*, son of a *archisynagōgos* and grandson of a *archisynagōgos*, who built the synagogue for purposes of reciting the law and studying the commandments, and the hostel, chambers and water installations to provide for the needs of itinerants from abroad, and whose father, with the elders, and Simonides, founded the synagogue.[3]

The temple in Jerusalem had a magnetic effect on Jews dispersed throughout the empire, but especially so among those who were freed slaves. When Pompey conquered Jerusalem in 61 BC, many slaves were taken to Rome. As these slaves and their descendants were freed, many of them, as devout Jews, wished to return to Jerusalem to be close to and, eventually, be buried near the temple.[4] For those dispersed Jews who made the Synagogue of the Freedmen their home, the gospel had a considerable impact there. Eventually, the first Christian missionaries come from this synagogue. Importantly, Saul (i.e., Paul), a native of the province of Cilicia (Acts 21:39), was a member of the synagogue and present when Stephen spoke to the Sanhedrin and was stoned outside the city (7:58; 8:1).

The Accusation (6:11–14)

The adverb "then" begins verse 11, indicating that Stephen's enemies took prompt action. They persuaded at least two men from the synagogue to offer testimony that Stephen spoke "blasphemous words." This had the effect of disturbing "the people"—previously open to the apostles' teaching and deeds (2:47; 4:21; 5:13, 26)—along with the elders and the teachers of the law. This also drew the attention of the Sanhedrin, and just like the apostles (5:18) Stephen is arrested and brought forward to face charges. Ironically, false witnesses testify against Stephen, contending that he spoke against the temple ("this holy place") and against the Mosaic law.[5] It is ironic because in bearing false witness, the law itself, in the Decalogue no less, is violated by the accusers (see Exod 20:16; cf. Prov 14:5 and 24:28). The early Christians' relationship to the temple and the law are the two points where the new sect ambiguously relates to the rest of Judaism. They are also the areas where Jesus conflicted with the elders and the teachers of the law, a fact highlighted by their reference to "*this* Jesus of Nazareth." The menace in the accusations can be heard in the references to "*this* fellow" and "*this* Jesus" (Acts 6:13–14), in which the demonstrative pronoun "this" carries a contemptuous and derogatory tone.[6]

---

3. Quoted in B. Chilton and E. Yamauchi, "Synagogues," in *DNTB* 1147. See also R. Riesner, "Synagogues in Jerusalem," in Bauckham, *Book of Acts in Its Palestinian Setting*, 204–6.
4. See Dunn, *Acts*, 86.
5. Compare this with the charges brought against Paul later in Acts 21:28; see also 21:21 and 25:8.
6. Barrett, *Acts*, 1:328.

The content of the charges relates to words spoken against the temple and against the law made by Stephen and, inferentially, by Jesus. The scholar F. F. Bruce notes that "Jesus had indeed said something about destroying the temple, and Stephen had evidently repeated his words.... That Jesus had indeed said something of the kind was apparently a matter of general knowledge in Jerusalem; it was recalled in mockery when he was exposed to public derision on the cross (Mark 15:29–30). But we search the Synoptic Gospels in vain for any information about the setting in which he uttered those words, or words like them."[7] The Gospel of John does refer to Jesus saying the words, "Destroy this temple, and I will raise it again in three days" (John 2:19), when he was challenged to answer by what authority he cleansed the temple. But here Jesus was referring not to Herod's temple in Jerusalem but to the "temple" of his body. Still, what is being picked up is that following Jesus means that while the temple precincts are still a good venue in which to pray and preach, Jesus has made the practices of the temple irrelevant. That is, Jesus has fulfilled what the sacrifices occurring in the temple anticipate (see 1 Pet 2:4–5). This kind of new thinking about the temple, which was the religious center for Jews living in Jerusalem, was simply too much for many of them to abide.

Before we proceed, it is helpful to observe an interesting note raised by James Dunn about the temple and the law, two key areas related to Israel's identity:

> Luke omitted the charge against Jesus (Mark 14:58) from his version of the trial of Jesus. This is odd, since Luke elsewhere tries to bring out points of parallel between Jesus and the heroes of his Acts.... What is operative here, however, is another factor in Luke's two-volume record, and one which shows that he had the second already in mind when he wrote the first. At several points he omits episodes in his Gospel because he evidently wanted to delay the break which they signified in the second volume.... The editing here ... is not motivated by the desire to draw a parallel between the death of Jesus and that of Stephen. It is motivated rather by Luke's attempt to portray the redefining of the Jesus movement's relation to Israel's traditionally key points of identity.[8]

Dramatic Pause (6:15)

There is a sense that this sentence (v. 15) is the deep breath before plunging into the long speech of Stephen that follows. The word translated "looked intently"[9] is a repetition of the word used in Acts 3:4 when the lame man

---

7. Bruce, *Acts*, 127.
8. Dunn, *Acts*, 88.
9. *Atenizō* is a favorite word of Luke; of this word's fourteen occurrences in the NT, twelve of them are in Luke-Acts. The other two occurrences are in 2 Cor 3:7, 13.

sitting at the gate called Beautiful gazed at Peter in hope of receiving a few coins. This time, however, the gaze is not hopefully expectant but reminiscent of the intense stare turned on Jesus after he delivered his first sermon in his home synagogue of Nazareth (Luke 4:20). What they see as they look intently at Stephen is a countenance "like the face of an angel." References to angels recur four times in Stephen's speech that follows (7:30, 35, 38, and 53). Again, it is ironic that angelic Stephen is accused of speaking against Moses, the same Moses who received the law on Mount Sinai through the words of an angel (7:38). Glorious angelic messengers regularly speak for God in the OT (besides those referred to in Stephen's speech, see also Ezek 8:2; Dan 10:5–6, etc.). The implication is that Stephen, with angelic face, is speaking for God before the Sanhedrin, just as Moses before had spoken to the people with a radiant face (Exod 34:29–35; cf. 2 Cor 3:7, 13) and as God's angels continue to do so.

LIVE the Story

Life is dangerous for many Christians who worship and work in the world. In the early part of the twenty-first century, this was especially so for Iraqi Christians who fled by the tens of thousands before the onslaught of ISIS, also known as the "Islamic State," to the region of Kurdistan and neighboring countries. One of the congregations that faced the brunt of persecution was St. George's Anglican Church in Baghdad. Reverend Canon Andrew White, fondly known as "the Vicar of Baghdad," led St. George's. Reverend White, is a humble and humorous Englishman, who lived and worked in the Middle East from 1998–2015, including his charge for St. George's. By the summer of 2014, St. George's congregation was a growing community of over a thousand people who served the region with a vibrant medical clinic, a food-relief ministry, and a foundation for religious reconciliation. Less than a year later in 2015, White reported that many people in his congregation left Baghdad. He reported that most of his congregation "sought refuge in Ninevah, the traditional homeland for Iraqi Christians. 'But it was there that ISIS came to kill them,' White told *MacLean's*. 'Most of my staff . . . relocated there to provide [for] their basic needs, their food, clothes, everything.'"[10]

Iraq was always a dangerous place for White to live and work, and over the years he was threatened, beaten, held at gunpoint, kidnapped, and kept as a hostage. By 2014, however, the situation became so severe, with the killings

---

10. Rachel Browne, "The Vicar of Baghdad and the Lost Christians of Iraq," in *MacLean's*, 17 Dec. 2014. See http://www.macleans.ca/news/world/the-vicar-of-baghdad-and-the-lost-christians-of-iraq/.

of several of his staff and death threats against him that he was ordered to leave Iraq by his boss, the Archbishop of Canterbury. After that time, he traveled the world to raise funds for Iraqi-Christian refugees and to increase awareness for the Foundation for Relief and Reconciliation in the Middle East. He constantly stayed in contact with his Iraqi congregation by phone and Facebook, but often the news he received was devastating. For example, shortly after leaving Iraq, he reported, "One of the first things I heard was that a young child who I had baptized as a baby was cut in half by ISIS. His name was Andrew, after me. I can't cope with the fact that our children, children I loved, are being massacred."[11]

If the story of Stephen is written for anyone, it is written for people like Andrew White and the Christians of Iraq. Stephen is a model of faithful witness and godly response for all believers who live amid oppression. Stephen, and people like Andrew White, are praiseworthy because of their wise and winsome witness in the face of opposition. More than that, they are praiseworthy because their characters reflect that of their Lord Jesus, who also faced false charges and injustice with humble strength. Anthony Bloom once noted, "The word 'humility' comes from the Latin word *humus* which means fertile ground."[12] What Stephen and Andrew White exhibit in their humility and weakness is the fertility of lives willing to be abandoned to the hands of God. Again, Bloom writes that we can think of this kind of humble weakness "in terms of a sail. A sail can catch the wind and be used to maneuver a boat only because it is so frail. If instead of a sail you put a solid board, it would not work; it is the weakness of the sail that makes it sensitive to the wind."[13] Amid opposition, Stephen humbly opened his life to let the Spirit blow in wisdom and wonders, holiness and angelic peace. May the Spirit continue to do this today in the *humus* that is Iraqi Christianity and every other Christian community facing threat of persecution.

---

11. Ibid.
12. Anthony Bloom, *Beginning to Pray* (Mahwah, NJ: Paulist, 1970), 35.
13. Ibid., 33–34.

CHAPTER 15

Acts 7:1–53

 LISTEN to the Story

¹Then the high priest asked Stephen, "Are these charges true?"
²To this he replied: "Brothers and fathers, listen to me! The God of glory appeared to our father Abraham while he was still in Mesopotamia, before he lived in Harran. ³'Leave your country and your people,' God said, 'and go to the land I will show you.'¹
⁴"So he left the land of the Chaldeans and settled in Harran. After the death of his father, God sent him to this land where you are now living. ⁵He gave him no inheritance here, not even enough ground to set his foot on. But God promised him that he and his descendants after him would possess the land, even though at that time Abraham had no child. ⁶God spoke to him in this way: 'For four hundred years your descendants will be strangers in a country not their own, and they will be enslaved and mistreated. ⁷But I will punish the nation they serve as slaves,' God said, 'and afterward they will come out of that country and worship me in this place.'² ⁸Then he gave Abraham the covenant of circumcision. And Abraham became the father of Isaac and circumcised him eight days after his birth. Later Isaac became the father of Jacob, and Jacob became the father of the twelve patriarchs.
⁹"Because the patriarchs were jealous of Joseph, they sold him as a slave into Egypt. But God was with him ¹⁰and rescued him from all his troubles. He gave Joseph wisdom and enabled him to gain the goodwill of Pharaoh king of Egypt. So Pharaoh made him ruler over Egypt and all his palace.
¹¹"Then a famine struck all Egypt and Canaan, bringing great suffering, and our ancestors could not find food. ¹²When Jacob heard that there was grain in Egypt, he sent our forefathers on their first visit. ¹³On their second visit, Joseph told his brothers who he was, and Pharaoh learned about Joseph's family. ¹⁴After this, Joseph sent for his father Jacob and his

---
1. Gen 12:1.
2. Gen 15:13, 14.

whole family, seventy-five in all. ¹⁵Then Jacob went down to Egypt, where he and our ancestors died. ¹⁶Their bodies were brought back to Shechem and placed in the tomb that Abraham had bought from the sons of Hamor at Shechem for a certain sum of money.

¹⁷"As the time drew near for God to fulfill his promise to Abraham, the number of our people in Egypt had greatly increased. ¹⁸Then 'a new king, to whom Joseph meant nothing, came to power in Egypt.'³ ¹⁹He dealt treacherously with our people and oppressed our ancestors by forcing them to throw out their newborn babies so that they would die.

²⁰"At that time Moses was born, and he was no ordinary child. For three months he was cared for by his family. ²¹When he was placed outside, Pharaoh's daughter took him and brought him up as her own son. ²²Moses was educated in all the wisdom of the Egyptians and was powerful in speech and action.

²³"When Moses was forty years old, he decided to visit his own people, the Israelites. ²⁴He saw one of them being mistreated by an Egyptian, so he went to his defense and avenged him by killing the Egyptian. ²⁵Moses thought that his own people would realize that God was using him to rescue them, but they did not. ²⁶The next day Moses came upon two Israelites who were fighting. He tried to reconcile them by saying, 'Men, you are brothers; why do you want to hurt each other?'

²⁷"But the man who was mistreating the other pushed Moses aside and said, 'Who made you ruler and judge over us? ²⁸Are you thinking of killing me as you killed the Egyptian yesterday?'⁴ ²⁹When Moses heard this, he fled to Midian, where he settled as a foreigner and had two sons.

³⁰"After forty years had passed, an angel appeared to Moses in the flames of a burning bush in the desert near Mount Sinai. ³¹When he saw this, he was amazed at the sight. As he went over to get a closer look, he heard the Lord say: ³²'I am the God of your fathers, the God of Abraham, Isaac and Jacob.'⁵ Moses trembled with fear and did not dare to look.

³³"Then the Lord said to him, 'Take off your sandals, for the place where you are standing is holy ground. ³⁴I have indeed seen the oppression of my people in Egypt. I have heard their groaning and have come down to set them free. Now come, I will send you back to Egypt.'⁶

³⁵"This is the same Moses they had rejected with the words, 'Who made

---

3. Exod 1:8.
4. Exod 2:14.
5. Exod 3:6.
6. Exod 3:5, 7, 8, 10.

you ruler and judge?' He was sent to be their ruler and deliverer by God himself, through the angel who appeared to him in the bush. ³⁶He led them out of Egypt and performed wonders and signs in Egypt, at the Red Sea and for forty years in the wilderness.

³⁷"This is the Moses who told the Israelites, 'God will raise up for you a prophet like me from your own people.'⁷ ³⁸He was in the assembly in the wilderness, with the angel who spoke to him on Mount Sinai, and with our ancestors; and he received living words to pass on to us.

³⁹"But our ancestors refused to obey him. Instead, they rejected him and in their hearts turned back to Egypt. ⁴⁰They told Aaron, 'Make us gods who will go before us. As for this fellow Moses who led us out of Egypt—we don't know what has happened to him!'⁸ ⁴¹That was the time they made an idol in the form of a calf. They brought sacrifices to it and reveled in what their own hands had made. ⁴²But God turned away from them and gave them over to the worship of the sun, moon and stars. This agrees with what is written in the book of the prophets:

> "'Did you bring me sacrifices and offerings
>   forty years in the wilderness, people of Israel?
> ⁴³You have taken up the tabernacle of Molek
>   and the star of your god Rephan,
>   the idols you made to worship.
> Therefore I will send you into exile'⁹ beyond Babylon.

⁴⁴"Our ancestors had the tabernacle of the covenant law with them in the wilderness. It had been made as God directed Moses, according to the pattern he had seen. ⁴⁵After receiving the tabernacle, our ancestors under Joshua brought it with them when they took the land from the nations God drove out before them. It remained in the land until the time of David, ⁴⁶who enjoyed God's favor and asked that he might provide a dwelling place for the God of Jacob. ⁴⁷But it was Solomon who built a house for him.

⁴⁸"However, the Most High does not live in houses made by human hands. As the prophet says:

> ⁴⁹"'Heaven is my throne,
>   and the earth is my footstool.

---

7. Deut 18:15.
8. Exod 32:1.
9. Amos 5:25–27 (see Septuagint).

> What kind of house will you build for me?
>   says the Lord.
> Or where will my resting place be?
> ⁵⁰Has not my hand made all these things?"[10]
>
> ⁵¹"You stiff-necked people! Your hearts and ears are still uncircumcised. You are just like your ancestors: You always resist the Holy Spirit! ⁵²Was there ever a prophet your ancestors did not persecute? They even killed those who predicted the coming of the Righteous One. And now you have betrayed and murdered him—⁵³you who have received the law that was given through angels but have not obeyed it."

Listening to the Text in the Story: Genesis 12–48; Exodus 1–3; 5:10; 15:4; 25:16; 32:1, 23; Deuteronomy 18:15; 1 Kings 8:27–30; Isaiah 66:1–2; Amos 5:25–27.

EXPLAIN the Story

Stephen's speech (7:1–53) is, chronologically, the first available Christian defense of the gospel in relationship to Judaism. After the high priest's question (v. 1), Stephen makes three clear points in his apology. First, *God's people* have a long history of not listening to him, whether out of jealousy toward one another or ignorance of God's ways (vv. 2–43). Second, *the temple* is not God's first earthly "house"—yet even so, God does not live in buildings made by human hands (vv. 44–50, esp. v. 48). And third, Stephen accuses the Jews of breaking the Mosaic *law* by killing Jesus (vv. 51–53). The response to Stephen's speech is swift and deadly. He is dragged outside the city and stoned to death, but his martyrdom precipitates two important results: (1) the further persecution of Jewish Christians, and (2) the geographic expansion of the church.

An Unusual Speech (7:1)

The high priest asks a simple question of Stephen: "Are these charges true?" That is, does Stephen speak against the temple and against the law of Moses? Stephen's response to the Sanhedrin is one of the most interesting speeches in all of Acts. It is the longest, by far, and the one most unlike the others in content. Indeed, in terms of scope and content, there is nothing quite like it

---

10. Isa 66:1, 2.

anywhere in the entire NT. The range of OT texts that Stephen draws on is broad, as can be seen in the passages listed above in "Listening to the Text in the Story." Simply put, this is a biblical *tour de force*. Yet, most intriguing of all is the simple reality that it does not seem to speak directly to the charges that are laid against him. Instead of addressing the charges, Stephen offers a qualified answer. Perhaps more accurately Stephen tells a story, a story about the patriarchs, the Mosaic law, and the dwelling place of God. This is a story that is intended to catch their attention and alert his audience to the fact that they are ignorant of God's purposes.

The Call of Abraham (7:2–8)

Stephen opens his speech in a nondefensive way by addressing his audience with the relational terms "brothers and fathers" (7:2).[11] The content of Stephen's response to the Sanhedrin is a condensed and selective summary of Israel's story of salvation. Not surprisingly, he begins with the father of his people, Abraham, the one who listened to and obeyed God's voice to "leave your country and your people . . . and go to the land I will show you" (7:3, quoting Gen 12:1). In beginning with Abraham, Stephen emphasizes the promise of the land, mentioning "land" (*gē*) five times in his opening remarks (Acts 7:3 [2x; NIV: "country"], 4 [2x], and 6). At the beginning (v. 5) he points out that Abraham was not given any inheritance of land in his own lifetime,[12] but that God promised to give it to his descendants. He mentions that God foretold to Abraham that his descendants would sojourn four hundred years as mistreated slaves in Egypt (Gen 15:13–14), but in the end they would "worship[13] me in this place" (Acts 7:7). After relating the promise of God to give the land to Abraham and his descendants, Stephen also highlights Abraham's obedient response to God's covenant of circumcision (7:8).

In this short section, Stephen's speech emphasizes the obedience of Abraham and the promise of the land. Here Stephen is putting the opening details of his argument in place. First, God graciously "gave" to his people promises and a covenant (vv. 5, 8). This theme of *grace* will be a recurring one (vv. 9, 25, and 38). The second building block is that *obedience* to God is not dependent on a place, whether a piece of land or something built with human hands.

---

11. Ben Witherington III, *The Acts of the Apostles: A Socio-Rhetorical Commentary* (Grand Rapids: Eerdmans; Carlisle: Paternoster, 1998), 264–65, notes that Stephen does not "distinguish himself from his audience until after the speech becomes overtly polemical."

12. The words *bēma podos*, used to express this, are literally "a step of a foot" (Acts 7:5). It is an idiom for a very small space (cf. Deut 2:5).

13. The word *latreuō*, translated in the NIV as "worship," can also be translated as "serve."

The Story of Joseph (7:9–16)

Stephen continues with his survey of the patriarchal period and takes a long step over the content of Genesis 21–36 to focus on Joseph (Gen 37) and how Israel went to Egypt. Here the first hint of disobedience is dropped: "The patriarchs were jealous of Joseph" (Acts 7:9a). The grace of God is highlighted again despite this resentful act, as Stephen continues with an important qualifier: "*But* God was with him and rescued him from all his troubles. He *gave* Joseph wisdom and enabled him to gain the goodwill of Pharaoh king of Egypt. So Pharaoh made him ruler over Egypt and all his palace" (7:9b–10). The promise of God given to Abraham is fulfilled, but so is the provision and providence of God to provide and protect his people by taking them to Egypt when they faced famine in Canaan. By emphasizing that the patriarchs were removed from the promised land and taken to Egypt, Stephen's speech continues the thread that underscores God's presence and blessing existing with his people wherever they are apart from a particular plot of land or specific buildings.

Moses (7:17–43)

The next section of Stephen's speech is the longest part and, importantly, the heart of the speech. The primary themes here are the repeated rejections of Moses and the disobedience of the people to God's law. This is important in Stephen's own defense in rebuffing the charges of speaking against the law and Moses. Within this section of the speech there are three movements: the birth of Moses (7:17–22); Moses's personal failure to deliver his fellow Israelites (7:23–29); and God's call of Moses (7:30–43).[14]

The Birth of Moses (7:17–22)

The first note in this subsection of the speech is God's action. Stephen highlights that the time "drew near for God to fulfill his promise to Abraham" (7:17). Now the biblical story has progressed from Genesis to Exodus. God has blessed the Israelites during their stay in Egypt, and their number has increased significantly from the seventy-five people who moved from Canaan. "A new king, to whom Joseph meant nothing" (v. 18; cf. Exod 1:8) begins to deal treacherously and dangerously with their ancestors.

Stephen notes that "at that time" Moses was born (Acts 7:20). Although God is not explicitly mentioned in bringing about the birth of Moses, several factors are noteworthy in this paragraph (vv. 20–22). First, the word translated

---

14. Schnabel, *Acts*, 355, makes an interesting suggestion that the Moses section in Acts 7 is divided into three forty-year periods (7:17–29; 7:30–34; 7:35–43), giving a chronological shape to this part of the speech.

as "time" is the word *kairos*. This is a Greek word where the emphasis is on a *purpose* in time rather than simply a chronological period.[15] In the purposes of God, Moses's birth was appointed for this time in order to "rescue" (cf. v. 25) the Israelites from the Egyptians. A second notable feature is that Moses was educated in "all the *wisdom* of the Egyptians" (v. 22). Moses, not unlike Stephen (cf. 6:10), is furnished with wisdom. Finally, a further and more important connection is made between Moses and Stephen. Moses was "powerful" in speech and action (7:22), not unlike Stephen who was full of grace and "power" (6:8).

Moses's Personal Failure to Deliver the Israelites (7:23–29)

This episode in Moses's life is told because it highlights the people rejecting their most esteemed prophet. An Israelite asks Moses: "Who made you ruler and judge over us?" (7:27, quoting Exod 2:14). Despite his wisdom, his powerful words and deeds, and his desire to rescue his own people from the mistreatment of the Egyptians, Moses's first attempt to do so results in failure and rejection. Thus, the paragraph begins by noting that he decided to "visit" his own people (Acts 7:23). Barrett argues that the word "visit" means more than a simple stopover to see the relatives.[16] Moses intends to step out of his royal environment and help his fellow Israelites. He thought that his own people would recognize him as God's instrument of deliverance, "but Moses was not God, had not yet been commissioned by God to act on his behalf, and his attempt failed."[17] Thus his own attempt to "rescue"[18] them failed (v. 25). In particular, the words that his fellow Israelites use to snub Moses when he tried to reconcile the two individuals who are fighting carries a harsh tone of rejection. They ask Moses: "Who made you ruler and judge over us?" (v. 27). The question is rhetorical, but the implied answer within Stephen's speech is simple: God has. The same question is raised again a little later in the speech (v. 35).

God's Call of Moses (7:30–43)

In this third and final section on the life of Moses, Stephen turns to his call on Mount Sinai. Here special attention is given to the way Israel rejected Moses a second time and refused to obey him and God's direction. Instead of accepting Moses's leadership, they fashioned an idol, brought sacrifices to it, and "reveled in what their own hands had made" (v. 41). Although it does not

---

15. The Greek word for time as it relates to chronology is *chronos*.
16. Barrett, *Acts*, 1:357.
17. Ibid.
18. The word translated "rescue" in the NIV is *sōtēria*, a word that can also be translated "salvation."

always come out in the NIV translation, it is notable how Stephen repeatedly mentions "this" Moses. "This" is the same Moses (v. 35) whom they had rejected, even though God *did* appoint him as their leader and redeemer. "This" one (v. 36, Gk. *houtos*; NIV: "he") led them out of Egypt with "wonders and signs."[19] "This" (v. 37) is the Moses who prophesied that God would raise up a mighty prophet from among them. "This" is the one (v. 38) who received the law to be given to Israel. Yet despite these clear indications, Moses is rejected a second time (v. 39), and this echoes the repudiation earlier in his life by his own people (v. 27).

In this way the opening sentence of this paragraph (v. 30) picks up the thread of Moses's life from Exodus 3:2, when the angel of the Lord appeared to him in the guise of a flaming bush in the desert of Sinai. The mention of an angel speaking to Moses reminds the reader of Stephen's face that resembled an "angel" (Acts 6:15). Moses, as retold in Stephen's speech, does not merely meet an angel; he meets "the Lord," who speaks to him. Literally, "the voice of the Lord happened" (7:31b). Flames and speech occur when the presence of the Lord is revealed, a fact realized on the day of Pentecost (2:3–4). The Lord declares, "I am the God of your fathers" (7:32, quoting Exod 3:6),[20] and these words reinforce the theme of continuity with the patriarchs with which Stephen began his speech. This is not only a theme that is important to Stephen's address but to the entire book of Acts. As we have noticed earlier in the speech of Peter (3:12–26) and will see later in the missionary work of Paul (e.g., 13:16–41), the church, "composed of Jews and Gentiles, stands in continuity with the saving plan of God, as revealed in the Jewish Scriptures."[21]

The next two sentences (vv. 33–34) draw our attention to Moses's commission from the Lord to return to Egypt. Stephen continues to shape his story and omits mention of Moses's own reluctance because of his stammering tongue (see Exod 3:13–4:17). Gaventa notes, "Including that reluctance would create a direct conflict with Stephen's earlier comments about Moses's powerful words and deeds. It would also create problems for Luke's parallel between Moses and Jesus, if the forerunner were found to be stammering and timid."[22]

As noted above, the final section intensifies the rhetoric (about Moses, beginning in Acts 7:35 with the repeated use of the Greek word *houtos* [vv. 35

---

19. Note how this connects to the work of Jesus and his apostles earlier in Acts (2:22, 43; 4:30; 5:12; 6:8).

20. This represents a change of order from the biblical account. In Exod 3, the Lord instructs Moses first to remove his shoes (v. 5) and then discloses himself as the God of the patriarchs Abraham, Isaac, and Jacob (v. 6).

21. Marshall, *Acts*, 45.

22. Gaventa, *Acts*, 126.

(2x; "this," "he"), 36 ("he"), 37 ("this"), 38 ("he")]) that places the focus squarely on Moses and indicates that Stephen's argument is about to become much more pointed.[23] The question about Moses's right to rule and judge is mentioned again (v. 35a). Here the answer is given unequivocally: "He was sent to be their ruler and deliverer *by God himself*" (v. 35b). In parallel with Jesus, the apostles, and Stephen, Moses "performed wonders and signs" in Egypt, at the Red Sea, and in the forty-year desert wandering (v. 36). The chronology is compressed and reaches a climax with Moses's prophecy: "God will raise up for you a prophet like me from your own people" (v. 37; quoting Deut 18:15). This is the same text that Peter used to draw his speech to a climax when he spoke to the onlookers at Solomon's Colonnade (Acts 3:22–23). All these words, declares Stephen (7:38), including the law received on Mount Sinai, were passed on to "us."[24]

The next sentence sharpens the pointed attack against disobedient Israel: "Our ancestors refused to obey [Moses]. Instead, they rejected him" (v. 39). This is a key moment in the speech. One of the primary accusations against Stephen was that he spoke "blasphemous words against Moses" (6:11). Stephen compresses all the disobedient grumbling against Moses in the desert by reminding his audience of the flagrant idolatry of Israel and the golden-calf incident in the wilderness (Acts 7:39–41; cf. Exod 32:1). In language reminiscent of Paul (Rom 1:24), Stephen notes that God rejected them and "gave them over" (Acts 7:42) to the worship of Molek[25] and the host of heaven (cf. Amos 5:25–27 LXX). Stephen draws a direct line between the rejection of Moses and the sin of the golden calf in Sinai with the idolatry Amos ascribed as the reason for the Babylonian exile. The repeated willingness of Israel to turn its back on God, emphasized in these two primary examples of idolatry, results in God turning his back on Israel. Dunn notes, "These two episodes were regarded within Israel as the two lowest points of Israel's story, the nadir of Israel's failures."[26] Regardless of any "high points" in the story of Israel, Stephen reminds his listeners that Israel's story has always arced toward disobedience.

---

23. Cf. Fitzmyer, *Acts*, 378; Witherington, *Acts*, 270.

24. There is strong manuscript support that Stephen said "you" (plural) and not "us" at this point in the speech. Which is more likely? In Greek pronunciation these two words probably were pronounced nearly identically, and translators are left to determine whether Stephen would have associated himself more closely with his hearers (using "us") or not. Since Stephen keeps the relationship close up until v. 51 (e.g., "our" in vv. 39, 44, 45), most translators and scholars prefer "us" as the likely reading.

25. Despite being expressly forbidden to do so, Israel worshiped Molek, the Ammonite god of sky and sun, and even sacrificed their children to this god (see Lev 18:21; 20:2–5; 1 Kgs 11:5, 7, 33; Isa 57:9; Jer 32:35; 49:1, 3; Zeph 1:5).

26. Dunn, *Acts*, 90.

The Tabernacle and the Temple (7:44–50)

Moses also gave the Israelites the tabernacle, a special *place* to meet with God. The NIV translates the reference to this earthly tent as "the tabernacle of the covenant law" (v. 44). Literally, it is a "tent of witness,"[27] a phrase describing the central place of worship for Israel prior to the building of the temple in Jerusalem. What the NIV helpfully points out by translating it as "the tabernacle of the covenant law" is that this probably refers to the Ten Commandments, which were kept in the ark (Exod 25:16) inside the "tabernacle of the covenant law" (Exod 38:21). Importantly, this "tabernacle" stands in contrast to the "tabernacle of Molek" mentioned in the quotation from Amos in the previous sentence. Stephen also points out that this place of meeting was mobile. That is, it traveled with the people in the wilderness, and Joshua brought it with them into the land when God cleared the land of pagans before them (Acts 7:45).

The tabernacle moved with the people of God until David's time. David asked if he might build a permanent place of meeting (Acts 7:46), but that job was reserved for his son Solomon, who built the temple (v. 47). Even though Solomon's temple was permanent and glorious, from this building's dedication Solomon proclaimed, "The heavens, even the highest heaven, cannot contain you. How much less this temple I have built!" (1 Kgs 8:27). It is interesting that in Solomon's dedicatory prayer he highlights the temple as being a place for the "Name"[28] of God. Although Stephen's speech does not highlight this, it is relevant to underscore that the disciples have been repeatedly admonished not to speak in the "name" of Jesus, and Stephen's own arrest was related to the charge that "Jesus of Nazareth" would destroy the temple. The point is that the "name" and the temple are intertwined. Solomon knew that God did not dwell in the house that his, or anyone else's, hands made. Stephen drives this point home at the end (vv. 48–50); God does not dwell in residences that human hands can make.[29] Instead, echoing Solomon's dedicatory prayer, he draws on the words from the prophet Isaiah to pronounce that God declares, "Heaven is my throne, and the earth is my footstool. . . . Has not *my hand* made all these things?" (vv. 49–50, quoting Isa 66:1–2).

---

27. The Greek is *hē skēnē tou martyriou* and comes from the LXX. It is translated here at Acts 7:44 variously as "the tent of testimony" (NRSV); "tabernacle of witness" (KJV); or "tent of witness" (ESV). All are attempts to help modern readers to grasp what is going on in the text.

28. The emphasis on the "Name" of God with the temple is emphasized strongly and repeated no less than fourteen times in Solomon's words to the people and then his prayer (see 1 Kgs 8:16, 17, 18, 19, 20, 29, 33, 35, 41, 42, 43 [2x], 44, 48).

29. The two rhetorical questions in v. 49 imply that no "house" could be adequate for God, the Most High.

The Conclusion (7:51–53)

Stephen has been selective in his retelling of Israel's salvation story. His most provocative words, however, are spoken in his conclusion: "You stiff-necked people!"—you resist God, reject his prophets, and break his law (see Acts 7:51–53). Throughout his speech Stephen has consistently included himself with his audience. He opened with the conciliatory words "brothers and fathers" and repeatedly referred to the people of God in the past using first-person pronouns (e.g., "*our* ancestors," v. 11). But at the end, the pronouns turn decidedly to the second-person plural "you": "*You* stiff-necked people. . . . *Your* hearts and ears are still uncircumcised. . . . *your* ancestors . . . *you* always resist the Holy Spirit. . . . *your* ancestors. . . . *you* have betrayed . . . *you* who have received the law" (vv. 51–53). Stephen's words are inflammatory and condemnatory—and biblical. "Stiff-necked people"[30] draws on a long litany of examples of stubbornness in the story of God's people in the Old Testament. Stephen accuses them of following the footsteps of their ancestors in not only being stubborn but also in being disobedient in their "uncircumcised" hearts,[31] grieving the Holy Spirit,[32] and persecuting the prophets[33] who spoke on God's behalf. The point is clear: like parents, like children. The parents killed God's prophets who predicted the coming messiah, and now, pathetically and unsurprisingly, the children have followed their forebears by disobediently betraying and murdering "the Righteous One"—Jesus (v. 52; see 3:13–14). They did this all despite the fact that they were the custodians of the law (v. 53) that had been given to them through angels. Their failure is climactic and complete.

In this fascinating speech it is noteworthy that Stephen never mentions Jesus by name. At one point (v. 37), he does mention a prophecy concerning him, and he refers to him as "the Righteous One" (v. 52). The point is that this is not primarily a NT salvation story, but an OT salvation story. The closest parallels to what Stephen does can be found in biblical texts like Joshua (24:2–15), the Psalms (e.g., Ps 105), or in extrabiblical texts like Judith (5:6–18). Psalm 106 and Nehemiah (9:6–37) are also interesting parallels because, like Stephen's speech, they deal with the rebelliousness of the people of God. Still, what are we to make of such a speech in Acts 7? It seems that Luke is offering a Christian use of a Jewish form, ready-made to "turn the

---

30. See Exod 33:3, 5; 34:9; Deut 9:6, 13; 10:16; 31:27; Judg 2:19; 2 Kgs 17:14; 2 Chr 30:8; 36:13; Neh 9:16, 17, 29; Ps 78:8; Prov 29:1; Isa 46:12; 48:4; Jer 7:26; 17:23; 19:15; Ezek 2:4; Hos 4:16.
31. Cf. Lev 26:41; Jer 4:4; 6:10.
32. Cf. Isa 63:10.
33. See 1 Kgs 19:10, 14; 2 Chr 36:16; Neh 9:26; Matt 5:12.

tables" on Judaism itself when the open struggle first makes its appearance against the Greek Christian community in Jerusalem.

In the overall narrative of Acts, this speech serves as a pivot for the expansion of the gospel geographically and as the first significant break with Judaism theologically. As such, the speech plays a significant role in Acts. First, it serves to counter the charges laid against Stephen in 6:11 that he spoke against Moses (he spoke against the law) and against God (he spoke against the temple). Second, the speech will serve as an apologetic to justify the turn that the Jewish-Christian church will make toward the gentiles because of the stubbornness of the Jewish leadership. In conjunction with this second aspect, it is also a polemic in the conflict with Judaism. The charge against Stephen that he attacked the temple, the focus of God's presence with his people, is answered late in the speech (vv. 44–50). Here, everything goes back to Moses. Even though God gave Moses the directive to construct the movable tabernacle while they were still wandering in the desert prior to entering the promised land, Stephen points out that the temple is not necessarily in the divine order of things. In this sense, he does speak against the temple. Regarding the charge about speaking against the law, however, this is denied vehemently (vv. 51–53). Rather, it is *they* who rejected Moses—following a long line[34] of others who rejected God's servants—by rejecting the Righteous One promised by Moses (Deut 18:15). Every other part of the speech is introduction to set up the reply to these two charges.

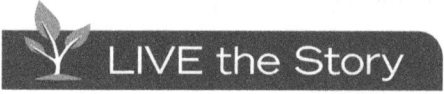

LIVE the Story

Knowing the Story

Marcion of Sinope was an important and popular teacher in the second-century church. He taught that the God of the OT, the God of law and justice, was radically different from the God of the NT, the God of grace and mercy and the Father of Jesus Christ. He rejected the OT as authoritative Scripture for Christians and instead proposed an alternative canon of Scripture that only included a modified version of Luke's Gospel and ten letters of Paul, the only "true" apostle. Marcion's select canon was determined by his gnostic thinking (i.e., the God of the OT is the creator of evil), and much of his teaching was characterized by an antilegalistic and anti-Jewish stance.[35] This view of

---

34. That is, the Egyptians (7:6–7), Joseph's brothers (7:9–10), the Israelites in the wilderness (7:35–41), and the ancestors who killed the prophets (7:52).

35. See Irenaeus, *Against Heresies* 1.27.2; Tertullian, *Against Marcion* 4.5–7 and 5.2–4; see also Richard N. Longenecker, "Three Ways of Understanding Relations Between the Testaments:

the canon acted as a catalyst for the early church to think seriously about what constituted their authoritative story, that is, what documents constituted "Scripture." In the end, the church came to recognize the twenty-seven documents of the NT alongside the Jewish Scriptures (i.e., the thirty-nine books of the OT).

While the early church rejected the Marcionite heresy, there is a sense in which some contemporary Christians are functional Marcionites. That is, some present-day Christians, including those who have been following Jesus for a long time, are ignorant of the OT story because they rarely hear it read in public worship and/or rarely study it in private devotion. As such, when it comes to hearing Stephen's speech in Acts, the shape, content, and argument of it are not easily understood or, worse, deemed irrelevant. It is crucial for pastors and teachers to ensure that those who they care for know that the OT is indeed essential to the story of Jesus and the story of the church. It is not helpful to be impatient or irritable about this situation. Rather, we preachers and teachers must winsomely and creatively engage people with the OT story in an integrative and comprehensive manner that connects with and climaxes in the story of Jesus.

When the church deepens its familiarity with the OT story, we see that the point of all engagement with Scripture—NT *and* OT—is not just to know its content but to be challenged and formed by it. In Stephen's speech, no less than in Peter's first sermon (Acts 2), engagement with the OT resulted in heart work. Granted, in response to Peter's sermon, when he declared how the OT story reached its climax with the crucified Jesus, his audience was "cut to the heart" and they asked, "What shall we do?" (2:36–37). In Stephen's case, when he concluded his retelling of the story of Israel with his declaration about the murder of "the Righteous One," his listeners were not cut to the heart in repentance. Rather, the hearing of the story stirred their hardened hearts into a rage. Interestingly, it was not Stephen who demanded a response, Scripture did. That too is as it should be when it comes to hearing the story of Scripture. We are not to be ignorant of our story, but we must not be indifferent to it either. It should challenge our comfortable thought patterns and incite action.

What God Is Doing and Why This Matters

Simple questions do not always generate simple answers. In the case of Stephen, he was asked a simple question: "Are these charges true?" He *could* have answered with a simple "no" or "I have never spoken against the temple

---

Historically and Today," in *Tradition and Interpretation in the New Testament*, ed. G. F. Hawthorne (Grand Rapids: Eerdmans, 1987); and E. C. Blackman, *Marcion and His Influence* (London: SPCK, 1948).

or against the law." Instead, Stephen took a deep breath and told a story, a carefully crafted story about God's dealing with his people. It is interesting that in responding to serious personal charges against him, Stephen shapes his apology not into something that he has done (or not done) but about what God has done. God is the primary subject in the story of Israel, including the role that Stephen plays in that story. Stephen models for us something quite significant in this. He understood both his significance and innocence within a larger narrative, and so he framed his words and actions against the larger backdrop of God's words and actions. His story begins and finishes with the glory of God, the triune God, actively at work in heaven and on earth: "The *God* of glory appeared to our father Abraham (7:2). . . . *God* sent him" (7:4). "*God* promised him. . . . *God* spoke to him" (7:5–6). "[*God*] gave Abraham the covenant" (7:8). "*God* was with [Joseph]. . . . [*God*] gave Joseph wisdom" (7:9–10). "*I am* the *God* of your fathers. . . . *I* have indeed seen. . . . *I* have heard. . . . *I* will send you" (7:32–34). "*God* turned away from them" (7:42). "But Stephen, full of the *Holy Spirit* . . . saw the glory of *God*, and *Jesus* standing at the right hand of *God*" (7:55).

There is much wisdom to be gathered from Stephen and his understanding of God and in Luke's recalling it at considerable length. First, and always foremost, we must pay attention to what God is doing. One of my great joys as a priest is the opportunity to come into someone's home or hospital room and point them to where God is active and present in their lives, in this moment. Of course, this must be done winsomely. But I often discover that many people, including many Christians, especially in times of grief or pressure, miss this very truth. Sherlock Holmes tells Watson in *A Scandal in Bohemia*: "You *see*, but you do not *observe*."[36] The poet Luci Shaw notes that "missing our cues, we fail to notice the fingerprints of the Creator in the ordinary textures and phenomena of living because we are distracted by daily urgencies."[37] As a minister I am also on the lookout for God's fingerprints. I remind myself before walking into any home or hospital room that God is present ahead of me; my role is to be attentive to that presence. Eugene Peterson, my guide in this way of thinking, encourages me deliberately to consider and say out loud words like this: God is present ahead of me at 1155 Laurier Street, look for him there; God is present ahead of me in room 143 at Union Hospital, look for him there. Look for God's presence, listen for God speaking, attend to God's glory—the Father, Son, and Holy Spirit at work—and then point that out as wisely as I can.

---

36. Arthur Conan Doyle, *The Adventures of Sherlock Holmes* (London: Octopus, 1981), 16.
37. Luci Shaw, *Breath for the Bones: Art, Imagination, and Spirit* (Nashville: Thomas Nelson, 2007), 117.

Secondly, we must grasp the wisdom that Stephen's understanding of God was large enough to cope with delayed promises and disobedient humans. Abraham was promised land by God, and yet in his lifetime he received no inheritance, "not even enough ground to set his foot on" (Acts 7:5). Abraham's descendants rejected Moses, God's prophets were persecuted, and even the Righteous One whom Israel longed for was betrayed and murdered by those he came to rescue. Stephen reminds us that all of us who consider ourselves to be "God's people" habitually have disobedient hearts, deaf ears, and deliberately ignore the Holy Spirit. In the story of the patriarch Joseph, his own brothers sold him into slavery. Joseph needed to wait twenty-two years before he saw how God would work this for their good.

In receiving this second strand of wisdom from Stephen, we must be pastorally sensitive and highly discerning. It does little good to tell a grieving widow or a young man who has just lost an eye in an accident that if they could only grasp the long view of God then they would know that "all things work together for good" (Rom 8:28 NRSV). Discernment and timing are key qualities in telling the providential story of God. Still, we must know God's story well enough to shape and show it in such a way, as Stephen did, that others might hear about God's ways. When this is done thoughtfully and sensitively, we may still even find that the gospel story is rejected or resented. Christians did not sweep the Roman Empire with the gospel because they were polite. As they spoke the truth in love, many of them also suffered the loss of their livelihoods or even their lives because they offended people. Yet their impact was chained to the dynamic that saw God at work in the world, climactically in Jesus—the Righteous One—who now stands at the right hand of God and fills us with the Holy Spirit to see truth accurately and to speak it boldly.

CHAPTER 16

Acts 7:54–8:3

 LISTEN to the Story

⁵⁴When the members of the Sanhedrin heard this, they were furious and gnashed their teeth at him. ⁵⁵But Stephen, full of the Holy Spirit, looked up to heaven and saw the glory of God, and Jesus standing at the right hand of God. ⁵⁶"Look," he said, "I see heaven open and the Son of Man standing at the right hand of God."

⁵⁷At this they covered their ears and, yelling at the top of their voices, they all rushed at him, ⁵⁸dragged him out of the city and began to stone him. Meanwhile, the witnesses laid their coats at the feet of a young man named Saul.

⁵⁹While they were stoning him, Stephen prayed, "Lord Jesus, receive my spirit." ⁶⁰Then he fell on his knees and cried out, "Lord, do not hold this sin against them." When he had said this, he fell asleep.

⁸:¹And Saul approved of their killing him. On that day a great persecution broke out against the church in Jerusalem, and all except the apostles were scattered throughout Judea and Samaria. ²Godly men buried Stephen and mourned deeply for him. ³But Saul began to destroy the church. Going from house to house, he dragged off both men and women and put them in prison.

Listening to the Text in the Story: Exodus 33:18–23; Leviticus 24:14, 16; Numbers 15:35–36; Deuteronomy 17:7; 1 Kings 21:13; Psalms 31:5; 35:16; 37:12; 110:1; Daniel 7:13–14.

 **EXPLAIN the Story**

The section following Stephen's speech focuses on three points. The first is the immediate and violent response to Stephen's words (7:54–60). The second is the introduction of a "young man named Saul" (7:58). The third is the widening persecution of the church after Stephen's death (8:1–3). Interjected within this short narrative are two prayers by Stephen (7:59, 60). The section begins with a description of the members of the Sanhedrin and their response to Stephen (7:54–56), followed by a description of Stephen's death by stoning (7:57–60). The brief account is rounded off with a sketch of the persecution of the broader church after Stephen's martyrdom (8:1–3).

The Sanhedrin Responds to Stephen (7:54–56)

Surprisingly, it is not Stephen's accusers who interrupt his speech; Luke himself interrupts it. He does so by inserting the Sanhedrin's reaction to Stephen's indictment (7:52–53). Luke begins with two vivid idioms to convey the intense rage of the members of the Sanhedrin: first, literally, "they were sawn through in/to their hearts," and secondly "they ground their teeth at him" (v. 54). The psalmist reminds us that it is the ungodly, the malicious, and the wicked that gnash their teeth against the righteous (Pss 35:16; 37:12). These idioms offer a biblical picture into the nature of the crowd. After this brief glimpse of the incensed crowd, the narration cuts back to Stephen (Acts 7:55). While the Sanhedrin is full of rage, Stephen is full of the Holy Spirit, and looking to heaven he receives a vision of Jesus. Luke first narrates what he sees (v. 55) and then records Stephen describing what he sees to the Sanhedrin (v. 56). He beholds the glory of God and Jesus, the Son of Man, standing at the right hand of God. An important point that Luke makes in this is to demonstrate that Stephen stands in continuity with the great patriarchs of Israel. The same glory that appeared to Abraham (v. 2) also is revealed to Stephen (v. 55). Of even more significance is that he stands in line with the great prophet and lawgiver Moses, who saw the glory of God (Exod 33:18–23; 34:5–8). In this, Stephen is portrayed as a faithful witness, divinely confirmed by the Holy Spirit, in what he says and what he sees. And what he says is that he sees God's glory, a glory that is not on earth in a building made by human hands but is located in heaven alongside his exalted Son.

In the final, climactic sentence of his speech Stephen explains what he sees: "Look . . . I see heaven open and the Son of Man standing at the right hand of God" (Acts 7:56).[1] Like other faithful visionaries (Peter in Acts 10:11; John in Rev 4:1), Stephen sees heaven opened. Throughout the speech his gaze has been fixed on his audience, but now, as he speaks his final words, his focus

---

1. Schnabel, *Acts*, 362, argues that "Stephen's statement about Jesus's identity as the Son of Man at the right hand of God (v. 56) is part of his speech, the intended climax that was interrupted by the Jewish leaders. . . . This connection is missed if a break is inserted between v. 53 and v. 54." Schnabel may be correct that the Jewish leaders interrupted the speech, but in the composition of the narrative it is Luke who has interrupted the speech and does so deliberately to heighten the climactic and final words of Stephen.

is turned heavenward. What he sees in heaven is a God-granted vision of the exalted Jesus. He describes Jesus as "the Son of Man," a familiar title in the Gospels that Jesus uses as a self-description. The occurrence of this title is unique in Acts, since it is the only one outside of the Gospels. It is connected to Luke's account in the Gospel (Luke 22:69) of Jesus's royal enthronement, and it also builds on the exalted figure portrayed in Daniel's prophecy (Dan 7:13–14). Importantly, the claim that is made about the Son of Man, which has already been made earlier (Acts 2:33–35; 5:31), is that Jesus, himself wrongfully condemned and killed, has been vindicated. Presumably Stephen could have made reference to Jesus's resurrection to express this. Instead, he simply asserts Jesus's royal and exalted status at the right hand of God (cf. Ps 110:1). Stephen claims that Jesus is "standing," rather than sitting. Psalm 110 refers to the Lord being invited "to sit at my right hand" (v. 1) in a posture befitting of royalty. It is unclear why Jesus is standing, and it has been variously interpreted.[2] Perhaps he is standing as a just judge who vindicates Stephen's claims, confirms his innocence, and receives his witness to the truth—just as Jesus proclaimed the Son of Man would do for those who publicly acknowledge him before others (Luke 12:8). Or, maybe, Jesus stands to "welcome home" his brother Stephen.

The Death of Stephen (7:57–60)

The members of the Sanhedrin cannot bear Stephen's speech any longer, and they cut off his words with shouts of anger. Indeed, they cover their ears to indicate that they regard his words as blasphemous. For this Jerusalem crowd, no human being, especially not Jesus who was hung accursed on a cross, could share the glory of God at his right hand. Yet despite the fact that they have brought Stephen forward in court to face charges of blasphemy, they provide no arguments with which to respond to Stephen's defense. As with Jesus, the Jewish leaders could produce only false accusers. Unable to offer verbal counterarguments, his opponents, like those arrayed against Jesus, resort to "noise, anger, and violence; their weapon is heat, not light."[3] And so they rush at him and together[4] drag him outside the city and stone him (Acts 7:57–58a).

---

2. Barrett, *Acts*, 1:384–85, lists no less than eleven different interpretations as to why Jesus is "standing." For example, some have suggested Jesus is standing as an indication that he is ministering as a priest in the heavenly temple, or that he is standing to speak on behalf of Stephen, or that he is standing to welcome Stephen, or that he is standing and about to come to the martyr at the time of his death.

3. Alexandru Neago, *The Trial of the Gospel: An Apologetic of Luke's Trial Narratives*, SNTSMS 116 (Cambridge: Cambridge University Press, 2002), 169, quoted in Schnabel, *Acts*, 363.

4. Luke uses one of his favorite words, *homothymadon* ("all [together]")—which he elsewhere uses to describe the unity of believers in prayer and peaceful fellowship (e.g., Acts 1:14; 2:46; 4:24; 5:12)—to depict the unity of the mob in brutality and bloodshed.

The appropriate biblical response to blasphemy is to take the offending party outside the city or camp and stone them (cf. Lev 24:14; Num 15:35–36). If the Sanhedrin had been meeting near or on the Temple Mount, then possibly the gate that Stephen would have been dragged out of was the one leading to the Kidron or Hinnom Valley. While some assume that this crowd's response is the act of an angry mob turned violent,[5] Schnabel is likely correct as he notes that "it is difficult to imagine that the members of the Sanhedrin would turn into an uncontrollable mob—after having successfully tried Jesus and after heeding Gamaliel's counsel at an earlier hearing."[6] Still, one has the sense that this is an act of injustice akin to the scoundrels who made unjust accusations against Naboth at the instigation of the evil queen Jezebel and then had him taken outside the city to be stoned (cf. 1 Kgs 21:13).

At the end (Acts 7:58b) Luke notes that the witnesses, responsible for the accusations against Stephen and thus duty bound to cast the first stones (Deut 17:7), remove their robes before beginning their gruesome task. This meant little more than that they needed to remove their heavy and bulky outer garments for the strenuous work of throwing rocks. Notably, Luke mentions the name of a young man,[7] Saul. Saul seems to be added (8:1, 3) to the narrative as a foreshadowing of his important role in the second half of Acts.

As Stephen is stoned, this faithful martyr utters two prayers (vv. 59–60): one for himself and one for his accusers. His first prayer, "Lord Jesus, receive my spirit," not only affirms Jesus as his "Lord," the active mediator of God's grace standing at the right hand of God, but it also echoes the prayer of his Lord, who called out with similar words to his Father when he was at the point of death (Luke 23:46). Both Jesus's prayer and Stephen's reach back further to a prayer of David (Ps 31:5). This is the prayer of a faithful person declaring dependence on God for refuge in the face of ruthless traps set for them. The second prayer is the final word Stephen will utter. This time he bends his knees in prayer and cries out with the petition, "Lord, do not hold this sin against them." Again, his prayer begins by addressing Jesus as his "Lord" and pleads on behalf of his enemies, just as Jesus both commanded (Luke 6:27–28) and modeled (Luke 23:34) in prayer. He intercedes that God might forgive his enemies for the "sin" of killing him, yet another faithful witness who had spoken the truth that God revealed to him. His final prayer is answered. One of his accusers, Saul, will be confronted by the Lord and converted to be a follower of the Way.

---

5. Dunn, *Acts*, 100.
6. Schnabel, *Acts*, 391.
7. "Young man" (*neanias*) is a term that covered a range of age for a man anywhere between twenty-four and forty years old (see BDAG 667).

The contrast between Stephen and his accusers in this poignant episode could not be sharper. While the mob is full of anger and seethes with aggression, Stephen is full of the Spirit and speaks with consolation. While the mob listens to the words of faithless witnesses, Stephen listens to the words of God and bears faithful witness to Jesus. While the mob closes their ears to the voice of truth, Stephen sees heaven opened and the glory of God revealed.

The Persecution of the Church (8:1–3)

The opening sentences of Acts 8 (vv. 1–3) offer a compact summary of the persecution that broke out against the Christians on the day Stephen was killed and serves to set up its far-reaching impact and consequences. Amid this summary, two more strands of information are introduced about Saul to go with the initial mention of him (7:58). First, the opening sentence indicates that Saul was not an innocent bystander at Stephen's stoning but that he "approved" of it. This is a detail about the inner intent of Saul, one that he will make later himself in his own words (cf. 22:20). Luke could only have known about this inner attitude firsthand from Paul. It also places Saul among those "experts in the law" who "approve" what their ancestors did in killing the prophets (cf. Luke 11:48). The next strand concerning Saul tells us that he had progressed from being an approving bystander in the stoning to death of one member of the church to an active perpetrator trying to destroy the church (Acts 8:3; cf. Gal 1:13; Phil 3:6). That is, he did not only try to apprehend Christians preaching in the temple or serving in the marketplace, but he purposely sought them out by going house to house to arrest them. Presumably he was granted permission and assistance from the Jewish leaders to do so because Luke notes that he forcibly "dragged"[8] both men and women[9] off to prison.

With a glimpse of the key perpetrator behind the persecution, we return to other dimensions in this summary (Acts 8:1). A lot of information is packed into this sentence. First, it tells us that Stephen's martyrdom was the spark for a "persecution" against the church in Jerusalem. While there have been glimpses of apprehension and hostility toward the apostles and the community of believers in Jerusalem before, this is the first overt program designed to harass and oppress the church. Second, Luke emphasizes that it was a "great" persecution; indeed, it was great enough to incite members of the community to flee the city for the regions of Judea and Samaria. That this was significant to

---

8. Later in the narrative as "Paul," he will be on the receiving end of this kind of treatment when he is stoned in Lystra by Jews and then "dragged" outside the city and left for dead (Acts 14:19).
9. See "Explain the Story" on Acts 5:12–16. It is a distinctive feature of Luke to include women in the story as equal recipients of the Spirit, the gospel, and in this case the target of persecution.

the whole story we cannot doubt, but the addition that "*all* except the apostles were scattered" is hyperbole in light of later passages (e.g., 9:26; 11:22; 15:4). Finally, the summary states that the apostles remained in Jerusalem. It should be noted that this does not imply that the apostles were spared somehow from the persecution. It only relates that they did not leave the city.

After beginning with this compact summary (Acts 8:1), the narrative briefly returns to Stephen in verse 2. Amid the broader act of persecution against the Jerusalem church, the martyr whose death sparked the conflagration is not forgotten. Rather, godly men, presumably at great personal risk,[10] came and buried the body of Stephen. While a "great" persecution erupted against the church, there was also "great"[11] mourning for the beloved Stephen.

LIVE the Story

Stephen was killed for his witness. "Witness for Jesus, man of fruitful blood, /Your martyrdom begins and stands for all" are the memorable first lines that Malcolm Guite wrote for his sonnet "Stephen."[12] Guite reminds us that Stephen's blood worked as gospel seed in the world, and because of its sowing the faith sprang out robust and more complete than it ever had before. Instead of subtracting from their number, Stephen's martyrdom produced a multiplied harvest that continues to widen and deepen to this day.

The most notable fruit of Stephen's martyrdom is highlighted at this point in Luke's narrative with the triple reference (7:58; 8:1, 3) to a new character: Saul. The day the Jewish witnesses took off their coats and laid them at the feet of a young man named Saul was the day a gate cracked open in his soul for Christ's light to pour through. When later he passed through a Jerusalem gate along the road to Damascus to persecute the followers of the crucified Jesus, he finally met the One whom he was persecuting and was blinded by his light. Stephen's witness and his prayers contributed to the conversion of Saul and the apostleship of Paul.

It is important for all of us who continue to read and attend to the book of Acts to view Stephen's prayerful witness as a model, even if we never face martyrdom. He submitted his life and words to God, who is revealed in his Son, Jesus. Jesus was the single and ultimate reason for all that Stephen did, and

---

10. This is reminiscent of Joseph of Arimathea, who came and buried the body of Jesus (cf. Luke 23:50–53).

11. The same adjective (*megas*) describes both the "great" persecution (Acts 8:1) against the church and the "great" (8:2) mourning for Stephen.

12. Malcolm Guite, *Sounding the Seasons: Seventy Sonnets for the Christian Year* (Norwich: Canterbury, 2012), 17.

when Stephen died it was *for* his Savior and *like* his Savior. He served others at table *like* his Savior, who before him had served others and washed their feet. He lived *like* his Savior by offering his all on behalf of others regardless of the opinion of the crowd. He prayed *like* his Savior by confidently asking God to receive him into his presence at the time of his death. He forgave *like* his Savior in forgiving those who were killing him. Stephen did not seek martyrdom; it was forced upon him. His words and actions challenged injustice and untruthfulness, and in doing so the unjust and untruthful pushed back. Stephen's path was the peaceful path of his Savior's, but *like* his Savior this way of living often creates confrontation and, in Stephen's case, a fruitful martyrdom.

Stephen Cherry, dean of King's College Chapel in Cambridge, expresses well both the confrontational nature of Christian witness and the way "God's redemptive, healing, and transformative mission" can be expressed through it:

> The Christian way is a path towards peace, but it is one that knowingly goes through the territory where injustice is challenged and untruthfulness is exposed. To put it more poetically, it involves visiting what Edwin Muir called the "fields of charity and sin." This means that the Christian path inevitably involves a profound seriousness about both spirituality and truth and also about relationships and justice.
>
> It also means that self-sacrifice and even martyrdom make sense within a Christian frame of reference. And it makes a very specific sense: Christian martyrdom is not a fast track to paradise or an escape to nirvana. It is a gift of the self to God's redeeming, healing and transformative mission. It is never sought. But it is always possible where love, compassion and truth encounter merciless evil.[13]

In all this, Stephen was a sympathetic servant ("like Savior, like disciple") and an engaging model of one empowered by the Spirit of the Lord.

---

13. Stephen Cherry, "'Spiritual But Not Religious'—or Is There More to It Than That?," *Another Angle*, 5 Oct. 2014, http://stephencherry.wordpress.com/page/2/.

CHAPTER 17

Acts 8:4-25

 LISTEN to the Story

⁴Those who had been scattered preached the word wherever they went. ⁵Philip went down to a city in Samaria and proclaimed the Messiah there. ⁶When the crowds heard Philip and saw the signs he performed, they all paid close attention to what he said. ⁷For with shrieks, impure spirits came out of many, and many who were paralyzed or lame were healed. ⁸So there was great joy in that city.

⁹Now for some time a man named Simon had practiced sorcery in the city and amazed all the people of Samaria. He boasted that he was someone great, ¹⁰and all the people, both high and low, gave him their attention and exclaimed, "This man is rightly called the Great Power of God." ¹¹They followed him because he had amazed them for a long time with his sorcery. ¹²But when they believed Philip as he proclaimed the good news of the kingdom of God and the name of Jesus Christ, they were baptized, both men and women. ¹³Simon himself believed and was baptized. And he followed Philip everywhere, astonished by the great signs and miracles he saw.

¹⁴When the apostles in Jerusalem heard that Samaria had accepted the word of God, they sent Peter and John to Samaria. ¹⁵When they arrived, they prayed for the new believers there that they might receive the Holy Spirit, ¹⁶because the Holy Spirit had not yet come on any of them; they had simply been baptized in the name of the Lord Jesus. ¹⁷Then Peter and John placed their hands on them, and they received the Holy Spirit.

¹⁸When Simon saw that the Spirit was given at the laying on of the apostles' hands, he offered them money ¹⁹and said, "Give me also this ability so that everyone on whom I lay my hands may receive the Holy Spirit."

²⁰Peter answered: "May your money perish with you, because you thought you could buy the gift of God with money! ²¹You have no part or share in this ministry, because your heart is not right before God. ²²Repent

of this wickedness and pray to the Lord in the hope that he may forgive you for having such a thought in your heart. ²³For I see that you are full of bitterness and captive to sin."

²⁴Then Simon answered, "Pray to the Lord for me so that nothing you have said may happen to me."

²⁵After they had further proclaimed the word of the Lord and testified about Jesus, Peter and John returned to Jerusalem, preaching the gospel in many Samaritan villages.

Listening to the Text in the Story: 2 Kings 17:21–24; Acts 6:5; 21:8.

EXPLAIN the Story

The primary result of the persecution of the early Christians in Jerusalem, led by Saul, is that they are scattered; as they scatter, the gospel goes with them. Outside of Jerusalem and the immediate territory of Judea, the next significant geographical step is Samaria. It is important to remember that the Jews and their distant "family" members, the Samaritans, while sharing many similarities and living in close proximity to one another, were bitter enemies in the first century. Nonetheless, the mission to Samaria was a direct mandate from Jesus. Furthermore, after Philip's mission to Samaria he is sent to meet an Ethiopian eunuch traveling to his distant home from Jerusalem (Acts 8:26–40). These two extensions of the gospel, to Samaria and Ethiopia, represent an initial fulfillment of Jesus's commission to his followers to be his "witnesses in Jerusalem, and in all Judea and Samaria, and to the ends of the earth" (1:8).

There are several thematic strands in the present narrative (8:4–25). First, the *great* persecution of the church in Jerusalem and Judea is a catalyst for a *great* expression of the power of God in Samaria. Secondly, the *dispersed* preaching of the word and the joyful reception of the Messiah by the Samaritans highlights a restoration of the *dispersed* "lost sheep of Israel" to the people of God. Finally, the apostles are sent to *authenticate* this first extension of the gospel outside of Jerusalem and Judea, but it is the Holy Spirit's presence that *authenticates* the witness. These themes are expressed in three movements: first, the mighty words and deeds of Philip in Samaria (8:4–8); secondly, the "conversion" of the great magician, Simon, through the great signs of Philip (8:9–13); and finally the apostolic confirmation of the Samaritan reception to the gospel along with the divine verification of the Holy Spirit (8:14–25).

The Mighty Words and Deeds of Philip in Samaria (8:4–8)

When Luke wrote Acts, he did not number his verses; in fact, there were no verses, no punctuation, and no spacing between the words, and everything was written in capital letters in the original Greek composition. Therefore, to signal a new subject, writers would use verbal signposts, often untranslatable in English. One of these untranslatable signposts occurs in verse 4 and again in verse 25.[1] Coupled with the repeated mention of the preaching of "the word," it creates a bracket to the overall section and ties the intervening verses together while preparing for the next transition in verse 26. All of this is to say that verse 4 is a transition to a new topic that will continue until verse 25.

Among those who were scattered and preaching "the word" was Philip. Who is Philip? A few scholars[2] have argued on the basis of some sources in the tradition of the early church[3] that this is "Philip" of Bethsaida (John 12:21), one of the twelve apostles of Jesus, who also goes by the name "the evangelist" (Acts 21:8). It is more likely, however, that Philip the apostle and Philip the evangelist are two different individuals. This is implied by the word "except" where we are told "all *except* the apostles were scattered throughout Judea and Samaria" (8:1). Furthermore, Philip "the evangelist," noted later (21:8), is described as being one of "the Seven" (6:5), which seems to distinguish him from "the Twelve" apostles. All in all, this points to Philip being one of the Greek-speaking Jewish Christians who were scattered by the outbreak of persecution in Jerusalem. He was thus one of those who went "down" (that is, he went north) to Samaria.

If Philip is one of the Seven, the next question to address from the present passage (v. 5) is the question of the location of where he went. At this point in the Greek text of Acts there are some manuscripts that refer to Philip going "to *the* [main] city of Samaria," while others tell of him going "to *a* city of Samaria." The issue here involves whether there is the presence or absence of the Greek article ("the") before the word "city." The oldest and best manuscripts suggest that there should be an article here so that we would understand Philip going "to *the* [main] city of Samaria," which, in this case, would either be Sebaste,[4] the ancient capital city of Samaria, or Neapolis, the ancient city of Shechem and the religious capital of the Samaritans. On the

---

1. The Greek words are *men oun*.
2. E.g., Arnold Ehrhardt, *The Acts of the Apostles: Ten Lectures* (Manchester: Manchester University Press, 1969), 36–40.
3. That is, Polycrates of Ephesus (ca. AD 190) in Eusebius, *Hist. eccl.* 3.31.3 and Clement of Alexandria (ca. AD 190), *Strom.* 3.6.16.
4. Carl S. Rasmussen, *Zondervan Atlas of the Bible* (Grand Rapids: Zondervan, 2010), 217, suggests that Sebaste was not likely the destination of Philip because in the first century it was predominantly gentile.

other hand, reading the text without the article, "to *a* city of Samaria," makes excellent sense in the context and seems to set up verse 8 that states "there was great joy in that [unnamed] city."[5] In the end, it is difficult to decide on the exact location of Philip's preaching in Samaria, but the NIV translators have gone with the reading that does not include the Greek article.

One final piece of background to this passage relates to who the Samaritans were and how they related to the Jews in the first century. The historical origins of the Samaritans are difficult to determine.[6] From the Samaritans' own perspective, their origins date to the distant past from the time of Eli in the eleventh-century BC when the nation's religious capital was moved from Mount Gerizim to Shiloh. The Samaritans viewed themselves as the "faithful" Israelites who continued to worship at Gerizim. From the Jewish perspective, the Samaritans were Israelites who intermingled with the Cuthaean people following the Assyrian conquest of the northern kingdom (cf. 2 Kgs 17:24–41). The Jews viewed this new people as syncretistic in their religion. Furthermore, they understood them not only to have intermingled Israelite faith with paganism but that they also intermingled with pagans in marriage. The Jewish historian Josephus recalled this tradition of Cuthaean intermarriage and the establishment of a temple on Mount Gerizim near Shechem and understood this new place of worship as an imitation of the one in Jerusalem (see *Ant.* 9.288–91; *J.W.* 1.63). Josephus routinely referred to the Samaritans as people who were "evil and enviously disposed to the Jews" (*Ant.* 11.114 [Whiston]). He even goes so far as to write that "when the Jews are in adversity, they deny that they are of kin to them, and then they confess the truth; but when they perceive that some good fortune has befallen them, they immediately pretend to have communion with them, saying, that they belong to them, and derive their genealogy from the posterity of Joseph, Ephraim, and Manasseh" (*Ant.* 11.341 [Whiston]).

Most scholars think these opposing Samaritan and Jewish views on their origins are too polarized. Most likely Samaritan origins come from the time when the region was conquered by Alexander the Great and ruled by his successors in the fourth-century BC. Sometime during this period, Shechem was resettled by "a group of religious purists who were descendants of the original Israelite population in the north who had not been exiled by the Assyrians."[7] Dissident priests from Jerusalem may also have supplemented these settlers and reestablished the temple on Mount Gerizim. Throughout the period when Samaria and Judea were controlled by competing Greek dynasties, the varying political

---

5. See Bruce M. Metzger, *A Textual Commentary on the Greek New Testament*, 2nd ed. (Stuttgart: German Bible Society, 1994), 311.
6. On Samaritan origins, see H. G. M. Williamson, "Samaritans," *DJG* 724–26.
7. Ibid., 726.

allegiances of Samaria and Judea and their different approaches to accepting or rejecting Greek culture further alienated the two peoples. A decisive rift occurred in 128 BC when the Jewish Hasmonean leader, John Hyrcanus, captured the capital and destroyed the sanctuary on Mount Shechem. With this event, Samaritan and Jewish regard for one another reached its lowest ebb and continued throughout the first-century AD.

It is not surprising that when Jesus wanted to shock a Jewish legal expert who asked him, "Who is my neighbor?" (Luke 10:29), he told the story of the "good Samaritan."[8] Jews did not even want to come near Samaria. In fact, Jewish pilgrims journeying from Galilee in the north to Jerusalem in the south routinely traveled out of their way to bypass Samaritan territory so as not to come into contact with its outcast people. Jesus, however, did not do this. Jesus healed a Samaritan leper (Luke 17:11–19), and he traveled through Samaria and engaged a Samaritan woman in conversation at a well outside her city of Sychar (John 4:5–42). Furthermore, unique to Luke's Gospel, there is a long insertion of Jesus's teaching as he travels through Samaria to Jerusalem (Luke 9:51–19:27). All of this is to say that the ground was well prepared in Samaria for Philip's proclamation of the Messiah (Acts 8:5) prior to his arrival. And who better to declare the good news to "outcast" Samaritans than Philip? Philip, a Greek-speaking Jewish Christian, was an outcast too. He was driven by persecution from his spiritual home in Jerusalem to the same territory where outcast Samaritans lived. Philip would proclaim the gospel as one who understood the feelings of those who were marginalized and hated.

Philip not only proclaimed Jesus as the Messiah (Acts 8:5), the anointed king, he also performed "signs" (8:6) of exorcism and healing—similar to Jesus (Luke 6:18) and his apostles (Acts 5:16). While this mission to Samaria marked an expansion of the gospel outside of Jewish boundaries, the actual message and ministry maintained strong continuities with the message and ministry of Jesus and the apostles. For example, this continuity is expressed with the note that there was "great joy" in this Samaritan city (8:8). Luke often highlights, both in the Gospel and in Acts, that the proclamation of the good news for "the poor," including those who were hated outsiders like the Samaritans, is accompanied with joy. In the beginning of the Gospel, the angel announced to the Bethlehem shepherds "good news of great joy" (Luke 2:10

---

8. Of course, few Jews would describe any Samaritan as "good," and it is important to note that Luke does not describe him as "good" either in the narrative (Luke 10:25–37). After all, the response to Jesus's question (i.e., "Which of these three do you think was a neighbor to the man?") by the expert of the law is, "The one who had mercy on him" (v. 37). The "expert" could not even mention *where* he was from! That is a part of the power of the story—and also the clear evidence that no one could possibly have made it up. When we use the language "*good* Samaritan," this is an indication that modern readers have missed Jesus's point.

NRSV). In the middle of the Gospel there is "rejoicing in heaven over one sinner who repents" (15:7; cf. v. 10, 32). At the end of the Gospel the disciples returned to Jerusalem "with great joy" (24:52). Not surprisingly, this attendant joy continues to resonate when the good news is proclaimed in Samaria.

The Conversion of Simon the "Great" (8:9–13)

The "great joy" experienced by the Samaritans from Philip's ministry also drew the attention of a notable local celebrity, one Simon, a sorcerer, also known as "Simon Magus" or "Simon the Great." The word "great" (*megas*) is a key word in this narrative,[9] and Simon's role is interesting. "This is . . . a story about power—different kinds of spiritual power, and its use and abuse."[10] Simon the powerful sorcerer is well known outside of the NT in early Christianity. For example, the early apologist and native of Samaria Justin Martyr (ca. AD 100–165) wrote about Simon Magus coming to Rome during the reign of Claudius. According to Justin, Simon had a significant following among Samaritans living in Rome who honored him as a "god" and revered him with an altar and statue dedicated to him.[11] The apocryphal *Acts of Peter* relates at length the supernatural battles between the apostle Peter and Simon Magus in Rome. Further, Irenaeus, a second-century apologist, regarded Simon Magus as a forerunner of the gnostic heresy.[12] These stories are later developments from the description in Acts. Still, what is clear is that there was a Simon from Samaria who had a negative impact on the early church that originated from his first encounter with Christianity through Philip. So, what is Simon's role in the narrative?

Early on (v. 9), Luke describes Simon as a man who practiced "sorcery," a practice that was abhorred and forbidden by the Mosaic law (see Deut 18:9–14). Indeed, it was a practice that often tripped up the Israelites and led them into idolatry and the demonic (e.g., Isa 47:9, 12; 57:3; Jer 27:9; Ezek 13:18). Nonetheless, Jewish magic flourished in antiquity and continued in Acts.[13] Sorcerers or magicians (whether they were Jewish or gentile) in the ancient world were not people who merely entertained on the street with

---

9. *Megas* occurs in Acts 8:7, 9, 10 (2x), 13. It also sounds similar to the other descriptor for Simon: the "magician/sorcerer" (*magos*) and could therefore also be a play on words.

10. Loveday Alexander, *Acts: The People's Bible Commentary* (Oxford: The Bible Reading Fellowship, 2006), 70.

11. See Justin's *The First Apology* 26.3; *Dialogue with Trypho* 120.6.

12. Irenaeus, *Against Heresies* 1.23.

13. See P. S. Alexander, "Incantations and Books of Magic," in Emil Shürer, *The History of the Jewish People in the Age of Jesus Christ*, ed. G. Vermes, F. Millar, and M. Goodman, rev. ed., 3 vols. (Edinburgh: T&T Clark, 1986), 3:342. Dunn, *Acts*, 109, rightly notes that "we should not assume that 'magic' had a consistently bad image in the ancient world. . . . Even within the New Testament 'the three wise men' who visit the child Jesus are actually 'magi' (there in the sense of astrologers), the same term used in Acts 13:6–8."

clever card or illusory tricks. Sorcerers sought to harness supernatural powers to achieve specific results or tasks (e.g., for protection, to alter one's fate, to gain favor with people, predict the future, to heal). The encounter with Simon is the first engagement in Acts between those who declared the gospel and those who practiced sorcery, but it will not be the last (see also Acts 13:4–12; 16:16–18; 19:18–19). Part of what Luke is doing with this initial confrontation is preparing his readers for future conflicts that explore the character of "spiritual power and the boundaries between magic and miracle."[14]

Luke's next sentence (v. 10) notes that all the people of this Samaritan city, "both high [literally "great"] and low," declared Simon to be "great." Interestingly, the narrative recalls that the Samaritans gave him their close "attention" (v. 10), that is, until Philip came with his great deeds and words, and they turned their "attention" (v. 6) to the evangelist. This indicates that prior to Philip, Simon had been as successful as the evangelist, and this creates a dynamic comparison between the two. Despite holding the amazement of the Samaritans with his sorcery for a "long time" (v. 11), Simon's powerful magic was no match for Philip's proclamation of the kingdom of God and the name of Jesus the Messiah (v. 12). Both Philip's preaching and the signs and wonders that attended his ministry indicate that his work was in continuity with others who proclaimed the good news in Acts (see 19:8; 20:25; 28:23, 31). Confronted with the reign of God and King Jesus, the Samaritans' interest in Simon and his sorcery evaporated, and they embraced the good news and were baptized. Although the NIV does not translate the word *kai*, the text deliberately intensifies the result of Philip's work by noting that even "Simon himself believed and was baptized" (v. 13; cf. NRSV; ESV). At this point in the narrative, it appears that Simon's conversion is authentic and sincere. Furthermore, Simon continued to follow Philip because his "great" signs and miracles amazed him. Here, the sorcerer's role in the story serves as a contrasting foil between the "great" works of the sorcerer and the "great" works and words of the evangelist. However, Simon's function in the narrative is not finished. In the next section another Christian leader, the apostle Peter, confronts Simon and exposes his inferior and false view of God.

The Affirmation of the Apostles and the Holy Spirit (8:14–25)

Philip's extraordinary missionary work in Samaria did not go unnoticed by the leadership in Jerusalem. Their response was to send their two primary leaders and spokesmen, Peter and John,[15] to affirm the gospel work by praying for

---

14. Alexander, *Acts*, 71.
15. In the early chapters of Acts, Peter and John are regularly paired together as twin spokesmen for the Jerusalem church (see Acts 3:1, 3, 4, 11; 4:1, 3, 7, 13, 19, 23). Interestingly their round-trip

the new believers and laying their hands on them so that they might receive the Holy Spirit. While Peter and John are the means of this authentication, the primary authenticator is the person of the Holy Spirit. Until this point, the Holy Spirit has not been mentioned in connection with Philip's Samaritan mission. After Peter and John pray for them to receive the Holy Spirit in (v. 15), the Spirit's presence is central to the story, with the Spirit explicitly mentioned several times (vv. 16, 17, 18, 19).

Much of the scholarly and popular interest in this part of Acts 8 has centered on Luke's understanding of conversion and the baptism of the Spirit. The issue at hand is that the Samaritans believed and were baptized (v. 12), but they do not receive the Spirit until some time later. James Dunn refers to this as "the riddle of Samaria" and observes, "In the context of the rest of the New Testament these facts appear to be mutually exclusive and wholly irreconcilable."[16] The two basic answers to this riddle are: (1) the Samaritans became Christians through the preaching of Philip; or (2) the Samaritans were not *really* Christians until Peter and John arrived with the Holy Spirit. Dunn concludes that the Samaritans were not yet Christians until Peter and John arrived. He comes to this conclusion because in Acts it is only the presence of the Spirit that marks a Christian. This is why the narrative includes the story of Simon in the first place. The Samaritans' response and Simon's response highlight the difference between authentic and inauthentic Christian faith.[17]

Dunn provides a very helpful insight on this passage. However, elsewhere in Acts, to be baptized—without explicit mention of the Spirit—is regarded as a mark of Christian belief (e.g., 2:41; 16:15; 18:8; 22:16). Furthermore, the passage expressly states that the Samaritans *and* Simon (8:13) believed the message of Philip's preaching. In the narrative following this one, the conversion of the Ethiopian eunuch, all of the same elements are present: Philip preaches the good news about Jesus (v. 35); the Ethiopian becomes a believer (although this is not explicitly stated); he is baptized (v. 38); and he continues on his way rejoicing (v. 39). The implication here is that the Ethiopian is a true Christian even though Luke did not state explicitly that he received the Spirit.[18] Still, Dunn is correct to note that something is not yet complete for the Samaritans until Peter and John arrive. That is, there were many converts through Philip's preaching, and after the Jerusalem church sends its delegation

---

visit from Jerusalem to Samaria in chapter 8 (vv. 14, 17, 25) is the last time the two are paired together in Acts.

16. James D. G. Dunn, *Baptism in the Holy Spirit: A Re-examination of the New Testament Teaching on the Gift of the Spirit in Relation to Pentecostalism Today* (London: SCM, 2010), 55.

17. Ibid., 66–67.

18. See the discussion by Gordon D. Fee, *Gospel and Spirit: Issues in New Testament Hermeneutics* (Peabody, MA: Hendrickson, 1991), 97–98, 110.

it is through their ministry that expressions of the Spirit occur (e.g., speaking in tongues)—expressions which could be *seen* ("Simon *saw* that the Spirit was given at the laying on of the apostles' hands," v. 18).

Yet for all of this, Luke does not take the opportunity of this Samaritan episode to offer an explanation for what true Christian conversion looks like. Rather, what Luke seems to indicate is that in this first reception of the good news outside Jerusalem, the apostles' presence is required to complete the process. Since the Samaritan mission is such a radical first step, all the parties involved need a divine affirmation of the legitimacy of this mission. This may be why outward expressions of the Spirit occur only after the coming of Peter and John and the laying on of their hands. Luke records the same affirmation when it comes to the mission being extended to gentiles like Cornelius (see Acts 10:44–48; 11:15–17). This narrative also reminds us that conversion is a process that occurs over time with appropriate responses to the Spirit to each new stage of perception and transformation.

Of course, besides the central role of the Spirit in the narrative there is also the matter of that other character, Simon Magus, who now takes center stage (8:18–24). As was mentioned above, Simon was an important figure in early-church records outside the NT. Simon, it seems, having basked in the adulation of others, is now reluctant to join the cast as an extra player in the drama; instead, he wants to be one of the primary players in the Samaritan production. The issue is one of power and authority, and Simon makes several crucial misjudgments.[19] First, he thinks he can obtain, or regain, power—he was, after all, known as "the Great Power of God" (v. 10)—by money (v. 18). Second, he assumes that the Holy Spirit is a thing to be managed and ordered about by Peter and John. In this he thinks the Spirit is an "authority"[20] to be controlled rather than God's personal presence to be received. The fourth-century bishop of Jerusalem Cyril put this eloquently by noting that Simon wanted power, not grace: "He did not say, 'Give me also the participation of the Holy Ghost,' but 'Give me this power,' with a view to selling to others what could not be sold—something he himself did not possess."[21]

A dialogue ensues between Simon and Peter (John is omitted) in the following sentences (vv. 18–24). Simon offers money (vv. 18–19) for the gift of the Holy Spirit; Peter replies with strong words of reproach (vv. 20–23); Simon

---

19. Gaventa, *Acts*, 138, refers to Simon's statement in v. 19 as containing a "trinity of profound errors." That is, (1) Simon's own "magic" is not even comparable to the power of the Spirit, (2) he thinks the Spirit is at the disposal of Peter and John, and (3) he thinks bribery is the avenue to obtain the Spirit's power.

20. The NIV translates the Greek word *exousia* in v. 19 as "ability," but more frequently translates it as "authority" as is done in Acts 1:7; 9:14; 26:10, 12.

21. Cyril of Jerusalem, *Catechetical Lecture* 16.10, in *ACCA*, 94.

then responds with a plea for prayer (v. 24). Peter's words of rebuke are harsh. His words, "may your money perish with you" (v. 20a), imply a curse against Simon.[22] Peter is aghast with the suggestion that the "gift of God" could be bought with money! Furthermore, Peter announces that Simon has no "share" (or "lot") in this ministry—echoing the language used of Judas earlier on (1:17). Peter's words are also similar to the words of Jesus spoken to Saul on the Damascus Road, where the purpose of gospel ministry is to "open [the] eyes" of unbelievers so that they can "turn . . . from darkness to light, and from the power of Satan to God, so that they might receive forgiveness of sins and a *place* [i.e., a "share"] among those who are sanctified by faith in [Jesus]" (26:18).

Unfortunately, Simon does not see or turn, and hence he does not receive forgiveness or a share. Simon's heart is "full of bitterness and captive to sin" (8:23). Peterson notes that "this terminology recalls Deuteronomy 29:18 . . . where the image of a root producing 'bitter poison' describes a person going after false gods and leading others to do the same."[23] In this case the bitter poison debilitates Simon. In the end, the once "great" Simon is reduced feebly to asking others to pray for him (Acts 8:24). Through this dialogue, Luke is able to do two things. First, he highlights that the presence of the Spirit is indeed what characterizes the genuine reception of the gospel, and secondly it offers Luke an opportunity to explain to his own generation at the time of the writing of Acts (at least twenty years after this episode) the proper relationship between Simon and the Christian church.

The narrative concludes with the note that Peter and John continue to proclaim "the word of the Lord and testif[y] about Jesus" (v. 25). This brackets the opening words of this section (v. 4) where those who were scattered from Jerusalem to Samaria by persecution preached "the word" wherever they went. As the apostles return to Jerusalem from Samaria, they continue proclaiming the gospel throughout their journey. The mission to Samaria is thus confirmed and consolidated by the apostles and, more importantly, by the Holy Spirit.

LIVE the Story

Modern Samaria

In the realm of sport, often the fiercest of rivalries occur between teams and their supporters who live in close proximity to one another. Since my childhood, I've known about the rivalries between the Green Bay Packers and Minnesota

---

22. This is implied by the use of the Greek optative mood for the verb "to be" (translated as "may") that indicates a wish or, in this case, a curse. See Parsons and Culy, *Acts*, 157.

23. Peterson, *Acts*, 289.

Vikings in football, or between the New York Yankees and the Boston Red Sox in baseball, or between the Montreal Canadiens and Boston Bruins in hockey. Still, this did nothing to prepare me for the experience of the intense rivalries that exist in England between football (i.e., soccer) clubs, especially those clubs who are neighbors. At least twice a year there are local "derby" matches between rival clubs of close geographic proximity, for example, Newcastle and Sunderland, or Manchester United and Manchester City, or Arsenal and Tottenham. These matches create intense competition and, unfortunately, sometimes even violence. Of course, this is merely sport, but we know of more serious and violent ethnic rivalries between neighbors in recent history in places such as Pakistan, India, Yugoslavia, Syria, Sudan, Rwanda, and Nigeria.

The point is that we need to be mindful of the disdain that can occur between those who often live in close proximity—even when they share much history, religion, or bloodlines in common—as did the Jews and Samaritans in the first century. In his book *Vanishing Grace*, Philip Yancey reminds us that we still live in a world shaped by realities of Jewish and Samaritan animosity:

> In Jesus's day the Samaritans lived just down the road from their cousins the Jews, and despite having much in common the two groups could not get along. Like estranged family members, they nursed grudges. To the Jews, Samaritans were heretics, plain and simple. John's Gospel reports, "Jews do not associate with Samaritans." Surprisingly, groups that are closest to each other may spark the strongest enmity. The world outside Rwanda and Yugoslavia had trouble just keeping straight the differences between Hutu and Tutsi or Bosniak, Serb, and Croat—even as the groups themselves were slaughtering each other over those differences. And now we look at Middle East violence and struggle to understand the rancor between Shiite and Sunni Muslims. People who are the-same-but-not-quite-the-same can somehow generate more hatred than two groups with more obvious otherness. That was true in Jesus's time. The Pharisees used the "S-word" when insulting Jesus, accusing him of being "a Samaritan and demon-possessed."[24]

The problem, both in first-century Palestine no less than in the contemporary Middle East, is that people are not so much different from one another as they are familiar and similar. Even as Christians, we are sometimes not very much different in our attitudes to the "Samaritans" of our day from those of Jesus's own disciples, James and John, who suggested that fire should be rained down upon Samaritan villagers who did not welcome Jesus (Luke 9:53–55).

---

24. Philip Yancey, *Vanishing Grace: What Ever Happened to the Good News?* (Grand Rapids: Zondervan, 2014), 25.

How then can we treat our opponents and enemies with the kind of love and respect commended by our Lord? As is often the case, we need to follow the words and example set by Jesus. Jesus rebuked the kind of "strike first" or "strike back" mentality when relating to the Samaritans of his day. To the Pharisees who accused him of being "a Samaritan and demon-possessed" (John 8:48), Yancey notes, "[Jesus] denied the accusation of demon-possession but did not protest the racial slur."[25] In fact, he went out of his way to talk to Samaritans, even a Samaritan woman at a well, and, uncharacteristic of Jews of his day, he traveled through Samaria on his way to Jerusalem. Remarkably, he made a Samaritan one of his most famous heroes in his parables, and he commanded his followers to preach the gospel in Samaria. This is what Philip did and, later, what Peter and John did as well in Acts 8. In an irony certainly not missed on Luke and careful listeners of his two-part story of Jesus, it is the same John who once wished to call down fires of judgment upon Samaritans to destroy them who now, in Acts 8, prays that Holy Spirit fire might fall upon them to confirm salvation. For good measure, on his way back to Jerusalem with Peter, John continues preaching the good news of salvation "in many Samaritan villages" (v. 25). Christians today are equally charged with both a rebuke and a commission from Jesus as we live in our "modern Samaria." We are rebuked for treating our enemies—whether they are crosstown rivals or international terrorists—without love. And we are commissioned to rain down prayer upon those whom Jesus loves. We are called to use the weapons of the Spirit upon those who oppose us.[26] When people think of followers of Christ, the first word that should come to their minds is *love*. Until this is the case, Christians will need to remind themselves of our Lord's words from the Last Supper: "My command is this: Love each other as I have loved you" (John 15:12).

Modern Simony

In the book of Acts, Christians are not the only ones who can exercise spiritual power. Simon Magus is only the first among others who implemented power and amazed people with his sorcery. Yet as the story in Acts 8 unfolds, even Simon believed and was baptized. It is important to remember, however, that Simon is not a fraudster but a foe. Simon is the first Christian heretic. Again, following on the discussion above, how does this story call us to live the story today? That is, in encounters with *simony*—the attitude that thinks the gifts of God are something to be exploited, bought, or traded—how do we discern the real thing? Real power from God transforms one spiritually and relationally.

---

25. Ibid., 27.
26. I remind the reader of the villagers of Le Chambon who "lived the story" under Nazi-occupied France; see "Live the Story" in Acts 5:17–42.

While Simon may have believed the message proclaimed by Philip, this belief did not penetrate his interior life and exterior actions. Authentic faith results in authentic worship. Eugene Peterson notes, "If [Simon] had presented himself before God as a worshiper, giving himself in humility and service, it would never have entered his mind to try to take God's gift and make a profession of using it. For the Holy Spirit is not a Power to be manipulated but a Power to be obeyed."[27]

Authentic faith, in contrast to the faith of simony, enacts a change of heart, a realignment of commitment and purpose to the kingdom of God and the reign of King Jesus. It impacts the way we use our money and our power. True spiritual power, modeled first by Jesus and then by his followers in Acts (e.g., Peter, Stephen, Philip), comes through laying down one's life for others, not by grasping for money and magic. In this sense, the encounter with Simon in Acts 8 is similar to the story of Ananias and Sapphira in Acts 5. In both the narrative is about the conflict of powers vying for the hearts and minds of individuals and not merely a story about the degree of an individual's personal conviction.

There are many spiritual powers in the world and many rivals like Simon seeking prestige and power that can be bought and manipulated. Yet for all this misdirection and misunderstanding, when authentic Spirit power is expressed, people turn and notice it just as readily today as they did in first-century Samaria. For example, Operation Mobilization relates this story of the Spirit's power from their publication *Walk the Talk in the Arab World* about an encounter in Algeria:

> A young man developed severe depression for two years. He had hardly slept for three months and his family tried everything: doctors, sorcerers, imams—all in vain. A Muslim neighbor told him, "I hear that, in a nearby town, there is a church where the pastor prays for people and they are healed. Why not try that?" He attended the service and then went forward for prayer. He left as a follower of Christ, and went home to sleep through the night from that point on. His family was amazed and asked what medicine he was taking. He replied that, in fact, he took none at all; he had gone to the Christians who prayed for him. His family said, "We all have different needs. Let us all go there and see what happens." He had a truck which he filled with people to take to church; nearly all of them trusted Christ that day. When [Operation Mobilization workers] went to his home to record his testimony, the whole family came and said, "Everyone of us has a story and we want to tell them."[28]

---

27. Peterson, *Conversations*, 1695.
28. Operation Mobilization, "Misconceptions, God Stories and Being There," in *Walk the Talk in the Arab World* (Winter 2015): 5.

CHAPTER 18

Acts 8:26-40

 LISTEN to the Story

²⁶Now an angel of the Lord said to Philip, "Go south to the road—the desert road—that goes down from Jerusalem to Gaza." ²⁷So he started out, and on his way he met an Ethiopian eunuch, an important official in charge of all the treasury of the Kandake (which means "queen of the Ethiopians"). This man had gone to Jerusalem to worship, ²⁸and on his way home was sitting in his chariot reading the Book of Isaiah the prophet. ²⁹The Spirit told Philip, "Go to that chariot and stay near it."

³⁰Then Philip ran up to the chariot and heard the man reading Isaiah the prophet. "Do you understand what you are reading?" Philip asked.

³¹"How can I," he said, "unless someone explains it to me?" So he invited Philip to come up and sit with him.

³²This is the passage of Scripture the eunuch was reading: "He was led like a sheep to the slaughter, and as a lamb before its shearer is silent, so he did not open his mouth. ³³In his humiliation he was deprived of justice. Who can speak of his descendants? For his life was taken from the earth."[1]

³⁴The eunuch asked Philip, "Tell me, please, who is the prophet talking about, himself or someone else?" ³⁵Then Philip began with that very passage of Scripture and told him the good news about Jesus.

³⁶As they traveled along the road, they came to some water and the eunuch said, "Look, here is water. What can stand in the way of my being baptized?"[37][2] ³⁸And he gave orders to stop the chariot. Then both Philip and the eunuch went down into the water and Philip baptized him. ³⁹When they came up out of the water, the Spirit of the Lord suddenly took Philip away, and the eunuch did not see him again, but went on his

---

1. Isa 53:7, 8.
2. Verse 37 is an addition to the text by later manuscripts in the Western tradition. Metzger, *Textual Commentary*, 315, notes, "Although the earliest known New Testament manuscript that contains the words dates from the sixth century (ms. E), the tradition of the Ethiopian's confession of faith in Christ was current as early as the latter part of the second century, for Irenaeus quotes part of it (*Against Heresies*, III.xii.8)."

way rejoicing. ⁴⁰Philip, however, appeared at Azotus and traveled about, preaching the gospel in all the towns until he reached Caesarea.

Listening to the Text in the Story: Leviticus 21:20; Deuteronomy 23:1; 1 Kings 8:41–43; Psalm 68:31; Isaiah 56:3–7; Zephaniah 3:10.

EXPLAIN the Story

Although Philip's presence faded at the end of the previous story in Samaria, his role in Acts is not finished. Once more Philip has an important part to play in the unfolding drama in Acts. Philip's role is key, but in this narrative we are again reminded that the primary initiator is not human, but divine. It is divine initiative that leads Philip to an unexpected place, at an unexpected time, to engage in an unexpected conversation. While there is much that is unanticipated in this episode, the story unfolds simply: first, the stage is set for Philip and the Ethiopian's encounter (8:26–29); second, Philip and the eunuch engage in a conversation that leads to an explanation of the good news about Jesus (8:30–35); and third, the eunuch is baptized, and they both go their separate ways (8:36–40).

The Stage Is Set for Philip and the Ethiopian (8:26–29)

The first phrase opens the episode with a surprising encounter: "Now an angel of the Lord said to Philip" (v. 26a). From the very beginning, God takes the initiative in the story and at all its crucial stages (see vv. 29, 39). This is not the only surprising element; the destination is also unusual. Philip is commanded to go south along "the desert road" from Jerusalem to Gaza. He is not instructed to move from Samaria to another populated location to continue his successful evangelistic ministry; rather, he is directed to a desert road. Further, the word translated as "south" can also be translated as "noon." While the directional sense of his journey is more likely in play than the time of day, the unusual nature of the situation is heightened by hinting that Philip is not only traveling to an odd location in a southerly direction but doing so at an unusual time of day for traveling in a desert. God's ways are inscrutable. Much like the prophet Elijah, Philip is addressed by the angel of the Lord (8:29; cf. 2 Kgs 1:15), directed by the Spirit on his journey (Acts 8:26–29, 39; cf. 1 Kgs 18:12), and finds himself running along a road with an important person (Acts 8:30; 1 Kgs 18:46).[3]

---

3. Cf. Peterson, *Acts*, 292.

Another interesting element is the simple mention of the word "road" (*hodos*), a word that can also be translated as "way." This word occurs frequently in Acts, but in this narrative it connects all the elements of the story. Philip is sent along the desert *road* (Acts 8:26, *hodos*), so that he can *explain the way* (v. 31; *hodēgeō*) to the Ethiopian. As they travel along *the way* (v. 36; *hodos*), they find water to baptize the eunuch. When they finally part, the new believer is sent on his *way* (v. 39; *hodos*) rejoicing. Already the narrative seems to be foreshadowing the next account when Saul is set upon his murderous pursuit of those who belong to "the Way" (9:2) before he himself meets Jesus along the *road* (9:17; *hodos*) to Damascus.

The specific person that Philip is led to is also unexpected. He meets an "Ethiopian eunuch, an important official in charge of all the treasury of the Kandake (which means 'queen of the Ethiopians')," who had "gone to Jerusalem to worship" (8:27). In going to preach to the Samaritans, Philip was reaching out to his near neighbor, but in meeting this man he is reaching out to someone from Ethiopia, or "Cush" as it is frequently translated in the OT, the proverbial "ends of the earth" (cf. Esth 1:1; 8:9; Ezek 29:10). In this sense there is a poignant and immediate symmetry between Jesus's command to go to "Samaria, and to the ends of the earth" (Acts 1:8). The listening reader may recognize the promises of Psalm 68:31 and Zephaniah 3:10 that describe how foreigners from as far away as "Cush" would one day bring offerings and submit themselves to God in Jerusalem.

It is unlikely that this Ethiopian would have found satisfaction from his pilgrimage. When Solomon dedicated the temple in Jerusalem, he envisaged a time when "the foreigner . . . [will] come from a distant land" to worship the Lord, the God of Israel (1 Kgs 8:41–43). Unfortunately, it would not be his ethnicity that would have barred him from the precincts of the temple but the fact that he was a eunuch: "No one who has been emasculated by crushing or cutting may enter the assembly of the Lord" (Deut 23:1; cf. Lev 21:20). Eunuchs were often important court officials, but they would have been restricted as worshipers in Jerusalem. Nonetheless, this man is reading an Isaiah scroll, purchased no doubt at considerable cost, as he travels in his chariot on the long journey home. Philip is directed again by divine agency, and this time "the Spirit" commands him to "go" and stay near the chariot, waiting for his opportunity (Acts 8:29).

The Good News Is Explained (8:30–35)

Before long a break occurs for Philip. As he puffs alongside the chariot, he hears the man reading from Isaiah. His next course of action is clever. He asks a simple question: "Do you understand what you are reading?" (8:30).

The question opens the door, and the Ethiopian replies with a question of his own—"How can I unless someone explains [*hodēgeō*] it to me?"—and an invitation for Philip to join him in his chariot.

The eunuch was reading from Isaiah (53:7–8); a direct citation of the text from the LXX is then recounted in the narrative. A key principle about biblical reading is discernible here: Scripture requires interpretation. The eunuch is reading from one of the most important portions of Scripture for Christians, about the servant of the Lord who, silent like a lamb before its shearer, suffers humiliation and injustice. The eunuch asks a second key question: "Who is the prophet talking about, himself or someone else?" (Acts 8:34). Jesus, walking with a pair of traveling companions along *the way* to Emmaus, launched into an interpretation about himself "*beginning* with Moses and all the prophets" (Luke 24:26–27). Philip also "*began* with [Isaiah 53]" and tells the eunuch about the good news of Jesus (Acts 8:35). Whereas Isaiah's suffering servant does not open his "mouth" (Acts 8:32; cf. Isa 53:7), Philip does open his "mouth"[4] and begins teaching. The Isaiah passage where they begin speaks very little about Christology or atonement, but it does address the issue of the Messiah's "descendants." This is important because it would not have taken Philip long to lead the Ethiopian eunuch to a magnificent passage just a few sentences further along the way in Isaiah that would burst with resonance for him:

> Let no foreigner who is bound to the LORD say, "The LORD will surely exclude me from his people." And let no eunuch complain, "I am only a dry tree." For this is what the LORD says: "To the eunuchs who keep my Sabbaths, who choose what pleases me and hold fast to my covenant—to them I will give within my temple and its walls a memorial and a name better than sons and daughters; I will give them an everlasting name that will endure forever" (Isa 56:3–5).

The eunuch may not have been welcomed as a "descendant" by those at the temple in Jerusalem, but Jesus, the One in whom all that the temple pointed to has been fulfilled, will welcome a foreigner *and* a eunuch like him as a son. This would indeed have been very good news. On the way from Jerusalem to Gaza, the eunuch, with reliable Philip to guide him, is yet another person who is set along "the paths of life" (Acts 2:28; Ps 16:11).

The Eunuch Is Baptized (8:36–40)

As they continued along the road, the eunuch became a believer of the good news about Jesus. In Luke's own narrative there is no confession of faith

---

4. The connection between the closed "mouth" of the suffering servant and the open "mouth" of Philip is more readily noticed in the Greek text where the word *stoma* ("mouth") occurs in 8:32 and 35.

related by the eunuch, but he understood the implications of his belief and asked a third and final question of Philip: "Look, here is water. What can stand in the way of my being baptized?" (Acts 8:36). Philip's answer comes by way of action: he baptizes the eunuch. After they "went down" into the water, when they "came up out of the water" the Spirit of the Lord took Philip from the eunuch's presence.[5] This is the final reminder of the divine initiative in this episode. At the first moment of encounter with Philip, the eunuch is perplexed; now, as he is left alone, he is no longer confused but rejoices in God's salvation—a hallmark of gentile response to the gospel.[6] Joyfulness is a frequent theme in both Luke's Gospel and in Acts,[7] and joy accompanies the eunuch along his journey. That seems fitting. A man who has become a follower of *"the Way"* continues on his *way* with joy. Later church tradition, as recorded by Irenaeus (*Against Heresies* 3.12.8; 4.23.2) and Eusebius (*Hist. eccl.* 2.1.13), recounts that this eunuch returned to his home in Ethiopia and proclaimed the good news about Jesus there, as an early extension of Jesus's great commission.

As for Philip, possibly a little confused by now, he finds himself next in Azotus, a coastal city about twenty-two miles north of Gaza (Acts 8:40). There, he continues his evangelistic ministry along the coast in these predominantly gentile cities and towns until he arrives in Caesarea. After this geographical note, Philip completely drops out of the frame of Acts until much later, where we find him still living in the city of Caesarea with his four prophesying daughters (21:8–9).

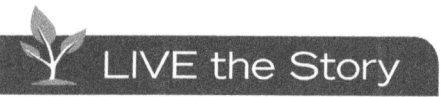

LIVE the Story

God Is the Primary Actor in the Story

The Ethiopian eunuch story bristles with interesting angles for reflection. The first and foremost aspect is the role that God plays in this episode. While we know (or should know) that God is the primary actor in every story, this narrative reminds us unequivocally that God is before us, behind us, and with us. Most mornings I meet together with my youngest son for morning prayer. We use a simple liturgy from the Northumbria Community called *Celtic Daily Prayer*. After praying through the Psalms and biblical lessons appointed for the day, we finish by singing a canticle, beginning with the words, "Christ,

---

5. Schnabel, *Acts*, 429n25, mentions 1 Kgs 18:12; 2 Kgs 2:16; Ezek 3:14 as parallel, sudden "translation" stories to this one of Philip.
6. Gaventa, *Acts*, 145.
7. E.g., Luke 2:10; 15:7, 10, 32; 24:52–53; Acts 3:8; 11:23; 13:48.

as a light illumine and guide me."[8] It continues, echoing the ancient prayer of St. Patrick's Breastplate:

> *Christ with me, Christ before me,*
> *Christ behind me, Christ in me,*
> *Christ under me, Christ over me,*
> *Christ to the right of me, Christ to the left of me,*
> *Christ in lying down, Christ in sitting, Christ in rising up,*
> *Christ in the heart of every person, who may think of me!*
> *Christ in the mouth of every one, who may speak to me!*
> *Christ in every eye, which may look on me!*
> *Christ in every ear, which may hear me!*[9]

That prayer captures well the theological shape of the Ethiopian eunuch story. The Lord is before Philip to illumine and guide the way for him: "An angel of the Lord said to Philip, 'Go south to the road—the desert road'" (Acts 8:26). With humility born by the Spirit, Philip approaches the chariot: "The Spirit told Philip, 'Go to that chariot'" (v. 29). Once there, he discovers Christ is in the heart and mouth of the one to whom he speaks and overshadows their conversation over the Scriptures: "Tell me, please, who is the prophet talking about?" (v. 34). When all is said and done, the Spirit leads him again on a new path: "The Spirit of the Lord suddenly took Philip away" (v. 39). We need regular reminding about the intimate ways God illumines and guides us all, whether we are riding in our modern "chariots" along deserted highways or walking down crowded city streets that can feel relationally arid. Despite what the surroundings may indicate and despite regular confusion about God and his ways, God is present to us: under us, over us, on our left and our right.

God Is the Initiator of Mission

A secondary theme from this passage that flows out of the first theological theme is that God is the initiator of mission. As the initiator, God can take so-called chance encounters and unexpected circumstances to work his purposes. Of course, this does not mean that we should not think strategically and plan carefully. However, as we will see time and again in Acts, God can, and frequently does, accomplish his purposes in unexpected ways. He can turn martyrdom into seed for the gospel; he can take an enemy like Saul and turn

---

8. *Celtic Daily Prayer: Prayers and Readings from the Northumbria Community* (New York: HarperCollins, 2002), 18.
9. *St. Patrick: His Writings and Life*, ed. and trans. Newport J. D. White (New York: Macmillan, 1920), 66–67.

him into an apostle to the gentiles; and he can reach a seeking, but confused, eunuch along a deserted patch of road. Beyond the book of Acts, the story of the church is replete with God breaking through into individuals' lives and then using those persons as catalysts to reach countless others. In the fifth century, a British Christian boy was taken captive by slavers to Ireland. As a slave he learned the language, customs, and territory of the island. Although the boy would later make his escape to freedom back home in England, he later returned as a man as the first Christian missionary to Ireland. That man was Patrick, and his influence on Ireland and Ireland's impact on the world for the gospel is still reverberating.

More recently, there are indigenous movements that are sprouting in the Arab world, three of which in Jordan involve thousands of people. Operation Mobilization (OM) reports, "They all began with one or two people. A short-term foreigner with no Arabic took a taxi and shared her testimony with the driver, who was genuinely interested in her words. They exchanged numbers and men on the [OM] team led him to Christ. Within weeks, several hundred people came to Christ through his effective witness."[10] Although we do not know for certain whether the man Philip led to Christ in Acts 8 is responsible for then bringing the gospel to the country we now know as Ethiopia, we do know that there has been a vibrant church in that region dating back to the early fourth century.[11] It is hard to account for that kind of history apart from the heart of God who initiates and sustains his global mission.

Outsiders Made Insiders

Finally, there is a fascinating personal angle to this story. It does not relate to any personal details about the Ethiopian offered in the story but to universal personal experience. Most of us at one time or another have experienced what it feels like to be a foreigner or somebody looking in from the outside through an invisible glass barrier on something we don't quite understand or don't feel a part of. Where others belong and appear so self-assured, we might often feel left out. Luke seems to delight in and champion the story of the misfit, the outsider, and the foreigner—people like the Ethiopian eunuch. Luke repeatedly shows how Jesus, and then his disciples, welcomes and includes those who often find themselves marginalized by the religious and cultural establishment: women (Elizabeth, Mary, Lydia, and Damaris), the poor (slaves, shepherds, and day laborers), the infirm (lepers and the lame), and foreigners (Samaritans, Ethiopians, and Romans).

---

10. Operation Mobilization, "Misconceptions, God Stories and Being There," in *Walk the Talk in the Arab World* (Winter 2015): 4.

11. The Ethiopian Orthodox Church dates its origins to the arrival of Frumentius (ca. AD 330).

Although Acts does not tell us directly, the Ethiopian is not a Jew by birth, but as a eunuch he could not even become a proselyte of Judaism. And yet for all this, he made the arduous journey to Jerusalem to worship there, even though as a eunuch he would have been barred entrance to the temple. Undaunted and at significant personal expense, he nonetheless obtained an Isaiah scroll and then attempted to read it on his own. For all of these cultural, religious, and personal barriers—and with no hope of gaining entrance into the people of God—he discovers the doors flung open wide in Jesus. Isaiah relates a question about the servant who was led like a sheep to slaughter and humiliated and deprived justice. "Who can speak of his descendants?" (Acts 8:33). In Jesus the Messiah, we now know that even "dry-tree" eunuchs—or anyone else who is an excluded outsider and misfit—may receive an inheritance as his descendants "better than sons and daughters . . . [and] an everlasting name that will endure forever" (Isa 56:3–5).

CHAPTER 19

Acts 9:1–19a

 LISTEN to the Story

¹Meanwhile, Saul was still breathing out murderous threats against the Lord's disciples. He went to the high priest ²and asked him for letters to the synagogues in Damascus, so that if he found any there who belonged to the Way, whether men or women, he might take them as prisoners to Jerusalem. ³As he neared Damascus on his journey, suddenly a light from heaven flashed around him. ⁴He fell to the ground and heard a voice say to him, "Saul, Saul, why do you persecute me?"

⁵"Who are you, Lord?" Saul asked.

"I am Jesus, whom you are persecuting," he replied. ⁶"Now get up and go into the city, and you will be told what you must do."

⁷The men traveling with Saul stood there speechless; they heard the sound but did not see anyone. ⁸Saul got up from the ground, but when he opened his eyes he could see nothing. So they led him by the hand into Damascus. ⁹For three days he was blind, and did not eat or drink anything.

¹⁰In Damascus there was a disciple named Ananias. The Lord called to him in a vision, "Ananias!"

"Yes, Lord," he answered.

¹¹The Lord told him, "Go to the house of Judas on Straight Street and ask for a man from Tarsus named Saul, for he is praying. ¹²In a vision he has seen a man named Ananias come and place his hands on him to restore his sight."

¹³"Lord," Ananias answered, "I have heard many reports about this man and all the harm he has done to your holy people in Jerusalem. ¹⁴And he has come here with authority from the chief priests to arrest all who call on your name."

¹⁵But the Lord said to Ananias, "Go! This man is my chosen instrument to proclaim my name to the Gentiles and their kings and to the people of Israel. ¹⁶I will show him how much he must suffer for my name."

¹⁷Then Ananias went to the house and entered it. Placing his hands

on Saul, he said, "Brother Saul, the Lord—Jesus, who appeared to you on the road as you were coming here—has sent me so that you may see again and be filled with the Holy Spirit." ¹⁸Immediately, something like scales fell from Saul's eyes, and he could see again. He got up and was baptized, ¹⁹and after taking some food, he regained his strength.

> *Listening to the Text in the Story*: Deuteronomy 21:23; 1 Corinthians 15:8–9; 2 Corinthians 11:22–33; Galatians 1:11–24; 3:13–14; Philippians 3:4–15.

EXPLAIN the Story

After describing episodes where nearby Samaritans and a gentile from the "ends of the earth" (the Ethiopian eunuch) receive the gospel, the next episode (ch. 9), the account of the conversion of Saul, is a crucial one. It is significant because Saul will be the Lord's "chosen instrument to proclaim [Jesus's] name to the Gentiles and their kings"—in a sense, to cover much of the gentile ground between Samaria and the ends of earth. So significant is this narrative that it is told three times in Acts (9:1–19a; 22:1–21; 26:2–23) and corroborated in Paul's letters (1 Cor 15:8–9; 2 Cor 11:22–33; Gal 1:11–24; Phil 3:4–15).

None of Saul's conversion narratives recounted by Luke in Acts are identical. Of course, there is much that *is* consistent between all three accounts, especially the key words of encounter between Jesus and Saul and his commission to take the gospel to the gentile world. There are, however, slight alterations in wording[1] or additional details,[2] which one would expect from retelling any story, along with several minor differences in the conversion stories, including: (1) Acts 26:14 states that "*we all* fell to the ground," while 9:4 and 22:7 note that only Saul "fell to the ground"; (2) Acts 9:6 and 22:10 cite Jesus directing Saul to get up and go to Damascus to receive further instruction, whereas 26:16–18 have more detailed instructions as a part of the original encounter; and (3) Acts 9:7 notes that Saul's traveling companions heard the voice, while

---

1. E.g., the narrative in ch. 9 is told from the third person, while the stories in chs. 22 and 26 are spoken from the first person.
2. E.g., the narratives in Acts 22:6 and 26:13 note that the blinding light from heaven shone "about noon" whereas Acts 9:3 only states "suddenly a light from heaven flashed." Or in 26:14 there are additional words from Jesus: "It is hard for you to kick against the goads."

in 22:9 Paul testifies that "my companions . . . did not understand the voice." Despite these differences, it is important to recognize that Luke included all three accounts in Acts with all their similarities and differences. As a credible historian of his time, he did not feel compelled to make all three accounts identical. "This tells us something about what a responsible historian like Luke saw as good practice."[3] Much like the Synoptic Gospels, Luke's variations and fresh angles of perspective need not imply inconsistency or historical inaccuracy.

There are two constants in the pre-conversion pictures of Saul in Acts and in Paul's own letters.[4] First, Saul persecuted the church. In the first account he is described as an approving onlooker at the killing of Stephen, and later he is directly involved as a persecutor (Acts 8:3; 9:1–2, 13–14; 22:4–5; 26:10–11). These details are corroborated in Paul's letters (1 Cor 15:9; Gal 1:13; Phil 3:6; 1 Tim 1:13). We are not told in Acts *why* he did so. Philippians offers clarity to this matter: "As for zeal [as a Jew], persecuting the church" (Phil 3:6). This indicates a theological motivation for Saul. Jesus frequently disagreed with Pharisees over theological and biblical issues. It is not surprising that after his ascension, Jesus's followers and their message continued to pose a threat to the theological security of zealous Pharisees like Saul. Further, before his Damascus Road encounter Saul had one great conviction of Jesus: because he died by crucifixion, God's curse was upon him (see Deut 21:23; cf. Gal 3:13–14).

Second, Saul was a Jew. This may be an obvious fact, but it is important to point out what kind of Jew he was. Saul was a *Hellenistic Jew*, and both of these elements are important. His thinking was thoroughly Jewish, and by his own testimony he was "a Hebrew of Hebrews . . . a Pharisee" (Phil 3:5). From Luke's recorded testimony (Acts 22:3) we learn he was trained under Gamaliel, a renowned Hillelite rabbi known for his liberal attitudes. There is no good reason to doubt this testimony of Luke's since it makes such good sense of the apostle Paul's later "liberalism" with regard to such crucial matters as circumcision and food sacrificed to idols. Saul was also a *Hellenistic* Jew. He was born in Tarsus—"a citizen of no ordinary city" (Acts 21:39). Tarsus was a place of learning and culture, in the same league with great cities like Athens and Alexandria, boasting a library of no less than two hundred thousand volumes. Saul would have spoken the Greek language fluently and understood Greco-Roman culture thoroughly. Furthermore, he was born a Roman citizen, an honor rarely granted to provincial subjects. His citizenship would have been registered in the public-record office in Tarsus. It granted him significant privileges of which he would, on occasion, avail himself. For example, his Roman citizenship would grant him the right to a fair trial, exemption from

---

3. Dunn, *Acts*, 117. Cf. Keener, *Acts*, 2:1598–618.
4. I am indebted to Gordon Fee for reminding me of these two "pictures" of Paul.

demeaning punishments like scourging, and the right to appeal a case against him to the very emperor of Rome.[5] A Hellenistic Jew with this background, education, and credentials would make a formidable apostle to the Gentile world. Yet, despite these exemplary qualities, the nature of his encounter with the risen Lord Jesus (9:1–19a) is so dramatic and unexpected that it would mark him for life and leave him to undertake his mission with uncommon humility and grace.

This crucial episode in Acts unfolds in three phases. First, Saul is given permission to pursue Christian Jews outside of Judea (9:1–2). Second, the risen Jesus confronts Saul as he nears Damascus (9:3–9). Third, after reaching Damascus, Jesus sends a disciple named Ananias to Saul to heal him and give him Jesus's words of commission (9:10–19).

Saul Pursues Followers of "The Way" (9:1–2)

The first short paragraph of this new narrative focusing on Saul begins by helping the reader catch up on the story relating to the campaign of persecution against the church hinted at earlier (8:1–3). Typical of Luke, we are not provided with any sense of how much time has elapsed between Stephen's martyrdom and Saul's brutal actions. While we are at a loss regarding the lapse of time, we do know that Saul is following in the steps of others in the history of Israel who used violence in their "zeal" to uphold the law of God.[6] Luke uses the present participle "breathing" (9:1) to describe Saul's ongoing and continuous threats against the followers of the Lord. The text suggests that after exhausting opportunities for pursuing Christians in Jerusalem and Judea, Saul looked for other prospective places to carry out his vicious campaign. Damascus was a reasonable choice. It was not too distant, it had a sizable Jewish population[7] where Christian Jews were likely to have fled, and although it was a city in the Roman province of Syria it had some municipal autonomy that would keep his activities off the radar of imperial authorities. Before departing for Damascus, Saul asked for extradition letters from the Jerusalem high priest to the synagogues of Damascus. The scholar F. F. Bruce points out that the Romans granted extradition rights to states, including Judea, which remained in force even after Judea was no longer a sovereign nation: "In 47 B.C. Julius Caesar confirmed those rights and privileges anew to the Jewish nation . . . and more particularly to the

---

5. See F. F. Bruce, "Paul in Acts and Letters," *DPL* 681–82.
6. Such precedents include Moses (Num 25:1–5), Phinehas (Num 25:7–11), Elijah (1 Kgs 18:40; 19:10, 14), and Mattathias, the father of the Maccabees (1 Macc 2:24–27).
7. According to Josephus, there were at least ten thousand Jews living in Damascus at the time of the Jewish revolt in AD 66 (*J.W.* 2.559–61; 7.368).

high-priesthood."[8] These letters granted Saul permission to round up Jewish refugees from Jerusalem and escort them back for punishment.

It is interesting that in this second sentence followers of Jesus are referred to as those who belonged to "the Way" (v. 2). This is the first time that Luke has used this title. Schnabel makes the excellent observation "that this term derives from Isa 40:3 and, more broadly, from other passages in Isaiah that speak of the way on which the Lord will travel when Israel is liberated from exile and restored to Zion."[9] That is, the disciples of Jesus understood that *the way* of the Lord proclaimed by John the Baptist (Matt 3:3; Mark 1:3; Luke 3:4; John 1:23) was complete, and they were now traveling on this completed road of the Lord. It is also an interesting title because the same word translated as "the Way" (*hodos*) occurs three times in the previous narrative as "road" or "way" (Acts 8:26, 36, 39; cf. *hodēgeō* ["explains"] in v. 31). Luke seems to be adding an ironic touch to his narrative. An Ethiopian eunuch pursuing truth finds his "way" as he meets Jesus on the road home from Jerusalem, while Saul pursuing those who belong to "the Way" meets Jesus "on the road" (9:17) as he travels from Jerusalem to Damascus.

Jesus Encounters Saul (9:3–9)

There is no preparation for Saul's encounter with Jesus. He was not looking for Jesus. He shows no mental distress or remorse, either with his current vocation or his own theological convictions at the time. What happened, however, was a radical turnabout, and while Paul the letter writer rarely records details of the Damascus Road encounter, both he and Luke are in complete agreement: he saw the risen Lord in person.[10] Given these items together, including the fact that his encounter occurred on the way to Damascus, it reflects well on Luke as a historian who seems to have his facts in good order.

Although we cannot be certain about either the route Saul took to Damascus or the location where the Lord appeared to him,[11] the journey was about 240

---

8. Bruce, *Acts*, 180–81; see also Josephus, *Ant.* 14.192–95. Bruce also cites an earlier letter around 142 BC delivered by a Roman ambassador to Ptolemy VIII of Egypt that demands "if any pestilent men have fled to you from their own country [Judea], hand them over to Simon the high priest, so that he may punish them according to their law" (1 Macc 15:21).

9. Schnabel, *Acts*, 290.

10. In Gal 1:16 Paul writes that God chose "to reveal [*apokalypsai*] his Son *in me.*" The "in me" is especially noteworthy: Paul was to serve as "exhibit A" among the newly formed people of God. In 1 Cor 9:1 he writes, "Have I not seen Jesus our Lord?" and in 15:8, "[Jesus] appeared to me [*ōphthē kamoi*]." This compares favorably with Acts 9:17, "[Jesus] appeared to you [*ho ophtheis soi*]" and Acts 26:16, "[Jesus said] I have appeared to you [*ōphthēn soi*]."

11. William M. Ramsay, *St. Paul the Traveler and Roman Citizen*, rev. ed. (Grand Rapids: Kregel, 2001), 43–44, suggests that Saul took the direct road to Damascus, "called 'the Way of the Sea' (i.e., the Sea of Galilee), crossing the Jordan by the 'bridge of Jacob's daughters' (as it is now called), a few miles above that sea. The old tradition places the scene of that remarkable event that followed at

kilometers (150 miles). Somewhere, "as he neared Damascus," a light from heaven flashed around him, and Saul fell to the ground. Luke adds the word "suddenly" to introduce the scene (v. 3). This may be for dramatic effect, but it also indicates the sovereign nature of the encounter. Saul did not seek this meeting, God did. The meeting is unexpected, but Saul's reaction to the flashing light is typical of other occasions when humans encounter the divine. In terror and alarm he fell to the ground and hid his face from the presence of the Lord.[12] He falls to the ground not necessarily because he is submitting to Jesus who is addressing him but because he is properly overwhelmed by the divine manifestation—a "knockout" blow of the highest order! He is addressed by the voice with a double vocative: "Saul, Saul." This resembles other biblical scenes where God addresses a person about to receive a unique calling.[13]

The voice from heaven asks Saul, "Why do you persecute me?" (v. 4). There is a certain edge to the question since the word "persecute" is in the present tense. For those of us familiar only with English tenses (i.e., past, present, future), where the emphasis is on "time," it is important to know that in Greek the present tense emphasizes more the *kind of action* than the time when an action occurs. That is, Saul is persecuting "me" in an *ongoing and continuous* manner. Further, the word "me" begins to prepare us for the revelation that the one whom Saul persecutes is none other than the one associated with "the Way" (v. 2). Saul replies to the question from heaven with a question of his own, "Who are you, Lord?" It is noteworthy that Saul addresses the voice from heaven as "Lord." The word "Lord" is more than mere polite address. For a Jew familiar with biblical stories of divine manifestations, Saul would know that the person behind the voice is none other than the "Lord," the Greek equivalent of the sacred, four-lettered Hebrew name "YHWH," the divine "I AM." This is remarkable since the reply he receives from heaven is "*I am* Jesus" (v. 5). For Christians used to viewing Jesus as divine, the second person of the Trinity, this may not strike them with the same force it would have for Saul. Saul's life up to this point was enveloped with "zeal" for the Lord; zeal focused on persecuting fellow Jews who regarded Jesus, one cursed by God, as the Messiah. The blow that this would have meant to his entire worldview is unimaginable. This may account for why the frequency of references to Jesus as the "Lord" in Acts spikes[14] in Saul's Damascus Road encounter. It may be a reminder of the new theological framework being shaped in Saul's mind.

Kaukab, where 'the Way of the Sea' crosses a very slight ridge about twelve miles south of Damascus. Here the first view of Damascus burst on the persecutor's sight."

12. See, e.g., Exod 3:6; Ezek 1:28; Dan 8:17; Rev 1:17.

13. E.g., note the calls of Jacob (Gen 46:2), Moses (Exod 3:4), and Samuel (1 Sam 3:10).

14. Luke uses the word "Lord" frequently to refer to Jesus in Acts (107x in total), but the usage of the word spikes to its highest number of eleven hits per a thousand words in the episodes related

The moment of Saul's encounter with Jesus as "the Lord" had tremendous impact on his thinking. Indeed, if his basic theology comes from his Jewish roots, then his essential Christian theology comes from his experience on the Damascus Road. At least two basic theological implications stem from this. The first implication is the centrality of the resurrection of Jesus (remembering that for him, this encounter on the Damascus Road is a resurrection appearance, not merely a vision), and thus a new understanding of the cross as well as the "curse" related to anyone who is hung on a tree (Gal 3:13; cf. Deut 21:23). That is, Saul would have to reimagine that God's "curse" (i.e., judgment) was upon humanity, not upon Jesus: God's *no* is not on Jesus but on those who rejected him. Saul would have to come to an entirely new understanding of Jesus. If God said *yes* in contrast to humanity's *no* to Jesus, then this would mean that Jesus who is speaking with him is "the Lord."

The second significant implication of Saul's encounter on the Damascus Road would be a whole new understanding of grace. God had accepted him freely—even though he was an enemy persecuting the Lord and his disciples. This moment would be the beginning of Saul learning about the transforming power of grace, and, eventually, this would mean a reorientation to righteousness based on the Mosaic law. This, of course, is what would open up the door to Saul's commission to proclaim the gospel to the gentiles. This is not to suggest that all this would be fully formed in this moment, but from the moment that Jesus commanded him to "get up and go into the city" (Acts 9:6) Saul would begin working out the profound implications of his encounter.

After the final words spoken by the voice from heaven, the scene shifts to the broader perspective of narrative. The event that Luke describes in vv. 3–6 was not an isolated experience for Saul; it affected those traveling with him. While Saul was on the ground, those who were with him "stood there speechless," hearing "the sound but did not see anyone" (v. 7). While his companions did not receive the full revelation that Saul did, they *did* experience something. This is important because it means Saul did not have a private experience—hallucinatory or otherwise. It was something that others experienced too. The phrase they "did not see anyone" is another implicit note that while his traveling companions did not see anyone, Saul certainly did "see" someone. The brilliance of *whom* he saw and *what* this meant for his entire theological orientation left Saul blind. The once fierce and feared Saul is helpless, and like a little child he must be led by the hand into the

---

to Saul's conversion in Acts 9:1–31. Kavin Rowe explores the significance of the title "Lord" superbly in his work on Acts (see *World Upside Down*, 103–16).

city (v. 8). He had set out, determined to pursue and prosecute those who followed "the Way," and now he cannot see his own way. For three days he was entombed in darkness, taking neither food nor drink, and thus had time to begin to rethink everything he knew about God, Jesus, and his misdirected zeal (v. 9). This was not the arrival to Damascus that he anticipated. The Lord will shortly commission Saul to take the light of the gospel to the nations, but first Saul must sit in darkness for three days. "He must be converted from his condition of embodying Israel's blind resistance to the straight way of God."[15]

Ananias Speaks for Jesus (9:10–19)

Even though Jesus revealed himself to Saul unbidden and personally, the Lord also called another disciple, Ananias, to become involved with Saul. This is instructive. Saul's reputation for brutality preceded him, but if he were to become a follower of "the Way" he would eventually need to meet fellow Christians in his journey. Saul's transformation required a visitation from the risen Lord Jesus; his first Christian companion would need no less than a vision from the same Lord. Visions are not uncommon in Acts (e.g., Cornelius in 10:3; Peter in 10:3–6, 11–17; Paul in 16:9 and 18:9–10), but they are not random. A vision is required for an unexpected task or a new direction. In this vision, the Lord called Ananias by name, and he responded, "Yes, Lord" (v. 10; cf. Gen 22:1–2; 46:2–3; 1 Sam 3:10–14; Isa 6). Ananias then received detailed instructions to go to a specific house on a specific street and ask for a specific person. In the middle of this vision, the most surprising notes are struck: Saul is praying (v. 11b), and he too has seen a vision where a man named Ananias will come to him and pray for his healing. What is surprising is that Saul has progressed beyond blindness and fasting (vv. 8–9) to prayer and insight (vv. 11–12).

Ananias's response to the Lord's instructions is resistance (vv. 13–14). He is aware both of what Saul has done in Jerusalem to harm the Lord's "holy people"[16] and why Saul has come to Damascus. Ananias is reasserting what we have already learned about Saul (Acts 8:3 and 9:1–2): Saul is an enemy. The Lord responds to Ananias with a sovereign command: "Go! This man is my chosen instrument to proclaim my name to the Gentiles and their kings and to the people of Israel" (9:15). The command from the Lord establishes a new identity for Saul. It pivots on the "name" of the Lord. Ananias only

---

15. Dennis Hamm, "Paul's Blindness and Its Healing: Clues to Symbolic Intent (Acts 9, 22, and 26)," *Bib* 71 (1990): 53–72, quoted in Schnabel, *Acts*, 445.

16. Lit., "saints" (*hagioi*), which serves as another new title for followers of Jesus in Acts. It will recur again in 9:32, 41; 26:10.

knows him as one who persecutes those who "call on your name" (v. 14), but now Saul will be known as the Lord's "chosen instrument" to "proclaim my name" (v. 15).

The scope of Saul's new commission, outlined in verse 15, is not as neat and programmatic as the commission Jesus offered in Acts 1:8 (Jerusalem, Judea, Samaria, and the ends of the earth), but in due course in the narrative of Acts, Saul will bear witness to the gentiles (13:46–28:31), their kings (25:23–26:32), and, of course, to the children of Israel dispersed throughout the empire (9:20; 13:5, 14; 14:1; 17:1, 10; 18:4, 19), as well as in Jerusalem itself (22:1–21). What is important to notice in this is that Saul's commission to the gentiles does not exclude or reject the Jews. In fact, as Paul the apostle will assert in his letter to Christians in Rome, the gospel is "first to the Jew, then to the Gentile" (Rom 1:16; cf. 2:9–10). There is also another element to Saul's identity that is highlighted beyond his verbal witness. Saul will also be called upon to "suffer for [Jesus's] name" (Acts 9:16). Almost to add emphasis, the Lord states that Saul in fact "must" suffer for his name. The narrative in Acts will bear this out as Paul is stoned, whipped, beaten, shipwrecked, and imprisoned for the "name"—testimony that is confirmed in Paul's own letters.[17]

Convinced of his own mission, Ananias now departs to find Saul to give him his commission (v. 17). He finds the house of Judas on Straight Street in Damascus, and without much ado places his hands on Saul and addresses him as "brother Saul." Ananias's gracious spirit toward a former enemy is remarkable. It is another witness to the transformative power of God's grace. But there is more. Ananias confirms that the Lord who met him on the way (cf. "the Way" in v. 2) to Damascus is indeed Jesus. Further, Jesus has sent Ananias to Saul so that Saul may be healed inside and out. His sight is restored "immediately" (v. 18) and "something like scales fell from Saul's eyes" (cf. Tob 11:10–13). The text does not state explicitly that Saul received the Holy Spirit or that he even repented. The text only states that he "got up and was baptized." Gaventa wisely notes, "This tiny anomaly should not prompt the conclusion that Luke believed Saul never received the Spirit or that some earlier text has been edited. Instead, Ananias's words together with Saul's actions comprise the whole event."[18] Saul gets up; he sees again; the Lord has conquered him. This completes the transformation of Saul the persecutor of Jesus, to Saul the commissioned proclaimer of Jesus.

---

17. Paul reflects that his ministry is commended to others in his "troubles, hardships and distresses" (2 Cor 6:4), and writes further that "we always carry around in our body the death of Jesus, so that the life of Jesus may also be revealed in our body" (2 Cor 4:10).

18. Gaventa, *Acts*, 153.

LIVE the Story

Saul's Story as Paradigm

Saul's Damascus Road encounter with the risen Jesus turns out to be a crucial event in world history. His experience changed not only the course of his life but the course of countless other lives as well. It is comparable to the transformative moment when Julius Caesar, on January 10, 49 BC, crossed the Rubicon River, the border between Gaul and Italy, leading the Thirteenth Legion. It was legally forbidden for Roman generals to lead an army into Italy, and in doing this Julius Caesar began a civil war that would transform the Roman state, not to mention world history. A few years later, the same proud and confident Julius Caesar informed the Roman Senate of his decisive victory over Pharnaces II of Pontus with the memorable words: *veni, vidi, vici*—"I came, I saw, I conquered." In a brilliant sermon entitled "The Humility of Faith,"[19] the Rev. Dr. David Widdicombe skillfully contrasts the words of Caesar and the experience of Saul. Whereas Caesar pronounced, "I came, I saw, I conquered," Saul's experience was, "I come, I cannot see, conquer me." The former words are "the pious certainties of a secular age and [the latter words express] the necessary humility of faith in a crucified and risen Lord."[20] In this sense, Saul's story is an essential paradigm for all Christians. The Lord Jesus Christ challenges all self-dependence, self-assertion, and self-satisfaction.

Conversion or Calling?

Scholars regularly use two words to describe the transformation of Saul: conversion and calling.[21] Was Saul's experience a *conversion*? No, and yes. On the one hand, Saul did not convert from one religion to another entirely new one. He still read the same Scriptures and prayed to the one God, the God of Israel. On the other hand, much changed. Saul's course was not a continuation in Judaism. In his own words, Paul describes that a "veil" had been lifted from his darkened heart so that he could see who Jesus really is (2 Cor 3:12–18). This meant he would read all the Scriptures in a new way. Now, he would "see" the promises to Abraham and his "seed" as pointing to Jesus (Gal 3–4). He would see that "the Son is the image [*eikōn*] of the invisible God" (Col 1:15). When Paul quotes Scripture, his new understanding of Jesus as "the Lord" can be discerned. For example, when he proclaims that "every knee should bow . . . every tongue acknowledge that *Jesus Christ is Lord*"

---

19. Rev. Dr. David Widdicombe, "The Humility of Faith," http://ecclesialuniversity.ca/the-humility-of-faith-a-sermon-on-acts-9-1-18.
20. Widdicombe, "Humility."
21. For a useful discussion, see J. M. Everts, "Conversion and Call of Paul," *DPL* 156–63.

(Phil 2:10–11), he is quoting Isaiah 45:23. In Isaiah 45 the "Lord" is the God of Israel, but Paul declares that the "Lord" is Jesus. Saul has emerged from the chrysalis of his former life in Judaism, transformed into something new. He started out his journey to Damascus as one man and arrived another. He did not alter paths in his journey, but like someone journeying through the center of the earth, he has descended into the core of darkness and, without changing direction, continues the journey that leads through the darkness to ascend into new light.[22]

Was Saul's experience a *calling*? This is the other descriptor often used to explain Saul's Damascus Road encounter. The language in both Acts and in Paul's letters indicates that the Damascus Road experience was much like a prophetic commission or calling. "Saul, Saul" echoes the callings of Moses, Samuel, and Elijah. The emphasis in the narratives in Acts falls on Saul's new commission as the Lord's "chosen instrument" (9:15) and as "a servant and as a witness" who is sent to the gentiles "to open their eyes and turn them from darkness to light" (26:16–18). His radical transformation included a new commission, a renewed calling to his fellow Israelites ("to the Jew first"), so that Israel might be the blessing to the families and nations of the earth that they were always meant to be. In this sense, Saul was still as zealous as he had always been. He was still willing to take to the road on dangerous missions, but this time not to *persecute* the church but to "*press on* toward the goal to win the prize for which God has called me heavenward in Christ Jesus" (Phil 3:6, 14).[23] He will pursue his calling as one transformed by grace. He will pursue his new course of life not with triumphalistic zeal but with grace-filled humility. He will boast no longer in the law but in his weaknesses.

What accounts for such a change in Saul? At the very least, he knew that the Lord called him to be his "chosen instrument" not because he suddenly realized that he was a sinner who needed to be justified by faith, or that he was conflicted about the truth claims of Judaism and realized Christians were right after all, or because God was handing out jobs to new converts and his just happened to be the apostle to the gentiles. There is so much more that happened with Saul the Pharisee on the Damascus Road that day than this. On that day he began to realize that all God wanted to do through Israel to bring blessing and healing and freedom to the world he was doing through Jesus, the resurrected Lord.[24] He understood that this was "good news" not just

---

22. See Scot McKnight, *Turning to Jesus: The Sociology of Conversion in the Gospels* (Philadelphia: Westminster John Knox, 2002).

23. The same Greek word, *diōkō*, can be translated either as "persecute" or "press on/pursue."

24. This basic point, helpfully I think, has been made often by N. T. Wright; for a detailed account see chs. 9 and 10 in *Paul and the Faithfulness of God* (Minneapolis: Fortress, 2013). For a shorter

for the people of Israel but for the whole world. He would then pursue this calling, using all the knowledge, gifts, and privileges he possessed. Yet he would also pursue it out of a deep humility because he knew he was transformed by an unmerited grace and empowered by the Holy Spirit. This meant he could pursue his calling with zealous humility, with indefatigable weakness, foolish wisdom, and cruciform glory. Saul is indeed a paradox. He experienced a conversion *and* a calling. His conversion was genuine, and his calling was transformative.

Surprise and Intimacy in the Call to Christ
Whatever terms we use to help us understand Saul's encounter on the Damascus Road, we must never lose sight of the reality that Luke's narrative in Acts underscores the element of surprise in the story. The transformational event was completely unexpected by Saul, as well as by everyone else who knew Saul, for that matter! God suddenly invaded and transformed this person from being his enemy to being his chosen instrument, his spokesperson to the world. This is instructive for us on several levels. First, it should remind us that God can transform anyone. Who are the people in your life or in the world who you think are beyond God's reach? Is it an estranged family member? A surly neighbor? A distant enemy? A rival at work? A radicalized Muslim? A bigoted Christian? When we read Acts 9, we should be struck, blind if necessary, by the fact that this is a story about what God can do with the person we think is beyond God's reach and grace.

Second, another important aspect to this story is the reminder that Jesus continues to encounter and call people by name. No follower of Christ is anonymous. All are personally confronted with truth. All must be personally led, brought out if you like, from darkness to light. This journey of faith may in fact first take us down into darkness before we come through. After his encounter with the risen Lord, Saul continued on his journey toward Damascus, albeit in deep darkness on its last stage, before he came through the darkness and was delivered by the filling and illuminating light of the Holy Spirit. This is a common experience for many Christians. To "ascend" to God, one must often first descend into darkness and defeat. This "journey" through darkness will require a complete rewiring of one's life. This can take a moment, a few days, or even years. As we each walk through this experience, we will witness a conversion from the inside out and, in the process, will often discover our calling. Our calling to be Christ's disciple is intimately linked to

---

discussion see his *What Saint Paul Really Said: Was Paul of Tarsus the Real Founder of Christianity* (Grand Rapids: Eerdmans), ch. 2.

our conversion. Malcolm Guite identifies this as the heart and meaning of the word *vocation*:

> A vocation is a calling, and to have a Christian vocation is to have been called, called by name. The Lord of life and love calls us out of nothingness into being, calls us out of darkness into light, and calls us, personally, to turn and begin our lives anew in him. All our lives, all our journeyings . . . are a response to that call. Our quest . . . begins at dawn and is an 'orientation': a turn towards the growing light. But this is not light as an abstract, it is light embodied in a person, and it calls to a vision and a realm beyond what is possible for us in this world.[25]

We pursue this new and called life, motivated by grace. We do so because we know that all this has come our way as a gift. God showered grace and kindness on us in Christ Jesus. As Paul would later describe in Ephesians, "For it is by grace you have been saved, through faith—and this is not from yourselves, it is the gift of God—not by works, so that no one can boast. For we are God's handiwork, created in Christ Jesus to do good works, which God prepared in advance for us to do" (2:8–10). A gracious calling led Paul to a lifework of helping people respond to this grace. We too, because of our own encounters with the risen Lord, receive the calling to live grace-filled lives that are winsome and inviting to others. God will see to it that each of us is equipped to share with others the inexhaustible riches and generosity of Jesus, the risen Messiah and ascended Lord.

---

25. Malcolm Guite, *The Word in the Wilderness* (London: Canterbury, 2014), 42.

CHAPTER 20

Acts 9:19b-31

LISTEN to the Story

¹⁹Saul spent several days with the disciples in Damascus. ²⁰At once he began to preach in the synagogues that Jesus is the Son of God. ²¹All those who heard him were astonished and asked, "Isn't he the man who raised havoc in Jerusalem among those who call on this name? And hasn't he come here to take them as prisoners to the chief priests?" ²²Yet Saul grew more and more powerful and baffled the Jews living in Damascus by proving that Jesus is the Messiah.

²³After many days had gone by, there was a conspiracy among the Jews to kill him, ²⁴but Saul learned of their plan. Day and night they kept close watch on the city gates in order to kill him. ²⁵But his followers took him by night and lowered him in a basket through an opening in the wall.

²⁶When he came to Jerusalem, he tried to join the disciples, but they were all afraid of him, not believing that he really was a disciple. ²⁷But Barnabas took him and brought him to the apostles. He told them how Saul on his journey had seen the Lord and that the Lord had spoken to him, and how in Damascus he had preached fearlessly in the name of Jesus. ²⁸So Saul stayed with them and moved about freely in Jerusalem, speaking boldly in the name of the Lord. ²⁹He talked and debated with the Hellenistic Jews, but they tried to kill him. ³⁰When the believers learned of this, they took him down to Caesarea and sent him off to Tarsus.

³¹Then the church throughout Judea, Galilee and Samaria enjoyed a time of peace and was strengthened. Living in the fear of the Lord and encouraged by the Holy Spirit, it increased in numbers.

Listening to the Text in the Story: 2 Corinthians 11:32–33; Galatians 1:13–24.

EXPLAIN the Story

The content of the narrative following Saul's conversion focuses on *reactions* to Saul's experience. It does describe some of Saul's actions—his preaching in Damascus synagogues, a dramatic escape, and time spent in Jerusalem—but the emphasis at this point in the story is on how others respond to Saul. In time we will hear much more about what Saul will do and say, but not now. At this point the spotlight is on how the Jews in Damascus react to the new Saul and how he flees his own persecutors (9:19b–25), then how both Christian and non-Christian Jews in Jerusalem react to him (9:26–30). The final verse of this subnarrative is in fact the summary for the entire second panel (6:8–9:31) in Acts, thus preparing the reader for a major shift in the story (v. 31).

Saul in Damascus (9:19b–25)

Luke makes a point of emphasizing that Saul did not take long to get on with his commission from Jesus "to proclaim my name" (Acts 9:15). After a few days with the disciples in Damascus, he immediately (*eutheōs*)[1] began to preach about Jesus (v. 20). Saul proclaimed that "Jesus is the Son of God"[2] (9:20) and that "Jesus is the Messiah" (9:22). These will certainly be two significant christological themes in Paul's letters,[3] and it is significant that Saul has brought "Son" and "Messiah" together in the person of Jesus, yet *how* Saul in Acts came to these theological conclusions in a few short days and *what* this all means are not elaborated. Rather, the questions that are highlighted by the Jews in Damascus relate to Saul personally: Isn't he the persecutor of Christians? Hasn't he come to arrest those who call on Jesus and bring them back to Jerusalem? Saul, both in terms of who he has become and what he is saying, baffles the Jews in Damascus.

The Jewish bafflement soon transforms into the same kind of murderous zeal that motivated Saul. Saul's deeds and words stir up a conspiracy to kill him, much like that which was plotted against Jesus and, as Saul would remember all too well, against Stephen. It has not taken long for Saul to see fulfilled the double promise that he would both proclaim Jesus's name and

---

1. NIV: "at once."
2. This is the only time that this title occurs in Acts; it occurs five times in the Gospel of Luke in reference to Christ (Luke 1:35; 4:3, 9, 41; 22:70).
3. Paul declares that it was the "Son" of God who was revealed to him on the Damascus road (Gal 1:16; see also Rom 1:4; 2 Cor 1:19). Paul frequently refers to Jesus as "Christ," in Greek, *Christos*. "Christ" is Paul's favorite title for Jesus. It should be remembered that *Christos* is the Greek translation of the Hebrew word for "Messiah." Both Messiah and Christ mean "Anointed One," a term with special significance in the OT in connection with Israel's king (e.g., see 1 Sam 24:6; 2 Sam 1:14; Ps 2:2), where the term is often a royal title.

suffer for Jesus's name (see Acts 9:15–16). We are not told how, but Saul learned about the plot. Paul elsewhere recalls this tense moment in his life, writing, "The governor under King Aretas[4] had the city of the Damascenes guarded in order to arrest me" (2 Cor 11:32). This is not a detail included by Luke. Both accounts agree, however, on the mode of Saul's escape: he was lowered by his followers in a basket through an opening in the wall (Acts 9:25; 2 Cor 11:33). Although there is agreement on this episode in both Acts and Paul's letters, Luke omits Paul's three-year stay in Arabia (cf. Gal 1:17–18).

Saul in Jerusalem (9:26–30)

It was not cowardice that led Saul to flee Damascus. If it were, he would not have left the proverbial "frying pan" of Damascus for the "fire" of Jerusalem. Rather, his motive was to continue his calling to preach the name of Jesus, not to avoid suffering. After his escape, Saul returned to Jerusalem—without Christian prisoners. He possibly stayed at his sister's residence in the city (see Acts 23:16). He soon discovered he was not only distrusted by followers of the Way but also by non-Christian Jewish leaders, especially those in the Hellenist synagogues. Saul was interested in meeting with the disciples of Jesus. They were still afraid of the Saul who once breathed "murderous threats against the Lord's disciples" (cf. 9:1). They imagined Saul had hatched a new conspiracy to flush them out, and they did not trust the news that Saul had become a disciple (9:26). Saul needed an advocate and bridge-builder, much like Ananias had been for him in Damascus, who would connect him to the disciples in Jerusalem. But who would believe him? Who would be generous enough in spirit to give him a chance? Again, it is a disciple, known for his generosity, who has already appeared briefly in the narrative (4:36–37) and now steps forward: Barnabas. Barnabas, true to his name as a "son of encouragement," encourages the apostles to listen to Saul's story.[5] The heavenly Jesus's "chosen instrument" requires an earthly connection to vouch for him; Ananias did it in Damascus, and Barnabas now does it in Jerusalem. Barnabas assures the apostles about the truthfulness of Saul's encounter with "the Lord" and about the boldness of his proclamation "in the name of Jesus" (9:27). Barnabas's testimony is effective.

Next we hear that Saul moved freely in Jerusalem and, much like the other apostles before him, spoke "boldly" in the name of the Lord (9:28; cf.

---

4. King Aretas was ruler over the Nabatean kingdom from 8 BC until AD 39. He may have ruled over Damascus through an ethnarch or governor at the time of Saul's stay in the city due to a policy of Emperor Caligula, who gave client-kings favorable terms of rule during his brief reign (ca. AD 37–41). Cf. Loveday A. Alexander, "Chronology of Paul," *DPL* 116.

5. Bruce, *Acts*, 193, suggests that "when Luke says that Barnabas brought Saul 'to the apostles,' the narrative of Gal 1:18–20 compels us to interpret this as a generalizing plural." That is, Paul's solemn declaration was that he only spoke with Cephas (Peter) and James the Lord's brother.

4:13, 29, 31). Again, as in Damascus, Saul appears to begin his work in the synagogues, but in Jerusalem his focus is on Greek-speaking ("Hellenistic") Jews. This is not surprising given his own Hellenistic background, and it may have been a ministry that was neglected after the death of Stephen. He may have debated Hellenistic Jews in the Synagogue of the Freedmen (6:9), the same synagogue where Stephen debated, likely with the same polarizing effect. Saul, like Stephen, was not only a follower of Jesus but was also a traitor to those who supported his zealous persecution of Christians. Soon, Saul's former coreligionist Jews in Jerusalem conspire to kill him, and when the believers learn of the plot they usher him to the port city of Caesarea and send him back to his home city, Tarsus, in Cilicia (9:30). Was this a snub? Was Saul offended by the Jerusalem church's reluctance to go through another season of suffering like they experienced after Stephen's martyrdom? No. Later in Acts we learn that he understood this as divine guidance, for in his defense in Acts 22 he refers to a vision he received at this time from the Lord in the temple instructing him to "leave Jerusalem immediately" (22:18) and focus on his mission to the gentiles (22:21). As a result, Saul "went to Syria and Cilicia" (Gal 1:21). We will not hear again of Tarsus's famous son in Acts until much later (Acts 11:25).

Summary and Transition (9:31)

The conversion of Saul and his early ministry as Jesus's "chosen instrument" is a pivotal moment in the narrative. The chronology is somewhat vague, but the general thrust of Saul's encounter and his resulting words and deeds can be substantiated in several of Paul's letters. Important for Luke's narrative is the fact that with Saul's transformation, the spearhead of the persecution against the disciples is blunted. For now, this important phase in Acts draws to a close, a phase that included key contributions and experiences by "Hellenist" (Greek-speaking) Jews, including the ministry and martyrdom of Stephen, the evangelistic work of Philip, and the call and early preaching of Saul. Now the narrative will return to focus on the contributions of the Aramaic-speaking apostles and how they become involved in the gentile mission.

After Saul's departure for Tarsus, he drops out from the narrative for some time, and other narrative threads are taken up again. In particular, Peter will resume center stage in the chapters that follow. Luke marks the transition with another summary verse (9:31; cf. 6:7; 12:24; 16:5; and 19:20). These verses appear as a brief pause, a time to "take a breath" before plunging into a new direction. The transitional summaries contain one or more of these elements: a geographical note, a word about church growth, and a reference to the word of God increasing. In this case, two of the three elements are mentioned—geography and growth, as Luke refers to the church in *Judea, Galilee, and Samaria* and that the church *increased in numbers*.[6] The disciples of Jesus have been harried and harassed in this panel. A period of peace is necessary to refresh and renew them. The peace was accompanied by a deep sense of reverence ("fear") for the Lord and encouragement from the Holy Spirit. These notes are not token references to Jesus and the Spirit. Their fear of their Lord is what makes them fearless before people, and the same Spirit who transformed them in Acts 2 from timid to bold disciples continues to imbue them with courage and strength.

LIVE the Story

Acts 9:19–30 describes Saul at a threshold moment, or what anthropologists refer to as a "liminal" stage, in his new life as a follower of Jesus.[7] There is no way of knowing this for sure, but if I were to guess, I think Saul would rate as a high "E" on a Myers-Briggs scale for extroversion. Not surprisingly, he brings all the "zeal for God" he had in his former unenlightened life (Gal 1:14; cf. Rom 10:2) to his new life as a disciple of Christ. Transitions can be awkward periods. For example, the transition from childhood to adulthood—fueled by hormones and sustained by gangly limbs and unbounded courage—is often characterized by some embarrassing moments. Just watching this transition can be uncomfortable. In Saul's transitional period, he brought all his intellectual and persuasive powers immediately to synagogue life, first in Damascus and later in Jerusalem, and it disrupted both Christian and non-Christian Jews alike. While he preached powerfully (Acts 9:22) and fearlessly (9:27), this nearly had disastrous results for Saul and created uneasiness for the believers, particularly those in Jerusalem. Saul may have continued to careen through synagogues and Christian households and never matured into the Lord's "chosen instrument," had it not been for two important factors: a friend and time.

Often new converts, especially if they are gifted, can either be pushed or push themselves into roles for which they are not yet ready. It is vital that new converts have a "Barnabas" to come alongside them. Barnabas, as a true "son of encouragement," was a sponsor for and support to Saul. As a respected and longtime member of the Christian community (see Acts 4:36–37), he was the one who introduced Saul and shared his story with others. We still need men and women today who will walk alongside new and immature believers,

---

6. Note that it is the singular "church," not plural "churches," of Judea, Galilee, and Samaria. Luke views the early Christian communities as one church.
7. See Alexander, *Acts*, 81.

who will take the time to hear their stories, listen for what the Spirit is doing in their lives, and help them make connections between what they know and who they know. Any mature Christian can be a "Barnabas" to a new believer. They need not be formal leaders in a congregation, but all mature and growing congregations need them. They are the links who assist those in the transitional stage from being a new believer to becoming a mature disciple. New believers require seasoned Christian friends to mature.

New converts need mature disciples to walk alongside them in their early days of faith, but they also require another element if they are to mature: time. Too often gifted new believers are identified for their potential leadership and are pushed into key roles too soon because the church constantly needs new leaders. The lament is often heard in Christian circles, "Where are the young leaders?" Unfortunately, impatient church leaders often rush many immature Christian men and women with leadership promise into roles and responsibilities that they are not mature enough to handle. The frequent and sad result is that these immature people, like teenagers, make awkward mistakes, use inappropriate language to express themselves, and then often find that they are cast aside. The impact on them is predictable. These young Christians, bursting with enthusiasm and potential, are often shipwrecked in their faith. Even worse, older and supposedly mature leaders will then tut-tut at the lack of character in this "next generation." None of this is helpful, neither the impatience nor the criticism. Instead we should remember that despite his gifts, energy, and unique calling from the Lord, Saul the new disciple was "sent off to Tarsus" (Acts 9:30) for a considerable length of time before being called into a leading missionary role. He was given space to grow into his calling. We must remember this no less in today's context. New believers require time to mature into their vocations.

PANEL 3

Acts 9:32–12:24

While the second panel in Acts (6:8–9:31) highlights the first *geographic* expansion of the gospel into Samaria, the third panel (9:32–12:24) focuses on the first expansion of the gospel among *gentiles*. The eunuch who returns to Ethiopia and Philip who evangelizes in Caesarea (8:39–40) are "advance parties" of the eventual sending out of the gospel "to the ends of the earth" (1:8). To demonstrate that this expansion does not occur apart from the approval of the Jerusalem-based apostles, Peter is reintroduced into the narrative. There has already been some indirect reference to ministry in the predominantly gentile coastal cities of Azotus and Caesarea through the work of the Hellenistic Jew and evangelist Philip (8:5). But it is through Peter, while visiting the Lord's people in the predominantly Jewish cities of Lydda and Joppa along the coastal plain (9:32–43), that the stage is set for the important movement of the gospel to the gentiles. The first gentile convert is no less than a Roman centurion living in the most Roman city in the region, Caesarea. Again, the initiative for this expansion is all divine: an "angel of God" instructs Cornelius to send for Peter (10:1–8); Peter is given a vision where he hears the voice of the "Lord" and the Spirit's directive to go with Cornelius's messengers (10:9–23a); the Spirit interrupts Peter's speech and is poured out on Cornelius and his household (10:23b–48). When Peter is called upon to explain his actions to the Jewish believers in Jerusalem (11:1–18), he repeats the story of the conversion of Cornelius's household and emphasizes that this was "God's way" (v. 17). Of course, when the Jewish believers heard this, "they had no further objections and praised God, saying, 'So then, *even* to Gentiles God has granted repentance that leads to life'" (v. 18).

Only after it is established that this expansion is God's initiative does Luke inform us that a church has been founded farther north in Syrian Antioch (11:19–30), the place where the disciples were first called "Christians" (v. 26). Antioch will become a base church for sending missionaries to the gentile world. God's "chosen instrument" (see 9:15), Saul, is reintroduced in this subsection of the panel along with his traveling companion, Barnabas. Unfortunately, the "time of peace" (9:31) that the church experienced is disturbed by King Herod, who persecutes the believers, executes the apostle James, the brother of John, and arrests Peter (12:1–24). Nothing, however, will impede the expansion of the gospel to the gentiles. Peter could not stand in the way of God (11:17), nor could the Jerusalem church (11:18), and not even political opposition from King Herod can slow it down. The panel draws to a close by contrasting the weakness of Herod's royal assertions and proclamations (12:23) with the will of the Lord and the power of God's word (12:24).

CHAPTER 21

Acts 9:32-43

LISTEN to the Story

³²As Peter traveled about the country, he went to visit the Lord's people who lived in Lydda. ³³There he found a man named Aeneas, who was paralyzed and had been bedridden for eight years. ³⁴"Aeneas," Peter said to him, "Jesus Christ heals you. Get up and roll up your mat." Immediately Aeneas got up. ³⁵All those who lived in Lydda and Sharon saw him and turned to the Lord.

³⁶In Joppa there was a disciple named Tabitha (in Greek her name is Dorcas); she was always doing good and helping the poor. ³⁷About that time she became sick and died, and her body was washed and placed in an upstairs room. ³⁸Lydda was near Joppa; so when the disciples heard that Peter was in Lydda, they sent two men to him and urged him, "Please come at once!"

³⁹Peter went with them, and when he arrived he was taken upstairs to the room. All the widows stood around him, crying and showing him the robes and other clothing that Dorcas had made while she was still with them.

⁴⁰Peter sent them all out of the room; then he got down on his knees and prayed. Turning toward the dead woman, he said, "Tabitha, get up." She opened her eyes, and seeing Peter she sat up. ⁴¹He took her by the hand and helped her to her feet. Then he called for the believers, especially the widows, and presented her to them alive. ⁴²This became known all over Joppa, and many people believed in the Lord. ⁴³Peter stayed in Joppa for some time with a tanner named Simon.

Listening to the Text in the Story: Leviticus 11:24, 39; 1 Kings 17:19-20, 23; 2 Kings 4:33-36; Matthew 9:18-19, 23-26; Mark 5:21-24, 35-42; Luke 11:41; 12:33.

EXPLAIN the Story

Two of the most significant narratives in the entire book of Acts are the accounts related to the conversions of Saul in chapter nine and Cornelius in chapter ten. Saul is God's "chosen instrument" to bring the gospel to the gentile world (9:15); Cornelius and his household are the firstfruits of the gentile mission. The question facing the reader of Acts is why Luke includes the two accounts of the healing of Aeneas in Lydda (9:32–35) and Tabitha (Dorcas) in Joppa (9:36–43)? This section (9:32–43) is a narrative bridge between these two important moments (i.e., Saul and Cornelius) in the history of the early church, but how so? At one level, by reintroducing the apostle Peter into the picture, Luke establishes the connection between the mother church in Jerusalem and the gentile mission. This is similar to what was done in Acts 8 with Philip's mission to the Samaritans. In this sense, by having Peter visit the homes of Jewish believers living in the coastal plain there is "a *geographic preparation* for the conversion of the first Gentile, the centurion Cornelius, in Caesarea."[1] These accounts also provide *thematic preparation* to the narrative that will follow through verbal links. Both Aeneas and Tabitha are commanded to "get up" (9:34, 40) from their places of brokenness and death, with the result that others turn and believe in the Lord (9:35, 42). In a similar way Peter is commanded to "get up" (10:13, 20) and be "healed" of his closed-mindedness so that others might come to know the good news that Jesus Christ is Lord of all (10:36). Finally, there is *theological preparation* that is being established as well. That is, the priority of charity for the weak and the outcast is reaffirmed as the theological platform from which to launch the global mission to the "outsiders," the gentiles.

The Healing of Aeneas (9:32–35)

This section is abrupt and creates questions for the reader: What has Peter been doing since leaving Samaria for Jerusalem (8:25)? How did "the Lord's people" in this area come to faith (9:32)? Were they converts through Philip's ministry or those who fled the persecution in Jerusalem? We will probably never know the answers to these questions, but from his description of Peter's tour of the country, Luke *does* want us to know about two communities: Lydda and Joppa. There were many other locations that could have been named, but these are the two cities he chose to highlight along the road northwest of Jerusalem in the Judean coastal plain, known also as the plain of Sharon. Lydda lies about forty kilometers (25 miles) away from Jerusalem,

---

1. Martin Hengel, "The Geography of Palestine in Acts," in Bauckham, *Palestinian Setting*, 61. Emphasis mine.

and the port city, Joppa, is another twenty kilometers (12 miles) away. Martin Hengel points out that "one of the firm convictions of present-day 'critical' exegesis is that the author of the two-volume work dedicated to Theophilus was not at all well versed in the geography of Palestine."[2] Whether this is true or not, when it came to Luke's understanding of the Judean coastal plain, his details are accurate. It is worth noting that in contrast to Azotus and Caesarea, the coastal towns visited earlier by Philip (8:40), the towns of Lydda and Joppa were almost entirely inhabited by Jews. This demonstrates that even though Lydda and Joppa are both cities on the borderland of Judean territory near gentile communities, for now Peter, described by Paul as the apostle of "the circumcised" (Gal 2:7), is visiting only "the Lord's people"[3] who are Jewish (Acts 9:32).

In Lydda he found a longtime resident named Aeneas who was paralyzed for eight years.[4] Peter speaks to him tersely, but not uncharitably, "Aeneas, Jesus Christ heals you. Get up and roll up your mat" (v. 34). Uncharacteristically Peter did not say, "In the *name* of Jesus Christ" or "in Jesus's *name*" (cf. Acts 3:6, 16; 4:10). His command "get up" (cf. 14:10) is received as an invitation to wholeness, and Aeneas responds "immediately" by getting up. Chrysostom makes the helpful observation that since Aeneas may not be a believer he is first offered healing, then faith: "At that time [the apostles] had not yet offered proof of their own power, and so it was unrealistic to demand faith from the man. . . . Therefore, just as Christ in the beginning of his miracles did not demand faith, neither did these."[5] We are not told what Aeneas, whose name means "praise" or "praiseworthy," says or does, even though we can imagine he experienced untrammeled joy. Nonetheless, the impact is praiseworthy and notable: "All those who lived in Lydda and Sharon saw him and turned[6] to the Lord" (9:35). The healing prepared the ground for proclamation and the establishing of new relationships with the Lord Jesus. News like this travels fast, even without social media, and it soon reaches the ears of believers in mourning twenty kilometers (12 miles) away in the port city of Joppa.

---

2. Hengel, "Geography," 28. See also G. Lüdemann, *Paul Apostle to the Gentiles: Studies in Chronology*, trans. F. S. Jones (London: SCM, 1984), 35n40.

3. Lit., "the saints" (*tous hagious*).

4. Margaret H. Williams, "Palestinian Jewish Personal Names in Acts," in Bauckham, *Palestinian Setting*, 110, notes that this name entered the Palestinian-Jewish vocabulary in the first-century BC and continued in use until at least the fourth-century AD.

5. Chrysostom, *Homilies on the Acts of the Apostles* 21, in *ACCA*, 115.

6. The word "turn" is a favorite description used by Luke to refer to repentance and conversion (e.g., Acts 3:19; 11:21; 14:15; 15:19; 26:20). Perhaps this is in keeping with the sense of "movement" throughout the whole narrative.

The Healing of Tabitha (9:36–43)

The short account of the healing of Aeneas in Lydda leads to the longer account of Peter's healing of Tabitha in Joppa. Joppa, Hebrew *Yapho* and modern Jaffa, had long been an important port city along the Mediterranean until it was superseded by Caesarea, the magnificent city built by Herod the Great in 10/9 BC in honor of his imperial patron, Caesar Augustus. Originally, Joppa was a Phoenician city—used by the likes of the prophet Jonah (Jonah 1:3)—that later was Hellenized and fortified by the Greek successors of Alexander the Great, the Ptolemies and Seleucids. It was then conquered by the Jewish military leader Simon the Maccabee, who drove out all the gentile inhabitants (1 Macc 12:33; 13:11). When Pompey conquered Palestine for the Romans in the first-century BC, it was not re-Hellenized like other coastal cities but remained largely Jewish.[7] When the Jews revolted against the Romans in AD 66, Joppa, unlike Azotus and Jamnia, supported the rebels, and when Cestius Gallus subsequently conquered the city it was destroyed, and more than eight thousand inhabitants were slaughtered (see Josephus, *J.W.* 2.508–9). Joppa, like many of the cities of the coastal plain, had known heartache. This time, the grief is for a good Jewish woman named Tabitha.

Kirsten Pinto Gfroerer reminds us that "the story of Tabitha, who is also known as Dorcas, a disciple of Jesus, is the story of the iconic nurture and release of the society of caritas in the life of the young Church."[8] Tabitha, whose Aramaic name means "gazelle" and who was also know by her Greek name Dorcas, is introduced as a "disciple." The word for "disciple" occurs dozens of times in Acts and hundreds of times in the NT, but Tabitha is the only woman to warrant the feminine form (*mathētria*) of "disciple" in the entire NT. She was not merely a good seamstress, but weaved mercy into all her good works—so much so that when she became ill and died, she was not only mourned but deeply missed. Tabitha is described literally in the Greek as one who was "full of good works and doing charity/giving alms" (Acts 9:36). The word translated as "helping the poor" in the NIV occurs only thirteen times in the NT, but eight of those occur in Acts (*eleēmosynē*; twice more in Luke). Jesus described this kind of generosity as flowing from "what is inside you" (Luke 11:41) and as a means for providing for oneself a heavenly purse (12:33). This kind of "inner charity" is then received by the poor and noticed in heaven. The next time the word *eleēmosynē* occurs is in the narrative that immediately follows. Cornelius is described as devout and God-fearing and as one who gave "generously [*eleēmosynē*] to those in need" (Acts 10:2)—so

---

7. Hengel, "Geography," 60.
8. Read this entire excellent sermon by Kirsten Pinto Gfroerer, "Caritas Get Up," The Ecclesial University, 30 July 2013, http://ecclesialuniversity.ca/caritas-get-up.

much so that his prayers and "gifts to the poor" (*eleēmosynē*) have come to God's attention (10:4, 31). It is interesting, again, that Luke seems to highlight those on the outside of the religious establishment of the day—a woman and a Roman—for doing the deeds prescribed by Jesus. This is another item in keeping with the "from Jerusalem to Rome" movement in the entire narrative.

After her death, according to the custom of burial preparation, Tabitha's body was washed[9] and placed in an upper room (9:37). Since Lydda was only about twenty kilometers (12 miles) southeast from Joppa, the disciples sent word, again according to custom, by way of *two* messengers to Lydda, urging Peter to come at once (v. 38). The average walking distance of a person living in the first century was about thirty-two kilometers (20 miles) a day; Peter could have traveled the distance from Lydda to Joppa in about half a day. Upon arriving, he is taken upstairs to where the body lay (v. 39). Women who were widows were often among the most vulnerable people in the ancient world, and those who received special care and provision from Tabitha are there to meet Peter. Their cries are not the traditional grief wails but are cries of demonstrable loss. The women show Peter robes and garments that Dorcas had made—the visible and tangible good works of her faith (v. 39). The grief is deep and substantive. The impact for these widows living without Dorcas is not only that they will be left without clothes to wear; the loss will also leave them emotionally cold and exposed.

Peter dismisses them from the room (v. 40). Although we are not provided with temporal details (i.e., how long he stays alone in the room), we are given intimate details of what Peter does next. He kneels down and prays. He then "turns" to her body—echoing the same word we have just heard about those who in Lydda and Sharon "turned" to the Lord after Aeneas's healing—and speaks directly to her by name: "Tabitha, get up." The command to Tabitha in Joppa echoes what he said in Lydda to Aeneas: "Aeneas . . . get up" (v. 34). Again, the result is instantaneous. She opens her eyes, sees Peter, sits up, and with his assistance stands on her feet (vv. 40–41). The healing of Tabitha echoes the account of Jesus's raising of Jairus's daughter,[10] and even further back in the OT story to healings performed by Elijah and Elisha.[11] Now that

---

9. Haenchen, *Acts*, 339, notes by way of a question that her "body is washed, but not—as was normal—anointed: in anticipation of the hoped-for restoration?" Gaventa, *Acts*, 160, observes that while washing a body was a common custom in antiquity, this intimate detail is never mentioned in any other biblical narrative.

10. Even the name Tabitha and the use of the Aramaic word for "little girl"—*talitha*—evoke a connection through alliteration and assonance. See Mark 5:21–24, 35–42; cf. Matt 9:18–19, 23–26.

11. Peter prays alone in the room for the dead woman (cf. 1 Kgs 17:19–20; 2 Kgs 4:33); Tabitha opens her eyes (cf. 2 Kgs 4:35); Peter takes her by the hand and presents her to others (cf. 1 Kgs 17:23; 2 Kgs 4:36).

Tabitha has been resuscitated, Peter calls the "believers" (lit., "the saints"), and especially the widows, back into the room (v. 41). Luke likely distinguishes between "believers" and "widows" not because they are distinct groups but because of the special care Tabitha had provided to the latter. As in Lydda, this news soon spreads throughout Joppa, and the result is that many believe in "the Lord" (v. 42; cf. v. 35).

The twin healing narratives of Aeneas and Tabitha end with two notes. First, Peter stays in Joppa "for some time" (v. 43). Luke is nonspecific about the length of time. But that Peter is still in the port city of Joppa places him on the geographic boundary of Judea and within striking distance of Caesarea farther north up the Mediterranean coast. Second, Peter takes up residence with "a tanner named Simon" (v. 43). Simon is one of the most common male Hebrew names in first-century Palestine. While Simon of Joppa is likely Jewish, he is by profession a tanner, a profession despised by both sophisticated gentiles and Jews. A tanner worked with animal carcasses to produce leather, and the smells associated with this trade were noxious. The trade was usually practiced outdoors and near water; thus it is no coincidence that Simon's home is located "by the sea" (10:6). Even more important for Jews concerned with religious purity, Simon may have been ritually unclean because of the nature of his work (see Lev 11:24, 39).[12] These two notes—his location on the edge of Judea and his residence with an unclean tanner—place Peter both geographically and theologically on the boundary between Jews and gentiles. The stage is set for the next dramatic step of the gospel.

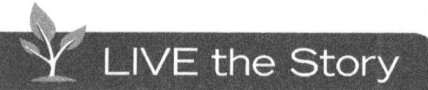

LIVE the Story

When I was a young man, there was often a distinction made between preaching the gospel so as to make converts and the "social gospel," which focused only on caring for the welfare of others and had no distinct connection to conversion. In the circles I lived in at the time, the priority was on the former. These days, I don't hear of this division nearly as much. Perhaps Christians in the West have become better about joining together that which Jesus never put asunder: caring for the poor *and* proclaiming the gospel. On this issue Henri Nouwen writes:

> What finally counts is not whether we know Jesus and his words but whether we live our lives in the Spirit of Jesus. The Spirit of Jesus is the Spirit of Love. Jesus himself makes this clear when he speaks about the

---

12. See Keener, *Acts*, 2:1724–26.

last judgment. There people will ask, "Lord, when did we see you hungry and feed you, or thirsty and give you drink?" and Jesus will answer, "In so far as you did this to one of the least . . . of mine, you did it to me" (Matthew 25:37, 40).[13]

This is what the healing of Aeneas points toward. As was noted above in "Explain the Story," we are not informed whether Aeneas was a believer before his healing, but after his restoration he became a living witness ("All those who lived in Lydda and Sharon *saw* him," Acts 9:35), and the result is that many people turned to the Lord. Aeneas's own role in all this may be indicated in the simple command from Peter to "get up and roll up your mat." Colloquially Aeneas is told to "get up and make your bed." His healing, and hence his ability to "get up," entails doing something. In this case, it was something as simple as making his bed and walking about so that others could see what Jesus Christ had done for him. His healing led to wholeness and fruitfulness; from his healing onward Aeneas was going to be able to spread out his own sleeping mat and help others who could no longer do it for themselves. His actions and the testimony of his own life became a twin proclamation of the good news of Jesus.

We see this connection between healing, care for the poor, and the gospel also played out in more detail in the story of Tabitha. Martin Hengel describes Peter's "journey to the coast" as "simply geographical preparation for the conversion of the first Gentile, the centurion Cornelius, in Caesarea." He does add that "the two miracle stories in Lydda and Joppa see to it that this amazing story . . . is not too isolated," as Luke's narrative reaches a boundary "both geographically and in the history of mission."[14] But Kirsten Pinto Gfroerer notes that there is more than this going on in the story. Tabitha's return to life offers us a witness to the historical moment when *caritas*—charity—burst forth again upon the earth; it is a theological foundation of love that is prepared before mission is extended to the "ends of the world." She writes:

> The book of Acts, and especially chapters nine and ten, offer an outline of the nature and the process by which the Church exploded unto the ends of the world. That the story of the widows and Tabitha is among these narratives gives priority and place to the fundamental ministry of charity in the life of the Church. Tabitha is raised from the dead in part to signify that the Word, Jesus Christ raised from the dead, will make charity possible and real; he will nurture it. In the life of this Word, the wounds

---

13. Henri Nouwen, *Bread for the Journey* (New York: HarperOne, 1997), entry for August 4.
14. Hengel, "Geography," 61.

of poverty and injustice, the wounds of orphans and widows, will be given what they need to heal, and time to do so.[15]

The point is that the ministry of charity—*caritas*—is not peripheral to the gospel; it is at the heart of the gospel and often is the foundation for the reception of the gospel in a person, a family, or a community.

A word of note may be in order to those of us—pastors, priests, etc.—who are privileged to be on the front lines of this ministry of charity. While the vocation of the pastor may sometimes be difficult,[16] the fact is that ministers of charity are privileged in many ways. That is, we *get* to visit with saints and sinners; we get to engage in interesting conversations, often without the preamble about who won the game last night or what the weather is doing. We get to engage with Tabitha-like people who are making a real difference in their communities; and we get to serve in doing, and affirming, good works of mercy. As Gfroerer reminds us, "Caritas, get up!" This is good work to get up to do. It is sometimes difficult work, but it is good work nonetheless. And we should be the first to affirm this work of *caritas* as foundational to mission and evangelism.

---

15. Gfroerer, "Caritas."

16. In her superb book *Gay and Catholic: Accepting My Sexuality, Finding Community, Living My Faith* (Notre Dame: Ave Maria, 2014), 78, Eve Tushnet reminds us that every vocation has a cross *as well as* a crown.

CHAPTER 22

Acts 10:1-48

 LISTEN to the Story

¹At Caesarea there was a man named Cornelius, a centurion in what was known as the Italian Regiment. ²He and all his family were devout and God-fearing; he gave generously to those in need and prayed to God regularly. ³One day at about three in the afternoon he had a vision. He distinctly saw an angel of God, who came to him and said, "Cornelius!"

⁴Cornelius stared at him in fear. "What is it, Lord?" he asked.

The angel answered, "Your prayers and gifts to the poor have come up as a memorial offering before God. ⁵Now send men to Joppa to bring back a man named Simon who is called Peter. ⁶He is staying with Simon the tanner, whose house is by the sea."

⁷When the angel who spoke to him had gone, Cornelius called two of his servants and a devout soldier who was one of his attendants. ⁸He told them everything that had happened and sent them to Joppa.

⁹About noon the following day as they were on their journey and approaching the city, Peter went up on the roof to pray. ¹⁰He became hungry and wanted something to eat, and while the meal was being prepared, he fell into a trance. ¹¹He saw heaven opened and something like a large sheet being let down to earth by its four corners. ¹²It contained all kinds of four-footed animals, as well as reptiles and birds. ¹³Then a voice told him, "Get up, Peter. Kill and eat."

¹⁴"Surely not, Lord!" Peter replied. "I have never eaten anything impure or unclean."

¹⁵The voice spoke to him a second time, "Do not call anything impure that God has made clean."

¹⁶This happened three times, and immediately the sheet was taken back to heaven.

¹⁷While Peter was wondering about the meaning of the vision, the men sent by Cornelius found out where Simon's house was and stopped

at the gate. ¹⁸They called out, asking if Simon who was known as Peter was staying there.

¹⁹While Peter was still thinking about the vision, the Spirit said to him, "Simon, three[1] men are looking for you. ²⁰So get up and go downstairs. Do not hesitate to go with them, for I have sent them."

²¹Peter went down and said to the men, "I'm the one you're looking for. Why have you come?"

²²The men replied, "We have come from Cornelius the centurion. He is a righteous and God-fearing man, who is respected by all the Jewish people. A holy angel told him to ask you to come to his house so that he could hear what you have to say." ²³Then Peter invited the men into the house to be his guests.

The next day Peter started out with them, and some of the believers from Joppa went along. ²⁴The following day he arrived in Caesarea. Cornelius was expecting them and had called together his relatives and close friends. ²⁵As Peter entered the house, Cornelius met him and fell at his feet in reverence. ²⁶But Peter made him get up. "Stand up," he said, "I am only a man myself."

²⁷While talking with him, Peter went inside and found a large gathering of people. ²⁸He said to them: "You are well aware that it is against our law for a Jew to associate with or visit a Gentile. But God has shown me that I should not call anyone impure or unclean. ²⁹So when I was sent for, I came without raising any objection. May I ask why you sent for me?"

³⁰Cornelius answered: "Three days ago I was in my house praying at this hour, at three in the afternoon. Suddenly a man in shining clothes stood before me ³¹and said, 'Cornelius, God has heard your prayer and remembered your gifts to the poor. ³²Send to Joppa for Simon who is called Peter. He is a guest in the home of Simon the tanner, who lives by the sea.' ³³So I sent for you immediately, and it was good of you to come. Now we are all here in the presence of God to listen to everything the Lord has commanded you to tell us."

³⁴Then Peter began to speak: "I now realize how true it is that God does not show favoritism ³⁵but accepts from every nation the one who fears him and does what is right. ³⁶You know the message God sent to the people of Israel, announcing the good news of peace through Jesus Christ, who is Lord of all. ³⁷You know what has happened throughout the province of

---

1. The NIV notes that one early manuscript reads "two"; other manuscripts do not have a number at all. There is substantial external evidence to support "three."

Judea, beginning in Galilee after the baptism that John preached—³⁸how God anointed Jesus of Nazareth with the Holy Spirit and power, and how he went around doing good and healing all who were under the power of the devil, because God was with him.

³⁹"We are witnesses of everything he did in the country of the Jews and in Jerusalem. They killed him by hanging him on a cross, ⁴⁰but God raised him from the dead on the third day and caused him to be seen. ⁴¹He was not seen by all the people, but by witnesses whom God had already chosen—by us who ate and drank with him after he rose from the dead. ⁴²He commanded us to preach to the people and to testify that he is the one whom God appointed as judge of the living and the dead. ⁴³All the prophets testify about him that everyone who believes in him receives forgiveness of sins through his name."

⁴⁴While Peter was still speaking these words, the Holy Spirit came on all who heard the message. ⁴⁵The circumcised believers who had come with Peter were astonished that the gift of the Holy Spirit had been poured out even on Gentiles. ⁴⁶For they heard them speaking in tongues and praising God.

Then Peter said, ⁴⁷"Surely no one can stand in the way of their being baptized with water. They have received the Holy Spirit just as we have." ⁴⁸So he ordered that they be baptized in the name of Jesus Christ. Then they asked Peter to stay with them for a few days."

Listening to the Text in the Story: Deuteronomy 10:17; Psalms 15:1–2; 107:20; Isaiah 52:7; 61:1; Ezekiel 4:14; Romans 2:11; Ephesians 2:11–22; Colossians 3:25; James 2:1; 1 Peter 1:17.

EXPLAIN the Story

Luke intends those who read Acts to see the conversion of Cornelius as the pivotal moment in the emerging mission of the church from its Jewish, Jerusalem-based beginnings to its worldwide outreach to the gentile world. This story is sometimes referred to as "the gentile Pentecost." We have no way of knowing the precise chronology of this event, but its placement in the narrative of Acts is significant. It occurs between the conversion of Saul (who is almost totally responsible for the gentile mission in Acts) in chapter nine and the story of the church in Antioch (the first predominantly gentile church in Acts, and the church that will be the base of operations for the gentile mission) in chapter eleven. This seems to emphasize two realities in Acts: first, the gentile mission had prior divine approval and, second, the believers in Jerusalem, in principle at least, accepted the mission.

Along with the conversion of Saul (the Lord's "chosen instrument," 9:15) the conversion of Cornelius and his household ranks as one of the most significant events in salvation history. The event, just like Saul's conversion, is retold three times: once in full detail (10:1–48); a second more compact summary (11:1–18); and a third time, the briefest recollection, in the account of the Jerusalem council (15:7–11). The first description of the conversion occurs in five discernible movements: first, the introduction and initial vision to Cornelius in Caesarea (10:1–8); second, Peter's vision and reception of Cornelius's messengers in Joppa (10:9–23a); third, Peter's arrival in Caesarea and Cornelius's reception of his guest (10:23b–33); fourth, Peter's address to Cornelius's household (10:34–43); fifth, and finally, the gracious giving of the Holy Spirit (10:44–48). The heart of this story is that God opens wide the door of salvation to everyone because Jesus Christ is not merely the Lord of the people of Israel but is "Lord of all" (v. 36).

Cornelius and His Vision (10:1–8)

Luke does not say Cornelius is the first gentile convert, but that he is the "first" is implied in several ways.[2] Many argue that the Ethiopian eunuch carries the badge of "first gentile convert" since he is Ethiopian and therefore probably not Jewish (8:27). However, the text implies that he was, or wished to be, a Jewish proselyte since he went on pilgrimage to Jerusalem to worship (8:27), and on his return journey he was reading from Isaiah (8:28). All this suggests that, for Luke, he was not a gentile convert but a "Jewish proselyte" to "the Way" of Christ.

Cornelius, on the other hand, is described as a gentile in a comprehensive way (10:1). The figure of Cornelius is set on a detailed *Roman* stage. He resides in Caesarea, not just a predominantly gentile[3] port city, formerly known as Strato's Tower, but now a city designed and rebuilt by Herod the Great to function as the seat of Roman administration in the province of Judea.[4] It was

---

2. A number of subsequent passages also imply that Cornelius and his household were the first gentile converts. For example, 10:34–35, 45 and 11:18 all indicate surprise from "the circumcised" that God accepted them. In 11:19–20 Luke specifically says that to this point the gospel had been shared with Jews only, but that in Antioch it was now also proclaimed to the gentiles, and James observes "how God *first* intervened to choose a people for his name from the Gentiles" (15:14) after hearing about Cornelius's reception of the gospel from Peter.

3. Caesarea was the location for many of Herod the Great's significant building projects (Josephus, *Ant*. 15.331–41).

4. Herod built Caesarea as a thoroughgoing Greco-Roman city complete with gymnasia, amphitheatre, statues, and imperial temple.

named after and dedicated to the Roman emperor Caesar Augustus. Cornelius is not only a gentile but a soldier, a "centurion." A Roman centurion was well respected and, from a military standpoint, was the most important leader of his "century" of men. It usually took a soldier twelve to twenty years of outstanding service to be appointed a centurion.[5] Finally, if all this were not enough to demonstrate Cornelius's gentile pedigree, he is described as a member of the "*Italian* Regiment." A regiment, or cohort, consisted of six hundred men. Historians remind us that there is no historical evidence outside of Acts to support the existence of an auxiliary cohort by this name stationed in Caesarea in the first century. Hengel, however, notes that "auxiliary cohorts could be posted anywhere in the Roman Empire according to need" and for now, "we know far too little about military conditions in [first-century] Palestine to be able to draw any clear conclusions."[6] The point for Luke's narrative, however, is that Cornelius is a gentile, living in a significant gentile city, and a prominent and privileged member of Roman society.

There is more to Cornelius than his external personage as a prominent Roman soldier. The next sentence fills out the picture of his interior life as "devout and God-fearing" (v. 2; *eusebēs kai phoboumenos*). This is language used throughout Acts (cf. 13:16, 26, 50; 16:14; 17:4, 17; 18:7)[7] for those gentiles who were attracted to Judaism but were unprepared to take the final step of circumcision[8] and become full proselytes.[9] As such, the description indicates that Cornelius and his family household were gentiles and not proselytes to Judaism. Therefore, even though Cornelius was "respected by all the Jewish people" in Caesarea (10:22), he would still be considered as unclean by Jews like Peter. This is the point that Peter's vision will address (vv. 10–16).

Cornelius is also distinguished for possessing the same generosity of spirit and deeds that earlier characterized the good woman Tabitha. Like Tabitha, Cornelius gave "generously" to the poor (v. 2, *eleēmosynē*; cf. 9:36).

---

5. See G. L. Thompson, "Roman Military," *DNTB* 993. For the important social position of a centurion, see A. N. Sherwin-White, *Roman Society and Roman Law in the New Testament* (Eugene, OR: Wipf & Stock, 2004), 156ff.

6. Hengel, "Geography," 63n111.

7. See also Josephus, *Ant* 14.110: "all the Jews throughout the habitable earth, and *those that worshiped God* [*seboumenōn ton theon*]."

8. This is not an inconsequential matter for a Roman centurion like Cornelius. The practice of regular bathing in the public baths was highly significant in his culture. B. W. R. Pearson, "Gymnasia and Baths," *DNTB* 435–36, writes that "[bathhouses] formed a central focus for social life in the Roman city, and as such people often spent a great deal of time at the bathhouse, even conducting business."

9. See Scot McKnight, "Proselytism and Godfearers," *DNTB* 835–47; Hemer, *Acts*, 444–47. While the words "proselyte" and "God-fearer" may almost be synonymous, Luke does seem to distinguish between gentiles who have become full proselytes to Judaism (e.g., Nicolas from Antioch, a "convert" [*prosēlytos*; Acts 6:5; cf. 2:11; 13:43]) and those who, like Cornelius, were God-fearers.

Many widows gave witness to Tabitha's charity, her *caritas*, but God himself bears witness to Cornelius's devout character and charity (10:4, 31). As was the case at all the key moments thus far in Acts when mission is undertaken, God is the initiator. God sent his Spirit on the day of Pentecost; God sent Philip to speak to the Ethiopian eunuch; and now God reveals himself to Cornelius. The narrative reads that on some unspecified day at three in the afternoon (lit., "the ninth hour"), Cornelius meets an angel of God. Cornelius is the only gentile in all of Luke-Acts to receive an angelic visitation. The angel speaks to him, and characteristic of those experiencing a vision from God, Cornelius stares in fear (v. 4). Much like Saul did (9:5), he asks, "What is it, Lord?" This is more than polite address in the narrative as it foreshadows Peter's declaration to follow (10:36).

The angel informs Cornelius that his "prayers" and "gifts to the poor" (v. 4, *eleēmosynē*) have ascended to God as a "memorial offering." There has been a long-standing division among ancient and modern interpreters over the role of Cornelius's piety and good deeds. Ancient interpreters like Augustine[10] and Bede[11] along with moderns like Fitzmyer[12] insist that Cornelius did not "merit" faith. Chrysostom[13] and Arator[14] among the ancient commentators and Barrett[15] among the modern suggest that there is a measure of "virtue" in Cornelius's good works. For Luke, the interest is not on what role Cornelius's prayers and piety may or may not have served as merit before God. Rather, Cornelius is portrayed as being responsible for what he does with what he knows from his association with Judaism. As such, he prays, and in the venerable tradition expressed in the OT (e.g., Prov 14:31; 19:17), in the sayings of Jesus (Matt 25:40; Mark 9:41), and later in the tradition of the early church (Heb 6:10), he cares for the needy, and this is approved by God and received

---

10. Augustine, *Predestination of the Saints* 1.7.12, in *ACCA*, 119, in the fourth century argued that "whatever . . . good works Cornelius performed, whether before he believed in Christ or when he believed or after he had believed, all to be ascribed to God. Otherwise, it might be assumed that human initiative is being lifted up."

11. Bede, *Commentary on Acts of the Apostles* 10.1, in *ACCA*, 119, from the seventh century writes that "he had faith, this man whose prayers and alms were able to please [God], and by his good deeds he earned the right to know God perfectly and to believe in the mystery of the incarnation of his only begotten, so that he might approach the sacrament of baptism. Therefore, through faith he came to works, yet through works he was strengthened in faith."

12. Fitzmyer, *Acts*, 448.

13. Chrysostom, *Homilies on the Acts of the Apostles* 22, in *ACCA*, 120, from the fourth century exclaims, "See how great the virtue of alms, both in the former discourse [i.e., Tabitha] and here! There, it delivered from temporal death; here, from eternal death, and opened the gates of heaven."

14. Arator, *On the Acts of the Apostles* 1, in *ACCA*, 120, from the sixth century writes, "Cornelius, born of Gentile stock, was highly respected in the city of Caesarea; his life, given over to godly works, sanctified him for the waters, and he, who did whatever faith was inclined to perform in those washed by baptism . . . began to believe through his actions."

15. Barrett, *Acts*, 1:503.

as a "memorial offering" (Acts 10:4). A memorial offering (see Lev 2:2, 9, 16; 6:15; Num 5:26; Sir 38:11) was a share of the grain harvest that symbolically reminded Israel that the entire harvest was God's, but that God only required a portion of it as a reminder of this reality. In using a memorial offering to refer to Cornelius's prayers and good deeds, this might be indicative of the fact that Cornelius and his household are a representative portion of the gentile "harvest" to come. God gives this first testimony to his approval of the mission to gentiles by providing two visions, first to Cornelius ("an angel of God," Acts 10:3; called a "holy angel" in v. 22), and then later to Peter (10:9–16).

The angel of God not only mentions Cornelius's prayer and service but gives him a command: send men to Joppa to bring back a man named Simon who is called Peter (v. 5). Joppa was about sixty kilometers (36 miles) south along the coast from Caesarea, a walking journey of about two days for the able-bodied. The angel provides Cornelius with both his Hebrew name, Simon, and his Greek name, Peter. Presumably, this is to distinguish Simon Peter from Simon the tanner. Simon the tanner's residence was located "by the sea"—a common location for a tanner who would need access to water for his trade. Cornelius responds to the command with the expected military obedience and efficiency of a centurion. He calls (v. 7) two servants from his household along with a "devout [*eusebēs*] soldier" who shared the same "devout" faith he did (v. 2). After relaying the vision to these three, they are dispatched to Joppa to find Simon Peter (v. 8).

Peter's Vision and Reception of Messengers (10:9–23a)

Peter's vision, just like Cornelius's conversion narrative, is recounted twice in the narrative (Acts 10:9–22; 11:5–14). The point of the doublet is to emphasize the vision's importance, both in the story of Acts and in the history of salvation. There is also a tight temporal connection between Cornelius's vision and Peter's vision: "About noon the following day as they were on their journey and approaching the city, Peter went up on the roof to pray" (10:9). He may have gone up onto the roof for privacy or to get away from the reek of the tanner's vats. Whatever the reason, Peter has no clue what is about to happen. While his thoughts stray from prayer to lunch, he falls into a "trance," literally becoming "outside himself" (*ekstasis*), and has a vision of food (vv. 11–12). He sees "heaven opened"—a familiar biblical signal that something extraordinary from God is about to be revealed (e.g., Ezek 1:1; Matt 3:16; Luke 3:21; John 1:51; Acts 7:56; Rev 4:1; 19:11)—and a large blanket descending with a wide variety of lunch options: all kinds of animals, reptiles, and birds were on it. After seeing the vision, he hears a voice. The heavens open—as they have previously in the narrative[16]—and the one who has ascended to the right hand of God in heaven speaks. What he hears from the Lord is the same command Peter gave in the previous chapter to Aeneas and Tabitha (9:34, 40): "Get up." This time Peter is on the receiving end of charity, and he is offered food to satisfy his hunger (10:13).

Peter does not, however, respond with the same obedience with which Aeneas and Tabitha did. Instead, like Ananias did when the Lord commanded him to go visit Saul in Damascus (9:13–14), he begins a debate in response to the divine directive: "Surely not, Lord!" (10:14). It is somewhat odd that Peter then adds that he has never eaten anything impure or unclean, words reminiscent of Ezekiel when the Spirit came to him near the Kebar River, which was gentile territory in the land of the Babylonians (Ezek 4:14).[17] An even closer historical echo occurs in the accounts in Maccabees.[18] First Maccabees recounts the intense persecution that occurred about a century before the birth of Christ when the Greek despot in control of Palestine, Antiochus IV (Epiphanes), oppressed the Jews. He despised the Jews and their religion and sought to obliterate them by imposing Greek culture and religion upon them. He tried to put an end to Jewish sacrificial worship and imposed the worship of Greek idols where they were to sacrifice swine and other unclean animals. Antiochus also forbade Jews from circumcising their sons (1 Macc 1:44–48). In all this, the Jews "were to make themselves abominable by everything unclean and profane, so that they would forget the law and change all the ordinances" (1:48–49 NRSV). Nonetheless, there were some who resisted. In summary of what this resistance looked like, the author of 1 Maccabees writes, "But many in Israel stood firm and were resolved in their hearts not to eat unclean food. They chose to die rather than to be defiled by food or to profane the holy covenant; and they did die" (1:62–63; cf. 4 Macc 5:36–6:30). The issues of food and purity were not merely questions of diet and fastidiousness; they were matters of Jewish identity, Jewish zeal for the law, and Jewish courage in the face of Greek persecution. All this would still resonate with Jews like Peter even a hundred and fifty years later under Roman rule.

Presumably Peter could have found something on the blanket buffet that would both satisfy his hunger and be ritually pure and clean for his Jewish palette. Gaventa alerts us to the issue, and solution, that is often raised by Peter's objection: "The question is why the dream concerns items of food when the

---

16. See Acts 2:2, 33; 3:21; 4:12; 5:31; 7:56; 9:4–6.
17. On Jewish dietary practices, see Lev 11 and Deut 14.
18. I was alerted to these by Nijay Gupta in his essay, "1 Maccabees and Romans 14:1–15:13: Embodying the Hospitable Kingdom Community," in *Reading Romans in Context*, ed. Ben Blackwell, John K. Goodrich, and Jason Maston (Grand Rapids: Zondervan, 2015), 152–54.

larger story concerns human beings. In a fundamental sense, such objections are misplaced because they ignore the character of Peter's experience. The function of the vision is to be suggestive, as is evident in v. 17; like dreams or visions in some OT narratives, its meaning is not immediately obvious (e.g., Gen 41; Dan 2:31–45; 4:1–27; 5:1–28)."[19] In particular, we might take seriously the implication of the numbers in the vision. For example, the vision has a sheet with "four corners" suggestive of the whole earth, God's created world, which is often described as having four corners, four elements, or four parts.[20] If God has created the whole earth, nothing he has made—including animals and humans—is unclean. More importantly, Peter is alerted to a reality that is in heaven, where all things are pure and clean, that is now coming to earth. If the sending of the Spirit from heaven is the "firstfruit" of new creation on the fallen earth,[21] here we glimpse another revelation of new creation—the kingdom of God coming to earth as it is in heaven.

We do not have long to wait before the implication of the dream is apparent in the larger narrative. The point is that Peter treats food the same way he treats people. Some foods are regarded as clean and pure, some as unclean and impure; some people are regarded as clean and pure, some as unclean and impure. Peter knows the boundaries. Up to this point in Acts, he has done nothing to transgress Jewish purity laws—especially regarding food.[22] The voice from heaven responds emphatically: the things that *God* declares ceremonially clean, *you*[23] should not consider unclean (Acts 10:15). The word "unclean" (*koinoō*) is a difficult word to translate. For example, it can mean either "consider" or "declare" something (ritually) unclean.[24] Alexander asks an important question about this: "So is it about labels [to declare unclean], or about reality [to consider unclean]? The answer is both, because, in a purity context, labels create reality. The next question is: whose labels? Who actually has the right to label some parts of God's creation 'pure,' fit for human consumption, and others not? Who gets to decide?"[25]

---

19. Gaventa, *Acts*, 165.

20. E.g., in the visions in Revelation the earth has four corners (Rev 7:1; 20:8) and four winds (7:1) and can be divided into four divisions (5:13: "in heaven and on earth and under the earth and on the sea"; or earth, sea, springs, heavens in 8:7–12; 14:7; 16:2–9). See Richard Bauckham, *Climax of Prophecy* (London: T&T Clark, 2005), 31.

21. See "Explain the Story" on Acts 2:1–41.

22. On the way food regulations served to distinguish Jews from non-Jews in the Greco-Roman world, see John M. G. Barclay, *Jews in the Mediterranean Diaspora* (Berkeley: University of California Press, 1996), 434–37.

23. The "you" is an emphatic pronoun, placed in front of the phrase and also in opposite position to "God." The point is Peter could not be more wrong in his judgment.

24. BDAG 552.

25. Alexander, *Acts*, 87.

The answer is not obvious to Peter at first. The vision occurs three times to help him in his deliberations. The answer is given when we consider the source of the vision and, importantly, the creatures themselves. The creatures—all of them—whether Peter regards them as clean or unclean, derive from and return to heaven. Heaven is an unusual place; it does not distinguish and differentiate the same way humans, like Peter, do on earth. Peter must grapple with the realities and labels on earth in relation to how they are in heaven. The issue is not primarily about food, although food issues will return for Peter (e.g., Gal 2:12), but about people. The issue will be about the people of God. Will this be a people distinguished by race, or by grace?

While Peter is perplexed[26] by this triple vision and the questions it raises, the men sent by Cornelius arrive at the gate of Simon the tanner's home. Peter is still wondering[27] about the meaning of the vision (Acts 10:19) when the Spirit speaks to him and commands him again to get up, go downstairs, and go with them, "for *I* have sent them" (v. 20). They may be Cornelius's messengers, but the Spirit claims to be the originator of their mission. Again, we are reminded that the divine initiative is at work throughout this narrative—the gentile mission is, after all, God's idea! Three men have arrived looking for him—one for each vision perhaps?

Although Peter is still sitting in predominantly Jewish Joppa, emotionally and intellectually he is in unfamiliar theological territory. Almost as if to focus our attention on the importance of this moment—not only in the lives of Peter and Cornelius but in the life of the church—Luke provides a significant amount of descriptive detail to the story in terms of the travel, dialogue, and hospitality. When the narrative shifts into this kind of slow motion, it is as if Luke is reminding the reader that this is an important moment, this is God's moment.[28] After initial greetings, Cornelius's messengers relate to Peter what we already know about their master: he is a righteous and God-fearing man (see v. 2). This time, however, we hear that he is "respected by all the *Jewish* people" (v. 22). Peter may be in unfamiliar theological territory and a guest in Simon the tanner's home, but he makes the overture toward gentile inclusion by actually inviting these gentile visitors to enter a Jewish home as *his* "guests" (v. 23). Hospitality in the ancient world was important. While Peter

---

26. Levison, *Inspired*, 103, notes that this verb, translated as "wondering" (10:17) by the NIV but also carrying the notion of puzzlement, is significant. He writes, "Peter searches for meaning in a vision that took place under ecstasy or sleep. He is not interested in physical transport or emotional catharsis or basking in ecstasy; he wants *meaning*."

27. The tension created by the vision for Peter is one that derives from his effort to reconcile God's word and instructions in the OT (see Lev 11) with the word and instructions now being received from the Lord in heaven.

28. Alexander, *Acts*, 88.

is not transgressing any purity law by inviting gentiles to be his guests, it is a significant move because hospitality generally also included *reciprocity*—the giving *and* receiving of hospitality. That is, he would in turn be invited as a guest into the home of Cornelius, a gentile—and this would involve the eating of gentile food and experiencing, potentially, other "impure" objects.

Peter Arrives to Cornelius's House (10:23b–33)

Peter, accompanied by fellow Jewish believers from Joppa, thus sets out with Cornelius's messengers "the next day" and arrives in Caesarea "the following day" (vv. 23–24). Cornelius is not timid about meeting Peter. He waits expectantly for the Jewish apostle with a gathered company of family and close friends. In an act of profound humility, the respected Roman centurion falls at Peter's feet in reverence. We must remember that the Romans regarded themselves as the rulers of the world. Imperial rule of the "civilized world" was assumed and asserted by Rome. The Romans took pride that they had conquered the world (Pliny the Younger, *Panegyricus* 51.3), that Rome was the greatest of all cities (Horace, *Odes* 4.3.13) and a light of the world and citadel for all nations (Cicero, *De republica* 2.4.10; *In Catalinam* 3.1; 4.11; *Pro Sulla* 33), and that they were chosen by the gods to achieve these aims (Pliny the Elder, *Natural History* 3.39; 27.3; 36.118). Roman rule, including Roman rule of the Jewish people, was an indication of the favor of the gods, especially the god Victoria. For a Roman, and a centurion at that, to bow[29] at the feet of a Jew was unusual. Peter, however, makes him get up and rebukes him, "I am only a man myself" (Acts 10:26). He knows that this kind of reverence is due only to God.

Peter then takes a last but climactic step by entering Cornelius's home. Inside he finds even more people waiting for him (v. 27). Peter's first words to the waiting crowd are not heartwarming; there is still a reluctant tone that carries over from his "surely not, Lord!" reaction when he first saw his vision (v. 14). In crossing the threshold, he declares to his gentile audience (a household of substance and reputation) that it is unlawful[30] for a Jew like him to

---

29. The verb *proskyneō* had a wide range of meaning in the ancient world, from "worship" to "obeisance" or "respect." It is difficult to know how Cornelius intended this gesture, but any debate about what this might have meant is brushed aside by Peter's abrupt response: "Stand up, . . . I am only a man myself." Peter, as a devout Jew, knows there is a clear boundary between what is offered to God and what is offered to human beings: only God is to be worshiped. A similar experience is related about Paul and Barnabas in Lystra in Acts 14:11, 15; see also Rev 19:10; 22:8–9.

30. BDAG 24 notes that this word refers primarily "not to what is forbidden by ordinance but to violation of tradition or common recognition of what is seemly or proper." What is "unlawful" does not refer to any written *torah* but to tradition. The Gospel of Luke (7:1–10) relates the story of another Roman centurion who is commended by Jewish elders as one who "loves our nation and has built our synagogue" (v. 5). Further, gentiles were even welcome in the temple, as the court of

"associate" or visit with a gentile. Although Peter had welcomed Cornelius's messengers as guests, it is often more difficult, especially for a Jew in the first century, to receive hospitality. When one is a guest, you must live by the "house rules." The expression "associate" (v. 27) implies that one is on intimate terms with another.[31] Another glimpse of this Jewish view occurs in John 18:28 where the Jewish leaders avoid entering a Roman residence, the palace of the governor, so that they are not made ceremonially unclean. But whereas the Jewish leaders there avoid impurity, Peter, albeit reluctantly, crosses the boundary. Why? Because "God" (Acts 10:28) showed him that no human ethnic group is unclean and that gentile inclusion is anticipated in biblical texts describing the messianic age (e.g., Isa 2:1–4). Peter, however, asks the real question: I would like to know why *you* (plural) sent for me?

As the master (Latin, *dominus*) of the house (*domus*), Cornelius answers. The substance of his reply to Peter's question (Acts 10:30–32) is almost a verbatim repeat of the initial description of the vision (vv. 3–6). Cornelius does add one new detail to the context: the vision is rooted in waiting prayer. It appears that Cornelius, much like the disciples of Jesus, observed set times for prayer since he recalls *praying* "at about three in the afternoon"—that is, the ninth hour—the time set for afternoon prayer.[32] He then recounts his vision and how Peter was the answer to his prayers. While Luke is careful to provide a thorough *Roman* context for Cornelius, he also reminds the reader of the charitable and prayerful background that has shaped Cornelius's life. God has already been at work in Cornelius's life before the apostle arrives. Again, we are reminded in the narrative that the people of God are ever and always following and catching up in witness, as it were, to the work of the Spirit of God. God has initiated this meeting between Peter and Cornelius. Cornelius acknowledges as much and closes by telling Peter that "we are all here in the *presence* of God" (v. 33). Further, as the household of a commanding officer and respected master, they are ready to hear "everything *the Lord has commanded* you to tell us" (v. 33). The mention of "the Lord" provides a significant framework for what will follow in Peter's speech.

---

the gentiles demonstrates. The point seems to be that gentiles were welcome within Judaism, but Jews must be careful in the welcome they receive from gentiles lest assimilation to gentile ways occurs (e.g., they might be served pork!).

31. The same word is used to describe Saul's intent to "join" the disciples in Jerusalem (Acts 9:26).

32. For centuries Jews prayed at set times in the day: at sunrise and sunset, at the third (9:00 a.m.) and ninth (3:00 p.m.) hours of the day when the sacrifices were offered (see Ezra 9:5; Dan 9:21; Jdt 9:1; Pss. Sol. 6:4; Josephus, *Ant.* 4.212). There was also the tradition of midday prayer (the sixth hour), giving three "hours" of prayer for the observant Jew, and subsequently Christians as well (Ps 55:17; Dan 6:10; Did. 8:3).

Peter's Speech (10:34–43)

For those who have been following Luke's narrative and not just dipping in at this juncture, much of what follows in Peter's words echoes earlier speeches (2:14–36 and 3:12–16). Many of the themes are similar: Jesus was anointed by God, performed powerful healings, was handed over to death by the Jews, raised by God on the third day, seen by witnesses, and proclaimed by his apostles. Unlike the prior speeches, there are no direct quotations of Scripture, but the address is replete with scriptural allusions and echoes (e.g., Deut 10:17–18; Pss 15:1–2; 107:20; Isa 52:7; 61:1; cf. Sir 35:12–13).[33] What is different is the initial setting for the speech. Despite his unenthusiastic response to Cornelius's messengers ("I'm the one you're looking for," 10:21) and his less-than-flattering opening words at the doorstep ("You are well aware that it is against our law for a Jew to associate with or visit a Gentile," 10:28), Peter hears Cornelius's account of his vision and is finally convinced "that God does not show favoritism but accepts from every nation the one who fears him" (10:34–35). The fact that God does not show favoritism is not a cold assertion. It implies that God is relational. If anyone wants God, God is open to receive him or her. This has been a long journey for Peter, both geographically and theologically. But the theme of inclusion is not a brief stop along the journey through Acts; it is a pivotal theme that extends throughout the book and across the New Testament (see Rom 2:11; Eph 2:11–22; Col 3:25; Jas 2:1; 1 Pet 1:17). The lesson of Peter's vision has finally taken root in Peter's head and heart.

The climactic moment in Peter's speech (v. 36) is built around allusions from a Psalm (107:20: "He [God] sent out his word") and Isaiah (52:7: "Those who bring good news, who proclaim peace"). First, the good news through Jesus is that the "message"—literally the "word" (Acts 10:36, *logos*)—sent by God brings earthly peace and reconciliation between Jew and gentile; this is the point of "no favoritism" (vv. 34–35). But there is more. Through Jesus Christ there is also peace on a cosmic level; this is the point of mentioning the overpowering of the devil (v. 38). Second, all this is possible because Jesus Christ is "Lord of all."[34] The importance of this second point can sometimes be obscured because of some translations (e.g., KJV, RSV, NET) and commentators that

---

33. E.g., compare "God does not show favoritism but accepts from every nation the one who fears him and does what is right" (Acts 10:34–35) with "the great God . . . shows no partiality. . . . and loves the foreigner residing among you" (Deut 10:17–18) and "who may dwell in your sacred tent? Who may live on your holy mountain? The one whose walk is blameless, who does what is righteous, who speaks the truth from their heart" (Ps 15:1–2). Additionally, compare "you know the message God sent to the people of Israel, announcing the good news of peace through Jesus Christ, who is Lord of all" (Acts 10:36) with "how beautiful on the mountains are the feet of those who bring good news, who proclaim peace, who bring good tidings, who proclaim salvation" (Isa 52:7).

34. This is a title for God (Josh 3:11, 13; Ps 97:5; Mic 4:13; Zech 4:14; 6:5; cf. Wis 6:7; 8:3) and for pagan gods (e.g., Plutarch, *Isis and Osiris* 355E).

regard "who is Lord of all"[35] as a parenthetical remark.[36] Kavin Rowe argues, persuasively I think, that the Greek word *houtos*, translated as "who" in the NIV, makes clear that this entire phrase is "hardly peripheral to Peter's point. Indeed, the use of [*houtos*] makes clear that the identity of Jesus Christ as [Lord of all] is made known in just such a way as to draw attention to its uniqueness. *This one* [emphasis his], and not someone else, is the Lord of all."[37]

While modern readers may sometimes miss the importance of this assertion, it would not have been lost on Peter's distinctly *Roman* audience. In Cornelius's world, the Roman emperor was regarded both as a god and the "Lord of all the world."[38] The point is that both Jesus Christ and the emperor were called "Lord," but Peter asserts that only Jesus is "Lord of all." Some recent scholarship has tried to suggest that this creates a sort of competition between Christians and the Roman Empire.[39] This is almost certainly not Peter's position. Again, Rowe states it well: "Jesus does not challenge Caesar's status as Lord, as if Jesus were somehow originally subordinate to Caesar in the order of being. The thought . . . is much more radical and striking: because of the nature of his claims, it is Caesar who is the rival; and what he rivals is the Lordship of God in the person of Jesus Christ."[40] The lordship of Jesus the Messiah is central to the proclamation of the gospel both to Jews (see Acts 2:36) and gentiles alike.

After the assertions of the climactic moment of Peter's speech (10:36), the remainder of the speech offers a succinct summary of the gospel with several notable elements. The next sentence (vv. 37–38) reaches back to the ministry of John the Baptist, picking up language from Isaiah (61:1), and highlights that Jesus of Nazareth is "anointed" by God with the Holy Spirit. It is noteworthy that this concise summary of the gospel is given with a Trinitarian frame. And as an interesting aside, especially within the context of Cornelius's household, it is that God chose as witnesses to the resurrected Lord those of *us* (that is, including Peter) "who ate and drank with" Jesus (Acts 10:41). Gaventa observes, "Although the sharing of food may be implied by Acts 1:4, none of the other speeches in Acts refers to this qualification of the witnesses, but it is especially appropriate for a story that concerns itself with hospitality for

---

35. Gk.: *houtos estin pantōn kyrios*.
36. Barrett, *Acts*, 1:522.
37. Rowe, *World Upside Down*, 105. One might add that what is being expressed is not just the uniqueness of Jesus as Lord of all but also the centrality of this assertion.
38. The evidence for this is substantial. By way of example, Rowe provides a sampling from the first-century Roman world (*World Upside Down*, 106).
39. For a broad review of this issue, see Scot McKnight and Joseph B. Modica, eds., *Jesus Is Lord, Caesar Is Not: Evaluating Empire in New Testament Studies* (Downers Grove, IL: InterVarsity Press, 2013).
40. Rowe, *World Upside Down*, 112.

gentiles, one in which the sharing of food plays an important role (see especially 11:3)."[41] Peter then continues with his customary and invitatory words that "everyone who believes in [Jesus] receives forgiveness of sins through his name" (10:43). But before Peter can mention the promised gift of the Holy Spirit, the Spirit finishes the speech in dramatic fashion.

The Holy Spirit's Response (10:44–48)
The Holy Spirit has led Peter and Cornelius to their dramatic encounter. It is thus only fitting that the Spirit has, so to speak, the last word. Peter is interrupted, and the gracious giving of the Spirit comes dramatically and noticeably upon all who were listening to his words (vv. 44–45). The outpouring "astonishes" Peter's circumcised associates who traveled with him from Joppa. Who could not be astounded? Who could ever think the Spirit could be managed or contained? The unexpected outpouring did, however, remind them of a similar experience in Jerusalem for Jewish believers: the outpoured Spirit led them to speaking in tongues (10:46; cf. 2:4) and praising God (10:46; cf. 2:11). In this sense, this "gentile Pentecost" thus parallels the day of Pentecost.

In a complete and unexpected reversal of the situation experienced in Samaria (8:12–17), the believers in Cornelius's house receive the Spirit and then are baptized (10:47–48). This should keep any contemporary theologian from attempting to schematize the work of the Spirit. Peter didn't. He simply acknowledged this as evidence of God's impartiality. So how could he, or anyone else for that matter, forbid uncircumcised gentiles from being baptized if God approved them? The episode draws to a close with the note that they asked Peter to "stay with them for a few days" (10:48). This meant Peter's participation was not limited to a grudging admission of their inclusion in the people of God, obligatory baptisms, and then a return to the status quo. Rather, this meant that Peter—along with his Jewish companions—would enter into full communal life with these gentiles. They would stay in their home, receive hospitality, and sit at table, eating and drinking together. This could only be possible because Jesus Christ was Lord of all.

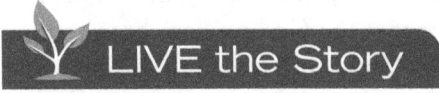

LIVE the Story

Divine Impartiality, Divine Initiative, and the Triune God
"I now realize how true it is that God does not show favoritism but accepts from every nation the one who fears him and does what is right" are Peter's

---
41. Gaventa, *Acts*, 171.

opening words to Cornelius's household (Acts 10:34–35). The impartiality of God that Peter proclaims has been in view since the beginning of the narrative when Jesus commissioned his disciples to be his witnesses in "Jerusalem . . . and to the ends of the earth" (1:8). God loves the world and accepts *everyone*—regardless of race or gender or age—who follows him and his ways. This is a profound truth. Unfortunately, Christians all too often overlook it. We tend to be slow learners to truth, much like Peter was. But, like Peter, we must learn. This is a dominant theme in Acts that is struck again and again from beginning to end. Peter proclaims Jesus as "Lord" in David's city, Jerusalem (2:36); he again proclaims Jesus as "Lord" in Caesar's city, Caesarea (10:36). Therefore, as a matter of divine impartiality, Jesus is "Lord of all"—of both Jews and gentiles alike. Just as the Jewish disciples waited and prayed in Jerusalem for the gift of the Spirit, so also gentiles waited and prayed in Cornelius's home for the gift of the Spirit. Now, as much as Jews and gentiles did in the first century, we are called to wait and pray for the renewing presence of the Spirit to fall afresh on us all, impartially and graciously.

While the mission of the *Jewish* apostles proclaiming the gospel to the *gentile* world connects the Christian movement in Acts, it is important to remember that this is always the result of the divine initiative at work. Cornelius feared God and did what was right, but unexpectedly an angel of God comes to Cornelius unbidden. Peter climbed on a roof to pray, but unexpectedly the Lord Jesus speaks to Peter in a vision unbidden. Peter journeyed to Caesarea and was welcomed into the home of Cornelius and invited to tell everyone assembled what the Lord commanded him, but unexpectedly the Spirit interrupts Peter's words and is poured out on the gentiles unbidden. There is much that we must do and say for God both at home and abroad, but Acts 10 reminds us what the entire narrative does as a whole: God acts first and invites us to participate alongside that work. God speaks first and invites us to participate alongside that word. Divine impartiality reminds us that God accepts people graciously; divine initiative reminds us that God acts as "first mover" and invites his people alongside to participate and live with him.

Another observation is also noteworthy regarding living the theology of this text. It is important to recognize that the God we have been reading about is revealed as triune. The triune God is in view, both in action and in proclamation, in this passage. In the action of the narrative, the angel of *God* comes to Cornelius (10:3), the ascended *Lord* Jesus opens heaven and addresses Peter (10:11–12), and the *Spirit* is poured out upon Cornelius's gentile household (10:44–45). In the proclamation of the narrative, Peter declares to his gentile audience "how *God* anointed *Jesus* of Nazareth with the *Holy Spirit* and power, and how he went around doing good and healing all who were under the power of the devil, because God was with him" (10:38). As we read these kinds of passages in Acts, or elsewhere in the NT, we can sometimes overlook the Trinitarian shape of the words and works being conveyed. I know from personal experience that I can confess Trinitarian belief, but I overlook Trinitarian behavior. The implicit reminder in the text is that the Trinity is more than a creed to be affirmed; it is a reality to be entered and explored. Perhaps equally significant, all this is *assumed* within three decades of the saving events themselves. Hence, this Trinitarian understanding of God is an established assumption that is in place centuries before it was articulated more explicitly by church councils (e.g., the First Council of Constantinople in AD 381) and by "doctors" of the church like Augustine.

Spirit-Led Mission

At the heart of Acts 10 is the proclamation by Peter that "Jesus Christ" is "Lord of all" (v. 36). Like the creedal reality of the Trinity, this is a Christian truth that is not only meant to be confessed but to propel mission. "Jesus is Lord of all," asserts Kavin Rowe, "presupposes the reality and success of Christian mission. Or, to put it another way, mission is that practice presupposed by all existing Christian communities, the fundament upon which their communal life was originally made possible. According to Acts, however, the basis for Christian mission is not internal to the notion of mission as such; rather, mission is the necessary response to the universal Lordship of God in Jesus Christ."[42] Mission, the act of carrying one's faith to others ignorant of that faith, was not something that pagans who lived alongside Jews and Christians in the first century Mediterranean world did. Martin Goodman comments on this with marked insight that "no pagan seriously dreamed of bringing all humankind to give worship in one body to one deity."[43] However, the early Christians did. Christians took their faith on the road and the high seas and traveled the extent of their known world, proclaiming the universal lordship of Jesus. They did not view Jesus as a local deity or the preserve of a specific ethnic group. They understood mission—sending—to be at the core of who they were. Mission is at the heart of the triune God. Jesus said, "As the Father has sent me, I am sending you" (John 20:21), and in the power and initiative of the Holy Spirit, mission was at the heart of the early church. And so it should continue to be at the heart of the contemporary church.

While the church has not always been actively engaged in cross-cultural mission over the centuries, there have been significant waves of mission in its

---

42. Rowe, *World Upside Down*, 116.
43. Martin Goodman, *Mission and Conversion* (Oxford: Clarendon, 1996), 32, quoted in Rowe, *World Upside Down*, 117.

history. For example, from the fifth to the eighth century, Celtic missionary monks engaged in extensive evangelization and education of western Europe after much of it had fallen into paganism after the collapse of the Roman Empire. In the twelfth century the Waldensians and the wider *Vita Apostolica* (lit., "the apostolic life") movement recaptured the early church impetus for preaching and evangelism with great impact on their culture. In the eighteenth century, John and Charles Wesley and George Whitefield sparked the First Great Awakening, an evangelistic and renewal movement that swept much of Europe and British America. In our own day, there is a dramatic awakening to the gospel in Asia with thousands of missionaries being sent from churches in South Korea alone. All this reflects the mission heart of the church in Acts.

Amidst this enthusiastic outreach, it is important to raise a note of caution. As we have noticed in Acts 10, mission is Spirit-led, *not* adventure-led. In the 1970s Francis Schaeffer critiqued Western culture, including the Western Protestant church, for its idolatrous pursuit of "personal peace and affluence."[44] Schaeffer's assessment of culture is also relevant to Christian mission. Much that is done in the name of "mission" by North American Christians seems to be an extension of this in the rise of short-term mission work. While many find short-term mission work fulfilling and life changing, for some this kind of mission effort can be unhelpful and burdensome—especially for the long-term workers who host them—and, at worst, feeds a sense of self-glorification. In comparison, when we see the first Christian missionaries at work, it involved long and prayerful discernment, usually great sacrifice, and often significant risk. Many of those sent on mission by the early church were celibate (e.g., Paul), endured hunger and often deprivation, imprisonment, and torture, and frequently worked with their own hands to support their mission. Most importantly, they responded to the divine initiative in mission—with the Spirit sometimes leading them into new fields and sometimes keeping them from their plans and intentions for mission (e.g., Acts 16:6–7).

I do not wish to be harsh toward those genuinely called to engage in short-term mission work. I do, however, think wisdom for our contemporary missionary efforts can be discerned from the story of Acts. In particular, for those considering short-term or long-term mission, a hard question should be asked: Is this mission Spirit-led and obedient, or is it adventure-led and self-indulgent? If we are to answer this question honestly, it will require much prayer and community discernment. Sarita Hartz points out helpful ways that short-term missions can make meaningful and lasting contributions. For example, she suggests that short-term missionaries should "pour into the [local,

---

44. Francis Schaeffer, *How Should We Then Live? The Rise and Decline of Western Thought and Culture* (Wheaton, IL: Crossway, 1976), 205.

long-term] missionaries," "seek to serve and not self-glorify," and "actually have a specific, needed skill to offer."[45] In the end, as is reflected in the variety of circumstances in Acts, some Christians who may have made excellent missionaries were called to stay in one place and were rooted in their local communities (e.g., Philip lived in Caesarea for twenty years; Cornelius and his household do not move), while others were identified and sent abroad for months, and sometimes years (e.g., Paul and Barnabas). We need both, but neither must be driven by ego or self-glorification. Instead, mission must be at the heart of all Christian life and must be articulated and lived as a response to the universal lordship of Jesus Christ, the leading of the Holy Spirit, and the gospel proclamation of the story of Jesus.

---

45. See Sarita Hartz, "What to Do about Short Term Missions," *A Life Overseas: The Missions Conversation*, 25 May 2015, http://www.alifeoverseas.com/what-to-do-about-short-term-missions/#.Vqd_AbF-lII.facebook. She adds seven thoughtful ideas for those considering short-term mission work.

CHAPTER 23

Acts 11:1–18

 LISTEN to the Story

¹The apostles and the believers throughout Judea heard that the Gentiles also had received the word of God. ²So when Peter went up to Jerusalem, the circumcised believers criticized him ³and said, "You went into the house of uncircumcised men and ate with them."

⁴Starting from the beginning, Peter told them the whole story: ⁵"I was in the city of Joppa praying, and in a trance I saw a vision. I saw something like a large sheet being let down from heaven by its four corners, and it came down to where I was. ⁶I looked into it and saw four-footed animals of the earth, wild beasts, reptiles and birds. ⁷Then I heard a voice telling me, 'Get up, Peter. Kill and eat.'

⁸"I replied, 'Surely not, Lord! Nothing impure or unclean has ever entered my mouth.'

⁹"The voice spoke from heaven a second time, 'Do not call anything impure that God has made clean.' ¹⁰This happened three times, and then it was all pulled up to heaven again.

¹¹"Right then three men who had been sent to me from Caesarea stopped at the house where I was staying. ¹²The Spirit told me to have no hesitation about going with them. These six brothers also went with me, and we entered the man's house. ¹³He told us how he had seen an angel appear in his house and say, 'Send to Joppa for Simon who is called Peter. ¹⁴He will bring you a message through which you and all your household will be saved.'

¹⁵"As I began to speak, the Holy Spirit came on them as he had come on us at the beginning. ¹⁶Then I remembered what the Lord had said: 'John baptized with water, but you will be baptized with the Holy Spirit.' ¹⁷So if God gave them the same gift he gave us who believed in the Lord Jesus Christ, who was I to think that I could stand in God's way?"

¹⁸When they heard this, they had no further objections and praised

God, saying, "So then, even to Gentiles God has granted repentance that leads to life."

Listening to the Text in the Story: Genesis 12:2; 17:4; 18:8; Isaiah 2:2; 11:10; 49:6; 60:3; Ezekiel 36:23; Joel 2:28; Malachi 1:11.

EXPLAIN the Story

Again, we are not given any indication as to how long Peter stayed in Caesarea in Cornelius's home.[1] Eventually, however, he was bound to return to Jerusalem and face the inevitable questions and critique from the "circumcised believers" there—questions Peter would no doubt have asked himself if he were the one waiting and not the one returning from a gentile household. This passage is another example of Luke's repeating important events in his narrative, and the conversion of Cornelius is not only important in so far as this attests to the gospel's progress to the gentile world but also is vital in terms of how the Jewish Christian church will respond to it.[2]

This section has three discernible movements: first, the initial response from and questions raised by the "circumcised believers" in Jerusalem and Judea (Acts 11:1–3); second, Peter's summary of his vision and the events in Caesarea (11:4–17); and finally, the brief but welcoming response by those in Jerusalem to the life-giving work of God among the gentiles (11:18). Notably, this section is framed by mention of the words and direction of the Lord (Jesus), God, and the Holy Spirit (vv. 8, 9, 12) while Peter is still in Joppa, and then again the double testimony of the Holy Spirit (vv. 15, 16), the Lord (vv. 16, 17), and God (twice in v. 17) when Peter is in Caesarea.

Questions Raised in Jerusalem (11:1–3)

News that gentiles had also received the word of God and the Holy Spirit spread fast from Caesarea to Jerusalem. It is important to recognize that Jews familiar with their own Scriptures were *not* put off with the fact the gospel was proclaimed to the gentiles or that they shared in the promises of God; after all, this was something promised in the Law (e.g., Gen 12:2;

---

1. There is a considerable expansion in 11:2 of Peter's stay in Caesarea in several Western manuscripts, but the NIV follows the shorter version as preserved in the older Alexandrian manuscripts. For a discussion on this, see Metzger, *Textual Commentary*, 337.
2. Longenecker, *Acts*, 396.

17:4; 18:8), the Prophets (e.g., Isa 2:2; 11:10; 49:6; 60:3; Ezek 36:23; Joel 2:28; Mal 1:11), and the Writings (e.g., Pss 2:8; 9:11; 22:27; 57:9; 105:1). The issue that the "circumcised" believers had with Peter's encounter with the "uncircumcised" is not *that* they received the word of God from Peter but the *circumstances* of the reception. The concern they had was that Peter went into a gentile home and ate with them; the issue is one of purity. Of course, this was the identical problem Peter had himself before going to Cornelius's home (see Acts 10:10–20).[3] This is a question about food, but more importantly, it is a problem about people. The sharing of meals and the sharing of life—table fellowship and care for one another's needs—has been a distinctive marker of early Christian community (2:42–47; 4:32–35; 6:1–5). The question is whether these intimacies will be shared now with gentiles. This is a live question for the Jewish Christian community, a community that we should remember now includes "a large number of priests" (6:7) familiar with purity laws and those used to strict observance of the law. How will Peter respond to this test to the unity within the early Christian church? While it is important that Peter responds to critique, Chrysostom notes that this passage is more than another opportunity for Peter to teach. It is a divine opportunity for others to learn: "Surely it was part of the divine plan for Peter to be accused, so that they too might learn. For Peter would not have spoken without cause."[4]

Peter Explains His Vision and the Events in Caesarea (11:4–17)

Just as the Greek-speaking, Jewish Christians stirred up trouble in Jerusalem among the Jews for their broad-minded attitudes (see Acts 6:8–7:56),[5] so now the leading apostle of the early church must account for his openness, especially his "open table" actions, among the gentiles to his fellow Jewish Christians in Jerusalem. The implications for the early church, including the early Jewish-Christian relationships with other Jews in Jerusalem, are significant. This move of the Spirit could fracture the early church and lead to further persecution in Jerusalem from non-Christian Jews.

Peter responds to the criticism of the "circumcised believers"[6] in Jerusalem by "starting from the beginning" (11:4). What follows next is almost a verbatim description of his early visionary experience (10:11–16), including a

---

3. Gaventa, *Acts*, 172, points out that the same verb Luke uses to describe how the Jerusalem believers "criticize" (*diakrinō*) Peter in Acts 11:2 is what the Spirit prohibits Peter from doing ("do not hesitate [*diakrinomai*] to go with them") in Acts 10:20.
4. Chrysostom, *Homilies* 24, in *ACCA*, 142.
5. That is, Stephen, in his speech, articulates the two primary ways in which early Christian Jews did not align with their contemporaries: their attitude to the temple and to the law.
6. *hoi ek peritomēs*, referring most likely to "Jewish Christians"; the same phrase is also used earlier in Acts 10:45 (cf. Gal 2:12).

word-for-word repetition of the words spoken from heaven to Peter (cf. 10:13 with 11:7; 10:15 with 11:9). There are a few minor variations in this repeated account. First, a number of commentators note the vividness of Peter's retelling of his vision from the first-person perspective in contrast to the comparative colorlessness of the earlier third-person account (10:11–12).[7] Second, and possibly even more important, while there are references to "heaven" and "earth" in both accounts, they are accounted for differently. In chapter 10 heaven "opened" (v. 11), whereas Peter simply remarks that a large sheet was let down "from heaven" in his account to Jerusalem (11:5). In chapter 10, a sheet loaded with animals, birds, and reptiles coming from heaven is lowered "to earth" (v. 11), whereas in his retelling he saw on the sheet from heaven the "animals of the earth" (11:6)—the varied creatures of God living in the world. These are slight alterations, but when Peter notes that a voice "from heaven" spoke to him, the emphasis is shifted from the *contents* of the sheet from heaven to the *commands* coming from heaven. This is an important element since Peter is seeking to draw his interrogators' focus from the question of legal purity to the issue of divine obedience.

After relating his vision, the focus shifts to the gentiles. The threefold vision from God is followed up with three men from Caesarea arriving where Peter is staying in Joppa (11:11). While the focus has moved from a heavenly vision to earthly messengers, the divine initiative is still at work. The *Lord* (v. 8) Jesus spoke to Peter about what *God* (v. 9) declares pure, and now the *Spirit* (v. 12) tells Peter to go with the gentile messengers. Peter agrees to go with the messengers to the gentile house in Caesarea, but he adds that he did not go alone. "Six brothers"[8] who can offer their eyewitness testimony to the proceedings in Jerusalem accompany Peter (v. 12). Peter also adds the message that the angel of God spoke to Cornelius (vv. 13–14; cf. 10:5–6), directing him to send for Peter from Joppa.

Finally, Peter's testimony recounts what happened after he entered the house and began to speak to the gentiles gathered there. He does not relay anything of what *he did* (beyond arriving) or what *he said* in the house. He also says nothing about eating or purity. Instead, he tells them that "the Holy Spirit came on them as he had come on us" (11:15). In all this, it is interesting that Cornelius is never mentioned by name in any part of Peter's retelling of this entire account. Cornelius is alluded to when Peter refers to "the man's house"

---

7. E.g., Longenecker, *Acts*, 397; Bruce, *Acts*, 221.

8. Bede notes that this is an appropriate number: "Because this world was formed in six days, the works accomplished [by Peter] were demonstrated through the six brothers who fittingly accompanied the teacher when, among the words of his exhortation, he described to his hearers the exemplary work that he had accomplished" (*Commentary on the Acts* 11.12, in *ACCA*, 143).

(v. 12), but for the most part Cornelius is left out of the explanation beyond the bare minimum required to tell the story. Cornelius is merely grouped together with an undifferentiated "them." Instead, most of the episode is recounted in terms of what the Holy Spirit *did* among them and a recollection of what Jesus *said* to them about the promised Holy Spirit (cf. Acts 1:5)—a promise that he now sees being renewed among gentiles. Interestingly, Peter does not connect the outpouring of the Spirit to *his* own "ecstatic" vision (*ekstasis* in 10:10; translated as "trance" by the NIV), but with the Spirit's action and Jesus's words. As Levison notes, "The logic of Peter's actions and explanation are framed by the words of Jesus—and not by his vision."[9] The conclusion for Peter is simple. If this is what the *Holy Spirit did* for them as the Spirit did for us, and it is affirmed by what the *Lord Jesus said*, then "who was I to think that I could stand in God's way?" (v. 17). The experience of the gentile community mirrors the experience of the Jewish community and thus confirms and corroborates the work of the Holy Spirit among all the peoples of the world. Again, it is worth noting that with this statement Peter attests to the triune affirmation of the Holy Spirit, the Lord Jesus, and God for what had occurred (vv. 15–17). Just as "the Lord," "God," and "the Spirit" were involved in preparing and leading Peter to Caesarea (vv. 8–12), so also "the Holy Spirit," "the Lord/Jesus Christ," and "God" (vv. 15–17) establish the acceptance of the gentiles into the people of God.

Jerusalem Responds with Praise (11:18)

Against this evidence, the circumcised believers have no further objections and offer their enthusiastic support to what God has done. As with earlier responses in Luke and Acts to the reception of the gospel and the work of God,[10] they respond with joyful "praise" to what God has graciously given to gentiles (11:18). With this short response, the present narrative comes to its conclusion. For Luke's purposes, this is a significant episode for his narrative. If it were not, he would not have repeated at length Peter's vision and the pouring out of the Holy Spirit on the gentiles. This, however, is not the end of questions relating to Jews and gentiles coming together as one in the church, and it will require further discussion later on at the so-called "Jerusalem Council" (ch. 15). For now, these practical issues give way to praise. Further, as important as the conversion of Cornelius and his household is to the overall narrative, we are not given any further information about them. How did they relate to Christian-Jewish brothers and sisters in nearby Joppa? Were there any consequences from their fellow Romans because of their conversion? Did they

---

9. Levison, *Inspired*, 103.
10. See Luke 2:20; 5:25; 7:16; 13:13; 17:15; 18:43; 24:52–53; Acts 4:21; 8:39.

eventually travel to Jerusalem and meet with believers there? All these questions and more are left unanswered by Luke. For him their role in the narrative is over, presumably because the narrative of Acts is not a biographical account about them any more than it is a biographical account about the apostles. The narrative of Acts is the story about God and the message of the gospel of the Lord Jesus Christ being spread through the world in the power of the Holy Spirit. Now that the divine initiative has been established in the mission to the gentiles and initial questions offered by Jewish Christians have been answered, the next passage turns to the extraordinary expansion of the gospel to the north in Antioch, Syria.

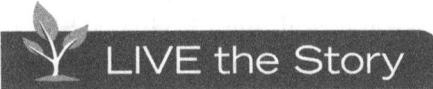

LIVE the Story

The Primary Actor Is God

An important aspect to this part of Luke's narrative is not simply the conversion of Cornelius and his household. To be sure, they are significant, but they are not the primary actors in the story. Again, as always, throughout Acts the primary Actor is the triune God, and he is gracious. God *gives* the same gift to gentiles as he does to Jews. God's free gift offered through faith in his Son cannot be earned; it can only be received and explored. God is gracious and thus also impartial and unpredictable. The work of the Spirit cannot be anticipated or contained by Jewish Christians in Jerusalem any more than the Sanhedrin in Jerusalem could control the work of God among the early Jewish church (cf. Gamaliel in Acts 5:39). This is an important reminder, especially for those who are responsible to lead the church today. To whom are leaders in the church responsible? Is it ultimately to God or to someone else? That is, in the earlier episode when Peter and John go to Samaria to investigate the reception of the gospel (8:14), they are sent almost as delegates of the church in Jerusalem to validate the work there. In the present instance, we might assume that Peter functions in the same role when he departs on his journey. But this is not the case. Peter is commissioned directly by the Lord, not by the church in Jerusalem. So the question is "partly about the patterns of authority that direct the ongoing life of the church. Are the apostles answerable to an organization called 'the church,' or to someone else?"[11] The apostles are those sent by God, the primary Actor in this drama, not those sent merely by a group of people—however much those people may have at stake in the work of God.

---

11. Alexander, *Acts*, 92.

Learning with a Critical Mind and Listening Heart

Part of "Living the Story" of Acts 11:1–18 relates to how we learn and listen as Christians. In this episode, even though Peter was the lead apostle—that is, up to this point in the narrative, he is the one who speaks on behalf of the early Christian community and leads them in decision-making and prayer—he is put under scrutiny to explain his actions in Caesarea. In the past Peter has had to explain his actions to the opponents of the church (see Acts 4:1–23; 5:17–32), but this is the first time he must explain himself to friends, to fellow believers. Good learners know that possessing a critical mind is vital, and a critical mind is one that asks thoughtful questions and seeks fulsome clarity. Further, to be transformed by a critical mind one must also learn with a listening spirit. While a critical mind is vital, a critical spirit is lethal for learning. Peter thought carefully about his heart-piercing, "ecstatic" experience of the Spirit (10:10–16) and came to learn new truth about what God was doing in the world. He then invites his fellow Jews in Jerusalem to learn and reflect critically on the work of the Holy Spirit experienced in their own hearts so that they might listen to God's new truth about the gentiles.

Jack Levison illustrates how this kind of learning and critical engagement occurs in Acts by following the thread of an old word that is given new meaning in the story of gentile inclusion, a new and necessary truth, in the people of God.[12] He notes the way the word *diakrinō*, used first in Acts 10:20, 11:12, and then in 15:9, progresses in meaning.[13] It begins with Peter being urged by the Spirit not to "hesitate" (*diakrinomenos*) to go with Cornelius's messengers. Later Peter uses the same word in his explanation to the Jewish followers of Jesus: "The Spirit told me to have no hesitation [*diakrinō*] about going with them" (11:12). Here, however, the meaning of the word means more than just go *without hesitation* but to go *without discriminating* between Jews and gentiles, between believers in Jerusalem and believers in Caesarea. Finally, the same word reoccurs in chapter 15 (v. 9), when the Christian community gathers together in Jerusalem to decide what Torah obligations will be required of non-Jewish followers of Jesus. Peter argues in the meeting that God "did not discriminate [*diakrinō*] between us [Jews] and them [gentiles]" (15:9). Peter critically engaged with his own experience of the Spirit and the Spirit's word for him not to "hestitate" or "discriminate" about his relationship to gentiles. "Peter transforms the word spoken to him in particular historical circumstances—the appearance of Cornelius's trio at his door—into a

---

12. Levison, *Inspired*, 105–6.
13. The verb also occurs in Acts 11:2, but Levison does not comment on this text.

theological agenda . . . .for the entire church of every age."[14] As we continue to move forward with this agenda, we must listen to the experience of the Spirit in our hearts *and* be open to learn new truth and comprehend it with critical minds. The day of Pentecost in Jerusalem and the gentile Pentecost in Caesarea model for us today the way to straddle *both* ecstatic experience *and* critical engagement.

---

14. Levison, *Inspired*, 106.

CHAPTER 24

Acts 11:19-30

 LISTEN to the Story

¹⁹Now those who had been scattered by the persecution that broke out when Stephen was killed traveled as far as Phoenicia, Cyprus and Antioch, spreading the word only among Jews. ²⁰Some of them, however, men from Cyprus and Cyrene, went to Antioch and began to speak to Greeks also, telling them the good news about the Lord Jesus. ²¹The Lord's hand was with them, and a great number of people believed and turned to the Lord.

²²News of this reached the church in Jerusalem, and they sent Barnabas to Antioch. ²³When he arrived and saw what the grace of God had done, he was glad and encouraged them all to remain true to the Lord with all their hearts. ²⁴He was a good man, full of the Holy Spirit and faith, and a great number of people were brought to the Lord.

²⁵Then Barnabas went to Tarsus to look for Saul, ²⁶and when he found him, he brought him to Antioch. So for a whole year Barnabas and Saul met with the church and taught great numbers of people. The disciples were called Christians first at Antioch.

²⁷During this time some prophets came down from Jerusalem to Antioch. ²⁸One of them, named Agabus, stood up and through the Spirit predicted that a severe famine would spread over the entire Roman world. (This happened during the reign of Claudius.) ²⁹The disciples, as each one was able, decided to provide help for the brothers and sisters living in Judea. ³⁰This they did, sending their gift to the elders by Barnabas and Saul.

Listening to the Text in the Story: Exodus 9:3; Joshua 4:24; Ezra 7:6; 1 Corinthians 12:28–29; Ephesians 4:11–12; 1 Peter 4:16.

EXPLAIN the Story

It is not always easy for contemporary readers to hear and make connections in a long story like Acts, especially if they are used to reading and thinking about the documents in the Bible in terms of chapter and verse. Nonetheless, it is important to remember that Luke never wrote chapters and verses. In order to tie the narrative together, like any good writer tries to do, he links themes, ideas, and characters together. At this point in Acts, with the gospel spreading beyond Judea into gentile territory in Syrian Antioch, the story picks up the great promise that Jesus's disciples would be his witnesses "to the ends of the earth" (Acts 1:8). The proclamation of the gospel to the gentiles is a central theme in Acts. When the mission to the gentiles launches in full force, it is a significant moment in the story of Acts. All along the way there have been preparatory hints of the mission to the gentiles. For example, we see this theme on the day of Pentecost with the comment about the gathering of the nations (2:5–12). It is in view in Peter's sermon when he mentions the anticipated blessing for "all peoples on earth" (3:25). It occurs again in the narrative of Saul's conversion when he is identified as God's "chosen instrument" to carry Jesus's name to the gentiles (9:15). Of course, the climactic moment of the gospel being declared to gentiles is when Peter comes to Cornelius's household and the Spirit descends on those gathered there as a "gentile Pentecost" (10:1–11:18). Beyond this grand thematic promise, the mention of "those who had been scattered by the persecution that broke out when Stephen was killed" (11:19) creates a verbal link with the pivotal episode at the beginning of the second panel (6:8–8:3). There is also here a reintroduction of characters we have met before: Barnabas (4:36; 9:27) and Saul (7:58; 8:1, 3; 9:1–30). In all these ways, Luke has prepared the reader for this phase of the story and signals that this is a new development with the introduction of a new name for followers of Jesus—"Christians"—in his account of the first gentile church of Antioch (11:26).

The account of this first gentile church in Acts develops in four steps. First, there is a description of how the Lord Jesus came to be proclaimed to the "Greeks" (11:19–21). Second, news of this community soon returned to the mother church in Jerusalem, whose leaders were keen to investigate what was occurring. So Barnabas is sent north (11:22–24). Third, Barnabas, apparently desiring assistance in equipping the Christians in Antioch, makes a journey farther north to retrieve Saul from Tarsus (11:25–26). Fourth and finally, as if to strengthen the connection between Jewish and gentile communities, prophets come from Jerusalem. While with these new Christians, one of the visiting prophets, Agabus, predicts an imminent famine in Judea.

The disciples in Antioch respond by collecting money from individuals in this new Christian community and sending relief to Jerusalem by way of Barnabas and Saul (11:27–30). Almost as if to bracket this episode is the word "hand." The "hand" (11:21) of the Lord was with the evangelists who brought the gospel to Antioch, and the church in Antioch returned the blessing by caring for their brothers and sisters by sending aid by the "hands" of Barnabas and Saul (11:30).[1] In this small way the Jewish and gentile "hands" of the church are united.

The Lord Jesus Is Proclaimed to Greeks (11:19–21)

The mention of those "scattered" (*diaspeirō*, v. 19) by the persecution that occurred after Stephen's martyrdom immediately ties this episode to the earlier narrative of persecution and scattering that occurred in Jerusalem (8:1). Amidst this turmoil sometime in the 40s of the first-century AD, some Jewish believers—especially Greek-speaking Jewish believers—fled north. Some went to Phoenicia, an area along the coast near Mount Carmel. Others traveled to Cyprus, an island nestled in the northeastern part of the Mediterranean Sea. Still others went to Antioch, the seat of Roman administration in the Roman province of Syria.

Syrian Antioch[2] was an important city in the empire, and before Roman domination it had been a primary city of Greek administration and culture since the time of Alexander the Great (ca. 333 BC). So important was Antioch by the first century that Josephus referred to it as the "third" city of the empire after Rome and Alexandria (*J.W.* 3.29). Antioch's population was large,[3] wealthy, and comprised of a diverse mix of cultures and peoples, including a large concentration of Jews numbering in the thousands (Josephus, *J.W.* 7.43). Of note is that the only named gentile proselyte to Judaism in all of Acts is Nicolas, who also happened to be a native of Antioch (Acts 6:5). When Jewish believers arrive in Antioch, they initially speak about Jesus only to fellow Jews. However, Jewish believers from the islands of Cyprus and Cyrene—the latter, an important city in North Africa[4]—are even bolder; they begin to tell "Greeks" about the Lord Jesus. In this case, "Greeks" refers to those who are

---

1. The NIV leaves the word "hand" (*cheiros*) untranslated. See ESV.
2. Syrian Antioch was located about twenty-five kilometers (15 miles) inland from the northeastern coast of the Mediterranean Sea on the Orontes River. Seleucus I (312–281 BC), one of the successors to Alexander the Great, founded it as his capital. It was one of *sixteen* cities similarly named in honor of his father Antiochus. Pisidian Antioch is another (Acts 13:14).
3. About 250,000–500,000 in the first century (cf. Strabo, *Geography* 16.2.5).
4. Cyrene Jews are mentioned several times in the NT, including Simon of Cyrene, who carried Jesus's cross (Matt 27:32; Mark 15:21; Luke 23:26); those who were present on the day of Pentecost in Jerusalem (Acts 2:10); and Cyrene Jews who worshiped in Jerusalem in their own Greek-speaking synagogue (6:9).

non-Jews, or "gentiles." Likely, the Greeks they spoke with would have been those present in Jewish synagogues as proselytes or God-fearers. This would set the stage for the later episode when a council in Jerusalem is called in order to discuss how the Jewish and gentile followers of Christ should relate to one another (15:1–35).

The boldness of the Cyprian and Cyrene Jewish believers should not be overlooked. Of course, the Twelve did proclaim Jesus boldly in Jerusalem, and Stephen, Philip, and Barnabas were not timid in their witness to Jesus. Nonetheless, it required heaven opening and the Lord speaking directly to Peter before he could be persuaded to share the good news about Jesus with gentiles. Yet these Cyprian and Cyrene believers do so without any specific divine imperative. This required a significant level of trust and confidence on their part. As such, "the Lord's hand" was with these bold disciples, and a great number of gentiles believed and turned to the Lord (11:21). By way of note, the "hand of the Lord" or "the Lord's hand" is used frequently in the OT to refer to the power and presence of Yahweh.[5] Here (Acts 11:20), it is clearly used to refer to the "Lord Jesus." There is a cluster of references to the "Lord" at the opening of this passage (vv. 20, 21 [2x], 23, 24). This might be coincidental, but the impression it gives, especially just after Jesus has been declared "Lord of all" in Cornelius's household (10:36), is significant. For Jews, "the Lord" is Yahweh; for the Greeks of Antioch, "the Lord" may have referred to the mighty gods Apollo and Artemis just as much as to "Lord" Caesar. Now, Jewish believers tell Greeks in Antioch that Jesus is "the Lord." Again, this is a testimony to the early and high view of Jesus by Jewish *and* Greek believers. That is, both Jews who had been strict monotheists and Greeks who acknowledged many gods and lords (cf. 1 Cor 8:5) now proclaim and worship the *Lord* Jesus.[6] The response to this message in mid first-century Antioch is a significant development in the story of Christianity.

Barnabas Sent to Investigate (11:22–24)

News about the spread of the gospel among gentiles in Antioch, even by ancient standards, would not have taken long to reach the ears of believers in Jerusalem. There were frequent pilgrims from various parts of the empire to Jerusalem, including from the large number of Jews who lived in Antioch. When the "word" of the gospel spread to Samaria, the Jerusalem church sent

---

5. E.g., Exod 9:3; Josh 4:24; 2 Kgs 3:15; Ezra 7:6; Luke 1:66.
6. Gaventa, *Acts*, 179, helpfully points out that the phrase "turned to the Lord" is an expression more often associated with gentile conversion than with Jewish conversion. The gentiles are called to repent of their idolatry and acknowledge that Jesus is the Lord; Jews are called to repent and acknowledge that Jesus is the Messiah.

Peter and John to verify the expansion (8:14). Now, when "the news" (lit., "the word," *logos*) reaches Jerusalem, they again send a trusted representative, Barnabas, to investigate what is occurring in Antioch (11:22). Barnabas has already appeared twice in Acts (4:36–37; 9:27). He is a person who has a track record of being reliable, discerning, and a natural bridge-builder between communities. In this case, since he was a prominent Levite from Cyprus (4:36), he may even have been known by some of the other Jews from Cyprus who were preaching in Antioch.

Upon his arrival, Barnabas could see the grace of God in operation in Antioch (11:23). Luke does not elaborate on what visible evidence this entailed. He may have witnessed marks of the Spirit—"signs and wonders," such as miracles and speaking in tongues. We can surmise that it would also include the marks of fellowship that were expressed whenever believers gathered elsewhere, including devotion to apostolic teaching, sharing meals together, praying, and caring for one another. That Jews and gentiles would do so together is indeed an unexpected gift—a "grace" from God. Again, as elsewhere in Luke's writings, the response in Antioch to God's grace in Jesus is *joy* (cf. Luke 1:14; 2:10; 24:52; Acts 8:8). Barnabas, that "son of encouragement" and Spirit-filled man, encourages the new believers in their faith. Luke, almost repeating verbatim what he just noted (11:21), mentions that a great number of people were brought to the Lord (11:24).

Barnabas Recruits Saul (11:25–27)

Good storytellers often introduce key actors through brief cameos before their characters take center stage. Luke has offered tantalizing glimpses of Saul of Tarsus on several prior occasions. He is introduced to the narrative when the crowd in Jerusalem stoned Stephen (7:58). He then is briefly reintroduced as a persecutor of the church in Jerusalem (8:1) before his dramatic conversion story on the way to Damascus (9:1–30). Important to this present section is the fact that Barnabas and Saul were well acquainted with each other. In fact, Barnabas is the one who initially introduced Saul to the apostles in Jerusalem (9:27). The last note we hear about Saul is that he was sent to his hometown of Tarsus (9:30), a city of Cilicia in the southeastern corner of the Roman province of Asia (modern Turkey). Someone who was designated as the Lord's "chosen instrument to proclaim [Jesus's] name to the Gentiles" (9:15) is bound to reappear now that the mission to the gentiles is under way. Furthermore, as a Greek-speaking Jew, a trained theologian (under Gamaliel; cf. 22:3), and someone already familiar with missionary preaching in a Greek cultural context, Saul would be a valuable colleague for Barnabas in his work in Antioch. As is so often the case in Acts, we are not given any time frame for how long Saul resided in Tarsus before being recalled by Barnabas. Nonetheless, Barnabas makes the nearly three-hundred-kilometer journey from Antioch to Tarsus, locates Saul, and then returns to Antioch (11:25–26a).[7] For once, Luke does indicate a measure of time. He notes that Barnabas and Saul gathered together with the Antioch church and taught the great crowd for "a whole year" (11:26). Their meeting with the church and their instruction to the great crowds may reflect two distinct activities by Barnabas and Saul.[8] With the church they engaged in teaching that equipped new believers; with the great crowds they engaged in evangelistic outreach.

Luke adds an important remark about those who gathered to be instructed about the Lord Jesus in Antioch. He notes that "the disciples were called Christians first in Antioch" (11:26). The term "Christian" is one of the most common names used today to indicate those who follow Jesus. Within the NT, however, the name "Christian" occurs only two other times (Acts 26:28 and 1 Pet 4:16). The origin of the name is uncertain, but most scholars suggest that it is based on a Latin word referring to "adherents to Christ." It was common in the first century to add the Latin suffix-*ianus* (plural:-*iani*) to the name of leaders (in English this comes out as, e.g., Herodians [Matt 22:16; Mark 3:6; 12:13] or Caesarians [Epictetus, *Discourses* 1.19.19]) in reference to their followers. We are not told *who* called the disciples in Antioch "Christians." Was it a self-designation by the church in Antioch? Was it something the Jewish disciples used to refer to gentile believers? Or did those outside the church (non-believing Jews or gentiles) coin it? The latter seems to be the most likely since the church already had other names to refer to itself.[9] It is improbable that non-believing Jews would give implicit credence that Jesus was *Christos*, the Messiah, by referring to his disciples as "Christians." Our best guess, then, is that non-believing gentiles referred to disciples of Jesus as Christians. In a large city like Antioch, with its numerous religions and cults, it would be natural to refer to those who often spoke about *Christos* as *Christianoi*, Christ's followers. Whatever the nature of its origin, at this point in Luke's narrative the mention of a new name, especially one that is associated with the first gentile church, serves to distinguish the disciples of Christ—Jew and gentile—from paganism and Judaism. While the name "Christian" is not popular in the NT, by the early second century it was used as a test. Pliny the Younger wrote a letter to Emperor Trajan (ca. AD 112),

---

7. Ramsay, *St. Paul*, 53, suggests that this journey from Antioch to Tarsus occurred in early AD 43.

8. See Schnabel, *Acts*, 523–24.

9. E.g., followers of Jesus referred to themselves as "disciples," "believers," "servants of Jesus Christ," "the Way."

describing how those accused of believing in Jesus Christ were asked whether or not they were "Christians" (*Letters* 10.96–97). Those who confessed that they were Christians were then executed, unless they were Roman citizens; as Roman citizens they were entitled first to a trial in Rome. In due course, the name "Christian" soon became a popular designation for followers of Jesus—and a dangerous one too.[10]

Christians in Antioch Send Relief to Jerusalem (11:27–30)

This last paragraph completes the travel loop made in this section from and to Jerusalem (via Phoenicia-Cyprus-Antioch-Tarsus-Antioch). This paragraph also adds that Barnabas was not the only envoy sent from the church in Jerusalem to Antioch. At some later point, "prophets" also came down. Prophets, including those who foretold the future and those regarded as false prophets, were not only recognized among first-century Jews (e.g., Josephus, *J. W.* 1.78–80; 2.112–13; 6.283–87, 300–309), but also by early Christians (e.g., Acts 13:1; 15:32; 1 Cor 11:4; 12:28–29; 14:29–37; Eph 4:11). One of these itinerant, Jewish-Christian prophets is Agabus,[11] whose Hebrew name means "grasshopper."[12] Agabus predicted that a severe famine—something often associated, ironically, with grasshoppers—would occur over the entire Roman world during the reign of Claudius, who ruled from AD 41–54. While local famines, including ones in Judea, are known from this time (ca. AD 47),[13] the reference to "the entire Roman world" might also reflect hyperbole on Luke's part. Nonetheless, these various famines could be linked to the same failed harvest in the Roman Empire's breadbasket, Egypt, which impacted different areas at various times. Whatever the actual circumstances of this famine, Agabus's prophecy would have given the young Syrian congregation time to collect an offering of silver or gold coin. This would likely occur at their regular gathering for worship and was determined not by a set amount but according to each person's ability—a practice that Saul would continue when he encouraged the collection from other gentile churches later in his ministry (see 1 Cor 16:1–2; 2 Cor 9:7). When the foretold famine in Judea arrived, the collected coin was entrusted to Barnabas and Saul, who delivered the gift to the Jerusalem elders. The elders would then use the money to purchase food and distribute it to believers living in Judea.

---

10. See Michael J. Wilkins, "Christian," *ABD* 1:925–26; cf. BDAG 1090.
11. Agabus will appear again later in Acts 21:10.
12. Williams, "Palestinian Jewish Personal Names," 84.
13. Helena, queen of Adiabene and a convert to Judaism, sent aid to Jerusalem when a famine struck the city during the reign of Claudius ca. AD 30 (Josephus, *Ant.* 20.51–53, 101). Other ancient historians mention various famines during the reign of Claudius; see Suetonius, *Claud.* 18.2; Tacitus, *Ann.* 12.43; Dio Cassius, *Roman History* 60.11.

The gift that is offered from gentile Christians in Syria to Jewish believers in Judea is significant. It is not merely an offer of assistance but forges bonds of affection and recognizes God's grace with human gratitude. As the gentiles share in "the grace of God" (Acts 11:23), their gift to their new family—the "brothers and sisters" (*adelphoi*) in Judea (v. 29)—in Christ is an extension of that grace. They do not "owe" the Judean church anything. Rather, together they share in God's gift to them all, and thus they give to others in ways reflective of that grace. Divine giving and human giving are intimately connected.[14]

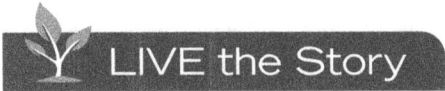

LIVE the Story

Leaving the Nest
In terms of the narrative, it is important for Luke first to tell about the conversion of the first gentile, Cornelius (and his household). His description of this is deliberate and extensive. Now the pace quickens, and another expression of the "gentile Pentecost" occurs in Syrian Antioch. Although this outreach did not require a direct revelation by way of a vision or dream as it did for Peter and Cornelius, it is still not orchestrated or overseen by the apostles or the mother church in Jerusalem. Rather, the believers who had been scattered by persecution shared "gospel gossip" wherever they went.

Persecution is never easy to experience, and it can be devastating to Christian communities.[15] In certain instances, however, its unintended consequences are gracious and good. We even witness examples of this in the working of creation. Every year our family watches purple martin birds migrate back to Saskatchewan and take up residence in the martin house we built for them in our back garden. Martins are acrobatic and elegant birds, and apart from nesting with their young, they spend most of their time in the air. By midsummer the mother birds start nudging their young out of the house and onto the ledge as they encourage them to fly on their own. The baby birds are very reluctant to leave their comfy home, let alone leap off the edge. Nonetheless, the mothers guide them out of the house and gently bump them to the edge. Occasionally, some of the baby birds grip tightly to the railing

---

14. This coincides with Paul's own connections between gift and grace. See John M. G. Barclay, *Paul and the Gift* (Grand Rapids: Eerdmans, 2015).

15. E.g., the persecution of Japanese Christians in the sixteenth and seventeenth centuries under the Tokugawa shogunate decimated the church there. More recently, the plight of Syrian Christians comes to mind. In the 1920s, Christians were believed to have constituted about 30 percent of the population. By 2015, due to the war and overt persecution, Syrian Christians made up only 10 percent of the population. See the BBC report, "Syria's Beleaguered Christians," BBC.com, 25 February 2015, http://www.bbc.com/news/world-middle-east-22270455.

and refuse to leap off and spread their wings to fly. I don't blame them! It is a long drop to the ground, and often there is a hungry cat waiting at the bottom for them. The mother birds will stand next to them on the ledge and leap off—over and over again—until the birds follow their example. Sometimes, however, there is a baby bird that won't budge. Instead, they grip the railing tightly with their claws. What happens next seems almost cruel, but it is a kind cruelness: the mother birds will peck at their feet until the baby birds can no longer bear the pain and they jump. I have never (yet) seen a baby bird hit the ground. Instead, they spread their wings and soar.

Persecution of Christians is indeed cruel. Still, in Acts 11 we see that the persecution also led believers to leave the Jerusalem "nest." From here, the gospel soared at great speed to various parts of the empire. Sometimes, for us what initially seems like an uncomfortable situation is just the nudge we need to move out of our complacency. Difficulty and persecution may be the nudge we need to take new steps. As we leave the comfortable surroundings of our home "nests," this passage nudges us to look for gospel opportunities and grace moments. When the mother church in Jerusalem sent Barnabas to Antioch to observe what was happening there, he "saw what the grace of God had done" and rejoiced (v. 23). Persecution was not comfortable, but it pushed the fledgling church to move and reach out.

The Fruit of Teaching and Prophecy

When the good news pushed out beyond the mother church, the new believers did what Christians do. They were open to apostolic teaching—a whole year's worth of it (v. 26)—and the ministry of prophets who spoke words inspired through the Spirit (v. 27). Later we will be told that there were "prophets and teachers" in Antioch (13:1), among whom Barnabas and Saul are numbered, and that this group of believers were receptive to the Spirit (13:2–4). The Antioch Christians were teachable and open to the Spirit's guidance. The words of teachers and prophets appear to be complementary. Both ministries are Christ's gifts to the church and enable healthy growth and equipping (cf. Eph 4:11–12). There is a tendency to try and prioritize one of these ministries over the other in church communities. Some communities gravitate to "solid teaching." This seems to entail good expository content related in a measured way by scholars who have been trained at the right schools. Other communities incline to Spirit-led "prophetic" ministry. This seems to involve a more spontaneous and edgy form of communication that is far from the curriculum and more directive in character. Of course, this may be a caricature, but my point is there is a tendency to drive a wedge between these ministries rather than to see them as mutually edifying. Good Christian teaching should be inspired, creative, and engaging; good Christian prophecy should be measured, informed, and reliable. In terms of direction, teaching often looks to the past so that, just like Theophilus, we might "know the certainty of the things [we] have been taught" (Luke 1:4). Christian teachers look to history to provide the church with rootage and context. Christian prophets listen to the Spirit to provide the church with direction and encouragement. Both ministries are necessary so that we might have confidence that we are in alignment with what Jesus taught and passed along to his first apostles and are traveling along a route that is marked by the Spirit.

The fruit of the combined ministry of prophets and teachers is outward facing and generous. The disciples in Antioch had a year to be informed about the arc and priorities of Jesus's teaching. When a Spirit-inspired prophet told the church in Antioch that there would be a famine throughout the Roman world, their first instinct was not to stockpile resources for their own needs. It is important to remember the predicted famine was spread across their entire world. There would be poor in Jerusalem *and* in Antioch. Yet the Antioch Christians recognized the connective tissue binding them to believers in Jerusalem. Jerusalem had sent them teachers (Barnabas, v. 22) and prophets (Agabus, vv. 27–28) who fed and nourished them in the faith. Now, when faced with famine, the disciples in Antioch chose freely and generously to help their brothers and sisters in Jerusalem. It is noteworthy that the prophet Agabus, who informed them of the famine, did not mention any encouragement or admonition to provide for the needs of others. So why would the Antiocheans respond like they did? They did so because they were well instructed about the shape and character of their faith by their teachers. In fact, it is a thematic emphasis of Luke's that the gospel is "good news to the *poor*" (Luke 4:18; 7:22; cf. 1:53). While this group includes anyone who is marginalized by society regardless of wealth, there is a special focus of concern for those who are economically deprived and physically in need (see 14:13; cf. 16:19–31). It should be no surprise then that when famine is predicted, the Antiochean Christians, rooted in and informed by the priorities of Jesus, instinctively and without explicit direction share what they have for those who shared the gospel with them.

Gratitude and generosity are the fruit of teaching and prophecy. This should be instructive for us today. Not only that teaching and prophecy are complementary ministries but that their fruit is expansive and gracious. Fruit is not intended to be hoarded or to sit long-term on the shelf. It is to be shared and eaten. The knowledge and teaching of the past that is communicated to us by the church in Antioch, where disciples were first called Christians, should fire and inspire the hearts and actions of Christians today. Grace and gifts received fuel grace and gifts passed along to others.

CHAPTER 25

Acts 12:1–24

 LISTEN to the Story

¹It was about this time that King Herod arrested some who belonged to the church, intending to persecute them. ²He had James, the brother of John, put to death with the sword. ³When he saw that this met with approval among the Jews, he proceeded to seize Peter also. This happened during the Festival of Unleavened Bread. ⁴After arresting him, he put him in prison, handing him over to be guarded by four squads of four soldiers each. Herod intended to bring him out for public trial after the Passover. ⁵So Peter was kept in prison, but the church was earnestly praying to God for him.

⁶The night before Herod was to bring him to trial, Peter was sleeping between two soldiers, bound with two chains, and sentries stood guard at the entrance. ⁷Suddenly an angel of the Lord appeared and a light shone in the cell. He struck Peter on the side and woke him up. "Quick, get up!" he said, and the chains fell off Peter's wrists.

⁸Then the angel said to him, "Put on your clothes and sandals." And Peter did so. "Wrap your cloak around you and follow me," the angel told him. ⁹Peter followed him out of the prison, but he had no idea that what the angel was doing was really happening; he thought he was seeing a vision. ¹⁰They passed the first and second guards and came to the iron gate leading to the city. It opened for them by itself, and they went through it. When they had walked the length of one street, suddenly the angel left him.

¹¹Then Peter came to himself and said, "Now I know without a doubt that the Lord has sent his angel and rescued me from Herod's clutches and from everything the Jewish people were hoping would happen."

¹²When this had dawned on him, he went to the house of Mary the mother of John, also called Mark, where many people had gathered and were praying. ¹³Peter knocked at the outer entrance, and a servant named Rhoda came to answer the door. ¹⁴When she recognized Peter's voice, she was so overjoyed she ran back without opening it and exclaimed, "Peter is at the door!"

[15]"You're out of your mind," they told her. When she kept insisting that it was so, they said, "It must be his angel."

[16]But Peter kept on knocking, and when they opened the door and saw him, they were astonished. [17]Peter motioned with his hand for them to be quiet and described how the Lord had brought him out of prison. "Tell James and the other brothers and sisters about this," he said, and then he left for another place.

[18]In the morning, there was no small commotion among the soldiers as to what had become of Peter. [19]After Herod had a thorough search made for him and did not find him, he cross-examined the guards and ordered that they be executed.

Then Herod went from Judea to Caesarea and stayed there. [20]He had been quarreling with the people of Tyre and Sidon; they now joined together and sought an audience with him. After securing the support of Blastus, a trusted personal servant of the king, they asked for peace, because they depended on the king's country for their food supply.

[21]On the appointed day Herod, wearing his royal robes, sat on his throne and delivered a public address to the people. [22]They shouted, "This is the voice of a god, not of a man." [23]Immediately, because Herod did not give praise to God, an angel of the Lord struck him down, and he was eaten by worms and died.

[24]But the word of God continued to spread and flourish.

Listening to the Text in the Story: Exodus 3:8; 18:4; Ezekiel 28:1–10; Luke 22:1, 7, 56; 24:11.

EXPLAIN the Story

The previous episode ended with the story returning to Jerusalem. This prepares the way for a shift of focus from the gentile mission back to the situation in Jerusalem. In this section we are given information about a renewed persecution of the church in Jerusalem instigated by King Herod—especially targeting the leadership—along with a theological explanation of Herod's demise. Herod knew enough about the church to suppress it by force. This marks the first trouble since Jesus's arrest that the disciples have with *secular* authorities. After the shift in Acts toward a full-swing gentile mission, this material offers a brief interlude in the narrative. Still, the contextual question remains: Why are these details included here? For Luke, this interlude seems to function in two ways. First, it brings the narrative of the church in Jerusalem to a close, sounding two notes in this regard.[1] It offers an encouraging note about the prayerfulness, piety, and the continued blessing of God on the Jerusalem church. The other note it signals is a change in leadership. From this point (v. 17) James takes the lead in Jerusalem, and Peter leaves the city (even though he will return for the council; ch. 15). Second, the interlude functions to perpetuate the theme of the triumphant spread of the gospel. Nothing can hinder its expansion: not the martyrdom of leaders (v. 2), nor imprisonment (v. 4), nor prideful power (vv. 22–23).

This transitional interlude is presented in four movements. First, it describes the outbreak of persecution by Herod Agrippa in which James, the brother of John, is arrested and executed, followed by Peter's arrest and imprisonment (12:1–5). Second, Luke describes, at considerable length, Peter's miraculous escape from prison with the aid of an angel (vv. 6–11). Third, it recounts the believer's response to Peter's deliverance (vv. 12–19a). Fourth, the episode concludes with the account of Herod's death (vv. 19b–23). With this, the third panel in Acts draws to a close by way of Luke's customary summary note (v. 24; cf. 6:7; 9:31; 16:5; 19:20).

Herod Agrippa Persecutes the Jerusalem Church (12:1–5)

The "King Herod" referred to at the beginning of this narrative is Agrippa I, the grandson of Herod I ("the Great"). Agrippa was sent with his mother to Rome when he was a child. In Rome he was raised in the company of Claudius—just mentioned a few sentences earlier (Acts 11:28)—and later became a close friend of Gaius (i.e., "Caligula"). Those connections would serve him well when Gaius and Claudius, in succession, became Roman emperors. After Gaius's accession in AD 37, he granted Agrippa the northern lands of Philip the tetrarch along with the title of king. After Gaius's assassination, Agrippa played a significant role in preventing a bloody civil war and in securing the ascendance of Claudius. For this service, Emperor Claudius granted Agrippa all the lands of his grandfather Herod along with the rank of consul. All told, Agrippa had good reason to be confident of his new position as king and consul. From what Josephus relates about him, he was careful in the observance of Jewish laws and was considered to be an equitable and generous ruler (*Ant.* 19.331).

Agrippa's kindness did not, however, extend to those who belonged to the church. According to Luke, he had one of the Twelve, James, the brother of

---

1. Of course, the narrative returns to Jerusalem later for the council (ch. 15), but the interest there is for the broader gentile church outside of Jerusalem.

John, executed (Acts 12:2). A couple of items are noteworthy. First, Agrippa targeted the leaders. This implies that they were well known in Jerusalem. Second, we are told that this was "met with approval among the Jews" (v. 3). This is an uncomfortable record in the narrative because it reflects a growing tension that existed between the majority who rejected Jesus as the Messiah and the minority who identified with Jesus as the Messiah. Already we know how this is reflected in the execution of Jesus in the Gospel of Luke, and it is also reflected in the narrative in Acts in the martyrdom of Stephen (ch. 7) and in the persecution led by Saul (8:1–3; 9:1–2). From what we know about despots in the ancient *and* the modern world, selective engagement in persecution of minorities as a way of pleasing the masses is not uncommon. What is odd is that those who approved of the persecution are referred to as "the Jews" when those who were being persecuted are also Jewish. Dunn, noting this tension, points out that "on the one hand, the new sect was in full continuity with Israel's hope and heritage. But on the other, there was a growing distinction between this movement and those with a more obvious claim to that heritage in national and religious terms."[2] This rupture will become more pronounced as the gentile mission widens and there is an influx of non-Jewish followers of Jesus.

The broad approval of Herod's execution of James instigates another attack against the leadership of the early church. He follows up by arresting Peter during the Festival of Unleavened Bread, the Passover. Of course, this is the same feast during which Jesus was arrested and executed (Luke 22:1, 7). Unlike Jesus, however, Peter's trial is delayed until after the Passover. Instead, he is imprisoned, likely in the Antonia Fortress adjoining the temple,[3] and guarded by sixteen soldiers (Acts 12:4). By pointing out the significant number of soldiers guarding Peter, Luke emphasizes the impossibility of his escape.[4] Another detail, "the church was earnestly praying to God for him" (v. 5), emphasizes the instinctive reflex of the church. They desired and expected God to receive and respond to their prayers as they have experienced numerous times before (Acts 1:24–25; 2:42; 4:24–30; 6:6; 8:15; 9:11; 10:2, 9). Of course, this expectancy also sets up a humorous incident that occurs at the house of Mary where they were gathered to pray (12:12–16).

Peter's Miraculous Escape from Prison (12:6–11)
Peter's miraculous escape from prison carries a striking quality to it. The timing (on the eve of his trial), the context (under heavy guard), and the means of his deliverance (an angel) all contribute to heighten the drama. Peter was

---

2. Dunn, *Acts*, 162.
3. Another option would be Herod Agrippa's palace near the Jaffa Gate.
4. The four squads correspond to the four watches of the night; see Barrett, *Acts*, 1:577.

delivered from jail in the night by an angel once before (5:19), but this time the details are spelled out at length. There is the quality of personal reminiscence to it all. Eyewitness features occur in the description: "A light shone in the cell" (12:7), the angel "struck Peter on the side" (v. 7), "the chains fell off Peter's wrists" (v. 7), the angel speaks to Peter directly (vv. 7, 8), they passed two rings of guards, and when they arrived at the iron gate to the city it "opened for them by itself" (v. 10). Despite all these specific details, the narrative adds that Peter "had no idea that what the angel was doing was really happening; he thought he was seeing a vision" (v. 9). Luke has no doubt that it was real, and soon Peter realizes this too (v. 11).

After Peter emerges from prison and stands alone and free in a Jerusalem street, he reflects on what has just occurred. First, he confesses that this is the Lord's doing (v. 11). The ascended Lord has dispatched an angel to deliver Peter again from prison. Interestingly, the wording of the Passover deliverance of Peter from the hands of the tyrant, Herod Agrippa, echoes that of *the* exodus Passover deliverance (cf. Exod 3:8; 18:4).[5] Second, Peter's escape foils "everything the Jewish people were hoping would happen" (v. 11). Again, the note is struck about the tension that exists between the early Jewish Christians and the non-Christian Jewish populace in Jerusalem (cf. v. 3). The more significant point that is made within the context of this narrative is that nothing can thwart the gospel and the Lord's plans for Peter.

The Believer's Response to Peter's Deliverance (12:12–19a)

A high level of personal detail continues in the narrative after Peter's deliverance from prison. The first detail is that Peter goes to the house of Mary, who is likely a widow of considerable means. She owned her own home, large enough to have an outer gate, and she had servants. In terms of the broader narrative in Acts, Luke notes that Mary is the mother of John Mark.[6] Again, as he has done several times before for other figures, Luke foreshadows John Mark's role by briefly mentioning him before reintroducing him in a more significant role later in the narrative (Acts 12:25; 13:5, 13; 15:36–39).[7] Luke mentions his common Hebrew name, John (Hebrew *Yehohanan/Yohanan*), and his second Latin name, Mark (Latin *Marcus*). The circumstances of his acquiring his second name are not provided, but it may relate to his travels among gentiles where they would have found the common Latin name easier to deal with than the unfamiliar Hebrew Yehohanan.[8]

---

5. Gaventa, *Acts*, 184–85; Keener, *Acts*, 2:1891–92.
6. John Mark is also considered to be the cousin of Barnabas (see Col 4:10).
7. Cf. Barnabas in 4:36 and later in 9:27 and 11:22–30; Saul in 7:58–8:1 and later in 9:1–30.
8. Williams, "Personal Names," in Bauckham, *Palestinian Setting*, 105.

The next detail provided in the aftermath of Peter's escape occurs at the outer gate. It is a humorous moment. Peter knocks at the gate, and a servant girl named Rhoda ("rose") arrives in response to the summons. Although it is assumed the young woman is Jewish, this may not be the case. Her name is a common slave name in the Greco-Roman world; Jews, however, did not take up this name until much later in the fifth century.[9] Whatever else, it is another interesting encounter that Peter has with a servant girl (*paidiskē*). The last time Luke records Peter's action with a servant girl is on the night he denied knowing Jesus (Luke 22:57). In that instance, fear was the dominant feeling of the night. On this occasion, joy is the dominant tone. Rhoda, overjoyed with the sound of Peter's voice, leaves him standing outside the gate and runs back to tell the others, who are inside praying for Peter's deliverance (Acts 12:14). When the others hear the breathless announcement of Rhoda, they dismiss her testimony and insist, "It must be his angel" (v. 15). Again, the testimony of a woman is initially dismissed only to be proven accurate (cf. Luke 24:11).

Peter continues knocking until they open the gate to see for themselves the escapee standing before them (Acts 12:16). A joyful din ensues. Peter motions for them to be quiet so that he can describe his rescue (v. 17). Although the narrative relates that an angel guided him out of prison, Peter asserts in language echoing the exodus that "the Lord had *brought him out*" (cf. Exod 3:8; 18:4). Peter then adds that they must tell "James and the other brothers and sisters about this" (Acts 12:17). Why Peter explicitly requests that they tell "James"—in this case James, the brother of Jesus—is unclear. It may be that Luke is signaling a transition of the leadership of the Jerusalem church from Peter to James. Besides this is the simple fact that James was not present at this prayer meeting, and since he was a leader in the church he needed to be alerted.

The danger for Peter is not finished. He departed from Mary's home "for another place" (v. 17). Whether it was another Christian home in Jerusalem or another location outside the city, we are not informed. Most likely it was a location outside the city since at the time when Luke wrote there was no need to avoid mention of the place Peter stayed (for fear of reprisals). The main point is that it was not safe for him to stay at Mary's place. Meanwhile, the situation at the prison was chaotic (v. 18). The soldiers awoke to find Peter gone. After a complete search was made, the next step taken by Herod was to interrogate the guards. They are doomed. In the Greco-Roman world of the time, the inevitable fate of guards who allowed their prisoners to escape is the death penalty (cf. Act 16:27–28).[10] The Greek text simply states that the

---

9. Ibid., 111.
10. Barrett, *Acts*, 1:588, points toward the legal precedent for this in the *Codex Justinianus* 9.4.4.

guards were led away (12:19, *apachthēnai*), but the implication is that they are led away to be executed according to the custom of the day (NIV thus rightly translates the verb as "be executed").

Herod's Death (12:19b–23)

Luke, as a good historian and a good storyteller, often provides historical details for his narrative. He could have merely described Herod's relocation to his capital in Caesarea, but he sets the stage by describing first the occasion of his stay (a dispute with the people of Tyre and Sidon), then the name of his chamberlain (Blastus, v. 20), who helps resolve the disagreement, and the power dynamics of the situation (the northern coastal cities depended on food from the king). With all this outlined, Agrippa emerges to preside over a public festival in Caesarea, dressed in magnificent garments (v. 21). Josephus corroborates and expands for us the details of this scene:

> [Herod] put on a garment made wholly of silver, and of a contexture truly wonderful, and came into the theatre early in the morning; at which time the silver of his garment being illuminated by the fresh reflection of the sun's rays upon it, shone out after a surprising manner, and was so resplendent at to spread a horror over those who looked intently upon him; and presently his flatterers cried out, one from one place, and another from another (though not for his good), that he was a god; and they added, "Be thou merciful to us; for although we have hitherto reverenced thee only as a man, yet shall we henceforth own thee as superior to mortal nature." Upon this the king did neither rebuke them, nor reject their impious flattery. But, as he presently afterwards looked up, he saw an owl sitting on a certain rope over his head, and immediately understood that this bird was the messenger of ill tidings, as it had once been the messenger of good tidings to him; and fell into the deepest sorrow. A severe pain also arose in his belly, and began in a most violent manner. He therefore looked upon his friends, and said, "I whom you call a god, am commanded presently to depart this life; while Providence thus reproves the lying words you just now said to me; and I, who was by you called immortal, am immediately to be hurried away by death. But I am bound to accept of what Providence allots as it pleases God; for we have by no means lived ill, but in a splendid and happy manner" (*Ant.* 19:344–47; Whiston).

The story of Herod Agrippa is a cautionary tale. In many ways, he led a charmed life. He was raised in Rome among the elite; successive emperors (Gaius and Claudius) befriended and honored him; he accrued titles (king and consul), lands, and riches. At the height of his power and popularity he is now acclaimed as a god (Acts 12:22). He accepts the flattery and is then struck down almost immediately by a severe stomach illness and dies soon thereafter. Because he did not give the "glory to God,"[11] Herod is punished for accepting divine acclamations (cf. Ezek 28:1–10). Again, it is worth noting the parallels of this cautionary Passover tale with the exodus of God's people from Egypt. When a king who imagines himself a god kills and imprisons God's people, they are delivered from the clutches of the boastful ruler, and an angel of the Lord strikes with deadly force.

A Summary Note (12:24)

With the demise of Herod Agrippa, the interlude and, indeed, the entire panel (Acts 9:32–12:24) draws to a close. In this pivotal panel the gospel reaches the gentiles, and a new phase of mission ensues with the expansion into Syria. As if to mark this new development, followers of Jesus are given another name: "The disciples were called Christians first at Antioch" (11:26). To signal the end of the panel and the shift to a new development in the narrative, Luke inserts another transitional marker (cf. 6:7; 9:31; 16:5; 19:20). Typically these markers include at least one of the following three elements: (1) a geographical note; (2) an indication about church growth; or (3) a reference to the word of God increasing. In this marker at 12:24 two elements are included: the reference to the "word of God" and the implication that it gained adherents.[12] A reference to geography is omitted, possibly because in the next two sentences geographical details are provided. The important matter to recognize is that Luke is alerting his readers to the end of one section and preparing them for the next progression.

LIVE the Story

The Passover deliverance account in Acts 12 reframes the ancient story of the exodus in the life of the first-century church. This narrative also reframes—or better, reimagines—two important aspects for believers in the twenty-first century church. It helps us reimagine angels and power. I was alerted to this in a short but well-written introduction to *McCausland's Order of Divine Service* for 2013 by Gary Thorne. Thorne was explaining how the Anglican prayerbook tradition is reenchanting a new generation.[13] What he notes about the

---

11. The Greek is *tēn doxan tō theō*, which is translated as "praise to God" in the NIV.
12. The opening phrase of the first transitional marker (6:7: *kai ho logos tou theou ēuxanen kai eplēthyneto*) is almost identical to the third marker (12:24: *ho de logos tou theou ēuxanen kai eplēthyneto*).
13. Gary Thorne, "Re-Enchanting a New Generation," in *McCausland's Order of Divine Service: The Christian Year 2013* (Toronto: Anglican Book Centre, 2011), 4–7.

difference between the sixteenth century and the twenty-first century can also be applied to the difference between the first and twenty-first centuries. The worldview of the first century is so foreign to our Western, twenty-first century worldview that most people find it virtually incomprehensible. In his book *A Secular Age*, the Canadian philosopher Charles Taylor addresses why it was "virtually impossible not to believe in God in, say, 1500 in our Western society, while in 2000 many of us find this not only easy, but even inescapable."[14] Taylor documents the gradual "disenchantment" of the cosmos to the materialist, autonomous, and self-centered world of modernity.

One dimension that has been lost in this disenchantment is the angelic sphere. Despite the fact that Hollywood endlessly produces films that include angels, it seems an actor hasn't earned their acting chops unless he or she has had a role as an angel (holy or otherwise)! Nonetheless, most people, even many Christians, dismiss any acknowledgment of angelic messengers and ministers. The world has become disenchanted. This is especially tragic when it comes to Christians. Followers of Jesus, of all people, should be alert to this transcendent dimension. Angels are, after all, hardly incidental to the story of God. A cursory look at the biblical narrative includes angels at almost every crucial juncture:

- Cherubim guard the entrance to Eden (Gen 3:24);
- An angel helps Hagar (Gen 16:7; 21:17);
- An angel calls out to Abraham to stay his hand (Gen 22:11);
- An angel accompanied Abraham's messenger to Mesopotamia when he went searching for a wife for Isaac (Gen 24:7);
- Jacob dreams about and meets angels (Gen 28:12; 32:1);
- An angel appeared to Moses from the burning bush (Exod 3:2);
- An angel went ahead of the Israelites as they approached the Red Sea (Exod 14:19);
- An angel opposed Balaam and his donkey (Num 22:22–35);
- Angels guide many of Israel's judges (e.g., Gideon [Judg 6:11–23]);
- Angels are called upon to praise the Lord in the Psalms (103:20; 148:2);
- Seraphim are found in Isaiah's vision (Isa 6:1–7; cf. Ezek 1:1–24);
- An angel speaks with Joseph, telling him that the child conceived in Mary's womb was of the Holy Spirit (Matt 1:20);
- An angel speaks to Zechariah as he ministered in the temple (Luke 1:11);
- The angel Gabriel announced the incarnation to Mary (Luke 1:26–38);

---

14. Charles Taylor, *A Secular Age* (Cambridge: The Belnap Press of Harvard University Press, 2007), 25.

- Angels announce the birth of Jesus to shepherds (Luke 2:9–15);
- Angels attend to Jesus in the wilderness (Mark 1:13);
- An angel sits at the entrance to the tomb and announces Jesus's resurrection (Matt 28:2–7);
- Angels explain the meaning of the ascension to the disciples (Acts 1:10–11);
- And, last but not least, Peter is twice delivered from imprisonment by an angel (Acts 5:19; 12:7–10).

The list could go on, but the point is that angels are not occasional characters in Scripture; they are integral to the biblical story.[15]

While disenchantment with angels and the supernatural is understandable for those shaped by our secular age, it is unacceptable for Christians. Nonetheless, there are indications that this is changing and that even non-Christians are being reenchanted by the Christian imagination of Christian writers and even dusty, old English prayer books. For example, when the pre-Christian C. S. Lewis struggled to reconcile his vivid imagination fueled by the fairy-tale world of George MacDonald with his cold, scientific materialism, he turned to his devout friend J. R. R. Tolkien. One evening in 1931, as the two strolled the gardens of Magdalen College, Oxford, Tolkien explained to Lewis how the two sides could be reconciled in the Christian account, in which God took on human flesh and entered his own story. This is the moment when the world became enchanted for Lewis. As the transcendent touched the material and enchanted Lewis's world, so may we continue to be enchanted by Christ and the Lord's angelic host, who visit humans, announce God's word, and deliver the saints from corrupt power.

Inasmuch as Acts 12 reenchants us with the thought of angels, so too it can reframe our attitude to political power. The comic genius of Monty Python expresses how many people in the contemporary world view the "myths" of the past. The charming legend of the transfer of Excalibur from the Lady of the Lake to King Arthur is wiped away by the prosaic worldview of modernity: "Strange women lying in ponds distributing swords is no basis for a system of government. Supreme executive power derives from a mandate from the masses, not from some farcical aquatic ceremony."[16]

---

15. See Scot McKnight, *The Hum of Angels: Listening for the Messengers of God around Us* (New York: WaterBrook, 2017).

16. Terry Gilliam and Terry Jones, dirs., *Monty Python and the Holy Grail* (Michael White Productions, National Film Trustee Company, and Python [Monty] Pictures, 1975), a scene alerted to me by Fr. Stephen Freeman in his blogpost, "Human Tradition in a Modern World," at *Glory to God for All Things*, 16 October 2015, https://blogs.ancientfaith.com/glory2godforallthings/2015/10/16/human-tradition-in-a-modern-world/.

Despite the profound impact of the modern project and its insistence that the world is devoid of the transcendent, we still abide with political rulers who act as if—and some who even proclaim that—they are divine. For those of us who have been enchanted or reenchanted by the gospel and the story of Acts, we know that executive power does not reside with kings, presidents, sheiks, or divinized tyrants. Ultimate power and praise belong to God. Herod Agrippa is merely one in a long line of Pharaoh-like rulers throughout history who demanded divine prerogative. His pageantry and pretension were all show, and his life is displayed for what it truly was: worm-eaten, diseased, and hollow. In contrast, the life of Christ, embraced and engaged in the believing community, pulsates with interior energy, joyfulness, and vibrant action.

Although not every misguided ruler receives so swift a judgment as Herod did, his story reinforces what is at stake for Christians. What is at issue is the answer to the question, Who is going to be Lord of our lives? Will it be the God who reveals himself in Jesus, who saves and gives us the glorious presence of his Spirit, or the "Herod" who imagines himself to be a god and persecutes us? Luke points us to the truth that the glory of God is recognized in humility and repentance, not received in flattery and boastfulness. We are invited to be reframed and reenchanted throughout Luke's narrative in Acts by the gospel and a worldview "charged with the grandeur of God."[17] In doing so, biblical enchantment exposes the emptiness of modernist assertions for what they are: cold, selfish, mechanistic, and brutal.

---

17. Gerard Manley Hopkins, "God's Grandeur," in *The Major Works*, ed. Catherine Phillips (Oxford: Oxford University Press, 2009), 128.

PANEL 4
Acts 12:25–16:5

The previous panel in Acts narrated the whole matter of the inclusion of the gentiles. At the heart of this are the conversions of the Roman centurion Cornelius and his household. With this key event, the church breaks out of its Jewish, Palestinian boundaries. The church is now wide open to the world. There are no limits to whom or where the good news in Christ is relevant. The church needed two "Pentecosts," much like Peter needed two conversions. Peter's first breakthrough moment to understanding who Jesus was occurred on the road to Caesarea Philippi (Matt 16:13–20); his second breakthrough to understanding who Jesus was occurred in Caesarea Maritima (Acts 10). The church's first Pentecost was in Jerusalem where Jews received the Spirit (Acts 2); the church's second Pentecost was in Caesarea where gentiles received the Spirit (Acts 10). Now, Luke returns to the geographical expansion of the gospel to the region of Asia Minor (modern-day Turkey).

Barnabas and Saul embarking on missionary journeys bracket this panel. Their first missionary journey is together (12:25–14:28); their second journey is apart (15:36–16:5). Between these journeys is the "Council at Jerusalem" (15:1–35)—one of the most significant meetings in apostolic history. Within this panel are two important developments. First, Syrian Antioch becomes the new hub for Christian mission (cf. 12:25–13:3; 14:26–28). Second, Paul becomes the principal leader in the narrative.[1] There are also several other important matters in this panel. In Pisidian Antioch (13:16–41) we hear an

---

1. Compare "when Barnabas and Saul had finished their mission" (12:25) with "Paul and his companions sailed to Perga" (13:13). Saul the colleague of Barnabas has become Paul the leader of the group.

example of missionary preaching in the context of a diaspora synagogue—that is, a synagogue outside of Judea and Galilee. We also observe the first real parting of the ways between the early Christian community and Judaism (13:44–52). This is noted in the missionaries' pronouncement to the Jews in Pisidia, "Since you reject [the gospel] and do not consider yourselves worthy of eternal life, we now turn to the Gentiles" (v. 46). The Jerusalem Council (15:1–35) is held in order to deal with the influx of gentile believers. The primary issue is whether circumcision should be required for them. On this occasion Peter (vv. 6–11) and James (vv. 13–21) offer their considerable support to what God was doing through the work of Paul and Barnabas.

One final note worth highlighting is the staggering distance that the apostle Paul travels in the narrative. Beitzel calculated the apostle's journeys by land and sea in Acts at about 13,400 miles (i.e., 21,500 km) as the crow flies.[2] This number would be larger if we also account for the circuitous routes Paul would often travel to reach his destinations. Given the perils associated with ancient travel and the many difficult circumstances he faced (cf. 2 Cor 11:23–27), we must not overlook the courage, stamina, and indomitable will that fired Paul. With these energies linked to the empowering presence of the Holy Spirit, it is a wonder to behold and consider.

---

2. Barry J. Beitzel, *The Moody Atlas of Bible Lands* (Chicago: Moody, 1985), 176.

CHAPTER 26

Acts 12:25–13:12

 LISTEN to the Story

²⁵When Barnabas and Saul had finished their mission, they returned from¹ Jerusalem, taking with them John, also called Mark.
¹Now in the church at Antioch there were prophets and teachers: Barnabas, Simeon called Niger, Lucius of Cyrene, Manaen (who had been brought up with Herod the tetrarch) and Saul. ²While they were worshiping the Lord and fasting, the Holy Spirit said, "Set apart for me Barnabas and Saul for the work to which I have called them." ³So after they had fasted and prayed, they placed their hands on them and sent them off.
⁴The two of them, sent on their way by the Holy Spirit, went down to Seleucia and sailed from there to Cyprus. ⁵When they arrived at Salamis, they proclaimed the word of God in the Jewish synagogues. John was with them as their helper.
⁶They traveled through the whole island until they came to Paphos. There they met a Jewish sorcerer and false prophet named Bar-Jesus, ⁷who was an attendant of the proconsul, Sergius Paulus. The proconsul, an intelligent man, sent for Barnabas and Saul because he wanted to hear the word of God. ⁸But Elymas the sorcerer (for that is what his name means) opposed them and tried to turn the proconsul from the faith. ⁹Then Saul, who was also called Paul, filled with the Holy Spirit, looked straight at Elymas and said, ¹⁰"You are a child of the devil and an enemy of everything that is right! You are full of all kinds of deceit and trickery. Will you never stop perverting the right ways of the Lord? ¹¹Now the hand of the Lord is against you. You are going to be blind for a time, not even able to see the light of the sun."
Immediately mist and darkness came over him, and he groped about, seeking someone to lead him by the hand. ¹²When the proconsul saw

---

1. Some manuscripts read *to* Jerusalem. Even though the reading with "to" has the better manuscript evidence, it makes little logical sense of the passage. Not surprisingly, this has vexed scholars. The NIV decided to go with a reading that made better sense of the narrative rather than with the "better" (i.e., the older manuscripts and the harder reading) textual tradition.

what had happened, he believed, for he was amazed at the teaching about the Lord.

Listening to the Text in the Story: Exodus 7:4–17; 9.3; Nehemiah 1:4; Luke 2:37; Romans 1:16.

EXPLAIN the Story

The opening passage of the second panel begins with a summary (12:25–13:3) and the first leg of Barnabas and Saul's journey from Antioch to Cyprus (13:4–12). This first step in mission establishes a pattern that will recur throughout Acts. First, the missionaries will begin in the Jewish synagogues, if they are available.[2] Second, the work of the missionaries is primarily a ministry of the "word," which for Luke means the proclamation of the gospel, the message of salvation.[3] Third, even though the emphasis of the ministry is the word, it is also a work of the Holy Spirit. Signs, therefore, accompany the word.[4] Still, even though the first demonstration of the Spirit's power on this mission leads to faith, it is "the teaching about the Lord" that amazes (13:12).

The Spirit Sends (12:25–13:3)

The way that the narrative of the first missionary travels into Asia is constructed suggests that Luke himself recognizes its special importance. Above all else, it is the activity of the entire community in Antioch cooperating with the Holy Spirit that is highlighted. That is, it is not just some individual missionaries who happen to think it is a good idea to take a journey. This can be seen in the way that the entire community's recognition is emphasized at the outset (13:3) and at the conclusion of the journey (14:26–27):

> So after *they* [i.e., the whole church] had fasted and prayed, *they* placed their hands on them and sent them off. (13:3)

> From Attalia they sailed back to Antioch, where they had been committed to the grace of God for the work they had now completed. On arriving there, they gathered *the church together* and reported all that God had done through them and how he had opened a door of faith to the Gentiles. (14:26–27)

---

2. Cf. Acts 13:5, 14; 14:1.
3. Cf. Acts 13:5, 7, 15, 44, 46, 48; 14:1, 3, 7, 21.
4. See especially Acts 14:3; cf. 13:12.

"Now in the church at Antioch there were prophets and teachers" (13:1). Within this community there were prophets and teachers spread throughout the various places where Christians gathered in the city. Five individuals are named: Barnabas, Simeon, Lucius, Manaen, and Saul. We already know the two who bracket this list of prophets/teachers, Barnabas and Saul, from earlier episodes. The middle three are new characters in the story. These three are listed with descriptive notes. Simeon is called "Niger," a Latin word meaning "dark-complexioned." Possibly he is from Africa. Lucius is certainly African as he originates from Cyrene, the district capital of the Roman province of Cyrenaica located in North Africa. Simon, who bore Jesus's cross, was also from Cyrene (Luke 23:26). Cyrene has already been referred to at earlier junctures in Acts: Jews from *Cyrene* were in Jerusalem at Pentecost (Acts 2:10); Jews from *Cyrene*, but residing in Jerusalem, argued with Stephen (6:9); and some individuals from this city were converted and proclaimed the gospel in Antioch (11:20; 13:1). Interestingly, the next person in the list, Manaen, is noted for being a *syntrophos* (v. 1; NIV: "brought up with") of Herod the tetrarch.[5] A *syntrophos* can refer to someone who is a fellow member of court.[6] It can also denote someone on more intimate terms, like a person raised as a companion or foster brother with another.[7] Luke seems to have special knowledge of the Herodian dynasty, and this detail is all the more noteworthy since the preceding episode described the persecution by and demise of Herod Agrippa.

It is not easy to know why Luke mentions these names, unless it is to note that all five of these individuals were available for service. The mention of them as "prophets" does, however, prepare the way for the Holy Spirit, who is the one who inspires the prophets of the Lord. While "they"—likely referring to the whole church and not just the five—were "worshiping the Lord and fasting," the Spirit speaks to the church (v. 2). The verb "worshiping" (*leitourgeō*) does not occur elsewhere in Luke-Acts. It is coupled with "fasting," another rare verb in Luke-Acts. Fasting is associated with prayer and disciplined seeking of God's will (see Luke 2:37; Acts 9:9–11; 14:23; cf. Neh 1:4), but it is not a well-attested practice in the early church. The purpose of mentioning these two activities is that the Holy Spirit speaks to the community about mission in the context of corporate worship.

That this is an important moment in the overall narrative of Acts is indicated by the unique activity of the Spirit. Nowhere else does the Spirit direct a church to a specific task like this. The Spirit elsewhere speaks to individuals (e.g., Acts 8:29; 10:19; 11:12; 21:11), but not to a community in this manner.

---

5. That is, Herod Antipas, son of Herod I and ruler of Galilee and Perea in AD 6–37.
6. Schnabel, *Acts*, 554; Gaventa, *Acts*, 190.
7. Cf. BDAG 976.

How does the Holy Spirit "speak"? The Spirit speaks through the ministry of prophets (13:1). In so doing, the Spirit identifies Barnabas and Saul as the candidates for mission. This is a tandem that has already worked well together. They were responsible for carrying the relief offering from Antioch to Jerusalem (12:25). Now, they will be responsible for carrying the gospel to the gentiles—a calling that has already been confirmed by the Lord earlier in the narrative (9:15–16). Further fasting and prayer is also required as a continuation of their preparation for mission (13:3). Finally, the community indicates their obedience to the will and clear leading of the Spirit by placing their hands on them (cf. 6:6) and releasing[8] them from their regular duties in Antioch for service elsewhere.

Bar-Jesus Opposes (13:4–12)

The first missionary outreach to the island of Cyrpus is met with success and opposition. There is much else that Barnabas and Saul do in terms of teaching in the Jewish synagogues on the island, but Luke chooses to focus his attention on the reception of the gospel by the Roman proconsul, Sergius Paulus, and the opposition expressed by one of his attendants, the Jewish sorcerer Bar-Jesus.

The journey begins with specific mention of the company being sent by the Holy Spirit (13:4). The Spirit's direct guidance is a significant mark in Saul's life. Technically, his first Spirit-led journey is the one he took with Barnabas to Jerusalem after the Spirit spoke through Agabus (11:28–30). Now the Spirit directs Barnabas and Saul, this time to Seleucia and then on to Cyprus (13:4). Saul will also be divinely guided on his second journey (16:6–10), third journey (20:22–24; 21:11–14), and during his voyage to Rome as a prisoner (23:11; 27:23–25). This Spirit activity is not only characteristic of his public life but his private life as well.[9]

The first brief stage of their journey is the twenty-five-kilometer trip from Antioch to its harbor city, Seleucia, downstream along the Orontes River. Cyprus, an island in the northeast corner of the Mediterranean Sea, is their first target beyond that. In some ways, this is not surprising since Cyprus is the home of Barnabas (4:36), and there would have been Jewish Christians on the island (11:19–20). This meant they had contacts, places to stay, and along with

---

8. Ramsay, *St. Paul*, 70, argues that the last word of v. 3 should not be translated as "sent them off." Rather, the Spirit sends them, and the church "releases" them. The Greek verb *apolyō* is used by a superior, a host, or a commanding officer to grant someone leave to depart. Simeon uses the same word when, after seeing the baby Jesus, he says to the Lord, "You may now dismiss [*apolyō*] your servant in peace" (Luke 2:29).

9. Cf. 2 Cor 12:1–7; cf. Ramsay, *St. Paul*, 69.

a number of Jews settled on Cyprus who would have established synagogues on the island (cf. 1 Macc 15:23), there were many places to begin their work.

The first city they come to on Cyprus is Salamis on the east side (13:5). If the missionaries traveled in the early part of the sailing season (i.e., March), they had fortuitous winds that would have allowed them to sail directly west. Once on land, they established a pattern of proclamation by first going to Jewish synagogues. The imperfect tense of the verb "proclaimed" suggests this is an ongoing and continuous rhythm for them (v. 5). Saul may very well be God's chosen vessel to the gentiles, but his calling never excluded the Jewish people. Paul would later write to the church in Rome that the gospel is "first to the Jew, then to the Gentile" (Rom 1:16). This approach describes his actions perfectly in Acts. Whenever possible, he approached his fellow Jews first with the gospel, usually in their synagogues.

Two additional items are worth mentioning at this point in terms of the narrative. First, Luke makes no comment about the reception of "the word" in the synagogues. His silence need not imply that there was no response in the synagogues; it may simply suggest that this is not where he wants to place his emphasis. Second, almost as an aside, he adds "John was with them as their helper" (13:5). John Mark's name first appears in the narrative when Peter miraculously escapes from prison in Jerusalem (12:12) and then again when he accompanies Barnabas and Saul back to Antioch (12:25). That he is secondary to the apostles is indicated by two things: (1) the mention that he is a "helper" (v. 5), and (2) Luke only mentions that the Holy Spirit sent "the two," that is, Barnabas and Saul, on the mission (v. 4).

Luke allocates a couple of sentences to the missionaries' arrival in Salamis and their preaching in the Jewish synagogues. He describes this as traveling "through the whole island" (v. 6). He then goes on to spend considerable space on what happens in Paphos. Paphos is located on the southwest coast of Cyprus and was the seat of Roman administration on the island. Without mentioning anything else about Paphos or their work there, we are introduced to one of the most interesting characters in all of Acts: Bar-Jesus. His Aramaic name means "son of Jesus/Joshua"—a common Jewish name (v. 6). He is described in three ways: (1) as a Jewish sorcerer (*magos*), (2) as a false prophet, and (3) as an attendant of the proconsul (vv. 6–7). Although Christ's followers have encountered magic before (8:9–24; cf. 19:11–20), Bar-Jesus is the only person in Acts denoted as a sorcerer or magician. Again, it is important to note that a sorcerer or magician need not imply negative connotations in the ancient world. To some, these individuals were more akin to "scientific advisors" of the day than conjurers of cheap tricks. They were regarded as important consultants both on religious and astrological matters. Emperor Tiberius retained a magician, Thrasyllus, as one of his advisors.[10] Not unusually, then, the Roman proconsul on Cyprus did as well.

More pejoratively, Bar-Jesus is noted to be a "false prophet" (13:6). Although he is not depicted as a representative of Judaism in any way, within the broader biblical narrative false prophets are dangerous individuals (e.g., 1 Kgs 22:1–38; Jer 28:1–17). In this case, the danger is that Bar-Jesus "opposed" the missionaries and their message (Acts 13:8). The immediate contrast is with Barnabas and Saul, who have just been described as "prophets and teachers" and divinely commissioned by the Holy Spirit (v. 2). Not unlike OT narratives, there will be a clash between prophets, and the conflict will reveal who is indeed empowered by the Spirit of God and who is a counterfeit.

The final designation of Bar-Jesus is that he was an "attendant" to the proconsul, Sergius Paulus (v. 7). That is, he is one of the entourage of the Roman emperor's political representative on the island. A *proconsul* was the governor of a senatorial province and was appointed directly by the emperor. Oddly, Luke also notes that Bar-Jesus's name can also be translated as "Elymas." This may be a nickname, since this name is not a translation of Bar-Jesus.

The other main character in this interesting scene in Paphos is the proconsul himself, Sergius Paulus. It would not have been unusual for a Roman administrator to welcome itinerant teachers into his court.[11] The assumption is that they had acquired a measure of notoriety in the city, and eventually this word was passed along to the proconsul. Sergius Paulus stands in direct contrast to Bar-Jesus. He is a highly regarded Roman official, eager to learn ("an intelligent man," v. 7), and open to the word of God. In contrast, Bar-Jesus is a fraudulent Jewish prophet, closed to the gospel, and opposed to the Spirit's messengers. Bar-Jesus, sensing that the proconsul's interest in the missionaries might marginalize his own role at court, attempts to dissuade Sergius Paulus from the faith. The climactic moment has arrived. Saul, equally discerning as a true prophet, is "filled with the Holy Spirit," looks "straight"[12] at Elymas, and pronounces the one named "son of Jesus" to be a "child [lit., "son"] of the devil" (vv. 9–10). The condemnation continues. He is declared to be what has already been mentioned of him. He is "full of all kinds of deceit and trickery" (i.e., the marks of a false prophet and sorcerer); he is an "enemy" inspired by the devil; and the proof of his identity is in his actions that make

---

10. Dunn, *Acts*, 175.

11. Technically, the proconsul "sent" (13:7, *proskaleō*) for the apostle, which in the Roman world was equivalent to a summons or command. The Holy Spirit spoke the same word—translated as "call"—to the apostles just a few verses earlier (13:2).

12. This word (*atenizō*) is used frequently in Acts of those who are about to be used by the Holy Spirit to perform a miracle (see 3:4; 14:9) or when some dramatic sign occurs (see 1:10; 6:15; 7:55; 11:6).

crooked the ways of the Lord (v. 10). Judgment is swift for Bar-Jesus, and he is plunged into a period of blindness (v. 11). Dunn points out that both the language ("the hand of the Lord") and the result (darkened to the "light of the sun") "recalls the language used in the ancient accounts of Moses' and Aaron's victory over Pharaoh and his magicians (Exod 7:4, 5, 17; 9:3)."[13]

Two things soften the judgment meted out against Bar-Jesus. First, his blindness will be only for "a time" (Acts 13:11). Second, the description of his malady ("immediately mist and darkness came over him, and he groped about, seeking someone to lead him by the hand") is reminiscent of the same circumstances Saul faced earlier (9:8). Physical blindness sometimes precedes spiritual enlightenment. While we are not informed whether Bar-Jesus will see either the sun or the truth again, we are told that the proconsul was struck by what he saw and "believed" (13:12). In the end, however, it is not the miracle that decides the matter for the proconsul; rather, he is "amazed at the teaching about the Lord."

One final note is worth mentioning. Careful listeners and readers of the narrative will have noticed that during this dramatic encounter Luke mentions a second name for Saul, "who was also called *Paul*" (v. 9). From this point on in the narrative he will no longer be referred to by the Jewish name Saul but by his Greco-Roman name, Paul. Why did Luke make the transition at this point? There is considerable scholarly discussion on this going back as far as Jerome, who suggested that Saul appropriated the name of his famous first convert, Sergius Paulus.[14] More likely, Saul already possessed this second name and used it when he was in the company of gentiles. Here it may be helpful to note that the Greek adjective *saulos* was a word that referred to a person's way of walking—and not in a complimentary way.[15] In this sense, the Hebrew name "Saul" may have created an initial barrier to Greek-speaking gentile audiences. Perhaps Paul wanted to ensure that the messenger didn't obscure the message.[16] Whatever his reason to change his name at this point, it seems to be about contextualization; now that he will be working among gentiles in a Roman context, he shifts to a fitting, Roman-sounding name.

Besides the shift in name from Saul to Paul, another significant shift occurs in the leadership pairing. Previously Barnabas's name always headed the pair when they were named. While there will be exceptions—most notably when

---

13. Dunn, *Acts*, 177.
14. Jerome, *On Illustrious Men* 5.4. For a more recent discussion, see C. J. Hemer, "The Name of Paul," *Tyndale Bulletin* 36 (1985): 179–83.
15. *Saulos*, according to LSJ, is a Greek adjective "descriptive of gait and carriage . . . applied to a tortoise" or to the "loose, wanton gait of courtesans or Baccantes." This seems to refer to a person with an effeminate way of walking.
16. Wright, *Acts*, 2:6–7.

they are back in Jewish company during the Jerusalem Council (15:12)—for the most part Paul will be named first when the pair are mentioned together from now on. This suggests the emergence of Paul's leadership in relationship to Barnabas. Thus, it will no longer be "Barnabas and Saul" but "Paul and his companions" (13:13) or "Paul and Barnabas" (13:43, 46, 50, etc.). Luke never discloses why this shift is made. It might be as simple as wherever Barnabas was well known—either among the churches in Jerusalem, in Antioch Syria, or on his home turf of Cyprus—he took the lead. Now that the mission moves into Asia Minor in the southern part of Galatia, the missionary team is working in settings and synagogues possibly more familiar to Paul, who was raised in the neighboring province of Cilicia. Paul was familiar with living as a Jew surrounded by gentile culture. He knew the context, understood the ways in which both Jewish and gentile people thought, and he could relate to their daily experiences. Perhaps it was simply a practical advantage, at least at first, for Paul to take the lead role in the missionary team.

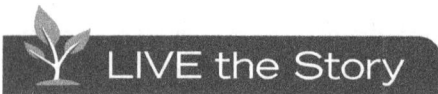

LIVE the Story

The Virtues of a Mission-Focused Church
In his superb book on the Holy Spirit and the mind of faith, Jack Levison reminds us why the Antioch church is such a vibrant community for mission. I can't imagine any Christian congregation or parish who wouldn't want advice or insight on how to be effective in mission. Luke's description of the first-century Christians in Syrian Antioch points us to the qualities of a church shaped by the Holy Spirit and active in mission.[17] Levison identifies four virtues, which he refers to as "qualities," that shaped the inward health in this community so that it might be fruitful in its outward mission. He notes that in these virtues we see a "direct correlation between the preparation of the church and the inspired word [for mission] it receives."[18] The first virtue of the mission-oriented church of Antioch is that it was a *listening and learning* community. Luke begins by mentioning that they were blessed with "prophets and teachers" (Acts 13:1). Teachers take the lead in forming a church with a learning heart. Prophets then take this embedded truth and discern outlets for their newfound knowledge. Knowledge without action is sterile, action without knowledge is foolish. Both prophets and teachers provided balance for the learning church in Antioch.

The second virtue of the church in Antioch was its *generosity*. We already

---

17. Levinson, *Inspired*, 109–12.
18. Ibid., 109.

know that this predominantly gentile church is generous with its treasure as it helped relieve the famine-stricken Jewish church in Jerusalem (11:29–30; 12:25). They not only sent money elsewhere but were open and hospitable in welcoming others (e.g., Barnabas from Cyprus, Saul from Tarsus, and Agabus from Jerusalem) into their own homes for short and extended periods of time of teaching and prophetic ministry. Possibly the most remarkable sign of their generosity is that they did not keep their best teachers and prophets to themselves. They sent their best—men like Barnabas and Saul—to share the gospel with others and likely even paid their travel expenses to do it.

A third virtue that marked the Antioch church for Spirit-directed, cross-cultural mission is that they were already *a multicultural community*. They were an ethnically and economically diverse community. Barnabas was a wealthy landowner originally from Cyprus. Simeon, "the black one," was probably from North Africa, while Lucius most certainly was from Africa (Cyrene). Manaen was acquainted with the royal court of the Herods. Saul was a well-educated Jew, born with Roman citizenship, who hailed from the vaunted Tarsus—"no ordinary city" (21:39). Unfortunately, our contemporary world is growing increasingly tribal and insular despite its burgeoning population. It is a place where countries are more interested in building barriers to keep people out rather than welcoming the "poor . . . huddled masses . . . homeless [and] tempest tossed."[19] We should not be surprised that if we want to break through cultural and economic barriers for the sake of the gospel, then our churches must be places that reflect cultural and economic diversity.

Finally, the church in Antioch was prepared to be a seedbed of mission because it was a community *engaged in the spiritual disciplines* of prayer and fasting. These are not extra or exotic disciplines. Prayer, engaged in corporately, and fasting, practiced corporately, is as basic to fruitful mission as healthy soil is to fruitful gardening. The Spirit, of course, gives the increase, but this takes root in the seedbed of prayer and fasting.

In mission we are either sending or supporting, and both are important. The church in Antioch was endowed with gifted and diverse leaders and teachers whom they supported, nurtured, and sent. They did not hoard them but sent out their very best. It is not easy to give up faithful and fruitful members in a congregation, and to share them in mission is also inconvenient. This is why our missionaries must be chosen in the context of trust, prayer, and fasting and also supported with trust, prayer, and fasting, along with whatever other resources can help them accomplish their task. The church in Antioch was willing to share and give to see the gospel declared to their world. In turn,

---

19. Words from the inscription on the Statue of Liberty in New York Harbor (Emma Lazarus, "The New Colossus," Nov. 2, 1883).

their best members were willing to do whatever it took to share the good news of Jesus—including changing their names if necessary—by becoming all things to all people so that they might win some.

Mission Will Be Opposed

The cost of sending and supporting mission is significant. Despite all our best plans, however, another harsh reality is that mission will often be opposed by individuals, communities, political powers, and spiritual powers. Opposition of various kinds is to be expected by those who engage in mission. The Antioch missionaries' initial opposition occurred in the form of a Jewish magician. As they continued with their mission into Galatia, they would encounter jealous Jewish leaders (13:45; 14:2) and hostile pagans (14:19). It is important not to be naive about opposition. We need not provoke it unnecessarily by our own ignorance or pride. Rather, wisdom calls us to do all that we can to let the winsomeness and truth of the gospel win over the imaginations of unbelievers. Still, having sent our best ambassadors to an unreached world, we will often face opposition that is unrelenting and irrational. Apart from the Spirit's presence and empowerment, this can be disheartening.

Yet for all the opposition we may experience, it is also important to embrace unexpected friends—like Sergius, a Roman proconsul—when they appear. Luke is aware that while the empire is certainly not neutral when it comes to the Christian faith (after all, it was the Roman governor Pontius Pilate who granted permission for Jesus to be scourged and crucified by his soldiers), those who pledge allegiance to the empires of this world are not all hardened to the gospel. In the first century, Roman centurions (e.g., Cornelius) and politicians (e.g., Sergius Paulus) discerned the truth and placed their trust in the Lord. In our own world it is common to dismiss people by branding them with superficial labels so as to dismiss their receptivity to the good news. We often exclude people because of their ethnicity, their economic status, their educational background, their political affiliation, or their social location. Luke reminds us to be open to "the other" in mission. Further, he demonstrates the subtle approach of the early church's mission in the Roman world. Sometimes partners can be found within existing social and political structures. Sometimes those working within those social and political structures are the church's greatest enemies. The point is not to foreclose opinions on people regardless of their gender, social standing, political persuasion, or position of power.

CHAPTER 27

Acts 13:13-52

 LISTEN to the Story

[13] From Paphos, Paul and his companions sailed to Perga in Pamphylia, where John left them to return to Jerusalem. [14] From Perga they went on to Pisidian Antioch. On the Sabbath they entered the synagogue and sat down. [15] After the reading from the Law and the Prophets, the leaders of the synagogue sent word to them, saying, "Brothers, if you have a word of exhortation for the people, please speak."

[16] Standing up, Paul motioned with his hand and said: "Fellow Israelites and you Gentiles who worship God, listen to me! [17] The God of the people of Israel chose our ancestors; he made the people prosper during their stay in Egypt; with mighty power he led them out of that country; [18] for about forty years he endured their conduct in the wilderness; [19] and he overthrew seven nations in Canaan, giving their land to his people as their inheritance. [20] All this took about 450 years.

"After this, God gave them judges until the time of Samuel the prophet. [21] Then the people asked for a king, and he gave them Saul son of Kish, of the tribe of Benjamin, who ruled forty years. [22] After removing Saul, he made David their king. God testified concerning him: 'I have found David son of Jesse, a man after my own heart; he will do everything I want him to do.'

[23] "From this man's descendants God has brought to Israel the Savior Jesus, as he promised. [24] Before the coming of Jesus, John preached repentance and baptism to all the people of Israel. [25] As John was completing his work, he said: 'Who do you suppose I am? I am not the one you are looking for. But there is one coming after me whose sandals I am not worthy to untie.'

[26] "Fellow children of Abraham and you God-fearing Gentiles, it is to us that this message of salvation has been sent. [27] The people of Jerusalem and their rulers did not recognize Jesus, yet in condemning him they fulfilled the words of the prophets that are read every Sabbath. [28] Though they

found no proper ground for a death sentence, they asked Pilate to have him executed. ²⁹When they had carried out all that was written about him, they took him down from the cross and laid him in a tomb. ³⁰But God raised him from the dead, ³¹and for many days he was seen by those who had traveled with him from Galilee to Jerusalem. They are now his witnesses to our people.

³²"We tell you the good news: What God promised our ancestors ³³he has fulfilled for us, their children, by raising up Jesus. As it is written in the second Psalm:

> "'You are my son;
>   today I have become your father.'[1]

³⁴God raised him from the dead so that he will never be subject to decay. As God has said,

> "'I will give you the holy and sure blessings promised to David.'[2]

³⁵So it is also stated elsewhere:

> "'You will not let your holy one see decay.'[3]

³⁶"Now when David had served God's purpose in his own generation, he fell asleep; he was buried with his ancestors and his body decayed. ³⁷But the one whom God raised from the dead did not see decay.

³⁸"Therefore, my friends, I want you to know that through Jesus the forgiveness of sins is proclaimed to you. ³⁹Through him everyone who believes is set free from every sin, a justification you were not able to obtain under the law of Moses. ⁴⁰Take care that what the prophets have said does not happen to you:

> ⁴¹"'Look, you scoffers,
>   wonder and perish,
> for I am going to do something in your days
>   that you would never believe,
>   even if someone told you.'"[4]

⁴²As Paul and Barnabas were leaving the synagogue, the people invited them to speak further about these things on the next Sabbath. ⁴³When the

---

1. Ps 2:7.
2. Isa 55:3.
3. Ps 16:10 (see Septuagint).
4. Hab 1:5.

congregation was dismissed, many of the Jews and devout converts to Judaism followed Paul and Barnabas, who talked with them and urged them to continue in the grace of God.

⁴⁴On the next Sabbath almost the whole city gathered to hear the word of the Lord. ⁴⁵When the Jews saw the crowds, they were filled with jealousy. They began to contradict what Paul was saying and heaped abuse on him.

⁴⁶Then Paul and Barnabas answered them boldly: "We had to speak the word of God to you first. Since you reject it and do not consider yourselves worthy of eternal life, we now turn to the Gentiles. ⁴⁷For this is what the Lord has commanded us:

"'I have made you a light for the Gentiles,
 that you may bring salvation to the ends of the earth.'"[5]

⁴⁸When the Gentiles heard this, they were glad and honored the word of the Lord; and all who were appointed for eternal life believed.

⁴⁹The word of the Lord spread through the whole region. ⁵⁰But the Jewish leaders incited the God-fearing women of high standing and the leading men of the city. They stirred up persecution against Paul and Barnabas, and expelled them from their region. ⁵¹So they shook the dust off their feet as a warning to them and went to Iconium. ⁵²And the disciples were filled with joy and with the Holy Spirit.

Listening to the Text in the Story: Psalms 2:7; 16:10; Isaiah 49:6; Habakkuk 1:5; Luke 2:30–34; Hebrews 13:22.

EXPLAIN the Story

This next phase of the journey begins with Paul and his traveling companions sailing from Paphos, on the island of Cyprus, to the southern coast of Asia Minor. When they reached Perga in Pamphylia, their helper, John Mark, returned home to Jerusalem while Paul and Barnabas made their way to Pisidian Antioch (13:13–14). They continue their pattern of first preaching in the Jewish synagogues (vv. 14–15). What then follows is a long and significant speech by Paul (vv. 16–41). This episode concludes with a description of the impact of his preaching on his Jewish and gentile audience before the Jewish

---

5. Isa 49:6.

leaders stirred up opposition and forced the missionaries out of their region (vv. 42–52). The heart of this episode in the overall story of Acts is Paul's first sermon preached to Jews and gentiles. The setting includes both Jews and gentiles (in the form of converts to Judaism, v. 43), but nothing in the opening sentences (vv. 14–15) prepares the reader for the gentile response to Paul's words. Still, everything about the sermon aims at reaching both Jews and gentiles (see vv. 16, 26, 43, 46).

The Journey to Pisidian Antioch and the Departure of John Mark (13:13–15)

This phase of the journey begins with a terse travel narrative. Paul and his companions sail from Paphos on the island of Cyprus to Perga in the Roman province of Pamphylia. Bypassing the port of Attalia, they sailed up the river inlet to Perga, one of the largest cities in the province. It appears they did not preach or stay long in Perga, despite its being an important city in southern Asia Minor (modern-day Turkey). The only detail Luke provides is that John, their helper, "left them to return to Jerusalem" (v. 13). We are not provided with any information as to *why* John departs. Was John afraid of the difficult journey ahead through the dangerous and difficult mountainous terrain in southern Galatia? Did he lose interest in the mission, or did Paul's displacement of his uncle Barnabas as the leader of their group disturb him? Did the change to their travel itinerary upset him? Whatever the reason, we can only surmise the cause of his departure. We do know, however, that Paul did not approve of his departure, and when Paul and Barnabas were about to embark on another journey to revisit believers in Asia, they had a vigorous disagreement on whether to take him again. Barnabas wanted to take him; Paul did not. The disagreement could not be resolved, and Paul and Barnabas parted company over the matter (Acts 15:36–41).

From Perga they made their way north through the demanding Taurus Mountains to Antioch in the region of Pisidia, located in the southern part of the Roman province of Galatia. The maps that are often included in Bibles usually have straight arrows connecting the cities visited by Paul. As anyone who has traveled through mountainous territory will know, straight roadways in such terrain are rare. For Paul and Barnabas, they likely used a winding, paved Roman road, the *Via Sebaste*, which connected Perga and Antioch. Although the mission was moving into unfamiliar territory, there were several relational connections they would have looked for in their new location. First, the Roman proconsul from Cyprus, Sergius Paulus, may have provided a possible connection for them. It is a well-known fact among ancient Greco-Roman historians that Pisidian Antioch was the hometown of Sergius

Paulus.[6] It is not too far-fetched to assume that he would have provided letters of introduction in his home city for his newfound brothers in the Christian faith. Second, as always, they would seek out connections in the local Jewish synagogue if there was one there. In keeping with the custom in first-century synagogues, they would gather to pray and listen to Scripture being read from the Torah and the Prophets. Paul and Barnabas would join them for this service of the word. They would have stood out clearly as newcomers to the community. They may even have been wearing clothes that distinguished them as teachers from Jerusalem, much like academics and clergy are still recognized by academic gowns and clergy collars.[7] After the Scripture lessons were read, an appropriate man in the synagogue would expound on the texts. One of the duties of the synagogue leaders was to select someone to give this address. The leaders in Antioch sent word by an attendant to invite Paul and Barnabas to offer a "word of exhortation" for the people. This phrase may have been in use in the first century to describe a synagogue sermon (cf. Heb 13:22). Paul accepted the impromptu opportunity granted him.

Paul's Synagogue Sermon (13:16–41)

This is Paul's first address that is recorded rather than simply reported in Acts (e.g., Acts 9:20, 27–28; 11:16; 13:5). It is also the only "missionary" sermon that is preserved in Acts. That is, it is a message that is preached to convey the content of the gospel to a non-Christian audience. This is different from his later speeches that also convey the gospel but are more apology than proclamation. The sermon has three stages, and linking each stage is a form of direct speech:

> "Fellow Israelites and you Gentiles who worship God" (13:16)
> "Fellow children of Abraham and you God-fearing Gentiles" (v. 26)
> "Therefore, my friends" (v. 38)[8]

Despite some appearances to the contrary, it is a sermon that is focused on telling the story of God's salvation ("this message of salvation," v. 26). To tell this story, Paul combines stories about Israel and the story of Jesus. Paul's synagogue sermon has points of overlap with the earlier addresses of Peter (2:14–39; 3:12–26) and Stephen (7:2–53). For example, both Peter and Paul quote from Psalm 16:10 (cf. Acts 2:27; 13:35) and make the point that King

---

6. Keener, *Acts*, 2:2037–38.
7. Alexander, *Acts*, 102, cites "a later rabbinic source (Lam.R. 1.1.4) [that] records a saying of R. Huna: 'Wherever a Jerusalemite went in the provinces, they arranged a seat of honour for him to sit upon in order to listen to his wisdom.'"
8. Gaventa, *Acts*, 196.

David died and was buried, but it was Jesus, the descendant of David, who was raised from the grave and "did not see decay." Further, both Paul and Stephen emphasize similar themes that emphasize how God acts to choose, deliver, and exalt the people of Israel. What is entirely unique about Paul's address, however, is that his sermon is aimed at reaching both "*Israelites* [i.e., Jews] *and* you *Gentiles* who worship God" (v. 16).

Paul's sermon combines elements from both the OT and the life of Jesus in explaining salvation history. While we do not know what lessons were read from the Law and the Prophets (v. 15), his word of exhortation draws on a range of OT quotations and stories that traverse both the Law (vv. 17–19, 32, 39) and the Prophets (vv. 20, 27, 32, 34, 40–41). He begins by describing how God delivered Israel from Egypt, led them through their wilderness wanderings, and finally settled them in Canaan (vv. 17–20). After all this, he eventually gave them kings. God first gave them Saul to be their king before he put David in his place, a man whose heart beat for God and who would do God's will (vv. 21–22). David, then, serves as the lead-in to the story of his even greater descendant, Jesus. From out of David's own descendants God produced a Savior for Israel, Jesus. John the Baptist served as his forerunner and the final prophet preparing the way for the coming king (vv. 24–25).

The second stage of the sermon is signaled by the personal address to his "fellow children of Abraham and you God-fearing Gentiles" (v. 26). He then launches into the second act of the story of salvation by focusing on the suffering of Jesus in terms of what "the people of Jerusalem and their rulers" did to him (v. 27). Although the people acted in ignorance, nevertheless they fulfilled what the prophets said in their corporate act of denial. After turning Jesus over to the Romans, they "asked" Pilate to have him executed (v. 28). This request may reflect a similar kind of disobedience at work when earlier in their history the people of Israel "asked" for a king (v. 21). Paul emphasizes that *they* crucified Jesus and laid him in a tomb, *but God* raised him from the dead (vv. 29–30). After this Jesus appeared to his followers, who continue to be his witnesses to the people of Israel (v. 31).

The sermon now focuses on Jesus's resurrection as the fulfillment of the promise to their ancestors and to David (vv. 32–37).[9] While Jesus's followers from Galilee are his witnesses in Jerusalem (i.e., the homeland), Paul declares, "We tell *you* the good news" (v. 32)—that is, to those living everywhere else.

---

9. This theme of God's salvation "promise" draws on an overarching theme in Luke-Acts. This promise theme is struck early in Luke's Gospel in Mary's song, the *Magnificat* (Luke 1:46–55), Zechariah's song, the *Benedictus* (1:68–79), and Simeon's *Nunc Dimittis* (2:29–32). It is also dominant at the end of Luke (24:49). Not surprisingly, the promise motif also is present in the opening words of Acts (1:4) and punctuates the narrative, especially in the speeches of Peter (2:30, 33, 39; 3:21), Stephen (7:5, 17), and Paul (13:23, 32, 34).

This is the pivot of the whole sermon, even though the argument is a bit hard to follow. Paul begins by citing Psalm 2:7, a well-known messianic text and Davidic psalm. In Paul's sermon this passage is portrayed as "fulfilled" in the resurrection (cf. Rom 1:3–4). He then picks up the "promise" of the resurrection in the next few sentences (Acts 13:34–35). Jesus, unlike King David, is the one who was not "subject to decay." This is substantiated by a citation from Isaiah (v. 34; Isa 55:3): "I will give you [those now hearing] the *holy* [*hosia*] and sure blessings promised to David." This is what God has now done, because in another place (Ps 16:10) he promised that his "holy one" (*hosion*) would not see corruption. He then goes on to explain that this was *not* true of King David but has been fulfilled in King Jesus (Acts 13:36–37).

In all of Paul's words about Jesus, he is not primarily offering instruction on *who* Jesus is (i.e., "Christology") but on how God has *acted* to bring about salvation through him. Paul, therefore, brings the final phase of the sermon—signaled again by direct speech (v. 38)—to a conclusion by highlighting what Jesus does both for Jews and gentiles. In his final words (vv. 38–41), Paul makes two distinct points. First, through Jesus *everyone* who believes is justified. Everyone, Jew or gentile, gets in on this salvation. For those keeping in mind Luke's first book along with this second volume, they will recall that this is the good news that has been proclaimed since Jesus's birth (Luke 1:77) and the beginning of John the Baptist's ministry (3:3). Second, Paul also issues a warning. Those who read Moses and the Prophets (cf. Acts 13:15) must be careful not to reject the wonderful work that God is doing (v. 41). Here, then, is the message of salvation: it is something unattainable from the law of Moses; it is available to *everyone* who believes; and all hearers must be careful lest they, like Habakkuk's audience, unwittingly fulfill Scripture (Hab 1:5) by scoffing at God's promise and then "perish" in their disobedience.

God's Message Divides and Draws Opposition (13:42–52)

"Outsider" and "insider" are two sides of the same coin. Miroslav Volf articulates this as "exclusion" and "embrace" in his heralded book of the same title. Initially, the synagogue congregation in Pisidian Antioch *embraces* the prophet-and-teacher tandem of Paul and Barnabas, only later to violently *exclude* them from their midst. Yet initially Paul and Barnabas are not only urged to return the following Sabbath to continue speaking about "these things" (Acts 13:42) but continue in conversation with "many of the Jews and devout converts to Judaism" (v. 43).

Just as crowds gathered to hear "the word of God" proclaimed by John the Baptist in the Judean wilderness (Luke 3:2–7), so now crowds gather to hear "the word of the Lord" proclaimed by Paul and Barnabas in the Jewish diaspora (Acts 13:44–45). Strong messages, however, elicit strong reactions—both positive and negative. This pattern is not unfamiliar to the broad scheme of Luke-Acts. Although many Jews responded positively to the apostles' message, Luke writes that "the Jews" (cf. 17:5, 13; 18:12; 20:3, 19) were filled with "jealousy" (13:45; cf. 5:17) and began to contradict Paul's teaching. The word translated "jealousy" (*zēlos*) can connote either intense negative feelings toward something or intense positive feelings toward something. While in this instance the emphasis seems to be on the former, the English "jealous" may not entirely catch the nuance of the Jewish opposition in Antioch. For example, elsewhere believers are described as "zealous" (*zēlōtēs*) for the law (21:20). Paul also reminds others that what drove him to persecute Christians before his own conversion was that he was "zealous" (*zēlōtēs*) for God (22:3; cf. Phil 3:6). "The Jews" then may hold their energetic opposition to Paul's message not only because they are "jealous" but also because they have a "zeal" for God and his law and believe them to be under attack.

As this episode concludes, Luke draws the situation to a neat rhetorical close. The word of God is first proclaimed to Jews; the Jews reject the message; we now turn to the gentiles (Acts 13:46). This may be a tidy way of summing things up, but there is more going on than simple Jewish rejection and gentile acceptance. "Many of the Jews" embraced the gospel (v. 43). Further, Paul will continue his pattern of preaching "to the Jew first" wherever he travels (Rom 1:16). What is clear is that Paul's vocation, first declared in Damascus (Acts 9:15), is now affirmed on his first mission. This vocation is affirmed by what "the Lord"[10] commanded in Isaiah: "I will make you[11] a light for the Gentiles" (Isa 49:6). The purpose of this "light"—as the quote from Isaiah continues—is so that salvation might reach "to the ends of the earth." The end of the earth is not so much a geographic location as it is a theological perspective related to the mission to all peoples and across every boundary. It is the fulfillment of Jesus's final command before his ascension (Acts 1:8). This theme reaches not only back to the beginning of Acts but reaches back into the Gospel where it is echoed in Simeon's words to Mary: "For my eyes have seen your salvation, which you have prepared in the sight of all nations: a light for revelation to the Gentiles, and the glory of your people Israel" (Luke 2:30–32). The salvation seen by Simeon when he first laid eyes on the infant

---

10. It is worth noting the ongoing ambiguity in Acts with the usage of the word "Lord." This could either be Yahweh, the divine name of the "Lord" frequently used in the OT, or the "Lord" Jesus. In the next sentences this overlap can be noticed, as mention is made of the "word of the Lord" being honored and increasing. The "word of the Lord" points to Scripture, but Acts often declares that Jesus is "Lord" (cf. 2:36; 4:33; 7:59; 8:16; 9:5, 17; 10:36; etc.).

11. The Greek word behind "you" is singular, but Paul regards himself and his companions, not Israel, to be the "light" for the gentiles.

Jesus now enlightens the gentiles in Antioch and its surrounding region. The gentiles—and "all who were appointed for eternal life" (Acts 13:48)—were delighted in this "word of the Lord."

The evangelization of the Phrygian region around Antioch must have taken some time. Luke in typical fashion is not interested in the lapse of time. He spends most of this discourse on the speech and actions over the course of two Sabbaths and then summarizes what must have taken months with a simple sentence, noting that the word of the Lord "spread through the whole region" (v. 49). This is his compressed conclusion to the positive reception of the missionary work. But just as there is an opposite side to every coin, so too is there a negative response to Paul and Barnabas. In this we are also reminded of Simeon's final words to Mary: "This child is destined to cause the falling and rising of many in Israel" (Luke 2:34). While many Jews and gentiles receive the word of the Lord, the declaration that Jesus is the Savior of Israel draws opposition. Some of the Jews,[12] supported by "the God-fearing women of high standing and the leading men of the city," incite persecution against Paul and Barnabas (Acts 13:50). Alexander notes that "the role of 'women of high standing' (v. 50) fits with what we know of the attraction of highly placed women to Judaism, here used (as often in Roman history) as a short cut to the sources of civic power."[13] The result is that the apostles are escorted to the border of the city's region and expelled. As they leave the region, they enact the formal sign of protest as "they shook the dust off their feet" (v. 51; see 18:6; cf. Matt 10:14; Luke 10:11). As the missionaries turn to Iconium, about 120 kilometers (75 miles) southeast of Antioch, they leave behind disciples full of joy and the Holy Spirit (Acts 13:52). The same Spirit who filled and empowered the church of Syrian Antioch now fills and empowers the believers in Pisidian Antioch.

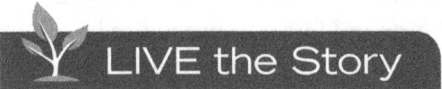

Signposts for Preaching and Teaching

Our family once spent a glorious holiday week in the city of Rome. Rome is an awesome city on so many levels. It has a multilayered history, it is full of artistic and architectural wonders, and its importance to the story of the

---

12. The Greek text simply refers to "the Jews" (*hoi Ioudaioi*), whereas the NIV interprets this as "the Jewish leaders."

13. Alexander, *Acts*, 108. Barclay, *Jews in the Mediterranean Diaspora*, 279–80, notes that an inscription dating from the middle of the first century in "Acmonia [in the province of Asia] indicates that an extremely prominent Gentile, Julia Severa, donated a synagogue building to the Jewish community."

Christian church is almost unparalleled. It is also a bewildering city. The traffic is horrendous. Motorcycles and scooters randomly weave through the maze of cars and trucks. And, of course, everyone speaks Italian and speaks it quickly! With all this, it can be difficult to find your bearings. Interestingly, this was even the case in the medieval times, when pilgrims from far-off lands made their way to Rome. In order to help pilgrims orient themselves to this large and important city, Pope Sixtus V (1585–90) moved four giant obelisks (that the Romans had previously brought from Egypt) into strategic locations throughout the city. While not all these long and narrow structures can be seen from any one vantage point, if you find one, there is a sight line to another. They function as large, ancient signposts to guide travelers.

In a manner similar to the way these obelisks functioned as signposts for pilgrims in Rome, Paul uses a system of "signpost" biblical events when preaching his first sermon for a synagogue congregation in Pisidian Antioch. The signposts so familiar to his listeners are the great events and characters of Israel's story: the exodus, the return to Canaan, the prophet Samuel, Kings Saul and David. As Paul walks through the biblical story with them, each one of these great events or persons functions as a marker that aligns and marks the Way of the gospel. This is instructive for us in our preaching and teaching. Of course, we must be aware of significant cultural differences between the first-century world and our own. Further, the examples of proclamation we have in Acts come by way of very short speeches or sermons. Even by the standards of many Anglicans I know who think a homily should be no longer than ten minutes, Peter and Paul's sermons in Acts are remarkably brief. In this, we must be aware that Luke has shaped, and possibly shortened, the addresses in service of his overall narrative. Still, we can be confident that they reliably convey what the apostles said, and we can learn helpful lessons from them.

What, then, can we learn from a sermon like Paul's in Acts 13? What are the instructive "signposts" they offer? First and foremost, we notice how Paul draws on the great biblical events and grounds their messages in the larger story of salvation. For Paul, Scripture, along with its signpost stories, was not a straitjacket but a springboard for the gospel. This is not to downplay the close reading of individual passages in Scripture. Detailed exegesis is vital. Yet every time we immerse ourselves in close readings of the text, we must also pull back and notice the connective tissue that binds it to the overall story. As Paul illustrates in Pisidian Antioch, his "word of exhortation" (Acts 13:15) encourages us to see how the story of Scripture—from the choosing of Abraham, the exodus, the promised land, and the Davidic kingdom—comes to a climax in God's fulfilling his promises to Israel and the world through Jesus (cf. vv. 23, 32–33). The story of Jesus does not begin with his birth in Bethlehem.

It begins in Genesis and is told every time the Law and the Prophets are read on the Sabbath.

A second signpost that Paul's sermon illustrates is the way Spirit inspiration is linked with study of Scripture.[14] Biblical teachers like Paul are not dispensers of data but are inspired reservoirs of the Spirit to bring new life. We must remember that Paul and Barnabas, before they were sent off on mission are described as teachers *and* prophets (13:1). Further, Luke highlights that they are sent and filled by the Holy Spirit for their mission, including the mission of proclamation (vv. 4, 9). For those called to roles of proclamation (e.g., preaching and teaching), preparation begins not only in the study of inspired Scripture but also in the power of the inspiring Holy Spirit. This is deeply humbling. As biblical preachers and teachers, we recognize that our effectiveness and fruitfulness depend not on slick presentation, clever turns of phrase, or novel insight. Our words are empty unless the Holy Spirit inspires our minds as we proclaim the faith.[15]

A final signpost for biblical preaching and teaching is the adaptability of Scripture. The core of the biblical message is consistent, but it requires sensitive adaptation to the contexts of our hearers. Preaching has a public responsibility. Peter and Paul's sermons in Acts have similar dimensions, yet both are shaped to the context of their listeners. They knew and understood their hearers. Peter is aware of the questions and perspective of his Jewish audience and the context of the day of Pentecost in Jerusalem (Acts 2). Paul is sensitive to the needs of his diaspora audience and the questions of God-fearing gentiles in southern Galatia (Acts 13). All good storytelling, especially the telling of *the* story of salvation, puts its hearers into the story. We all know good storytellers who do this well. One of the best storytellers I've ever heard was my Grandpa Katzberg. He died when I was a young boy, but I have vivid memories of him and his storytelling. He was a joyful man, brimming with laughter and self-deprecating humor. He had a full head of hair and lush eyebrows. He always carried a comb in his shirt pocket, and he would let us grandchildren crawl on his lap and comb his hair into crazy styles. Amid all the laughter, he would often ask us if we wanted to hear a story. Of course we did! He was a master bard. Most of his stories were biblical stories. Yet what he did so masterfully was not only tell great stories of the Bible but would put us *into* the stories. We would be put standing in the valley of Elah as one of the Israelite soldiers when David challenged Goliath. We would be put as Jehu's charioteer as he chased down the evil King Joram. We sat on the hillside

---

14. Cf. Levison, *Inspired*, 169–70.
15. Again, on this entire issue, see the important work of Jack Levison, *Inspired: The Holy Spirit and the Mind of Faith*.

in Galilee as Jesus preached his Sermon on the Mount. We ate the fish and bread Jesus multiplied for the five thousand. We watched with excitement and awe as the resurrected Jesus invited Thomas to take his finger and examine his nail-scarred hands. In all this, Grandpa Katzberg did what good biblical preachers and teachers still do: he put us in the story.

Renewing Disdain for the Church

I don't personally know any preachers who court conflict through their sermons. We do not seek conflict, but it is important to remember that Jesus, the Prince of Peace, often brings contempt. The mission and message of Jesus is uncomfortable and controversial. Jesus, after all, is the one who said, "Do you think I came to bring peace on earth? No, I tell you, but division" (Luke 12:51; cf. Matt 10:34). Whenever the early church proclaimed Jesus as God incarnate, the one sent so that through his death and resurrection forgiveness of sins could be recognized and received, this message invited decision and, frequently, incited division.

As a parish priest, I often court disdain, if not outright division, when I preach at the high points of the Christian year. One of the most uncomfortable sermons for me to preach is the early service on Christmas Eve. While I am grateful that our building is normally quite full of a diverse and committed group of worshipers at most services throughout the year, the nave is packed for our family service on Christmas Eve. I normally recognize a number of the faces that evening from the regular congregation, but there are often many more who are unknown to me. The surplus of worshipers is a mixed group. There are some who are lonely and seeking solace on a cold night at a dark time of the year. Others are family members of our regular parishioners who are home for the holidays, often visibly uncomfortable at being made to "come to church" just because it is Christmas. Some others make their annual pilgrimage, described so aptly by my fellow priest David Widdicombe, in order "to renew their disdain for the church." Amid this varied group, I try to preach a message that is a faithful and winsome proclamation of Jesus, the Word made flesh. Many find this assertion disdainful.

In my part of the world in the lead-up to Christmas, there are many vague, general references made about God. Words like "peace" and "joy" and "love" are ubiquitous. People seem comfortable at this time of the year to talk about God, using broad concepts and big ideas, but this keeps everything generic and at a safe distance. God, in this kind of language, is more akin to *Star Wars* and its view of the Force at work in the universe than to a Person at work in our life. But that is not true to experience, and it is not true to the Christ of Christmas. We can't love people in general, and we can't love God in general either. We are unavoidably particular. We live somewhere, with specific people, with neighbors who have names. Everything by which we know God is particular too. The God we know makes himself specifically known by becoming a human being. The message of Christmas brings us to the very heart of the Christian faith. That is, Jesus is God who became a man. Not, Jesus is God who became "man" in general.[16]

Acceptance of this particular message, this specific "good news," is troublesome and sometimes disdainful to my culture—including some of the very people who come to a Christmas Eve service. Why? Acceptance of the particular mission and message of Jesus means the rejection of "the etiquette of the generic"[17] in the Christmas season along with its vague and abstract notions about God. But this difficult acceptance is the necessary, solid, and particular reality of Christmas and the Christian faith. This specific and, for some, initially disdainful truth flattens the niceties, generalities, and idolatries of our cultural norms. This disdainful truth also paves the way for a relationship with the particular and personal triune God, made known to us in the man, Jesus.

---

16. This is articulated eloquently by Fr. Stephen Freeman in his blogpost, "A Particular Scandal," *Glory to God for All Things*, 19 May 2014, https://blogs.ancientfaith.com/glory2godforallthings/2014/05/19/a-particular-scandal/.

17. A pointed phrase used by Freeman, "Particular Scandal."

CHAPTER 28

Acts 14:1-7

LISTEN to the Story

¹At Iconium Paul and Barnabas went as usual into the Jewish synagogue. There they spoke so effectively that a great number of Jews and Greeks believed. ²But the Jews who refused to believe stirred up the other Gentiles and poisoned their minds against the brothers. ³So Paul and Barnabas spent considerable time there, speaking boldly for the Lord, who confirmed the message of his grace by enabling them to perform signs and wonders. ⁴The people of the city were divided; some sided with the Jews, others with the apostles. ⁵There was a plot afoot among both Gentiles and Jews, together with their leaders, to mistreat them and stone them. ⁶But they found out about it and fled to the Lycaonian cities of Lystra and Derbe and to the surrounding country, ⁷where they continued to preach the gospel.

Listening to the Text in the Story: Leviticus 20:2; 24:14; Deuteronomy 13:6–11; 17:2–5; 21:18–21; Romans 1:1; 1 Corinthians 1:1; 9:1; 2 Corinthians 1:1; Galatians 1:1.

EXPLAIN the Story

This short paragraph has three movements to it. The first (14:1–2) describes the reception and subsequent resistance Paul and Barnabas experienced when they visited Iconium. The second movement (vv. 3–5) expands on the work of "signs and wonders" they performed along with the resistance they received from both the gentiles and Jews of the city, including a plot to stone them. The final movement (vv. 6–7) explains what Paul and Barnabas did when they found out about the plot: they fled to Lystra and Derbe! While in these new locations they continued to proclaim the good news in these cities and their surrounding environs.

Reception and Resistance (14:1–2)

After leaving the region of Pisidia, Paul and Barnabas traveled to Iconium, present-day Konya, about 120 kilometers (75 miles) southeast of Antioch but still within the region of Pisidia. Whereas Antioch was a key city of Roman administration, Iconium was a relatively unimportant city in the region. Upon arriving in the city, the missionaries follow the same pattern established at the beginning of their journey: they spoke first in the Jewish synagogue (v. 1). As often the case elsewhere in the synagogues spread throughout the Roman Empire, there were both Jews and gentiles present. As on Cyprus and in Antioch, a number of Jews and "Greeks" (i.e., anyone non-Jewish) responded positively to the message about the Lord Jesus. Also true to pattern is the resulting opposition from "the Jews" to the missionary teaching (v. 2). Again, this did not refer to all the Jews in Iconium—Luke has just stated that a "great number of Jews . . . believed" (v. 1).

Resistance Intensifies (14:3–5)

Luke does not give any specific record as to what Paul and Barnabas teach while in Iconium. Since he has just related the long speech of Paul in the previous narrative (13:16–47), the implication is that their teaching follows the general content of that earlier message. Paul's speech in Antioch is a paradigm for all his subsequent synagogue messages preached in diaspora settings. Without giving a specific length of time, Luke does add that the reception and resulting opposition to their message required them to spend "considerable time there" (14:3a). Another interesting addition is that "the Lord . . . confirmed the message of his grace by enabling them to perform *signs and wonders*" (v. 3b). The implication here is that Paul and Barnabas carry on the same bold ministry of word and deed established by Jesus—"a man accredited by God to you by miracles, wonders and signs"—and mirrored in his followers sent to proclaim his word (2:22; cf. 2:43; 4:29–30; 6:8; 13:12). The words of grace are reinforced and verified by deeds of power.

Before long a plot is uncovered to mistreat and stone "the apostles."[1] Stoning was an accepted form of punishment in the law for misdeeds or blasphemy (see Lev 20:2; 24:14; Deut 13:6–11; 17:2–5; 21:18–21). In this instance it is not simply a mob that tries to instigate the punishment. Both "Gentiles and Jewish

---

1. Interpreters struggle to account for the term "apostles" in 14:4 and 14 with Luke's early description of qualifications for "apostles" (see 1:21–22). Some suggest that Luke has not been careful in how he edits his source material (e.g., Haenchen, *Acts*, 420; Hans Conzelmann, *Acts of the Apostles*, Hermeneia [Philadelphia: Fortress, 1988], 108). Barrett, *Acts*, 1:666–67, suggests Paul is an apostle, as in "envoy," of the church in Antioch, Syria. Peterson, *Acts*, 405, suggests that Luke may be aware of Paul's insistent claim to be the apostle to the gentiles (e.g., Rom 1:1, 5; 1 Cor 9:1–6; Gal 1:1). Cf. Keener, *Acts*, 2:2124–25.

leaders"—presumably synagogue leaders and Greek officials—support the action against the apostles. By now we recognize a pattern forming: synagogue proclamation, a measure of Jewish and God-fearing gentile reception, emerging opposition, and Jewish/gentile leaders joining together in action against Paul. Paul does not always emerge from these plots unscathed (see Acts 14:19), but in this instance he and Barnabas learn of the plan and manage to escape.

To Lystra and Derbe (14:6–7)

From Iconium, on the edge of the region of Phrygia, they flee to the Lycaonian cities of Lystra and Derbe (v. 6). Lycaonia was another of the local regions in the southern part of the Roman province of Galatia. William Ramsay states that the reference of Paul and Barnabas fleeing to Lystra and Derbe is "remarkable." It is remarkable because here "we have one of those definite statements involving both historical and geographical facts, which the student of ancient literature pounces upon as evidence to test accuracy and date."[2] It is only in the period between AD 37–72 that Lystra and Derbe were part of the Roman administration of Lycaonia in contrast to the non-Roman part ruled by King Antiochus. Ramsay argues the following:

> The subsequent narrative makes it clear that Paul visited only Lystra and Derbe. Why, then, should the author mention that Paul proceeded "to Lystra and Derbe and the region in which they lie"? The reason lies in his habit of defining each new sphere of work according to the existing political divisions of the Roman Empire. It is characteristic of Luke's method never formally to enunciate Paul's principle of procedure, but simply to state the facts and leave the principle to shine through them. And here it shines clearly through them, for he made the limit of Roman territory the limit of his work, and turned back when he came to Lystra. He did not go on to Laranda, which was probably a greater city than Derbe at the time, owing to its situation and the policy followed by King Antiochus. Nor did he go to the uncivilized, uneducated villages or towns of Roman Galatia, such as Barata.[3]

Luke uses an economy of words to convey a principle, usually missed by modern readers, that Paul was guided to go to the Roman world, especially its great cities, in his mission as God's "chosen instrument" to the gentiles (cf. Acts 9:15). This will help us understand why later in the narrative Paul's work can be considered finished once he has declared the gospel in the heart of the empire, in the capital city of Rome.

---

2. Ramsay, *St. Paul*, 100.
3. Ibid., 101.

LIVE the Story

Sometimes unbelievers assert that if they could only "see" a miracle performed in Jesus's name, then they would believe in the truth of the gospel. The evidence from the biblical record runs against the grain of this claim. The Israelites witnessed "signs and wonders" in the exodus as they left Egypt, and yet many of them failed the test of obedient belief when they reached the Sinai wilderness. When Jesus performed signs and wonders as part of his "new exodus" ministry in Galilee, many people refused to believe despite what they saw. In the same way, despite their message of grace being confirmed with "signs and wonders" (Acts 14:3), many people refused to believe—and even opposed—Paul and Barnabas. Again and again we see demonstrated in the biblical story that signs and wonders do not necessarily produce faithful belief. More often than not, signs and wonders seem to illuminate or even instigate opposition to obedient faith. The gospel, along with its demonstrative witness in signs and wonders, sharpens this reality. The fact is many people do not want more of God in their lives. It is often far more appealing and far easier simply to maintain the status quo of belief and behavior.

How often do we turn to the path of maintaining the status quo—even when it creates strange bedfellows for us? This was certainly the case in Galatia. In Iconium, even though "the people of the city were divided" in their response to the apostles' message, it is ironic that it also created a strange unity of opposition. Polytheistic gentiles and monotheistic Jews joined together to plot against the Christian missionaries. Both rejected the preaching directing them to "the Lord," Jesus. The challenge to both sides of this united opposition was the call to an allegiance to an invisible kingdom despite visible signs and wonders. The challenge for many first-century Christians was how to live in the face of this kind of multidimensional opposition and rejection. For many of us today, however, the question is nuanced differently. Many of us live off the cultural legacy where Christianity has been the maintainer of the status quo. Loveday Alexander reminds us that this requires careful reading of texts like this one for today:

> For us in the 21st century, it is impossible to read these narratives without an awareness of the centuries of Christian ascendancy that reversed the power structures and made Jews, not Christians, a persecuted minority in Europe. Luke could not have imagined the situation that led to the Holocaust, but we have to be careful not to perpetuate any reading of his narrative that demonizes 'the Jews' as the enemies of 'the apostles' and allows Christians to ignore or even support persecution of the Jews.[4]

---

4. Alexander, *Acts*, 109.

Another relevant question is how we choose to welcome or exclude others. While Jesus and his earliest followers prioritized care for the poor and the outsiders (e.g., women, slaves, barbarians), Christians in contemporary Western countries are now often in positions of power and influence to welcome refugees coming from war-torn countries abroad. As refugees clamor to escape brutal regimes and persecution, we can be tempted to maintain the status quo of our own communities. Much of this effort is driven by the fear of scarcity. The fear is that we don't have enough resources, enough jobs, enough housing, or enough. . . . These are complex problems, but we must repeatedly return to our founding story that roots us in "the message of [the Lord's] grace" (Acts 14:3) so that we might meet the complex challenges and questions of our day not with rejection but with love—a love that is rooted in the extravagant and abundant grace of God.

CHAPTER 29

Acts 14:8-20

LISTEN to the Story

⁸In Lystra there sat a man who was lame. He had been that way from birth and had never walked. ⁹He listened to Paul as he was speaking. Paul looked directly at him, saw that he had faith to be healed ¹⁰and called out, "Stand up on your feet!" At that, the man jumped up and began to walk.

¹¹When the crowd saw what Paul had done, they shouted in the Lycaonian language, "The gods have come down to us in human form!" ¹²Barnabas they called Zeus, and Paul they called Hermes because he was the chief speaker. ¹³The priest of Zeus, whose temple was just outside the city, brought bulls and wreaths to the city gates because he and the crowd wanted to offer sacrifices to them.

¹⁴But when the apostles Barnabas and Paul heard of this, they tore their clothes and rushed out into the crowd, shouting: ¹⁵"Friends, why are you doing this? We too are only human, like you. We are bringing you good news, telling you to turn from these worthless things to the living God, who made the heavens and the earth and the sea and everything in them. ¹⁶In the past, he let all nations go their own way. ¹⁷Yet he has not left himself without testimony: He has shown kindness by giving you rain from heaven and crops in their seasons; he provides you with plenty of food and fills your hearts with joy." ¹⁸Even with these words, they had difficulty keeping the crowd from sacrificing to them.

¹⁹Then some Jews came from Antioch and Iconium and won the crowd over. They stoned Paul and dragged him outside the city, thinking he was dead. ²⁰But after the disciples had gathered around him, he got up and went back into the city. The next day he and Barnabas left for Derbe.

Listening to the Text in the Story: Genesis 1:1; Exodus 7:1; Deuteronomy 11:14; 1 Samuel 12:21; Job 5:10; Psalms 4:7; 146:6; Romans 1:20; 2 Corinthians 11:25; 2 Timothy 3:11.

EXPLAIN the Story

After narrowly escaping a second round of persecution in Iconium (the first being in Pisidian Antioch), Paul and Barnabas left the region of Phrygia for the cities of Lycaonia to the southeast. While preaching in Lystra, a man, crippled from birth, listened to Paul's preaching and is healed (14:8–10). Paul, discerning[1] that the man had the faith to be healed,[2] dramatically tells him to "stand up." The man jumped to his feet, healed, to the amazement of the crowd around him (14:11–13). As Paul challenges the religious worldview of the astonished crowds (14:14–18), the amazement soon turns to resentment when some Jews travel from Pisidian Antioch and Iconium to incite a Lystran mob against them (14:19–20).

Dramatic Healing of a Lame Man (14:8–10)

The entire scene in Lystra is reminiscent of the account in 3:1–10 of God healing the man lame since birth sitting outside the Gate Beautiful in Jerusalem by Peter: Peter and Paul proclaim the good news (2:42; 14:7); Peter and Paul "looked" intently (3:4; 14:9; *atenizō*) at the man, and God dramatically heals him (3:6; 14:10); immediately the man jumps up and walks to the amazement of the surrounding crowds (3:10; 14:11). The sharp theological edge of both stories is that the healings result in direct confrontation with the religious establishment and, more importantly, the very basis of the people's worldview. Peter's call to turn from their disobedience and accept God's appointed Messiah, Jesus, had disturbed the priests and guards in the temple in Jerusalem (4:1–3); Paul's call to turn from "worthless things" and embrace "the living God" disturbs all those who worshiped "the gods" in the temple of Zeus just outside the city of Lystra (14:11–13, 15).

Confused Worship in Lystra (14:11–18)

The initial response of the crowds in Lystra to the healing appears positive (14:11). The crowds shout something in their local Lycaonian dialect, which may explain why the religious acclamations progress as far as they do. Luke tells us that the crowds proclaim the apostles to be Zeus and Hermes; the gods have taken on human form in their midst. The crowds' first impulse is to worship them and offer sacrifices (vv. 11–13). Numerous scholars observe that ancient people,

---

1. Luke uses a favorite word, *atenizō* ("to look directly/steadfastly"), to indicate Paul's discernment. This is reminiscent of Peter who "looked straight" (*atenizō*) at the cripple begging at the Gate Beautiful (Acts 3:4).
2. It is worth noting that the word translated "to be healed" is *sōzō*, which also can and does often mean "to save" (e.g., Acts 2:21, 40, 47; 4:12; 11:14; 15:1; 16:30, 31).

especially those in the Hellenized region of the Roman province of Galatia, believed the gods could appear in human form. Greek and Latin stories of the gods taking on the guise of humans to walk among them were well known.[3] One particular story is relevant for this episode in Lystra. Ovid recounts the story of Jupiter (the Latin name of Zeus) and Mercury (the Latin name of Hermes), who disguised themselves as mortals and visited a thousand homes in nearby Phrygia, searching for a place to rest (*Metamorphoses* 8.611–724).[4] All the homes denied them entrance except one: a humble dwelling inhabited by a poor elderly couple, Baucis and Philemon. When the gods reveal their true identity, they reward the welcoming and pious couple and punish the inhospitable and impious residents who rejected them. While it is impossible to know whether Luke is aware of the account from Ovid, as Kavin Rowe remarks, "the Lystrans' eagerness to honor Barnabas and Paul makes excellent sense in light of their religious prehistory: Zeus and Hermes had been sighted in the interior of Asia Minor before."[5]

When Paul and Barnabas recognize that the Lystrans are worshiping Barnabas as Zeus and Paul as Hermes,[6] their first impulse is to rend their clothes in the traditional prophetic response to blasphemy of this kind. Next, much like Peter did when meeting a prostrate Cornelius (Acts 10:26), Barnabas and Paul declare their humanness: "We too are only human, like you" (14:15). Beyond telling the crowds to stop what they are doing, they also urge them "to turn" from lifeless practices and vain gods—that is, from these "worthless things."[7] In effect, they are asking them to demolish their belief system and their understanding of the world. In a manner similar to Philip's challenge to the Ethiopian eunuch traveling on his "way" home, Paul challenges the Lystrans to cease going their own dead-end "way" (*hodos*; 14:15–16; cf. 8:39) and join with others who follow "the Way" (cf. 9:2). In place of Zeus—the chief of the Greek gods, the giver of rain and fertile crops—they are to worship the living God, the true Creator (Gen 1:1). The Creator has left them clues in creation itself (cf. Rom 1:20), and he is the one who sustains the earth with rain (cf. Deut 11:14; Job 5:10; Ps 65:10) and gives abundant crops (cf. Ps 4:7). Again, Rowe articulates this well: "As Luke would have it, the [end] of the pagan religious

---

3. Cf. Homer, *Odyssey* 17.483–87. Gaventa, *Acts*, 207, also points to Dan 2:46; Josephus, *Ant.* 10.211–12; Chariton, *Chaereas and Callirhoe* 1.1.16; 1.14.1; 3.2.15–17; Xenophon of Ephesus, *Ephesian Tale* 1.12.1.

4. Cf. Barrett, *Acts*, 1:677; Luke Timothy Johnson, *The Acts of the Apostles* (Collegeville, MN: Liturgical Press, 1992), 248.

5. Rowe, *World Upside Down*, 20.

6. This may appear backward to modern readers, but the identification of Barnabas as the leading god, Zeus, and Paul as the messenger god, Hermes, is likely due to the simple fact that Paul did most of the speaking.

7. Greek *mataia* is often used in the LXX to refer to the vain fashioning of idols and the false worship of other gods. Cf. Lev 17:7; 2 Kgs 17:15; 2 Chr 11:15; Isa 44:9; Jer 10:3; Ezek 8:10; Amos 2:4.

impulse is not in need of a different or additional name; rather, the impulse itself requires a fundamentally new direction, from dead worship to the living God."[8]

Paul Is Stoned (14:19–20)

At first the apostles' words do little to dissuade the crowds. Not surprisingly, when some Jews from Antioch and Iconium arrive and begin inciting the gathered admirers—perhaps even explaining the implications of Paul's radical critique of their religion and way of life—they help rework them from an amazed crowd to a violent mob. Paul may be God's "chosen instrument" (Acts 9:15) to share the light of Christ with the gentile world, but not all gentiles are interested in the message he proclaims. In fact, it is hard to imagine the Lystran gentiles turning so fierce had they not understood what turning away from their own "ways" and following "the Way" implied. They may have grasped that they were being asked to turn from their core religious, political, and personal beliefs. They were to put off all their familiar practices and pick up new ones. For them, it was too much. Instead, they chose the easier option. Just as Paul endorsed the stoning of Stephen when confronted with his radical theological critique (Acts 8:1), now the Lystrans stone Paul when challenged by his critique of their beliefs. After stoning him and dragging him outside the city, they leave him for dead (cf. 2 Cor 11:25; 2 Tim 3:11).

A few of the Lystran gentiles must have accepted the apostle's message and followed him since Luke adds that after leaving Paul for dead outside the city "the disciples . . . gathered around him" (14:20). This group may have included the lame man who was healed. We will learn later, however, of one notable disciple who comes from Lystra, Timothy (16:1). Timothy will become a traveling companion and close associate of Paul, undertaking many important missions in the early church. Without extra comment, Luke notes that Paul "got up and went back into the city" (14:20). The next day, he limps out of the city with Barnabas and travels to Derbe, the last city they were to visit on this missionary journey. Derbe, about a hundred kilometers (60 miles) further southeast from Lystra, sat on the edge of the Roman province of Galatia.

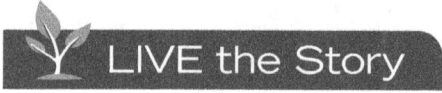

LIVE the Story

Idolatry—Ancient and Modern

In his important work on Acts, Kavin Rowe demonstrates that as Christian missionaries confronted the pagan world with the gospel, they were not only

---

8. Rowe, *World Upside Down*, 22.

challenging pagan religion but were critiquing the very fabric of pagan cultural life. He writes:

> To affirm that God has "created heaven and earth" is, in Luke's narrative, simultaneously to name the entire complex of pagan religiousness as idolatry and, thus, to assign to such religiousness the character of ignorance. Pagan religion, regardless of the specific differences engendered by time and locale, knows only the cosmos; it does not know God.
>
> This is not to say that Luke conceives idolatry in a facile manner, as if it were one simple thing, an uncomplicated realm of error. . . . Because "religion" in antiquity was not a category separable from the rest of life—as modern usage generally implies—this difference in the perception of divine reality amounts to vastly more than a mere difference in a discrete sphere of faith and ritual. . . . As both classic and more recent studies have shown, to take an ancient religion seriously in its various dimensions is to see that it "ran through all [of life's] phases." Ancient religion . . . is a pattern of practices and beliefs inextricably interwoven with the fabric of ancient culture. . . . Hence, to call into question pagan religion is to critique pagan culture: tear out the threads of pagan religiousness and the cultural fabric itself comes unraveled.[9]

Rowe's assertion is important for understanding why the Christian message was so subversive and threatening to pagan priests and crowds in Lystra (Acts 14), to owners of a mantic slave and colony magistrates in Philippi (Acts 16), to philosophers and political authorities in Athens (Acts 17), and to magicians and craftsmen in Ephesus (Acts 19). For those of us living in the modern "enlightened" world, where church and state are often separated and where the whole notion of religion is resigned to the private sphere, we might assume that cultural idols are no longer an issue. In this assumption we would be fatally wrong.

Westerners can be smug in their secularity. For example, when my wife worked in Nepal in the 1980s, she was traveling with a number of North Americans along a highway. As they were driving along the highway, they came across a big rock in the middle of the road. It wasn't so large that it could not have been moved. Instead, however, the road was paved around it because it was a sacred rock to the Nepalese. The Westerners noticed it, of course, and smirked at the locals for keeping it in place. After all, there was a big rock right in the middle of the road! The locals rarely even noticed it was there. It was simply a given. To visitors, however, it was clearly visible. The point is that

---

9. Ibid., 50–51.

every culture has its big rocks in the middle of the road. What are our "big rocks" that are sacred to us in our local cultures? What are the idols that are readily noticed by foreigners but overlooked and assumed by us? What might conversion to "the living God" from our idols mean for us?

For the early Christians, conversion to "the living God" was more than just a private and interior change of heart. It was more than rebranding—that which we once called Zeus and Hermes we now call the God of Israel and his Son, Jesus. Rather, it was an entire structural overhaul of one's worldview. It was a rejection of idolatry, "worthless things," and an embrace of the living God. This impacted every aspect of how one understood and lived in the world. It was more than a philosophical reform. It was a reinterpretation of all reality. This required identifying idols and destroying them. It meant rebuilding one's whole understanding of who "God" is. It meant exchanging the dead worship of "worthless things" made by human hands—whatever they may be and whatever they may be called—with worship of "the living God," the Maker of all things, the heavens and earth and sea and everything in them.

So, what are our cultural idols? Even more basic, what is idolatry in our context? If our assumptions about idolatry are one dimensional or ignorant, we will live blind to them. The Jewish tradition was clear on what idolatry was. An idol was something made by humans and invested with a significance that it could not carry, that is, as if it could help or "save" humans in some way. Isaiah describes how a blacksmith might shape a metal into an image or a carpenter might carve a form and then worship it, bowing down and praying to it (Isa 44:9–20; cf. Wis 13–15). Isaiah ascribes a blindness, ignorance, and shame to this kind of practice (Isa 44:9). Paul uses similar language when describing how those in his own day exchanged the glory of the invisible God for created visible things (Rom 1:21–25). Idols in the biblical tradition are "empty" and vain, disconnected from ultimate reality, and exhibit disobedience to the Creator God. Idolatry inverts reality by investing the "made" as something greater than the "Maker."

In the modern, enlightened, secular world we still maintain the long practice of idolatry by humanity, yet in different forms. Frederick Buechner winsomely describes idolatry as "the practice of ascribing absolute value to things of relative worth."[10] What are some of the idols that we worship and bow down to in our culture? In our day, idolatry is often less visible and diffuse than first-century Lystra, but no less invasive. For many in our culture, our idols—those things that we grant absolute value—might be money, nationalism, patriotism, family, "authentic sexual experience," morality, drugs, body

---

10. Frederick Buechner, *Wishful Thinking: A Theological ABC* (New York: Harper and Row, 1973), 40.

image, or even the ideal of "perfection" (e.g., the perfect house, the perfect job, the perfect spouse). At an individual level, each of us has our shame triggers that often have us turning toward an idol for help. When we feel that life is out of control, we turn to the idols of food, pornography, or entertainment as ways to avoid reality. When we awake from these virtual idolatries, we do so guilty and ashamed. At a corporate level, there are systems of idolatry that we worship too. Buechner observes:

> It is among the unreligious that idolatry is a particular menace. Having ushered God out once and for all through the front door, the unbeliever is under constant temptation to replace him with something spirited through the service entrance. From the moment the eighteenth-century French revolutionaries set up the Goddess of Reason on the high altar of Notre Dame, there wasn't a head in all Paris that was safe.[11]

Antidotes to Idolatry

As Christians, we must not be naive to idols, those "big rocks in the middle of the road" that our culture reveres. It is a temptation to live as if they don't exist or as if they are a part of normal paths along the Way. What then is the antidote for us? What is the switch that will thrust our idols into the light in all their overt and covert forms in our culture and within our hearts? To begin with, *God-focused worship* is one of the fundamental solutions. This means gathering together with other Christians with the focus set squarely on God, not us. As Robert Webber encourages as an antidote to "worship narcissism," we must teach Christians that the important question to ask after having gathered together as the church in worship is not, "What did I/you get out of it?" but, "Was God pleased with what we did today?"[12] It is about God, the lordship of Jesus Christ, and the empowering presence of the Spirit—not us!

Related to our rigorous attention to God through worship is *resistance to the cult of personality*. The Lystrans were willing to fall at the feet of Barnabas and Paul and declare them to be gods because of their stunning deeds and their eloquent words. Lest we think that only ignorant pagans fall at the feet of created beings, we should be reminded of the many times that even God-fearing people in the biblical story mistakenly fell at the feet of angels or apostles in worship (e.g., Acts 10:25–26; Rev 19:10; 22:8–9). More than once in our grand story—either past or present—Christians have fallen astray in supernatural excitement and misplaced devotion for God with devotion to

---

11. Ibid., 41.
12. Robert E. Webber, *The Divine Embrace: Recovering the Passionate Spiritual Life* (Grand Rapids: Baker, 2006), 94.

those who reveal God to us. This is idolatrous. Why do even we, as Christians, have such a hard time getting this right? Eugene Peterson concludes that we do so because it is easier:

> It is easier to indulge in ecstasies than to engage in obedience. It is easier to pursue a fascination with the supernatural than to enter into the service of God. And because it is easier, it happens more often. We have recurrent epidemics of infatuation with religion. People love being entertained by miracles. A religion of angels is a religion of supernatural excitement, of miraculous ecstasy. It is heady stuff. Around it for very long, any of us are apt to get swept off our feet and carried along in the general delirium. Revealing angels[13] have always proved more popular than the revealed God.[14]

Alongside attentiveness to God-focused worship and resistance to the cult of personality, another important antidote to help resist idolatry is *inspired biblical teaching*. Even though the healing of the lame man amazes the Lystran crowds and they are eager to believe that Zeus and Hermes had taken human form, Luke highlights the place the spoken word has over the amazing deeds that were performed. This is a common theme in the overall narrative in Acts. In this regard, Levison notes:

> Throughout the book of Acts . . . spectacular events that border on magic take second place to the sanity of the inspired interpretation of scripture. The holy spirit [*sic*] amazes throngs of people because it catalyzes the impressive and entirely unexpected abilities of scriptural interpreters. The inspired interpretation of scripture, more than mission in a general sense or miracles or speaking in incomprehensible tongues, is the principal effect of the holy spirit in the book of Acts.[15]

Inspired interpretation of Scripture need not be flashy, novel, or eloquent. It must, however, be nourishing. That is, it must promote spiritual growth. This growth is concerned not with size—as if just getting bigger was an indicator of health. Rather, spiritual growth is concerned with maturity. Paul describes this growth as becoming "in every respect the mature body of him who is the head, that is, Christ" (Eph 4:15; cf. Col 1:10; 2:19).

Finally, each of us must also be attentive to *guarding against the infection of idolatry*. Again, much like the role of inspired interpretation of Scripture with its focus on growth and maturity, the focus here is less on looking out for the

---

13. And I might add, even revealing apostles, or revealing evangelists, or revealing speakers.
14. Eugene Peterson, *Reversed Thunder: The Revelation of John and the Praying Imagination* (San Francisco: Harper & Row, 1988), 186.
15. Levison, *Inspired*, 152.

bad as learning how to taste the good. I've heard it told that banks do not train their tellers to discern counterfeit money by becoming familiar with different examples of fake bills. Rather, they require their employees to become familiar with the feel of authentic money. Once they do that, they will routinely discern the feel of true money. The same principle applies to food and wine. Give people good food and good wine, and their tastes will learn to discern bad food and bad wine. So how do we discern spiritual growth in our lives? What are some of the "taste tests" to recognizing maturity and development? My good friend and one of the associate priests in my parish, Cal Macfarlane, has four questions that are simple yet effective tools for discerning spiritual growth:

- Is my heart becoming softer to the things of God?
- Am I more thankful today than yesterday?
- Am I patient in suffering?
- Is fear diminishing in my life?

To the extent that we answer yes to these questions is an indicator whether we are maturing in our faith. The tools that Christians have used throughout the centuries to grow into mature followers of Jesus are the standard rhythms of private prayer (especially praying the Psalms), Bible reading, periods of fasting and feasting, bringing the teaching and example of Jesus into everyday life, giving of one's treasure as offering trust, and the receiving of holy Communion.[16] None of these practices, either individually or taken together, is the goal itself. They are only a set of tools to help and promote growth. Yet the Holy Spirit uses them to grow each of us into the full stature of Christ. As we worship God honestly and attentively in the company of fellow believers, as we receive nourishing and inspired interpretation of Scripture, and as we assist and discern the life of the Spirit in us, we will be protected from idolatry in its visible and invisible forms. Of course, when we do fall, when we are overcome in false worship, there is always the welcome relief of confession and forgiveness. In God's grace we always find steadfast love and infinite mercy when we come to him with contrite and repentant hearts.

---

16. This is what classically is known as framing a "Rule of Life."

CHAPTER 30

Acts 14:21-28

 LISTEN to the Story

²¹They preached the gospel in that city and won a large number of disciples. Then they returned to Lystra, Iconium and Antioch, ²²strengthening the disciples and encouraging them to remain true to the faith. "We must go through many hardships to enter the kingdom of God," they said. ²³Paul and Barnabas appointed elders for them in each church and, with prayer and fasting, committed them to the Lord, in whom they had put their trust. ²⁴After going through Pisidia, they came into Pamphylia, ²⁵and when they had preached the word in Perga, they went down to Attalia.
²⁶From Attalia they sailed back to Antioch, where they had been committed to the grace of God for the work they had now completed. ²⁷On arriving there, they gathered the church together and reported all that God had done through them and how he had opened a door of faith to the Gentiles. ²⁸And they stayed there a long time with the disciples.

Listening to the Texts in the Story: Luke 21:12–19; 1 Corinthians 16:9; 2 Corinthians 2:12; Colossians 4:3.

 EXPLAIN the Story

The next episode describes Paul and Barnabas's final destination on their first missionary journey, Derbe, and how they retrace their steps through Galatia (14:21–25) before returning to their sending church, Syrian Antioch (vv. 26–28). It is a brief recounting of the return trip. After leaving Lystra, Paul and Barnabas traveled southeast about a hundred kilometers (60 miles) to Derbe at the edge of the province of Galatia. Very little is discussed about this city or its church beyond the fact that the apostles' preaching was effective in winning a "large number of disciples" (14:21a). Derbe is notable for being visited by

Paul on his first and second missionary journeys (see 16:1), and likely on his third as well (18:23). One of his later traveling companions, Gaius, is also a native of Derbe (20:4).

A Return Journey through Galatia (14:21–25)

After preaching in Derbe, Paul and Barnabas did not continue eastward and take the short route to Syrian Antioch through the Cilician Gates in the Taurus Mountains. Instead they retraced their steps through Lystra, Iconium, Pisidian Antioch, the regions of Pisidia and Pamphylia, visiting Perga near the southern coast. Eventually they arrived in the port city of Attalia from which they sailed back to Antioch. All told, they traveled about two-thousand kilometers (1,200 miles) on their journey.[1] Although Luke is brief in his description of this return trip through Galatia (14:21b–25a), several important elements emerge. First, mention is made of strengthening the new disciples and encouraging them to remain true to their new faith (v. 22). The obvious reason for this is that in each of the cities where new churches were founded there also arose opposition (13:50), threats (14:5–6), and violence (14:19). A decision to follow Christ in these places was not without cost. It is not surprising that Luke records a simple line of admonition, echoing Jesus's own words (Luke 21:12–19), from the preachers: "We *must*[2] go through many hardships to enter the kingdom of God" (Acts 14:22). Hardships—translated variously in Acts as "suffering" or "troubles" or "persecution"—are part of the cost of traveling "the Way" with Jesus, the crucified Messiah. They are not a requirement to "enter" the kingdom, but they are the expected consequences of traveling with Jesus. Paul and Barnabas remind believers that these should be expected and that they are part of God's "map," so to speak, for believers. Hardships are not only the lot of leaders like Stephen or Paul but also are part of the expected experience of every believer. Like bumps, breakdowns, and bandits along the road, they accompany disciples along the route "through" to the kingdom. Reference to "the kingdom" is infrequent but not unimportant in Acts.[3] The reference to the kingdom seems to be strategic. It occurs in the opening words of Jesus (1:3) and the closing words of Paul (28:31) as a summary of the proclaimed truth of the Christian faith.[4]

---

1. Cf. Rasmussen, *Atlas*, 225–27.
2. The Greek word is *dei*. Gaventa, *Acts*, 209, helpfully reminds us that "elsewhere in Luke-Acts, *dei* signals something that is part of the divine plan, such as the suffering and death of Jesus. . . . The implication seems to be that the persecution of believers is to be understood as consistent with God's plan, not that it is an entrance requirement that believers must meet by virtue of their own conscious choice."
3. "Kingdom" is referred to eight times in Acts: 1:3, 6; 8:12; 14:22; 19:8; 20:25; 28:23, 31.
4. Barrett, *Acts*, 1:686.

In addition to providing encouragement in the faith for the new believers in Galatia, a second element is also mentioned: Paul and Barnabas appointed "elders" (*presbyteroi*) for each church (14:23). Until this point, the only mention of "elders" in Acts (cf. 4:5, 8, 23; 6:12; 11:30) refers to Jewish elders in Jerusalem—both those inside and outside of the believing community. The "elders" in this sense suggests not merely those who are older but those who were recognized as leaders. While Paul and Barnabas had a leadership role as the founding apostles of the Galatian churches, there was also the need to establish resident leadership in these new churches—not least because they will experience "hardships." It is Paul and Barnabas—the subjects of the verb "appoint"—who select the elders. Notably, they select elder*s*; that is, *plural* leadership for the congregations. In a manner reminiscent of their sending church in Syrian Antioch, the missionaries join with the church in "prayer and fasting" (14:23; cf. 13:3) before presenting the new leaders to the Lord in whom they had come to believe. With this, new spiritual disciplines accompany the forming of new leadership for the disciples. Located in strategic cities of southern Galatia, these new churches are equipped to influence many people living and traveling along one of the major thoroughfares of Asia Minor.

Back in Syrian Antioch (14:26–28)

The final paragraph of this section draws the first missionary journey to a close (14:26–28). From Attalia they sail back to Syrian Antioch and give an accounting of their travels. Again, Luke reminds us of what God graciously does *through* them (v. 27; cf. 15:4). God always acts first. From first to last God is the initiator of mission through the early church. Although Paul and Barnabas regularly began their preaching of the gospel in the Jewish diaspora synagogues of Cyprus and Galatia, the real story of their mission was the open "door of faith to the Gentiles" (v. 27). In his letters, Paul will employ the "open door" metaphor to describe how God made the way possible for the story of a Jewish Messiah to be received by gentiles (1 Cor 16:9; 2 Cor 2:12; Col 4:3; cf. Rev 3:8).[5] As they recount how a large number of gentiles began entering the church through their ministry, this news will not be contained to Antioch. Soon the "mother church" in Jerusalem will hear the story too. Before long, this will raise the question of how gentile converts should relate to the Mosaic law, especially with regard to the issue of circumcision. After Paul and Barnabas stay with the disciples in Antioch "a long time" (v. 28), they will travel to Jerusalem to participate in a discussion of the issue of gentile inclusion. The open door to the gentiles also opens the proverbial "can

---

5. Dunn, *Acts*, 194.

of worms" for Jewish believers on *how* the gentiles are to come through this door. The issue of gentile inclusion is what Luke turns to next in the following narrative, the so-called "Council at Jerusalem."

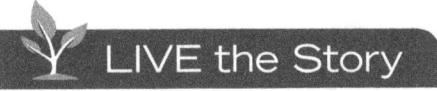

LIVE the Story

Encouragement and Equipping

There are plenty of meaty details in this short description of the work of Christian mission. Paul and Barnabas do not evangelize and leave; they also return so that encouragement and equipping can occur. *One part of the encouragement* is to remind the believers in southern Galatia that following Christ is costly. Grace is abundant, free, unmerited, and without regard to work or worth. Yet those who receive the gift of grace should expect hardships to follow. The hardships are not inevitable, but they will often accompany those who follow a Messiah who suffered abuse from his countrymen and was crucified by imperial decree. Jesus and Paul's own examples remind those who follow the way of the kingdom that they will often experience sufferings akin to their king and his companions. This is part of Christian discipleship. It should be encouraging to know that as we participate in the suffering of our king, we will also share in his glory (e.g., Phil 3:10).

One part of the equipping is to establish local leadership. We are not given much detail at this point in Acts about the qualifications and virtues of this leadership. One detail given is that Paul and Barnabas appointed elders in each church. Each church received *plural* leadership. This seems consistent with Paul's epistles, where plural leadership is the consistent model. This stands in contrast with much of our experience of church leadership in North America, where there is far too much expectation that each church has a singular, omnicompetent leader. The assumption is often that there must be just one person who makes the final decision on matters because he or she is the gifted and ordained one. Here we might be reminded of the wooden sign that sat on President Truman's desk that read, "The BUCK STOPS here!" This emphasis on singular leadership plays off the hyper-individualism of our culture. We crave for strong individuals who will boldly lead us with resolve and assurance. This kind of singular leadership can often generate enthusiasm, decisive judgment, and rapid success. This is important if one is playing a game of football or fighting a war, but not as helpful if one wants to nurture relationships and build community. At its worst, the concentration of individual power gives room for the cult of personality, misinformed judgment, and abuse of authority. While plural leadership is no guarantee that perfect decisions will be made or all abuses will be avoided, it often fosters sober decisions and tempers abuse. Plural leadership can speak with unity and model love and community. After all, our ultimate model is our triune God—one God, three Persons working in love and unity and perfect communion.

What God Does through Us

When Paul and Barnabas arrive back in Syrian Antioch, they called the church together to tell them "all that *God had done* through them and how *he had opened* a door of faith to the Gentiles" (Acts 14:27). This is the consistent message of the entire narrative. God is first. God acts. God opens. It is a reminder to us all that we are subordinate to God, and everything we do comes through him. This is not to denigrate us. It just gives us perspective. But even more than that, these words reflect an indescribable sense of joy and achievement. After prayer and fasting, the church in Antioch sent this small band on mission, and look at what God has done through them! A door has been opened to the gentile world. They launched out in faith, and their trust in God has borne fruit. By all accounts, when the small party left the church in Syrian Antioch, the church had no idea what would happen to them. Now that Paul and Barnabas have returned, they recognize they have been used by God to establish something remarkable. How often does that happen for us? We start a small project, extend a kindness, or offer a simple invitation, and God makes something extraordinary out of our efforts. God can take a few loaves and fish and feed a multitude. God can take a few obedient followers and open a door to the world.

CHAPTER 31

Acts 15:1-21

 LISTEN to the Story

¹Certain people came down from Judea to Antioch and were teaching the believers: "Unless you are circumcised, according to the custom taught by Moses, you cannot be saved." ²This brought Paul and Barnabas into sharp dispute and debate with them. So Paul and Barnabas were appointed, along with some other believers, to go up to Jerusalem to see the apostles and elders about this question. ³The church sent them on their way, and as they traveled through Phoenicia and Samaria, they told how the Gentiles had been converted. This news made all the believers very glad. ⁴When they came to Jerusalem, they were welcomed by the church and the apostles and elders, to whom they reported everything God had done through them.

⁵Then some of the believers who belonged to the party of the Pharisees stood up and said, "The Gentiles must be circumcised and required to keep the law of Moses."

⁶The apostles and elders met to consider this question. ⁷After much discussion, Peter got up and addressed them: "Brothers, you know that some time ago God made a choice among you that the Gentiles might hear from my lips the message of the gospel and believe. ⁸God, who knows the heart, showed that he accepted them by giving the Holy Spirit to them, just as he did to us. ⁹He did not discriminate between us and them, for he purified their hearts by faith. ¹⁰Now then, why do you try to test God by putting on the necks of Gentiles a yoke that neither we nor our ancestors have been able to bear? ¹¹No! We believe it is through the grace of our Lord Jesus that we are saved, just as they are."

¹²The whole assembly became silent as they listened to Barnabas and Paul telling about the signs and wonders God had done among the Gentiles through them. ¹³When they finished, James spoke up. "Brothers," he said, "listen to me. ¹⁴Simon has described to us how God first intervened to choose a people for his name from the Gentiles. ¹⁵The words of the prophets are in agreement with this, as it is written:

> ¹⁶"'After this I will return
>   and rebuild David's fallen tent.
> Its ruins I will rebuild,
>   and I will restore it,
> ¹⁷that the rest of mankind may seek the Lord,
>   even all the Gentiles who bear my name,
> says the Lord, who does these things'[1]—
>   ¹⁸things known from long ago.
>
> ¹⁹"It is my judgment, therefore, that we should not make it difficult for the Gentiles who are turning to God. ²⁰Instead we should write to them, telling them to abstain from food polluted by idols, from sexual immorality, from the meat of strangled animals and from blood. ²¹For the law of Moses has been preached in every city from the earliest times and is read in the synagogues on every Sabbath."

Listening to the Text in the Story: Exodus 20:3; Leviticus 17–18; Isaiah 45:21; Jeremiah 12:15; Amos 9:11–12; Matthew 11:29–30; Romans 14–15; 1 Corinthians 8–10; Galatians 2:1–10.

EXPLAIN the Story

Jesus Christ commissioned his disciples to "be my witnesses in Jerusalem, and in all Judea and Samaria, and to the ends of the earth" (Acts 1:8). It is true that his disciples did not immediately embark on this commission, and when they did, as in the case of Peter's mission to Caesarea, they sometimes did so reluctantly. Still, if Jesus Christ is indeed "Lord of all" (10:36), then Christian mission to the whole world is the necessary response to this claim. After Peter declared the universal lordship of Jesus to Cornelius and his household, Luke describes how the early church in Antioch got on with this mission to "the world" by sending out Paul and Barnabas. By all accounts, this first mission journey to the gentile world was a success. Yet its very success brought the early church to a crossroads.

The apostolic council in Jerusalem is a crucial moment in the story of the early church. The stakes were high. The decision the early church would make here would shape who they would be (*identity*) and how they would be

---

1. Amos 9:11, 12 (see Septuagint).

together (*unity*).² In this council, the leadership of the early church would deal with the watershed ethnic question: What is to be the basis of the inclusion of gentiles in the newly constituted people of God? The issue of diversity and inclusion had been hinted at in earlier stages of the narrative. To begin with, tensions emerged when disagreements occurred in Jerusalem between the Hebraic and Hellenistic Christians (6:1–4). This was a tension between Jews with different cultural backgrounds. Later, when "the word of God" spread outside Judea, the apostles sent Peter and John from Jerusalem to investigate what had occurred among their neighbors and ethnic cousins in Samaria (8:14–25). Here the question of inclusion stretched the early church, but Samaritans still had a measure of ethnic connection with the Jewish Christians, however strained it may have been. Yet when Peter shared the gospel to the receptive household of a Roman centurion, Cornelius, it led Jewish Christians to criticize even this leading apostle (11:1–18). Granted, this was only one household, but the hole was in the dike. Now, with reports of gentiles accepting the gospel preached by Paul and Barnabas throughout cities on Cyprus and in Galatia, the dam burst. A resolution to this question of the widening movement's connection to its Jewish heritage must be made. As Dunn observes, "It was . . . imperative, before Paul's mission became more extensive and less under Antioch's (and Jerusalem's) oversight, to address the problems caused by the success of Paul's mission for what was still essentially a Jewish sect, and to show how harmony between Jew and Gentile within the new movement could be maintained without sacrificing the continuity with and through Jerusalem."³

How Luke describes them reaching this objective is straightforward. Luke sets the stage for the council by describing a confrontation between Jerusalem Christians and those in Antioch that results in an Antioch delegation being sent to Jerusalem to speak with the apostles and elders there (15:1–5). While Barnabas and Paul will have their say (v. 12), the bulk of the testimony comes from Peter (vv. 6–11). James draws the arguments to a conclusion and, based on a reflection from Scripture, offers directive recommendations for the council (vv. 13–21). The following section describes how this decision was implemented (vv. 22–35).

Luke's accounting of the Jerusalem Council has vexed scholars who, for well over a century, have tried to reconcile or relate the details of Luke's account in Acts (15:1–21) with Paul's description of a similar event in his letter to the Galatians (2:1–10). Scholars are divided on whether these are two accounts

---

2. Dunn, *Acts*, 195.
3. Ibid.

of the same event[4] or two separate events altogether.[5] It is unnecessary here to untie all the knots in this complex debate.[6] In the end, Luke's historical account and Paul's personal account of the so-called "Jerusalem Council" are likely reconcilable. This is possible if the historian (Luke) and the participant (Paul) are allowed to express their accounts of the same event within the framework of different overall concerns and thus different points of view.[7]

The Situation in Antioch and Jerusalem (15:1–5)

Luke's version of the Jerusalem Council begins by describing the event that instigated the meeting. First, "certain people came down from Judea" (Acts 15:1) and began to teach that gentile believers must be circumcised to be "saved." Although there have been hints about this kind of Jewish pushback earlier (cf. 10:45; 11:2; 13:45), this is the first open argument for this theological position. The "certain people" were not likely sent to Antioch as authorized representatives from the Jerusalem church (cf. 15:24). We will learn that these people were of the "party of the Pharisees" who demanded that gentiles be circumcised and keep the Mosaic law (v. 5).[8] This suggests that they were a distinctive group or party from the "apostles and elders" (v. 2). Whether they were official representatives (or not) from Jerusalem, the point is that they

---

4. There are a number of factors that indicate both Acts 15 and Gal 2 are recording the same event. The similarities include: (1) both events occur in Jerusalem; (2) both events involve the same individuals (Paul, Barnabas, Peter, James, and "the apostles"); (3) the same issue of circumcision is in play; (4) both fit together at about the same time—Paul suggests it is seventeen years after his conversion (Gal 1:18; 2:1) and Luke places the council before the mission to Philippi, Thessalonica, and Corinth (ca. AD 49–51); (5) the problem is "in house," that is, by "some of the believers who belonged to the party of the Pharisees" (Acts 15:5) and "some false believers" (Gal 2:4); (6) the same solution is offered in both accounts—there is to be no circumcision of gentiles.

5. There are arguments that suggest Acts 15 and Gal 2 are recording different events, including: (1) in Acts this is Paul's *third* visit to Jerusalem as a Christian, whereas in Galatians it is his *second* visit; (2) Luke writes that "Paul and Barnabas were *appointed* . . . to go up to Jerusalem" (Acts 15:2), while Paul writes that "I went in *response to a revelation*" (Gal 2:2); (3) Luke presents an open council, with much debate, on the issue of circumcision raised by the church in Antioch, whereas Paul suggests that the issue was raised after he arrived in Jerusalem in a private discussion with the leaders in Jerusalem.

6. For guidance through the complicated scholarly debate, see Alexander, "Chronology of Paul," *DPL* 115–23. For longer discussions and differing conclusions, see R. Jewett, *A Chronology of Paul's Life* (Philadelphia: Fortress, 1979), and Hemer, *Acts*, 244–76.

7. That is, Luke the historian is offering a historical narrative that has a broad view of the story of the early church, and this may account for his more stylized rendering of individual episodes. Paul, on the other hand, is writing to the Galatians in which the occasion of the letter—some of the Galatian Christians turning to a "different gospel" (Gal 1:6)—set the agenda for his description of the Jerusalem meetings.

8. Circumcision is traced back to Abraham (Gen 17:9–14; cf. Lev 12:3). While other people groups also practiced it, it became one of the distinctive markers of Jewish identity (1 Macc 1:15; Josephus, *Ant.* 1.192; Tacitus, *Hist.* 5.5.2); see Gary Gilbert, "Acts," in *The Jewish Annotated New Testament*, ed. Amy-Jill Levine and Marc Zvi Brettler (Oxford: Oxford University Press, 2011), 227.

had firm biblical ground and historical precedence to advocate that gentiles be circumcised.[9]

After these people began to advocate their position in Antioch, Paul and Barnabas respond with a fierce protest[10] against their view (v. 2). Here we have the making of the two sides of the debate: "certain people" from Judea on one side and Paul and Barnabas on the other. The outcome of this disagreement is that the church in Antioch wishes the matter to be settled in Jerusalem. They determine that Paul, Barnabas, and some other believers will go up to Judea. While the NIV rearranges the phrases so that it reads better in English, the order is interesting in the Greek text:

1. "to the apostles and elders"
2. "to Jerusalem"
3. "about this question"

The implication of this order suggests that this is an issue that requires apostolic authority. Further, Luke seems to emphasize that the call for a "council" was at the impetus of the church in Antioch, not Jerusalem. Thus, he then reports about their delegations' journey "up to"[11] Jerusalem. After they had been sent on their way by the church, the Antioch delegation travels through Phoenicia and Samaria (15:3). As they journeyed through locations with Christian residents, they explained in detail about the breakthrough of the gospel to the gentiles. News of this brought great joy to the brothers and sisters who heard about it (v. 3). Luke seems to be driving home the point that there are other Jewish Christians who are delighted to hear about the fruitfulness of the gentile mission.

Upon arriving in Jerusalem, Paul, Barnabas, and the other members of the Antioch delegation were welcomed by "the apostles and elders" (v. 4a). Who were these apostles and elders? The apostles are likely "the Twelve" (cf. 1:26; 6:2)—or at least some combination of them that included Peter. The "elders" (*presbyteroi*) is a more general title, used frequently to refer to recognized leaders in Jewish communities, including synagogues and the community of Qumran (e.g., Exod 17:5; Ruth 4:2; Luke 7:3; Acts 4:5; 6:12; Josephus, *Ant.* 12.406; 1 QS VI, 8; etc.). Here it is used to refer to leaders of the church in Jerusalem, likely mirroring the structure of the synagogue. Paul and Barnabas

---

9. On the biblical ground, see Gen 17:9–14; Exod 4:24–26; Lev 12:3; Josh 5:2–9; for historical precedence, see Esth 8:11–12, 17; Jdt 14:10; Josephus, *Ant.* 13.257–58; *J. W.* 2.454; 1 Macc 1:60–61; 2 Macc 6–7.

10. "Sharp dispute" is how the NIV translates the Greek *stasis*—a word elsewhere in Acts used to convey a riot or violence (19:40; 23:10; 24:5; cf. 23:7).

11. That is, their journey south. Most North Americans tend to think of a journey south as one that is "to go down."

report to Jerusalem "everything *God* had done through them" (v. 4b). This report highlights that it is God who has taken the initiative in the gentile mission, not them. This report is met with a response: "*But* [*de*; NIV "then"] some of the believers who belonged to the party of the Pharisees stood up and said . . ." (v. 5). Their demand is twofold: first, gentile Christians "*must be* circumcised" if they are to belong to the covenant people of God, and second, gentile Christians *must keep* the law of Moses—the covenant requirements for the people of God.

Peter, Barnabas, and Paul Give Witness (15:6–12)

After establishing the setting for the meeting in Jerusalem, Luke describes some of the deliberations of the council proper. We are not provided with any precise number of people present at this gathering or how long the debate lasted. Luke appears not to be interested in the details of the proceedings. Rather, he is interested in the results and the opinions of the figures that support the church in Antioch. Nothing else that the party of the Pharisees may have said in their defense is recorded. We only read that "after much discussion" (v. 7a) several named individuals offer their opinion on this issue. The first is Peter, the leading apostle and the first one to declare the gospel to gentiles (i.e., Cornelius's household, 10:27–48).

Peter's address (15:7b–11) is an abbreviated summary of the Cornelius narrative. Of particular note is the emphasis that is placed on God's action. He stresses the fact that "*God* made a choice among you that the Gentiles might hear from my lips" (v. 7b). This was then sealed by the gift of the Holy Spirit to "them"—exactly as he gave to "us" (v. 8). This is the same point affirmed in the Cornelius narrative (chs. 10–11). In making this choice and in granting this gift, God made it clear that there should be no distinction between "them" and "us." The assertion that God "purified their hearts by faith" (15:9) speaks directly to the issue at hand. The gentile Christians are not "purified" by circumcision or by keeping the law. Instead of beginning with outward identity markers, God begins with inward matters by cleansing the center—the heart (cf. Ps 51:10). Peter continues that adding external demands of the law for the gentile converts is tantamount to putting God to the "test" (Acts 15:10). In this, the Jerusalem church may well have heard the echo of warning from the situation with Ananias and Sapphira (5:9–10) and even further back historically to the time of Israel in the wilderness (Exod 17:2; Deut 6:16; Ps 78:41). Furthermore, this demand to keep the law turns out to be a "yoke"—and not the kind of yoke that fits but the kind that is burdensome and impossible to carry. In fact, Peter adds that these demands crushed both "our ancestors" and us (cf. Gal 5:1). The crushing burden of the Mosaic law does not refer only to circumcision—after all, no first-century Jew would regard circumcision in itself as a "yoke." The issue of the burden of the law is one that pitted Jesus repeatedly against the Pharisees in the Gospels. Jesus invites his Jewish hearers to change yokes (Matt 11:29–30), and it is the "weary," not the strict Pharisees, who come to him (Matt 11:28; 23:4; cf. Luke 11:46). Peter's personal experience illustrates this. Peter and his fellow disciples were not strict keepers of the law when they followed Jesus. They ate with people regarded as unclean (Matt 9:11), they did not fast (Luke 5:33), they picked grain on the Sabbath (6:1–2), and they ignored the ritual regulations of the "elders" (Mark 7:1–5). Peter sums up his position with a phrase reminiscent of Paul's own language: "We believe it is through the grace of our Lord Jesus that we are saved, just as they [i.e., gentiles] are" (Acts 15:11; cf. Gal 2:16; Rom 3:24; Eph 2:5–8). These are Peter's final recorded words in Acts.

After Peter's address, Barnabas and Paul offer their opinion (Acts 15:12). The order of their names is noteworthy. Now that they are back in Jerusalem among fellow Jews, Barnabas resumes his place as group leader. Their testimony, situated between Peter and James, is brief, and they are only narrators of what God has done (cf. v. 4). They do add, however, the note of "signs and wonders" that accompanied the gentile mission (cf. 14:3). This reference to "signs and wonders" links the mission to the gentiles with the mission of Jesus (2:22) and the apostles' ministry among the Jews (2:43; 5:12; 6:8). Interestingly, in this short account by the missionary duo there is no mention of any specific Pauline theological reflection on this matter.

The Address of James (15:13–21)

That it is James—not Peter—who draws the arguments to a conclusion and offers the directive advice to the Jerusalem gathering is noteworthy. At the very least it suggests he has become an important figure in the early church in Jerusalem. In many ways, however, James is an enigma. Both in Luke's record of him in Acts and in Paul's reference to him in his letters, he is referred to as someone who is well known. In the Gospel of Mark, we learn that he is a brother of Jesus (Mark 6:3). On the one hand, James is not what could be described as a convinced disciple of his older brother (Mark 3:31–35; cf. John 7:1–10). On the other, he is mentioned as one of the first to meet the risen Jesus (1 Cor 15:7), and he joins his mother Mary in gathering together with the company, prayerfully waiting in Jerusalem after the ascension (Acts 1:14). Three years after his conversion, Paul mentions that he went up to Jerusalem to see Cephas (i.e., Peter) and "James, the Lord's brother" (Gal 1:18–19). By the time we come to the council (Acts 15), James is the recognized leader in the Jerusalem church.

How did this come about? Why James and not Peter? This is a difficult question to answer since it lies beyond Luke's interests. The evidence in Acts suggests that Peter is the primary spokesperson in the early stages of the church's development in Jerusalem. After the persecution of Stephen, Peter appears more frequently *outside* of Jerusalem in places like Samaria (Acts 8:14), Lydda (9:32), Joppa (9:38), and Caesarea (10:1–48). When he does return to Jerusalem, he speaks not as their leader but as one summoned to explain his actions (11:1–18). Peter remains in Jerusalem long enough to be arrested by Herod and, later, to be miraculously released (12:3–10). When he finally does arrive at the door of Mary, the mother of John, to announce his release, he tells them how the Lord delivered him from prison and then says, "Tell *James* and the other brothers and sisters about this." Then "he left for *another place*" (v. 17). Peter does not return to Jerusalem until the council is summoned (15:6–7), and after his testimony he disappears from the narrative. Between Peter's journeys and his arrest by Herod, James assumes leadership of the Jerusalem church. Apparently, while many of the Hellenistic Jewish Christians leave Jerusalem amid the early period of persecution after Stephen's martyrdom, James remains in the city. Perhaps to avoid persecution, he and other Jewish Christians may have put more emphasis on their Jewishness—especially in their observance of the Mosaic law. This seems to be corroborated by the picture we have of James from his own letter, along with evidence outside the NT by the early-church chronicler, Hegesippus (ca. AD 110–180), as recorded in Eusebius.[12] Eventually, James was arrested and executed by the Sanhedrin shortly before the Romans sacked Jerusalem during the Jewish revolt (Josephus, *Ant.* 20.200).

It is this James, the leader of the Jerusalem church, who addresses the gathered Christian council. In his address he makes two key points. First, after referring to Peter and the gentile conversion in Cornelius's household (Acts 15:14), he emphasizes that this is the activity of God. Again, as we noticed earlier in Peter's address (vv. 7, 8, 9, 10), the priority is placed on the initial act of God. It is God's idea to include the gentiles, to choose them as his "people" (cf. Deut 14:2; Ps 135:4). The call of the gentiles is not in addition to Israel's call but inclusive of Israel's call.

Second, Scripture supports God's action. That is, "the words of the prophets are in agreement with this" (Acts 15:15)—*not* God's action is in agreement with the prophets. The authority of Scripture relies on the authority of God, not God on the authority of Scripture. In this instance, it is the combined testimony of several prophets who look for the renewal of Israel: the bulk of the text is from Amos 9:11–12 along with introductory words echoing Jeremiah (12:15)

---

12. Eusebius, *Hist. eccl.* 2.23.4–18.

and with closing words echoing Isaiah (45:21).[13] The emphasis begins with the language from Jeremiah that envisages God's "return" to restore Israel from its hostile captors. The citation continues with the promise that God will also "rebuild David's fallen tent" (Acts 15:16; Amos 9:11). As in earlier Lukan texts (Luke 1:32–33; Acts 1:6), the language of "rebuilding" points to a restoration of Israel.[14] This time, however, the rebuilding is not of a physical house made by human hands but a people for his name. The consequence of this rebuilding, which is the real point of the Amos citation, is "that the rest of mankind may seek the Lord, even all *the Gentiles who bear my name*, says the Lord, who does these things" (Acts 15:17; Amos 9:12). Here the text in Acts follows the LXX translation of Amos 9:12, not the Hebrew of Amos 9:12. The reason for this is simple: the point of gentile inclusion is not found at all in the Hebrew.[15] The citation ends with an allusion to Isaiah's famous passage denouncing idols with the closing phrase: "Things known from long ago" (Acts 15:18; Isa 45:21). The final point in this is that it is all according to God's ancient plan.

Taken together in Luke's arrangement, the testimony of the prophets draws together and interprets the arguments of Peter, Barnabas, and Paul. God has done the dramatic and miraculous work of drawing gentiles into the story of salvation so that they might also be a people for his name. The ground is now prepared for the implications of James's words (Acts 15:19–21). He concludes that the gentiles who are turning to God should not be burdened (v. 19). Because it is God who has *returned* (*anastrephō*, v. 16) and is "rebuilding" the fallen tent of David, the church, they must not get in the way of the gentiles who are *turning* (*epistrephō*, v. 19) to God. If anyone, including gentiles, turns to God, then that should be enough for Jews to accept and welcome them in fellowship. The implication of this is that the traditional identity marker for inclusion, circumcision, is of no consequence.

There are, however, certain things that James suggests that gentiles be asked to abstain from. These elements have come to be referred to as "the apostolic decree"—things that will be repeated in a formal letter to be read to the gentiles (vv. 23–29). There are several issues that arise with this decree. First, besides the fact that the decree occurs three different times in Acts (15:20, 29; 21:25) there is a complicated textual history of the precise wording in its first occurrence (15:20). There are three basic but slightly different forms of the wording in different Greek manuscripts.[16] The Alexandrian text has four

---

13. Richard Bauckham, "James and the Jerusalem Church," in Bauckham, *Palestinan Setting*, 352–62.
14. Gaventa, *Acts*, 219.
15. In fact, the Hebrew of Amos 9:12 is the opposite in that it anticipates the dispossession and defeat of the gentiles.
16. See Metzger, *Textual Commentary*, 379–83.

prohibitions: food offered to idols, sexual immorality, animals strangled, and blood. Another variant, the Western text, omits "what is strangled" and adds at the end a negative version of the golden rule ("and do not do to others whatever they do not wish to be done to them"). In effect this variant transforms the decree into a moral code. Another variant, likely due to a scribal error, omits the reference to sexual immorality.

While the history of this text is varied and interesting, the more important question is what this decree means.[17] In James's opinion, gentiles need not be circumcised nor follow the Mosaic law. This does *not* mean that gentile Christians can live as they please without any moral constraints. In fact, all the NT epistles have descriptions of what Christian behavior entails as believers follow and imitate the Lord—especially as believers consider the needs of fellow brothers and sisters in Christ above their own "rights."[18] In this vein, James lists four things that should be avoided by gentile Christians (v. 20).[19] First, they should abstain from food "polluted by idols." In the gentile world, much of the food available in the marketplace had first been dedicated to various pagan gods. In fact, most of the meat available for purchase throughout cities in the Roman Empire had initially been sacrificed to idols in pagan temples. Paul's careful description of the implications of this for the church in Corinth is an example of what barriers faced Christians who wished to share meals together (1 Cor 8–10). Beyond eating, however, much of the civic, economic, and political life (e.g., going to theatre, participating in trade guilds, civic celebrations) included making sacrifices to idols. This prohibition would impinge on all those involvements for gentile converts.

Second, James calls on them to abstain from "sexual immorality." The Greek word here, *porneia*, refers to various kinds of unsanctioned sexual activity in the Jewish tradition: adultery, fornication, incest, and prostitution (cf. Lev 18:6–30; Rom 1:29; 1 Cor 5:1; 6:13; etc.). Gaventa reminds us that the Jewish tradition also associates sexual immorality with idolatry (Jer 3:1–10; Ezek 16:15–46; Hos 5:3–4; Wis 14:12, 24; Sib. Or. 4:1–39; Jub. 22:16–23; 1 Cor 10:7–8; Rev 2:14, 20).[20] This very problem seems to have overtaken some gentile Christians in Corinth who engaged in sexual activity with prostitutes, possibly even with temple prostitutes (1 Cor 6:15–17; 10:7–8).[21]

---

17. For a comprehensive list for the proposed backgrounds against which to interpret the decree, see Keener, *Acts*, 3:2260–69.

18. A point drawn from Alexander, *Acts*, 120.

19. For a further discussion on the enduring signficance of the law for Christians, see Bauckham, "James and the Jerusalem Church," 415–80.

20. Gaventa, *Acts*, 221; cf. Dunn, *Acts*, 205–6.

21. See Gordon D. Fee, *The First Epistle to the Corinthians*, New International Commentary on the New Testament (Grand Rapids: Eerdmans, 2014), 249ff.

The third and fourth prohibitions are more difficult to interpret: "The meat of strangled animals"[22] and "from blood." These two items seem to be linked and point to eating meat that had not been properly butchered according to Jewish tradition—a tradition going back as far as the time of Noah (Gen 9:4; cf. Lev 3:17; 7:26; 17:10–13; 19:26; Deut 12:16, 23). Here the concession relates especially to table fellowship between Jewish and gentile Christians. F. F. Bruce suggests that this points to these two elements, along with the previous two items, as providing the necessary conditions for both groups to enjoy one another's company as followers of Christ: "It is natural that, when the stumbling block of circumcision had been removed, an effort should have been made to provide a practical *modus vivendi* [Latin, "a way of living"] for two groups of people drawn from such different ways of life. The *modus vivendi* was probably similar to the terms on which Jews of the dispersion found it possible to have a measure of fellowship with God-fearing Gentiles."[23]

The view that these four prohibitions are directed primarily to dietary proscriptions in order to facilitate table fellowship has been a long-standing interpretation among commentators. There are, however, some problems with this view. First, it does not seem to make sense of the prohibition against sexual immorality (*porneia*). It is also difficult to imagine how someone like the apostle Paul would receive this addition of "food laws." It would mean that in practice Paul either completely ignored James and the council on this matter (cf. 1 Cor 10:23–33) or else he changed his mind on this position after his mission to the gentiles extended further. Another interpretative angle may be more coherent. James's prohibitions, instead of being an additional "food law" for gentile Christians, may relate more specifically to gentiles associating with pagan temples and idolatry. In this case, all four prohibitions make sense—including the point about sexual immorality and animal sacrifices that were made without letting blood. Pagan animal sacrifices went beyond worship of the gods in pagan temples. Economic life for anyone who worked in the trade associations as well as civic celebrations included sacrifices made to the guild god(s), local patron gods, or even to the emperor. Further, since the leftover parts of pagan-temple animal sacrifices were also sold in the marketplace, the prohibitions would have carried over into that context as well. The intent then would be to remind gentile Christians against the seductive threat of idolatry that enveloped gentile Christians in the Roman world.

The conclusion to James's speech, indicated by the explanatory "for" (*gar*), gives the impression that these four prohibitions were so basic and well-known

---

22. The Greek word *pniktos*, translated by the phrase "the meat of strangled animals," does not occur in the LXX or any other Jewish writings; cf. BDAG 838.

23. Bruce, *Acts*, 295–96.

points of wisdom derived from the law of Moses proclaimed for centuries that even gentiles would be aware of them (Acts 15:21). In particular, the very first commandment from the Decalogue—"You shall have no other gods before me" (Exod 20:3)—establishes the primary basis for the enduring proscription against idolatry. Beyond this, Christopher Seitz argues that these four particular injunctions reflect "a close reading" and interpretation of Leviticus 17–18. Seitz answers what James likely had in mind as he referred to the preaching of "the law of Moses" (Acts 15:21):

> A close reading of Leviticus 17–18 gives the answer, and precisely those sections that would be relevant in the context of a discussion of conduct for Gentile believers, whom the prophets Amos, Jeremiah, and Isaiah foresaw, as was declared at [Acts] 15:15. . . . It is . . . a penetration into the Law of God as this now takes form in the context of Gentile conversion. Gentile Christians are to avoid specific contact with blood, pollutions of idols, and *porneai* because long ago the Law of Moses saw fit to describe Israel's life in such a way that it anticipated Gentile association. The synagogue is one such prominent context in the period in question, once the diaspora has become a general reality. So those gathered in Jerusalem dispatch men to work with Paul and Barnabas and send them out with a letter that summarizes their admonitions for Gentile Christians (15:28). The Holy Spirit gave a goodly insight into how Scripture, and the Law of Moses as such, was to function in a context the prophets long ago anticipated. Far from setting Scripture aside, the logic of Scripture's word is sought for a context of Gentile association occasioned by the work of the one Cross of Jesus Christ in the power of the Holy Spirit.[24]

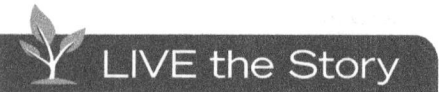

LIVE the Story

The Difficult Walk of Unity

From time to time one hears people wistfully hearken back to some "good old days" in the story of the church when apparently everyone got along and there was a general agreement on what was good, true, and beautiful. If pressed as to when this time of general unity and bliss actually existed, people have a hard time identifying such a season and often bail out and say something like, "You know, in the early church." The book of Acts, however, tells a

---

24. Christopher Seitz, "Evaluating 'This Holy Estate': Misunderstanding Acts 15," *Covenant*, 12 June 2016, http://livingchurch.org/covenant/2016/06/12/evaluating-this-holy-estate-misunderstanding-acts-15/.

different story about the early church. In fact, there are numerous examples of disagreement and tension that Luke relates. For example, the confrontation with Ananias and Sapphira (Acts 5), the complaints of the Hellenistic Jewish widows (Acts 6), and the fallout between Paul and Barnabas (Acts 15). Amid these examples (and others), the most significant moment of tension occurs when "certain people came down from Judea to Antioch and were teaching the believers: 'Unless you are circumcised, according to the custom taught by Moses, you cannot be saved'" (Acts 15:1). This precipitated the first "synod" of the church in Jerusalem. The word *synod* is a Greek compound word that means "to walk together" (*syn* = "with/together" and *hodos* = "walk/way"). It is not always easy to walk together, and this situation in the early church illustrates this. At stake was the fundamental unity of the church. How should Jewish and gentile Christians walk together in their common faith in Christ Jesus? Would gentile Christians be required to be circumcised and keep the law of Moses (v. 5)? Or will the grace they shared through the Lord Jesus (v. 11) be enough to knit them together? After debate and discussion, they decided on the latter course of action—along with some minimal requirements that would help them refrain from idolatrous influences in the culture around them.

Helpful Virtues for Resolving Conflict in the Church

What can we learn from the way the early church resolved one of their first major issues of tension and disagreement? For the early church, they *required* gentile believers to follow specific stipulations. Levison observes that the meeting in Jerusalem points to at least three key practices or "collective virtues" the Jerusalem Council inhabited.[25]

First, they acknowledged their *common experience of the Holy Spirit* (v. 8; cf. vv. 28–29). When faced with a similar circumstance related to ethnic tensions in Ephesus, Paul also begins by appealing to the "unity of the Spirit through the bond of peace" (Eph 4:3). Of course, for our own context, this assumes that we can recall the evidence for the experience of the Spirit in our midst. Can we? Can we remember how the Spirit transformed people? Has the Spirit purified hearts and lives from the inside out? If we all share the same experience of the Spirit—the Spirit that Jesus prayed would come to reveal truth and give peace to his followers after his departure (John 14:26–27)—then we must begin there in framing our shared understanding on how we are united as Christ's body. But that is not all. James will later conclude, "It seemed good to the Holy Spirit *and to us*" (Acts 15:28). The Holy Spirit's leading is primary,

---

25. Levison, *Inspired*, 112–15.

but discernment also includes the gritty conversation and debate between people. This leads us to the next observation.

Second, and only after acknowledging the Spirit's presence among them, the early church then incorporated debate and *reasoned argument* into the situation. The debate or "sharp dispute" (*stasis*, v. 2) actually began in Antioch before the council met in Jerusalem. The intense investigation and conversation continued in Jerusalem, and Peter took the lead in the discussion. Peter's argument was simple. If the shared experience of the Spirit is evident, then why would we—as mere humans—try to "out-god God" (Acts 15:10, *The Message*)? The yoke of Moses was not a yoke that fit properly for either their Hebrew ancestors or themselves. Why would they then think it would fit properly on gentiles?

Third, after appealing to the experience of the Spirit and reasoned argument, James offers an *interpretation of Scripture*—drawing on the prophets Amos, Isaiah, and Jeremiah, as well as Moses's instruction in Leviticus—to inform the question at hand (vv. 15–21).

These three practices do not guarantee quick or easy resolutions for every conflict the church may experience, either at a global or local level. After all, the unfortunate schisms and the various denominations that have emerged in the church testify to this sad reality. As Christians, we want to "get it right" when it comes to following God's leading. It is shortsighted to assume that those "certain people" coming down from Jerusalem were being hypocritical in their attitudes toward gentile believers. If anything, the evidence suggests they were trying to be biblical. Like many contemporary Christians, they were seeking a helpful framework for a biblical ethic, a biblical way of being followers of Jesus in the world. It is regrettable that denominational distinctives are deepening, widening, and renewing schisms in our efforts to "get it right," even though we have a model for helping resolve conflicts in the church from Acts 15. In short, purity by schism has never worked well for the church. Schism and division only mean our circles get drawn tighter and our call for "unity of the Spirit" rings hollow. Further, our instant access to news and information via global networks only exacerbates the situation and ratchets up anger and strife; this has not made it easy to live the "grace" we say we believe (v. 11).

Conflict, anger, and schism are all evidence that we need, as ever, the Spirit's presence to engage in the spiritual warfare we face. If we are going to live and struggle for what really matters, we must draw on the power of the Spirit that will allow us to see what is important, how to reason well, and how best to interpret and apply Scripture. Richard Rohr suggests that a good place to start is with silence:

Inside of silence—especially extended silence—we see that things find their true order and meaning somewhat naturally. When things find their true order, we know what is important, what lasts, what is real, what Jesus would call the reign of God or the Kingdom of God, or in other words, the big stuff. All the rest is passing. All those things you were emotional about last Wednesday that you cannot even remember are . . . emptiness. They have no lasting substance, and in that sense they are not real. . . . Feelings are first of all always about "me," which gives us good self knowledge but also traps us in the very self if we do not use them to go further. My metaphor for Jesus's Kingdom of God is simply The Big Picture. In The Big Picture, what matters? When you are on your deathbed, what will matter? Will you be thinking about what you are thinking about now? Will you be arguing about what you are arguing about now? To pull back from the tug of emotion and ego that wants to be right, wants to win, wants to put the other down, wants to humiliate the enemy, is the very heart of spiritual warfare. This is where we need to put our energy first, instead of obsessing about theoretical or real moral issues that usually ask little of us personally.[26]

As we engage in the spiritual warfare that is conflict in the church, it is important we begin by turning to the resources God gives us in our common experience of the Spirit, in Spirit-renewed thinking, and in Spirit-inspired Scripture. If we do so, we might be able to grasp the "Big Picture" and begin to see the marks of the unity of peace that Jesus envisioned and what the early church strove for in their life together.

---

26. Richard Rohr, *Silent Compassion: Find God in Contemplation* (Cincinnati: Franciscan Media, 2014), 20.

CHAPTER 32

Acts 15:22-35

 LISTEN to the Story

²²Then the apostles and elders, with the whole church, decided to choose some of their own men and send them to Antioch with Paul and Barnabas. They chose Judas (called Barsabbas) and Silas, men who were leaders among the believers. ²³With them they sent the following letter:

The apostles and elders, your brothers,
To the Gentile believers in Antioch, Syria and Cilicia:

Greetings.

²⁴We have heard that some went out from us without our authorization and disturbed you, troubling your minds by what they said. ²⁵So we all agreed to choose some men and send them to you with our dear friends Barnabas and Paul— ²⁶men who have risked their lives for the name of our Lord Jesus Christ. ²⁷Therefore we are sending Judas and Silas to confirm by word of mouth what we are writing. ²⁸It seemed good to the Holy Spirit and to us not to burden you with anything beyond the following requirements: ²⁹You are to abstain from food sacrificed to idols, from blood, from the meat of strangled animals and from sexual immorality. You will do well to avoid these things.

Farewell.

³⁰So the men were sent off and went down to Antioch, where they gathered the church together and delivered the letter. ³¹The people read it and were glad for its encouraging message. ³²Judas and Silas, who themselves were prophets, said much to encourage and strengthen the believers. ³³After spending some time there, they were sent off by the believers with the blessing of peace to return to those who had sent them. [34]1

---

1. Later Greek manuscripts insert this verse: "But it seemed good to Silas to remain there." Another text extends the verse even further by reading, "But it seemed good to Silas that they remain, and Judas journeyed alone." Metzger, *Textual Commentary*, 388, notes "the insertion, whether in the longer or the shorter version, was no doubt made by copyists to account for the presence of Silas at Antioch in ver. 40."

³⁵But Paul and Barnabas remained in Antioch, where they and many others taught and preached the word of the Lord.

Listening to the Text in the Story: Leviticus 17–18; Luke 6:13; 9:35.

EXPLAIN the Story

The Jerusalem Council evokes two responses. First, a response in the mode of a formal letter from the believers in Jerusalem as to the requirements they commend to gentile believers in Antioch, Syria, and Cilicia (15:22–29). The second is a response from the believers in Antioch who are encouraged by the message from Jerusalem (15:30–35).

The Jerusalem Letter (15:22–29)

After the council heard the arguments of Peter, Barnabas, and Paul along with the summary recommendation of James, the community was settled and unified in its convictions. Luke indicates the diversity of the support by noting that "the apostles and elders, with the *whole* church" chose representatives to carry a letter to Antioch. Antioch's key delegates—Paul and Barnabas—are included along with two witnesses from the Jerusalem Council: Judas, called Barsabbas ("son of the Sabbath"), and Silas. They are individuals of significance; they are "leaders" among the brothers and sisters (v. 22); and they are *chosen ones*. The use of the word "chose" helps sharpen the sense that they are not random or insignificant. The same word was used to signify those Jesus "chose" as his twelve apostles (Luke 6:13); it is the same word used by the voice from heaven saying, "this is my Son, whom I have *chosen*" (Luke 9:35). This is an important word in the Gospel of Luke, and it continues to be used at important junctures in Acts (1:2, 24; 6:5; 13:17).[2]

The letter recorded in Acts is shaped by all the typical elements of a Greco-Roman letter, including: the name of the writers, the name of the recipients, a word of greeting, the body of the letter, and a closing word of farewell. The wording of the recipients is interesting in that it is expressly addressed to *gentile* believers in Antioch, Syria, and Cilicia—that is, not gentile *and* Jewish believers. This seems to reinforce that the letter is speaking to something related specifically to the gentile context (i.e., idolatry) and not

---

2. Cf. Gaventa, *Acts*, 224.

something related to gentile and Jewish Christian life together (i.e., "table fellowship").

The body of the letter opens with the apostles and elders of Jerusalem distancing themselves from those individuals who incited the controversy with the gentile believers in Antioch in the first place (v. 24; cf. v. 1). Whereas these individuals troubled their "minds" (Greek, *psychas*) without Jerusalem's authorization, now Barnabas and Paul, men who have given[3] their lives (*psychas*) for the "name of our Lord Jesus Christ," are sent with Jerusalem's full authority (vv. 25–26). Along with Barnabas and Paul, they also "chose" to send two confirming witnesses from Jerusalem: Judas and Silas. We will not hear again of Judas, but Silas will later become Paul's traveling companion (v. 40). The Holy Spirit, however, provides the ultimate authorization and confirmation of the content of the letter: "It seemed good to the *Holy Spirit* and to us" (v. 28). This echoes the divine initiative related earlier in the council by Peter (v. 8), Barnabas and Saul (v. 12), and James (v. 14). The intent of the community in Jerusalem is not to "burden" their gentile brothers and sisters beyond what they have discerned from the Spirit. The body of the letter concludes with the four prohibitions that will help guard them from the prevailing culture's idolatrous ways. These safeguards that were previously narrated by James (v. 20), presented now in the official decree in a slightly different order (v. 29), are meant to keep the gentile believers from the bodily practices Jews associated with idolatrous worship. Further, these guidelines reflect a close reading of Leviticus 17–18, where the law of Moses describes key elements of Israel's life and their association with gentiles.

Sent off to Antioch (15:30–35)

The two pairs of witnesses—Barnabas and Paul from Antioch along with Judas and Silas representing Jerusalem—make the return journey with the letter in hand. After gathering the congregation at some unnamed location in the city, the letter is read out loud to believers. The letter has the desired impact: the church in Antioch rejoices upon hearing the exhortation (v. 31). The source of conflict and debate is resolved for them. Gentile believers do not have to be circumcised, and they are not required to become proselytes. Presumably, the injunctions from the letter—abstaining "from food sacrificed to idols, from blood, from the meat of strangled animals and from sexual immorality" (v. 29)—were practices that they were already keeping.[4] In many ways, the news that they are accepted as full members in the people of God

---

3. Greek *paradidōmi*. The NIV translates this as "risked." It is part of an idiomatic phrase literally translated as "who have handed over their souls."

4. Cf. Schnabel, *Acts*, 651.

generates the same kind of "joy" as their initial reception of the gospel. Beyond delivering and reading the letter, Judas and Silas remain with the brothers and sisters for a ministry of the word to further encourage and strengthen them (v. 32). Luke adds that Judas and Silas were also "prophets" (v. 32). This additional note drives home the reality that this letter from Jerusalem is inspired and sanctioned by the Spirit, who speaks through the prophets. Further, their prophetic ministry would likely also affirm the teaching of the letter in a way that reinforces for the Antioch Christians that they are the Lord's people alongside their Jewish brothers and sisters in Jerusalem. Unity and peace are restored. After "spending some time"[5] with the believers in Antioch, Judas and Silas are sent home with the same peace with which they were themselves sent. As for Paul and Barnabas,[6] they have come full circle. Along with the others—presumably Niger, Lucius, and Manaen (cf. 13:1)—they resume their "word" (*logos*) ministry by teaching and preaching in Antioch (15:35). While this marks only the halfway mark of the entire narrative, there is a sense of finality to this stage (cf. 28:31). The ministry of teaching and preaching exemplifies the primary work of the witnesses of Jesus.

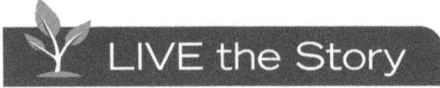

LIVE the Story

Bruised, Battered, but Not Beaten by Schism

When "certain people" (Acts 15:1) came down from Judea to Antioch and insisted on circumcision as a required practice for gentile Christians there, it so disturbed and troubled (v. 24) believers that it resulted in angry argument (*stasis*, v. 2) in the early church. We must not underestimate the tension this created. It could have gone wrong in so many ways. In the end, after intense debate and rigorous investigation was linked with the experience of the Holy Spirit ("it seemed good to the Holy Spirit *and* to us," v. 28), an inspired arrangement was worked out. It is not surprising that such a pivotal display of tension, godly leadership, and spiritual discernment occurs in the middle of Acts. If the Spirit cannot help to resolve the gritty realities of life together, then why bother? Thankfully, the Spirit does. The Spirit works both with and through the gifts of godly leaders—Peter, Barnabas, Paul, and especially James—who model what it takes to weather the storms of controversy. In these inspired leaders we witness those who are willing to engage in fierce argument without ever giving up on the goal of unity. They embody a peacefulness that is conciliatory without ever being weak.

---

5. Again, Luke is vague on chronology. The stay could be a few days or a few months.
6. Note that the order of the names is now switched back to "Paul and Barnabas."

Jack Levison summarizes well these exemplary early Christians who faced controversy and compromise with unswerving conviction and inspired leadership:

> The spirit [*sic*] in this story takes believers to the mat, where they wrestle until the match is over, until they come to a communal compromise, until they take others' experiences seriously, until arguments are angrily laid out, until scripture is carefully considered. Bruised, battered, but not beaten by schism, the church then rolls on and rolls out a compromise that, in the end, seems good to the holy spirit and to them because, however difficult it may have been to arrive at, this compromise enlarges the boundaries of the church.[7]

Attempts at ecclesial purity through schism inevitably leave us diminished, not enlarged. Compromise is not the "easy way out"; rather, it is often brutal. But it is essential if we are going both to grow numerically and, more importantly, grow in maturity as followers of Jesus. By their bruised and battered example, the early church reminds us both how to seek compromise and to live in peace.

Words That Create Community

Some of us still send handwritten letters, affixed with a stamp, and placed in a mailbox. Within a few days those letters arrive, carried by faithful postal workers, and are read by their recipients. I write about two hundred of these letters each year, generally to friends and parishioners. I write to encourage them and tell them they are remembered and loved. For the most part, people are pleased to receive them. When the church in Jerusalem sent their letter to the gentile Christians in Antioch, it too was received with joy because of its "encouraging message" (v. 31). Likely, the "requirements" outlined in the letter did not come as much of a surprise. After all, gifted teachers and prophets carefully instructed these gentile Christians in the Scriptures (cf. 13:1). It would not have come as any surprise that they should avoid those practices that would pollute them with idolatry. What probably inspired gladness was the fact that they were included in the family of God, as gentiles. That is, they were not required to take on the marks of Judaism after receiving the defining mark of the Holy Spirit. What a relief! They were included in the story of God, the God who was at work in the world. This letter did its proper work: it created community and it deepened relationship. That's what words do when they are made flesh in the actions and attitudes of those who speak them. Henri Nouwen comments on this kind of good word-work:

---

7. Levison, *Inspired*, 123.

The word is always a word for others. Words need to be heard. When we give words to what we are living, these words need to be received and responded to. A speaker needs a listener. A writer needs a reader.

When the flesh—the lived human experience—becomes word, community can develop. When we say, "Let me tell you what we saw. Come and listen to what we did. Sit down and let me tell you what happened to us. Wait until you hear whom we met," we call people together and make our lives into lives for others. The word brings us together and calls us into community. When the flesh becomes word, our bodies become part of a body of people.[8]

Whether we write letters like the church in Jerusalem to a distant congregation or just write a note to a friend, our words written authentically and honestly can help create community. Social media is a great tool and should not be overlooked, but often the simplest gestures, like a handwritten letter, can do wonders to call people together and incarnate the gospel in meaningful and life-giving ways.

---

8. Nouwen, *Bread for the Journey*, entry for June 25.

CHAPTER 33

Acts 15:36–41

LISTEN to the Story

³⁶Some time later Paul said to Barnabas, "Let us go back and visit the believers in all the towns where we preached the word of the Lord and see how they are doing." ³⁷Barnabas wanted to take John, also called Mark, with them, ³⁸but Paul did not think it wise to take him, because he had deserted them in Pamphylia and had not continued with them in the work. ³⁹They had such a sharp disagreement that they parted company. Barnabas took Mark and sailed for Cyprus, ⁴⁰but Paul chose Silas and left, commended by the believers to the grace of the Lord. ⁴¹He went through Syria and Cilicia, strengthening the churches.

Listening to the Text in the Story: Deuteronomy 29:27; Jeremiah 39:37; Acts 12:12, 25; 13:13; Colossians 4:10; Philemon 24; 2 Timothy 4:11; 1 Peter 5:13.

EXPLAIN the Story

Despite being agents of unity between the Jewish and gentile Christians in Jerusalem and Antioch, Luke records an account of disunity between Paul and Barnabas as they intended to revisit the churches they established on their first mission together. This short account (Acts 15:36–41), along with the next two short accounts (16:1–5; 16:6–10), functions as a transitional bridge in the overall narrative. A significant moment occurs here as Luke introduces a significant new phase in the movement of the gospel. Although there are six identifiable "panels" in Acts, this is not simply a transition between panels but a transition from one half of the narrative to the second half. Gaventa writes:

> As at the beginning of the book, here Luke recalls earlier events (15:36, 38, 40; 16:4–5; cf. 1:1–5, 16–17, 21–22), identifies the personnel of the

mission (15:40; 16:1–3; cf. 1:12–14, 15–26), and defines the role of the witnesses (16:10; cf. 1:8, 21–22). Perhaps most important, both halves begin with the insistence that neither Peter nor Paul is the proper focus of attention or director of the action, but God alone. Here God's role comes to expression first through the Spirit, which frustrates the plans of Paul and his companions, and then through a vision that directs the witnesses to Macedonia (16:6–10; cf. 1:7; 2:1–4, 22–24).[1]

Typical of Luke, he does not specify how long Paul and Barnabas waited in Antioch before they decided to set out again. He does note that it was Paul who initiated the proposal of a return mission to Barnabas (v. 36). The intent of this "second missionary journey" is simple: they wanted to see how the fledgling congregations were doing. No doubt they also intended to deliver to them the content of the Jerusalem letter and its implications for gentile believers.

Unfortunately, when they began to make concrete plans together, including who would accompany them on their journey, this is where the simplicity ended. Barnabas proposed that they take John Mark, his younger cousin (cf. Col 4:10), with them again. Paul demurred. He did not think this was a wise suggestion. Luke tells us that this was because Mark deserted them in Pamphylia on their first mission and did not continue with them (Acts 13:13). We are not given further details about Paul's misgivings. That is, did he think the problem was with Mark's character? Was it an issue with his physical fitness? Maybe it was both. Whatever the reason, Paul would have none of it, while Barnabas insisted. This created a "sharp disagreement" (*paroxysmos*) between the two. This is a rare word in the NT, but it is used twice in the Greek OT where it expresses God's intense indignation over his people's rebellion (cf. Deut 29:28; Jer 39:37). In the end, Barnabas separated from Paul, took Mark with him, and sailed back to Cyprus. For Barnabas, this was a return to his home soil (Acts 4:36). Barnabas will not return in the narrative of Acts after this incident, but Paul mentions him in his letter to the Corinthian church (1 Cor 9:6).

Paul chose a new partner, Silas,[2] to replace Barnabas. Silas was recently introduced into the narrative (Acts 15:22). He is a Jewish Christian, possibly a Roman citizen (16:37), and likely from Jerusalem since he was sent as one of their council's envoys to Antioch. Paul may have come to know him well on their journey to Antioch and in the time he spent teaching and preaching there. In terms of his suitability for mission, he is a "leader" among the

---

1. Gaventa, *Acts*, 229.
2. Luke consistently uses the Aramaic version of his name, Silas, whereas Paul refers to him in his letters by his Latin name, Silvanus (cf. 2 Cor 1:19; 1 Thess 1:1; 2 Thess 1:1; see ESV [NIV renders it "Silas"]).

believers (15:22), a "prophet" (15:32), and able to articulate how gentiles relate to a Jewish Messiah. Paul will travel with him at least as far as Corinth (18:5), although no further mention of him is made in Acts after this point. For now, however, he embarks on his first extended journey with Paul. Whereas Barnabas and Mark returned to visit new believers on the island of Cyprus (Barnabas's home), Paul and Silas go over land northward through Syria and Cilicia (Paul's home) to build up the congregations there (15:41). Syria and Cilicia, along with Antioch, are the explicit locations addressed in the Jerusalem letter (15:23). Paul and Silas would walk north on foot through the Amanus Mountains out of Syria on their way into Cilicia.[3] Likely they would travel through Tarsus, Paul's hometown, before heading northwest through the Cilician Gates, the well-known pass in the rugged Taurus Mountains. Eventually they would arrive in Derbe (16:1). Luke does not offer any details on the founding of churches in Syria—outside of Antioch—or Cilicia, but in his letter to the Galatians Paul mentions that some of his earliest missionary efforts were spent in these territories (Gal 1:21). Despite the disagreement with Barnabas, Paul appears to have still maintained a warm relationship with the sending community in Antioch. Along with his new partner, he begins his second missionary journey with the same grace-full commendation with which he began the first (Acts 15:40; cf. 14:26).

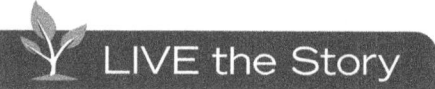

LIVE the Story

Failure happens, often in ministry as much as anywhere else. Failure stings, and in some cases the shame of it can impact us so deeply that we give up on the very callings we receive from God. One way to put failure in context is to reflect on the story of John Mark in the biblical record. His story might help those who struggle with the darkness of failure to emerge into the light of grace.

John Mark has a checkered history in the biblical narrative. Before we ever hear about his abandoning Paul and Barnabas partway through their first missionary journey (Acts 13:13), or being at the center of a controversy that fractured the missionary duo's relationship (15:37–39), there is a possible glimpse of him in the Gospel of Mark. It is likely that John Mark wrote the Gospel of Mark.[4] He may even be the young man referred to in the Gospel who ran away naked when the soldiers reached out to seize him after Jesus's

---

3. Cf. Rasmussen, *Atlas*, 227.
4. According to well-established church tradition, "Mark became Peter's interpreter and wrote accurately all that he remembered, not, indeed, in order, of the things said or done by the Lord. For he had not heard the Lord, nor had he followed him, but later on . . . followed Peter, who used to give teaching as necessity demanded" (Eusebius, *Hist. eccl.* 3.39.15 [Lake, LCL]).

arrest (Mark 14:51–52). Would anyone else but the author have included such an embarrassing detail if they had not experienced it personally?[5] This is conjecture, but it does add to our unflattering, early picture of John Mark. At the least, at first look John Mark appears to be a coward and a quitter.

Despite this initial negative portrayal of Mark, it is important also to recognize that disgrace did not define him or his ministry. Failure, for Mark or for us, need not be the last word. While Mark is not mentioned again in Acts after he and Barnabas embark for Cyprus (Acts 15:39), he is mentioned elsewhere in the NT. The apostle Peter acknowledges him at the conclusion of his first epistle: "She who is in Babylon[6] . . . sends you her greeting, and so does my son *Mark*" (1 Pet 5:13). If John Mark is the one who wrote the Gospel of Mark to the church in Rome, following the direction of Peter, then it is not surprising that he is mentioned in Peter's company in Rome. Neither is it surprising that, along with the encouragement that came from his kind cousin, Barnabas, it is the apostle Peter who would also be the one to take Mark under his wing. Who better to understand the heart of a coward and quitter than Peter! Peter, who denied his Lord three times, would grasp the inner dynamic of one who may have struggled with feelings of inadequacy and failure.

It is also important to recognize that John Mark's relationship with that other leading apostle, Paul, did not end in the bitter disagreement in Antioch (Acts 15). A considerable time after the episode in Antioch, Paul, now in prison, would write his letters to the Colossians (Col 4:10) and Philemon (Phlm 24). In these two letters we discover that John Mark has somehow rejoined Paul's company. His role as one of Paul's coworkers was not peripheral either. In the final letter Paul may have ever written, 2 Timothy, John Mark reemerges in the story. When Paul wrote his urgent letter to Timothy, he was again in prison, but this time when his circumstances were dark and his emotional resources thin. Paul is discouraged and cold, and most of his coworkers have abandoned him (2 Tim 4:9–10). In the midst of destitution and discouragement, he asks Timothy to "do your best to come to me quickly. . . . *Get Mark* and bring him with you, *because he is helpful to me in ministry*" (4:9, 11). Remarkable! Paul *asks* for Mark to join him at one of his most difficult times in his life. Again, we recall this about Mark: he may have been the one who ran away naked on the night Jesus was arrested; he was the

---

5. Most contemporary scholars think not, but the tradition that this might in fact be Mark is tantalizing. See Ben Witherington, *The Gospel of Mark* (Grand Rapids: Eerdmans, 2001); 382; R. H. Gundry, *Mark: A Commentary on His Apology for the Cross* (Grand Rapids: Eerdmans, 1993), 882; Morna Hooker, *The Gospel According to Saint Mark* (Peabody, MA: Hendrickson, 1991), 352.

6. Likely an oblique designation for the city of Rome; cf. the Christian tradition where "Babylon" refers to Rome in Rev 14:8; 17:5, 18; 18:2. See Peter H. Davids, *The First Epistle of Peter* (Grand Rapids: Eerdmans, 1990), 202.

assistant who abandoned Paul and Barnabas on their first missionary journey; and he was the one who caused a major rift between Paul and Barnabas. Yet for all this, John Mark not only became a trusted "son" to the apostle Peter and helped pen one of the earliest Gospels to be written, but in time he also became one of Paul's most reliable and appreciated coworkers. We are not given the details of how this transformation occurred with John Mark. The biblical story does not give us the details between these interesting glimpses of his character. At best we have to use a holy imagination to fill in the gaps. What we do know, however, is that failure did not have the last word; it did not define his life and ministry. The one who was once a coward and a quitter had become a trusted writer and a reliable coworker.

Mark's story reminds us all that failure, shame, and disappointment need not define our lives, give ultimate shape to our ministries, or abort our God-given callings. Grace is infinite, and our God is the God of second (and third, fourth, fifth, etc.) chances. Jesus restored the apostle Peter after his triple denial (John 21:15–19). Jesus also took the first step and forgave Saul with all his anger and unbelief (Acts 9:1–16) and gave this chief sinner a renewed direction for his life (1 Tim 1:12–16). As recipients of great grace, Peter and Paul understood forgiveness and restoration. If you don't have friends, families, or colleagues who extend grace to you at your point of greatest need and failure, look to Mark. Although not formally recognized as such, he has good reason to be looked to as the patron saint of second chances.

CHAPTER 34

Acts 16:1-5

 LISTEN to the Story

¹Paul came to Derbe and then to Lystra, where a disciple named Timothy lived, whose mother was Jewish and a believer but whose father was a Greek. ²The believers at Lystra and Iconium spoke well of him. ³Paul wanted to take him along on the journey, so he circumcised him because of the Jews who lived in that area, for they all knew that his father was a Greek. ⁴As they traveled from town to town, they delivered the decisions reached by the apostles and elders in Jerusalem for the people to obey. ⁵So the churches were strengthened in the faith and grew daily in numbers.

Listening to the Text in the Story: Genesis 34; Exodus 34:15–16; Numbers 25; Deuteronomy 7:1–4; Nehemiah 9–10.

 EXPLAIN the Story

Along with his new traveling companion, Silas, Paul travels through Derbe and Lystra in the southern region of Galatia. In Lystra, we are introduced to Timothy—described as a "disciple"—who is the son of mixed marriage between a Jewish mother and a Greek father.[1] Presumably Timothy and his mother became believers through Paul and Barnabas while on their first missionary journey. From Paul's own letters, we know that Timothy would become a respected "brother" (Col 1:1) and "co-worker" (1 Thess 3:2; cf. 1 Thess 1:1; 2 Thess 1:1; Phil 1:1; Col 1:1; Phlm 1). So close was their relationship that Paul referred to him as his true and beloved "son" in the faith (cf. 1 Tim 1:2; 2 Tim 1:2). In short, Timothy would in time become Paul's closest partner in ministry and his dearest friend. This young man would prove to be an excellent traveling companion who, as the child of a

---

1. His mother is identified as Eunice in 2 Tim 1:5.

mixed marriage, demonstrated "his survival capacity in the testing conditions of the frontier church in Lystra."[2]

There is a debate among scholars whether Timothy would be considered a gentile (on account of his father),[3] or since he is not circumcised (Acts 16:3), an apostate Jew (on account of his mother).[4] Despite the fact that intermarriage was banned in the Pentateuch (Gen 34; Exod 34:15–16; Num 25; Deut 7:1–4; cf. Neh 9–10), it occurred frequently enough to be commented on by the likes of Philo and Josephus.[5] Luke does not choose to indicate the legality of Timothy's ethnic status; instead, he highlights his commendable reputation. The same word (*martyreō*) used to refer to the respect conferred to Jesus (Luke 4:22), the Seven (Acts 6:3), and Cornelius (10:22) is applied to Timothy by those who knew him in Lystra and the neighboring city of Iconium.

Paul wishes to bring Timothy along with them on their mission. Before doing so, however, he circumcises Timothy. This seems like an odd action on the heels of the Jerusalem Council and their conclusion that gentiles need not be circumcised in order to demonstrate their full inclusion in the people of God. What is Paul's motivation? Luke provides a simple reason: "Because of the Jews who lived in that area, for they all knew that his father was a Greek" (16:3). The motive is less about adherence to "the law" and more about mission. They were embarking on a mission to deliver the "decisions" (*dogmata*, v. 4) from the apostles and elders in Jerusalem for gentile converts "to obey," and in so doing to strengthen the faith of the new Christians (vv. 4–5). In contrast to his decision not to circumcise another one of his young Greek coworkers, Titus (cf. Gal 2:3), Paul does decide to circumcise Timothy. This is a reasonable course of action. Longenecker offers helpful insight on the distinction:

> While Paul stoutly resisted any imposition of circumcision and the Jewish law upon his Gentile converts, he himself continued to live as an observant Jew and urged his converts to express their Christian faith through the cultural forms they had inherited (cf. 1 Cor 7:17–24). As for Timothy, because of his Jewish mother, he was a Jew in the eyes of the Jewish world. Therefore, it was both proper and expedient for Paul to circumcise him. As Paul saw it, being a good Christian did not mean being a bad Jew. Rather, it meant being a fulfilled Jew. Paul had no desire to flout

---

2. Alexander, *Acts*, 123.

3. See S. J. D. Cohen, "Was Timothy Jewish (Acts 16:3)? Patristic Exegesis, Rabbinic Law, and Matrilineal Descent," *JBL* 105 (1986): 251–68.

4. Bruce, *Acts*, 352; and Witherington, *Acts*, 475–76.

5. John Barclay, *Jews in the Mediterranean Diaspora*, 107–8, 324–25, 410–13, provides a helpful analysis on intermarriage and Jewish ethnic bonds in the diaspora.

Jewish scruples in his endeavor to bring both Jews and Gentiles to salvation in Christ.[6]

In terms of the overall narrative in Acts, this short transitional episode serves to remind the reader that the inclusion of the gentiles does not entail the exclusion of the Jews. The mission to the "ends of the earth" does not mean abandoning witness to "Jerusalem" (cf. 1:8). Further, it serves to anticipate the charge later in the narrative that Paul's mission undermines the teaching of Moses (cf. 21:21).

The short episode draws to a close with one of the familiar panel summary "markers" in Acts (cf. 6:7; 9:31; 12:24; 19:20). While other markers include a geographic note and/or a reference to the word of God increasing, this summary statement only mentions that the churches grew stronger in faith and larger in size. This marks the end of an important phase in Luke's narrative. The gospel has reached and been received by the gentile world. The primarily Jewish church has understood and accepted the Spirit's leading and teaching about God's Savior and Messiah. Jesus is "Lord of all" (cf. 10:36). As gentiles turn from idolatry to the living God, they must be taught and strengthened in obedience to the faith, but they are received and constituted by grace.

LIVE the Story

Among several theological insights raised in this passage (e.g., the inclusion of the gentiles in the people of God; the relationship between law and grace), one key aspect worth identifying is the importance of flexibility in mission. Paul will circumcise Timothy because it relates to the mission of teaching and building up churches. While "neither circumcision nor uncircumcision has any value," what matters is something deeper than skin; what matters is deep interior realities of faith expressed in love (cf. Gal 5:6). Paul will fight for freedom from the Mosaic law for the gentiles, but he will also not deliberately place stumbling blocks to the gospel in front of his fellow Jews. Timothy must have not only accepted Paul's requirement that he be circumcised but understood his rationale as well. It is often assumed that Timothy is a young man. Regardless of what his age was when he entered Paul's company, he demonstrates a number of vital character traits needed in a leader. First, we are told that he has a solid reputation (Acts 16:2). This doesn't just happen; it requires "a long obedience in the same direction."[7] Second, as a son from

---

6. Longenecker, *Acts*, 455.
7. Friedrich Nietzsche, *Beyond Good and Evil*, quoted in Eugene Peterson, *A Long Obedience in the Same Direction* (Downers Grove, IL: InterVarsity Press, 2000), 13.

a mixed marriage living in the tough frontier town of Lystra, he must have developed inner reserves of strength. Finally, his willingness to be circumcised as an adult in support of the greater good of the gospel indicates his maturity, teachability, and flexibility.

Another important theological insight is that mission is not merely about making converts but nurturing strong disciples. Paul likely strengthened believers in ways of discipleship that reflected the basic rhythms outlined earlier in Acts (2:42–47). That is, believers were built up by the teaching of the apostles. They were nurtured in the disciplines of corporate life together (e.g., hospitality, caring for the poor, forgiveness, holiness). They were nourished by participating in "the breaking of bread"—the Lord's Supper. They were taught how to answer God by learning their "prayers" (e.g., the Psalms; the Lord's Prayer; Mary's Song; Simeon's Song).[8] Luke routinely ignores time signatures, but we should not overlook that he does emphasize the importance of pastoral oversight and the formation of disciples. Paul and his companions on mission are not just focused on evangelism; they are also focused on teaching, correcting, and strengthening.

---

8. For excellent contemporary resources in forming these rhythms of discipleship, see Rowan Williams, *Being Christian: Baptism, Bible, Eucharist, Prayer* (Grand Rapids: Eerdmans, 2014) and idem, *Being Disciples: Essentials of the Christian Life* (London: SPCK, 2016).

PANEL 5
Acts 16:6–19:20

The fifth "panel" in Acts narrates the movement of the gospel as it travels to Europe for the first time. Just as the Holy Spirit initiated the mission at the beginning of the previous panel (13:3–4), so also at the beginning of this panel it is the Spirit who leads Paul and his companions forward (16:6–10). This portion of the story includes Paul's so-called second and third missionary journeys. Significant distances are traveled in this panel, and Paul makes numerous stops along the way, including a two-year layover in Ephesus (19:10). Although Paul and his coworkers begin by retracing their steps in the regions of Phrygia and Galatia, they soon come to the Roman province of Macedonia (modern continental Europe). The focus of this section is devoted to the proclamation of the gospel in significant cities of the Roman Empire, including Philippi (16:11–40), Athens (17:16–34), Corinth (18:1–18), and Ephesus (18:24–19:20).

This panel has several notable features. To begin with, this is the first time that the narrative shifts to the first person, the "we passages" in Acts (16:10–17; cf. 20:5–15; 21:1–18; 27:1–28:16). Another important element is that Antioch remains the sending church and center for the Christian mission led by Paul, even though he delivers reports to those in Jerusalem (cf. 18:22). Finally, it is noteworthy that in this panel believers increasingly find themselves in conflict with secular authorities. In Philippi, the magistrates are obliged to apologize to Paul and Silas for their public mistreatment and their unlawful imprisonment (16:16–40). In Thessalonica, a Christian leader, Jason, and members of his household are dragged before city officials (17:5–9). In Corinth, Paul is brought before the Roman proconsul Gallio on charges of sedition—even though Gallio dismisses the charges brought by the Jews (18:12–17).

CHAPTER 35

Acts 16:6–10

 LISTEN to the Story

⁶Paul and his companions traveled throughout the region of Phrygia and Galatia, having been kept by the Holy Spirit from preaching the word in the province of Asia. ⁷When they came to the border of Mysia, they tried to enter Bithynia, but the Spirit of Jesus would not allow them to. ⁸So they passed by Mysia and went down to Troas. ⁹During the night Paul had a vision of a man of Macedonia standing and begging him, "Come over to Macedonia and help us." ¹⁰After Paul had seen the vision, we got ready at once to leave for Macedonia, concluding that God had called us to preach the gospel to them.

Listening to the Text in the Story: 2 Corinthians 2:12; Colossians 4:14; 2 Timothy 4:11; Philemon 24; 1 Peter 1:1.

 EXPLAIN the Story

This short paragraph is the third transitional paragraph that bridges the end of the last panel (Acts 12:25–16:5) to the new panel (16:6–19:20). The last panel ended with Paul and his companions back in Antioch with their sending church (15:35). The first transitional paragraph describes the plan to return and visit believers they had met on their first journey through Cyprus and Galatia (15:36–41). Unfortunately, before that journey begins, Paul and Barnabas have a sharp disagreement on taking Mark. The result is that Paul and Barnabas each form new teams and go their separate ways. The second transitional paragraph recounts Paul's new team, including Silas and Timothy, making their way overland through southern Galatia (16:1–5). This third transitional paragraph is a fascinating account of Paul and his companions' diagonal journey across Asia Minor (16:6–10). It is a compact narrative, yet brimming with interesting details.

Travel through Phrygia and Galatia (16:6)

Luke first tells us that the missionaries travel through the outback regions of Asia Minor: Phrygia and Galatia. They travel northwest through these two regions because the Holy Spirit kept them from preaching in Asia. Just to be clear, "Asia" in this passage does not refer to the modern continent of Asia but to the Roman province of Asia. Presumably Paul and his companions intended to travel directly west after leaving Pisidian Antioch. Instead, they were directed north through Phrygia and Galatia. Galatia could refer either to the Roman province of Galatia (formed in 25 BC) or to a large region in central Asia Minor. Phrygia was not a Roman province but a region straddling the northeast corner of the province of Asia and the northwest corner of Galatia. These two regions constituted the mountainous interior of Asia Minor. It was some of the wildest territory, both topographically and socially, in the ancient world.[1] The Romans never fully pacified these rough and tumultuous territories, and instead tried to contain them by establishing veteran Roman soldiers in settlements throughout the region and maintaining the Seventh Legion in the south of Galatia. The local people remained fiercely independent and maintained their tribal languages and cultural identity well into the Byzantine era (ca. fourth-century AD).

The Spirit Restrains and Leads (16:7–9)

As Paul and his companions traveled the northward highway, they would have come to the city of Dorylaeum and from there continued northwest through the region of Mysia (still in the province of Asia) either to Nicaea or Prusa in the Roman province of Bithynia—one of the regions addressed in the apostle Peter's first epistle (1 Pet 1:1). Again, however, the Spirit forbids them to enter Bithynia. Instead they travel west to the port city of Troas and stay there for at least a night. Troas was a prosperous Roman colony strategically situated along the east-west trade route.[2] The distance traveled on foot between Timothy's hometown of Lystra in southern Galatia and Troas is at least five hundred kilometers (300 miles), depending on the route they took. This would take at least twenty days of solid walking. About this journey, Luke simply writes, "Paul and his companions traveled throughout the region of Phrygia and Galatia" (Acts 16:6).

It is fascinating to imagine the travel of this missionary band, but the exegetical and theological interest of this short narrative is with the manner of the Spirit's leading. Twice Luke refers to them as "having been kept" and "not allow[ed]" by divine directive from preaching in or entering into a region

---

1. See J. A. Harill, "Asia Minor," *DNTB* 134–35.
2. Rasmussen, *Atlas*, 227.

(16:6, 7). How was this communicated? Was it a word of prophecy? Was it a growing consensus discerned by the group as they walked along the road? We are not given the specifics of this leading beyond that it was so. When they finally reach Troas, a definitive and clear directive is given to Paul in a vision. Visions occur at pivotal moments in Acts when direction is required or a new initiative from the Lord is given (cf. 9:10, 12; 10:3; 18:9). After days of "dusty discernment" by the Spirit on the long road from Lystra to Troas, Paul is given clear direction. In the night Paul sees in his vision "a man of Macedonia standing and begging him, 'Come over to Macedonia and help us'" (v. 9). The *group* concluded[3] that the call was not from a Macedonian person, but from God (v. 10). Luke relates that "the Holy Spirit" (v. 6), "the Spirit of Jesus" (v. 7), and "God" (v. 10) had directed their path and their preaching. Again, this is another fascinating example of the triune God leading the early Christians at the very heart of mission and new initiative in the narrative (cf. 11:15–17).

The First "We Passage" (16:10)

One final exegetical note is the initial appearance—subtle and unannounced—of the first-person plural "we" (*hēmas*) in the narrative (16:10). In effect, the author unobtrusively steps into the story that he is narrating. The insertion of "we" in the story will continue only for a few sentences (vv. 10–17) even after the travelers arrived in Philippi. The "we passages" will reappear at several intervals later in the story (i.e., at 20:5 [again in Troas] through to 21:19 [in Jerusalem], and again at 27:1 almost to the end of the story in 28:16 [from Caesarea to Rome]). This unadorned pronoun has garnered significant scholarly interest.[4] The simplest interpretation is that the author of Acts is offering firsthand testimony of his presence at this juncture in the story. For centuries, biblical readers have assumed that this is the physician Luke, a resident of Troas, who has joined the missionary company. Luke is mentioned in several of Paul's own letters (Col 4:14; Phlm 24; 2 Tim 4:11). More recently, scholars have suggested that this represents a "diary" or a written source used by the author in stitching together this book. Other more suspicious readings have even proposed that this is a deception invented by the author to create an authentic feel to the narrative, a "firsthand" assurance of someone claiming (falsely) to be a participant and thus to write with authority.

In the end, despite the many theories and speculative arguments, we will

---

3. The Greek participle translated as "concluding" is plural (*symbibazontes*).
4. There are many detailed discussions of this matter. Two thorough treatments, which reach different conclusions yet set out the issues well, can be found in Hemer, *Acts*, 312–64, and Stanley E. Porter, "The 'We' Passages," in David W. J. Gill and Conrad Gempf, eds., *Graeco-Roman Setting*, vol. 2 of *The Book of Acts in Its First Century Setting*, ed. Bruce W. Winter (Grand Rapids: Eerdmans; Carlisle: Paternoster, 1994), 545–74.

never know for certain who is included in this "we" since neither Luke, Paul's sometime traveling companion, nor anyone else attached their name to this document. The simplest answer is that whoever wrote Acts—and I see no good reason to go against the tradition that Luke did so—is offering a firsthand description. Several reasons point in favor of this. First, the nature of this inclusion is subtle, without fanfare, and emerges at a relatively unimportant travel section in the narrative. It is hard to imagine how this would validate the account or add authoritative weight to it if written falsely. Further, recent studies demonstrate that all the "we passages" in Acts are consistent with the vocabulary, style, and grammar of the rest of Acts.[5] In the end, what we do know is that "there is a new vividness and immediacy about the next phase of the story, especially in relation to travel."[6]

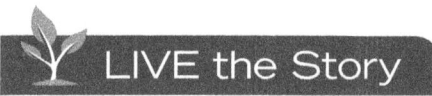

LIVE the Story

Luke is explicit about the Spirit's leading. The Spirit led Jesus into the wilderness (Luke 4:1) and empowered his ministry (4:14, 18); the Spirit empowered Paul and his companions in mission (Acts 13:2, 4) and again led them through the wilds of Phrygia and Galatia (16:6). We too can be confident that the Spirit leads us in our lives. Of course, the question many might ask about this is how? How does the Spirit lead? Sometimes this leading may come through dramatic visions in the night like Paul experienced in Troas. It is also important to remember that long before this pivotal vision is granted to Paul, he and his companions walked hundreds of miles over rough, mountainous territory across the heart of Anatolia (modern Turkey). Along those dusty and dangerous roads Luke only tells us obliquely that "the Holy Spirit [kept them] from preaching the word in the province of Asia. When they . . . tried to enter Bithynia . . . the Spirit of Jesus would not allow them to" (16:6–7). I suspect that in the days and weeks that they walked along these roads they often wondered where the Spirit might be leading them. It may not have been clear to them at all. Yet they walked *together*. They walked in company with one another—thinking and talking, praying and praising, discerning and listening—as they went.

---

5. I am indebted to my friend Mikael Tellbe for these observations. See Mikael Tellbe, *Paul between Synagogue and State: Christians, Jews, and Civic Authorities in 1 Thessalonians, Romans, and Philippians*, Coniectanea Biblica: New Testament Series 34 (Stockholm: Almqvist & Wiksell, 2001), 221n49. Cf. D. Schmidt, "Syntactical Style in the 'We'-Sections of Acts: How Lukan Is It?," in *Society of Biblical Literature 1989 Seminar Papers*, ed. David J. Lull (Atlanta: Scholars Press, 1989), 300–308; and Witherington, *Acts*, 480–86.

6. Alexander, *Acts*, 126.

For most of us, much of the time, the Spirit leads us quietly and obliquely. Hopefully we recognize that we have brothers and sisters as companions alongside us for when the way seems hard and the direction unsure. It is easy to trust the Spirit's guidance when the way is clear, but it is not so easy when we are being led down seemingly endless and unfamiliar roads. This is why fellow pilgrims are necessary. Paul never travels alone. He is always in the company of others. In the individualized culture of the West, it can be tempting to think we must do everything, or at least try to do everything, on our own. "The Lone Ranger"—the notion of a person who works mostly alone—is still a powerful imaginative story in the American mindset. It is not, however, a Christian mindset. Tertullian, an early Christian writer and apologist known as the father of Latin Christianity, is attributed with the adage, *unus Christianus, nullus Christianus*—"one Christian is no Christian." We may be called individually to Christ, but we are not solitary Christians. No one can be an authentic Christian in isolation. There is always a "one another" or "together" dimension to our relationship with Christ. Whether we are apostles or prophets, young or old, married or single, house builders or homemakers, professors or poets, resting or working, worshiping or washing dishes, failing or succeeding, we live and grow in communion with others in the body of Christ. In community, in the fellowship of other believers, we learn to know the fellowship and leading of the Spirit. Occasionally the Spirit may direct us individually through dramatic vision or prophetic word. More often, however, we are led through a growing and deepening conviction that is discerned as we walk and talk, as we pray and play, along the road of life together with others.

CHAPTER 36

Acts 16:11-15

 LISTEN to the Story

¹¹From Troas we put out to sea and sailed straight for Samothrace, and the next day we went on to Neapolis. ¹²From there we traveled to Philippi, a Roman colony and the leading city of that district of Macedonia. And we stayed there several days.

¹³On the Sabbath we went outside the city gate to the river, where we expected to find a place of prayer. We sat down and began to speak to the women who had gathered there. ¹⁴One of those listening was a woman from the city of Thyatira named Lydia, a dealer in purple cloth. She was a worshiper of God. The Lord opened her heart to respond to Paul's message. ¹⁵When she and the members of her household were baptized, she invited us to her home. "If you consider me a believer in the Lord," she said, "come and stay at my house." And she persuaded us.

Listening to the Text in the Story: Luke 24:44; Acts 10:2; 13:16, 26; 18:7.

 EXPLAIN the Story

Luke devotes a considerable amount of space to the mission in Philippi. This first section of Philippian mission introduces two specific details about this Macedonian city: first, it is distinctively *Roman* (vv. 11–12), and second, its first convert is Lydia (vv. 13–16).

Philippi—a Piece of Italy on Macedonian Soil (16:11–12)

Paul and his companions set sail westward from Troas (v.11). After dropping anchor for the night in Samothrace, a small island about halfway on their journey through the north end of the Aegean Sea, they arrived in Neapolis (modern Kavalla in Greece). From there, they walked ten kilometers (6 miles) inland to Philippi. Philippi was located along the Via Egnatia—an important, eleven-hundred-kilometer Roman road running from Dyrrachium in the west (on the coast of modern Albania) to Byzantium in the east. This strategic route connected Rome with its eastern provinces. Importantly, Luke describes Philippi as "a Roman colony and the leading city of that district of Macedonia" (v. 12). This is the only occurrence of the word "colony" (*kolōnia*) in the NT. Why would Luke mention this when there were other cities that Paul had recently visited—such as Troas, Lystra, and Pisidian Antioch—that were also colonies? He seems to be pointing out something distinctive about the status of Philippi. There is a distinct *Roman* quality to this city in Macedonia.

We know that Philippi had been the scene of an important victory for Antony and Octavian over Brutus and Cassius, the assassins of Julius Caesar, in 42 BC. The victory made possible the creation of the Roman Empire under Octavian (i.e., Augustus). To honor this historic location, Philippi was set apart as a Roman colony. A group of Antony's veterans then settled in this Greek city and began to shape a Roman character in Philippi, now composed of Thracians, Greeks, and its new Roman citizens. The Roman character of Philippi deepened a few years later. Mikael Tellbe notes:

> In 31 BCE, Octavian established a military outpost at Philippi, filled the city with Roman citizens, and gave it the *ius Italicum*, the highest privilege possible for a Roman provincial municipality, which meant that the colony was considered to be Italian soil. In the following year the city was officially named after the Julian family, *Colonia Augusta Iulia Philippensis*, which would forever remind its citizens of their great emperors Julius Caesar and Augustus.[1]

For a city to be recognized as a Roman colony was not only an honor but also conferred significant benefits on its citizens. They were exempted from taxes, tributes, and duties. They were also governed by Roman political structure and civil law. A city like Philippi would acknowledge its special status and honor the emperor by establishing the imperial cult in it and maintaining a robust worship of the emperor. By the time Paul and his companions arrived in Philippi, this colony had an entrenched Roman identity: "the city was administered the same way Rome was, the official language was Latin, and its citizens were subject to the *ius Italicum* [Italian justice]."[2] In short, the citizens of Philippi were fiercely loyal to Rome and expressed their devotion in various ways, especially through their endorsement of and participation in the imperial cult. Luke seems to want to underscore the civic pride of this city for a reason.

---

1. Tellbe, *Paul between Synagogue and State*, 212.
2. Ibid., 219.

In the next section, we will see why when Paul and his companions encounter difficulties with the civic—and very Roman—authorities (Acts 16:20–21).

Lydia's "Open Heart" (16:13–15)

Paul's usual pattern when beginning missionary activity in a city was to make connections with the local Jewish synagogue. In this instance, when the Sabbath came, they left the city and went looking for "a place of prayer" (*proseuchē*; v. 13). "A place of prayer" can be another way of referring to a synagogue, but here it seems more likely that there was no synagogue in Philippi. Luke does not mention the presence of any Jews or Jewish community in the city. In fact, there is scant literary or archeological evidence for Judaism at all in Philippi during the first century. Luke does, however, mention that there were an unspecified number of women gathered by the River Gangites, west of the city (v. 13).[3] They sat down with these women and engaged them in conversation. Only one woman, Lydia, is named (v. 14). She is described first as a dealer in purple cloth who was originally from Thyatira, a city in the western region of the province of Asia, known for its production of and trade in textiles and dyed cloth. This alerts us to the fact that she is a woman of means since she was dealing with a high-end product in the expensive commodity of purple cloth. She is also a "worshiper of God." (v. 14b). This short phrase indicates that she was a gentile who was committed to the God of the Jews and, when possible, involved in the Jewish community (cf. Acts 10:2; 13:16, 26; 18:7). How Lydia came to be a "worshiper of God" is not disclosed. She may have come to this commitment when she was in Philippi or possibly when she was still in Thyatira where a more robust Jewish community may have existed.[4]

Lydia's conversion is told simply and eloquently: "The Lord opened her heart to respond to Paul's message" (v. 14c). In prayer and worship she is a soul seeking God. With a sense of holy imagination Tom Wright suggests that "perhaps, indeed, it was partly through Lydia's prayers that Paul had received his vision from Troas. Anyway, the word Paul preached was in Lydia's case tapping at a window that was already open."[5] In any case, the light of Christ came flooding in, and she is baptized, presumably in the river they are sitting alongside, along with a number of members from her household. In a poignant

---

3. Synagogues and Jewish places of prayer were often located near water to make prescribed washing and cleansing easier (cf. Josephus, *Ant.* 12.106; 14.258; Philo, *Flaccus* 122).

4. W. M. Ramsay, *The Letters to the Seven Churches, Updated Edition* (Peabody, MA: Hendrickson, 1994), 234, writes: "Seleucus I, the founder of Thyatira, is mentioned by Josephus [*Antiquities*, 12.33] as having shown special favor to the Jews and made them citizens in the cities which he founded in Asia."

5. Wright, *Acts*, 2:63.

response to her conversion, she invites Paul and his companions to come stay in her house. Her words are touching and bold: "If you consider me a believer in the Lord, come and stay at my house" (v. 16). As much as she is persuaded by the gospel to join the company of believers, she now persuades the bearers of the gospel to join her in the company of her home. This woman of means and an open heart now opens her home as the gathering place for the newborn church in Philippi.

LIVE the Story

We seem to have an insatiable appetite for mystery stories. The enduring interest in the work of Sir Arthur Conan Doyle (*Sherlock Holmes*), Ellis Peters (*The Cadfael Chronicles*), Agatha Christie (*Poirot*), G. K. Chesterton (*Father Brown*), J. K. Rowling (*Harry Potter*)—both the written work and TV or film adaptations—attests to our love of mystery and the never-ending questions of "who did it?" and "why?" I think that the evangelistic thrust of the church must also include a detective instinct. We must observe the clues of God at work—especially in people who are often overlooked. We must follow our intuition and explore trails that may uncover the mystery of the Spirit's presence.

Evangelism itself involves paying attention to mystery. We are surrounded by mystery, but like fish in water who never notice they are even wet, much of the time we fail to notice that we are immersed in it. Paul and his companions, however, paid attention to mystery; they looked for the clues of where God was already at work. As was often their practice, they looked for a prayer meeting on the Sabbath. Often, they just attended the one occurring in the local synagogue. In Philippi, possibly because there was no synagogue to visit, they heard there was a group of people gathered for prayer just west of the city along the River Gangites. What they found was a small group of women there. In a cultural context where Jewish men may have disdained such a meeting, Paul and his companions did not. Possibly the women were Jewish and married to Greek men. If so, Timothy would certainly be the first one to point out that God could be at work amid such relationships. Whatever the case, they engaged in conversation with a woman by the water—just as Jesus had done in Samaria years before (John 4). In this case, however, the woman, Lydia, was a successful businesswoman. She was originally from Thyatira in Asia, but now she resided in this leading city in Macedonia and dealt in expensive purple textiles. What Luke chooses to highlight even more than her business acumen is her openness to God. She is prayerful and a "worshiper of God." These qualities formed an open door in her heart that the gospel message entered with ease. The Lord opened her heart (Acts 16:14) much like the Lord opened the minds of the disciples walking along the Emmaus Road (Luke 24:45). Yet it required an openness and interest on the part of Paul and his companions to look for this prayerful and godly woman.

Had Paul and his companions ignored or disdained these women, they may never have made inroads and developed warm relationships in Philippi. We know from Paul's own letters that the people of this community became some of his most faithful supporters and were his friendliest church.[6] Despite its "poverty," it was generous in deeds (cf. 2 Cor 8:2). How often do we overlook those who are open to the good news? Might there be cultural or gender biases in us that cause us to overlook certain people (e.g., as Paul could have overlooked Lydia)? Without vision and open eyes, the world becomes small and dark. Without vision, the church may look at people without God's perspective. God's vision enlarges our capacity to enter into mystery and the cosmic dimensions of his purposes. God's world is always larger than our world. Look with God's eyes and truly see.

---

6. In terms of Greco-Roman culture, the expression of reciprocity through giving and receiving was the hallmark of true friendship. When Paul left Macedonia, "not one church shared with [Paul] in the matter of giving and receiving" except the Philippians (Phil 4:15).

CHAPTER 37

Acts 16:16-40

 LISTEN to the Story

¹⁶Once when we were going to the place of prayer, we were met by a female slave who had a spirit by which she predicted the future. She earned a great deal of money for her owners by fortune-telling. ¹⁷She followed Paul and the rest of us, shouting, "These men are servants of the Most High God, who are telling you the way to be saved." ¹⁸She kept this up for many days. Finally Paul became so annoyed that he turned around and said to the spirit, "In the name of Jesus Christ I command you to come out of her!" At that moment the spirit left her.

¹⁹When her owners realized that their hope of making money was gone, they seized Paul and Silas and dragged them into the marketplace to face the authorities. ²⁰They brought them before the magistrates and said, "These men are Jews, and are throwing our city into an uproar ²¹by advocating customs unlawful for us Romans to accept or practice."

²²The crowd joined in the attack against Paul and Silas, and the magistrates ordered them to be stripped and beaten with rods. ²³After they had been severely flogged, they were thrown into prison, and the jailer was commanded to guard them carefully. ²⁴When he received these orders, he put them in the inner cell and fastened their feet in the stocks.

²⁵About midnight Paul and Silas were praying and singing hymns to God, and the other prisoners were listening to them. ²⁶Suddenly there was such a violent earthquake that the foundations of the prison were shaken. At once all the prison doors flew open, and everyone's chains came loose. ²⁷The jailer woke up, and when he saw the prison doors open, he drew his sword and was about to kill himself because he thought the prisoners had escaped. ²⁸But Paul shouted, "Don't harm yourself! We are all here!"

²⁹The jailer called for lights, rushed in and fell trembling before Paul and Silas. ³⁰He then brought them out and asked, "Sirs, what must I do to be saved?"

³¹They replied, "Believe in the Lord Jesus, and you will be saved—you

and your household." ³²Then they spoke the word of the Lord to him and to all the others in his house. ³³At that hour of the night the jailer took them and washed their wounds; then immediately he and all his household were baptized. ³⁴The jailer brought them into his house and set a meal before them; he was filled with joy because he had come to believe in God—he and his whole household.

³⁵When it was daylight, the magistrates sent their officers to the jailer with the order: "Release those men." ³⁶The jailer told Paul, "The magistrates have ordered that you and Silas be released. Now you can leave. Go in peace."

³⁷But Paul said to the officers: "They beat us publicly without a trial, even though we are Roman citizens, and threw us into prison. And now do they want to get rid of us quietly? No! Let them come themselves and escort us out."

³⁸The officers reported this to the magistrates, and when they heard that Paul and Silas were Roman citizens, they were alarmed. ³⁹They came to appease them and escorted them from the prison, requesting them to leave the city. ⁴⁰After Paul and Silas came out of the prison, they went to Lydia's house, where they met with the brothers and sisters and encouraged them. Then they left.

Listening to the Text in the Story: Psalm 119:55, 62; Jeremiah 20:2; 29:20; Esther 3:8; Mark 5:7; Luke 8:28; 2 Corinthians 11:25; Ephesians 5:19; 1 Thessalonians 2:2.

EXPLAIN the Story

The more we read about Paul, his travels, and his mission, the more we hear parallels with Peter's experience and mission. After proclaiming the gospel to the populace and performing acts of healing in public settings (Acts 3:6–10; 5:16; 16:18), both Peter and Paul begin to attract the attention and ire of political authorities (4:1–2; 5:17; 16:19–20). Encounters with political authorities are confrontational and end in beatings (5:40; 16:22–23) and temporary imprisonment (4:3; 5:18; 12:4–5; 16:24). While in jail, there is divine intervention in the night that affords escape (5:19; 12:7–10) or potential escape (16:25–28). These are exciting stories that make for vivid reading!

Along with being full of intrigue and drama, the action in the narrative serves to highlight the powerful impact of the gospel. In the story in Philippi, the work of deliverance through a sign (an exorcism) and a wonder (an earthquake) challenges a community and transforms the lives of an individual slave girl and the household of a jailer. All told, this section is an interesting interlocking of personal narratives: Paul and Silas encounter a slave girl (16:16–18); the slave girl's owners confront Paul and Silas and drag them before the local political authorities (16:19–21); the local authorities order the beating and imprisonment of Paul and Silas (16:22–24); Paul and Silas are afforded the opportunity to escape in the night, but instead stay in confinement in order to comfort the jailer (16:25–28); the jailer, with trembling gratitude, receives the good news of salvation from Paul and Silas (16:29–34); in the morning Paul and Silas confront the officers and magistrates with news that alarms them (16:35–38); the officials attempt to appease Paul and Silas and escort them out of the prison, requesting them to leave the city (v. 39); after a brief visit back at Lydia's house to meet and encourage the brothers and sisters, Paul and Silas leave Philippi (v. 40). This is a detailed description of events, certainly important for Luke if for no other reason than he was present to witness its unfolding for himself. From hints in the narrative, it appears that Luke may even have stayed behind in Philippi when Paul and his companions continued their way south into Greece. Given these dramatic events, it is not surprising that the Philippian church became Paul's loyal partner in ministry and a source of deep friendship for the apostle and his companions.

A Slave Girl with a Spirit of Divination (16:16–18)

The first-person plural "we" (v. 16) continues in this new section signaled by an indeterminate time signature ("once when we were going to the place of prayer"). The occasion of prayer—possibly occurring at the same location where they had previously met Lydia (vv. 13–14)—sets the stage for a dramatic encounter to follow. A young slave girl[1] who had a spirit by which she could predict the future met the missionary group. The Greek text states that she had a "pythonic spirit" (*pneuma pythōna*). The lineage of this spirit can be traced back to the Greek city of Delphi in the region of Pytho. Here, the Delphic oracle resided at the foot of Mt. Parnassus in a temple guarded by a serpent, a python. The prophetess of Delphi, also known as Pythia, was famous across the Greco-Roman world for her ability to discern the future. Later the word *python* came to be associated with a spirit of divination that would grant a person the ability to offer guidance on specific questions—for a generous

---

1. In Greek the word is *paidiskē*. In the literature of the NT, this word referred to the slave class (cf. Matt 26:69; Acts 12:13; etc.).

fee, of course.² For example, people might enquire from such soothsayers about the success or failure of a business venture, a journey, or a marriage.

Here, in Philippi, was a young woman who offered this profitable pythonic service for her owners. Upon meeting Paul and his companions, however, this slave girl went off script. Instead of predicting the future, she kept on following the visitors—for many days—and became an ironic voice of witness to the gospel by shouting, "These men are servants of the Most High God, who are telling you the way to be saved" (v. 17). The pythonic spirit was simply speaking the truth, to a degree, not unlike other spirits when they encountered the "Son of the Most High God" (e.g., Mark 5:7; Luke 8:28).³ Beyond the Jewish connotations associated with "the Most High God," pagans also addressed Zeus or other deities with this title. In the pagan context of Philippi, this kind of public support was not only annoying but was also theologically confusing.⁴ In the end, Paul becomes exasperated with this "support" from a demonic spirit. Paul turned the tables on the spirit (not the girl), invoked the powerful "name of Jesus," and commanded it to leave her (cf. Acts 2:38; 3:6; 4:30; etc.).

The Slave Owners' Indignation and Accusations (16:19–21)

In Acts, Luke denigrates "spiritual" or religious activities that yield financial gain (8:18; 19:19, 25; 20:33). Not so non-Christians—especially slave owners who were also privileged Roman citizens in Philippi. The slave girl's owners did not greet her deliverance from the pythonic spirit with joy. Their source of profit was gone. Indignant, they seized Paul and Silas and dragged them before the civic authorities in the marketplace. While the cause of their ire was a business issue, the accusation was racial and political: "These men are Jews, and are throwing our city [*polis*] into an uproar by advocating customs unlawful for us *Romans* to accept or practice" (vv. 20–21). Here we begin to understand why Luke highlighted the Roman character of the Greek city Philippi (cf. 16:12). Paul and Silas are accused of disturbing the peace and for promoting Jewish (and thus anti-Roman) customs among the populace. Roman "peace" meant profit for its citizens. When that profit was jeopardized, the peace is jeopardized. Coupled with this is the charge related to race and civic identity.

The secondary ethnic charges should not be surprising as Paul and Silas face political and civic challenges by Greeks who identify deeply as Romans.

---

2. Barrett, *Acts*, 2:784–85.

3. It is important to note that Paul and his companions have not engaged in any proselytizing and thus far in their stay in Philippi have related only to God-fearing gentiles who converted to Christianity.

4. P. R. Trebilco, *Jewish Communities in Asia Minor*, SNTSMS 69 (Cambridge: Cambridge University Press, 1991), 130–31.

What might their accusers assume these Jewish missionaries would be promoting their Roman citizens to adopt? At the very least, they would assume them to be advocating monotheism and circumcision—both of which were repugnant to Romans. Beyond that, the customs might also include the keeping of non-Roman holidays (e.g., Sabbath), food laws, exemption from Roman military involvements, etc. Brian Rapske makes the important note that "in law, Roman conversion to Judaism was a punishable offence."[5] Whether these laws were always applied in this era, the fundamental issue is that Jewish visitors were being accused of disrupting the welfare of the Roman state by local Roman citizens. This was serious and demanded severe, swift retribution in a Roman colony such as Philippi. Paul's actions and message were calling into question some of the very foundations of Roman identity and society. Race, religion, money, and politics are often intertwined with devastating implications (cf. Esther 3:8).

Governing Authorities Respond with Beatings and Imprisonment (16:22–24)

When the slave owners' accusations are made vehemently and publicly, the crowds hearing them react forcefully (v. 22). There is no clear indication that the crowd is behaving like an illegal mob, but they do side in solidarity with the accusers in the charges made against Paul and Silas. The magistrates agree with the accusation.[6] They must take seriously the charges of disturbing the peace and proselytizing from locally known Roman accusers against visiting Jewish missionaries. What is somewhat odd is that Paul does not reveal his own Roman citizenship up front. Rapske makes a helpful observation on this count:

> Paul's failure to assert his citizenship at the earliest possible time is the surface cause of the negative assessment of the magistrates. To declare his citizenship then would compromise his Jewishness, his Gospel message, and the fledgling Philippian church; to submit would, though preserving his religious integrity, give a false impression of his status and result in a public physical and social assault. Paul chose the latter course because, though a Roman, he had resolved to honour his religious and missiological commitments.[7]

---

5. Brian Rapske, *Paul in Roman Custody*, vol. 3 of *The Book of Acts in Its First Century Setting* (Grand Rapids: Eerdmans; Carlisle: Paternoster, 1994), 118.

6. At this point in the narrative, Luke exchanges the more generic word "authorities" (*archontes*, v. 19) for "magistrates" (*stratēgoi*, vv. 20, 22, 35–36, 38). The latter is the common title for the highest official (Latin *duumviri*) in a Roman colony.

7. Rapske, *Paul in Roman Custody*, 115.

With the information that they have in hand and with tensions escalating, the magistrates have Paul and Silas stripped and beaten with rods by their *lictores*, their attending assistants who carried bundles of rods to symbolize their authority to enact corporal punishment. This was both painful and demeaning for Paul and Silas. This punishment was formally known in Roman legal terminology as *admonitio*.[8] This beating could be administered with varying degrees of severity from using a rod or military staff (*fustigatio*), a whip (*catigatio*), or a chain (*verberatio*). In this case it was with a rod, the memory of which Paul would retell in his own letters (2 Cor 11:25; 1 Thess 2:2). Beyond the beating, which was significant enough to have opened wounds (Acts 16:33), they were thrown in the local jail, and the magistrates ordered the jailer to keep them secure. The jailer received the orders and did his best to enforce them by placing the two in the innermost cell, in stocks. This was the worst place in prison. "The context indicates that this was intended to demoralize, humiliate and punish them. Paul and Silas are therefore shut up in a place reserved for dangerous low class felons."[9] Reminiscent of Jeremiah before them, these two missionaries who took away the prophetic voice of the pythonic spirit endured the punishment of a prophet by being put in stocks (Jer 20:2).

Paul and Silas Singing in Their Stocks (16:25–28)

We have no certainty as to where the prison was located in Philippi or what kind of stocks were used to restrain them.[10] What we do know is that being bound in stocks would have resulted in extreme discomfort for the prisoners and was considered a form of torture, reserved for the most grievous felons and slaves. From a legal and social standpoint, Paul and Silas were treated as the lowest of the low. The Roman magistrates fulfilled their duty by putting the accused in their proper place, soothing the offended citizenry, and obliging the observant populace. Yet despite their beating, imprisonment, and torture—all of which was in order insofar as Roman law was concerned[11]—Paul and Silas remain composed. This would give credibility to Paul's later exhortation to the Philippian church to "conduct yourselves in a manner worthy of the gospel of Christ. . . . For it has been granted to you on behalf of Christ not only to believe in him, but also to suffer for him, since you are going through the same struggle you saw I had" (Phil 1:27, 29–30). Paul and Silas do not merely endure their misfortune stoically but do so joyfully.

---

8. BDAG 902.
9. Rapske, *Paul in Roman Custody*, 126.
10. Rapske, *Paul in Roman Custody*, 127, describes several types of wooden or iron stocks that were used to restrain prisoners in the Roman period.
11. Sherwin-White, *Roman Society*, 82–83.

About midnight they "were praying and singing hymns to God, and the other prisoners were listening to them" (Acts 16:25). They were trained in biblical disciplines (cf. Ps 119:55, 62; Eph 5:19).

Suddenly an earthquake—not uncommon in this part of the world, but timed perfectly for a potential prison break—shook the foundation of the prison. The doors swung open, and the prisoners' chains and stocks were loosed. The jailer must have lived close to the prison because he could see the prison doors were open after waking from his sleep.[12] The text suggests he assumed the worst: the prisoners had escaped. In his role as a jailer, allowing prisoners to escape meant his own life was forfeit (cf. Acts 12:19). Before he could fall upon his own sword, however, Paul shouted out to inform him that he and all the other prisoners were still there. Whereas Peter was miraculously delivered from his imprisonments (cf. 5:19; 12:7–10), Paul voluntarily chose to remain in his. By doing so, Paul's decision to stay in jail led to freedom for the jailer and his household.

Salvation Comes to the Trembling Jailer (16:29–34)

The jailer is cut to the heart by the mercy extended to him by Paul and Silas. The jailer's response is to fall "trembling" before Paul and Silas and to ask them, "Sirs, what must I do to be saved?" (vv. 29–30; cf. 2:37). The answer is simple and immediate. Paul and Silas tell him to put his entire trust in the Lord Jesus (v. 31). Further, they add that this new life of salvation extends to his household as it did for Cornelius and his household (vv. 31–32; cf. 11:14). Like Cornelius, the jailer then welcomed the prisoners into his home (vv. 33–34). This hospitality was risky and not without social cost (a jailer caring for a political prisoner?). Again, after considering juridical texts from the Greco-Roman period, Rapske concludes that the jailer's actions were illegal and could have led to punitive consequences for him.[13] Although Luke does not give us the details of what the missionaries then taught the jailer and his household, we are informed that they were instructed in the "word of the Lord" (v. 32)—a summary phrase implying that they understood what the lordship of Jesus meant and demanded (cf. 2:21; 4:12; 8:25; 13:44; etc.). Without further instruction, they were immersed into the life of Jesus's death and resurrection acknowledged in baptism (see 2:38; 10:48). In a wonderful symmetry, before being "washed" in baptism by Paul and Silas, the jailer washes their wounds (16:33). After the washings, they shared a common meal

---

12. Rapske, *Paul in Roman Custody*, 262–63, suggests that the Philippian jailer was a public slave. Despite being a slave, he still was privileged with this senior civic post. This not only positioned him above other slave peers but also brought him wealth and public standing.

13. Ibid., 390–92.

(v. 34). The font and the table are brought together as salvation is brought to this household. The good news of Jesus and the salvation offered in him are greeted with "joy," a recurring theme in Luke's two narratives (Luke 2:20, 28; 13:13; 15:6, 7, 9, 10; 24:52–53; Acts 2:47; 3:8; 8:8, 39).

Governing Authorities Tremble (16:35–40)

At daybreak, the Roman magistrates sent their official police (Greek *rhabdouchoi*; Latin *lictores*) to release Paul and Silas. These may have been the same officers who had carried out the previous day's order to have Paul and Silas "beaten with rods" (*rhabdizein*, v. 22). All the actions suggest a scenario carried out carefully according to Roman law and order: the magistrates deliver Roman judgment, the officers enforce the sentence, the magistrates order the release, and the officers convey the message to the jailer.

There is, however, a twist in the tale. Up until now, Paul has either not chosen to or not been able to speak directly to the Roman magistrates or their police. In the quiet of the morning light, he tells them that they have unlawfully beaten and imprisoned them, even though the two of them are Roman citizens. Therefore, Paul informs them that, no, they will not quietly skulk away. Instead, they demand that the magistrates come to them and escort them out of the city. As Roman citizens unjustly treated in public, they will have nothing less than a public vindication. When the Roman magistrates hear that Paul and Silas are Roman citizens, the officials "were alarmed" (v. 38). Cities, including a Roman colony like Philippi, could be punished for mistreating Roman citizens.[14] The magistrates hurry over "to appease" (v. 39, *parakaleō*) and escort them out of prison and ask them to leave their city. The officials want no further trouble in their town.

Before Paul and Silas leave the city, they return to where they began their sojourn in Philippi in the company of Lydia. In her home they meet with the believers and "encourage" (v. 40, *parakaleō*) them. No doubt these new believers were not only encouraged by their words but also by their example. The missionaries not only told them about Jesus, who suffered at the hands of the Romans and was later vindicated, but they also model for them the pattern set by the Lord by suffering the mistreatment of Roman "justice" themselves. Paul will reflect on this theme of imitation when he writes his letter to the Philippians. In that letter he will invite them to conduct themselves in a manner worthy of the gospel (Phil 1:27) by imitating the examples set out by Christ (2:5–11) and his followers (3:17).

---

14. Tacitus (*Ann.* 12.58), Suetonius (*Aug.* 47), and Cassius Dio (*Roman History* 54.7.6) all record incidents of punishment for cities that abused Roman citizens. See also references cited by Longenecker, *Acts*, 466; Gaventa, *Acts*, 241.

One final observation in this passage is required. As Paul and Silas depart from Philippi, the first "we passage" in Acts ends (16:10–40). The narrative returns to describing how "they" continued on their way to Thessalonica (17:1). Presumably, Luke stays for some indefinite time in Philippi. His presence and encouragement would no doubt provide stability to the new believers as they negotiated what their new "citizenship" in Christ would look like (cf. Phil 3:20). This would have been important in a colony like Philippi where Roman citizenship was held in high regard.

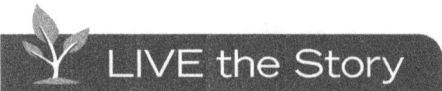

LIVE the Story

Gospel Impact for Individuals

Acts 16 relates a confrontation between the gospel and the state. While that is indeed the larger context, the effect of the gospel is described in the personal stories of two unnamed slaves: a girl and a jailer. Her owners exploit the slave girl for the money she can offer; the civic authorities exploit the slave jailer for the services he provides, even though he is privileged among his slave peers. Slavery in the ancient world was possessive and exploitive—it reached into the heart of humanity and shaped religious allegiances, economic circumstances, communities, and household life. Slavery, regrettably, continues to this day. Human trafficking—often for sex—exists in every country, often unseen. Its effects are devastating. It exploits the most vulnerable individuals (not unlike the Philippian slave girl) and yet implicates communities and political authorities (not unlike the Philippian magistrates). In the power of the gospel, courageous Christian organizations continue the work of Paul and Silas in bringing about seismic change for individuals enslaved by sex traffickers and corrupt officials in communities from Philadelphia to the Philippines, from Honolulu to Honduras.[15] The gospel is a powerful force to reshape the hidden, dark, and misshapen places of human society.[16]

The powerful name of Jesus brings deliverance for the sex slave workers of the twenty-first century world just as it did for the young slave girl in first-century Philippi. Unfortunately, Luke doesn't offer us any information about what happened to the Philippian slave girl after her release from the

---

15. As examples, International Justice Mission (www.ijm.org) and A21 (www.a21.org) are two organizations doing heroes' work in the world.

16. In a recent article for *Christianity Today*, Allison J. Althoff writes about "the hope dealers of Honduras" who work tirelessly to thwart corruption, assassination, sex trafficking, and drug addiction in the murder capital of the world. See "The Hope Dealers of Honduras," *Christianity Today* 57.7 (Sept. 2013): 17, http://www.christianitytoday.com/ct/2013/september/hope-dealers-of-honduras.html.

pythonic spirit. Yet there is a sense from the narrative that she would have been provided with support and refuge. The reason for this hope is that the gospel did not only transform the lives of individuals but of entire households. We know that Lydia's and the jailer's households believed in the Lord. The profound change that this would entail for them is significant. Among many things, it meant that their households became places of prayer, hospitality, and mission. In a city where demonic possession was present (Acts 16:16), where slavery and all its exploitive aspects were prevalent, and where the emperor was worshiped as Lord and Savior, the newly acquired core practices (e.g., a community rejecting demonic practices, worshiping Jesus as Lord and Savior, and regarding slaves and free people equally as brothers and sisters) of these Christian households would stand out. Beyond simply standing out, however, there was also the distinct threat of harassment and persecution. After all, Paul and Silas had just been beaten, tortured, and imprisoned; if that was how their leaders where treated, then their followers might expect the same. This is not surprising, given the example set by their suffering king, Jesus.

The Gift of Presence

As it did in the first century, the church today often challenges the religious, economic, and political life of its surrounding culture. The church does so by its very existence and the practices generated by the example of its Lord. Yet despite the cost of discipleship, the church continues to grow. In Philippi it grew even after Paul and Silas left. How? They flourished because they were not left alone or powerless. The church in Philippi knew from experience the power of Jesus to open hearts (16:14), to exorcise demons (16:18), and to shake the very ground beneath them (16:26). They knew the personal *presence of Jesus*, they had the *fellowship* of one another's company, and *Luke*—the probable author of this document—remained with them to cheer and to guide. These realities—God's presence, God's people, and God's leaders—remain for the church today as it dares to minister in the dangerous cities of the world, like Bangkok and Minsk, where sex traffickers continue to exploit their "slaves" for profit. These resources are still available for Christians who work like slaves for their corporate owners in the ruthless business cities of the world, such as London and New York. In whatever context Christians find themselves serving Christ, in his presence we find freedom and fellowship. There may be persecution, but there is also power to sustain the people of God and to challenge the authorities, whether they are political or pythonic.

CHAPTER 38

Acts 17:1-9

LISTEN to the Story

¹When Paul and his companions had passed through Amphipolis and Apollonia, they came to Thessalonica, where there was a Jewish synagogue. ²As was his custom, Paul went into the synagogue, and on three Sabbath days he reasoned with them from the Scriptures, ³explaining and proving that the Messiah had to suffer and rise from the dead. "This Jesus I am proclaiming to you is the Messiah," he said. ⁴Some of the Jews were persuaded and joined Paul and Silas, as did a large number of God-fearing Greeks and quite a few prominent women.

⁵But other Jews were jealous; so they rounded up some bad characters from the marketplace, formed a mob and started a riot in the city. They rushed to Jason's house in search of Paul and Silas in order to bring them out to the crowd. ⁶But when they did not find them, they dragged Jason and some other believers before the city officials, shouting: "These men who have caused trouble all over the world have now come here, ⁷and Jason has welcomed them into his house. They are all defying Caesar's decrees, saying that there is another king, one called Jesus." ⁸When they heard this, the crowd and the city officials were thrown into turmoil. ⁹Then they made Jason and the others post bond and let them go.

Listening to the Text in the Story: Psalm 118:26; Luke 1:32; 2:11; 19:38; 24:26, 46; Romans 16:21; 1 Thessalonians 2:2, 14–15; 3:1–5.

EXPLAIN the Story

From Philippi, Paul and his companions continued along the Egnatian Way for about 160 kilometers (100 miles) to Thessalonica via Amphipolis and Apollonia. It was the natural route for Paul and his companions to follow since this highway linked all the major cities in this province. Luke offers a compact summary of their brief three-week stay in the seaside Roman colony of Thessalonica. The city was roughly halfway along this main road. The episode is only two short paragraphs long. The first paragraph summarizes their synagogue preaching and its subsequent positive response (vv. 1–4). The second paragraph describes the negative response to their preaching from local Thessalonian Jews and their ensuing effort to provoke trouble for the Christians with the civic authorities (vv. 5–9). It is a remarkable passage that draws our attention not only to the ongoing Christian mission in Macedonia but also to the cultural and political tensions this mission incites.

Preaching in the Thessalonian Synagogue (17:1–4)

Thessalonica was the most important city in the Roman province of Macedonia and initially was the capital city of the second district.[1] Cassander, one of Alexander the Great's generals, founded the city in 315 BC. It was located at the northern edge of the Thermaic Gulf. In 146 BC it became the capital of the unified province of Macedonia, and in 42 BC it was declared a free city for its support of Antony and Octavian in their war with Brutus and Cassius. By all counts it was well populated, ethnically diverse, and an important commercial hub along the Egnatian Way—a key part of a highway network connecting Rome with Byzantium.[2]

Unlike Philippi, Thessalonica had a Jewish synagogue. As was Paul's "custom" whenever he found a local synagogue in a new location, he began his preaching in Thessalonica in the synagogue, doing so over three successive Sabbaths (Acts 17:2; cf. 13:5, 14; 14:1). We are not given many details of Paul's sermons. Rather, Luke only provides a simple summary and a sermon excerpt describing two aspects about the Messiah: "He reasoned with them from the Scriptures, explaining and proving that the Messiah *had to suffer and rise from the dead*," and he said, presumably more than once, "*This Jesus I am proclaiming to you is the Messiah*" (17:2–3). Luke is vague about how Paul explained these two points about the Messiah. What he does note is that "some" Jews and a "large number of God-fearing Greeks and quite a few prominent women" were persuaded and "joined"[3] Paul and Silas. For the mixed congregation of Jews and God-fearing gentiles, this was certainly "news," though it wasn't entirely received by everyone as "good" news. Yet for Luke's readers who have followed the overall narrative carefully thus far,

---

1. The Romans divided Macedonia into four administrative districts in 168 BC and then unified them into one province in 146 BC.
2. J. W. Simpson, "Letters to the Thessalonians," *DPL* 932.
3. Commentators often point out that this verb is in the passive voice. This seems to indicate that it is God who joins them to the Christian company, hence the "divine passive" voice. See Johnson, *Acts*, 306; Gaventa, *Acts*, 244; Schnabel, *Acts*, 705.

the message of the suffering Messiah has been a consistent message taught by the risen Jesus (cf. Luke 24:26, 46) and his followers (cf. Acts 2:22–36; 3:18). Jesus is indeed the King, the anointed descendant of David, heralded by angels (Luke 1:32; 2:11). Yet his kingdom is greater and distinct from that of temporal and earthly kingdoms. It is powerful but not oppressive; it is regal yet accessible to common people (e.g., poor shepherds [Luke 2:15–20], elderly saints [2:25–38], fishermen). Jesus is the King, but he is unlike any other the world has ever seen.

There Is Another King, Jesus (17:5–9)

Despite the mention that a significant number of aristocratic "prominent women" joined Paul and Silas as believers, they did not have the kind of political clout required to quell the actions of certain "jealous" Jews in the city.[4] They had good reason to be. The number of Jews, God-fearing Greeks, and prominent women shifting their allegiances diminished their synagogue. As Dunn observes, "We should note that the Jewish community in a major city was not a small despised group but of sufficient social status to attract significant numbers of Gentile adherents."[5] The Christian conversions stoked a jealousy similar to the one that occurred in Jerusalem (Acts 5:17; cf. 13:45). But in Thessalonica these so-called "jealous" Jews did not have recourse to temple police to help them arrest the disturbers. Instead, they gathered a mob from the marketplace to incite violence against the Christians in the city. This seems like an odd tactic given the aversion that secular authorities had to civic disturbances. The retribution the Jews were seeking against Paul and Silas could just as easily rebound on them. Nonetheless, they rushed to Jason's home in search of the missionaries to have them face mob justice.[6] The crowd was made up of "bad characters" that started a "riot"—hardly a respectable gathering of the local citizenry. We know little about Jason other than these few details: he was likely a fellow Jew (cf. Rom 16:21), he was a person of sufficient financial means to maintain a house large enough to provide hospitality, and he was a supporter of Paul and Silas.[7] Not finding Paul and Silas, the Jews change their strategy from "mob justice" to "civic justice" and

---

4. The Greek word is the verb *zēloō* and may indicate the "zeal" of Jews to maintain their ethnic distinction and strict adherence to the Mosaic law. Paul had expressed this kind of zeal before his Damascus Road conversion, and it had driven him to similar violent actions (see Acts 8:1; 9:1–2; Phil 3:6; 1 Tim 1:13).

5. Dunn, *Acts*, 227.

6. Greek *dēmos*. According to BDAG 223, this word can mean "a convocation of citizens called together for the purpose of transacting official business." This gathering, however, does not have the marks of "official business."

7. It was a frequent Jewish practice in the diaspora to substitute "Jason" (*Iasōn*) for the Jewish name "Joshua" (see BDAG 465).

drag Jason and some fellow believers before the city's leaders.[8] It is an ironic and risky move on their part. It is ironic because they accuse the believers of inciting rebellion when their initial action in fomenting a mob resulted in a riot (Acts 17:5). It is risky because the civic leaders could turn on them for causing the disturbance.

When they bring the bedraggled Jason and his company in front of the city officials of Thessalonica, their jealous motives may have remained, but they have shifted their strategy from the general melee of a mob to specific political accusations. As noted by Tom Wright, "Here things follow a very similar pattern to what we see in the gospel accounts of Jesus's trial: a Jewish charge, easily transformed into a pagan one."[9] Amid the raucous fray three accusations are made: (1) these outsiders who have caused trouble "all over the world" (v. 6) are now doing so in our city; (2) they are "*all* defying Caesar's decrees [*dogmata*]"; and (3) they are declaring another king, Jesus. Rowe makes the excellent suggestion that "it is actually better to take these discrete elements in reverse and read them as inseparable aspects of one well-calculated charge of sedition: by proclaiming another king, the Christians act against the decrees of Caesar and thereby turn the world upside down."[10] Rowe's point is simple and relativizes the unanswerable questions about what global upheavals the accusers might be referring to and what decrees of Caesar are being contravened. We may never know what troubles or decrees are being referred to, but the political charge is unambiguous: Paul and Silas proclaim a rival King.

It is well known that there was widespread aversion among Roman emperors to acknowledge themselves as "king" (Latin *rex*), but the reality is that from east to west in the empire, writers and the populace referred to the emperor as "king."[11] In contrast to this king, Luke's readers would be in agreement that Jesus is indeed another king. The royal pedigree of Jesus, the anointed (i.e., "messiah") king, has been on display from the beginning and throughout Luke's two-part narrative. The angel Gabriel proclaims Jesus to be the one who will sit on the *throne* of David, *reign* over the house of Jacob, and possess an eternal *kingdom* (Luke 1:32–33). Jesus repeatedly spoke about the kingdom of God inaugurated in and through his ministry. As he entered Jerusalem riding on a donkey, Jesus is heralded as the "king" (19:38; cf. Ps 118:26). Further, Jesus is

---

8. These local leaders, *politarchas*, were the court of arbitration in a free city like Thessalonica, where severe punishments could be meted out against traveling Jews like Paul and Silas. See Sherwin-White, *Roman Society*, 96.

9. Wright, *Acts*, 2:75.

10. Rowe, *World Upside Down*, 96.

11. Rowe, *World Upside Down*, 98, points to evidence from writers both in the eastern empire (e.g., Lucian, *Eunuch* 3; Dio Chrysostom, *1–4 Regn.* [*Or.* 1–4], *Regn. tyr.* [*Or.* 62]) and the western empire (e.g., Seneca, *Clem.* 1.4.1).

accused of acclaiming himself to be the Messiah, a king (Luke 23:2). Despite Jewish misgivings, Pilate ordered that a sign be hung over the crucified Jesus, reading: "This is the *king* of the Jews" (23:38). Therefore, the accusations of the unbelieving Jews of Thessalonica are accurate. Jesus is declared to be the Messiah, the anointed king, by the likes of Paul and Silas (Acts 17:3). Yet Luke would also disagree with the kind of political implications made by the Jewish accusers. Jesus's kingship is not a rival to Caesar's; if anything, Caesar's claims are rival to Jesus's lordship. It is worth noting Rowe's analysis at length:

> For Luke, [Jesus's] kingdom is obviously not a "human kingdom" in the straightforward simplistic sense, and in this way the Christian mission does not threaten Rome as did, for example, the Parthian kingdom. Yet, against every Gnosticizing impulse, the vision in Acts is of a kingdom that is every bit as much a human presence as it is a divine work. That is, the kingdom of which Jesus is King is not simply "spiritual" but also material and social, which is to say that it takes up space in public. The very fact of the disturbance in Thessalonica—that *this* is what happens—attests to the publicly disruptive consequences of the conversions (17:4). There is no such thing, at least in Acts, as being a Christian in private.
>
> The tension that surrounds the earthly nature of the kingdom mirrors that of the charges against Christians in Thessalonica. For the opponents' accusations are at one and the same time both true and false. They are false in that they attempt to place Jesus in competitive relation to Caesar. Such a positioning can only lead to a politics of revolt. The accusations are true, however, in that the Christian mission entails a call to another way of life, one that is—on virtually every page of Acts of the Apostles—turning the world upside down.[12]

In a manner similar to the outcome in Philippi (Acts 16) and despite the public and political "turmoil" (17:8), the civic authorities make no formal charge of sedition. If the charge of sedition had been proved to be true, then this would have defied the "decrees of Caesar"—whatever they may be—that there was a contender to imperial rule. Finally, if this did add up, it would indeed trouble the *Pax Romana* ("Roman peace"). As we know from "trouble" both before and after this period, the Romans gave no quarter to rivals: from Brutus and Cassius's sedition (ca. 44–42 BC) to the Bar Kokhba revolt (ca. 132–135 AD) and every major or minor uprising in between,[13] Roman rulers crushed rebellion.

In the end, the charges against the Christians in Thessalonica are stayed.

---

12. Rowe, *World Upside Down*, 101–2.
13. Cf. Acts 5:36–37 where Gamaliel mentions the uprisings of Theudas and Judas the Galilean.

Nonetheless, the vulnerable situation of the young Thessalonian church is far from resolved. Jason and "the others" are required to post bail of some unspecified amount. More importantly, the Christian community in the city is now identified and on watch. Without much ado, Paul and Silas leave the city for Berea (v. 10; cf. 1 Thess 2:15). Paul does not, however, leave and forget this young church. He remains anxious about this community, and in response to his concerns for the "strong opposition" (cf. 1 Thess 2:2, 14) they continued to face after his departure, he sends Timothy back to inquire about them (1 Thess 3:1–5). When Timothy returns to Paul with a favorable update from Thessalonica, Paul's care for them continues, and when he has a long layover in Corinth, this concern will impel him to write them a letter, 1 Thessalonians. This letter is the earliest document in the NT.

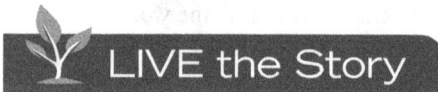

LIVE the Story

Many of us in the world today live under some form of democratic government. In fact, many uncritically assume the notion that liberal democracy is the best form of government. That is, when a country like Iraq is "liberated" from its oppressive dictator, few people in the West would advocate that we replace him with another king. For this reason, despite whatever interest people may have in contemporary royal families, few of us aspire to be governed by a king. It is not part of our governing DNA. So what are contemporary Christians to do with the royal theology we find in Scripture? That is, we worship, follow, and proclaim *King* Jesus. At the very least it requires enormous imaginative energy to maintain this allegiance under the enshrined ideals of liberal democracy. How do we live with this democratic worldview and yet follow Jesus who we proclaim to be "Lord of all" (Acts 10:36)? What are the habits of the heart and the core practices of Christians who are Christ's royal subjects?

The initial place we can look to find an answer is to the first Christians who lived under the rule of "king" Caesar in the Roman Empire. Their world was full of powerful visual imagery that asserted that "Caesar is Lord and Savior of the world" from various quarters, including public art, statuary, victory columns, and especially the imperial temples that filled public spaces in every major city in the empire (e.g., Ephesus, Corinth, Antioch, Tarsus, Thessalonica).[14] Even the coins they used to buy their food reminded them of the regal power of their emperors. Those who lived under the rule of the Romans were constantly bombarded with images designed not only to remind

---

14. See Paul Zanker, *The Power of Images in the Age of Augustus* (Ann Arbor: The University of Michigan Press, 1990).

them who governed them but also to shape their imaginations about their power and authority. Amid all this, the church endured, and even thrived, as a countercultural community following another king. How so?

Countercultural Habits of the Heart

We love and serve King Jesus with all that we are. That is, with what can be seen (bodies) and what cannot be seen (the "heart," soul, mind). It is not helpful to draw too sharp a distinction between the seen and unseen when it comes to human beings. With this in mind, Luke acknowledges that the early Christians experienced inner transformations of their "heart" that fueled and sustained their core practices. For example, when those in Jerusalem heard Peter's Pentecost sermon, Luke tells us that "they were cut to the *heart* and said to Peter and the other apostles, 'Brothers, what shall we *do*?'" (Acts 2:37). The razor-sharp message of the gospel "cut their heart," and they did something in response to the inner transformation. Soon afterward we hear that these early believers continued to gather together in the temple and "broke bread in their homes and ate together with glad and sincere *hearts*" (2:46); these believers "were one in *heart* and *mind*" (4:32). These internal changes in people, shaped by the declaration of Jesus as Lord, continued as the mission extended beyond Jerusalem and into the gentile world. When the Roman centurion Cornelius accepted the good news and declared his allegiance to the Lord Jesus, the church recognized his change of heart: "God, who knows *the heart*, showed that he accepted them by giving the Holy Spirit to them, just as he did to us. He did not discriminate between us and them, for he purified their hearts by faith" (15:8–9). When the mission reached Europe and gained a foothold in Philippi, the first convert, Lydia, responded because "the Lord opened her *heart* to respond to Paul's message" (16:14). After opening her heart to the Lord, she opened her home in hospitality to the missionaries (16:15). Their corporate actions were shaped by changes to the "heart"—the core (from the Latin word *cor*, which means "heart") of who they were.

This initial transformation of the heart was not an end but only the beginning of a life oriented around King Jesus. To nurture and sustain this inner life, especially in a culture bombarded by images of many "gods" and many "lords"—including "Lord Caesar"—they needed imaginative resources. They required inner pictures and inner stories that would quell and supersede the dramatic images and cultural voices surrounding them. The resources they drew on were likely the same ones that the people of God had drawn on for centuries. They *prayed* the prayers of Israel in the Psalms. They *listened* to the story of Scripture as their own stories, and since many of them could not read they *learned* the stories "by heart." To learn the biblical story "by heart" means to weave it into the very fabric of one's soul. Prayer, Scripture, and baptized imaginations are not simple steps for developing kingdom hearts, as if virtue and maturity in Christ are matters of theological calculus. Rather, they are habits of the heart of those attuned to King Jesus and his rule.

Countercultural Core Practices

The habits of the heart formed by King Jesus lead to countercultural, core ("heart") practices. Practice flows from being, from the heart. In the case of the early Christians in Acts, Kavin Rowe identifies three interrelated practices that shaped their pattern of life: confessing Jesus as Lord of all, mission, and the formation of community.[15] If Jesus is indeed the king and Lord of all, then this news must be heralded. As Christians spread out declaring this good news in mission, communities were formed to sustain the life of those whose hearts had been transformed. Mission and community formation continue to be the necessary response to the truth that Jesus is *the* king. Neither mission nor community formation are marginal extras to the Christian life in the first century or the twenty-first century.

For a detailed description of the key aspects that shaped the community life of the early church, see the discussion on Acts 2:42–47. All those elements (teaching, fellowship, breaking bread, prayer) are essential to living the story well in our day. All the core practices of the church—confessing Jesus as Lord, mission, community life—are lived in specific places and in time. It is that last facet—time—that we might discover a fruitful avenue to explore how we live out our "core" (i.e., our "heart") practices today. Although it is often unnoticed, the very way we denote the days of the week and the months of the year reflects the lords and gods of the Greco-Roman world. The seven days of the week are based on the planets, often associated with the gods of Greek astrology and later associated with Nordic gods: Sunday (Sun), Monday (moon), Tuesday (Mars), Wednesday (Mercury), Thursday (Jupiter), Friday (Venus), and Saturday (Saturn). Our months are Roman too. Some of the months are named for Roman and Greek gods, such as Mars (March), Aphrodite (April), and Maia (May); others are named after Roman rulers like Julius Caesar (July) and Augustus Caesar (August). Our year begins on January 1, and January is named for Janus, the Roman god of gates and doorways. Of course, advertising directives further shape a pagan worldview by heralding shopping periods in our culture. The few vestiges of Christian seasons have been co-opted by our culture in efforts to induce people to buy things. A successful "Christmas season" has nothing to do with declaring Christ and everything to do with consumer spending.

---

15. Rowe, *World Upside Down*, 102–37.

While it is impractical for us to disassociate ourselves as Christians from pagan names that mark our days and months, we can practice Christian celebrations in such a way that we reframe secular time with sacred time and counter our culture's appetite for consumption. A way forward in living out hearts transformed by King Jesus is to rediscover the gift of the Christian year. The Christian year is modeled on the practices of the Israelites, who celebrated feasts and marked time by them. For example, Easter is linked with the Feast of Passover and Pentecost with the Feast of Weeks/Firstfruits. A conversation with a local minister attuned to the church year or a consultation of prayer books,[16] books on the liturgical year,[17] or some helpful websites[18] are all good places to start. Personally, our family life was transformed when we were given Martha Zimmerman's book *Celebrating the Christian Year: Building Family Traditions around All the Major Christian Holidays*.[19] Martha helped introduce us to the Christian year and gave us practical ways of teaching our children how to enter the larger story of God's work in the world. It helped us see the significance of the times and seasons not by what our culture dictates but by infusing our days with meaning derived from the life, death, and resurrection of Jesus and his followers in the church.

Time is a gift. It is something to be received with gratitude and lived well. As we do this, we will better align our hearts and core practices to King Jesus as all that we are—hearts and bodies—is transformed by his rule. Helpfully, the Christian year ends with a Sunday called "the Reign of Christ/Christ the King." This sets us up for the Advent season—the beginning of the Christian "new year"—as we watch and wait for royalty again. After all, we are not simply awaiting the coming of a baby. The celebration of Christmas is about the arrival of a king: "Joy to the world, the Lord is come. Let earth receive her *King*!"

---

16. E.g., the *Book of Common Prayer* or *Celtic Daily Prayer*.

17. E.g., Bobby Gross, *Living the Christian Year: Time to Inhabit the Story of God* (Downers Grove, IL: InterVarsity Press, 2009) or Joan Chittister, *The Liturgical Year: The Spiraling Adventure of the Spiritual Life* (Nashville: Thomas Nelson, 2010).

18. See the blog by Corey Widmer, "Telling Time Differently as Christ Followers," *Third Church*, 31 Oct. 2016, http://www.thirdrva.org/blog/telling-time-differently-as-christ-followers) and the informative video "The Story . . . as Told through the Christian Calendar," Christ Church Anglican, 20 Nov. 2013, https://vimeo.com/79923336.

19. Although no longer in print, used copies are available through book distributors.

CHAPTER 39

Acts 17:10–15

LISTEN to the Story

¹⁰As soon as it was night, the believers sent Paul and Silas away to Berea. On arriving there, they went to the Jewish synagogue. ¹¹Now the Berean Jews were of more noble character than those in Thessalonica, for they received the message with great eagerness and examined the Scriptures every day to see if what Paul said was true. ¹²As a result, many of them believed, as did also a number of prominent Greek women and many Greek men.

¹³But when the Jews in Thessalonica learned that Paul was preaching the word of God at Berea, some of them went there too, agitating the crowds and stirring them up. ¹⁴The believers immediately sent Paul to the coast, but Silas and Timothy stayed at Berea. ¹⁵Those who escorted Paul brought him to Athens and then left with instructions for Silas and Timothy to join him as soon as possible.

Listening to the Text in the Story: Luke 16:29; 1 Thessalonians 2:14, 17.

EXPLAIN the Story

Luke provides this short paragraph (Acts 17:10–15), describing the reception of the gospel in Berea as a bridge between the traumatic events in Thessalonica (17:1–9) and the trial at the Areopagus in Athens (17:16–33). There are two movements explained in the narrative: (1) the initial receptivity in the city through Paul's preaching in the synagogue (vv. 10–12), and (2) the subsequent opposition led by Jews who arrived from Thessalonica that forced another hasty departure of Paul, this time for Athens (vv. 13–15). A pattern is emerging on this journey through the Greek provinces. Paul preaches to receptive audiences, but this is soon followed by opposition—often from unnamed "Jews"—that leads to disturbances and confrontations with local gentile authorities.

After the traumatic experience faced by Jason before the mob and magistrates in Thessalonica, the believers dispatched Paul and Silas as fast as they could under the cover of darkness (v. 10). The NIV translation does not include the word "immediately" (*eutheōs*), but it is there in the Greek text. The point is clear: they left hurriedly and stealthily. It was not an easy separation for Paul. When he wrote to the church soon after his exodus, he expressed that the separation was like being "orphaned" from them (1 Thess 2:17). Paul and his colleagues departed along the Via Egnatia (a major Roman highway in the travel network linking Rome with Byzantium) and traveled eighty kilometers (50 miles) southwest until they arrived in Berea. As was his custom, Paul looks for a synagogue (cf. Acts 13:5, 14; 14:1; 16:13; 17:1) and begins his preaching there (17:10–11). In comparison to Thessalonica, the Jews of Berea were of "more noble character" (*eugenēs*). Their noble conduct was evidenced by their lack of "jealousy" and in their enthusiasm in receiving the message. They diligently examined what Paul taught against the testimony of "the Scriptures" (i.e., the Law and the Prophets; cf. Luke 16:29). Luke does not offer any indication as to how long Paul spent in Berea. However long he stayed (weeks? months?), his influence extended beyond the synagogue to include the residents of the city as well. Elsewhere, many of the receptive gentiles seemed already to have some connection with Judaism as God-fearing Greeks (see 13:43, 50; 16:14; 17:4). Here, the receptive gentiles are described only as "prominent Greek women and many Greek men" (v. 12).

Unfortunately, news of Paul's work in Berea reached the ears of Thessalonian Jews who remained opposed to the Christian mission, and they traveled there to stir up trouble. Some of us might be surprised that people would go to this length of walking eighty kilometers (50 miles) only to make trouble. There is precedent though. Paul in his "zeal" did so when he left Jerusalem to pursue troublesome Jewish Christians in Damascus (9:1–2). While Paul may not have appreciated the antagonism of his fellow Jews, he would at least have understood it. In the end Paul, in similar circumstances to those he found himself in at Thessalonica, is forced to leave Berea "immediately" (*eutheōs*; 17:14). As he had done at Philippi, where he may have left Luke,[1] he instructed Silas and Timothy to remain with the young church in Berea while he traveled to the coast and then on further south to Athens (likely by sea) in the province of Achaia (17:14–15). The efforts of Paul, along with his colleagues Silas and Timothy, seem to have been fruitful and enduring since a large enough church was established there to send out its own ministers, like Sopater (20:4).

---

1. That is, if one assumed that Luke is the author of Acts. In the narrative the "we" portion ends in Philippi (cf. Acts 16:10–17 with 17:1).

Initially, it may seem odd that Paul leaves Silas and Timothy behind and then, upon reaching Athens, informs his Berean traveling companions to instruct Silas and Timothy "to join him as soon as possible" (17:15). Paul's own letter may help to clear this up. Apparently, his plan was to return to Thessalonica, and he was waiting for news that the opposition had abated before he could return (1 Thess 2:17–3:1). Besides offering comfort to the Berean believers, Silas and Timothy may also have been waiting for news from Thessalonica on whether matters with the civic authorities had calmed down enough to allow for their return. Paul did not seem to have left Berea with a specific plan in mind (it was "the believers [who] . . . sent Paul to the coast," 17:14). It was only when he arrived in Athens that he resolved to seek clarity about the situation in Thessalonica.

LIVE the Story

Do you know someone named "Eugene" or "Eugenie"? Their names are derived from the same Greek word (*eugenēs*) Luke used to describe the Jewish people in Berea (Acts 17:11). The word is translated as "noble character." The implication of this noble character is that the people possessing it are open-minded, they ask thoughtful questions, they are investigative, and they let the evidence take them where it leads. That is, they enjoy a vital quality required for wise learning: they are critically minded, without having a critical spirit. This is the nugget in this short narrative nestled in Acts. The next narrative will bring the reader to Athens, the most esteemed city in the ancient world for its love of learning—its "philosophy" (lit., "love of wisdom"). The school of Athens was the Harvard of its day. This is where you went to find the best scholars, the sharpest intellects, and the most inquiring minds. Yet for all its vaunted fame for wisdom, Luke describes the Stoic and Epicurean philosophers of Athens as scoffers when it came to Paul's new teaching (17:32). They were closed-minded. They had a reputation for seeking wisdom, yet they failed to live up to their reputation. Instead, little-known Berea is praised for its noble character and open-mindedness. There is a lesson for us all in this. Even though there are great scholars and intellects at the top-rated universities of the world, wisdom can be found wherever people face new questions and ideas with open, critical minds. Open minds and receptive spirits are fertile ground for biblical faith to flourish. Signs and wonders might accompany biblical faith, but it is the miracle of the open mind and listening heart that produces much of the highest praise in Acts. After all, it requires a unique openness to receive the mystery of the proclamation about a crucified Messiah. God often chooses the people and places the world overlooks, the Bereas, to expose the hollow pretensions of the "greats" of the world (1 Cor 1:23–27).

Chrysostom, the renowned ancient commentator, who noticed that Paul did not perform any miracles in either Thessalonica or Berea, did not overlook this. Instead, the "great miracle" that God enacted through his apostle was the miracle of faith in the heart of human beings. He writes:

> Why didn't [Paul and his colleagues] perform miracles? For if [Paul] stayed a long time where he was stoned (i.e., at Lystra), all the more could he have stayed [in Thessalonica and Berea]. What was the reason then? Because God did not always want them to perform miracles. For it is no less a miracle for them, persecuted as they are, to prevail without performing miracles. Therefore, just as now he prevails without miracles, often then he wished to prevail in the same way. And so the apostles did not chase after miracles either, as he himself says, "We preach Christ crucified" [1 Cor 1:23]. To those who seek miracles, to those who seek wisdom, we offer [the crucified Lord], which is not able to persuade even with miracles, and we persuade them. This is a great miracle.[2]

May we seek to be like the Bereans—the Eugenes and Eugenies of the world—as we hear, mark, learn, and inwardly digest the book of Acts and all of God's word.

---

2. Chrysostom, *Homilies on the Acts of the Apostles* 37, in *ACCA*, 213.

CHAPTER 40

Acts 17:16-34

 LISTEN to the Story

¹⁶While Paul was waiting for them in Athens, he was greatly distressed to see that the city was full of idols. ¹⁷So he reasoned in the synagogue with both Jews and God-fearing Greeks, as well as in the marketplace day by day with those who happened to be there. ¹⁸A group of Epicurean and Stoic philosophers began to debate with him. Some of them asked, "What is this babbler trying to say?" Others remarked, "He seems to be advocating foreign gods." They said this because Paul was preaching the good news about Jesus and the resurrection. ¹⁹Then they took him and brought him to a meeting of the Areopagus, where they said to him, "May we know what this new teaching is that you are presenting? ²⁰You are bringing some strange ideas to our ears, and we would like to know what they mean." ²¹(All the Athenians and the foreigners who lived there spent their time doing nothing but talking about and listening to the latest ideas.)

²²Paul then stood up in the meeting of the Areopagus and said: "People of Athens! I see that in every way you are very religious. ²³For as I walked around and looked carefully at your objects of worship, I even found an altar with this inscription: TO AN UNKNOWN GOD. So you are ignorant of the very thing you worship—and this is what I am going to proclaim to you.

²⁴"The God who made the world and everything in it is the Lord of heaven and earth and does not live in temples built by human hands. ²⁵And he is not served by human hands, as if he needed anything. Rather, he himself gives everyone life and breath and everything else. ²⁶From one man he made all the nations, that they should inhabit the whole earth; and he marked out their appointed times in history and the boundaries of their lands. ²⁷God did this so that they would seek him and perhaps reach out for him and find him, though he is not far from any one of us. ²⁸'For in him we live and move and have our being.' As some of your own poets have said, 'We are his offspring.'

²⁹"Therefore since we are God's offspring, we should not think that the divine being is like gold or silver or stone—an image made by human design and skill. ³⁰In the past God overlooked such ignorance, but now he commands all people everywhere to repent. ³¹For he has set a day when he will judge the world with justice by the man he has appointed. He has given proof of this to everyone by raising him from the dead."

³²When they heard about the resurrection of the dead, some of them sneered, but others said, "We want to hear you again on this subject." ³³At that, Paul left the Council. ³⁴Some of the people became followers of Paul and believed. Among them was Dionysius, a member of the Areopagus, also a woman named Damaris, and a number of others.

Listening to the Text in the Story: Psalm 50:8–13; Isaiah 42:5; 66:1–2; Jeremiah 10:16; Romans 1:22–23; 1 Thessalonians 1:9–10.

EXPLAIN the Story

After leaving Berea and arriving in Athens, Paul waits in this famous city for Silas and Timothy to rejoin him. Paul was not idle. He continued to follow his well-established mission pattern by seeking out the local synagogue to engage in dialogue about Jesus. There is a new twist, however, in Athens. Paul not only engages with Jews and God-fearing Greeks in the synagogue but also goes to the marketplace, the heart of economic and cultural life of the city. In the marketplace he confronts philosophers from two of the great intellectual traditions of the day: Epicureanism and Stoicism. When he meets them, they impel him to make a public presentation at the Aeropagus. From here, Paul delivers one of his most famous speeches.

This portion of the narrative falls into three parts. The first section (vv. 16–21) sets the stage for the speech as the result of cultural confrontation. In this paragraph we observe Paul in distress, in debate, and in dialogue. The second section (vv. 22–31) moves into the speech proper. The speech itself has five movements to it: an introduction (vv. 22–23); an assertion about the creator God and his transcendence (vv. 24–27a); an argument for God's immanence (vv. 27b–28); a final critique of idolatry (v. 29); and a conclusion (vv. 30–31). The closing section (vv. 32–34) recounts the response to Paul's speech.

Setting the Stage (17:16–21)

The first phrase (v. 16a) of this paragraph suggests that Paul's attention was still focused on situations in the north in Thessalonica and Berea. While he waited for his colleagues to arrive, he began to turn his attention to his surroundings in Athens. He was deeply disturbed by what he saw. The Athens he observed was no longer the administrative capital of Greece—that honor belonged to Corinth—but it still retained an esteemed reputation for its cultural heritage and philosophical schools. Yet this was not what distressed Paul. Paul's "distress"[1] is inflamed by the city's widespread idolatry. For a seasoned traveler and one familiar with Hellenistic culture, this is striking. His response takes him beyond his regular pattern of engaging with Jews and God-fearing gentiles in the local synagogue. In addition to this, he goes to the marketplace—the agora—to argue *every single day*[2] about the core realities of life (v. 17).

Paul's marketplace conversations eventually brought him into confrontational debate with the elite thinkers of Athens: Epicurean and Stoic philosophers. Our contemporary caricatures of these two ancient Greek schools are unhelpful—the notion that an "Epicurean" is a binge-drinking glutton or that a "Stoic" is an unfeeling robot. As modern interpreters, we must remember that these were two of the most respected intellectual traditions that had existed in Athens since the fourth-century BC as rigorous moral, albeit rival, schools of philosophy.[3]

The Epicureans and Stoics of first-century Athens should be distinguished from the idolatrous Athenians—to an extent. In broad terms, both schools rejected populist idolatry and scorned superstitious beliefs about the gods. Both schools also advocated materialism. They thought that matter—including god(s)—constituted everything that existed. Further, they were both monistic in their theology (i.e., they believed in only one god, while at the same time tolerated popular views on "the gods"). In broad terms, Epicureans were the deists of their day; if God (or possibly "gods") exists, he does so at a distance without care or concern for the cosmos or humanity. Stoics, on the other hand, were the pantheists of their day; god exists everywhere and permeates everything as a productive "fire"[4] or *pneuma* ("breath" or "spirit"). Probably the Epicureans are the "some" (v. 18a) who accuse Paul of being a "babbler"—a derogatory term suggesting that he is like a scavenger bird who randomly

---

1. The Greek word *paroxynō* is sharp; it occurs only one other time in the NT (1 Cor 13:5), and in both instances it carries a sense of indignation and anger.
2. The temporal phrase *kata pasan hēmeran* is emphatic with the addition of the adjective *pasan* ("every"); see Parsons and Culy, *Acts*, 333.
3. For succinct summaries, see D. J. Furley, "Epicurus," *OCD* 532–34; N. C. Croy, "Epicureanism," *DNTB* 324–26; J. Annas, "Stoicism," *OCD* 1446; J. C. Thom, "Stoicism," *DNTB* 1139–40.
4. Annas, "Stoicism," *OCD* 1446.

picks up scraps of ideas without any sustained understanding of broader truth. For them, Paul is a philosophic poser and peddler of foreign religion. The Stoics were likely the "others" (v. 18b) who consider him to be a preacher of "foreign gods." The fact that they think he speaks about foreign "gods" (rather than "god") suggests that they may have mistaken him for preaching about two gods: Jesus and Anastasia.[5] Together, the concerted Epicurean-Stoic opposition against Paul focuses on his message that he is introducing *foreign gods* (v. 18), *new* teaching (v. 19), and *strange* ideas (v. 20). Importantly, these charges represent more than simply points of philosophical disagreement; they are serious charges. It has long been recognized that both the *place* (i.e., the Areopagus) and the *content* of the indictments are reminiscent of the charges leveled against the Greek philosopher Socrates centuries earlier (see Plato, *Apol.* 24b–c). In Socrates's case, the trial ended with him being found guilty and forced to drink a fatal dose of hemlock. In short, Athens is known for enforcing the death penalty on those who proclaim "new gods."

Before the speech proper commences (in v. 22), Luke adds an interesting aside. In fact, the NIV goes so far as to put this sentence in parentheses. Luke remarks: "All the Athenians and the foreigners who lived there spent their time doing nothing but talking about and listening to the latest ideas" (v. 21). The impact of this sentence almost blunts the charges the Epicureans and Stoics level against Paul. How can they be upset with him advocating foreign gods, new teaching, and strange ideas if this is what "all the Athenians" in fact desire and seek out?[6] In this sarcastic aside, Luke cleverly provides a counterbalance to the charges and prepares his readers for an articulate response from Paul. In this, Luke will demonstrate Paul to be a respected "philosopher" advocating ancient teaching and wise ideas about the one true God who is far from foreign; in fact, this God has long been worshiped—albeit in ignorance—in Athens.

In the end, the Epicureans and Stoics "grasp"[7] Paul and bring him to the traditional place of investigation in Athens: the Areopagus (v. 19).[8] Commentators have long debated whether this reference to the Areopagus refers either to a *place* of meeting northwest of the Acropolis in Athens or to the formal *council* that met on the hill to judge in moral and religious matters.

---

5. The word "resurrection" is translated from the feminine Greek noun *anastasis*. The Greeks often understood gods as existing in male and female pairs.

6. This opinion was widespread in the first century; see also Josephus, *Ag. Ap.* 2.130; Strabo, *Geogr.* 9.1.16.

7. The NIV translates this Greek word as "took" (*epilambanomai*). In Acts, this word more often carries the notion of "seize"—as if the person taken does not have a choice in the matter, especially when it comes to people facing a mob, civic tribunal, or recognized authorities (see Acts 16:19; 18:17; 21:30, 33; 23:19).

8. The Areopagus or "Hill of Ares" (Ares is the Greek god of war; Mars is the Roman equivalent, hence the older designation, "Mars Hill"; see BDAG 129).

Kavin Rowe suggests that "by writing that Paul was seized . . . and brought before the Areopagus council, Luke thus draws on the Mediterranean cultural encyclopedia to situate Paul's speech within an overtly political context. The speech is not simply a peaceful philosophical dialogue with his curious opponents. It is, instead, so the attuned reader understands, a moment in which Christian preaching—once again—has drawn the attention of the governing authorities."[9]

In this opening paragraph, Luke sets the stage extremely well for Paul's ensuing speech. Again, Rowe observes, "Instead of a romantic view of Athens as the place of university-like debate, Luke portrays the city's rampant idolatry—Paul is rightly vexed—as the context in which the Christian preaching of the resurrection of Jesus (1) is distorted and (2) results in a potentially life-threatening situation for Paul vis-à-vis the political authorities."[10]

Paul's Areopagus Speech (17:22–31)

Paul's Areopagus speech is one of the most notable speeches in all of Acts. Historians, theologians, cultural critics, preachers, and apologists (just to name a few) are interested in it because it represents an example from the early church of significant cultural engagement. It is considered to be one of the high points of confrontation between "Jerusalem" (the biblical world) and "Athens" (the secular/pagan world). Whatever one's interest may be, it is a stimulating and fascinating address. Some commentators have regarded it as the forerunning work of the early-church apologists (e.g., Justin Martyr, Tatian, Tertullian). In this sense, it is viewed as a speech devoid of many biblical themes and reflects more the thought world of Greek philosophy (especially Stoicism) adapted to a Jewish-Christian agenda.[11] Other scholars have suggested the ideas behind Paul's speech are entirely based on the OT and their development in Second Temple Judaism.[12] Most writers today tend to steer a modified approach insomuch as the speech reflects the ideas of Hellenistic Judaism as it engaged with—and often accommodated—the theology and culture of its Hellenistic world.

The speech develops in five stages. In the first step (vv. 22–23), Paul makes his introduction. He begins by acknowledging that the Athenians are "religious" (v. 22), but they are ignorant of the true God they worship (v. 23). He draws this conclusion by observing their own admission at one of the altars

---

9. Rowe, *World Upside Down*, 31.
10. Ibid., 33.
11. For this position, see Martin Dibelius, *The Book of Acts: Form, Style, and Theology* (Minneapolis: Augsburg Fortress, 2004), 119, and the commentaries by Conzelmann and Haenchen.
12. See Bertil Gärtner, *The Areopagus Speech and Natural Revelation* (Lund: Gleerup, 1955).

in the city where they acknowledge they worship "an unknown god." Since they are ignorant of whom this god is, Paul intends to inform them. As of yet there is no known literary or historical evidence for an altar existing in ancient Athens with the inscription "to an unknown god." There is, however, literature that tells us about "altars to unknown *gods*" in Athens.[13] Luke may have made a mistake (turning the plural "gods" into the singular "god"), but since the ignorance of "god" (singular) on the part of the Athenians is the very focus of the entire speech, it makes more sense to view this as rooted in actual history, even if it is a history whose evidence is yet to be uncovered.

In the second step of the speech (vv. 24–27a) Paul begins his assault on idolatry, but in terms that would have kept his Epicurean and Stoic listeners engaged. Paul's first assertion is that the God whom they do not know is in fact the creator of the world and everything in it. Further, this creator God is the "Lord." The creator and Lord of all, therefore, does not need a temple made by human hands (cf. 1 Kgs 8:27; Acts 7:58) or require a ritual devised by human minds (Acts 17:24b–25a). Paul's statements that God is the creator and the Lord of all are rooted in biblical theology. The idea of God as the creator of "heaven and earth" is asserted in the first words of Scripture (Gen 1:1; cf. Isa 42:5; Jer 10:16), along with Paul's own letters (e.g., 1 Cor 8:6; Col 1:16). If it is granted that God is creator and Lord of all, then Paul sees fit to draw out several implications: God does not dwell in human-built temples (Acts 17:24b; cf. Isa 66:1–2); God is self-sufficient (v. 25a; cf. Ps 50:8–13); and God is the source of everything (v. 25b; cf. Gen 2:7).

While God, the creator and Lord, needs nothing from humans, humans need him. In fact, he created the whole race of humanity from one person—Adam—so that humanity might inhabit the earth and that they might seek him (vv. 26–27a). Paul emphasizes God's unique activity in creation—a theme that recurs in Acts, especially to demonstrate God's providential work of salvation (e.g., 2:22–24; 11:15–18; 15:7–11)—but this time in a broader way. The point Paul makes is that God, in his goodness, is thoroughly involved in the human drama by setting "appointed times [*kairous*]" in history and establishing national "boundaries"[14] so that humans might "seek him." "Seek[ing]" God here has little to do with the Athenian penchant for telling and hearing something new and has everything to do with the goal that humanity would "trust and obey."[15] In all of this, humanity is not abandoned merely to grope for God

---

13. Bruce, *Acts*, 335, cites Pausanias, *Description of Greece* 1.1.4 and Philostratus, *Life of Apollonius* 6.3.5 as examples of this.

14. The Greek word is *horothesia*; this is a rare word and only used this one time in the NT.

15. Note the biblical example of David, who seeks the face of the Lord (2 Sam 21:1; cf. 2 Chr 7:14; Ps 24:6).

in dark ignorance. God is there to be sought and discovered. Unfortunately, Paul's hopeful aspiration that humans might then seek out God is tempered by his conditional phrase "*perhaps* [they would] reach out for him and find him" (v. 27a). This type of condition[16] offers only the remotest possibility of the action actually happening. Yet as Dunn notes, "This Creator God has not created a hunger for God within humankind only to leave it unsatisfied."[17]

Paul continues with a third step in his speech (vv. 27b–28). Even though he is reserved in his hope that humanity might reach for God and find him, nonetheless this "unknown God" is not far from unbelieving gentiles. Why? Paul infers that humans all have existence "in him" because we are all part of his creation. To support his point, he appeals to two sayings by Greek poets. The first is an unknown source—"for in him we live and move and have our being" (v. 28). The second is a third-century BC Stoic poet, Aratus, who wrote, "We are his offspring" (*Phaen.* 5). Although Paul cites Greek sources, including a Stoic,[18] his argument is a biblical one. Paul employs his accusers' own insights and authors in such a manner that his argument encompasses the Greek world within his larger biblical framework.

Paul concludes his speech (vv. 29–31) with a final indictment against idolatry and an evangelistic appeal. Thus far he has argued that people's failing to find God cannot be blamed on God's *distance* from them. God has left observable signs in creation, in history, and within humanity itself. Humanity's very existence points to God. But now, he flips the argument. Given all this, we cannot then turn and fashion God out of lesser things made of gold or silver or stone (v. 29). Paul takes biblical concepts—God is creator, God is the Lord of all—to argue against idolatry. In all this, his Epicurean and Stoic listeners would have agreed with him. But then he takes the argument one step further and turns his sights directly on them. In contrast to the Stoic (i.e., pantheistic) view of reality, he declares that this "unknown god" of the idolaters is also the creator of the universe. This means God is not only immanently a part of all things but also transcendent above all things. In contrast to the Epicurean (i.e., deist) view of reality, who thought it was not necessary or even possible to relate to the distant, uncaring, and transcendent god, he warns that this "unknown God" has also appointed a day of radical involvement in judgment (v. 31). This leaves the marketplace idolater alongside the scholarly philosopher as both equally ignorant and equally guilty in relationship to this *known* God. As such, "God . . .

---

16. Greek grammars refer to this as a "fourth class condition." See Daniel B. Wallace, *Greek Grammar Beyond the Basics: An Exegetical Syntax of the New Testament* (Grand Rapids: Zondervan, 1996), 484.

17. Dunn, *Acts*, 236.

18. Paul may have been familiar with the work of Aratus since they both came from Cilicia.

now . . . commands all people everywhere to repent" (v. 30). Repentance, that complete turn from one's headlong run into error, is available still, but the day of reckoning is coming. Paul's final assertion of "judgment day" is supported by his closing phrase. There will be an appointed day for judgment because God has already appointed the judge, the one he raised from the dead. While he does not say the name "Jesus," that is certainly his point. The resurrection of Jesus is the pivotal event in human, not just Athenian, history and demands a decisive change for everyone. It requires repentance from idolatry, abandonment of practices associated with pagan worship, and the acceptance of a new way of life. This is radical, confrontational, and deeply challenging.[19]

The Response (17:32–34)

The response to Paul's speech is mixed, but with considerably less intensity (both in agreement and disagreement) than he experienced elsewhere on previous occasions (see 13:43, 45; 14:4, 11; 17:4–5). The crux of Paul's argument is the resurrection of the appointed judge, Jesus. With this, some sneered in derision, while others offered to hear him again on this matter (v. 32). Apparently, despite the grave charges leveled against Paul, his speech—offered in the very place where others, like Socrates, stood accused of similar offenses—provided enough clarification to demonstrate that his teaching was not "foreign . . . new . . . [or] strange" (cf. vv. 18–20). It is not clear whether Paul is vindicated or whether the ruling against him is postponed. Further, Luke does not parse out which philosophers scoffed and which ones were sympathetic. The Epicurean view of materialism and the final dissolution of everything into atoms at death would have ruled out for them any possibility of resurrection or a future judgment. Some of his Stoic listeners may have appreciated the rationality associated with Paul's argument and his theme of divine providence—the latter may have sounded much like their view of fate. In the end, however, his bold declaration of Jesus's resurrection and the coming judgment requires neither punishment from the council nor compromise from Paul. While we have no way of knowing who the scoffers and the sympathizers were, we are told that "some . . . believed" (v. 34). Included among this number are a man named Dionysius and a woman named Damaris.[20] Luke adds that Dionysius was a court "member of the Areopagus." All told, despite all the scholarly and popular interest given to Paul's speech over the centuries, from the episode itself it appears that there was little immediate fruit resulting from the apostle's efforts.

---

19. Rowe, *World Upside Down*, 39.
20. Bruce, *Acts*, 343–44, suggests that Demaris was unlikely to have been a God-fearing gentile before hearing Paul's speech as one of the many bystanders at his hearing. Chrysostom, *On the Priesthood* 4.7, concluded that she was Dionysius's wife.

LIVE the Story

Strange Ideas and the Need for Apologetics

In 2006 my family and I were living in England. At that time, there was great interest in Dan Brown's recent and best-selling novel, *The Da Vinci Code* (2003), and its film version (2006) starring Tom Hanks. For many, the plotline of this mystery was absorbing. Millions of people purchased the book and attended in droves the screening of the film. Unfortunately, even though Brown's story is a work of fiction, many people read the book and watched the film as if the story were a work of *fact*. They were enthralled by his alternative Christian account that the Merovingian kings of France were direct descendants of Jesus of Nazareth and Mary Magdalene. This assertion had been made before,[21] but this time it received widespread acclaim and interest, so much so that the "strange ideas" of the book's fictional plotline began to be assumed to be true by many people. I was grateful that amid the peeked attention, our regional BBC station sought out our local Anglican bishop, Tom Wright, for his opinion on *The Da Vinci Code*. Besides being a churchman, Bishop Tom is one of the world's finest scholars of the New Testament and early Judaism. He is also a superb apologist. In about the same amount of time that it takes to read Paul's speech answering for the "strange ideas" he was declaring, Bishop Tom offered a winsome and measured response to questions about the so-called "history" of *The Da Vinci Code*. Bishop Tom was not condescending, but he clearly and thoughtfully set the record straight.[22]

I have no idea whether that short BBC interview answered the questions of its viewers, but I was grateful the church had a spokesperson like Bishop Tom. He is a reputable, charming, and articulate person who thinks extremely well on his feet—much like the apostle Paul. We need apologists like him. The Western world is becoming increasingly post-Christian, and basic biblical knowledge and understanding of Christian history is also disappearing. People are being "taught" the Christian story by Hollywood and from titles picked out from the fiction section of bookstores. The need for thoughtful and educated Christian apologists is as great today as it has ever been. C. S. Lewis recognized this decades ago when he preached about "Learning in War-Time" in the Church of St. Mary the Virgin, on October 22, 1939. He said:

---

21. See, e.g., Lynn Picknett and Clive Prince, *The Templar Revelation: Secret Guardians of the True Identity of Christ* (London: Transworld, 1997).
22. Bishop Tom also invited viewers to come to an extended evening for questions and answers with him at a local pub. Apparently, it was "standing room only" for that discussion.

If all the world were Christian, it might not matter if all the world were educated. But, as it is, a cultural life will exist outside the Church whether it exists inside or not. To be ignorant and simple now—not to be able to meet enemies on their own ground—would be to throw down our weapons, and to betray our uneducated brethren who have, under God, no defence but us against the intellectual attacks of the heathen. Good philosophy must exist, if for no other reason, because bad philosophy needs to be answered. The cool intellect must work not only against the cool intellect on the other side, but against the muddy heathen mysticisms which deny intellect altogether. Most of all, perhaps, we need intimate knowledge of the past. Not that the past has any magic about it, but because we cannot study the future, and yet need something to set against the present, to remind us that the basic assumptions have been quite different in different periods and that much which seems certain to the uneducated is merely temporary fashion. A man who has lived in many places is not likely to be deceived by the local errors of his native village: the scholar has lived in many times and is therefore in some degree immune from the great cataract of nonsense that pours from the press and microphone of his own age. The learned life then is, for some, a duty.[23]

Since the time of Paul's Areopagus apologetic speech, many learned Christians have taken up the duty of replying to the critiques of pagan philosophers and popular objectors. In many ways, Paul set the benchmark for those who would follow him in attentiveness and response to one's cultural context. Paul was attuned to his world and how the gospel illumines and challenges it. In the early church, besides Paul and the other apostles, it was learned Christians (many of them laypeople) like Justin Martyr (ca. AD 100–165), Tatian (ca. AD 120–180), Irenaeus (ca. AD 130–202), and Tertullian (ca. AD 155–240) who offered reasoned arguments against the charges of pagans outside the church and defended the faith against heresy within the church. In modern times, besides the Anglican layman C. S. Lewis and the Anglican bishop and scholar Tom Wright, a number of people have emerged to offer thoughtful articulations of the Christian faith both in the marketplace and for the academy, including G. K. Chesterton, Peter Kreeft, Francis Spufford, Ravi Zacharias, Lee Strobel, Alvin Plantinga, Charles Taylor, Tim Keller, Philip Yancey, and many more. While none of us can read and respond to everything, it is important—whether we are called upon to speak to congregations or simply speak to our neighbors or fellow employees—that we are familiar with

---

23. C. S. Lewis, *The Weight of Glory and Other Addresses* (New York: HarperCollins, 1980), 58–59.

the work of our contemporary Christian apologists. They help provide us with the basics for "the reason for the hope that [we] have" (1 Pet 3:15). As such, we can prepare ourselves by reading selectively from the rich resources available in the work of ancient and modern apologists.

Some Ways to Proclaim the "Unknown God" Today

As I mentioned above, I am deeply grateful for those who have the gifting that enables them to speak extemporaneously in public as they articulate or defend the gospel. This is not, however, a gift that I have. I am thankful for those in the church—from Paul to Tom Wright—who do this well. Still, I think there are other ways with which to proclaim the "unknown God" today. I agree with Augustine that the human heart is restless until it finds rest in God. But there are other ways to reach restless hearts and minds besides reasoned debate. In addition to rational argumentation, there are also appeals that can be made imaginatively and relationally.

Again, C. S. Lewis offers us a way forward. In his acclaimed book *Planet Narnia*, Michael Ward makes a strong case for how Lewis used imaginative apologetics even more effectively than rational apologetics.[24] In 1948 Lewis famously lost a debate regarding his work of apologetics *Miracles*, at the Socratic Club in Oxford to the young philosopher Elizabeth Anscombe. After this defeat, Lewis revised his book *Miracles*, but then turned to focus his attention on a seven-part fairy tale, *The Chronicles of Narnia*. Some people thought that Lewis was so shaken by his loss in the debate that "he became a child, a little boy who was being degraded and shaken by a figure who, in his imaginations, took on witch-like dimensions."[25] Ward, in contrast, argues that "Lewis . . . turned to romance not as a retreat from apologetics after his debate with Anscombe, but precisely as a way of explaining his case to himself in imaginative form."[26] That is, his loss in the debate "fertilized" his apologetic efforts to help others understand God through symbol and imagination. Lewis already knew that reasonable argument was often ineffective in bringing people to knowledge about God. He suggested this through his own poem "The Apologist's Evening Prayer":

> From all my lame defeats and oh! much more
> From all the victories that I seemed to score;
> From cleverness shot forth on Thy behalf

---

24. See chapter 10, "Primum Mobile," in Michael Ward, *Planet Narnia: The Seven Heavens in the Imagination of C. S. Lewis* (Oxford: Oxford University Press, 2008). See also Holly Ordway, *Imaginative Apologetics and the Christian Imagination* (Steubenville, OH: Emmaus Road, 2017).
25. A. N. Wilson, *C. S. Lewis: A Biography* (London: Collins, 1990), 220.
26. Ward, *Planet Narnia*, 219.

> At which, while angels weep, the audience laugh;
> From all my proofs of Thy divinity,
> Thou, who wouldst give no sign, deliver me.
>
> Thoughts are but coins. Let me not trust, instead
> of Thee, their thin-worn image of Thy head.
> From all my thoughts, even from my thoughts of Thee,
> O thou fair Silence, fall, and set me free.
> Lord of the narrow gate and needle's eye,
> Take from me all my trumpery lest I die.[27]

Whereas non-Christians can often parry direct apologetic arguments, the indirect proclamation of the gospel through the imagination often allows truth to be conveyed and received. Lewis agreed: "Symbolism exists precisely for the purpose of conveying to the imagination what the intellect is not ready for."[28] In this, Lewis followed the opinion of his master, George MacDonald, who wrote: "It is not the things we see the most clearly that influence us the most powerfully."[29] The enduring popularity—among both children and adults—and apologetic impact of *The Chronicles of Narnia* seems to bear this out. Lewis, along with MacDonald and friend J. R. R. Tolkien, demonstrate that fairy tales and the imagination can create apologetic bridges for the gospel that can penetrate to the hearts of individuals reading them. There is just as much scope—if not more—for imaginative apologetics as there is for rational apologetics. As such, pastors and priests should nurture the creative life of artists and enlist them as fellow apologists in communicating not just the good and the beautiful but also the true.

Not all of us are gifted debaters or imaginative artists, but all of us can be good friends. There is a significant place for rational apologetics and imaginative apologetics, but all of us can engage in *relational apologetics*. As humans, we are made to connect socially. We need friends—and not just the Facebook kind. Andrew Solomon in his article "Depression Is a Disease of Loneliness" writes that in our era "Facebook has made 'friend' into a verb."[30] In this, he argues that we confuse the "ambient intimacy of websites with the authentic intimacy that comes with sharing your life's challenges with someone who cares. . . . We are imprisoned even in crowded cities and at noisy parties."

---

27. C. S. Lewis, *Poems* (New York: Harcourt, 1992), 129; used with permission.
28. C. S. Lewis, "Letter to Sister Penelope," in *The Collected Letters of C. S. Lewis Vol. II*, ed. W. Hooper (Grand Rapids: Zondervan, 2004), 565.
29. George MacDonald, "The Imagination: Its Functions and Its Culture," in *Orts* (London: Sampson Low, Marston, Searle, & Rivington, 1882), 28, quoted in Ward, *Planet Narnia*, 225.
30. Andrew Solomon, "Depression Is a Disease of Loneliness" in *The Guardian*, 16 August 2014, https://www.theguardian.com/commentisfree/2014/aug/16/depression-disease-loneliness-friends.

Mental illness, depression, or loneliness are often exacerbated because people lack true friends.

While literature, film, poetry, music, and art can help show us what relationship looks like, we have resources within the Christian tradition to offer the good news of God through the simple power of friendship. God loves the entire world, but our incarnate Lord demonstrated the Father's love by loving individuals, like John, "the disciple whom Jesus loved" (John 13:23). As Mac Stewart observes, "The witness of Christ himself seems to suggest that the best preparation for loving the world at large, and loving it duly and wisely, is to cultivate intimate friendship and affection towards those who are immediately about us."[31] Aelred of Rievaulx (AD 1110–1167) offers one of the most robust arguments for the importance of relationship in the Christian tradition in his masterful work *Spiritual Friendship*. In conversation with his friend Walter, when asked what practical advantage there was to spiritual friendship, Aelred replied: "[I]n human affairs nothing more sacred is striven for, nothing more useful is sought after, nothing more difficult is discovered, nothing more sweet experienced, and nothing more profitable possessed. For friendship bears fruit in this life and in the next."[32] In a world that can hardly conceive of love in ways that don't include sexual expression, one of the greatest gifts Christians can offer our neighbors starving for intimacy is friendship. We can share intimacy and affection with others that is rooted in discipleship—a mutual love for the God who loves us—and in so doing offer a relational apologetic for the claims of the gospel. Friendship does not require extended education, expertise, or sophisticated argumentation. It does require leisurely time, attentive listening, and openness. These are the slow disciplines of friendship. They are simple, but they are also costly. Yet for sharing a costly grace, they are indispensable and often the most effective and fruitful tools in extending "the reason for the hope that [we] have" (1 Pet 3:15). Imaginative and relational apologetics are two ways to proclaim "the unknown God" to people around us today who are craving knowledge and intimacy. While not all of us are gifted in debate, most of us can cultivate creativity and friendship with those who live near us and work with us.

---

31. Mac Stewart, "I Have Called You Friends," *Covenant*, 9 Dec. 2015, http://livingchurch.org/covenant/2015/12/09/i-have-called-you-friends/.

32. Aelred of Rievaulx, *Spiritual Friendship*, trans. Mary Eugenia Laker (Kalamazoo, MI: Cistercian, 1977), 2.9. See also the chapter on friendship in C. S. Lewis, *The Four Loves* (New York: Harcourt Brace, 1960).

CHAPTER 41

Acts 18:1-17

 LISTEN to the Story

¹After this, Paul left Athens and went to Corinth. ²There he met a Jew named Aquila, a native of Pontus, who had recently come from Italy with his wife Priscilla, because Claudius had ordered all Jews to leave Rome. Paul went to see them, ³and because he was a tentmaker as they were, he stayed and worked with them. ⁴Every Sabbath he reasoned in the synagogue, trying to persuade Jews and Greeks.

⁵When Silas and Timothy came from Macedonia, Paul devoted himself exclusively to preaching, testifying to the Jews that Jesus was the Messiah. ⁶But when they opposed Paul and became abusive, he shook out his clothes in protest and said to them, "Your blood be on your own heads! I am innocent of it. From now on I will go to the Gentiles."

⁷Then Paul left the synagogue and went next door to the house of Titius Justus, a worshiper of God. ⁸Crispus, the synagogue leader, and his entire household believed in the Lord; and many of the Corinthians who heard Paul believed and were baptized.

⁹One night the Lord spoke to Paul in a vision: "Do not be afraid; keep on speaking, do not be silent. ¹⁰For I am with you, and no one is going to attack and harm you, because I have many people in this city." ¹¹So Paul stayed in Corinth for a year and a half, teaching them the word of God.

¹²While Gallio was proconsul of Achaia, the Jews of Corinth made a united attack on Paul and brought him to the place of judgment. ¹³"This man," they charged, "is persuading the people to worship God in ways contrary to the law."

¹⁴Just as Paul was about to speak, Gallio said to them, "If you Jews were making a complaint about some misdemeanor or serious crime, it would be reasonable for me to listen to you. ¹⁵But since it involves questions about words and names and your own law—settle the matter yourselves. I will not be a judge of such things." ¹⁶So he drove them off. ¹⁷Then the crowd there turned on Sosthenes the synagogue leader

and beat him in front of the proconsul; and Gallio showed no concern whatever.

Listening to the Text in the Story: Matthew 28:20; Luke 1:28; Romans 16:3–4; 1 Corinthians 1:14; 4:3–5, 12, 18–21; 9:1–2; 16:19.

EXPLAIN the Story

After Athens (17:16–34), Paul's mission brings him to Corinth, the political capital of the imperial province of Achaia and one of the leading economic and cultural cities of the Roman Empire. Luke describes his eighteen-month stay here with only a few short paragraphs. The Corinthian narrative begins by reestablishing a common pattern: proclamation in the synagogue that is followed by resistance from the Jews (Acts 18:1–8). Once again, in common with their experience elsewhere on this mission in Greece, the Christians are brought before the political authorities; in this case it was Gallio, the proconsul of Achaia (vv. 12–17). However, between facing Jewish resistance and the proconsul, the two sections are bridged by an account of a reassuring vision to Paul from the Lord (vv. 9–11).

Synagogue Proclamation and Resistance (18:1–8)

Corinth was an important city in the Roman Empire and in the life of Paul.[1] The Romans destroyed Corinth in 146 BC for leading a Greek rebellion, but after lying dormant for over a century, it was reestablished as a Roman colony by Julius Caesar in 44 BC. By the time Paul arrived in the mid-first century, it had roared back to prominence to become a leading city alongside Alexandria and Rome itself. It soon eclipsed Athens as the most important Greek city in the empire. Its strategic crossroad location straddling the narrow isthmus that connected the Peloponnese with Greece ensured its status. It was the master of the two harbors on either side of the isthmus: Cenchreae leading east to Asia Minor and Lechaeum leading west to Italy. Because merchants preferred to portage their goods across the narrow isthmus rather than sailing the dangerous route around the Peloponnese, this meant Corinth controlled the flow of traffic east and west, north and south.[2] Its location brought with it political importance, incredible wealth, and a swelling immigrant population from

---
1. See S. J. Hafemann, "Letters to the Corinthians," *DPL* 172–73.
2. Rasmussen, *Atlas*, 229.

across the empire. Politically it was a coveted seat for Roman consuls, who could pad their coffers handsomely from this profitable city during their two-year terms. Along with many economic boomtowns came vice and corruption. Despite the propensity for vice, the opportunity for riches ensured that a diverse group of people came here to work and trade. As such, it attracted a mix of ethnicities—including a large number of Jews.

It is not surprising, then, that when Paul arrived in Corinth he found a sizable Jewish community and a synagogue. In particular, he meets a Jew, Aquila, from Pontus (a province adjacent to the Black Sea), and his wife, Priscilla. This couple became important friends and coworkers of Paul (cf. Rom 16:3–4; 1 Cor 16:19). They were a dynamic and learned duo who had recently arrived from Italy after Claudius had expelled all the Jews from Rome (Acts 18:2). The Roman historian Suetonius cites that the expulsion was due to the disturbances Jews were causing at the instigation of "Chrestus" (*Claud.* 25), which probably is a corruption of the word "Christ" (i.e., the Messiah). The proclamation of Jesus—the Christ—in Rome by his followers created tensions among the Jewish community there. This is a foreshadowing of the incident with a Roman ruler that will soon occur in Corinth too (Acts 18:12–17). Besides sharing the same ethnicity with them, Paul also shared a common trade with them as a "tentmaker" (v. 3).

The word "tentmaker" (*skēnopoios*) occurs only this one time in the NT. It is unlikely that an urban city like Corinth would require tentmakers or that a highly mobile traveler like Paul would have been able to carry the heavy tools required for weaving tent cloth.[3] Another possibility is that this trade relates to the technical work of making theatrical stages out of leather or tent cloth, a skill that was in high demand in the metropolitan areas where Paul stayed.[4] Paul lived with Aquila and Priscilla, likely near the marketplace, and shared with them not only common labor (1 Cor 4:12) but also a common vocation as preacher of the gospel. As was his pattern elsewhere, Paul did his best to convince Jews and Greeks (likely God-fearing gentiles) about Jesus every Sabbath (Acts 18:4; see 13:5, 14; 14:1; 16:13; 17:2; 19:8).

Silas and Timothy arrive from Macedonia (18:5). Their arrival afforded Paul the luxury of devoting himself to preaching and teaching. We are not informed what made this possible. Was it a financial gift from the Macedonian churches (cf. 2 Cor 11:9; Phil 4:15)? Or was it something else? Either way, what Luke does tell us is that Paul focused on informing Corinthian Jews that Jesus was "the Messiah" (*Christos*). The title Messiah evokes all the royal dimensions of Jesus's identity. The response to Paul's intensified preaching

---

3. Brian Rapske, "Acts, Travel and Shipwreck," in Gill and Gempf, *Graeco-Roman Setting*, 7.
4. See BDAG 928.

was intensified opposition from the Jews of Corinth. The opposition became so acute that Paul left the synagogue, shaking the dust off his clothes as a symbol of separation, and absolved himself of any bloodguilt by using the foreboding words, "Your blood be on your own heads!" (Acts 18:6). These are strong words of reproof and echo the words at Jesus's presentation before the Jews by Pilate (Matt 27:24–25) and indictments made earlier in Acts by Peter (Acts 2:23, 36; 3:14, 15; cf. 5:28) and Stephen (7:52). With that, as far as his mission in Corinth is concerned, he turns his attention to the gentiles.[5]

In turning to direct his attention to the gentiles, Paul did not move the base of his operation very far. In fact, Paul set up base "next door" in the house of Titius Justus, a "worshiper of God" (18:7). Luke often highlights the gentile adherents to the gospel like Titius (e.g., the Ethiopian eunuch, 8:26–28; Cornelius, 10:1; Lydia, 16:14). The move next door from the synagogue did not help moderate tensions with the Jewish synagogue—especially after the synagogue leader Crispus and his entire household also put their trust in the Lord (18:8). Crispus, along with many other Corinthians, believed and was baptized—a fact remarked by Paul in a letter to the Corinthian church (1 Cor 1:14).

The Lord Speaks in a Vision (18:9–11)

Visions, while not frequent in Acts, do occur at important points in the narrative. Visions are vital components in the calling of Paul (Acts 9:10, 12), in the gospel being preached to Cornelius (10:3, 17, 19; 11:5), and in the mission to Macedonia (16:9–10). Paul receives a vision in which the Lord Jesus speaks directly to him (18:9–10). In this instance, the Lord gives *comfort*: "Do not be afraid." The Lord gives *affirmation*: "Keep on speaking." The Lord gives *assurance*: "I am with you." The Lord makes a *promise*: "No one is going to attack and harm you." All these commands and assurances echo the words spoken by the Lord (Yahweh) to Joshua (Josh 1:9), Isaiah (Isa 41:10; 43:5), and Jeremiah (Jer 1:8, 19). In common with those prophets, Paul too is facing opposition. Although stated only indirectly, the opposition created anxiety and fear. Yet like the prophets before him, Paul is commanded to keep on speaking. The vital words of encouragement are, "I am with you" (Acts 18:10). The simple preposition "with" (*meta*) that joins the Lord and his servant makes all the difference. "With" the Lord, no opposition can stand against the apostle. Further, the Lord assures him that he is not alone; indeed, there were many of the Lord's people in Corinth. Paul would need this assurance in his Corinthian ministry not only for the courage he would require amid opposition

---

5. He returns to his regular pattern of preaching to the Jews when he arrives in his next point of mission in Ephesus (Acts 18:19; cf. 13:46; 28:17–28).

coming from outside the Christian community during his lengthy stay there but also for the coming tidal wave of opposition that he would experience from within the Christian community itself (cf. 1 Cor 4:3–5, 18–21; 9:1–2). Still, Paul needed this direct encouragement to sustain him during his year and a half there (Acts 18:11), his longest stay in any place thus far during his mission. The church in Corinth would continue to loom large in Paul's life, and this community would require considerable time, teaching, and written correspondence.

Before Gallio (18:12–17)

The protection promised by the Lord is soon put to the test when "the Jews of Corinth made a united attack on Paul" (v. 12). The attack takes the form of a charge brought against him before Gallio, proconsul of Achaia. Lucius Annaeus Novatus Gallio, brother of the famous Roman philosopher Seneca, was the proconsul of Achaia ca. AD 51–52. We are able to date his governance of this Roman province due to an inscription found in Delphi.[6] This has been a helpful date for New Testament studies since it provides a fixed point from which to begin determining the dates of Paul's letters and missionary excursions. The "place of judgment" before Gallio referred to by Luke (v. 12) is either a specific place near the Corinthian marketplace or simply wherever the proconsul happened to be at the time. Wherever the proconsul was, that was where the place of judgment would be. A proconsul was appointed directly by Caesar and spoke and acted for him.

The Jewish charge against Paul carries some ambiguity to it. They accuse Paul of "persuading the people to worship God in ways contrary to the law" (v. 13). The ambiguity relates to two words: "God" and "law." If one listens from the perspective of Gallio, the question that arises is "which god?" since there were many gods worshiped in Corinth at the time. Further, they accuse Paul of advocating ways contrary to the "law." Is this the legal decrees of the empire—including decrees acknowledging the Jewish religion as a "legal religion" (*religio licta*)[7]—or the "law" of the Jews? From Gallio's remark a few sentences later (v. 15), he regards the question as one related to "your own law." It seems, however, that the Jews of Corinth intended to distance their own legally recognized religion from the "worship of God" Paul was

---

6. The inscription is known as the *Delphic* or *Gallio Inscription*. See Jerome Murphy O'Connor, *St. Paul's Corinth: Texts and Archaeology* (Collegeville, MN: Liturgical Press, 2002), 161.
7. Josephus, *Ant.* 14.190–265, provides a number of examples of the legal privileges bestowed upon the Jews by the Romans. For example, they were exempt from service in the army, they had the right to assemble according to the customs of their forefathers (i.e., observance of special days, food laws, etc.), and they were exempt from sacrificing to other gods that other citizens were required to participate in.

advocating. The Jews of Corinth may have wished to make this clear because they were aware of the public disturbances following Paul in cities he visited in Macedonia and Achaia. These Jews, possibly better than anyone else, recognize the implications of Paul instructing recently converted gentiles on how to live. If gentiles committed themselves to Jesus the Messiah in significant numbers (cf. the "many" referred to in vv. 8 and 10), then Corinthian culture would be disrupted. The Jews would want to demarcate themselves clearly from this movement. After all, Claudius had recently expelled the Jews from Rome because of disturbances related to "Chrestus." The same thing could happen in Corinth because of Christ.[8] The Jews knew that following Jesus entailed not just disembodied beliefs but a way of life that ran counter to Roman culture and custom.

Yet, for all the insight the Jews of Corinth may have had about Paul and his teaching, it was not something shared by Gallio. He did not have the foresight to recognize the future collapse of Roman culture, and there were no immediate indicators—public disturbances, book burnings, loss of business, etc.—to suggest this was anything more than an internal dispute about "words and names and your own law" (v. 15).[9] In the end, he did not consider this charge worth his time or effort and "drove" them off (v. 16). These proceedings occurred in a public context, and as is often the case crowds had gathered around out of interest to see what was going on. Gallio's abrupt dismissal of the Jewish charges and inaction seems to have incited action from the watching gentile crowd. They turn on Sosthenes, likely the synagogue leader, and beat him in front of the proconsul without Gallio seeming to care at all (v. 17). Despite Paul experiencing the safety promised by the Lord (v. 10), this brush with a Roman consul will not be the last time in Acts that the apostle will face Roman rulers. Paul is safe from attack, for now.

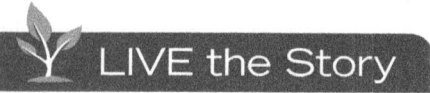

LIVE the Story

Our stop in Corinth with Paul is part of a longer journey through the major Greek cities of his day: Philippi, Thessalonica, and Athens. For those sensitive to this wider context and storyline, we discern patterns in the action and messages. In terms of actions, we notice that when Paul arrives to a new place he seeks out meeting places (synagogues and marketplaces). He then preaches about Jesus and usually experiences initial reception followed by eventual opposition. Further, he often finds himself brought before the secular

---

8. Rowe, *World Upside Down*, 60.
9. Ibid., 62.

authorities (magistrates, councils, or proconsuls) to answer political charges before leaving for the next city down the road. In terms of messages, we hear him proclaim that Jesus is "Lord" (Philippi), "king" (Thessalonica), and "judge" (Athens). By the time Paul reaches Corinth, we are used to the pattern of action and accustomed to the transcendent and triumphant messages. As the narrative unfolds in Corinth, we might be lulled into thinking this is all following to type: meeting place, proclamation, opposition, defense, and departure. In the middle of all this, however, there is a surprise. Between the opposition and Paul's defense, the Lord speaks. Jesus comes to Paul in a night vision to speak intimate words of comfort and encouragement. These words remind us that Paul is a human apostle, not a robotic mouthpiece. While the narrative pattern might be routine for the reader, for Paul living out this vocation the experience was physically, emotionally, and spiritually bruising. He may well have been tired from the opposition and fearful for his security. Amid his mission journey, he needed these words from the Lord: "Do not be afraid; keep on speaking, do not be silent. For I am with you, and no one is going to attack and harm you" (Acts 18:9–10).

In the simple phrase "I am with you," the most important word is the four-letter preposition "with." The God who is "I AM" comes alongside the human "you." The English word "with" is used to translate at least two different Greek prepositions—*meta* and *para*—and Latin prepositions—*apud* and *cum*. Prepositions, like "with," are quiet, unobtrusive words. Malcolm Guite comments on this:

> I sometimes think that Christianity is not so much a *propositional* religion as a *prepositional* religion: everything turns on the prepositions, the tiny little words that define and change relationships. So much of pagan religion was about God's aboveness, immortals over against mortals, eternity in contradistinction to time, about transcendence, disconnect and otherness. But Christianity brings these little words: *in*, 'Christ in you, the hope of glory' (Colossians 1.27); *for*, 'if God is for us, who is against us?' (Romans 8.31); *through*, 'we make our prayer to the Father through the Son and in the Spirit'; and most supremely in . . . *with*, 'God with us.'[10]

In the English language the legacy of Greek and Latin prepositions are still visible as prefixes in compound words like "*meta*physics," "*para*ble," and "*com*pany." More intimately, we hear about God "with us" in the comfort of the Holy Spirit—the "*Para*clete"—who Jesus promised would come *alongside* us and be *with* us to help, comfort, and guide us into truth (John 14:16, 26).

---

10. Malcolm Guite, *Waiting on the Word: A Poem a Day for Advent, Christmas and Epiphany* (Norwich: Canterbury, 2015), 88.

"With" is a powerful and empowering word in the phrase "I am with you." It echoes promises made to Isaac (Gen 26:24), Jacob (28:15), Joseph (48:21), Joshua (Josh 3:7), David (1 Chr 17:2), Isaiah (Isa 43:5), Jeremiah (Jer 1:8), and Mary (Luke 1:28).

Paul needed to hear "I am with you"—and so do we. Our own shortcomings, circumstances, and challenges often make us feel alone and ashamed. Brené Brown, an acclaimed writer and researcher on shame resilience, observes that when we zoom the camera in tight on ourselves often all we can see are our flawed selves and our difficult situations. In this we can feel isolated and afraid. We ask ourselves, *Am I the only one exhausted? Am I the only one with a muddled family situation? Am I the only one facing criticism from my congregation or colleagues? Am I the only one paralyzed by anxious thoughts? Something is wrong with me. I am alone.*[11] The promise of Jesus—"I am with you always" (Matt 28:20)—helps us zoom out so that we can see the picture of our lives differently. We realize that we are not alone. The Lord is present to us in our need and our loneliness.

Lest we think that all we need to hear is that Jesus is with just me, the Lord concludes by telling Paul: "I have many people in this city" (Acts 18:10). Paul never travels alone. He ministers in the company of colleagues such as Aquila and Priscilla, Silas and Timothy. He stays in the homes of Christian friends like Lydia and Titius Justus. The Lord reminds Paul, and all of us, that we are part of a larger company. Our culture seems to adore the image of the Lone Ranger, the Superman—the iconic individual who stands alone. The Lord knows us all by name and meets us personally, but we live, work, and serve in community. We are part of the *body* of Christ. Each of us has a unique part, but none of us can function in isolation. Sometimes Christian leaders fall prey to an "Elijah complex." We can be tempted to think, "I am the only one left" (1 Kgs 19:14). Not true, says the Lord. There are thousands of others in the people of God who have not bowed to the idols of our day (cf. 1 Kgs 19:18). Cultural messages, both ancient and modern, try to shape and distort our thinking about ourselves and the people of God. Critical awareness and reality checks are vital to keeping perspective and preserving meaning and purpose in our lives.

Brown, drawing on the work of Jean Kilbourne and Jackson Katz, points out the impact that media has on many of us in our society. Kilbourne and Katz research the relationship of media images to personal and societal problems such as eating disorders, addiction, violence, sexual abuse, pornography, masculinity/femininity, and loneliness. Kilbourne writes:

---

11. Brené Brown, *The Gifts of Imperfection* (Center City, MN: Hazelden, 2010), 68.

Advertising is an over $200 billion a year industry. We are each exposed to over 3000 ads a day. Yet, remarkably, most of us believe we are not influenced by advertising. Ads sell a great deal more than products. They sell values, images, and concepts of success and worth, love and sexuality, popularity and normalcy. They tell us who we are and who we should be. Sometimes they sell addictions.[12]

In the patterns and messages that shape our context and try to sell us an identity, we need to hear the words of Jesus, "I am with you," to jar us to our senses and, as necessary, comfort and relieve us from our loneliness and fear. We need not wait for a vision in the night. We can read and receive the words written in Acts, and those found throughout the story of God, in the clear light of day. Read the words slowly. Let them wash over you; let them penetrate the layers of cultural conditioning; and let them soak into your soul. You are not alone. Fear not. The Lord is *with* you, and he has placed you in a *com*munion of saints that is continents wide, centuries deep, and reaches to the heavens.

---

12. Jean Kilbourne, "Lecture Series: What Are Advertisers Really Selling Us?," http://www.jeankilbourne.com/lectures/, quoted in Brown, *Gifts of Imperfection*, 69.

CHAPTER 42

Acts 18:18-28

LISTEN to the Story

¹⁸Paul stayed on in Corinth for some time. Then he left the brothers and sisters and sailed for Syria, accompanied by Priscilla and Aquila. Before he sailed, he had his hair cut off at Cenchreae because of a vow he had taken. ¹⁹They arrived at Ephesus, where Paul left Priscilla and Aquila. He himself went into the synagogue and reasoned with the Jews. ²⁰When they asked him to spend more time with them, he declined. ²¹But as he left, he promised, "I will come back if it is God's will." Then he set sail from Ephesus. ²²When he landed at Caesarea, he went up to Jerusalem and greeted the church and then went down to Antioch.

²³After spending some time in Antioch, Paul set out from there and traveled from place to place throughout the region of Galatia and Phrygia, strengthening all the disciples.

²⁴Meanwhile a Jew named Apollos, a native of Alexandria, came to Ephesus. He was a learned man, with a thorough knowledge of the Scriptures. ²⁵He had been instructed in the way of the Lord, and he spoke with great fervor and taught about Jesus accurately, though he knew only the baptism of John. ²⁶He began to speak boldly in the synagogue. When Priscilla and Aquila heard him, they invited him to their home and explained to him the way of God more adequately.

²⁷When Apollos wanted to go to Achaia, the brothers and sisters encouraged him and wrote to the disciples there to welcome him. When he arrived, he was a great help to those who by grace had believed. ²⁸For he vigorously refuted his Jewish opponents in public debate, proving from the Scriptures that Jesus was the Messiah.

Listening to the Text in the Story: Numbers 6:1–21; Isaiah 40:3–5; Luke 3:2–6; 7:27; Romans 16:1; 1 Corinthians 1:12; 3:3–9; 16:19; Galatians 1:6–9; 3:1–5; 5:7–12; 6:12–16.

EXPLAIN the Story

As we near the end of this fifth panel in Acts (19:20; cf. 6:7; 9:31; 12:24; 16:5), the focus shifts to Ephesus, the important and prosperous capital city of the province of Asia.[1] It was also the home of the renowned temple of Artemis, a fact that will prove to be important at the beginning of the next panel (19:23–41). This section (18:18–28), despite its short length, contains a considerable amount of travel. The travel entails a full circle that begins and ends in Corinth (i.e., Corinth—Ephesus—Caesarea—Jerusalem—Antioch—Galatia—Phrygia—Ephesus—Corinth). In terms of content, this segment also provides the first (18:24–26) of four distinct "reports of witness" in Ephesus (cf. 19:1–7; 19:8–10; 19:11–20)[2] that serve to set the stage for the opening scene of the final panel (19:21–28:31) in Acts: the riot in Ephesus. The first report of witness is by a newcomer to the narrative, Apollos.

This portion of narrative develops in four paragraphs: Paul and his companions travel from Corinth to Antioch (vv. 18–22); Paul makes a return visit to churches in Galatia and Phrygia (v. 23); Apollos is introduced and receives instruction from Priscilla and Aquila (vv. 24–26); and finally, Apollos departs on mission to Achaia (vv. 27–28).

Paul and His Companions Travel (18:18–22)

After the incident with the proconsul Gallio (ca. summer AD 51), Paul remained in Corinth an unspecified number of days. He then began the long journey back to his sending community in Antioch Syria, accompanied by his new associates, Priscilla and Aquila, and likely other travel companions (v. 18). Although we are not given any specific time when Paul began his journey, we might assume that, since his travels required significant time on the Mediterranean Sea, he began his journey during the "safe season" for sea travel. Rapske cites ancient sources that attest to three distinct seasons for sea travel: the "safe season" from May 27 to September 14; the "risky season" from September 14 to November 11; and the "dangerous season" from November 11 to March 10.[3]

The first short stint of the journey began by traveling a short distance east on foot from Corinth to Cenchreae, a small harbor city on the Saronic Gulf, the home of a deacon, Phoebe (Rom 16:1). In Cenchreae, he had his hair

---

1. For a brief and helpful overview of this important first-century city, see C. E. Arnold, "Ephesus," *DPL* 249–52. For a longer, but readable, discussion of key historical details about Ephesus and its important history in the first century, see Paul Trebilco, "Asia," in Gill and Gempf, *Graeco-Roman Setting*, 302–57.
2. Gaventa, *Acts*, 262.
3. Rapske, "Acts, Travel and Shipwreck," 22.

cut off "because of a vow he had taken" (v. 18a). The "vow" may have been a "Nazirite vow" (see Num 6:1–21), a voluntary "vow of dedication." Some have suggested that this indicates that Paul, despite being an apostle to the Gentiles, still observed Jewish law and remained a "true Jew."[4] Another possibility is that this is Paul's expression of gratitude to the Lord for his safekeeping during his long stay in Corinth (cf. Acts 18:9–10).[5]

Without further elaboration about the meaning of Paul's vow, the narrative moves along and the company arrives in Ephesus, about a four-hundred-kilometer journey across the Aegean Sea. Ephesus was one of the largest and most important cities in the Roman Empire. It was the administrative capital of the province of Asia and home to one of the seven ancient wonders of the world, the temple of Artemis. Priscilla and Aquila would not accompany Paul any farther on his journey. However, before Paul continued on his way, he did what has now become an established practice of his upon arriving at a new city: "He . . . went into the synagogue and reasoned with the Jews" (v. 19; cf. 13:5, 14; 14:1; 16:13; 17:1, 10, 17; 18:4). This initial conversation was well received, and they encouraged him to stay. Paul declined, possibly out of haste to take advantage of the season of safe sea travel, but promised to return, "if it is God's will" (v. 21).

With his promise given to the Ephesians, Paul then embarked on the longer one-thousand-kilometer (six-hundred-mile) sea voyage to Caesarea. He then went "up" to Jerusalem to greet the church there and report on his mission to the gentile world before he went "down" to his sending church in Antioch. Although some readers of Acts may be inclined to think of traveling "up" as going north, travelers like Paul, who were used to praying the Psalms of "ascent" (Pss 120–134) as they walked the road to Mount Zion, understood that their journey to Jerusalem was "up." Luke does not offer any details of this brief visit to Jerusalem (ca. AD 51–52). It is, however, important to recognize that he mentions it. If the narrative's goal is simply to describe Paul's return to his community in Antioch, it makes no sense to mention travel there via the extended leg to Jerusalem. But between Paul's Nazirite vow and the greetings offered to the church in Jerusalem, these are important markers in the narrative. They remind the reader that even though the gentile mission is in full swing, it is a mission that is "first to the Jew, then to the Gentile" (Rom 1:16). The newly formed community around King Jesus, the Messiah, is a people made up of those who are Jews and gentiles.

---

4. Barrett, *Acts*, 2.860.
5. I. H. Marshall, *Acts*, TNTC (Grand Rapids: Eerdmans, 1999), 300.

A Return Visit to Galatia and Phrygia (18:23)

This sentence is a narrative bridge between Paul's work and the first report of witness of the mission in Ephesus. It also marks Paul's so-called "third missionary journey." Luke writes that after a period of reporting and resting in Antioch, Paul retraces his steps through the regions of Galatia and Phrygia. We assume he visited cities like Derbe, Lystra, Iconium, and Pisidian Antioch. The focus of these return visits is less on proclamation and more on consolidation. Paul focuses on "strengthening" the disciples in these different places (cf. Acts 14:22; 15:32, 41). The strengthening they need is related to the resolve required to maintain their trust in Christ and their dependence on the Spirit in the face of false teaching and persecution, threats that were real for Christians in these areas (cf. Gal 1:6–9; 3:1–5; 5:7–12; 6:12–16).

Priscilla, Aquila, and Apollos (18:24–26)

The scene now shifts back to Ephesus (Acts 18:24), where a new character is introduced, Apollos. In the space of two sentences, Luke provides eight pieces of data about him. First, despite his gentile-sounding name,[6] he is a Jew. Second, he is a native of Alexandria in Egypt. Alexandria was home to a large and often well-educated Jewish community. Third, he was a "learned man" (*anēr logios*). This can also be translated as an "eloquent man" (cf. KJV, NRSV, ESV), which may suggest that he was trained in rhetoric and the sophist tradition that flourished in Alexandria at this time.[7] Fourth, he was well versed in Scripture (i.e., the OT). Fifth, he had been "instructed in the way of the Lord" (v. 25). The expression "the Way" occurs frequently in Acts (cf. 9:2; 19:9, 23; 22:4; 24:14, 22) as a title for the movement to which they belonged. This also echoes the work of John the Baptist, who is the forerunner of Jesus and the prophet who prepared "the way for the Lord" (Luke 3:2–6; 7:27; cf. Isa 40:3–5). Sixth, Apollos spoke with "great fervor" (*zeōn tō pneumati*), lit. "with fervor in the Spirit." Schnabel observes that "since this comment is placed between the description of Apollo's having been instructed in the 'Way of the Lord' and his teaching about Jesus, the reference to 'spirit/Spirit' . . . should be understood as a reference to the Holy Spirit."[8] Seventh, he had been taught "accurately" (Acts 18:25) about Jesus, with the qualification, and eighth note, that "he knew only the baptism of John." This last piece of information has led to much speculation as to why it is mentioned. Some suggest Luke intended it as a corrective to those

---

6. The Greek god Apollo was the son of Zeus and brother of Artemis.
7. B. B. Blue, "Apollos," *DPL* 38.
8. Schnabel, *Acts*, 785.

Christians who continued to follow John the Baptist.[9] Others think that it was an effort to unite various communities of believers under one Pauline umbrella.[10] Gaventa helpfully notes, however, that "the problems with all of these proposals are considerable, since Apollos does not appear identified exclusively with John the Baptist, and since he also knows 'the Way of the Lord' and teaches accurately about Jesus."[11]

Apollos applied all his gifts and abilities to teach "boldly" in the synagogue in Ephesus (v. 26). This same boldness also marked the proclamation of other preachers in Acts (e.g., Peter and John, 4:13; Paul and Barnabas, 13:46). Nonetheless, when Priscilla and Aquila heard him, they noticed some unnamed deficiency in his teaching and brought him to their home, a key "house church" in the city (cf. 1 Cor 16:19), to teach him "the way of God more adequately" (Acts 18:26). Luke does not include what deficiency the duo made up, but we can assume that it involved filling out teaching that went beyond "the baptism of John" (cf. v. 25). There are two notable features in this detail. First, Apollos had a teachable attitude. Second, Priscilla is included alongside her husband, Aquila, as among the early church's teachers. When the pair is initially introduced to the narrative, it is Aquila who is mentioned first (18:2). Now, in Ephesus, where this couple will have a significant teaching ministry, Priscilla's name is listed first (18:19, 26). This is reminiscent of the shift in order when Paul's name is listed first after he took the lead teaching role from Barnabas (cf. 11:26, 30; 12:25; 13:2, 7, 42, 43, 46, 50; etc.).

Apollos's Mission to Corinth (18:27–28)

Apollos, strengthened by the instruction from Priscilla and Aquila, desires to move along to teach believers in Achaia. Apollos's teaching efforts in Corinth (the capital of Achaia) are corroborated in Paul's correspondence with the Corinthians. At first, his presence is welcome. His rhetorical training, zeal, and scriptural understanding make him a formidable advocate in demonstrating that Jesus was the Messiah—especially against fellow Jews in public debates. Unfortunately, followers of Apollos contribute to some of the problems in Corinth, including "divisions," that Paul would later need to address in Corinth (1 Cor 1:12; 3:3–9), although Paul is careful not to cast the blame on Apollos. For now, however, Apollos's arrival in Corinth brings the travel narrative full circle from when the freshly shorn and newly avowed Paul left Corinth months earlier (Acts 18:18).

---

9. E.g., Johnson, *Acts*, 338.
10. E.g., Fitzmyer, *Acts*, 637.
11. Gaventa, *Acts*, 265.

LIVE the Story

Collaborative ministry is one of the distinctive features in Acts. While there are a few instances where individuals work on their own, for the most part ministry is shared. John accompanies Peter, and various combinations of colleagues accompany Paul. Despite the leadership role Paul takes midway through the book of Acts, time and again we see him alert for and open to new colleagues. He is not burdened with the need to do everything alone and is confident in his own calling and abilities not to be threatened by other gifted leaders—whether they are older (e.g., Barnabas) or younger (e.g., Timothy), men (e.g., Silas) or women (e.g., Priscilla), Jewish (e.g., Aquila) or gentile (e.g., Luke). His openhanded and humble leadership seemed to have rubbed off on his friends. When Apollos breaks on the scene in Ephesus, Paul's colleagues Priscilla and Aquila recognize the massive potential in this man from Alexandria. They were not jealous of his eloquence, intelligence, and boldness. They recognized, as did the great reformer, John Calvin, Apollos's commendable combination of doctrine and zeal:

> Doctrine without zeal is either like a sword in the hand of a madman, or else it lieth still as cold and without use, or else it serveth for vain and wicked boasting. For we see that some learned men become slothful; other some (which is worse) become ambitious; other some (which is of all the worst) trouble the Church with contention and brawling. Therefore, that doctrine shall be unsavory which is not joined with zeal. But let us remember that Luke putteth the knowledge of the Scripture in the first place, which must be the moderation of zeal, for we know that many are fervent without consideration."[12]

Apollos is a balanced individual, and Calvin points out that Luke emphasizes what this balance looks like. For their part in the story, Priscilla and Aquila identify this in Apollos. Yet they too have remarkable gifts of their own. They are discerning and bold not only in their willingness to welcome Apollos into their company but also in their readiness to confront him and explain "to him the way of God more adequately" (v. 26). It speaks to the wisdom of Priscilla and Aquila that they provided this instruction in the privacy of their own home so as not to expose Apollos to public embarrassment. It speaks to the humility and teachability of Apollos that he received it.

Collaborative ministry is risky. It requires wisdom and discernment, knowledge and boldness, and healthy doses of humility and teachability.

---

12. Calvin, *Acts*, 2.18.25.

Collaborative ministry is also creative. It can create space for new ideas and fresh approaches. Collaborative ministry is also encouraging and comforting. We live with the hopeful expectancy that Jesus may return today, but we must also plan for ministry that is long term and sustainable. This is possible only if we serve and work in diverse teams of godly men and women. This passage in Acts (18:18–28) describes a long journey from Corinth to Antioch and back again. Christian ministry is also a long journey. Like Paul, each of us needs traveling companions. We need fellow pilgrims who will encourage us when the road is hard and who can correct us when we veer off course. For example, despite his towering theological prestige and massive insight into Scripture, even the great John Calvin sometimes missed the mark. Just after his helpful comments on Apollos's character and Luke's emphasis on biblical knowledge and zeal, Calvin then makes an unhelpful statement. He remarks that Priscilla offers Apollos instruction in her own "house" so that "she might not overthrow the order prescribed by God and nature." He suggests that Priscilla, as a woman, could not have done so publicly because this would have overthrown God's "order" for women ministers.[13] Yet Acts does not suggest this at all. As Beverly Gaventa correctly observes, "The narrator's comment that Priscilla and Aquila 'took him aside' (v. 26) implies only that they did not publicly confront him in the synagogue and does not require the conclusion that her teaching was confined to the domestic arena."[14]

We need collaborative ministry—both the living presence of colleagues who walk with us day after day in the demanding and rewarding work of church ministry, and the voice of writers and commentators who speak to us from the pages of their books. Collaborative ministry is not always efficient or easy. Yet, for all the risk and energy it requires, it is our biblical model; it is "the way of God" (v. 26) and the way of wisdom. It protects us from self-importance and releases ministries that might otherwise lie dormant. In the end, it is a gift to be received with gratitude from the Spirit who equips and leads us all.

---

13. Ibid., comments on Acts 18:26.
14. Gaventa, *Acts*, 265.

CHAPTER 43

Acts 19:1-20

 LISTEN to the Story

¹While Apollos was at Corinth, Paul took the road through the interior and arrived at Ephesus. There he found some disciples ²and asked them, "Did you receive the Holy Spirit when you believed?"

They answered, "No, we have not even heard that there is a Holy Spirit."

³So Paul asked, "Then what baptism did you receive?"

"John's baptism," they replied.

⁴Paul said, "John's baptism was a baptism of repentance. He told the people to believe in the one coming after him, that is, in Jesus." ⁵On hearing this, they were baptized in the name of the Lord Jesus. ⁶When Paul placed his hands on them, the Holy Spirit came on them, and they spoke in tongues and prophesied. ⁷There were about twelve men in all.

⁸Paul entered the synagogue and spoke boldly there for three months, arguing persuasively about the kingdom of God. ⁹But some of them became obstinate; they refused to believe and publicly maligned the Way. So Paul left them. He took the disciples with him and had discussions daily in the lecture hall of Tyrannus. ¹⁰This went on for two years, so that all the Jews and Greeks who lived in the province of Asia heard the word of the Lord.

¹¹God did extraordinary miracles through Paul, ¹²so that even handkerchiefs and aprons that had touched him were taken to the sick, and their illnesses were cured and the evil spirits left them.

¹³Some Jews who went around driving out evil spirits tried to invoke the name of the Lord Jesus over those who were demon-possessed. They would say, "In the name of the Jesus whom Paul preaches, I command you to come out." ¹⁴Seven sons of Sceva, a Jewish chief priest, were doing this. ¹⁵One day the evil spirit answered them, "Jesus I know, and Paul I know about, but who are you?" ¹⁶Then the man who had the evil spirit jumped on them and overpowered them all. He gave them such a beating that they ran out of the house naked and bleeding.

> [17]When this became known to the Jews and Greeks living in Ephesus, they were all seized with fear, and the name of the Lord Jesus was held in high honor. [18]Many of those who believed now came and openly confessed what they had done. [19]A number who had practiced sorcery brought their scrolls together and burned them publicly. When they calculated the value of the scrolls, the total came to fifty thousand drachmas. [20]In this way the word of the Lord spread widely and grew in power.

Listening to the Text in the Story: 1 Corinthians 14; 16:8–9; Galatians 3:5; 4:6; Colossians 2:1; Revelation 2–3.

EXPLAIN the Story

Paul attempted to evangelize in the province of Asia earlier in the story, but the Holy Spirit kept him from doing so (Acts 16:6). Now, he makes good on his promise to spend an extended period in Ephesus after his first brief stop on his return to Antioch (18:21). In this section of the narrative, Luke describes three more "reports of witness" in Ephesus in addition to the initial report about the work of Apollos (18:24–26). First, there is a report of Paul's interaction with a small group of unnamed "disciples" (19:1–7). Next, Luke offers a summary of Paul's three-month teaching ministry in the synagogue (vv. 8–10). Finally, a more detailed report is provided of Paul's longer two-year ministry in Ephesus—including examples of authentic and inauthentic power encounters that occur in the city and elevate the profile and awe of the name and word of the Lord (vv. 11–20). Each of these reports contributes toward the dramatic confrontation between the followers of the Way and the followers of Artemis that will open the final panel (19:21–28:31) in Acts.

Paul Arrives in Ephesus (19:1–7)

It was only a matter of time before Paul reached Ephesus, the capital of the province of Asia, for an extended period of work there. Much like Corinth, it was a wealthy, important, and strategic city in the empire. In addition to its economic, religious, and political significance, it was one of the largest cities in the empire with a population of approximately two hundred thousand to two hundred fifty thousand people, rivaled only by Rome and Alexandria. It was also the hub of a number of important land and sea routes. Two great highways from the east—"the common highway" and the ancient "Persian

Royal Road"[1]—converged in this port city on the eastern shore of the Aegean Sea. Paul would likely have traveled on one of those land routes as he made his way through the interior of the province of Asia on his way to Ephesus.

When Paul arrived in Ephesus, he encountered a small group of "disciples" (19:1). No other information is provided about them. The word "disciples" is a common descriptor for believers in Acts (e.g., 6:1; 9:19; 11:26; 13:52; 14:28). However, Paul's question on meeting them—"Did you receive the Holy Spirit when you believed?" (19:2)—and their ignorance about the Spirit suggests that they were not Christians. The Spirit is, after all, the *sine qua non* for authentic Christian experience. As Gordon Fee notes, "Everywhere in Luke-Acts it is the presence of the Spirit that marks off the people of the Age to Come. That is exactly the point of Paul's question in Acts 19:2. [They] were obviously not Christians because the one essential ingredient was missing."[2]

Paul probes further and asks them what baptism they received. They reply, "John's baptism" (v. 3). Again, we are not told where or how they encountered this teaching. Regardless, Paul does not look down on them for this. He acknowledges the important anticipatory work of John the Baptist as a forerunner to Jesus, work that is highlighted elsewhere in Acts (e.g., 1:22; 10:37; 11:16; 13:24–25)—not least of all in the previous report about Apollos (18:25). Like Apollos, these disciples are open to further instruction, and once their ignorance was amended, they were "baptized in"[3] the name of the Lord Jesus by Paul. When Paul laid his hands on them, they received the Spirit like other believers in Acts, with audible signs of tongues and prophecy (19:6). Descriptions of audible experience of tongues (and prophecy) occur elsewhere in Acts only two other times (2:4 and 10:46). There is no reason to suggest, however, that this was an uncommon experience elsewhere in the early church (e.g., Gal 3:5; 4:6), including Paul's own life (see 1 Cor 14). It should be noted, however, that the specific mention of the manifestation of speaking in tongues occurs at significant junctures in the overall narrative. In each of these instances, a new and important work of the Spirit is exhibited: (1) when the Jews received the Spirit on Pentecost (Acts 2:4); (2) when the first gentiles, Cornelius and his household, receive the Spirit in Caesarea (10:46); and now, (3) when this unnamed band of disciples receive the Spirit in the strategic city of Ephesus.

---

1. Trebilco, "Asia," 308.
2. Gordon D. Fee, *Gospel and Spirit: Issues in New Testament Hermeneutics* (Peabody, MA: Hendrickson, 1991), 114. See also Dunn, *Acts*, 255, who also points us to Paul's own letters at Rom 8:9; 1 Cor 12:13; Gal 3:2–3.
3. Or "into" (*eis*) the name of Jesus. Bruce, *Acts*, 364, notes that this is "the same form of words as is used of the Samaritan believers in 8:16," and this may suggest "an intentional parallel here between the imposition of Paul's hands on these men and the imposition of Peter's (and John's) hands on the Samaritan converts."

Paul Teaches and Debates in the Synagogue (19:8–10)

After the first two Ephesian "witness reports" where listeners respond openly to Christian instruction from Priscilla, Aquila, and Paul, the next report relates an uneven response. Paul, as was his routine on arrival to a new city, sought out a local synagogue[4] and engaged those present in reasoned dialogue and persuasive speech "about the kingdom of God" (19:8 cf. 17:17; 18:4; etc.). We are not given the content of his proclamation beyond the compressed summary that it was about the kingdom of God. Readers who have followed the Gospel of Luke alongside this narrative would recall the extensive instruction from Jesus about the kingdom of God. All things considered, Paul was given a generous hearing—in comparison to other shorter hearings (e.g., Pisidian Antioch, 13:45–51; Iconium, 14:1–2)—since his audience listened for three months. In the end, however, another pattern resumed: resistance forms, and rumors spread about "the Way" (19:9). Luke has not used this title, "the Way," to refer to the Christian movement since much earlier in the narrative (9:2). The *negative* response to "the Way" may simply have seemed an appropriate manner with which to refer to Christians in Ephesus after two recent *positive* responses to instruction about "the way" (18:25, 26).

Since Paul's bold speaking in the Ephesian synagogue was creating friction that would have disturbed Sabbath gatherings, Paul turned away from that setting and moved elsewhere, with a group of disciples accompanying him, to teach for two more years in the city. Whereas in Corinth he only moved next door to the house of Titius Justus, in Ephesus he established a daily routine of discussions in "the lecture hall" (*scholē*) of Tyrannus (v. 9). The word *scholē* normally referred in ancient literature to a place used for leisurely intellectual pursuits. Despite extensive historical investigation, we do not know whether "Tyrannus" ("tyrant") was a notable lecturer at this venue or the owner of the lecture hall itself.[5] What we are informed about is that due to Ephesus's strategic location and as a result of Paul's extended period of preaching, "all the Jews and Greeks who lived in the province of Asia heard the word of the Lord" (19:10). This need not imply that the entire population of the province heard the gospel preached in Ephesus but only that from this place the gospel spread throughout the region. Paul echoes this in one of his own letters, which he wrote while in Ephesus, where he acknowledges that a "great door . . .

---

4. It is worth noting that when Paul proclaimed to the unresponsive Jews in the synagogue in Corinth, "From now on I will go to the Gentiles" (Acts 18:6), this meant only in Corinth, not for his ongoing ministry.

5. Trebilco, "Asia," 311–12. Longenecker, *Acts*, 495, wryly notes, "Since it is difficult (except in certain bleak moments of parenthood) to think of any parent naming his or her child 'Tyrant,' the name must have been a nickname given by the man's students or tenants."

opened" to him in Ephesus (1 Cor 16:8–9). During this two-year period, other associates of Paul carried the gospel from Ephesus into the interior of Asia so that the church became well established in this province (see Col 2:1; cf. Rev 2–3; Ign., *Eph.*; Ign. *Phld.*).

Power Encounters in Ephesus (19:11–20)

The final Ephesian "witness report" (19:11–20) is the longest of the four reports. Besides drawing this "panel" (Acts 16:6–19:20) to a close, this report's description of "power encounters" sets up the opening scene of the final panel in Acts (19:21–28:31). The scene that is to follow (19:21–41) describes a dramatic confrontation between the followers of Artemis and the followers of the Lord. The seeds of this confrontation with the "great goddess Artemis" and the economic benefits that accompany her "good name" (v. 27) are planted in the accounts of God's miraculous power at work through Paul (vv. 11, 20), including the high honor being bestowed on "the name of the Lord Jesus" (v. 17) and significant economic developments resulting from this new belief (v. 19). In short, religion, politics, and economics are all at play in these two interrelated scenes (vv. 11–20 and 21–41). This is a conflict of powers.

The first demonstration of power in this scene belongs to God. Luke writes, "*God* did extraordinary miracles [*dunameis*] through Paul" (v. 11). This is an example of one of the ways Paul continued to be the Lord's "chosen instrument" (9:15) to proclaim the name of Jesus Christ to the gentiles. Sometimes this proclamation was through persuasive speech (19:8); sometimes this witness was through powerful miracles. When God works authentically and powerfully, even the most insignificant objects—a sweaty "handkerchief" (*soudarion*) Paul would have used to wipe his brow or a work "apron" (*simikinthion*) tied around his waist—could be the means God could use to cure illnesses or drive away evil spirits.[6] The emphasis, however, is *not* on the object or the vessel but on the source of the power: God. God is the subject of the verb; God is the one who "did" these things *through* Paul.[7] The power derives from God, not from a person or a relic.

In contrast to authentic miracles performed by God through Paul, what follows is a description of the feeble efforts of "seven sons of Sceva, a Jewish chief

---

6. Trebilco, "Asia," 313, notes that "in the ancient world evil spirits were often, though not always, seen as the cause of sickness. The practice of exorcism was thus quite common and a notable example comes from Ephesus. A few decades after Paul's visit, a great plague . . . struck the city; according to Philostratus, the people summoned Apollonius of Tyana and asked for his help. He perceived that the sickness was due to a demon . . . who was visiting the city. As soon as the demon was killed, the plague left the city."

7. Cf. the miracles associated with touching the fringe of Jesus's cloak (Luke 8:44) and through Peter's shadow (Acts 5:15).

priest,"[8] who were attempting to drive out evil spirits in Ephesus.[9] Whereas the effectiveness of Paul, and even items of clothing that touched him, is derived from God, these Jewish exorcists attempted to drive out demons by incantation, by magic. They would invoke "the name of Jesus whom Paul preaches" (v. 13). This implies they had no firsthand knowledge of Jesus. Like Simon Magus in Samaria (8:18–24), who thought spiritual power could be bought and manipulated by magic,[10] these seven exorcists tried manipulating the name of Jesus to exorcise an evil spirit possessing a man in Ephesus. The evil spirit in the man called their knowledge and their incantation for what it was: derivative and ineffectual (v. 15). In an ironic comparison, seven men were "overpowered" by one evil spirit (v. 16), whereas mere handkerchiefs touched by Paul drove out multiple "evil spirits" (v. 12).

Luke continues by adding that when "this"—presumably both the effectiveness of Paul's ministry and the ineffectiveness of the seven sons of Sceva's ministry—became known both to Jews and gentiles living in Ephesus, they were "seized with fear" (19:17; cf. 5:5, 11). Further, "the name of the Lord Jesus" (19:13) that the Scevan exorcists were invoking was not brought into disrepute because of their embarrassing encounter with the evil spirit; rather, "the name of the Lord Jesus" was elevated with high honor (v. 17). The names of deities, and the bonds of affection those names have for their followers, will become central in the next episode (v. 27). For now, however, the honor accorded to Jesus resulted in more than just a personal confession from the new believers; it also enacted a public response. We learn that a significant number of the new believers in Ephesus had "practiced sorcery" (v. 19). Trebilco alerts us to relevant historical background at play in first-century Ephesus:

> Magic seems to have flourished in Ephesus, and the city gave its name to the well known [Ephesian Letters]. The genuine Ephesian Letters were six magical terms which were thought to be words of power which could, for example, ward off evil demons and so could be used as written amulets or spoken charms. Inscriptions from Ephesus also contain references to magicians and curses. The magicians' books . . . which were burned may have contained the famous Ephesian Letters and the sort of material

---

8. There is no Jewish high priest in the historical record with the name "Sceva." Peterson, *Acts*, 538, notes that the word *chief priest* (*archiereus*) is regularly used in the plural in Luke's Gospel (e.g., 9:22; 19:47; 20:1, 19) and in Acts (4:23) to refer to the broader group of the Jewish aristocracy or the members of that class making decisions related to the priests and the temple. Sceva could be part of that wider high-priestly body. Cf. Barrett, *Acts*, 2:909.

9. Josephus, *Ant.* 8.45–46, suggests that the Jews, ever since King Solomon, had special powers to exorcise demons.

10. See also the corrupt combination of Judaism and magic with Bar-Jesus (Acts 13:6–11).

preserved in the magical papyri, such as thaumaturgic [magical] formulae, incantations, hymns and prayers.[11]

Book burning was not unheard of in antiquity. Rulers or authorities who regarded books as offensive, seditious, or unsafe would seize and publicly burn them as a way of expressing rejection of their content.[12] What is unique in the case in Ephesus is that the new Ephesian believers *voluntarily* burned their own books in public. At a valued price of fifty thousand drachmas,[13] the cost of these books was considerable. Paul's powerful demonstrations by word, the miraculous healings and exorcisms performed through him, and now a public book burning by new believers drew the Christian faith into the center of Ephesian cultural, religious, and economic life. It would not be long before the followers of the "great goddess Artemis" would respond to uphold the honor of their beloved deity (v. 27).

Before we hear about that dramatic response, however, Luke inserts his fifth and final "marker" (v. 20; cf. 6:7; 9:31; 12:24; 16:5) to signal a major transition in the narrative. In Acts, these transitional markers contain one or more of the following three elements: (1) a geographical note; (2) an indication about church growth; or (3) a reference to the word of God increasing. In this final marker (19:20) only the last two elements are present. The reference to the "power" (*ischuō*) of the Lord may be a final taunt that looks backward at the seven sons of Sceva who were "overpowered" (v. 16, *ischuō*) by the evil spirit. It is also a look forward to the upcoming confrontation with the cult of "the great goddess Artemis." Whatever the case, neither evil spirits nor honored goddesses nor any other "power" in Ephesus—religious, political, or economic—are able to match the power of the Lord.

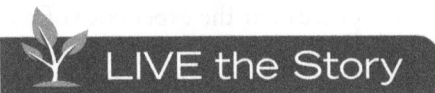

The Spirit and Experience

Many Christians in the Western world have a deficient *pneumatology* (the study of the Holy Spirit). We write and think a lot about *theology* (the study of God) and *Christology* (the study of Christ), but the Holy Spirit—the third person of the Trinity—is routinely ignored. Sometimes, unintentionally I'm sure, we even depersonalize the Spirit. This is easy to do because many of the images in Scripture for the Spirit are impersonal. For example, the images of

---

11. Trebilco, "Asia," 314.
12. Again, Trebilco, "Asia," 315, provides examples from Seutonius, *Aug.* 31; Livy, *History of Rome* 39.16; Diogenes Laertius, *Lives of the Philosophers* 9.52, and Cicero, *Nat. d.* 1.63.
13. A drachma was a Roman silver coin worth about a day's wages.

fire, oil, and *wind* are impersonal. Furthermore, the "gender" of the Greek word for Spirit, *pneuma,* is neuter, and even this may subconsciously influence those of us who read biblical Greek to regard the Spirit as an impersonal force instead of a *person* who groans, grieves, and loves. Even among those who do speak and teach about the life of the Spirit, the emphasis tends to focus on individual experience (how the Spirit works in, through, and for *me*). Further, among some interpreters who write about the Spirit in Acts, the question about when and how people should experience the manifestations of the Spirit—especially speaking in "tongues"—can get them bogged down in debate. I cannot single-handedly redress this deficiency, nor can I resolve long-standing debates. I can, however, highlight a clear emphasis in the story of Acts and point to resources that have helped balance my own thinking and experience of the Spirit.

First, what is clear in Acts 19 is that the work and experience of God the Holy Spirit is as important as the work and experience of God the Father and God the Son. We know that the work of the Spirit is often inscrutable. For some reason, when Paul and his companions first wished to preach in the province of Asia—of which Ephesus was the capital—the Spirit "kept" (16:6; "forbidden" in KJV, NRSV, ASV, and ESV) them from doing so. Now, when they finally arrive for an extended and focused period of ministry in Asia, the first question Paul asks a dozen unnamed disciples is, "Did you receive the Holy Spirit when you believed?" (19:2). Clearly the experience of the Spirit's presence was of foremost importance for Paul. The work of the Spirit (vv. 2, 6) sits in the narrative on a par with the work of the Lord Jesus (vv. 4, 5, 10, 13, 15, 17, 20) and the work of God (vv. 8, 11). Without coaching or teaching, after Paul placed his hands on them "they spoke in tongues and prophesied" (v. 6). Neither the leading of the Spirit to Ephesus nor the experience of the Spirit in Ephesus is predictable, but the experience and work of the Spirit are *central.* This is instructive for us as well. We cannot demand or calculate all the Spirit can and will do in our lives, but we are right to expect the Spirit to be at the very heart of our experience of salvation.

Furthermore, the experience of the Spirit, while intensely personal, is most often encountered corporately. The Spirit was experienced corporately on the day of Pentecost by Jesus's disciples in Jerusalem (Acts 2); the Spirit was experienced corporately in the "gentile Pentecost" in Cornelius's household in Caesarea (Acts 10); the Spirit was experienced corporately at the Jerusalem Council to guide the early church as gentiles came to faith (Acts 15); and the Spirit was experienced corporately among the twelve unnamed disciples in Ephesus (Acts 19). These experiences are often ecstatic and involve "fire," speaking in tongues, and even apparent drunkenness. Yet not all corporate experience of the Spirit was this dramatic in the ancient church, and neither is it today. The Spirit *nudges* us in our daily encounters with one another (e.g., Philip and the Ethiopian eunuch, 8:29); the Spirit *whispers* to us in the sweetness of common sense in meetings and deliberations (e.g., Paul and his companions navigating their way on mission, 16:6–7); the Spirit *hints* to us through the gentleness of new ideas or initiatives (e.g., in corporate worship and teaching, 13:1–4).

Our modern eyes and ears that are trained to read and hear through individualized filters do not always notice this *corporate* dimension in the Spirit's presence. This requires patient and deliberate attentiveness. Jesus instructed the early disciples to return to Jerusalem to prepare in unified prayer and watchful waiting (1:14–15). The church in Antioch was committed to communal disciplines of generosity, prayer, fasting, worship, prophetic teaching, and study (11:27–30; 13:1–3). We assume that the twelve people Paul met in Ephesus were not randomly gathered together without any purpose; in fact, the only thing we do know about them is that they were called "disciples"— that is, they were gathered together as learners. While we must not avoid individual devotions or private prayer,[14] repeated emphasis on the corporate dimension of Christian preparation for the work of the Spirit is an element that requires reinforcement in the contemporary church—especially the hyper-individualized church of the Western world.

The Spirit and Comprehension

Even though the experienced reality of the Spirit is a dynamic that must not be ignored or downplayed,[15] we also must recognize that the Spirit is the source of robust reflection and theological *comprehension*. This is not a matter of prioritizing comprehension over experience or experience over comprehension; it is a matter of recognizing and living out a biblical balance. The work of contemporary theologian Jack Levison is extremely helpful for us today in this regard.[16] Levison encourages a balanced appreciation of *both* ecstasy and *comprehension*. He points out that all three instances of speaking in tongues in Acts (chs. 2, 10, and 19) also combine comprehensible "praise/prophecy" with the ecstasy of tongues. As such, he notes:

---

14. After all, Cornelius's own preparation for receiving the Spirit—generous almsgiving and constant prayer (Acts 10:2)—bears all the marks of a soldier's individual diligence and discipline.
15. Of course, this is not an issue for the vibrant Pentecostal movement in the church in the Global South.
16. See Jack Levison, *Filled with the Spirit* (Grand Rapids: Eerdmans, 2009); idem, *Fresh Air: The Holy Spirit for an Inspired Life* (Brewster: Paraclete, 2012); and idem, *Inspired: The Holy Spirit and the Mind of Faith* (Grand Rapids: Eerdmans, 2013).

> Luke has composed a remarkable triad of speaking in tongues, which lead to the simultaneous embrace of ecstasy and comprehension. When the earliest believers are filled with the holy spirit [*sic*], they speak the praiseworthy acts of God in comprehensible foreign languages. When Gentiles speak in tongues, they participate actively in praise, as had the followers of Jesus during Pentecost. When a group of disciples speak in tongues, they prophesy—an activity that is, throughout Acts, practical and understandable. Three times Luke unites in a single moment a form of inspiration—speaking in (other) tongues—that rides the edge of ecstasy while proclaiming in clear and comprehensible ways words of praise and prophecy.[17]

What Levison is acknowledging is that we need not prioritize incomprehensible ecstasy over comprehensible teaching and prophecy. Both aspects, he argues, contribute to the virtues of learning and the development of the mind of faith. Unfortunately, readers of Acts often emphasize one aspect over another and fail to maintain a biblical balance.

Evil Spirits and the Power of God

A final note of reflection related to this passage has to do with the other "spirits" that are at work in our world in addition to the Holy Spirit. Despite biblical admonition to the contrary, it is ironic that many Christians limit reality "to the things that are seen" (cf. 2 Cor 4:18). However much attention evil spirits may (or may not) be given in Christian circles today, we can be sure that neither Luke nor the pagan inhabitants of first-century Ephesus ignored them. Because most people in the ancient world were aware of malevolent spirits, the work of exorcists and magicians was respected. Important elements of their work included magical formulae, special incantations, and amulets that were used to drive away or ward off evil spirits. To modern readers raised on scientific rationalism, this all sounds like a bit of nonsense. Of course, many people—regardless of how "rationalistic" their outlook may be—have expressions that indicate they believe in malevolent forces that need to be held in check. For example, even if it is in a light-hearted manner, many people refer to certain practices as "bad luck" (e.g., walking under a ladder, encounters with black cats). In the sphere of sport (for many people a substitute religion) some of the most bizarre expressions of this occur when athletes, and often their supporters, engage in certain superstitious rituals (e.g., wearing certain clothing or putting on their equipment in a certain order) in the hope of securing victory. A darker danger emerges, however, when people attempt to appeal to magic or spirits in a desire to manipulate circumstances for their

---

17. Levison, *Inspired*, 96.

own benefit. C. S. Lewis offers a cautionary tale in the account of Lucy Pevensie's experience with the magician Coriakin's book on the Island of the Duffers in *The Voyage of the Dawn Treader*. Lucy is tempted by the power of spells, including "an infallible spell to make beautiful her that uttereth it beyond the lot of mortals," a spell that would let her know what her friends thought about her, and a spell "to make hidden things visible." When she recites this final spell, she is confronted with Aslan, not a tame lion, who has been present all along. In asking by magic to make things visible that are invisible, Lucy recognizes that "there might be lots of other invisible things [good and evil] hanging about . . . [and] I'm not sure that I want to see them all."[18]

Lucy's experience is a fictitious story, but it illustrates a similar dynamic at work in the experience of the debacle of the seven sons of Sceva. The contrast between these seven sons and the apostle Paul is dramatic. Paul did successful healings and exorcisms because he was a follower of Jesus and could call upon the name of Jesus with legitimate and powerful effect. In contrast, the seven sons of Sceva attempted to invoke Jesus's name as one would an incantation from the Ephesian Letters. They were relying on technique, manipulation, and derivative power to exorcise an evil spirit. As Dunn accurately notes, one lesson is clear in all this: "Spiritual power can be self-destructive in the wrong hands or where attempts are made to use it illegitimately. Only the one who follows in close discipleship upon Jesus and is led by his Spirit can act thus in his name. . . . At the same time we should recall that Luke did retain the tradition of Luke 9.49–50: it is Christ, not his disciples, who determines just who can act in his name."[19]

This story reminds us that we are dependent on God to work when praying for healing and encounters with evil spirits. We must be open to the power of the Spirit to heal and deliver people from the grip of evil. This implies that we must not be ignorant or naive about evil spirits in the world. Luke's accounts of Jesus (see Luke 4:33–37; 6:18; 7:21; 8:2, 26–39; 9:37–43; 11:14; 13:32; Acts 10:36–39) and his disciples (Acts 5:16; 8:7; 16:16–18) are indications that the power of God is available to heal and deliver. What the seven sons of Sceva remind us of is that the power of God is not an impersonal force to be manipulated. Rather, all our efforts to alleviate the sick and the oppressed are dependent on God. Like Paul, God may do extraordinary miracles *through* us (19:11), but it is always the power of God, not a formula, that is the source. In truth, all our prayers—for ourselves and for others—fall under the rubric of the prayer our Lord taught us: "Thy will be done" (Matt 6:10 KJV). It is God's purpose and power that enact miracles, not our own will or words.

---

18. C. S. Lewis, *The Voyage of the Dawn Treader* (New York: HarperCollins, 1999 [reprint]), 158.
19. Dunn, *Acts*, 260.

PANEL 6
Acts 19:21–28:31

The final, and longest, "panel" or movement in Acts begins by stating Paul's intention to go to Jerusalem and to Rome (19:21–22). These two great cities are the geographical focal points of this section, but before Paul goes to either of them he must first attend to matters in Asia, Macedonia, and Greece (19:23–20:38). Shortly after arriving in Jerusalem, Paul is arrested after a disturbance occurs in the temple (21:1–36). What follows is a series of addresses (21:37–23:11), a plot to kill Paul (23:12–35), and several trials before Roman and Jewish rulers (24:1–26:32). In the process of his trials, Paul appeals to have his case heard by Caesar (25:11), and eventually his request is granted. His journey to Rome is not without incident; he will face a violent storm, a shipwreck, and a venomous snakebite before reaching his destination (27:1–10). The story of Acts ends with Paul under house arrest in Rome, still awaiting his audience before the emperor (28:11–31) but also continuing to proclaim and teach "with all boldness and without hindrance" (v. 31). Luke does not explain what becomes of Paul in Rome; it seems that was never his intent to tell us that. Neither Paul, nor any other apostle or early-church figure, is the primary actor in this story. The primary actor is God, and the goal of this story was to tell how the gospel was proclaimed in Jerusalem, Judea, Samaria, and to the ends of the earth (1:8). In the Roman Empire all roads did indeed lead to Rome. In effect, with the gospel reaching the capital of the empire, it had reached their "world," and so the narrative can, fittingly, end.

Amid all the travels and trials of this final panel, two primary themes emerge. First, more and more of Paul's fellow Jews reject Jesus and the good news of the kingdom of God. In Luke's account, it is the accusations of his own people that lead to Paul's arrest and subsequent trials. Paul's final words—in fulfillment of Isaiah 6:9–10—attest to this unfortunate reality of rejection: "Therefore I want you [Jews] to know that God's salvation has been sent to the Gentiles, and they will listen!" (28:28). Second, the narrative shape of the ending of Acts, much like the beginning of Acts, imitates the life of Jesus. Just as both the Gospel of Luke and the book of Acts begin with a Spirit conception and birth, so too both narratives end with arrests and trials before Jewish and Roman rulers. Of course, there is no mention of Paul's execution, but the trajectory of the story points in this direction. That is, like Jesus's own experience and despite declarations of innocence from Roman authorities (23:26–30; 25:24–27; 26:31–32), Paul's own death is imminent (20:25, 38). Yet, also like Jesus, neither imprisonment nor death can chain or silence the bold proclamation of the gospel.

CHAPTER 44

Acts 19:21-41

 LISTEN to the Story

²¹After all this had happened, Paul decided to go to Jerusalem, passing through Macedonia and Achaia. "After I have been there," he said, "I must visit Rome also." ²²He sent two of his helpers, Timothy and Erastus, to Macedonia, while he stayed in the province of Asia a little longer.

²³About that time there arose a great disturbance about the Way. ²⁴A silversmith named Demetrius, who made silver shrines of Artemis, brought in a lot of business for the craftsmen there. ²⁵He called them together, along with the workers in related trades, and said: "You know, my friends, that we receive a good income from this business. ²⁶And you see and hear how this fellow Paul has convinced and led astray large numbers of people here in Ephesus and in practically the whole province of Asia. He says that gods made by human hands are no gods at all. ²⁷There is danger not only that our trade will lose its good name, but also that the temple of the great goddess Artemis will be discredited; and the goddess herself, who is worshiped throughout the province of Asia and the world, will be robbed of her divine majesty."

²⁸When they heard this, they were furious and began shouting: "Great is Artemis of the Ephesians!" ²⁹Soon the whole city was in an uproar. The people seized Gaius and Aristarchus, Paul's traveling companions from Macedonia, and all of them rushed into the theater together. ³⁰Paul wanted to appear before the crowd, but the disciples would not let him. ³¹Even some of the officials of the province, friends of Paul, sent him a message begging him not to venture into the theater.

³²The assembly was in confusion: Some were shouting one thing, some another. Most of the people did not even know why they were there. ³³The Jews in the crowd pushed Alexander to the front, and they shouted instructions to him. He motioned for silence in order to make a defense before the people. ³⁴But when they realized he was a Jew, they all shouted in unison for about two hours: "Great is Artemis of the Ephesians!"

> ³⁵The city clerk quieted the crowd and said: "Fellow Ephesians, doesn't all the world know that the city of Ephesus is the guardian of the temple of the great Artemis and of her image, which fell from heaven? ³⁶Therefore, since these facts are undeniable, you ought to calm down and not do anything rash. ³⁷You have brought these men here, though they have neither robbed temples nor blasphemed our goddess. ³⁸If, then, Demetrius and his fellow craftsmen have a grievance against anybody, the courts are open and there are proconsuls. They can press charges. ³⁹If there is anything further you want to bring up, it must be settled in a legal assembly. ⁴⁰As it is, we are in danger of being charged with rioting because of what happened today. In that case we would not be able to account for this commotion, since there is no reason for it." ⁴¹After he had said this, he dismissed the assembly.
>
> *Listening to the Text in the Story*: Romans 15:26; 1 Corinthians 15:32; 16:1–4; 2 Corinthians 1:8; 8:9; 2 Timothy 4:14.

EXPLAIN the Story

The opening scene of this final panel in Acts picks up from where the last panel ended, in Ephesus. The proud followers of the goddess Artemis react to the growth and power of the word of the Lord in Ephesus. After a brief orientation as to Paul's broad travel plans (vv. 21–22), the narrative focuses on the upheaval in Ephesus that occurs because of Paul's preaching. A speech, a riot, and then another speech round out this episode. A silversmith named Demetrius sparks a defense of his beloved goddess Artemis (vv. 23–27) that spreads across Ephesus and eventually explodes in the heart of the city's largest structure, the theater of Ephesus (vv. 28–34). Only the town clerk, the highest-standing civic official, can quell the uproar and prevent a riot (vv. 35–41). This is a fascinating episode that combines all the vital spheres of life—economic, religious, and political—that were present in a world-renowned city like Ephesus.

Spirit-Led Orientation (19:21–22)

After the narrative marker (19:20) that brings the previous "panel" to a close, the new panel opens with a theological orientation that will set the broad geographical focal points for the final panel: Jerusalem and Rome (vv. 21–22). The NIV states, "Paul decided to go to Jerusalem" (v. 21a). The phrase could also be translated "Paul resolved in the Spirit to go . . ." (NRSV). The choice is between reading the Greek words *en tō pneumati* (lit., "in the spirit") as an idiom referring either to Paul's inner process of deciding his next travel plans or as referring to the leading of the Holy Spirit. While the former is possible, it seems more likely that Luke, as he conveyed at the beginning of the previous panel (16:6–7), is signaling divine initiative and guidance. Rarely in Acts does the singular usage of the word "spirit" (*pneuma*) refer to anyone else other than the Holy Spirit, and when it does the context and/or modifying words make that clear.[1] Further, the Spirit often leads or speaks to guide and direct the disciples (e.g., 1:2; 8:29, 39; 11:12, 28; 13:2, 4; 15:28; 16:6–7; 20:22–23; 21:4, 11; 28:25). Another indication that this is the divine Spirit who is leading Paul is suggested by his final comment, "I *must* visit Rome also" (19:21b). The word "must" (*dei*) is a verb used frequently in Acts (e.g., 1:16, 21; 3:21; 4:12; 5:29; 9:6, 16; etc.) to indicate a divine imperative. It is the Spirit, not merely his own desire, who is guiding Paul back to Jerusalem and then on to Rome.

Besides naming Jerusalem and Rome as the two primary focal points in this last panel of the narrative, Paul also indicates that he will pass through Macedonia and Achaia. Why does Paul wish to revisit churches in Macedonia (e.g., Thessalonica, Philippi) and Achaia (e.g., Corinth, Athens)? Paul would certainly want to provide encouragement and further teaching, but there might be something more than this. Although Luke never mentions it in Acts, from Paul's own letters he indicates that these visits provided opportunities for these new, and mostly gentile, churches to contribute to a financial collection Paul is gathering for the impoverished Jewish church in Jerusalem (see Rom 15:26; cf. 1 Cor 16:1–4; 2 Cor 8–9). Like he often does, Paul relies on trusted companions and coworkers—in this case Timothy and Erastus[2]—to go on ahead to prepare the way for his coming and most likely make a start on gathering the collection (cf. Acts 19:22).

Demetrius's Defense of Artemis (19:23–27)

Luke opens this episode with the phrase, "About that time there arose a great disturbance about the Way" (v. 23).[3] Riots are not unheard of in large cities—whether ancient or modern. The root cause of this one in Ephesus was economic, but this observation must be set within a broader framework.

---

[1]. E.g., the spirit of Stephen (7:59); the pythonic spirit (16:16, 18); "his [Paul's] spirit" (17:16; see ESV); an evil spirit (19:15); a spirit (23:9).

[2]. Erastus may be a native of Corinth and the same "Erastus" mentioned in Rom 16:23 and 2 Tim 4:20.

[3]. Gaventa, *Acts*, 270, notes that references to "the Way" often occur in connection with resistance and persecution (cf. 9:2; 19:9; 22:4).

To understand the vigorous defense of the cult of Artemis in Ephesus, one needs to appreciate the bond between city and goddess reflected in its economic, civic, cultural, and political spheres.[4] The origins of the Greek goddess Artemis (Roman "Diana"), daughter of Zeus and sister of Apollo, were believed by the ancient Greeks to originate in a grove known as Ortygia near Ephesus where Artemis was born. Although some early Christian apologists thought Artemis was a fertility goddess, it is more likely that she was regarded as "great" because of her lordship over supernatural powers along with the generosity and protection she bestowed on her followers.[5] Trebilco notes that she was "acclaimed as Lady [*kuria*], Saviour [*sōteira*] . . . and the Queen of the Cosmos [*basilēis kosmou*]. She was described as greatest [*megistē*], holiest [*hagiōtatē*], and most manifest [*epiphanestatē*]."[6]

Two magnificent festivals were held each year in Artemis's honor. In addition to these, there were biweekly Artemis processions through Ephesus's streets that brought traffic in the city to a standstill. Her temple, known as the Artemisium, stood outside the city wall and was the star attraction of the city. It was enormous. It measured 130 by 70 meters, making it four times the size of the Parthenon in Athens. Some ancient historians argued its majesty was rivaled in the world only by Mount Olympus, the earthly home of the gods.[7]

The Artemisium was not only a temple for prayer and worship but was also the largest bank in Asia. Large sums of money were on deposit from people in Ephesus and farther afield. The temple of Artemis was a magnetic draw for people and their wealth from all over the Roman world. Pilgrims would not only visit the temple but would purchase shrines from local craftsmen—miniatures of the goddess and temple, often made of silver—and use them as votive offerings in the temple or as memorials in their homes.

The reputation and significance of the city and its temple cannot be underestimated. In some ways, Ephesus and her temple was to many Greeks what Jerusalem and her temple was to most Jews. As such, we can understand the town clerk's question, "Doesn't all the world know that the city of Ephesus is the *guardian* of the temple of the great Artemis?" (Acts 19:35). That is a key point. The citizens of Ephesus did not only host the goddess Artemis, they *guarded* her temple. As such, the Ephesians coveted the status and wealth the goddess brought them, and they would go to great lengths to defend her

---

4. For a thorough and readable overview of these dynamics, see Trebilco, "Asia," 316–57. See also his monograph, *The Early Christians in Ephesus: From Paul to Ignatius* (Eerdmans: Grand Rapids, 2004).

5. The ancient Greek historian Strabo (*Geogr.* 14.1.6) wrote that the goddess received her name because she kept her followers *artemeas*, i.e., safe and protected.

6. Trebilco, "Asia," 317–18.

7. Antipater, the epigramist; see Trebilco, *Early Christians in Ephesus*, 20.

honor. R. E. Oster describes the unique bond between Ephesus and Artemis this way:

> The quintessence of Artemis was forever related to the well being of Ephesus. Notwithstanding the individualistic and personal significance of the goddess, the principal force of her cult was upon the interrelated components of the city's urban life, e.g., the civic, economic, educational, patriotic, administrative, and commercial facets. . . . There was no other Graeco-Roman metropolis in the Empire whose 'body, soul, and spirit' could so belong to a particular deity as did Ephesus' to her patron goddess Artemis.[8]

The speech and actions of Demetrius and his fellow silversmiths and artisans are understandable. The significant loss of livelihood along with the potential denigration of their goddess because of Christian preaching was a strong motivator. It did not take Demetrius long to get a hearing among his fellow artisans who fashioned miniature replicas of Artemis and her temple. After all, Demetrius accurately, if not fully, comprehended Paul's message that "gods made by human hands are no gods at all" (v. 26; cf. 17:29; Rom 1:23). If "the Way" of the Christians was true, then the Ephesian Artemis way of life was wrong. A clash between Lady Artemis, "who is worshiped throughout the province of Asia and the world" (v. 27), and Jesus, the Lord of all, who was gaining followers "in Ephesus and in practically the whole province of Asia" (v. 26), was inevitable. Two deities of this magnitude and majesty could not coexist; the place wasn't big enough for both.

Uproar in the Theater (19:28–34)

The speech of Demetrius ignited a hymn-like chant from his hearers: "Great is Artemis of the Ephesians!" (v. 28). This is not only a song of praise to their goddess but also a song of resistance aimed at the Christian outsiders and their Lord. Before long the spirited defense of Demetrius and his fellow artisans engulfed the "whole city . . . in an uproar" (v. 29).[9] In their rage, the Ephesians appear to seize whatever Christians were closest at hand. In this case it was two of Paul's traveling companions: Gaius from Corinth (see Rom 16:23; 1 Cor 1:14) and Aristarchus from Thessalonica (see Acts 20:4; 27:2). The rioters were not well organized, but it was unsurprising that this large crowd dragged their quarry to the city's local theater (19:29). The theater was built into the western slope of Mt. Pion and was massive; it was capable of seating about twenty-four thousand people. Paul, upon hearing this news, wished to

---

8. R. E. Oster, "Ephesus as a Religious Center under the Principate, I. Paganism before Constantine," in *ANRW* 2.18.3 (1990): 1728, quoted in Trebilco, "Asia," 329.

9. Paul alludes to serious conflicts in Ephesus/Asia in his letters (1 Cor 15:32; 2 Cor 1:8).

join his colleagues but was restrained from doing so (v. 30). As a sign of the significant inroads the gospel had made into Ephesian society is the remark that a group of "officials of the province" sent Paul a message, "begging him not to venture into the theater" (v. 31). These "officials" (*asiarchēs*), whether Christian or not, were wealthy aristocrats who took an interest in Paul and his well-being.

Many of those present in the theater seemed simply to have been swept up in the flow of the crowd, much like they would have been for an Artemisan festival or procession day. Instead of this being a reasonable "assembly" (*ekklēsia*, v. 32; cf. vv. 39, 40), it is a riotous rabble. An initial attempt was made to quell the uproar. Luke states that some Jews in the crowd pushed a certain Alexander forward (v. 33). Possibly he was a person well known to the artisans of the city (perhaps he is the Ephesian metalworker Paul refers to in 2 Tim 4:14?), pushed forward to clarify the position of the Jewish community. Or he may have been a Christian Jew who was thrust forward as a scapegoat. Whatever his identity, when the crowd realized he was a Jew, any quiet that was gained was soon lost to renewed chants of "Great is Artemis of the Ephesians!" (v. 34; cf. v. 28). This response from the worshipers of Artemis may reflect an inability or unwillingness to make a distinction between Jews, Christian Jews, and gentile Christians. The crowd continued their chant in a mesmerized frenzy for almost two hours (v. 34).

The City Clerk Brings Back Order (19:35–41)

A speech by the silversmith Demetrius ignited the uproar in Ephesus about "the Way." Now a speech from an unnamed but high-ranking civic authority extinguishes the uproar. It is interesting that in this entire episode, there is no recorded word from the followers of "the Way." The city clerk, the only one powerful enough to subdue the crowd, appeals to them with a double-edged argument. The first edge is theological. He argues that people everywhere know Ephesus is the "temple guardian" (*neōkoros*) of Artemis, whose image "fell from heaven" (v. 35). The clerk seems to counter the claim that their goddess is "made by human hands" (v. 26). Rather, he argues, Artemis's origins are divine. The phrase "fell from heaven" (*diopetēs*) can be translated literally as "fallen from Zeus." This theological assertion is, according to the clerk, a fact that is undeniable.

The second edge of the clerk's speech is legal. On this note, he points out that the men they are accusing of wrongdoing have neither "robbed temples" (recall that the temple of Artemis was also a bank) nor "blasphemed our goddess" (v. 37).[10] Here the legal argument is directed against the economic

---

10. Jewish writers, like Josephus and Philo, were keen to demonstrate that their people living in the diaspora (i.e., outside Judea or Galilee) were neither violators of pagan temples nor blasphemers

(cf. vv. 25, 27) and sacrilegious (cf. v. 27) accusations of Demetrius and his associates. The clerk continues that even if this were true, the proper forum for dealing with these legal matters is not in a theater before rabble but in a lawful assembly (*ekklēsia*) before proconsuls (vv. 38–39). He alerts them to the real peril. The real "danger" (see v. 27, *kindyneuō*) is not a loss of business or the dishonor of Artemis. Rather, the "danger" (v. 40, *kindyneuō*) is from the Roman Empire that responds harshly to civic riots, even ones in important cities like Ephesus. "A city could lose the respect of Roman officials, guilds which caused trouble could be disbanded, city officials could be punished, and a city could even lose its freedom."[11] The town clerk does not want to jeopardize the city's relationship with Roman proconsuls and the benefits and advantages that came to cities (and its local officials) that maintained good relations with the empire. This warning seemed to have sunk in for the Ephesians. The rioting crowd is now dismissed formally as a civil "assembly" (*ekklēsia*; v. 40).

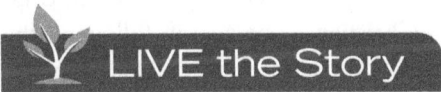

LIVE the Story

Discerning the Spirit's Leading

For all the times that Acts is appealed to for its dramatic demonstrations of the Spirit, it is remarkable how often the Spirit's manifestation appears quietly in the narrative. At the beginning of this account, the Spirit's presence is so restrained that even the NIV translators grapple with how to relate the meaning of the Greek phrase *etheto ho Paulos en tō pneumati* (19:21; lit., "Paul decided in the S/spirit"). In the end, they chose to translate this phrase related to Paul's travel deliberations with two words: "Paul decided." As such, the clause reads, "Paul *decided* to go to Jerusalem" (v. 21). This is a valid and understandable translation, although I think it is more likely that this overlooks the presence of the Holy Spirit in the narrative. After all, Luke offers his readers little insight as to *how* Paul made his decision "in the Spirit." The way the Spirit prompts Paul is quiet. There is no vision, no dream, and no dramatic word of prophecy. All we are told is Paul somehow discerned the Spirit's leading in much the same way that many of us do today most of the time.

While we might crave to know the logic—the "how to"—of the Spirit's leading, I'm grateful for the ambiguity. If we were provided with instructions or steps that Paul took to discern this leading, we would be tempted to rely

---

of foreign gods; see Josephus, *Ag. Apion* 2.237; *Ant.* 4.207; Philo, *Moses* 2.205; *Spec. Laws* 1.53.

11. Trebilco, "Asia," 344. Trebilco goes on to cite examples of Roman discipline against cities that allowed riots like Cyzicus, Prusa, and Pompeii.

on a procedure rather than the person of the Spirit. In doing so, we might even make an idol out of the method. Human beings, including the people of God, are adept at making idols. Given the choice between extended periods of quiet listening to the Spirit or short transactions with "the divine," we most often choose the latter. It is easier to take the impersonal route—pay the priestesses of Artemis, buy a votive idol made of silver, use a marketing strategy, or follow ten "easy steps" to discern the "will of (a) god" than it is to take the relational way of the Spirit. We are seduced by visible, flashy, and loud advertisements guaranteeing instant "results." Yet much of the time, decisions "in the Spirit" are discerned through extended periods of silence or gentle conversations with fellow believers. We are not told how Paul made his decisions "in the Spirit," and we are the better for it. God may provide a dream in the night, a flash of light along the road, or a spoken word from a reliable prophet, but we should not crave these. Instead, we should lean into the everyday tools and disciplines cultivated by followers of Jesus for centuries as we discern the leading of the Spirit, including prayer, fasting, Scripture, and conversation with wise Christians. The goal in following the Spirit's leading is not an impersonal transaction, a fast-food fuel, and accurate marketing data but lives characterized by a long obedience, relational maturity, and *personal* discernment.

The Challenge of the Gospel

Loveday Alexander writes, "If the preaching of the gospel is having any real effect, sooner or later it will start to touch the political and economic structures with which our lives are entwined—and then, watch out for fireworks!"[12] This was the case in first-century Ephesus and in centuries since. The gospel of Jesus is not a religion, it is not a new set of ideas, and it is not a new ethic. The gospel of Jesus is a way, a way of being. The Jesus "Way" touches everything we *are*. When non-Christian individuals or societies recognize this, there is often resistance. Think about this. If someone declared that everything about you—what you did for work, the people you cherished, the celebrations you enjoyed, the cultural identity you inhabited—had to be rethought and reoriented in view of the reality of Jesus, what would you do?

Throughout history, when individuals and/or larger groups recognized the implications of the gospel, they often pushed back. The citizens of first-century Ephesus, the vikings of Scandinavia, and the leaders of Soviet Russia are all examples of those who resisted gospel claims. It may take decades or even centuries, with many failures and by much perseverance, before people

---

12. Alexander, *Acts*, 151.

submit to the lordship of Christ. In some instances, after initial footholds of acceptance, the gospel Way may still flounder. The story of the gospel in Japan—poignantly told by the Christian novelist Shusaku Endo in his book *Silence*[13] and powerfully depicted in Martin Scorsese's film adaptation of Endo's work—is one such example.[14] Initially, the witness of Jesuit missionaries in sixteenth-century Japan was well received. Within a generation of the first missionaries arriving in 1549 the church swelled to more than three hundred thousand believers. Before long, sadly, the Japanese warlords of the Tokugawa era resented the cultural incursions of these foreigners and brutally purged their country of Christians. In his foreword to Makoto Fujimura's book *Silence and Beauty*, Philip Yancey writes:

> In 1597 [the Japanese warlords] arrested twenty-six Christians—six foreign missionaries and twenty Japanese Christians, including three young boys—mutilated their ears and noses, and force-marched them some five hundred miles. Upon arrival in Nagasaki, the focal point of Japan's Christian community, the prisoners were led to a hill, crucified and pierced with spears. The era of persecution had begun, on what became known as Martyrs Hill. . . . In one of history's cruel ironies, the second atomic bomb exploded directly above Japan's largest congregation of Christians, many of whom had gathered for mass at the cathedral. (Clouds obscured the intended city, forcing the bombing crew to select an alternate target.) In the end, more Christians died in the atomic destruction of Nagasaki than in the centuries of persecution that followed the deaths of the twenty-six martyrs in 1597, for over the years by far the majority of believers had apostatized.[15]

Complex circumstances like these should temper a triumphalistic reading of history—after all, even in the case of the gospel of Christ challenging the citizens of Ephesus, the cult of Artemis remained dominant there for another two centuries. On the other hand, grappling with these stories need not lead to a defeatist reading of history either. The gospel has and does transform individuals and cultures. The reality of the Way of Jesus does, however, mean that we must recognize both the sobering challenge and the joyful impact of the gospel. The gospel cannot be compartmentalized into "personal faith" that has no impact on the broader implications of economics or politics. The complex question of the gospel in our day impels us to ask whether our

---

13. Shusaku Endo, *Silence*, trans. William Johnston (New York: Taplinger, 1969).
14. Martin Scorsese, dir., *Silence* (Hollywood: Paramount Pictures, 2016).
15. Philip Yancey, "Foreword," in Mako Fujimura, *Silence and Beauty: Hidden Faith Born of Suffering* (Downers Grove, IL: InterVarsity Press, 2016), Kindle edition.

businesses, our cultural loyalties, and our political ideologies are idolatrous or reflect the Way of the Lord Jesus. This requires hard, and often uncomfortable, work and reflection. It is much easier to pigeonhole our commitment to Christ than to let it touch the "real life" issues of career and commerce, culture and politics, celebration and patriotism.

In my city in Saskatchewan, unlike first-century Ephesus, we do not have goddesses/gods named Artemis or Apollo. But like Ephesus, one can detect the idols by identifying what we worship. The *Oxford English Dictionary* tells us that *worship* derives from the Old English word *weorthscipe*: "worthiness, acknowledgment of worth." Behind this word we recognize that where we attach ultimate "worth-ship" is at the heart of our "worship." In my neighborhood, it is easy to see what idols are given this kind of worth. They go by names like "Convenience," "Control," and "Choice." Let's consider Choice, the last idol in this list. On a basic consumerist level, this is expressed in our shopping demands. For example, despite living in a climate that is entombed in winter much of the year, we expect the choice of soft fruit (strawberries, raspberries, blueberries, etc.) and exotic vegetables year-round in our grocery stores regardless of the cost to the farmer or to the environment. On a deeper level, this can express itself in the freedom to "choose" one's gender or to choose to regard a life in the womb as an impersonal fetus or a personal baby. At the heart of these choices is the focus on the autonomous self: self-defined, self-asserting, and self-authenticating. Without reference to the will of God, the givenness of creation, or a sense of interdependency with others, Choice takes the place of ultimate worth. In the end, one is consumed and devoured by Choice. Before long, we have transformed God's good gift of freedom into an unseen but powerful idol in our lives. If this happens, we betray the reality of our faith by failing to recognize the challenge the gospel holds for the idols—visible and invisible—that we bow before in our "worth-ship."

And yet the gospel is good news because it speaks to the heart of betrayal in all of us. Again, as Yancey reminds us, "It was for traitors that Jesus died." He continues, in telling us why Endo's enduring novel *Silence* dwells on the experiences of failure and shame:

> [It is] because these leave the most lasting impact on a person's life. Jesus's most poignant legacy was his undying love, even for—*especially for*—those who betrayed him. When Judas led a lynch mob into the garden, Jesus addressed him as "friend." On Calvary, while stretched out naked in the posture of ultimate disgrace, Jesus roused himself to cry out for his tormentors, "Father, forgive them." To those scandalized by the apparent apostasy of [the Jesuit characters in *Silence*], Endo points to the two great

founders of the Christian church: Peter denied Christ three times, Paul led the first persecution of Christians. The entire Bible can be seen, in fact, as a story of betrayal, beginning with Adam and proceeding through the history of the Israelites, culminating in the cross.[16]

The Jesus Way is challenging—on every level—and yet the message of the cross, in all its foolishness, ambiguity, and hiddenness also has the beauty and power to transform, heal, and sustain individuals, societies, people groups, and, indeed, nations.

---

16. Yancey, "Foreword," Kindle edition.

CHAPTER 45

Acts 20:1-16

 LISTEN to the Story

¹When the uproar had ended, Paul sent for the disciples and, after encouraging them, said goodbye and set out for Macedonia. ²He traveled through that area, speaking many words of encouragement to the people, and finally arrived in Greece, ³where he stayed three months. Because some Jews had plotted against him just as he was about to sail for Syria, he decided to go back through Macedonia. ⁴He was accompanied by Sopater son of Pyrrhus from Berea, Aristarchus and Secundus from Thessalonica, Gaius from Derbe, Timothy also, and Tychicus and Trophimus from the province of Asia. ⁵These men went on ahead and waited for us at Troas. ⁶But we sailed from Philippi after the Festival of Unleavened Bread, and five days later joined the others at Troas, where we stayed seven days.

⁷On the first day of the week we came together to break bread. Paul spoke to the people and, because he intended to leave the next day, kept on talking until midnight. ⁸There were many lamps in the upstairs room where we were meeting. ⁹Seated in a window was a young man named Eutychus, who was sinking into a deep sleep as Paul talked on and on. When he was sound asleep, he fell to the ground from the third story and was picked up dead. ¹⁰Paul went down, threw himself on the young man and put his arms around him. "Don't be alarmed," he said. "He's alive!" ¹¹Then he went upstairs again and broke bread and ate. After talking until daylight, he left. ¹²The people took the young man home alive and were greatly comforted.

¹³We went on ahead to the ship and sailed for Assos, where we were going to take Paul aboard. He had made this arrangement because he was going there on foot. ¹⁴When he met us at Assos, we took him aboard and went on to Mitylene. ¹⁵The next day we set sail from there and arrived off Chios. The day after that we crossed over to Samos, and on the following day arrived at Miletus. ¹⁶Paul had decided to sail past Ephesus to avoid

spending time in the province of Asia, for he was in a hurry to reach Jerusalem, if possible, by the day of Pentecost.

Listening to the Text in the Story: 1 Kings 17:21; Mark 5:39.

EXPLAIN the Story

After opening the final panel in Acts with an episode in Ephesus, told from the perspective of nonbelievers (19:21–41), Luke returns the narrative's focus to the concerns and the encouragement of Christ's disciples as Paul and his companions travel from Ephesus to Jerusalem (20:1–21:17). As Gaventa points out,[1] this narrative alternates between accounts of detailed travel and dramatic events:

20:1–6	Travel from Ephesus to Macedonia-Greece-Macedonia-Troas
20:7–12	Eucharist and Eutychus in Troas
20:13–16	Travel from Troas to Assos-Mitylene-Chios-Samos-Miletus
20:17–38	Paul's farewell address in Miletus
21:1–9	Travel from Miletus to Kos-Rhodes-Patara-Tyre-Ptolemais-Caesarea
21:10–14	Prophetic declaration by Agabus in Caesarea
21:15–17	Travel from Caesarea to Jerusalem

This travel narrative is full of extraordinary details. Luke provides abundant and specific elements for the reader to consider, including *in-depth setting descriptions* (e.g., "many lamps in the upstairs room," 20:8; "third story," 20:9; "passing to the south of [Cyprus]," 21:3; "at Tyre, where our ship was to unload its cargo," 21:3; "all of them, including wives and children . . . on the beach we knelt," 21:5), *specific time signatures* (e.g., "three months" stay, 20:3; "after the Festival of Unleavened Bread, and five days later," 20:6; "the first day of the week," 20:7; "talking until daylight," 20:11; "by the day of Pentecost," 20:16; "stayed with them seven days," 21:4; "stayed with them for a day," 21:7); a number of *named traveling companions* and believers (e.g., Sopater, Aristarchus, Secundus, Gaius, Timothy, Tychicus, Trophimus, Eutychus, Philip, Agabus, Mnason), and *extended addresses* from Paul exclusively to believers (to those

---

1. Gaventa, *Acts*, 276.

in Troas and to those in Miletus). All this information suggests the memories of a person who was an eyewitness to the travel and events. Not surprisingly, at this point in the narrative the account shifts from the third person ("he/them" narration) to the first-person perspective ("we/us," 20:5). Also worthy of note is the fact that Paul wrote two of his most significant epistles while on this journey through Macedonia (2 Corinthians) and Corinth (Romans). All in all, this detailed travel narrative (20:1–21:17) is a fitting summary to Paul's mission. That is, Paul was not only interested in establishing communities of "the Way" but also in encouraging and equipping those communities for when he was no longer present with them.

The journey of Paul and his companions starts with a travel episode beginning in Ephesus and ending in Troas (20:1–6); this is followed by a dramatic story from the life of the community in Troas (vv. 7–12); after this event, Paul and his companions resume their travel by departing from Troas and going to Miletus (vv. 13–16). Initially the focus of the travels is on returning to revisit communities that Paul founded, but by the time he reaches Miletus, and from then on, the goal is fixed on Jerusalem alone (20:16; cf. 20:22; 21:4, 11, 12, 13, 15, 17).

Ephesus to Troas (20:1–6)

Paul departed Ephesus probably in the summer of AD 56. His route from Ephesus took him north to the port city of Troas. From there, he likely took a ship across the northern tip of the Aegean Sea to the Macedonia port of Neapolis, retracing the stages of his first visit to this area (cf. 16:11). The point of this trip, however, was not for establishing new congregations but to strengthen existing ones. That this is a primary purpose of the journey is articulated at the beginning. A note of "encouragement" (*parakaleō*) is struck twice at the outset of Paul's travel, first as he leaves Ephesus after the clamor in the city had ceased (20:1), and then as he travels through Macedonia and into Greece (v. 2). It is interesting that while on this journey through Macedonia, Paul writes one of his most famous letters to the church in Corinth (2 Corinthians), a letter that is full of notes of "comfort/encouragement."[2] Besides the theme of encouragement in this travel account, another theme is also struck: Jewish opposition to Paul. This note of opposition is mentioned after Paul arrives in Greece where he spends three months (winter AD 56–57)—likely in Corinth—"speaking many words of encouragement" (Acts 20:2). It appears that he had intended to sail from Greece to Syria, possibly on a pilgrim ship full of fellow Jews, but because "some Jews had plotted against

---

2. The word *parakaleō* occurs eighteen times in 2 Corinthians, more than any other of Paul's letters. Only Acts (twenty-two times) contains more occurrences of this word.

him" (v. 3), these plans were changed and he retraced his steps north back through Macedonia.[3] This theme of Jewish opposition foreshadows much of what will follow in the narrative. Later we will hear about the hostility Paul faces from Jews in Jerusalem, hostility that has been revealed by the Spirit not only to Paul himself (vv. 22–23) but also through fellow believers (21:4) and the prophet Agabus (21:11).

As Paul makes his way north through Macedonia, eight men accompany him. Seven of them are named. Some of them are new to the narrative (i.e., Sopater from Berea, Secundus from Thessalonica, and Gaius from Derbe). Some of them are already familiar and show up in Acts and in Paul's letters, including Aristarchus from Thessalonica (19:29; 27:2; Col 4:10; Phlm 24), Timothy from Lystra (Acts 16:1; 17:14–15; 18:5; 19:22; Rom 16:21; 1 Cor 4:17; 2 Cor 1:1; Phil 1:1; Col 1:1; 1 Thess 1:1; 2 Thess 1:1; 1 Tim 1:2, 18; 6:20; 2 Tim 1:2; Phlm 1), Tychicus from Asia (Eph 6:21; Col 4:7; 2 Tim 4:12; Titus 3:12), and Trophimus from Asia (Acts 21:29; 2 Tim 4:20). The eighth member of this company is quietly introduced by the pronoun "us" (Acts 20:5). This unnamed colleague, traditionally known as the physician Luke, first appeared in the narrative when Paul received his "Macedonian call" in Troas (see commentary discussion on 16:10) and traveled with him to Philippi. It appears Luke remained in Philippi since the "we passages" end after Paul leaves that city. The "we passages" resume when Paul revisits Philippi and apparently invites Luke back into the traveling company where he remains until they arrive in Jerusalem (21:18). Some interpreters suggest that these traveling companions represent the churches that had contributed to the collection Paul organized for the church in Jerusalem.[4] This is not stated explicitly in the text, but it is alluded to later in Acts when Paul states that he has returned to Jerusalem "to bring my people gifts for the poor and to present offerings" (24:17). Beyond that, these individuals represent a living witness to the fruit of his missionary work across Galatia (Timothy and Gaius), Asia (Tychicus, Trophimus, and Luke), and Macedonia (Sopater, Aristarchus, and Secundus).

After sending the seven named colleagues ahead to Troas (Acts 20:5), Paul and Luke wait to leave Philippi—probably sailing from Neapolis (cf. 16:11)—until after the Feast of Unleavened Bread (i.e., Passover, v. 6) in the spring of AD 57. Troas is an important place for Paul. It was the place of a significant vision (16:9–10), and it will once more be the place of a powerful event. Of note is that the Passover marks the time of Jesus's journey to Jerusalem and

---

3. Ramsay, *St. Paul*, 220, suggests that it would have been more dangerous for Paul on an enclosed ship with conspirators than it would be on the open road.
4. E.g., Barrett, *Acts* 2:947; Peterson, *Acts*, 556.

his subsequent arrest and trial at the end of Luke's Gospel (22:1); the Passover also marks Paul's journey to Jerusalem and his subsequent arrest and trials at the end of Acts.

Eucharist and Eutychus (20:7–12)

The final night of Paul's seven-day[5] stay in Troas included an extended meeting with believers on "the first day of the week" (20:7)—that is, on Sunday. Longenecker notes that this is "the earliest unambiguous evidence we have for Christians gathering together for worship on that day (cf. John 20:19, 26; 1 Cor 16:2; Rev 1:10)."[6] Both the late time of day and the location of the meeting room on the third floor[7] suggest these believers came from a lower social stratum. Paul's audience had likely worked all day, and their meeting place was in an upstairs room, the cheaper and less desirable rooms. The largest and most expensive apartments were on the ground level, whereas the upper, cheaper rooms—often without heating, running water, or toilets—were rented by those who were less well off. They had gathered to "break bread" (Acts 20:7), which, reflecting Paul's teaching in 1 Corinthians (1 Cor 10:16–17; 11:17–34), indicates it was a gathering to remember the Lord's Supper, a Eucharist. At such meetings, besides gathering together for fellowship, food, and worship, there was also time for teaching. Despite these intentional elements, there is an unstructured sense to the Troas meeting, and because Paul intended on leaving them the next day, he continued speaking until midnight.

Besides the specific detail about the lengthy conversation, Luke couples this with several eyewitness comments. First, he notes that there were "many lamps" lit in the meeting place (Acts 20:8). There isn't any specific indication in the text that this contributed to a somnolent atmosphere, but he adds another note that a young man named "Eutychus"—a common Greek slave name meaning "fortunate/lucky"—was sitting in an open window and becoming increasingly drowsy while Paul talked on at length. Luke suggests that sleep takes a character role in the drama that unfolds, for the sentence literally reads, "a deep sleep fell upon him" (v. 9). Sound asleep, unlucky Eutychus fell from the third-floor window and was picked up dead. Paul ran down the stairs and, reminiscent of the actions of Elijah (1 Kgs 17:21) and Elisha (2 Kgs 4:34), he threw himself on the young man and put his arms around him. He advised

---

5. Ramsay, *St. Paul*, 224, offers a helpful suggestion that "Paul would not voluntarily have spent seven days at Troas: the length of a coasting voyage was too uncertain for him to waste so many days at the beginning, when he was hastening to Jerusalem."
6. Longenecker, *Acts*, 509.
7. The second storey in British usage.

the onlookers not to be alarmed[8] and declared him to be alive (Acts 20:10). The joyful company, no doubt renewed with energy and excitement, returned upstairs to their meeting room for a late-night snack[9] and further teaching. Paul continued teaching until dawn and then left Troas. This dramatic episode ends with another note of encouragement (*parakaleō*, v. 12; cf. vv. 1, 2) for the believers, including Paul who was also comforted to see Eutychus recovered.

Troas to Miletus (20:13–16)

Paul lingered in Troas to bid his farewell while sending his traveling companions on ahead by ship to the port town of Assos. While the company sailed the long way around the projecting Cape Lectum, Paul walked the shorter thirty-kilometer (eighteen-mile) route overland—a normal day's walk for a seasoned traveler like Paul (v. 13). Paul rejoined the sailing party at Assos, and they continued south along the Ionian coast until arriving at Mitylene (v. 14). Ships at this time would have stopped every evening. Ramsay informs us why: "The reason lies in the wind, which in the Aegean during the summer generally blows from the north, beginning at a very early hour in the morning. In the late afternoon it dies away; at sunset there is a dead calm, and thereafter a gentle south wind arises and blows during the night."[10] At first light they set sail for Chios, Samos a day later, and then Miletus (v. 15).

Luke then informs his readers "Paul had *decided* to sail past Ephesus" (v. 16). This has led some to conclude that Paul hired an entire ship for his personal use and then, to avoid being delayed in Ephesus, which was north of Miletus, chose to visit with a community he knew well and with whom he enjoyed warm relations. This may be a misreading of Paul's "decision." That is, the decision may not be related to avoiding believers in Ephesus but may be a decision about travel plans. The reason for leaning toward this interpretation is that it would be unlikely for Paul to pay the entire fare for a privately chartered ship, one whose stops he could choose at will. Instead, he likely paid the fare to board one of the many cargo vessels or transships that worked in the Aegean Sea. Much like a modern air traveler, one cannot determine the layovers a plane might make, but one can choose the routes. As such, it might be quicker to take a route that seems longer on a map, but with fewer stops. In such a scenario, what Paul "decided" was *not* intentionally to sail past his friends in Ephesus, but to decide—among the options open to him—to choose a faster

---

8. The word translated "alarm" (*thorybeō*) in v. 10 is the verb related to the noun translated "uproar" in v. 1 (*thorybos*).

9. Longnecker, *Acts*, 509, notes that the compound phrase "broke bread and ate" (v. 11) signifies an ordinary meal, not the Lord's Supper.

10. Ramsay, *St. Paul*, 222–23.

way to make Jerusalem within fifty days in time for Pentecost. This may have required taking a ship sailing *past* Ephesus and docking in Miletus. He could then afford to wait several days for the Ephesian elders to join him, and he could spend a full day devoted to conversation with his friends.[11]

With his travel decisions made in such a way as to offer the speediest travel possible, Paul was determined to reach Jerusalem by Pentecost to participate in this important festival. Pentecost (cf. 2:1) was the great festival when Jews celebrated the firstfruits of the harvest season. Paul may have been determined to participate in the feast not merely out of Jewish devotion but out of a vocational conviction. One of his great callings as the apostle to the gentiles was to bring unity to the people of God, now comprised of *both* Jews *and* gentiles. By delivering the financial gift he was carrying from the gentile church to the impoverished Jewish "home church," he was providing another means of establishing a common bond in Christ between them all. For Christians—both Jew and gentile alike—Pentecost was a special festival. It was the occasion when the Spirit was poured out "on *all* people" (Acts 2:17). What better symbol of the church's unity formed by the Spirit across ethnic lines than the delivery and acceptance of this gift during another Pentecost season.

The Comfort of Good Storytelling

Storytelling is one of the most basic urges humans possess. In particular, we seem especially to enjoy recounting and reading travel adventures. From Moses's account of the exodus to Homer's *Iliad*, from Dante's *Divine Comedy* to Tolkien's *Lord of the Rings*, road-trip narratives fascinate us. We are pilgrim people and drawn to pilgrimage, whether it is with our feet or with our imaginations. Of course, the best stories are the ones in which we have a part, even if it is only a minor role. What young child doesn't warm with inner delight when he or she hears a story told with them as a character in it? Who doesn't like to be put into the story? Or, short of that, hear a story told so well that they can imagine themselves in it? This is, in fact, what Luke does. He puts himself in

---

11. Ramsay, *St. Paul*, 224, offers this solution to Paul's journey and why he would have sailed past Ephesus, waited in Miletus for three days, and still managed to reach Jerusalem by Pentecost. Alternatively, Rapske, "Acts, Travel, Shipwreck," 16–17, suggests that Paul's sail past Ephesus and then the calling of elders to Miletus served a dual purpose. First, Paul would have avoided the risk of offending the church in Ephesus by relating to their elders without the added time pressure of having to relate to the entire church. Second, the location of Miletus would have served as an "effective buffer" that would prevent Paul's travel plans from being delayed further by the extended and affectionate hospitality of this community.

the story—most likely because he was actually there. Because of that, the story has added depth and color. For us as readers we are invited to put ourselves in the story. For those of us who are called upon to tell the story of Acts by way of teaching and preaching, we are further invited to put our audience into the story. Of course, we must do so sensitively as well as creatively. It is notable, however, how often Luke names characters—even if we never hear about them in the pages of Christian history. Rather than write that Paul was accompanied by "friends" or "coworkers," he names people like Sopater and Secundus—the only time in all of Acts or the NT—as having a part in the story.[12] The point is that they not only appear in the story but that they have something to contribute to the story, however secondary or significant that part may be.

The reasons why these stories connect with us are not only because of the personal touches Luke uses or the imaginative impact that they convey. We connect with them because they are stories that comfort us. The word translated "encouragement" (*parakaleō*) is a favorite verb of Luke. He uses it more often than any other writer in the NT and includes it three times in this episode (vv. 1, 2, 12). It could also be translated as "comfort"—literally, "with strength."[13] Luke retells how Paul's presence in these communities was a comfort to believers, as God worked through him in teaching and healing. For individuals like Sopater, Secundus (20:4), and Eutychus (20:9) who only appear once in the pages of Scripture, the story of the gospel mattered because they were included in it. This could not help but strengthen their faith. For many of us, it might be difficult to imagine the great apostle to the gentiles—one of the true heroes of the faith—being an example for us. For people like me—those who are local ministers and teachers trying to live the gospel with authenticity—it matters that there are individuals who are included and contribute to Acts simply because of their willingness to do the ordinary work of being a traveling companion or a weary listener. While God is indeed gathering a people for his name, the story of salvation includes individuals. God notices those who may appear insignificant or uninteresting to the world, and Luke reminds us of this about God by putting some of these people in the story. Among the many theological purposes of Acts, I think Luke encourages us not only to see ourselves in the grand narrative of Scripture but also to include others—by name—in it too. As we see others and ourselves in this pilgrim story, this "road-trip" account of people along "the Way," our hearts are comforted. We are encouraged to take the next step, however hard it may be, in the fellowship with other travelers.

---

12. Hemer, *Acts*, 236, does suggest that Sopater may also be the same person identified by the longer name Sosipater in Rom 16:21.

13. Latin, *com* (expressing intensive force) + *fortis* ("strong").

Eutychus and Eucharist

As I spoke about the account of Eutychus with my wife over coffee one day, she thought this episode merited the heading, "It's happened to us all." Who among us hasn't felt the effects of drowsiness—even when hearing a master teacher? I am only guessing, but I can imagine a few chuckles occurring when this story began to be told in the Greek-speaking early church. A young man whose name, in Greek, means "lucky," plunges to his death out of a third-story window after falling asleep listening to the great apostle. Of course, there are different ways to read that. For example, either he was "unlucky" to have fallen in the first place, or he was "lucky" enough to have someone like Paul there to take prompt action to save his life. The point is that the irony of his name and the circumstances of his fall would have been appreciated by Luke's listeners as another one of the many engaging events in his overall narrative.

The humor of this episode, much like many of the humorous episodes that occur in our own life, need not diminish the meaningfulness of Eutychus's resuscitation. Interpreters throughout the ages recognize the significance of this story. For some, it indicates the eagerness of Paul's Troas friends to listen to their teacher even late into the night (Chrysostom); for some it is a cautionary tale against slothfulness (Arator); and for others still, it is an example of how the loving help of a preacher may assist one to return to the "heights of virtue" (Bede).[14] Another meaningful reminder that commentators have recognized is that this episode occurs in the context of the breaking of bread (v. 7), that is, in remembrance of Jesus's last meal with his disciples. On that night of meeting and eating, Jesus "took bread, gave thanks and broke it, and gave it to [his disciples], saying, 'This is my body given for you'" (Luke 22:19). The episode of Eutychus's healing opens and closes with the thanksgiving meal—a Eucharist—for "which Christians down the ages have gathered on the first day of the week to celebrate" as "the victory of life over death."[15]

As we continue to gather around the table of the Lord to give thanks for his triumph over death for us, it is also appropriate to acknowledge the power to save and heal that still exists in this context. Jesus in fact *commanded* us to remember him in the breaking of bread: "*Do* this in remembrance of me" (Luke 22:19). As this act of remembrance is observed and obeyed by disciples in first-century Troas or twenty-first century Toronto, and everywhere in between, the story of Eutychus and a Eucharist reminds us of our resurrected Lord's power to heal and restore.

---

14. See *ACCA*, 245–46.
15. Alexander, *Acts*, 155; cf. Fitzmyer, *Acts*, 667–68.

CHAPTER 46

Acts 20:17-38

LISTEN to the Story

¹⁷From Miletus, Paul sent to Ephesus for the elders of the church. ¹⁸When they arrived, he said to them: "You know how I lived the whole time I was with you, from the first day I came into the province of Asia. ¹⁹I served the Lord with great humility and with tears and in the midst of severe testing by the plots of my Jewish opponents. ²⁰You know that I have not hesitated to preach anything that would be helpful to you but have taught you publicly and from house to house. ²¹I have declared to both Jews and Greeks that they must turn to God in repentance and have faith in our Lord Jesus.

²²"And now, compelled by the Spirit, I am going to Jerusalem, not knowing what will happen to me there. ²³I only know that in every city the Holy Spirit warns me that prison and hardships are facing me. ²⁴However, I consider my life worth nothing to me; my only aim is to finish the race and complete the task the Lord Jesus has given me—the task of testifying to the good news of God's grace.

²⁵"Now I know that none of you among whom I have gone about preaching the kingdom will ever see me again. ²⁶Therefore, I declare to you today that I am innocent of the blood of any of you. ²⁷For I have not hesitated to proclaim to you the whole will of God. ²⁸Keep watch over yourselves and all the flock of which the Holy Spirit has made you overseers. Be shepherds of the church of God, which he bought with his own blood. ²⁹I know that after I leave, savage wolves will come in among you and will not spare the flock. ³⁰Even from your own number men will arise and distort the truth in order to draw away disciples after them. ³¹So be on your guard! Remember that for three years I never stopped warning each of you night and day with tears.

³²"Now I commit you to God and to the word of his grace, which can build you up and give you an inheritance among all those who are sanctified. ³³I have not coveted anyone's silver or gold or clothing. ³⁴You

yourselves know that these hands of mine have supplied my own needs and the needs of my companions. ³⁵In everything I did, I showed you that by this kind of hard work we must help the weak, remembering the words the Lord Jesus himself said: 'It is more blessed to give than to receive.'"

³⁶When Paul had finished speaking, he knelt down with all of them and prayed. ³⁷They all wept as they embraced him and kissed him. ³⁸What grieved them most was his statement that they would never see his face again. Then they accompanied him to the ship.

Listening to the Text in the Story: 1 Samuel 12:3; Jeremiah 26:2; 42:4; Ezekiel 3:17–19; 22:27; Zephaniah 3:3; Ephesians 1:14; Philippians 3:1–19; Colossians 1:12; 2:4–23; 3:24; 1 Timothy 1:3–10, 19b–20; 4:1–3, 7; 6:3–10, 20–21; 2 Timothy 2:14–18; Titus 1:3.

EXPLAIN the Story

Paul's farewell speech to the Ephesian elders is not only a fitting goodbye to this group of friends, it is also an appropriate conclusion to his missionary journeys. This speech, while a fitting testament, is far from triumphalistic. It reflects humility and humanity, tears and trials, service and suffering. There are numerous extended speeches by Paul in Acts: to a Jewish synagogue in Pisidian Antioch (Acts 13); to the Areopagus in Athens (ch. 17); to a Jerusalem crowd (ch. 22); to the council in Jerusalem (ch. 23); and during his trials (chs. 24, 25, 26). This address to the Ephesian elders is Paul's only speech delivered exclusively to believers. It is reminiscent of the final and solemn declarations of OT luminaries—such as Jacob, Joshua, Samuel, Jeremiah, and Ezekiel. The address strikes many similar themes that occur elsewhere in Paul's own prison letters—themes of suffering, pastoral concern, and warning. This episode begins with a request for the Ephesian elders to come to Miletus (vv. 17–18a). After their arrival, Paul offers his emotional address to the elders (vv. 18b–35). The scene closes with a description of a tearful goodbye as Paul is accompanied to his departing ship (vv. 36–38).

The Ephesian Elders Are Called to Miletus (20:17–18a)

Paul's ship sailed south past the port of Ephesus to Miletus. As was noted in the previous section (Acts 20:13–16), this may not have been a decision intended to *avoid* being delayed in Ephesus. It may have been simply the fastest route Paul and his companions could secure as they attempted to make Jerusalem before the Feast of Pentecost—especially after being delayed a full week in Troas near the outset of their journey (v. 6). Paul would know many people in Ephesus after his three-year stay in that city. It would not have been feasible for everyone from the church there to travel the fifty kilometers (30 miles) south to Miletus. In this circumstance, he bids an unspecified number of church leaders—"elders" (*presbyteroi*)—to join him. The term is a common designation for a leader and here does not simply refer to an elderly person. The word is derived from the OT (e.g., Josh 20:4; Ruth 4:2) and was used in many Jewish (e.g., Luke 7:3; 9:22; Acts 4:5; 1QS VI, 8) and Christian communities (e.g., Acts 11:30; 14:23; 15:2, 4, 22, 23; 16:4; 1 Tim 5:17; Titus 1:5; Jas 5:14; Rev 4:4). All told, this stopover in Miletus would have entailed at least three days: a day to send a messenger by ship to the port of Priene, and then by foot (along the coast road) to Ephesus; a day return with the elders; and a day devoted to speaking with the elders in Miletus.

Paul's Farewell Speech to the Ephesian Elders (20:18b–35)

Paul's solemn farewell to the elders unfolds in several stages, with each successive stage opening with a short "[and] now" (*kai nyn*, vv. 22, 25, 32). First, Paul reminds them of how he lived and spoke among them (vv. 18b–21) in the *past*. Next, he tells them how the Spirit is leading him toward Jerusalem in the *present* (vv. 22–24). After this, he issues firm pastoral admonitions in view of the *future* (vv. 25–31). He finishes with a closing benediction (vv. 32–35). Although there is a sense of chronological movement in the address (past-present-future), throughout each stage the message is punctuated with references to Paul's example among them in the past. These reminders of his example not only confirm what he accomplished among them but provide a model for how the elders are to continue to serve the Ephesian church.

Paul's farewell words are simple and emotive. He begins by reminding them what they know from experience about him. He confesses, "You know how I lived" (v. 18), and how "I . . . preach[ed] . . . taught. . . . declared" (vv. 20, 21). His tears (vv. 19, 31, 37; cf. 2 Cor 2:4) speak to the deep emotional engagement of his ministry. The lordship of Christ (vv. 19, 21) brackets and roots the pathos of this service. Like the earnest service of the prophets of old, Paul has held nothing back in the verbal content that accompanied his personal connection with them. Just as Jeremiah was sworn not to omit a word from the Lord to the people of Judah (Jer 26:2; 42:4), Paul urged the Ephesians to radical life change before God and radical trust in Jesus. A further sense of the solemnity of his proclamation is conveyed by the Greek verb *diamartyromai* that is used several times in the speech and translated as "declare" (Acts 20:21;

cf. v. 26 [*martyromai*]), "warns" (v. 23), and "testifying" (v. 24). At the heart of this word is *martys*—a word that means "one who witnesses." It describes elsewhere those who bear costly testimony to Christ, even as far as becoming a *martyr* (e.g., Acts 1:22; 22:15; 26:16; Rev 2:13; 17:6).

Paul is aware of the potential cost of his witness. In fact, he alerts them ("and now," Acts 20:22) to the fact that in this present moment the Spirit "compels" (v. 22) him to go to Jerusalem and "warns" (*diamartyromai*, v. 23) him that there are hard times and imprisonment ahead.[1] Paul will testify to this by frequent reference to his circumstances "in chains" in several of his letters (e.g., Eph 6:20; Phil 1:7, 13, 14, 17; Col 4:18; Phlm 13; 2 Tim 2:9). The point in mentioning this awareness is not to emphasize his suffering but the fact that this is part of the Spirit's leading and is directly related to his calling given to him by the Lord Jesus (Acts 20:24; cf. Gal 1:1; Titus 1:3). Paul is aware that the present leading of the *Spirit* is rooted in the prior call from *Jesus* (see Acts 9:15) so that he might testify to *God's* grace. Once again, the Trinitarian shape of gospel declaration—whether it is Paul's or that of others—is reflected in the narrative of Acts (e.g., 1:4, 6–8; 2:33, 38–39; 5:29–32; 10:38).[2]

After speaking about his past ministry in Ephesus and the present leading of the Spirit, the speech shifts—with another climactic "now" (v. 25)—to an extended focus on pastoral admonitions that will be important for the future. The first future reality he alerts them to is the fact that they will not see him again. He has faithfully discharged his task of proclaiming to them *who* and *what* they need to know: King Jesus and his kingdom. The phrase "the kingdom of God" (shortened to "the kingdom" at v. 25) is the phrase used periodically in Acts to summarize the content of the Christian faith (e.g., 1:3; 8:12; 19:8; 28:23, 31). For his part, echoing the solemn charge God gave to Ezekiel, Paul is "innocent of the blood of any of you" (20:26; cf. Ezek 3:17–19). That is, anyone who has heard him speak will not be able to argue that they could not affirm Jesus as their Lord because Paul did not explain to them this good news. Paul held nothing back; he discharged all that he had to give—the whole will of God (Acts 20:27; cf. v. 20: "anything that would be helpful to you"). Now the baton of pastoral leadership is passed to the elders.

Paul draws on a preeminent "pastoral" image to describe their future task, that of flock and shepherds (vv. 28–29). These are familiar images from the OT (e.g., Ps 78:52, 70; Isa 40:11; Mic 5:4). Jesus also drew on images of sheep and shepherds to describe his ministry. Interestingly he applied both

---

1. Dunn, *Acts*, 272, notes how Paul's missions both begin (13:2, 4; 16:6–7) and end with the Spirit's direction.
2. See Simon Gathercole, "The Trinity in the Synoptic Gospels and Acts," in *The Oxford Handbook of the Trinity*, ed. G. Emery and M. Levering (Oxford: Oxford University Press, 2011), 55–68.

images to himself in that he is both the "good shepherd" (John 10:11–16) who cares for his sheep and also "the Lamb of God," the Passover lamb, who takes away the sin of the world (1:29; cf. Luke 22:7–20).[3] Paul then emphasizes the task facing the Ephesian elders with two imperatives: "Keep watch" (v. 28) and "be on your guard!" (v. 31). The fundamental requirement for shepherds is alertness, starting with themselves and then extending to those they are shepherding. But what should they be alert to? They are to be alert to the conduct of their life and the content of their teaching (1 Tim 4:16). This is made clear by the following sentence where malicious figures are mentioned— "wolves"—who will try and destroy the "flock" (Acts 20:29; cf. Ezek 22:27; Zeph 3:3; Matt 7:15). There will not only be wolves from without, but also wolves from within, "even from your own number." The threat is then spelled out as those who will "distort the truth" (v. 30). The threat, and eventual impact, of false teaching is echoed in many of Paul's letters, including those written from prison. Paul writes powerfully and pastorally to warn against false teaching (e.g., Phil 3:1–19; Col 2:4–23), some of which originates within the church in Ephesus (e.g., 1 Tim 1:3–10, 19b–20; 4:1–3, 7; 6:3–10, 20–21; 2 Tim 2:14–18).

The final climactic peak in Paul's speech—indicated again by the word "now" (v. 32)—expresses his benediction for them. Paul reminds them that although he is leaving, God remains. The future is secure for them, whatever wolves may come. Paul reinforces this encouragement with words familiar in many of his own letters, including: "grace" (*charis*, a word included in the benedictions of almost every Pauline letter), "build up" (*oikodomeō*; 1 Cor 8:1; 10:23; 14:4 ["edifies"], 17 ["edified"]; 1 Thess 5:11), "inheritance" (*klēronomia*; Gal 3:18; Eph 1:14, 18; 5:5; Col 3:24), and "sanctify" (*hagiazō*; Rom 15:16; 1 Cor 1:2; 6:11; Eph 5:26; 1 Thess 5:23; 1 Tim 4:5; 2 Tim 2:21).[4] Again, Paul appeals to his own example of life and work to urge that the elders lead not because of what they can get but for what they can give (Acts 20:34). Paul, whenever possible, took pride in providing for his needs by working with his own hands (Acts 18:3; cf. 1 Cor 4:12; 9:15–18; 1 Thess 2:9). However, even more important than his own example in this regard are the words of Jesus. Paul cites the Lord Jesus himself to drive his point home: "It is more

---

3. The language of v. 28 is challenging, and many manuscripts read "the church of the Lord" instead of "the church of God." The first option is explainable, as scribes may have wanted to avoid the impression that the crucifixion involved God's own blood. Either way, this is unusual language for Acts, but it does reflect Pauline themes evident in his letters (e.g., Rom 3:25; 5:9; Eph 1:7). Gaventa, *Acts*, 288, suggests, "Perhaps the phrase comes about here under the influence of the reference to blood in v. 26. Paul's innocence with respect to the blood of the elders prompts an identification of Jesus's death as an outpouring of blood."

4. Longenecker, *Acts*, 513–14.

blessed to give than to receive" (v. 35). These words are not recorded in any of the canonical Gospels, "but its spirit is expressed in many other sayings of Jesus which they record."[5] As Dunn adds, "This simply reminds us that not everything taught by Jesus has been preserved, and that there are a number of such sayings preserved outside the canonical Gospels which may well go back to Jesus himself."[6] With these words of Jesus, Paul's speech comes to a fitting, and an abrupt, end.

A Tearful and Prayerful Goodbye (20:36–38)

This entire episode has been anointed with tears. Tears are mentioned at the beginning (Acts 20:19), in the middle (v. 31), and now at the end (v. 37) of the speech. Not every reader or interpreter of the NT views the apostle Paul as a warm and affectionate person. Still, this is not the impression Luke provides as the travel-worn apostle bids a final goodbye to his Ephesian friends and coworkers. Luke does not tell us what they prayed. It seems more fitting that the final words recorded between them are the words of Jesus (v. 35) rather than their prayers for one another. Still, he narrates what he saw. And what he witnessed was a small group of believers—unnoticed by the world of its day apart from perhaps an impatient captain urging them to board his vessel—kneeling, praying, and weeping. It is a tender scene. There is mutual affection between Paul and his friends created and sustained by their common fellowship with the Lord Jesus. This is a fitting conclusion with which to end Paul's missionary travels. After he reaches Jerusalem, his travels will no longer be as a missionary but as a Roman prisoner. For now, there is an elegiac tone to the scene, as if they were saying farewell to a friend at the funeral.

LIVE the Story

Paul—An Example We Can Follow

Luke narrates extraordinary occurrences in the life of Paul. Besides Paul's Damascus Road experience with the risen Jesus, he describes exciting missionary journeys, nighttime visions, and remarkable exploits. In Ephesus alone, God did astonishing things through Paul. The handkerchiefs he used to wipe his sweaty brow and bits of his work apron became instruments used to heal the sick and drive out demons (19:11–12). It can be somewhat intimidating—no less for Christian elders in the twenty-first century than for the

---

5. Bruce, *Acts*, 395; cf. Matt 10:8; Luke 6:38; 11:9–13; John 13:34. Paul, while not often directly quoting Jesus, is aware of Jesus's teaching (see Rom 14:14; 1 Cor 7:10; 11:24–25; 1 Thess 4:15).
6. Dunn, *Acts*, 275.

Ephesian elders in the first century—to hear Paul's Miletus address and recognize that he repeatedly turns to his own example to exhort his listeners. This is not uncommon for Paul. In fact, it resonates with Paul's own letters where he offers himself (e.g., 1 Cor 11:1; Phil 3:17; 2 Thess 3:9) and others (e.g., 1 Thess 1:7; 1 Tim 4:12; Titus 2:7) as models for imitation. "Follow me" is one of the first imperatives Jesus extends to disciples, and Paul, like his Lord, is willing to offer the same invitation. Incarnate models are important if we are going to live the story of salvation. Living examples do with their bodies what Scripture does with words.

As helpful as Paul's example may be, however, it can also be daunting. The call to follow Paul's example may feel like a novice skier at the bottom of a hill watching an Olympic racer who comes flying down a dangerous run, stops in front of the skier with a spray of ice and snow, lifts their goggles and says, "Now you try that!" Really? Me? I'm an ordinary person. How can I possibly imitate a pro? In answering this question, it is important to recognize what Paul does and does *not* appeal to when he offers his life as an example. That is, he does *not* point to his unique encounter with Jesus on the Damascus Road. He does *not* point to his visionary experiences. He does *not* point to miracles God did through him. Instead of these things, Paul signals his observable *character*, his open *communication*, and his singular *commitment* to God as those qualities to be pursued by those who follow his example. Now *these* are things that all of us *can* and *should* imitate.

Paul's Character

Paul begins by reminding his Ephesian friends what they know about his character. Rather than appealing to his unique call *from* the Lord, he reminds them of his humble service *to* the Lord (v. 19). He regards this service, despite incurring trials and hardships, as part of the joyful task of letting others in on the extravagance of God's grace (v. 24). Instead of appealing to the miracles induced through his sweaty handkerchiefs and dirty aprons, he reminds them how hard he worked with his own hands to provide for his needs and those of others (vv. 34–35). Paul was aware that local residents often considered itinerant teachers like him to be hucksters—people who were out to defraud others of their hard-earned money. The same can still be said of some Christian leaders who seem more interested in wealth and image than in character and godly conduct. Yet, he reminds the elders, "I have not coveted anyone's silver or gold or clothing" (v. 33). The word *love* never appears in this address (in fact, it never appears in Acts!), but the quality of the conduct he describes bears the marks of one who loved those he served (v. 38). This love toward his family in Christ may also account for the references to "tears" in his address

(vv. 19, 31) and the weeping (v. 37) as Paul departed. This kind of emotional connection between people is not formed at a distance. These bonds of affection are the result of intimate and frequent connection, the kind that happens in homes, at table, and over long conversation. Paul demonstrated his character through humble service, long obedience, diligent work, and personal engagement. These are not easy qualities to imitate, but they were attainable for the Ephesians and continue to be a model for Christian leaders today.

Paul's Communication

The first thing Paul highlighted as exemplary was his character—*"you know how I lived"* (v. 18). The second thing he highlighted was his communication—*"you know* that I have not hesitated to preach" (v. 20). In fact, Paul seems to pull out every related verb he can think of to describe how he articulated truth to the Ephesians: preach (*anangellō*, vv. 20, 27); teach (*didaskō*, v. 20); declare (*diamartyromai*, v. 21; *martyromai*, v. 26); proclaim (*kēryssō*, v. 25); and warn (*noutheteō*, v. 31). In every way, Paul endeavored to use whatever verbal means he had available to him to tell others what would be helpful for them in knowing the whole will of God (v. 27). Paul is concerned that after he departs false teachers will emerge who will "distort the truth" (v. 30). He does not explain how they will do so, but he does flag up one mark of concern: they will "draw away disciples *after them*" (v. 30). Paul's communication continually drew disciples closer to God; false teachers continually draw disciples to themselves. This is an important warning for us as Christian preachers and teachers today. Does our speech attract people to us, or does it attract them to God? Paul's example is clear. His job is to testify to the good news of *God's* extravagant generosity, not to the eloquence of his speech.

Paul's Commitment

Athletic metaphors can be helpful. In the arena, out on the field, or in the starter's block, an athlete is exposed, and details about them and their performance are observable. Athletes don't carry extra baggage when competing. Good athletes have singular vision and commitment. There may be a significant investment of resources to train an athlete, but once in the race the aim must be on just one thing. In his farewell address to the Ephesians, Paul employs an athletic image to illustrate his commitment (Acts 20:24; cf. Phil 3:12–14; 2 Tim 4:7). Like a runner in a race, his "aim" is to finish well. For him, finishing the race means testifying to the good news of God's grace (v. 24). His desire was that everyone—Jews *and* Greeks—turn to God (v. 21). From this one vision there may be many fruitful by-products, but the focus remains on one thing. The motivation in all of this is what must be the aim in all our work: to invite people into a close relationship with God as experienced in the community of his people. This is why Paul's words to his dear friends conclude with "now *I commit you to God* and to the word of his grace, which can build you up and give you an inheritance *among all those who are sanctified*" (v. 32). This is a commitment we can trust; this is the community where we can learn the whole will of God. This is an example and a commitment that disciples can follow wherever and whenever we are sent to serve as "shepherds of the church of God" (v. 28).

Paul is an "apostle"—literally "one who is sent." This was a designation that Jesus gave him and an identity he embodied everywhere he went. More than that, as Eugene Peterson encourages us, this relates to all of us as we seek to imitate Paul:

> [Apostle] defines something basic about our nature as Christians. This is not a static thing. It's not a matter of nomenclature, putting the right name on us. For each and every one of us, the Christian life is apostolic. God is sending us to reach others with the gospel, sometimes at great distances geographically or emotionally. Now, remember where we are in Paul's life [in Acts 20]. He was near the end, with a lot of adventure and accomplishment behind him. But instead of sitting back, he set sail. And, in doing so, he set an example for all of us.[7]

---

7. Peterson, *Conversations*, 1721.

CHAPTER 47

Acts 21:1-17

 LISTEN to the Story

¹After we had torn ourselves away from them, we put out to sea and sailed straight to Kos. The next day we went to Rhodes and from there to Patara. ²We found a ship crossing over to Phoenicia, went on board and set sail. ³After sighting Cyprus and passing to the south of it, we sailed on to Syria. We landed at Tyre, where our ship was to unload its cargo. ⁴We sought out the disciples there and stayed with them seven days. Through the Spirit they urged Paul not to go on to Jerusalem. ⁵When it was time to leave, we left and continued on our way. All of them, including wives and children, accompanied us out of the city, and there on the beach we knelt to pray. ⁶After saying goodbye to each other, we went aboard the ship, and they returned home.

⁷We continued our voyage from Tyre and landed at Ptolemais, where we greeted the brothers and sisters and stayed with them for a day. ⁸Leaving the next day, we reached Caesarea and stayed at the house of Philip the evangelist, one of the Seven. ⁹He had four unmarried daughters who prophesied.

¹⁰After we had been there a number of days, a prophet named Agabus came down from Judea. ¹¹Coming over to us, he took Paul's belt, tied his own hands and feet with it and said, "The Holy Spirit says, 'In this way the Jewish leaders in Jerusalem will bind the owner of this belt and will hand him over to the Gentiles.'"

¹²When we heard this, we and the people there pleaded with Paul not to go up to Jerusalem. ¹³Then Paul answered, "Why are you weeping and breaking my heart? I am ready not only to be bound, but also to die in Jerusalem for the name of the Lord Jesus." ¹⁴When he would not be dissuaded, we gave up and said, "The Lord's will be done."

¹⁵After this, we started on our way up to Jerusalem. ¹⁶Some of the disciples from Caesarea accompanied us and brought us to the home of Mnason, where we were to stay. He was a man from Cyprus and one of

the early disciples. ⁱ⁷When we arrived at Jerusalem, the brothers and sisters received us warmly.

Listening to the Text in the Story: 1 Kings 22:11; Psalms 40:6–8; 50:5; Isaiah 20:2–4; Jeremiah 13:1–11; Matthew 20:19; 26:35; Luke 18:32; 22:42; 1 Thessalonians 5:21.

EXPLAIN the Story

In this section the usage of the first-person plural ("we") narrative resumes (v. 1) and continues until Paul reaches Jerusalem (v. 18). This explains the eyewitness color and content that comes through in these "we" portions. For example, there are vivid details about the journey ("sighting Cyprus and passing to the south of it," v. 3), people ("all of them, including wives and children," v. 5), and anecdotal features ("where our ship was to unload its cargo," v. 3; kneeling to pray "on the beach," v. 5). Luke also resumes the narrative pattern—travel/event/travel—that he established when Paul began the journey to Jerusalem from Ephesus (20:1).

Following the tearful goodbye in Miletus, the company continues their journey southeast by ship around the corner of Asia, past the island of Cyprus, until they reach the coastal ports in Phoenicia and Palestine (21:1–9). After arriving in Caesarea, Luke recounts a dramatic address from the Jerusalem prophet Agabus (vv. 10–14). Paul travels the final hundred-kilometer leg overland by foot, or possibly by horse,[1] from Caesarea to Jerusalem (vv. 15–17). All told, this so-called "third missionary journey," which began in Antioch (18:23) and ends in arrest in Jerusalem, traverses more than 4,300 kilometers (about 2,700 miles) in the course of approximately three years. After Paul's arrest, he will be transported back to Caesarea where he will remain imprisoned for several years (ca. AD 57–59) before finally appealing to Caesar for judgment.[2]

From Miletus to Caesarea (21:1–9)

The note of remorse continues as the Ephesian elders escort Paul and his companions to the ship where, at the last, Luke writes, "After we had torn

---

1. Chrysostom, *Homily* 45, in *ACCA*, 261–62, infers this. Cf. Ramsay, *St. Paul*, 230.
2. See Alexander, "Chronology of Paul," *DPL* 115–23.

ourselves away from them" (v. 1).³ Their travel from Miletus continues off the southwest coast of Asia in a southeasterly course with stops on the island of Kos,⁴ then the larger island of Rhodes, before reaching Patara, a seaport in the province of Lycia. From there they likely boarded a larger merchant cargo vessel that did not need to hug the coastline, but could take the shorter route traversing the Mediterranean Sea (about 650 kilometers/400 miles), bypassing the large island of Cyprus, on its way to Phoenicia. They landed first in Tyre, an important port and trading center. In Tyre, while the merchant ship unloaded over the course of seven days, the traveling party sought out disciples in the city. Since they had made good time in crossing the Mediterranean, they could afford to wait until the ship was ready to sail and still make Jerusalem before Pentecost (cf. 20:16).

The church in Tyre—in the region of Phoenicia and part of the Roman province of Syria—was likely founded after the dispersion of Hellenists from Jerusalem that occurred after Stephen was killed (cf. 11:19). No one in the group appears to know anyone in the church in Tyre since they had to seek out fellow believers there. It is a testimony to the importance of hospitality among early Christians that these nine strangers were hosted for an entire week. Few travelers would willingly stay in ancient boarding houses or wayside inns. Brian Rapske alerts us why by observing that "the available literary and archeological sources generally witness to dilapidated and unclean facilities, virtually non-existent furnishings, bed-bugs, poor quality food and drink, untrustworthy proprietors and staff, shady clientele, and generally loose morals."⁵ These generalizations provide context for the frequent appeals in the NT encouraging hospitality between Christians, known or unknown (e.g., Rom 12:13; 1 Tim 3:2; Titus 1:8; Heb 13:2; 1 Pet 4:9; 3 John).

As the company leaves Tyre, the goodbye on the beach is reminiscent of the farewell in Miletus (Acts 20:36–38). As such, the believers gather together and kneel to pray (21:5). Another important similarity that carries through in Tyre is the voice of the Spirit. As Paul noted in Miletus, "I only know that in every city the Holy Spirit warns me that prison and hardships are facing me" (20:23). This is echoed now in Tyre where the Spirit affirms this reality to these unnamed disciples. The prophetic voice of the Spirit is gaining focus in the narrative by first speaking in every city, then through this group of "disciples" in Tyre (21:4), soon to be narrowed to Philip's "four unmarried daughters

---

3. Bruce, *Acts*, 397, suggests we give the passive of the Greek verb *apospaō* ("to tear away") its "full force," noting that "the same verb is used in the active voice in 20:30 in the pejorative sense of enticing people to follow false teaching."
4. Hippocrates founded his famous medical school in the fifth-century BC on this island.
5. Rapske, "Acts, Travel and Shipwreck," 15.

who prophesied" (v. 9) in Caesarea, until finally the prophetic Spirit reaches a sharpened point in the singular prophet, Agabus from Jerusalem (vv. 10–11). In Tyre, in light of the Spirit's revelation, the disciples urge Paul not to continue on to Jerusalem (v. 12). This evokes the "tests" that Jesus received from his own disciples when he revealed to them the suffering and hardship that awaited him in Jerusalem. The warnings are well intended, but they illustrate what Paul will relate in his own letters (e.g., 1 Thess 5:19–21), namely, that prophecies inspired by the Spirit must not be regarded with contempt, but they also must be tested so that the Spirit's intention is appropriately discerned.[6]

After their weeklong stay in Tyre, the company continued south on the ship to Caesarea, briefly stopping at Ptolemais (Acts 21:7). In Caesarea, the administrative seat of the province of Judea, Philip "the evangelist"[7] reemerges in the story after a twenty-year absence (v. 8). Philip first entered the story as one of "the Seven" chosen to care for the Hellenistic-Jewish widows in Jerusalem (6:5). We next encounter him as he evangelizes in Samaria and along the Judean coast until he eventually settles in the port city of Caesarea (8:40). While enjoying the hospitality of Philip's home, Luke mentions his four "unmarried" (i.e., virgin) daughters who are also recognized prophets (21:9). The ancient historian Eusebius, recording the words of Polycrates (ca. AD 130–196), bishop of Ephesus, notes that Philip and his famed daughters moved to Hierapolis in Asia. Apparently, Philip's daughters lived long and esteemed lives as prophets there.[8] In Acts, these women do not deliver any specific words in the narrative. Their inclusion, however, is not incidental. Besides standing in the long tradition of women prophets such as Miriam (Exod 15:20), Deborah (Judg 4:4), and Anna (Luke 2:36), they are a reminder that these are the last days when the Spirit is poured out on all people, with the result that "your sons and *daughters* will prophesy" (Acts 2:17). Further, the mention of the presence of four young prophets sets up the event to follow when Agabus, speaking on behalf of the Spirit, will deliver a dramatic prophetic message to Paul.

The Holy Spirit Speaks through Agabus (21:10–14)

Much as Philip reemerged in the narrative after a long absence, so too the prophet Agabus returns. The last time Agabus spoke "through the Spirit" (11:28) was in Antioch when he predicted a severe famine during the reign of Claudius. Once again, Agabus came down from Judea to speak (21:10; cf. 11:27). This time, he not only speaks a word of prophecy but enacts it.

---

6. Ramsay, *St. Paul*, 228.
7. This distinguishes him from Philip "the apostle."
8. Eusebius, *Hist. eccl.* 3.31.2–5 in *ACCA*, 259–60.

Acting in a similar manner to former Hebrew prophets (e.g., 1 Kgs 11:29–39; 22:11; Isa 20:2–4; Jer 13:1–11), Agabus took Paul's belt[9] and tied up his own hands and feet. This dramatic gesture was to indicate how the Jews in Jerusalem would bind Paul and hand him over to the gentiles. Technically the prophecy is not accurate. The Jews in Jerusalem who would seize Paul did not hand him over willingly to the Roman commander (Acts 21:33). Several things are, however, noteworthy in this scene. First, while the words are spoken by Agabus, the text explicitly notes that this is what "the Holy Spirits *says*" (v. 11). "To speak" is a personal verb. "To speak" is also an active verb. It is important to notice that the person of the Holy Spirit frequently speaks and directs the action throughout Acts (e.g., 8:29, 39; 10:19; 11:12; 13:2, 4; 15:28; 16:6–7; 20:23; 28:25).

Second, Luke illustrates the importance of the discernment of prophetic messages for the church. The disciples plead with Paul not to go on to Jerusalem in light of the Spirit's revelation (21:12). Even so, while the Spirit may reveal truth about Paul's future to his friends, they are willing to relinquish Paul to his commitment by confessing, "The Lord's will be done" (v. 14). Yet even in Paul's tenacity, there is tenderness in the scene. As Ramsay memorably expresses, "Even the weeping entreaties of his dearest friends could not break his resolve, though they might break his heart."[10]

Finally, the scene echoes the passion of Jesus before his arrest in Jerusalem in the following elements: the prediction that Paul will be handed over to the gentiles (v. 11; cf. Luke 18:32), the weeping and anguish among friends (v. 13; cf. Luke 22:44), and the commitment to suffer if it is the Lord's will (v. 14; cf. Luke 22:42). All these aspects reinforce the theological parallels that Luke makes between the life of Jesus and the life of Paul, an observation that theologians have made since at least the time of Origen (ca. AD 200–250).[11]

From Caesarea to Jerusalem (21:15–17)

The last stage of the travel narrative entails a two- or three-day journey (about a hundred kilometers, or sixty miles) from Caesarea to Jerusalem. The retinue escorting Paul for this last leg was substantial. In addition to his eight companions, "some" of the disciples from Caesarea accompanied them. Upon arriving in Jerusalem, they all stay with an otherwise unknown Christian

---

9. This belt (*zōnē*) was a long piece of cloth or leather wrapped around the waist that could also be used to hold money or other small items (e.g., writing instruments); see BDAG 431.
10. Ramsay, *St. Paul*, 229. This echoes Jerome's much earlier sentiment found in *Letters* 14.3: "The battering ram of natural affection, which so often shatters faith, must recoil powerless from the wall of the gospel." See *ACCA*, 261.
11. See Origen, *Commentary on Matthew* in *ACCA*, 260–61. Cf. Bruce, *Acts*, 402; Peterson, *Acts*, 581.

named Mnason (v. 16). Two details are mentioned about Mnason. First, like Barnabas he was a native of Cyprus (4:36), and also like Barnabas he may have been a wealthy diaspora Jew who has returned to Jerusalem. His financial means is suggested by the fact that his household could room and board a large company of visitors. Second, Mnason was one of the "early disciples" (v. 16). Alongside Philip and Agabus, this mention of Mnason as an early disciple builds another bridge between Paul and the early church in Jerusalem—some of whose members may still have been suspicious of this former persecutor.[12] The importance of this connection will become evident in the next episode when Jerusalem Christians begin asking Paul about his rumored mission strategy (see 21:20–25).

Beyond these two anecdotal notes about Mnason, little else is known about this man. The travel narrative finally concludes with a simple statement that the brothers and sisters of the Jerusalem church warmly welcome the visiting company (v. 17). With this, the return journey to Jerusalem that was initially contemplated at the beginning of this panel (19:21) and embarked on from Ephesus (20:1) is now complete.

LIVE the Story

Christian Hospitality

When my congregation is blessed to host visiting theologians, scholars, teachers, or other guests, we normally try to lodge them in parishioner homes rather than putting them in hotels. Although there is the matter of cost savings for us, it is both a duty and a joy to welcome visiting Christians into our homes. We view this as a fundamental Christian practice.[13] In *Meeting God in Paul*, Rowan Williams writes:

> "[The] language of welcoming, of receiving or accepting, is something which Paul clearly likes to use. It comes out very strongly, for example, in the later chapters of the letter to the Romans [e.g., 14:3; 15:7; etc.]. . . . 'Welcome,' 'acceptance,' 'receiving': the words blend into each other but the central theme is clear: God has received us into the community that he wills and designs; and so our attitude to one another must be consistent with God's, an attitude of welcome or acceptance."[14]

---

12. Peterson, *Acts*, 576.
13. For a recent discussion on the topic of Christian hospitality, see Joshua W. Jipp, *Saved by Faith and Hospitality* (Grand Rapids: Eerdmans, 2017).
14. Rowan Williams, *Meeting God in Paul* (Louisville: Westminster John Knox, 2015), 30–31.

Hospitality is a universal phenomenon, and it was important in both the first-century Greco-Roman and Jewish cultures. Hospitality for Romans and Jews, however, was prescribed rigidly according to class, ethnicity, or gender. One could not welcome just anyone into their home and sit at table with them. (This is why Peter resisted the Spirit's leading to visit Cornelius in his home; see Acts 10:9–17, 28.) In contrast, notions about hospitality were to be radically different for those who understood themselves to be one in Christ Jesus. Table fellowship was not restricted according to race, or class, or gender (cf. Gal 3:28).

As Paul and his companions traveled throughout the Roman Empire, they relied on the hospitality of other Christians, even from Christians with whom they had no personal connection—as they did in cities like Tyre (Acts 21:4) or in the home of Mnason (v. 16). What this signaled was that there was a deeper commonality that went beyond the normal ties of friendship or kinship. What they were demonstrating in action was that the gospel had the ability to draw together remarkably different groups of people. As the newly constituted people of God, their fundamental identity marker was their common relationship in Christ. This is why Paul would write to the Roman believers, "In Christ we, though many, form one body, and each member belongs to all the others" (Rom 12:5; cf. 1 Cor 10:17; 12:12–14; Eph 4:4).

Christian hospitality is a powerful indicator of the gospel's effectiveness. In the first-century world, the gospel transformed masters and slaves into brothers and sisters; it transformed strangers into friends. While hotels and restaurants certainly have their place, a welcoming home and generous hospitality are a profound witness to the universal welcome of God and an effective means for breaking down barriers and establishing relational ties. Christ is the ultimate bridge-builder. Whether we are hosting known Christian theologians or unknown Christian visitors, God is vividly present when we open our doors. It is in our power to welcome Christ when we open our home. The fourth-century theologian John Chrysostom writes:

> Perhaps one of you will say, "If Paul was given to me as a guest to welcome, I would receive him readily and with great enthusiasm." But look, it is possible for you to welcome Paul's master as your guest, and you refuse. "For he who welcomes," says he, "the least among you welcomes me." Inasmuch as the brother is "the least," so much the more is Christ present through him. For he who welcomes the mighty often does so for the sake of vainglory, but he who welcomes the lowly does so honestly, for the sake of Christ. . . . Even if [a guest] is not Paul but a brother who believes and even if he is the least, Christ is present through him. Open your house, take him in.[15]

---

15. Chrysostom, *Homilies on the Acts of the Apostles* 45, in *ACCA*, 262.

Our world is becoming more and more fragmented and isolated along lines of race, culture, and status. Christian hospitality is one of the most important means we have to testify to the welcome we all share in Christ. Between Christians who come from divergent backgrounds or who normally reside far from one another, hospitality offered and received is a signal of our unity in Christ. When we extend hospitality even further beyond the household of God, our welcome and acceptance of others is a powerful and profound witness to the good news in Christ.

The Spirit, Suffering, and Hope

At the beginning of Advent in 2016, Scott, one of my parishioners, received news from his doctor that he had a serious form of cancer. After a routine checkup, some abnormalities were discovered, and upon further investigation oncologists revealed that cancerous lesions and tumors were in every major organ of his body. The doctors advised him and his wife, Karen, that he would not likely live to see Christmas and should put his affairs in order. Before his diagnosis, most people observing Scott would have seen a successful, fit, and charming middle-aged man. He is highly respected in the community and the beloved principal for one of the finest high schools in the province. After his diagnosis, as well-wishes poured in, many people asked Scott, "Why you? The community needs you, the school needs you, and the parish needs you. Besides, you look so healthy, and you are so deeply loved. Why would God allow this to happen to you?" Yet Scott, in his typically self-effacing manner replied, "Why *not* me?" As of this date, Scott, against all odds, continues to remind people that his ultimate hope does not rest in the health or comfort of his body; his hope is rooted in Christ and the promise of resurrection. Scott added, "Who knows what my testimony in walking through this crisis will mean for others and the gospel? Maybe this will be the most important lesson I teach my students."

The reason I relate Scott's story is because there are not many well-known Christian leaders in my immediate circles who, like the apostle Paul, are given advance notice by the Spirit that they will be arrested, handed over to pagan rulers, and face the possibility of execution for their faith. I have no doubt that there *are* Christian leaders today who do experience similar circumstances and trials like Paul in communities and regimes that are opposed to the gospel. Like Paul, their callings may involve the double vocation of being God's personal representative to the nations *and* to know how much suffering also accompanies this call (cf. Acts 9:15–16). Yet even apart from specific vocations like that, every Christian, like Scott, will face death. Some of us may be given the news in advance in a doctor's office, while some of us won't. But all of us will die, and all of us are called to live in such a way that our obedience to Christ allows the gospel to shine through us. It is important to remind ourselves that we belong to a kingdom that is not of this world. This kingdom is a future reality that is already present whenever and wherever people submit to God's reign and confess, "The Lord's will be done" (21:14).

There must have been something consoling for Paul in knowing that the future suffering that awaited him did not thrust itself upon him without God's awareness. The Spirit made known his upcoming arrest and suffering repeatedly as the apostle made his way to Jerusalem. The Spirit's awareness reminded him that the unholy trinity—the flesh, the world, and the devil—did not determine his ultimate reality. God did. God was at the center of his life, and the Lord's will took precedence. As Paul lived from that center, so we too must live from this core conviction so that when we are confronted with the good intentions and well-meaning questions—"Why you?"—from our friends and family, we will not be deflected from God's will. Paul could be confident that only God—not Jewish leaders or Roman rulers nor any threat of suffering or death—determined his ultimate future. All of us, like my friend Scott, can be confident that neither the diagnosis of a terminal illness nor the reality of our own death threatens our final existence. All of us are presented with the opportunity—either through the normal stresses of daily life or the intense stress of persecution and suffering—to reflect the light of the gospel and the hope of the resurrection. The tuning of our hearts to this truth will help us face death like another Christian woman I know. As she headed into hospice care, she asked her husband, "Now, help me live my dying well."

Sympathy in Mission

The Holy Spirit spoke to fellow believers about Paul's future circumstances, and the response on their part was deep concern. In fact, many of them had misgivings about Paul's course to continue to Jerusalem. While we might interpret these misgivings and Paul's decision to be at cross-purposes, there is something else that the knowledge given by the Spirit afforded them. It offered them an invitation for connection and participation in Paul's life and mission. These communities from Philippi to Jerusalem knew what was going to happen to Paul. For many of them, this may have been the last physical contact they would have with him. As hard as it was, this knowledge allowed them to grieve with him and to pray for him. As they parted, they would continue to be connected to him through prayer. Their prayers would not only be for the welfare of their beloved apostle and friend, but they could pray for the success of his gospel witness before rulers and kings—including Caesar himself.

The communities Paul founded may have eventually heard news of his condition and trials, but they did not have live updates or instant tweets from the apostle or Luke. What they did have, however, was the connection that comes through sympathy. Paul invites them to enter his suffering through the connective tissue of prayer. He did not model an individualistic stoicism as he walked toward his future. In fact, it is not Christian to think we suffer alone. Rather, by allowing others to participate in his suffering, Paul invited them to ongoing and active participation in his life and work. He allowed others to connect and engage in the larger work of the body of Christ and to the witness of the gospel. This engagement with others makes room for a healthy attitude toward suffering and death and, through the Spirit in prayer, for participation in mission.

In the end, Paul's Christlike witness to gentiles, Jews, and rulers is also a witness to believers about the fellowship of the Spirit and the God of hope. This is an enduring example to each of us since we will all die someday, perhaps even after prolonged suffering. As we face death, we do not have to do so alone. We are united with fellow Christian pilgrims who are all walking the same journey—whether we all acknowledge it or not. More importantly, we are united with Christ. He entered into our mortal life so that he could be united with us and exchange our death with his resurrection life.

CHAPTER 48

Acts 21:18-26

 ## LISTEN to the Story

¹⁸The next day Paul and the rest of us went to see James, and all the elders were present. ¹⁹Paul greeted them and reported in detail what God had done among the Gentiles through his ministry.

²⁰When they heard this, they praised God. Then they said to Paul: "You see, brother, how many thousands of Jews have believed, and all of them are zealous for the law. ²¹They have been informed that you teach all the Jews who live among the Gentiles to turn away from Moses, telling them not to circumcise their children or live according to our customs. ²²What shall we do? They will certainly hear that you have come, ²³so do what we tell you. There are four men with us who have made a vow. ²⁴Take these men, join in their purification rites and pay their expenses, so that they can have their heads shaved. Then everyone will know there is no truth in these reports about you, but that you yourself are living in obedience to the law. ²⁵As for the Gentile believers, we have written to them our decision that they should abstain from food sacrificed to idols, from blood, from the meat of strangled animals and from sexual immorality."

²⁶The next day Paul took the men and purified himself along with them. Then he went to the temple to give notice of the date when the days of purification would end and the offering would be made for each of them.

Listening to the Text in the Story: Numbers 6:1–21; Philippians 3:6.

 ## EXPLAIN the Story

Paul was familiar with Jerusalem. Although he grew up in Tarsus, he received education in Jerusalem under Gamaliel. After his conversion, he visited the city several times. On his last visit, he did so in fulfillment of a Nazirite vow he had taken in Cenchreae (Acts 18:18–22). This time, however, much has changed.

In terms of the Jerusalem church, James and "the elders" are in leadership—without any mention of Peter—and the church has grown substantially in size. The political climate in Jerusalem is also different. The mood is tense under the rule of governor Felix. This may account for the "zealous" fervor of the Jews in Jerusalem, including the "many thousands" of new Jewish believers. As Paul returns to Jerusalem, he must walk a tightrope in his efforts to demonstrate he is an observant Jew *and* to build bridges between the growing gentile and Jewish branches of the church.

This episode unfolds in three parts: first, a brief description of the greeting and report by Paul (21:18–19); second, the response by the Jerusalem leadership requesting that Paul demonstrate his commitment to the law and respect for the temple in order to dispel misinformation circulating about him (vv. 20–25); and third, another brief account, but this time describing Paul's submission to the request by the Jerusalem leadership (v. 26).

Greeting and Reporting (21:18–19)

The day after his arrival in Jerusalem, Paul meets with the Jerusalem church leadership. Several observations are noteworthy about this reunion. First, it is clear that James is the leader of the church. James, the brother of Jesus, has been taking a leading role for some time now, according to Luke's narrative (see 12:17; 15:13–21). There is no mention of Peter or other apostles at this gathering, but they may have been included within "the elders" (*presbyteroi*). Second, there is a clear indication that Paul must render a detailed account of what he has been doing the past few years. Since his split with Barnabas (15:39), this is all the more important since it was Barnabas who introduced him to the Jerusalem community in the first place and vouched for his credentials. It is vital for Paul to demonstrate that what he has been doing among the gentiles is from God. Hence, in Luke's description the emphasis is not simply on what Paul has done but what "*God had done . . . through* his ministry" (21:19). Again, we see the divine initiative taking precedence in the narrative and in Paul's report of his ministry (see 14:27; 15:4, 12). One final note is that the "we" perspective is dropped (cf. 16:10–17; 20:5–15; 21:1–18; 27:1–28:16). The narrative now resumes the account in the third person. Presumably, Luke is still with Paul in Jerusalem, but for literary reasons the focus has now shifted exclusively to Paul.

Paul and the Law (21:20–25)

The initial response to Paul's report seems positive: "They praised God" (v. 20a). However, the mood soon shifts. The leadership[1] now addresses Paul

---

1. For literary purposes, the leadership ("they") speaks with one voice.

with new realities in Jerusalem. To begin with, the church has grown by "many thousands of Jews" (v. 20b). This is all good. The shift begins with the ominous phrase that follows: "And all of them are *zealous* for the law" (21:20c).[2] Paul understands "zeal" for the law (see 22:3; cf. 2 Macc 4:2; Gal 1:14). Zeal for the law is not simply a matter of religious observance. It also has a sharp political dimension to it. Paul's pre-Christian zeal induced him to march off to Damascus in a rage to arrest Christian Jews (Acts 9:1–2; cf. Phil 3:6). The zealots in Judea were part of a revolutionary movement keen to overthrow Israel's oppressors, the Roman Empire. We know from the writings of the Jewish historian Josephus that revolutionary sentiment was building at this time under the rule of governor Felix (see Josephus, *J.W.* 2.247–70).[3] Jewish fundamentalist zeal targeted real or perceived collaboration or compromise with the gentile rulers. When Paul arrived to present a gift from the gentile church and to describe his ministry among the gentiles, the mood in Jerusalem was far from conducive to anything "gentile." The Jerusalem leadership is caught in the tension between a growing nationalistic fervor and a growing church of "zealous" Jewish believers.

In addition to this tense political and social situation, the Jerusalem leadership explains to Paul about rumors that are being spread by fellow Christian Jews regarding his teaching. Whereas Paul reported what God was doing among the gentiles in bringing them into the people of God, the leadership had a story to tell too. They know that his work among the nations also involves evangelism among the Jews. Wherever Paul traveled in the Roman Empire, if there was a Jewish synagogue in the vicinity, this is where he began his work. The Greek word Luke uses to describe what is being "informed" about Paul is *katēcheō* (v. 21). While this word does mean "to inform," it can also convey a sense of theological instruction (see Luke 1:4; Acts 18:25). In this instance, what is being informed—or misinformed—is that Paul is teaching that "all" diaspora Jews should "turn away" (*apostasia*) from observing the law of Moses. We have heard these charges before in the accusations made against Stephen (6:14; 7:48–49; cf. John 2:19). Specifically, they report that Paul instructs Jews not to circumcise their sons or walk according to their ancestral customs (e.g., the keeping of purity laws related to food and hospitality). Nowhere in Acts does Luke describe any occasion when Paul requires or instructs Jews who follow Messiah Jesus to turn from the law. As Alexander notes, Luke implies

---

2. Dunn, *Acts*, 284, suggests the reason why Luke does not mention the gentile collection Paul brought was because it was not welcome and may have been rejected. He writes, "Such a reaction would be understandable in light of 21.20–21: it would hardly be possible for the Jerusalem leadership . . . to receive a gift from someone regarded with such suspicion and hostility among the Jerusalem believers."

3. Felix ruled as procurator of Judea from AD 52–59.

the contrary: "Paul's decision to circumcise Timothy (16:3), his continued insistence on visiting synagogues, his keenness to keep Passover and Pentecost (20:6, 16), and the vow at Cenchreae (18:18) all build up a picture of a Paul who is happy to be regarded—at least when it suits him—as a faithful, Torah-observant Jew."[4]

To dispel the misinformation and make it absolutely clear that the charge of apostasy is false, the Jerusalem leadership requests that Paul, the apostle to the gentiles, demonstrate his commitment to the Mosaic law and the temple. The hope is that this expression of piety will satisfy the scrupulous Jewish believers' concerns. Another purpose was to demonstrate their connection to Paul and his mission. What could serve both purposes? At hand were four Jewish Christians who were about to complete their voluntary Nazirite vows (21:23). To do so was a costly undertaking (see Num 6:14–15). It also presented an opportunity for bridge-building. The Jerusalem leaders request (the two verbs are imperatives) that Paul *purify* himself with them and *pay* their Nazirite expenses (Acts 21:24). In this, he would demonstrate his devotion to the law and his charity to fellow Jews.[5] While these actions were aimed toward the opinion of scrupulous Jewish believers, James and the elders also reiterated their commitment to the gentile mission. They did so by reaffirming the decision from the Jerusalem Council about the requirements for gentile believers (v. 25; see 15:19–29). This is not to remind Paul of something he did not know but to confirm that this is not an issue related to the conduct of gentile believers.[6]

Paul's Submission (21:26)

Without expressing any verbal response from Paul to the requests made by the Jerusalem leadership, Luke describes what the apostle did. As he had submitted to the Spirit's leading to Jerusalem, so he also submitted to the Jerusalem leadership's request. Paul joined the four men as they completed their own dedication rite. As a pious Jew returning from travels in gentile lands, Paul was required to undergo a seven-day ritual of purification before entering the temple. In addition to signaling when his purification rite would end, he also informed an appropriate temple priest that he was paying the offertory expenses of the four impoverished Nazirites. This was an ingenious plan by the Jerusalem leadership and a noble and costly gesture on the part of Paul. The plan and the gesture, however, did not have the intended results.

---

4. Alexander, *Acts*, 163.
5. Josephus, *Ant.* 19.294, recounts how Herod Agrippa I a few years earlier undertook the expenses for impoverished Nazirites.
6. Dunn, *Acts*, 287.

LIVE the Story

Compromise. It is a word that sticks in the throat of most people I know. We tend to think about compromise as being dispassionate, indecisive, or weak willed—all characteristics that most North Americans disapprove of by their opinion if not by their actions. Freedom. Now there is a word that gets our hearts racing and gets our heads up! Freedom is considered by most to be a virtue. It inspires thoughts of heroic action and untrammeled joy. When Paul considered his own freedom and its use, however, he wrote this to the Corinthians:

> Though I am free and belong to no one, I have made myself a slave to everyone, to win as many as possible. To the Jews I became like a Jew, to win the Jews. To those under the law I became like one under the law (though I myself am not under the law), so as to win those under the law. . . . I have become all things to all people so that by all possible means I might save some. I do all this for the sake of the gospel, that I may share in its blessings." (1 Cor 9:19–23)

This use of "freedom" seems to be at work for Paul when he submits to the request of the Jerusalem leadership to demonstrate to Jewish Christians—especially those "zealous for the law" (Acts 21:20)—that he is a person who lives in obedience to the law. Paul uses his freedom as an act of compromise so that he might build bridges between the Jewish and gentile missions as he returns to the "home church" to tell them about his ministry in the gentile world.

Unfortunately, misinformation of what he was doing and how he was doing it had already reached "home," and this news did not please many in the Jerusalem church. Given the political climate in Jerusalem in AD 57 and the growing resentment against all things gentile, Paul is facing opposition both from Jews outside the church and those inside the church. We can understand why he urged the Roman church, prior to this journey to Jerusalem, to "pray that I may be kept safe from the unbelievers in Judea and that the contribution I take to Jerusalem may be favorably received by the Lord's people there" (Rom 15:31).

Paul is working at the difficult point of gospel boundaries: boundaries of ethnicity and integrity, culture and generosity, inclusion and exclusion. Many missionaries returning home after serving overseas face similar challenges to Paul. That is, they must try to articulate to their "home church" how God has used them to share the gospel elsewhere. The difficulty comes in trying to help the home church understand how the gospel is contextualized in ways that may seem like compromise or even apostasy to the sending church.

In returning home, missionaries may start telling their stories about how God worked in unexpected ways. It can be complicated, however, to come home to one's "Jerusalem" and tell your friends and family that Bengali Christians need not change their dress or start eating pork or pray in a certain way to be considered true believers. There can be pressure to "prove" that they are sharing theological truth accurately and rightly. Prabhu Singh describes the challenge of contextualization that exists even within the boundaries of a single country, albeit a country as diverse and complex as India. He writes:

> Sadhu Sunder Singh, the famous Indian evangelist from a Sikh background, gave a succinct description of contextualization in the Indian context. He said, 'It is giving the water of life in an Indian cup.'. . . . There are at least 4,693 cups within India that need the water of life. . . . As a trained missiological anthropologist, it is refreshing for me to see a new sense of openness among mission leaders and practitioners to contextualizing the gospel among peoples of different cultures and faiths in this new era. For instance, a southern Indian agency, serving in Punjab for many years, had earlier encouraged new believers from a Sikh background to cut their long hair and shave their beards as an evidence of their new faith. However, during a recent visit, I saw many followers of Jesus wearing their turban, as the agency seems to be more open to indigenous cultural forms. Perhaps this is one of the reasons for the exponential growth of the church in that region, as locals begin to realize that a Punjabi need not become a 'madarasi' (colloquial term for South Indian) in order to be a follower of Jesus.[7]

There are significant challenges of using one's "freedom" in sharing the gospel in another culture and in communicating "contextualization" to one's home church. The dangers of assumed compromise and miscommunication are real and difficult. Paul faced these challenges as he worked among the gentiles in their lands and when he returned home to his own people in Jerusalem. It was hard work for the missionary Paul, and it is hard work for missionaries today. Sometimes missionary efforts—either on the mission field or back home—are not successful. After all, this is why Paul could honestly comment, "I have become all things to all people so that by all possible means I might save *some*" (1 Cor 9:22). The view "some, not all" may sound like a compromise. It is a difficult compromise, but it can also be a freeing compromise if it is a gospel compromise. Not everyone—either on the mission

---

7. Prabhu Singh, "Surfing the Third Wave of Missions in India: Contextual Challenges and Creative Responses," in *Lausanne Global Analysis* 6.2 (March 2017), https://www.lausanne.org/content/lga/2017–03/surfing-the-third-wave-of-missions-in-india.

field or back in the home church—will understand the challenge of using our gospel freedom in creative and diverse ways to lead people to faith in Christ. For some, it is not even worth the effort of trying. And yet this is the challenge of our faith. Or, as G. K. Chesterton wrote, "The Christian ideal has not been tried and found wanting. It has been found difficult; and left untried."[8]

---

8. G. K. Chesterton, "The Unfinished Temple," in *What's Wrong with the World* (London: Cassell and Co., 1910), Kindle edition.

CHAPTER 49

Acts 21:27-36

 ## LISTEN to the Story

²⁷When the seven days were nearly over, some Jews from the province of Asia saw Paul at the temple. They stirred up the whole crowd and seized him, ²⁸shouting, "Fellow Israelites, help us! This is the man who teaches everyone everywhere against our people and our law and this place. And besides, he has brought Greeks into the temple and defiled this holy place." ²⁹(They had previously seen Trophimus the Ephesian in the city with Paul and assumed that Paul had brought him into the temple.)

³⁰The whole city was aroused, and the people came running from all directions. Seizing Paul, they dragged him from the temple, and immediately the gates were shut. ³¹While they were trying to kill him, news reached the commander of the Roman troops that the whole city of Jerusalem was in an uproar. ³²He at once took some officers and soldiers and ran down to the crowd. When the rioters saw the commander and his soldiers, they stopped beating Paul.

³³The commander came up and arrested him and ordered him to be bound with two chains. Then he asked who he was and what he had done. ³⁴Some in the crowd shouted one thing and some another, and since the commander could not get at the truth because of the uproar, he ordered that Paul be taken into the barracks. ³⁵When Paul reached the steps, the violence of the mob was so great he had to be carried by the soldiers. ³⁶The crowd that followed kept shouting, "Get rid of him!"

Listening to the Text in the Story: Ezekiel 44:6–8; Luke 23:2,18; 2 Timothy 4:20.

 ## EXPLAIN the Story

The story of Paul's arrest has been anticipated for a long time in Acts. In one sense, it can be traced back to the stoning of Stephen (Acts 7:54–8:1).

As Stephen was accused of "speaking against this holy place and against the law" (6:13) and then later dragged out of the city to be killed by his fellow Jews, a young man named Saul was present and "approved of their killing him" (8:1). This same Saul was confronted by the Lord on the road to Damascus and announced to be Jesus's "chosen instrument to proclaim [the Lord's] name to the Gentiles and their kings and to the people of Israel. . . . [and to] suffer for my name" (9:15). Eventually, Paul the apostle, after traveling throughout much of the eastern empire, decides to return to Jerusalem (19:21). As Paul nears Jerusalem, the Holy Spirit warns him "that prison and hardships are facing [him]" (20:23; cf. 21:10–14). At last, the anticipated arrest of Paul occurs. After his arrest and incarceration he will be given a platform not only to proclaim the Lord's name before gentiles and his fellow Jews (22:1–21; 23:1–6) but also before rulers in Judea (Felix, Festus, Agrippa) and eventually, he hoped, before Caesar in Rome (25:11–12; 27:24; 28:19).

The account of Paul's arrest in Jerusalem near Passover in AD 57 unfolds in three stages. First, he is identified and accused by Jews, likely from Ephesus, while he was at the temple (21:27–29). Next, Paul is seized, dragged from the temple, and then mob justice ensues until the uproar attracts the attention of the Roman tribune (vv. 30–32). Finally, Paul is arrested, chained, and even carried up the steps to the Antonia Fortress (vv. 33–36).

Asian Jews Identify Paul (21:27–29)

The temple in Jerusalem was not only a place of worship; it was a national symbol and the ancient seat of government. The temple was more than a place of prayer and devotion; it was a place of power and politics and, as such, often a place of protest. Protests often occurred during Jewish festivals, especially Passover, when the city swelled with pilgrims. At these times, the Romans were vigilant for any disturbances that might strike (cf. Josephus, *J.W.* 5.244), and even more so during this period of heightened tension under the governorship of Felix. The previous narrative ended with Paul, accompanied by four Jewish Christians, giving notice in the temple of the date of the end of their purification rite (Acts 21:26). Soon after, Paul was back in the temple where Jews, likely from Ephesus and in Jerusalem as Passover pilgrims, identified him. This is not surprising. Luke informed us earlier that Paul was well known by Jews and Greeks throughout the province of Asia from his two-year stay in Ephesus (19:10).

The sight of Paul in the temple by these Asian Jews was not a welcome one.[1] They began shouting and stirred up the crowd with accusations that Paul has been traveling all over the world, speaking "against our people and our law

---

1. Fitzmyer, *Acts*, 696, notes that Jewish agitation against Paul has been building for some time; cf. 13:50; 14:2, 5, 19; 17:5–9; 18:12–17.

and this place" (21:28). These accusations are reminiscent of the ones spoken against Jesus (Luke 23:2) and Stephen (Acts 6:13; see commentary on 6:8–15). The charges intensify with the insistence that he even has brought Greeks into the temple precincts and "defiled this holy place" (cf. Ezek 44:6–8).

The Jews were scrupulous about their holy place, even though they were under Roman domination. There was a part of the temple—the outer court of the gentiles—where non-Jews could visit. Gentiles, however, were forbidden from passing beyond that into the court of Israel. There were signs "declaring the law of purity, some in Greek, and some in Roman letters, that 'no foreigner should go within that sanctuary'; for that second [court of the] temple was called 'the Sanctuary'" (Josephus, *J.W.* 5.194 [Whiston]). Gentiles who broke this barrier and profaned the temple could be subject to the death penalty administered by the Jews.[2] Unfortunately, the Asian Jews concluded that the Jewish Christians Paul had brought into the temple to fulfill their purification rites were gentiles. Luke explains this conclusion as a case of mistaken identity. Paul had been seen earlier walking around Jerusalem with gentiles, including Trophimus, another recognizable person from Ephesus and one of his traveling companions (cf. Acts 20:4; 2 Tim 4:20). It was assumed that Paul had also taken him into the temple.

Paul Is Seized by the Mob (21:30–32)

Regardless of the confusion over identity, the crowd in the temple is ignited. The news travels swiftly, and soon "the whole city" is in an uproar. In much the same way that happened earlier with Stephen in Jerusalem (7:54–60) and Paul when he was in Ephesus (19:28–32), mob justice erupts. Paul is dragged from the holy precincts, and the Levites close the gates of the temple to prevent the disturbance from drifting back into the sanctuary. Paul was in significant danger, and Luke emphasizes this by alerting us to the violence of the crowd and the vulnerability of Paul. As they were trying to kill Paul, the uproar did not go unnoticed by the watchful Roman commander and soldiers at the Antonia Fortress.

The Antonia Fortress was part of a larger temple building project by Herod the Great. The paranoid Herod knew that the temple would be a prime place for political uprisings, and so he built a large garrison along the northeast corner of the temple walls to provide protection. He named it in honor of his patron, Mark Antony. It was a heavily fortified structure, built on the highest hill in Jerusalem with the highest tower in the city. Parapets connected it to the temple walls. All of this provided the Roman cohort (approximately eight hundred to a thousand men) garrisoned there with easy sightlines to

---

2. Philo, *Embassy* 212; Josephus, *J.W.* 6.126.

observe the temple and city. Josephus described this "tower of Antonia" (*J. W.* 5.238–45) in detail and concluded, "The temple was a fortress that guarded the city, as was the tower of Antonia a guard to the temple; and in that tower were the guards of those three" (5.245 [Whiston]). Word of the disturbance below "reached" (*anabainō*, lit. "went up") the Roman commander, a tribune (Gk.: *chiliarchos*, equivalent to a modern military colonel), who was in the guard tower.[3] He immediately "ran down" the steps (Acts 21:32; cf. vv. 35, 40) connecting the garrison to the temple together with officers and soldiers. When the mob saw the commander and the soldiers arrive, they stopped beating Paul and the uproar momentarily abated.

The Roman Commander Arrests Paul (21:33–36)

It may strike some modern ears as odd that it is Paul, the one who is being beaten up, who is arrested and not the ones who are giving the beating! This reminds us that the Roman soldiers were not in Jerusalem to ensure that justice was carried out. Rather, the soldiers were there to keep the Roman peace. Keeping the peace in rebellious provinces like Judea meant dealing with those who were the cause of disturbances. In this instance, it was clear to the tribune that the quickest and most efficient way to quell the disturbance was to arrest one person, not the many who were shouting and doing the beating. Of course, the tribune was not aware of the upcoming twist when Paul would reveal that he was not a Jewish ruffian but a Roman citizen (22:27). For now, however, Paul was bound with two hand chains connected to two soldiers. This was a very heavy guard, but it was warranted given the dangerous circumstances (21:35).[4] Without any way of determining the cause of the disturbance amid the ongoing uproar, the tribune decided to take Paul back to the fortress for a private interrogation. When Paul and his guard reached the steps joining the temple to the fortress, the violence was so intense that the soldiers had to carry Paul. As they carried him up the stairway, the crowd shouted, "Get rid of him!" (v. 36; cf. Luke 23:18).

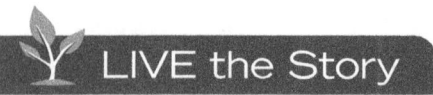

LIVE the Story

Boundary issues are complex. Boundaries can be protective. For example, most of us have heard about the importance of "setting good boundaries" in our life and ministries as a way of protecting us from burnout, resentment,

---

3. The tribune is later identified as Claudius Lysias (Acts 23:26), and he will play a key role in the unfolding drama after Paul's arrest.
4. Rapske, *Paul in Roman Custody*, 140.

misunderstanding, breech of confidence, etc.[5] Simply put, boundaries are "our lists of what's okay and what's not okay."[6] Boundaries can also be contested. As such, they are often sites of conflict, whether they are religious, cultural, political, or geographic boundaries. Robert Frost explores the tensions and contradictions of boundaries in his poem "The Mending Wall," a poem that includes the now famous line, "Good fences make good neighbors." In the poem, Frost asks the important question: "*Why* do they make good neighbors? . . . Before I built a wall I'd ask to know / What I was walling in or walling out, / And to whom I was like to give offense."[7]

Paul recognized the complexity associated with boundaries—maybe better than most. In this episode in Acts, Paul was accused of speaking "against *our* people and *our* law and *this* place" and of bringing gentiles across the boundary of the court of gentiles into the court of Israel. This was a boundary that was zealously defended by Jews in the first century. They had good theological grounds to guard the integrity of their holy place. The Levites who shut the gates (Acts 21:30) behind the mob as they dragged Paul out of the temple may even have been thinking about the admonitions of the prophet Ezekiel (see Ezek 44:6–7). First-century Jews also had good historical precedent for guarding the boundaries of the temple. The Greek king Antiochus desecrated the temple by sacrificing a pig on the altar, and he renamed the temple after "Olympian Zeus" in 168 BC (1 Macc 1:54–59; 2 Macc 6:1–12). Just over a hundred years after that incident, in 63 BC the Roman general Pompey entered the holy of holies itself after his legions captured Jerusalem (Josephus, *J.W.* 1.152–53). Therefore, first-century Jews had good reason to try to maintain the boundaries in their temple, and the pre-conversion Saul of Tarsus would have been just as zealous as anyone to protect them.

Luke is clear that the accusation made against the apostle Paul by the Jews about taking a gentile into the temple was based on a misunderstanding. Still, from what we know from both Luke-Acts and Paul's own letters, the gospel is about crossing boundaries and breaking down barriers between people. Jesus is repeatedly depicted as opening doors of welcome and fellowship to those who were considered outsiders and unfit to belong as full and equal members in the people of God, including women, shepherds, the poor, and sinners. Jesus's last command to his disciples before his ascension was that they were to be witnesses who cross boundaries (Jerusalem, Judea, Samaria, and to the

---

5. For a good discussion on the importance of healthy boundaries, see Brené Brown, *Rising Strong* (New York: Spiegel & Grau, 2015), 120–28.

6. Brown, *Rising Strong*, 126.

7. Robert Frost, "The Mending Wall," https://www.poetryfoundation.org/poems/44266/mending-wall (emphasis original).

ends of the earth). While gentile visitors to the temple in Jerusalem were met with a sign that read, "No foreigner [*allophulos*] should go within that sanctuary" (Josephus, *J.W.* 5.194 [Whiston]), Peter told the household of Cornelius, "You are well aware that it is against our law for a Jew to associate with or visit a Gentile [*allophulos*]. But God has shown me that I should not call anyone impure or unclean" (Acts 10:28). These same themes of breaking down barriers and welcoming the outsider run throughout Paul's own letters. Paul says over and over that "in Christ" we find the place where all—regardless of nationality, race, status, or gender—can meet on one level (e.g., 1 Cor 12:13; Rom 14–15; Gal 3:28; cf. Isa 14:1; 65:1). While the temple gates may have been shut behind Paul (Acts 21:30), he would later write from prison:

> But now in Christ Jesus you who once were far away have been brought near by the blood of Christ. For he himself is our peace, who has made the two groups one and has destroyed the barrier, the dividing wall of hostility, by setting aside in his flesh the law with its commands and regulations. His purpose was to create in himself one new humanity out of the two, thus making peace, and in one body to reconcile both of them to God through the cross, by which he put to death their hostility. He came and preached peace to you who were far away and peace to those who were near. For through him we both have access to the Father by one Spirit. Consequently, you are no longer foreigners and strangers, but fellow citizens with God's people and also members of his household, built on the foundation of the apostles and prophets, with Christ Jesus himself as the chief cornerstone. In him the whole building is joined together and rises to become a holy temple in the Lord. (Eph 2:13–21)

Jesus came to destroy boundaries between peoples: racial boundaries, class boundaries, gender boundaries. In a world where humans seem more and more obsessed with erecting barriers between people and nations, Paul reminds us that the gospel is about breaking down barriers between people and creating a new, living, and holy "temple." This new creation starts with the church. As Rowan Williams writes, "The one thing you know for certain about your tiresome, annoying, disobedient, disedifying fellow Christians is that God has welcomed them; that becomes your challenge."[8] That is a challenge! It is also complex and difficult to do. I would even suggest it is impossible—apart from the reality and work of our triune God. For it is only through *Jesus* that we all share in the same *Spirit* and have equal access to the *Father*.

---

8. Williams, *Meeting God in Paul*, 30–31.

CHAPTER 50

Acts 21:37–22:21

 LISTEN to the Story

³⁷As the soldiers were about to take Paul into the barracks, he asked the commander, "May I say something to you?"

"Do you speak Greek?" he replied. ³⁸"Aren't you the Egyptian who started a revolt and led four thousand terrorists out into the wilderness some time ago?"

³⁹Paul answered, "I am a Jew, from Tarsus in Cilicia, a citizen of no ordinary city. Please let me speak to the people."

⁴⁰After receiving the commander's permission, Paul stood on the steps and motioned to the crowd. When they were all silent, he said to them in Aramaic:

¹"Brothers and fathers, listen now to my defense."

²When they heard him speak to them in Aramaic, they became very quiet.

Then Paul said: ³"I am a Jew, born in Tarsus of Cilicia, but brought up in this city. I studied under Gamaliel and was thoroughly trained in the law of our ancestors. I was just as zealous for God as any of you are today. ⁴I persecuted the followers of this Way to their death, arresting both men and women and throwing them into prison, ⁵as the high priest and all the Council can themselves testify. I even obtained letters from them to their associates in Damascus, and went there to bring these people as prisoners to Jerusalem to be punished.

⁶"About noon as I came near Damascus, suddenly a bright light from heaven flashed around me. ⁷I fell to the ground and heard a voice say to me, 'Saul! Saul! Why do you persecute me?'

⁸"'Who are you, Lord?' I asked.

"'I am Jesus of Nazareth, whom you are persecuting,' he replied. ⁹My companions saw the light, but they did not understand the voice of him who was speaking to me.

¹⁰"'What shall I do, Lord?' I asked.

"'Get up,' the Lord said, 'and go into Damascus. There you will be told all that you have been assigned to do.' ¹¹My companions led me by the hand into Damascus, because the brilliance of the light had blinded me.

¹²"A man named Ananias came to see me. He was a devout observer of the law and highly respected by all the Jews living there. ¹³He stood beside me and said, 'Brother Saul, receive your sight!' And at that very moment I was able to see him.

¹⁴"Then he said: 'The God of our ancestors has chosen you to know his will and to see the Righteous One and to hear words from his mouth. ¹⁵You will be his witness to all people of what you have seen and heard. ¹⁶And now what are you waiting for? Get up, be baptized and wash your sins away, calling on his name.'

¹⁷"When I returned to Jerusalem and was praying at the temple, I fell into a trance ¹⁸and saw the Lord speaking to me. 'Quick!' he said. 'Leave Jerusalem immediately, because the people here will not accept your testimony about me.'

¹⁹"'Lord,' I replied, 'these people know that I went from one synagogue to another to imprison and beat those who believe in you. ²⁰And when the blood of your martyr Stephen was shed, I stood there giving my approval and guarding the clothes of those who were killing him.'

²¹"Then the Lord said to me, 'Go; I will send you far away to the Gentiles.'"

Listening to the Text in the Story: Exodus 3:15; Isaiah 6:1–13; Acts 9:1–29; 26:9–20; Romans 9:1–5; 10:2; Galatians 1:14–16; 2:2, 7; Philippians 3:6, 12.

EXPLAIN the Story

As a character in the narrative, Paul has been silent since his arrival in Jerusalem (21:17). In the previous two episodes (21:17–26, 27–36), Paul is at the heart of the action, but he does not speak. Now, after a disturbance has erupted around Paul and as the Roman tribune escorts him to the barracks for interrogation, Paul speaks. He begins with a simple question that leads to a short conversation with the tribune (21:37–40) before a longer address to the crowd (22:1–21). Paul introduces his speech as "his defense," but he does far more than defend himself. That is, he compactly tells his story. He reviews his *past* (22:1–5), he talks about his encounter with Jesus that has invaded his *present* (vv. 6–11), and he describes his commission that shapes his vocation moving forward into the *future* (vv. 12–16)—whether that future is in Jerusalem among fellow Jews (vv. 17–20) or "far away" among the gentiles (v. 21).

Paul's Conversation with the Tribune (21:37–40)

The immediate backdrop to Paul's brief conversation with the Roman tribune (Claudius Lysias; see 23:26) is the mob violence against Paul (21:35). The exchange between Paul and the tribune, however, is not insignificant, as it sets up Paul's address and illuminates several points in the episode. First, it clarifies—in one respect—a misunderstanding held by the tribune. Paul was *not* the Egyptian revolutionary who had slipped from the grasp of Governor Felix. Felix quelled a revolt led by an "Egyptian false prophet," but the leader of that insurrection eluded him (Josephus, *J.W.* 2.261–63 [Whiston]). It was because of these extreme Judean nationalists, whom the Romans regarded as "terrorists" (i.e., the Sicarii, lit. "dagger men"; Gk.: *sikarioi*), that the Roman guard would be on heightened alert—especially during Jewish festivals (see Josephus, *J.W.* 2.254–65). Rapske points out that Paul's response to the tribune's question was pointed:

> [Paul] had a clearly positive and informative thrust: when he said he was a Tarsian, he did so in a proud and overtly Hellenistic way. . . . [His] assertion that he was both a Jew and a Tarsian was probably more than simply a legal self-description. It may have amounted to an offended rebuttal. To be mistaken for an Egyptian was a social slur of no small degree. Jews who lived in Alexandria resented being identified as Egyptians. The offensiveness of the designation would have been compounded if, as in this case, a Jew who boasted his religious faithfulness was identified as an Egyptian false-prophet.[1]

Second, some readers may be surprised that Paul does not assert his Roman citizenship at this time. It is unlikely that Paul has a low view of his Roman citizenship or wishes to "keep his powder dry" for a later confrontation with the tribune. Rather, his assertion of his Jewish identity[2] and Tarsian citizenship has everything to do with his context and the accusations he faces in Jerusalem.

---

1. Rapske, *Paul in Roman Custody*, 137. Gaventa, *Acts*, 305, notes the implied insult as well and provides the following evidence as indictors of this: Strabo, *Geogr.* 17.1.12; Philo, *Dreams* 1.240; 2.255; *Alleg. Interp.* 2.84; 3.13, 37–38, 81, 87.

2. Dunn, *Acts*, 290, offers an important reminder regarding Paul identifying himself as a Jew: "This self-designation . . . undermines the impression which some have taken from Luke's references to the hostility of 'the Jews' elsewhere (e.g., 13.50; 17.5; 20.3, 19), that Christian identity had become wholly divorced from Jewish identity. Here the leading proponent of Gentile Christianity identifies

Paul's concern is not for his safety from his accusers and a dignified treatment from the Romans (cf. Acts 16). As Rapske notes:

> Perhaps even more than at Acts 16, there are at Acts 21 religious disadvantages to an early disclosure of Roman citizenship. The Jerusalem context is predominantly Jewish and Paul's loyalty to Judaism is the issue. . . . A claim of Roman citizenship, if not interpreted by the Jews (and perhaps even by the Tribune!) as conceding the truth of the charges, would nevertheless have evoked highly destructive distinctions between himself and his Jewish hearers. In such a context as this, "Jew" and "Roman" are strictly antithetic. That Paul would not have been so careless of such consequences as to disclose publicly his Roman citizenship is even confirmed by the manner of his Tarsian citizenship disclosure at Acts 22. . . . whereas Paul presents himself *in Greek* to the Tribune as a *Jew* who is a *citizen* of Tarsus, to the Jews Paul presents himself *in Aramaic* as a *zealous Jew* who, though born in Tarsus, was raised in Jerusalem.[3]

This context explains why Paul asserts different citizenships and identity markers at different times. The reason and character of Paul's disclosure of his Roman citizenship (22:25–28) are not due to a blunder on Paul's part. It is the fact that he is a Christian Jew facing accusations in Jerusalem from non-Christian Jews.

Paul's Defense (22:1–21)
Paul offers his defense from the "steps" (21:40) leading up to the Antonia Fortress overlooking the temple and all Jerusalem. Some Jews from the province of Asia have accused him of teaching "against our *people* and our *law* and this *place*" and defiling "this holy place" (21:28). While we can only imagine Paul's state of mind after being beaten by the crowd and manhandled by Roman soldiers, his defense itself is remarkable in its restraint. Without anger or malice, he addresses the crowd by telling his personal story—a story whose center is not himself but the resurrected Lord Jesus.

Paul's Past (22:1–5)
Paul begins by addressing the crowd with the typical opening and endearing words reminiscent of many of the speeches in Acts, including the speeches of Peter and Stephen before unbelieving Jews: "Brothers and fathers" (22:1; cf. Acts 2:29; 7:2; etc.). As he did with the tribune, he begins clarifying his Jewish

---

himself straightforwardly as (still) a Jew: Jewish and Christian identity still overlap and here merge in the person of Paul himself."

3. Rapske, *Paul in Roman Custody*, 142.

identity and impeccable credentials. His identity is first reflected in the Aramaic language he speaks (21:40; 22:2). Aramaic—or possibly Hebrew—was the language spoken in first-century Palestine. His defense opens by indirectly answering the charges leveled against him. His first assertion relates to his place and his people. He affirms that he is a Jew. Although he was born in Tarsus in Cilicia—a city renowned as a center for Greek culture—he stresses that he was "brought up" (22:3a, lit. "nourished," *anatrephō*) in Jerusalem. In terms of his teaching, he could boast that his educational pedigree derived from Gamaliel (cf. 5:34), an esteemed teacher of the law in the first century. Gamaliel, possibly a descendant of the great rabbi Hillel, was known as "the elder" and was the first to be acknowledged with the title Rabban ("our Master") rather than the ordinary Rabbi ("my Master").[4] Sitting at the feet of such a master, Paul contended that he was "thoroughly"[5] trained in the "law of our ancestors" (22:3b).

After briefly describing himself in relationship to his people and his education, Paul continues to thicken his bonds with the crowd by emphasizing that he "was just as zealous for God as any of you are today" (v. 3c; see Rom 10:2; Gal 1:14). Interestingly, the word translated by the NIV as "I was" (in the past tense) is actually a present participle and could also be translated as "I continue to be zealous for God."[6] Of course, that zeal is now directed in a different way: Paul is zealous for the gospel of God—not just the law. As a person zealous for God, he understood the moods and beliefs that touched off this uproar in Jerusalem. He illustrates his zeal by telling them how he *persecuted* followers of "this Way" to their death (possibly alluding to Stephen's stoning, see 8:1 and Phil 3:6) and *arrested* them (see Acts 8:3)—facts that can be attested by the high priest and the Sanhedrin. His zeal for God was ultimately expressed in his pursuing "these people" (v. 5) of the Way even so far as Damascus to bring them back to Jerusalem for punishment (see 9:1–2).

Paul's Encounter with Jesus (22:6–11)

In mentioning his zealous pursuit of Jewish Christians in Damascus, Paul pivots to his encounter with the risen Jesus, the defining moment of his life. This is the second of three accounts of the Damascus Road experience in Acts (see 9:1–29; 26:9–20), but this time it is told from Paul's first-person perspective. Paul's personal retelling of his encounter with Jesus resembles the descriptive

---

4. Paul L. Maier, "Chronology," *DLNT* 185.
5. Greek *akribeia*; this term was used by Josephus to describe the Pharisees (which Paul identifies himself as in Phil 3:5) and their "exacting" interpretation of the law (Josephus, *J. W.* 2.162; *Life* 191).
6. I am grateful to Dr. David Miller for alerting me to this grammatical note. See also Gaventa, *Acts*, 306.

account earlier in Acts. Two notable differences, however, are present.[7] First, in this speech Paul notes that his fellow travelers to Damascus "did not hear [*akouō*] the voice" (22:9) from heaven, while in 9:7 it says that "they heard [*akouō*] the sound" but did not see anyone. The NIV at 22:9 resolves this by translating the word as "understand": "They did not *understand* the voice." While this may ease the tension between the two texts, it also lends historical credibility to Luke as a historian in that he could relate both accounts without trying to harmonize them perfectly.[8] The second difference is the insertion of Paul's question: "What shall I do, Lord?" (v. 10a). It is this question, unlike the earlier account (9:6), that triggers Jesus's instructions to Saul to go to Damascus and be told "all that you have been assigned to do" (v. 10c). Theologically, however, Paul makes the same point that Luke described earlier. In his zeal for the law, Saul persecuted the Lord, not just Jesus's followers.

Paul's Commission (22:12–16)

The same divine initiative that was behind Paul's encounter with Jesus is also highlighted when Paul describes the commission that orients his ministry. Just as his encounter with Jesus was unexpected—which Paul would describe in his own letters as an unbidden "grace" (Gal 1:15–16) that "took hold" (Phil 3:12) of him—so also his vocation is given to him without prior notice. In his description of his commission, he is intent on emphasizing both Jewish piety and God's providence. He does so first by noting that the agent of the divine instructions, Ananias, was a *"devout* observer of the law and highly respected by *all* the Jews living" in Damascus (Acts 22:12). This might address some of the concerns of his audience in Jerusalem (see 21:28–29). As Bruce notes, "It was important to stress on the present occasion that the commission which Paul received from the risen Christ was to a large extent communicated through the lips of this pious and believing Jew."[9] Further, he retells how Ananias informed him that *God* had chosen Paul to "know" God's will and to "see" the Righteous One and to "hear" words from his mouth (22:14). The title the "Righteous One" occurs only two other times in Acts; both Peter and Stephen are reported as using it once each as they address their respective, non-believing Jewish audiences (3:14 [Peter]; 7:52 [Stephen]). Without referring to Jesus as "the Christ/Messiah," which may have inflamed his Jewish listeners, this title evokes messianic themes from Isaiah (53:11) and Jeremiah (23:5–6; 33:15) in which God's "righteous" servant enacts God's will. In a

---

7. Two other additions to the account from Acts 9:3–5 include the time signature "about noon" (22:6) and Jesus's identification of himself as "Jesus of Nazareth" (v. 8).
8. See Dunn, *Acts*, 294.
9. Bruce, *Acts*, 417.

similar manner, Paul is called on not merely to know God's will and to see and hear God's Righteous One but is also to give testimony and act on all he has seen and heard (Acts 22:15). In a manner echoing the commission of Moses himself, it is the "God of our ancestors" who has sent Paul to be his witness to the people of Israel (Acts 22:14; cf. Exod 3:15). Beyond this, however, he is to bear witness not only to the house of Israel but "to all people" (Acts 22:15).[10] As a new and visible identity marker of his commitment to God's call and to the words of "the Righteous One," Paul is to be baptized (v. 16).

Paul's Ongoing Vocation (22:17–21)

The final and climactic movement in Paul's speech describes his initial visit to Jerusalem after his commission in Damascus (cf. Gal 2:2, 7). While Luke has described this visit of Paul's earlier in the narrative (see Acts 9:26–30), the information Paul relates here in the speech is new. Yet as he did elsewhere in the speech, Paul also picks up themes of Jewish piety and divine initiative. In this instance he notes that while he was at prayer in the temple the Lord spoke to him in a trance (vv. 17–18). Again, this scene echoes the experience of another commissioning of an important prophet in Israel, Isaiah. Isaiah was also in the temple (Isa 6) when he is given a vision of the Lord and answers the call to "go and tell [the] people" (v. 9a). Earlier in Acts it was Peter who fell into a trance before his direct calling to bring the gospel to the gentile house of Cornelius (see Acts 10:10; 11:5). In Paul's temple trance, the "Lord"—presumably the Lord Jesus (see 22:8, 10)—speaks again and gives him two commands. First, he must "leave Jerusalem" (v. 18). The reason is simple: the people will not accept Paul's testimony. Again we note the similarities of rejection between Paul and Isaiah after their commissioning from the Lord (see Isa 6:9–10). Paul retells how he appealed to the Lord by recalling his previous activity as a persecutor (Acts 22:19–20). The implication seems to be that the Jews will accept his witness because they know his past and recognize "that his change of attitude must be based on the most compelling grounds."[11]

It is with the retelling of the Lord's second command—"Go; I will send you far away to the Gentiles" (v. 21)—that Paul's speech comes to an end. More accurately, he is cut off by the resumed and angry shouts of the crowd (v. 22). This command, with its mention of mission to the gentiles, appears to remind his audience of the accusation that Paul had brought "Greeks into the temple and defiled this holy place" (21:28). Dunn adds that this hostility may also have "called in question their own traditional self-understanding as

---

10. Gaventa, *Acts*, 308, notes that "the term 'witness' links Paul with the mission given to the apostles in 1:8 and their activity throughout Acts (e.g., 1:22; 2:32; 3:15; 5:32; 10:39; 13:31)."

11. Bruce, *Acts*, 419.

the chosen people of God."[12] Paul has done his best to articulate that he was still a "zealous" Jew, committed to the Law and the Prophets—indeed his commission echoed the calls given to Moses and Isaiah—and respectful of the temple. Paul's own efforts to affirm this before "zealous" Christian Jews (21:20) also supports the picture Luke is framing of Paul (see 21:20–26). Yet for all this respect for and affirmation of Jewish identity, Paul asserts that it is God's initiative, not his own, that has brought about his mission and ministry to the nations. Unfortunately, as will be discussed in the next section, with mention of the gentile mission any hope of further defense before the crowd is lost, as is any chance for the tribune to be better informed about the nature of Paul's wrongdoing. The speech is over, the frenzy resumes, and Paul is hustled into the Roman barracks (22:22–29).

LIVE the Story

Emotional Context

As readers of Acts and followers of Jesus seeking to live out the gospel story, it is important for us first to understand this story. This is why we read the text carefully and look for connections in the broader narrative of Acts, the rest of Scripture, and other helpful ancient documents. The historical context helps us recognize the political tensions at play in first-century Jerusalem during the time of Governor Felix and why Paul stood on steps leading up to a Roman fortress overlooking the temple. The literary context helps us understand the connections between the three accounts of Paul's conversion (chs. 9, 22, and 26) and how this speech relates to Paul's mission to the gentile world (chs. 13–20) and the tension it created for both Christian and non-Christian Jews in Jerusalem. Context is important.

One other context that is important not to overlook in this narrative is the emotional context. Paul was emotionally invested in his ministry. He was a passionate and "zealous" person. His own letters speak of Paul's anguish over his own people, the people of Israel (Rom 9:1–5). Paul's "synagogue first" mission strategy and his efforts to forge strong bonds of unity between Jewish and gentile Christians through the collection for the Jerusalem poor bear further testimony to his emotional investment. For these reasons alone, we should be aware of the emotional elements at this point in the story. Before Paul makes his speech, we ought to remember that he has just been beaten by a mob, shackled by Roman soldiers, and jostled through heaving and shouting

---

12. Dunn, *Acts*, 297.

crowds on a hot day near the festival of Pentecost. As Paul turned on the steps going up to the Antonia Fortress, he would have looked disheveled. Along with everyone else, he would be sweating profusely. He might have had a split lip, a bloodied nose, and swelling around his eyes from punches to his face. For those who were present on that day, or those who heard Luke's account being read for the first time in the first century, they would have been attuned to this emotionally charged scene. For those of us today who read this story from our bonded-leather NIVs with a cup of coffee at hand for quiet morning devotions or hear it in well-ordered liturgies with fellow believers gathered for worship, it is vital to keep the emotional context of the scene imaginatively in view. Along with historical and literary contexts, emotional context will help us understand and, by God's grace, live the story well.

I Am Not Throwing Away My Shot

My daughter and son—even though they are Canadians—love the American musical *Hamilton*. I don't know the musical or its story very well, but I've certainly heard "My Shot" sung often enough around our home to associate it with Paul's speech in Acts 22. Why, after all, would Paul—bloody, bruised, and cuffed—want to address those who have just been trying to kill him? I think Paul thought this (or something similar to it in Aramaic): "I am not throwing away my shot!" Despite his calling to be the apostle to the gentiles, he loved his fellow Jews. They were his people, his family. If we are brave enough, most of us will take our "shot" when love is on the line. We dare to speak the truth of our own stories when a family member is about to disengage from us; we dare to speak the truth when we have fallen in love with someone; we dare to speak the truth when a friend lies in a hospital room with terminal cancer. We don't throw away our shot.

Not every conversation requires bold truth telling, but if we are going to live the gospel story well, we need to recognize Paul's speech for the remarkable witness it is. What he did was to tell his personal story as a part of God's larger story in the world. His story, like yours and mine, is important. As Frederick Buechner writes in his own memoir, "My story is important not because it is mine, God knows, but because if I tell it anything like right, the chances are you will recognize that in many ways it is also yours."[13] The early church father Chrysostom also commented on the importance of telling our stories—like Paul—by what we *say* and what we *do*:

> [Paul] truly became a witness to [Jesus], and a witness as one should be, both by what he did and by what he said. We too must be such witnesses

---

13. Frederick Buechner, *Telling Secrets* (San Francisco: HarperOne, 1992), 30.

and not betray what we have been entrusted. I speak not only of doctrines, but also of our way of life. Look, what he knew, what he heard, he bore witness to this before all, and nothing hindered him. We too have heard that there is a resurrection and then a thousand good things; therefore, we ought to bear witness to this before all.[14]

Paul is passionate with his words, but he isn't angry. He offers a reasonable defense, but he isn't cynically defensive. He is assertive, but he isn't vengeful. How did he maintain this kind of balance? How did he tell and live this story so well? What gave him the courage to take "his shot"?

The first thing Paul did was to understand his past. There is enough shame and regret in everyone's past that we might simply want to ignore or forget it. Paul doesn't do that. He recognizes one of the most creative and restorative dimensions of the gospel is the ability to use the substance of the past in the present. When he says, "I was/am just as zealous for God as any of you today," he is sympathizing with his fellow Jews. More than that, he is taking all that is meaningful from the past—even the difficult lessons learned—and carrying it into the present so that he can build bridges with those he loves.

A second thing Paul does is to recognize how God takes the initiative in our lives. There is no part of heaven or earth, past, present, or future, in which God is not involved and leading the way. Jesus is ahead of us all to meet us on the road. The Lord brings devout friends and family—like Ananias—into our lives to heal us, direct us, teach us, and bless us.

A third thing Paul did was openly welcome his future and obediently do all God commanded him to do. This included the sorrow and the joy, the suffering and the glory. He could do this because his life was rooted in resurrection realities. The person he thought was cursed and dead had risen from the grave—reigning and speaking as Lord. Before Christ's second coming, few of us may see the risen Lord and hear audible words from his mouth. Yet all of us, if we are prayerful enough to listen and look, can know and see and hear the things God has done for us in the past and is doing in the present so that we can look hopefully to the future. As the Spirit continues to empower us all, this should give us the courage to "take our shot" when our backs are pressed against the wall and love is on the line. Don't throw away your shot. Decide to tell your story even though it might be difficult and daunting. It is important.

---

14. Chrysostom, *The Acts of the Apostles*, in *ACCA*, 271.

CHAPTER 51

Acts 22:22-29

 LISTEN to the Story

²²The crowd listened to Paul until he said this. Then they raised their voices and shouted, "Rid the earth of him! He's not fit to live!"
²³As they were shouting and throwing off their cloaks and flinging dust into the air, ²⁴the commander ordered that Paul be taken into the barracks. He directed that he be flogged and interrogated in order to find out why the people were shouting at him like this. ²⁵As they stretched him out to flog him, Paul said to the centurion standing there, "Is it legal for you to flog a Roman citizen who hasn't even been found guilty?"
²⁶When the centurion heard this, he went to the commander and reported it. "What are you going to do?" he asked. "This man is a Roman citizen."
²⁷The commander went to Paul and asked, "Tell me, are you a Roman citizen?"
"Yes, I am," he answered.
²⁸Then the commander said, "I had to pay a lot of money for my citizenship."
"But I was born a citizen," Paul replied.
²⁹Those who were about to interrogate him withdrew immediately. The commander himself was alarmed when he realized that he had put Paul, a Roman citizen, in chains.

Listening to the Text in the Story: John 19:15; Acts 16:35–40; Philippians 2:6–8; 3:20.

 EXPLAIN the Story

In the same way that Paul's brief conversation with the tribune (21:37–40) served as a prelude to Paul's speech (22:1–21), Paul's short conversation with the tribune afterward functions as its sequel (22:22–29). Luke frames Paul's speech by beginning with his identity as a Jew and then afterward revealing his Roman identity. This movement within Paul's speech reflects the shape of the narrative as a whole that begins "in Jerusalem . . . and [goes] to the ends of the earth [i.e., Rome]" (1:8). These two dimensions—Jerusalem/Jew and Rome/gentile—shape not only this immediate episode but are twin characteristics and loyalties that run throughout Acts and the history of the early church.[1]

This sequel scene continues the thematic issue of Paul's identity as it plays out with a Jewish audience and then a Roman audience. After hearing Paul's defense that describes his Jewish identity (22:3–5) and his Christian calling (vv. 6–21), the crowd is left far from persuaded. In fact, they resume their shouts to get rid of him (22:22; see 21:36). Their violent outburst is reminiscent of the cries of the crowd against Jesus: "Take him away! Crucify him!" (John 19:15).

In contrast to the Jewish audience that understands Paul's speech and violently rejects it, his Roman audience does not understand his words and requires further clarification. Since it was impossible to gain this knowledge amid the tumult, the tribune orders Paul to be taken up and into the Antonia Fortress for interrogation. In the Roman world it was expected that commoners and slaves would only speak truthfully under torture. Consequently, the commander directs the soldiers to flog and interrogate Paul (Acts 22:24). "And torture it would have been, since the Roman scourge was usually a flail with knotted cords, or possibly in a severe flagellation with pieces of metal or bone inserted into the leather straps."[2] The prospect of this torture was terrifying. In contrast to many modern commentators[3] who suggest that Paul suddenly appeals to/claims/reveals his Roman citizenship at this point, Rapske points out the following:

> Paul only *insinuates* [emphasis his] it. This would surely have been a matter of surprise to a Roman reader. Paul does not cry out 'I am a Roman.' Rather, he poses a hypothetical [question] in the second person . . . for clarification on a question of Roman trial procedure. . . . Paul's insinuation of, rather than insistence upon, his rights encourages two conclusions: first, Paul will not so stridently insist upon his Roman rights as to undercut his religious commitment to Judaism before Roman eyes. In other words, the fact that he is a Christian Jew affects the way he claims his Roman rights. This is not to say, however, that Paul puts little stock or is ambivalent about his Roman citizenship. Second, while his

---

1. Cf. Dunn, *Acts*, 291–92.
2. Dunn, *Acts*, 298.
3. E.g., Haenchen, *Acts*, 632; Longenecker, *Acts*, 527; Bruce, *Acts*, 419.

self-disclosure may make a difference in his treatment, its manner suggests that Paul is still prepared to suffer or even die without complaint (cf. Acts 21:13) if it is disregarded.[4]

Paul, as in Philippi (Acts 16), is aware of his rights as a Roman citizen. It is unlawful, before a formal trial, for a Roman citizen to be flogged, tortured, or injured.[5]

This question caught the attention of the centurion overseeing Paul's interrogation, and he immediately reported it to the tribune. It may seem implausible to modern ears that this simple question was taken seriously by the Roman soldiers, but the consequences for them were significant if Paul was indeed a Roman citizen (see commentary on 16:35–40). When the tribune returns and asks Paul directly whether he is a Roman citizen—which Paul affirms—his follow-up comments are more than a game of social comparison. The tribune is probing Paul because how he proceeds could very well threaten his own future. The tribune is an important Roman officer in Jerusalem and one of the leading authorities in the city. He is a first-generation Roman citizen. "His name Claudius Lysias (Acts 23:26; 24:22) and the cost of his citizenship (22:28) indicate that he was probably Greek and had received the franchise early in the Emperor Claudius' reign."[6] Paul's claim to citizenship was far superior since his came by way of birth.[7] This revelation caused his interrogators to withdraw in worry. In Roman law, "the harm done to a plaintiff was judged more serious and worthy of a more harsh penalty where the plaintiff was the defender's better. . . . That Paul was a citizen from birth . . . threatened great damage to Claudius Lysias' person and career."[8] As Paul's identity provoked fear earlier in Philippi (16:38–39), so too in Jerusalem it arouses "alarm" (*phobeō*) for the tribune. As Rowe reminds us, Cicero had stated that "to bind a Roman citizen is a crime, to flog him is an abomination, to slay him is almost an act of murder" (*Verr.* 2.5.65).[9] The tribune's fear is heightened because he is not only in danger of violating the rights of a Roman citizen but of a citizen who is his better.

---

4. Rapske, *Paul in Roman Custody*, 143.
5. Gaventa, *Acts*, 310, points toward Roman sources: Livy, *History of Rome* 10.9.3–6; Cicero, *Verr.* 2.5.66. See also C. S. Wansink, "Roman Law and Legal System," *DNTB* 987; Rowe, *World Upside Down*, 67.
6. Rapske, *Paul in Roman Custody*, 144. Bruce, *Acts*, 421, suggests that this was likely the result of a citizenship bribe that, during the principate of Claudius, reached "scandalous proportions."
7. Wright, *Acts*, 2:163, notes that scholarly speculation abounds as to how this came about. There is evidence that some Jews received their Roman citizenship up to a hundred years before Paul. It is possible that Roman citizenship was passed down to Paul through three or four generations.
8. Rapske, *Paul in Roman Custody*, 145.
9. Rowe, *World Upside Down*, 68.

LIVE the Story

It is a sad comment of human history that every age from Roman times to the present has used torture to extract information from suspected insurrectionists whether they are ancient *sicarii* or modern terrorists. From whips to water boards, from the Antonia Fortress to Abu Ghraib, cruel means of interrogation are a systemic problem within human forms of "justice." Tom Wright asks why Paul didn't press his advantage of Roman citizenship before the tribune in such a way as to challenge the entire corrupt legal structure of his day. Should it not all be abandoned since it was rotten to the core? He writes:

> Forget it. As with the fashionable idea that the New Testament writers approved of slavery itself, on the grounds that if they hadn't they would have protested against it, such suggestions proceed, to be honest, from the comfortable armchairs of people who have never faced the realities of life under pressure on the ground, or have never tried in imagination to live even for a minute in the real world of antiquity. *Of course* [emphasis his] Paul and the others disapproved of slavery. Their controlling narrative, the great Jewish Exodus story, was precisely a story about a God who, as the supreme revelation of his own character, rescued people from slavery. Of course they disapproved of torture; their even greater controlling narrative, the story of the cross and resurrection of Jesus, focused specifically on the cruelty and injustice of his torture and death, and on the victory over the entire system which was declared when he rose from the dead. Yes, there is a time for protest, and a time to drive through reforms whether people are truly ready for them or not. But yes, too, the far greater reform is to teach whole communities so to live by these controlling stories that an inner revulsion will stop them from ever going near such practices again. Would that these stories were having that effect throughout today's world.[10]

As a priest entrusted with leading a congregation in worship, I regard it with the utmost seriousness to teach my community how to live by these "controlling narratives" of the exodus and the cross and resurrection. In addition to articulating this in sermons, this is taught through the litanies ("For all in danger, for those who are far from home, prisoners, exiles, victims of oppression: grant them your salvation"),[11] the affirmation of the baptismal covenant ("Will you strive for justice and peace among all people, and respect

---

10. Wright, *Acts*, 2:164–65.
11. *The Book of Alternative Services of the Anglican Church of Canada* (Toronto: Anglican Book Centre, 1985), 114.

the dignity of every human being? *I will, with God's help*"),¹² and the prayers of the people ("For prisoners and captives, and for their safety, health, and salvation, let us pray to the Lord. *Lord, have mercy*").¹³ As Loveday Alexander adds, we should also remember to "pray for soldiers, police officers, prison guards, and all whose jobs give them control over the lives of others."¹⁴ In short, we live the story as we pray the story.

Living this story, however, often involves us in more than just praying for others. As those who know that the exodus and new-exodus narratives involve redemption from suffering and slavery, we also know that sometimes they require that we endure affliction. This is not a popular notion in our culture, but Christians take their cue from their Lord on how to live the cruciform life. Paul would reflect on this at length when he wrote a letter to the Philippian church. He informed them that the paradigm for believers is Christ Jesus—the one who condescended in coming to our world, who became incarnate, and who took the nature of a slave and became obedient to death—even death on a cross (Phil 2:6–8). As believers think of themselves the way King Jesus thought of himself, they will reflect the qualities of citizens of heaven (3:20). This was the citizenship that counted most for Paul when the Roman tribune questioned him in the Antonia Fortress. Paul's commitment was motivated by the love of his Savior and exemplar, Jesus Christ. Christ's love is a transformative love, a love that confounds the world. It is a love that extends to one's enemies—those who respond with threats, torture, and sometimes murder of those who love them. Paradoxically, this love eventually conquered the Roman world. The Roman tribune in Jerusalem had no framework to understand this conquering love while he held Paul in custody. Yet for all the danger that imprisonment offered for Paul, he knew that his faithfulness to Jesus was part of a larger, more powerful, and transformative reality than any Roman prison could be. In an era when citizenship mattered significantly, Paul's understanding of citizenship—and where one placed their ultimate allegiance—continues to be important for Christians, wherever they may happen to live.

---

12. Ibid., 159.
13. Ibid., 237.
14. Alexander, *Acts*, 169.

CHAPTER 52

Acts 22:30–23:11

 LISTEN to the Story

³⁰The commander wanted to find out exactly why Paul was being accused by the Jews. So the next day he released him and ordered the chief priests and all the members of the Sanhedrin to assemble. Then he brought Paul and had him stand before them.

¹Paul looked straight at the Sanhedrin and said, "My brothers, I have fulfilled my duty to God in all good conscience to this day." ²At this the high priest Ananias ordered those standing near Paul to strike him on the mouth. ³Then Paul said to him, "God will strike you, you whitewashed wall! You sit there to judge me according to the law, yet you yourself violate the law by commanding that I be struck!"

⁴Those who were standing near Paul said, "How dare you insult God's high priest!"

⁵Paul replied, "Brothers, I did not realize that he was the high priest; for it is written: 'Do not speak evil about the ruler of your people.'"¹

⁶Then Paul, knowing that some of them were Sadducees and the others Pharisees, called out in the Sanhedrin, "My brothers, I am a Pharisee, descended from Pharisees. I stand on trial because of the hope of the resurrection of the dead." ⁷When he said this, a dispute broke out between the Pharisees and the Sadducees, and the assembly was divided. ⁸(The Sadducees say that there is no resurrection, and that there are neither angels nor spirits, but the Pharisees believe all these things.)

⁹There was a great uproar, and some of the teachers of the law who were Pharisees stood up and argued vigorously. "We find nothing wrong with this man," they said. "What if a spirit or an angel has spoken to him?" ¹⁰The dispute became so violent that the commander was afraid Paul would be torn to pieces by them. He ordered the troops to go down and take him away from them by force and bring him into the barracks.

¹¹The following night the Lord stood near Paul and said, "Take courage!

---

1. Exod 22:28.

As you have testified about me in Jerusalem, so you must also testify in Rome."

> *Listening to the Text in the Story*: Exodus 22:28; Leviticus 19:15; Ezekiel 13:10–15; Matthew 23:27; John 7:51; Philippians 1:27.

EXPLAIN the Story

The previous section ended by describing the Roman tribune being "alarmed" (*phobeō*, 22:29) at having put Paul, a Roman citizen, in chains. Despite his fears, we should not suppose that he would simply release Paul and that would be the end of the trouble. The realities of Roman rule in Palestine were not that simple. Once Roman rulers have been brought into the picture, especially in such a politically unstable place like Jerusalem, the matter is far from over when it comes to maintaining the Roman peace. In the narrative, we have already heard by prophetic words (20:22; 21:10–11) and Paul's intentions (19:21) that the apostle will be arrested, handed over to the gentiles, endure hardship and trials, and eventually make his way to Rome. While the present episode is another step in that overall direction, the specific intent is to describe the tribune's attempt to understand what crime Paul has committed. What ensues is a second occasion where the tribune witnesses a theological conversation and dispute between Jews that he cannot understand.

The scene is introduced with the tribune asking Paul to stand before the Sanhedrin (22:30); the scene ends with the Lord standing near Paul (23:11). In between, Paul makes two assertions (vv. 1, 6) that provoke violent exchanges within the Sanhedrin. The first heated exchange is between the high priest and Paul (vv. 2–5); the second is between some Sadducees and Pharisees (vv. 6–10).

The Tribune Brings Paul to Stand before the Sanhedrin (22:30)

Whatever "fear" the Roman commander experienced at Paul's declaration of Roman citizenship, he is still in a position of power and control. He does "release" Paul—but only "the next day" (22:30). Paul may have been "released" from his chains, but he was not free to go as he pleased. The tribune was determined to discover what "the Jews"[2] were accusing Paul of. It is worth remembering that the Roman tribune in Jerusalem is a man of considerable political

---

2. It is important to remember that in Luke's recurring references to "the Jews" this never refers to "all Jews." In fact, Paul emphasizes that he is a "Jew" (21:39; 22:3) and, as a Jew, he (along with others

and military power. As such, he could summon the Sanhedrin to assemble for a meeting with Paul. The Sanhedrin was the supreme religious, judicial, and political council in Jerusalem at this time. Early Jewish sources inform us that it had seventy-one members, including the high priest, as well as any former high priests, and various elders and scribes.[3] This body is featured in several important episodes in the NT. Jesus (Mark 14:53–65), Peter and John (Acts 4:1–22; 5:27–40), and Stephen (6:12–7:53) all stood before the Sanhedrin. Now the tribune brought Paul for his turn to stand before this council, not as part of a formal trial but more as an evidence-gathering inquiry (cf. 23:28).[4] This inquiry places Paul, alone, between Roman and Jewish judicial gaze.

The Violent Exchange between Paul and the High Priest (23:1–5)

Luke begins by noting that Paul courageously gazed (v. 1, "looked straight") at the Sanhedrin and opened with a single assertion. His declaration is terse and direct, with only a simple "my brothers" (23:1) to preface his address in contrast to his opening "brothers and fathers" from the day before (22:1). As such, this choice of language is "less brotherly than it might appear,"[5] and its curtness may have set the tone for the exchanges that would follow. Paul also uses a rare word, *politeuomai*, translated as "fulfilled my duty,"[6] to describe his behavior. This verb is used only one other time in the NT (Phil 1:27)[7] and it carries political connotations in the sense that it has to do with one's "citizenship." That Paul would use this word here is unsurprising given that he has been expressing his Jewish identity in terms of his Tarsian and Roman citizenship (21:39; 22:3, 25–29). Now, however, he declares that he has not lived by the standards of Tarsus or Rome but by the standard of God. He made this clear in his speech the previous day by highlighting that he was "zealous for God" before meeting the risen Lord and then obedient to God afterward. In this way he asserts that "in all good conscience" he has fulfilled his duty to God all his days (23:1).

Paul's assertion angers the high priest Ananias. He commands someone standing near Paul to bring a stop to his words by striking his mouth (23:2).

---

like Ananias from Damascus; see 22:12) is zealous for God, committed to the law, and respectful of the temple and the traditions of his fellow Jews.

3. See G. H. Twelftree, "Sanhedrin," *DJG* 729–31.
4. I.e., outside the ordinary trial procedures referred to in Roman law by a category known as *extra ordinem* (outside the ordinary). See Wansink, "Roman Law," 986–88.
5. Dunn, *Acts*, 303.
6. Cf. "lived my life" (NRSV; ESV); "I have lived" (KJV).
7. The noun form, *politeuma*, is used only once (Phil 3:20). The verb (e.g., 2 Macc 6:1; 11:25; 3 Macc 3:4; 4 Macc 2:8, 23; 4:23; 5:16; Philo, *Virtues* 161; *Spec. Laws* 4.226; Josephus, *Ant.* 12.142; *Life* 12) and its cognate noun (e.g., 2 Macc 12:7; Josephus, *Ant* 1.13; *Ag. Ap.* 2.257) occur elsewhere in Jewish literature from the Second Temple period.

While the outrage may have come from a perceived blasphemy, this temperament is not out of character from what we know of the high priest Ananias. Ananias, the son of Nedebaeus, was appointed high priest by Herod of Chalcis (grandson of Herod the Great) and reigned from AD 47/48–59. As high priest he collected taxes, controlled the temple and Sanhedrin, and was the primary representative of the Jews before Rome. Josephus describes Ananias as politically astute but also greedy and prone to violence (*Ant.* 20.205–7, 213). Theologically he was likely a Sadducee; politically he was pro-Roman. Jewish nationalists despised him both for his avarice and his political loyalties. Not surprisingly, after the outbreak of the Jewish War (AD 66), rebels burned him out of his home and, eventually, killed him (*J.W.* 2.426–29, 441). If the picture Josephus paints of Ananias is at all close, Paul's biting words to him in response to the strike on his mouth—"God will strike you, you whitewashed wall" (Acts 23:3)—are more appropriate than they might first appear. They echo Ezekiel's critique of Israel's false prophets whose words are compared to flimsy and cracked walls with a veneer of "whitewash" to hide their faults (Ezek 13:10–15; 22:28; cf. Matt 23:27). As judge for Israel and the council of the Sanhedrin, Paul adds that the very law Ananias represents was violated when he had him struck. The law required that Paul receive a fair trial before he received any punishment (see Lev 19:15; cf. John 7:51).[8]

Those standing nearby this exchange alert Paul to the fact that he has just spoken harshly to "God's high priest" (Acts 23:4). Paul gathers himself and acknowledges his own oversight of the law in speaking against a ruler of the people (Exod 22:28). Is Paul being ironic[9] with his reply (i.e., a "true" high priest would not have acted this way)? Perhaps Paul's poor eyesight is to blame for his failure to recognize who spoke? The simplest explanation may be that since Paul had only been in Jerusalem intermittently for the past number of years (the last time in about AD 51, about six years earlier), he didn't recognize the current high priest. In the end, whether he is ironic, shortsighted, or just ignorant, Paul is portrayed as being more obedient to the law than the sitting high priest!

The Violent Exchange between Sadducees and Pharisees (23:6–10)

The second declaration Paul makes also sparks a violent response, but this time between members within the Sanhedrin. Significant theological divisions marked first-century Judaism, and the Sanhedrin was no different. The Sadducees, centered in Jerusalem and from the Jewish aristocracy, held to a strict

---

8. Schnabel, *Acts*, 927, observes that while Lysias may not have regarded the meeting with the Sanhedrin as a trial, after being struck on the mouth Paul certainly does (Acts 23:3, 6; cf. 24:20–21).

9. See Augustine, *Epistles* 138. Calvin, *Acts*, 2.23.1–5, also views Paul's words as ironic and regards them as a "taunting excuse" of Ananias.

literal reading of the Scriptures and elevated the Torah far above the Prophets and Writings. They did not believe in the idea of the resurrection of the dead. The Pharisees, in contrast, did believe in the resurrection. Paul, recognizing the sharp theological disparity existing within the Sanhedrin (v. 6a), exploited the division by declaring, "My brothers, I am a Pharisee, descended from Pharisees. I stand on trial because of the hope of the resurrection of the dead!" (v. 6b; cf. Phil 3:5). When he said that, mayhem ensued among this distinguished body: "A dispute broke out . . . the assembly was divided [v. 7]. . . . there was a great uproar [v. 9]. . . . [and] the dispute[10] became . . . violent [v. 10]."

Some may regard Paul's tactic as a cynical or cunning move.[11] That is, when he recognized that he would not get a fair hearing at this inquiry, he threw out this declaration to generate chaos between his opponents. While Paul does not specify that it is Jesus's resurrection at issue, what he is doing with this declaration is turning the question back to his own agenda. This is not a matter of theological minutia for Paul. For him, resurrection—especially the resurrection of Jesus—is of primary importance, as his previous day's testimony attests (see 22:6–10, 14–15, 18–21). As Alexander notes, Paul "reminds his audience—and Luke's readers—that there is a real theological issue at stake here (v. 9). The Pharisees believed (unlike the Sadducees) that God was still revealing himself to his people. The real question was, were they prepared to accept that the apostolic testimony to Christ was part of this continuing self-revelation?"[12]

Paul may have been content to sit back and watch the Sadducees and Pharisees experience a little of what he had experienced the previous day, but the tribune would have none of it. The commander understood that the increasingly violent dispute could well mean danger for Paul and so had him returned to the barracks (23:10). Just like the previous day's experience, allowing Paul to speak to his own people, in their own language, about their own concerns, led only to violent clashes and no clearer knowledge for the tribune.

The Lord Stands Near Paul (23:11)

At significant junctures in Acts, the Lord himself appears and speaks directly (see 1:4–8; 9:3–16; 10:13–15; 18:9–10). This is another significant point in the narrative. Paul was made to stand alone before the Roman tribune and the Jerusalem Sanhedrin; now, alone in his room in the Antonia Fortress, the Lord stands with him. At this moment, the Lord speaks to Paul and tells him

---

10. The Greek word *stasis* can also carry the meaning "riot," "revolt," or "rebellion." It is ironic that what happens in the Sanhedrin between Sadducees and Pharisees is the very thing that they will later accuse Paul of before Felix (Acts 24:5).

11. E.g., Richard Pervo, *Acts*, Hermeneia (Philadelphia: Fortress, 2008), 574; Rowe, *World Upside Down*, 70.

12. Alexander, *Acts*, 171.

to be resolute. The last few days have been intense and difficult. He has been falsely accused, beaten by a mob, chained by Roman soldiers, stretched out to be whipped, and forced to defend himself in the Sanhedrin. No doubt Paul was depleted physically, emotionally, and spiritually. Alone and back under Roman guard in the barracks, he would need courage. More than just encouragement, however, the Lord's words mark a significant shift in the narrative.[13] Paul's testimonial work in Jerusalem is complete; he "*must*" (*dei*) now also testify in Rome. Luke, as he does often in his twin narratives, employs the divine "must" to indicate providential guidance.[14] Paul is reminded that the Lord is shaping and directing the drama of his life and the drama of human history. Although it may have been difficult to comprehend, this is connected to the way in which Paul will "finish the race and complete the task the Lord Jesus has given [him]—the task of testifying to the good news of God's grace" (20:24) not only in Jerusalem, but also in Rome.

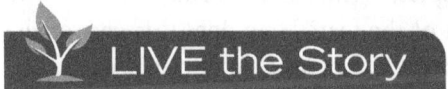

LIVE the Story

Pay Attention When the Narrative Slows Down

Acts is a long document. Sometimes Luke will describe the events of a long period—weeks, months, or even years—in a brief sentence or two (e.g., Acts 11:26; 18:11; 19:8–10; 20:3). Like any good storyteller, he will also slow down the narrative and describe in detail the experience of just a few hours or days. When storytellers slow down the narrative, it is their way of telling the audience, "This is important, pay attention." Although we might come to read Acts with a variety of theological agendas, when a writer like Luke deliberates over a few specific episodes, we must try to understand what *his* agenda is and, in that, what is the agenda of the Spirit who inspired him to write.

We are amid one of Luke's "slow motion" narratives now. Luke takes more than two full chapters to describe the events of just a few days. Again, the parallels with Jesus's passion narrative are evident. This, in a sense, is Paul's Jerusalem passion narrative. Paul set his face toward Jerusalem earlier in narrative (19:21; cf. Luke 9:51), and the reader is reminded that the Spirit has alerted him to the hardships that are awaiting him (Acts 20:22–24; cf. Luke 9:22). After Paul's arrival in Jerusalem, he faces serious inquiry from his fellow Christian Jews about his mission to the gentiles and is forced to prove his loyalty "to the law" (Acts 21:17–26). Within a week of this, Paul is

---

13. Cf. Rowe, *World Upside Down*, 70.
14. See, e.g., Luke 2:49; 4:43; 9:22; 17:25; 22:37; 24:7, 26, 44; Acts 1:16; 3:21; 4:12; 5:29; 9:6, 16; 14:22; 17:3; 19:21; 27:24.

accused and accosted in the temple precincts by a mob (21:27–36), and after the intervention of Roman soldiers (21:37–40), he addresses that same crowd (22:1–21). Later that evening he is taken to the barracks and is stretched out to be whipped as a part of standard Roman "questioning" when he reengages his Roman captors in an intense conversation (22:22–29). The next morning Paul is made to stand alone before the highest Jewish ruling body, the Sanhedrin, and after several passionate exchanges, violence erupts in the council (23:1–10). In the night the Lord appears to Paul (23:11), and the next morning a plot to kill Paul will be uncovered, and he will be hastily transferred to Caesarea under heavy Roman guard (23:12–35). In all this Luke is bringing to the foreground multiple and important themes. These include tension within the early Christian and non-Christian Jewish community over the inclusion of the gentiles in the people of God, the question of Christian mission and its relationship to the state, and the centrality of the resurrection of Jesus. Amid all these important topics, events, and exchanges, how do we dig deep into this particular section of the text? How does this part of the story of Acts compel us to live the story of the gospel in our own world and in our own lives?

Jesus Stands with Us When the Burdens Are Great

One way to dig deeper into this section of Acts is to recognize that this episode speaks to all those who have been persecuted, falsely accused, or forced to deal with legal systems that are uncaring (at best) or cruel (at worst). Most of my life has been privileged. No police officer or soldier has pulled me over because of the color of my skin as they sometimes do for my First Nations friends in Canada or my African-American friends in the United States. No violent mob has threatened my community as we have gathered together in worship as they sometimes do in Iraq, Egypt, or in Odisha (northeastern India). No state-sponsored agents have brutally interrogated me because of my Christian faith as they sometimes do to Christians in Myanmar (aka Burma) or North Korea.[15] Yet, because I am aware that my Christian brothers and sisters do face these injustices and trials (not unlike what Paul faced), I pray that in their loneliness and struggle they might know that the Lord stands near them. I pray that they might know, in meaningful and true ways, the simple words from Jesus: "Take courage!" (Acts 23:11). This courage comes from their union with Christ. The burden of Christian witness is heavy, and getting

---

15. For the details of persecution of Christians that is occurring on a massive and unprecedented scale in our world today, see the important article by John L. Allen Jr., "Today's Attack in Egypt Is the Latest Strike in the War on Christians in the Middle East," *The Spectator*, 9 April 2017, https://blogs.spectator.co.uk/2017/04/todays-attack-egypt-latest-strike-war-christians-middle-east/#.

mixed up with Jesus of Nazareth does anything but remove us from tension, uncertainty, chaos, and trial. At the heart of the gospel, however, is the promise that we do not carry our burdens alone. We are yoked together with Christ (Matt 11:28–30).

Philip Yancey reminds us that following Christ and bearing witness draws us into the burdens of Jesus. For example, these include caring for creation and the stewardship of resources, standing against racism and religious persecution, and attending to questions of justice and violence. He cites the work of two Quakers to drive home this point:

> The Quaker philosopher Elton Trueblood writes: "In many areas the gospel, instead of taking away people's burdens, actually adds to them." He cites John Woolman, a successful Quaker merchant who lived a comfortable life until God convicted him of the offense of slavery. Woolman gave up his prosperous business, used his money to purchase slaves' freedom, wore undyed suits to avoid using dye produced by slave labor, traveled on foot in solidarity with slaves who were not permitted to ride in carriages, and refused to eat sugar, rum, molasses, and other products tainted by slave labor. Largely because of this "quiet revolutionary," by 1787 not a single American Quaker owned a slave. Trueblood writes: "Occasionally we talk of our Christianity as something that solves problems, and there is a sense in which it does. Long before it does so, however, it increases both the number and the intensity of the problems. Even our intellectual questions are increased by the acceptance of a strong religious faith. . . . If a man wishes to avoid the disturbing effect of paradoxes, the best advice is for him to leave Christian faith alone."[16]

As Paul gave witness to Jesus in the tough circumstances of accusation, hardship, and confinement in Jerusalem, he could do so because he knew Jesus stood next to him. He was yoked together with the Lord. This is what union with Christ means. It does not mean problems or confusions or chaos are taken away. In fact, they may be multiplied. But if circumstances for you happen to be light and easy, remember that for many of your fellow believers—members of the one body to which we all belong—living the story of the gospel is difficult today. For them and for ourselves, we pray for courage. We remember that the Lord stands near us all. For, as Frederick Buechner notes, "God himself does not [always] give answers. He gives Himself."[17]

---

16. Philip Yancey, *Reaching for the Invisible God: What Can We Expect to Find?* (Grand Rapids: Zondervan, 2000), 91.
17. Frederick Buechner, *Telling the Truth: The Gospel as Tragedy, Comedy, and Fairy Tale* (San Francisco: HarperCollins, 1977), 43.

CHAPTER 53

Acts 23:12-35

 LISTEN to the Story

¹²The next morning some Jews formed a conspiracy and bound themselves with an oath not to eat or drink until they had killed Paul. ¹³More than forty men were involved in this plot. ¹⁴They went to the chief priests and the elders and said, "We have taken a solemn oath not to eat anything until we have killed Paul. ¹⁵Now then, you and the Sanhedrin petition the commander to bring him before you on the pretext of wanting more accurate information about his case. We are ready to kill him before he gets here."

¹⁶But when the son of Paul's sister heard of this plot, he went into the barracks and told Paul.

¹⁷Then Paul called one of the centurions and said, "Take this young man to the commander; he has something to tell him." ¹⁸So he took him to the commander.

The centurion said, "Paul, the prisoner, sent for me and asked me to bring this young man to you because he has something to tell you."

¹⁹The commander took the young man by the hand, drew him aside and asked, "What is it you want to tell me?"

²⁰He said: "Some Jews have agreed to ask you to bring Paul before the Sanhedrin tomorrow on the pretext of wanting more accurate information about him. ²¹Don't give in to them, because more than forty of them are waiting in ambush for him. They have taken an oath not to eat or drink until they have killed him. They are ready now, waiting for your consent to their request."

²²The commander dismissed the young man with this warning: "Don't tell anyone that you have reported this to me."

²³Then he called two of his centurions and ordered them, "Get ready a detachment of two hundred soldiers, seventy horsemen and two hundred spearmen to go to Caesarea at nine tonight. ²⁴Provide horses for Paul so that he may be taken safely to Governor Felix."

²⁵He wrote a letter as follows:

²⁶Claudius Lysias,
To His Excellency, Governor Felix:

Greetings.
²⁷This man was seized by the Jews and they were about to kill him, but I came with my troops and rescued him, for I had learned that he is a Roman citizen. ²⁸I wanted to know why they were accusing him, so I brought him to their Sanhedrin. ²⁹I found that the accusation had to do with questions about their law, but there was no charge against him that deserved death or imprisonment. ³⁰When I was informed of a plot to be carried out against the man, I sent him to you at once. I also ordered his accusers to present to you their case against him.

³¹So the soldiers, carrying out their orders, took Paul with them during the night and brought him as far as Antipatris. ³²The next day they let the cavalry go on with him, while they returned to the barracks. ³³When the cavalry arrived in Caesarea, they delivered the letter to the governor and handed Paul over to him. ³⁴The governor read the letter and asked what province he was from. Learning that he was from Cilicia, ³⁵he said, "I will hear your case when your accusers get here." Then he ordered that Paul be kept under guard in Herod's palace.

Listening to the Text in the Story: Acts 4:23.

EXPLAIN the Story

The story of Acts is riveting, and the last few chapters of the narrative have been dramatic. Since Paul arrived in Jerusalem (21:17), fellow Christian Jews have challenged him; he was accused and accosted by a Jewish mob; he delivered an impassioned speech to a riotous crowd; he was dragged into Roman custody and nearly tortured; and, after all this, he was forced to face the Jewish legal and religious leadership in the Sanhedrin. In each successive episode, Paul becomes more isolated and alone as the dramatic tension increases. The parallels with Jesus's passion are profound. For readers who have listened to Luke's two-volume account and discerned the correspondences between Jesus and Paul, they may not have been surprised that the next step for Paul would be a plot to have him killed. The drama is intense! Yet for all of Paul's isolation, he is not alone. Between Paul and his violent plotters stands the risen Lord (v. 11)—and a young man, Paul's nephew. This episode describes the plot to have Paul killed (vv. 12–15), how the plot was uncovered (vv. 16–22), and how the plot was foiled (vv. 23–35).

The Plot (23:12–15)

The years leading up to the Jewish War (which began in AD 66) were violent and politically unstable in Judea. *Sicarii*—revolutionary "dagger men"—stalked the crowds that flocked to Jerusalem, especially during festival seasons, and drew curved knives hidden in their cloaks to stab their political enemies suddenly and then blend into the crowd. Nationalistic fervor was on the rise, and anyone perceived to be a threat to Jewish identity or to be in collaboration with the Romans was considered to be an enemy by radicals. In this environment, just ten years or so before the war (AD 57), it would be unsurprising that Paul was perceived to be a traitor worthy of elimination.[1]

The forty or so Jewish men who plotted Paul's assassination are not identified as *sicarii*, but they have similar intentions. To emphasize the passion and steadfastness of these men, Luke tells us three times (vv. 12, 14, 21) that they had committed themselves by an oath not to eat or drink until they had killed Paul. This oath (*anathematizō*) is a self-inflicted curse of destruction if they do not fulfill their promise to destroy Paul. Of course, when the plot is foiled, there is the black humor of how this oath might be fulfilled.[2]

Given what we know about the character of the high priest Ananias (see comments on 23:1–5), it is not surprising that these firebrands sought assistance from members in the Jewish leadership like him. The plot brings together two parties from the previous violent episodes: a group of men from the Jerusalem mob and some members from the Sanhedrin. The text says the plotters approached "the chief priests and the elders" to assist them in their plan (v. 14). "The chief priests and the elders" were the same ones who brought Peter and John before the Sanhedrin earlier in the narrative (see 4:1–23). In the intervening decades, however, much has changed from the mild threats made against Peter and John and the violent plans made against Paul. Interestingly, no mention is made of the scribes or Pharisees involved in the plot since they may have been favorably disposed to Paul from the previous day's events.[3]

---

1. Dunn, *Acts*, 306.
2. Longenecker, *Acts*, 533, notes that they would not have to starve themselves if they failed. In the Mishnah, the rabbis permitted four types of oaths to be broken: "Vows of incitement, vows of exaggeration, vows made in error, and vows that cannot be fulfilled by reason of constraint" (m. Nedarim 3:1–3).
3. Gaventa, *Acts*, 319.

In the end, the plot against Paul was a simple one: while he was en route from the Antonia Fortress northwest of the temple to the hall of the Sanhedrin southwest of the temple, they would overwhelm Paul's Roman escort and kill him.

The Plot Is Uncovered (23:16–22)

Without any prior mention of family either in Acts or anywhere else in the NT, a nephew of Paul's is introduced to the narrative. Luke has introduced unexpected characters in his narrative before (e.g., Rhoda in 12:13; Jason in 17:5–8; Dionysius and Demaris in 17:33).[4] This time, it is an unnamed relative of Paul's (23:16). That Paul would have a sister in Jerusalem is not out of the question. Paul may have been born in Tarsus, but he was "brought up" in Jerusalem (22:3). It is therefore unsurprising that another family member also settled in Jerusalem. His intermittent visits here after his conversion (cf. 9:26–30; 11:30; 15:2) would afford him opportunities to call on and possibly stay with his sister and her family when he was in the city. Somehow, the young nephew gathered information about the plot and brought the news to Paul.

After the turbulent meeting with the Sanhedrin, Paul is brought back to the Antonia Fortress and placed in protective custody. Luke does not describe his confinement as including chains again, but centurions are close at hand (23:17). It is likely that he is being held securely in "the senior officers' quarters in the fortress."[5] All this does not necessarily mean that he can freely receive guests or relatives. How then does his nephew gain access to the barracks to unveil the plot to kill Paul? While the term "young man" (*neanias*) can refer to a youth between twenty and forty years of age, Rapske argues that he may be younger than this and that the repeated emphasis of his "youth" (vv. 17, 18, 22) may account for why he was able to gain access to the fortress. He did so not because he was identified as a nephew of Paul—in fact his identity as a relative is kept secret from the Romans. Rather, "being so young, Paul's nephew was deemed entirely harmless by the soldiers," whereas an "adult male would probably have been denied access for security reasons."[6] Given his urgent news, the youth is granted access to the tribune. The commander takes Paul's nephew "by the hand" (v. 19) and listens to his information about the plot. The plot is credible to the tribune—especially given Paul's previous brushes with violence and the ongoing political turmoil within the city—and after dismissing the youth with the warning "don't tell anyone" (v. 22), he takes immediate action to ensure Paul's safety (vv. 23–35). The Lord's promise to Paul to keep him safe

---

4. Peterson, *Acts*, 622.
5. Rapske, *Paul in Roman Custody*, 148.
6. Ibid., 149.

(v. 11) is beginning to be fulfilled through the sharp ears of a young man and by this unbelieving Roman commander. Again, we are reminded that Paul's life is under God's care—even as it involves human agents.

The Plot Is Foiled (23:23–35)

The commander moved quickly to ensure Paul's security against the assassination plot. A significant proportion of the garrison was mobilized to relocate Paul from the danger in Jerusalem to Caesarea, the seat of Roman administration in the province of Judea and the residence of the governor, Felix. The tribune commanded the centurions to make ready two hundred soldiers, seventy horsemen, and two hundred *dexiolaboi* (v. 23).[7] The word *dexiolabos* is unique, and its meaning is unclear. Literally it means "taking by the right hand." This word occurs only here in all our known ancient Greek literature. Most translations, including the NIV, assume that it refers to "spearmen" because Roman javelins were thrown with the right hand. Another suggestion is that it refers to two hundred "led horses" (i.e., led by the right hand).[8] If this suggestion is correct, these horses would be the remounts for the men so that they could travel the hundred kilometers (60 miles), a significant distance for soldiers to do at speed, from Jerusalem to Caesarea.[9] Whatever the word meant, the details are clear: this is a large military escort mobilized in haste—by the "third hour of the night" (i.e., around 9:00 p.m.)—and able to travel with speed.

Some commentators think the number of soldiers recorded is an exaggeration envisioned by Luke to emphasize the importance of Paul[10] or the benevolence[11] of the Roman authorities. More recently, historians have recognized that "the textual details concerning the third hour, the provision of mounts, and the numbers involved in Paul's transport, because of their precision and because they are not strictly material to the text, suggest accurate reporting rather than Lukan romancing."[12] The escort may seem excessive to modern readers, but the growing political unrest in Jerusalem suggests that the numbers are realistic. The tribune acted, as a competent Roman officer

---

7. These would be from a garrison of almost a thousand men—a garrison comprised of both cavalry and foot soldiers.

8. F. J. Foakes Jackson and Kirsopp Lake, *The Acts of the Apostles: English Translation and Commentary*, vol. 4 of *The Beginnings of Christianity* (London: Macmillan, 1933; repr., Grand Rapids: Baker, 1979), 293.

9. The range of a legion's march was traditionally fixed at twenty-four Roman miles per day. Antipatris, the first stop on their journey to Caesarea, was about forty miles away. This would be impossible for soldiers to reach on foot, even if they were lightly armed spearmen.

10. E.g., Conzelmann, *Acts*, 194.

11. Haenchen, *Acts*, 650.

12. Rapske, *Paul in Roman Custody*, 154.

should amid tense circumstances, to relocate a Roman citizen like Paul with safety and speed.

Along with the heavily armed escort, the Roman tribune sent along a formal legal letter to Governor Felix. Luke includes the letter for his readers. Some commentators suggest that in writing that the commander sent a letter "as follows" (v. 25, *echousan ton typon touton*) or "of this type" should be read as Luke acknowledging "that what follows is only the general purport of the letter."[13] The logic is that Luke could not have known the private correspondence between the tribune and the governor. In light of recent discoveries of Roman judicial proceedings from this era, however, others have suggested that this could very well be a copy of the official letter written by Claudius Lysias. The Romans were scrupulous recordkeepers, and copies of these legal documents were retained and made available to defendants.[14]

The letter itself follows the standard form of ancient letter writing with the following elements: (1) sender; (2) recipient; (3) greeting; and (4) body of the letter. The letter contains interesting details. To begin with, this is the first mention of the full name of the Roman tribune, Claudius Lysias (v. 26), who has been so important in the preceding episodes. Lysias is a Greek name, and it suggests the tribune was a Greek who worked his way up the ranks in the Roman military. At some stage he purchased his Roman citizenship (cf. 22:28) from someone in Emperor Claudius's government. After receiving citizenship, he took on the name Claudius in honor of the emperor.[15] The second name mentioned in the letter is that of Governor Felix, who served as governor of the Roman province of Judea from AD 52–59/60. Despite Lysias's laudatory greeting—"to His Excellency"—history has not looked favorably on his administrative and political abilities. The Roman historian Tacitus, a near contemporary of Luke, looked down his aristocratic nose at this former slave who, along with his brother Pallas, had risen through the ranks to become a favorite of Emperor Claudius. Even though the emperor had elevated Felix to be procurator of Judea, Tacitus wrote that he "practiced every kind of cruelty and lust, wielding the power of a king with all the instincts of a slave" (*Hist.* 5.9).[16]

The body of Lysias's letter offers a modified summary of the events of the past few days in relation to Paul (23:27–30). In it, Lysias presents his version

---

13. Longenecker, *Acts*, 536; cf. Dunn, *Acts*, 308.
14. See Bruce W. Winter, "Official Proceedings and the Forensic Speeches in Acts 24–26," in Bruce W. Winter and Andrew D. Clarke, eds., *The Book of Acts in Its Ancient Literary Setting*, vol. 1 of *The Book of Acts in Its First Century Setting*, ed. Bruce W. Winter (Grand Rapids: Eerdmans; Paternoster: Carlisle, 1993), 309.
15. Longenecker, *Acts*, 536.
16. Cornelius Tacitus, *Histories, Books IV–V*, trans. C. H. Moore, LCL (Cambridge: Harvard University Press, 1914), 191–93. See Josephus, *J.W.* 2.247; *Ant.* 20.137, 162–63.

of the story so as to cast himself in the most favorable light possible while at the same time providing a legal account of the events. He recounts the riot in the temple grounds (cf. 21:27–30), his "rescue" of Paul (21:31–33), and his discovery of the plot against Paul (23:17–22). Of course, he ignored informing the governor that he did not "rescue" Paul because he had learned he was a Roman citizen but because he was trying to control a violent outburst in Jerusalem. Nor does he tell him that he first chained Paul and only learned about his citizenship when Paul was stretched out to be "questioned" (i.e., whipped!) by his soldiers. Those details (i.e., chaining and torture), forbidden by Roman law against its citizens, could have jeopardized his career. The important part of the letter is "I found that the accusation had to do with questions about their law, but there was no charge against him that deserved death or imprisonment" (v. 29). That Lysias would refer the case to his superior in Caesarea is not unusual; after all, this is where a legal case like this should be heard. The twin declarations of Paul's innocence under Roman law and the controversy over Jewish law will recur as the story of Acts continues (24:1–21; 25:8–12; 26:30–32). One additional piece of new information is that the tribune has ordered Paul's accusers to come and present their evidence to Felix against Paul (v. 30).

With Paul securely guarded and Lysias's letter in hand, the party makes their way to the city of Caesarea Maritima, a Roman colony and the seat of Roman administration. Luke provides an abundance of detail about this military transfer. Although the actual route from Jerusalem to Antipatris, their first stopover, is not given,[17] this is the logical place to rest.[18] This would have put the longest (about sixty-five kilometers, or forty miles) and most dangerous part of the journey behind them as they made their way northwest through the Judean hills. The hills would provide excellent opportunities for an ambush if one was coming. After reaching Antipatris, the rest of the journey was much more flat and safe for the fifty kilometers (30 miles) remaining to Caesarea. The accompanying infantry returned to Jerusalem, while the cavalry continued on safely with Paul.

Once arriving in Caesarea, the prisoner and Claudius Lysias's letter were delivered to Governor Felix. Despite his known administrative incompetence, Felix asked the correct question of Paul concerning which province he was from. The question is a matter of legal jurisdiction. Upon learning that Paul was from Cilicia, he could have extradited Paul there. Rowe clarifies why Felix

---

17. Rasmussen, *Atlas*, 219, notes that the detachment could either follow the easterly old Beth Horon road or take the road that ran farther north through Gophna and Thamna.

18. This is the same route taken by Cestius Gallus and his army in October of AD 66 at the beginning of the Jewish War; see Rapske, *Paul in Roman Custody*, 154n9.

chose not to do so: "'Sometimes' the provincial governor 'has power even in relation to non-residents, if they have taken direct part in criminal activity.'... [Further, the exercise of the governor's authority] was particularly apropos to criminal activity that affected public order and to charges that fell outside the normal legal *ordo*."[19] After deciding to hear Paul's case, Felix ordered that Paul be kept under armed guard in Herod's "palace" (Greek: *praitorion*; Latin: *praetorium*). This palace was the grand coastal structure built by Herod the Great and later expropriated by the Romans as the residence for their Judean provincial governors. It would have ample facilities to accommodate prisoners, like Paul, as they awaited trial.[20] This entire episode—the account of the tribune's orders, the formal legal letter, the troop's movements, and Felix's preliminary questions—is not only interesting for its detailed description but also demonstrates Luke's competence and accuracy as a historian.

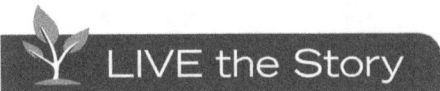

LIVE the Story

Unlikely Courage

The episode describing the plot against Paul's life comes after the Lord's encouraging promise in the night (23:11). At this point in the narrative, Paul had no idea how he would be delivered from his difficult situation in Jerusalem to "testify" in Rome. In Acts thus far, God has used different means to work his purposes through his witnesses amid trouble. Peter was delivered from prison by an angel (Acts 12), while on another occasion an earthquake in Philippi was instrumental for Paul and Silas (Acts 16). What would God do this time? Despite the parallels with other episodes in Acts, there are no "dittoes" with God. God is too creative and unpredictable to repeat himself in the story of Acts or in the story of our lives. If God were predictable, life would not require trust, and trust requires the courage to risk. Paul is not told how God will bring him to Rome; he is only given the simple and risky command: "Take courage!" At the height of this dramatic and tense moment in the narrative, God does not use a mighty angel or a mighty deed. God uses an unnamed boy, Paul's young nephew.

The theological point I want to make by emphasizing the age of Paul's nephew is that the means God uses to initiate the process of Paul's deliverance and his movement to Rome begins with a young boy. While the Lord stood near to Paul and told him to take courage, the one who stood between Paul

---

19. Rowe, *World Upside Down*, 72.
20. On the "first phase" (i.e., the first five days) of Paul's guarded custody in Caesarea, see Rapske, *Paul in Roman Custody*, 155–58.

and his assassins was a brave child. God used a sharp-eared and keen-witted boy with the courage to enter the Antonia Fortress to assist Paul. Paul was in a vulnerable situation. He did not know how his situation would unfold. He only knew that the Lord was with him, and with him working out the details, he could take courage. In this instance, the details were worked out by a brave youth acting on information he had overheard. This was an unexpected source of courage. We are not given any warning of this in the narrative. This young boy suddenly enters the story and acts his part bravely. His action turns out to be the means God uses to bring about his purposes for Paul. Neither Paul in the first century, nor Christians in the twenty-first century, can anticipate what means God will use to help his people and advance the kingdom. This story reminds us that he can use unlikely courage—even the courage of a young boy—to move the gospel story forward.

On the Front Lines

Luke does not inform us whether the youth who helped his uncle Paul by disclosing a plot against him was a Christian. I think it is unlikely that his close relationship with his uncle would mean he would have no understanding about Paul's gospel. In short, I think Paul's nephew was a believer. While we may be uncertain about this young person's personal engagement with the gospel, we do know that this was a dangerous situation he was stepping into. If the forty men who wanted to kill Paul learned about this young boy's actions, it is not beyond the realm of possibility that they would have wanted to silence and kill him too. It is unfortunate that we do not know more about Paul's nephew. Still, his brave example is one of many unheralded stories of love in action, of Christians who risked their lives on the front lines in the care of others.

Brian Stewart, one of Canada's most experienced and respected foreign journalists, eloquently spoke for courageous unnamed Christians, such as Paul's nephew, in his address for the 160th convocation of Knox College.[21] Stewart is a Presbyterian. He doesn't often explicitly articulate his faith in his work for the secular news agency, the Canadian Broadcasting Corporation. Most of the time, he just honestly and professionally tells the stories from the world's most troubled conflicts and worst tragedies. His reporting from El Salvador to Ethiopia has earned him global respect and numerous awards. One story that has not gained the broad recognition he thinks it deserves is the story of Christians showing up first "on the front lines." That is, his long years of global correspondence in some of the most dangerous places on earth

---

21. Brian Stewart, "On the Front Lines," Christianity.ca, convocation address delivered on 12 May 2004, https://www.christianity.ca/page.aspx?pid=11235.

have convinced him that Christians consistently show up where help is needed most. His excellent address is worth reading in full, but here is a sample to whet the appetite:

> I've been struck by the rather blithe notion, spread in many circles including the media, and taken up by a rather large section of our younger population that organized, mainstream Christianity has been reduced to a musty, dimly lit backwater of contemporary life, a fading force. Well, I'm here to tell you from what I've seen from my "ring-side seat" at events over decades that there is nothing that is further from the truth. . . . I've found there is *no* movement, or force, closer to the raw truth of war, famines, crises, and the vast human predicament, than organized Christianity in action. And there is no alliance more determined and dogged in action than church workers, ordained and lay members, when mobilized for a common good. It is these Christians who are right "On the Front Lines" of committed humanity today, and when I want to find that front, I follow their trail.

The "front lines," of course, are not limited to war zones and African famines. The front lines run through every country, city, and community. Wherever we are called to serve and offer courageous witness, what Paul's nephew and Brian Stewart remind us of is that we are not alone. We may feel isolated and alone, but we are not. We serve on the front lines with many other Christians—most of them unknown to us—and in that company of Christ's body we can indeed take courage.

CHAPTER 54

Acts 24:1-27

 LISTEN to the Story

¹Five days later the high priest Ananias went down to Caesarea with some of the elders and a lawyer named Tertullus, and they brought their charges against Paul before the governor. ²When Paul was called in, Tertullus presented his case before Felix: "We have enjoyed a long period of peace under you, and your foresight has brought about reforms in this nation. ³Everywhere and in every way, most excellent Felix, we acknowledge this with profound gratitude. ⁴But in order not to weary you further, I would request that you be kind enough to hear us briefly.

⁵"We have found this man to be a troublemaker, stirring up riots among the Jews all over the world. He is a ringleader of the Nazarene sect ⁶and even tried to desecrate the temple; so we seized him.[1] ⁸By examining him yourself you will be able to learn the truth about all these charges we are bringing against him."

⁹The other Jews joined in the accusation, asserting that these things were true.

¹⁰When the governor motioned for him to speak, Paul replied: "I know that for a number of years you have been a judge over this nation; so I gladly make my defense. ¹¹You can easily verify that no more than twelve days ago I went up to Jerusalem to worship. ¹²My accusers did not find me arguing with anyone at the temple, or stirring up a crowd in the synagogues or anywhere else in the city. ¹³And they cannot prove to you the charges they are now making against me. ¹⁴However, I admit that I worship the God of our ancestors as a follower of the Way, which they call a sect. I believe everything that is in accordance with the Law and that is written in the Prophets, ¹⁵and I have the same hope in God as these men

---

1. There is an expanded version of this passage ("but Lysias, the commander, came and with much violence seized him from our hands, commanding his accusers to come before you") that appears in a number of copies of the Western text at vv. 7–8a. These words are included in the Received Text, and this explains their inclusion in the KJV/NKJV. The additional words are not, however, included in the best and earliest manuscripts. See Metzger, *Textual Commentary*, 434.

themselves have, that there will be a resurrection of both the righteous and the wicked. ¹⁶So I strive always to keep my conscience clear before God and man.

¹⁷"After an absence of several years, I came to Jerusalem to bring my people gifts for the poor and to present offerings. ¹⁸I was ceremonially clean when they found me in the temple courts doing this. There was no crowd with me, nor was I involved in any disturbance. ¹⁹But there are some Jews from the province of Asia, who ought to be here before you and bring charges if they have anything against me. ²⁰Or these who are here should state what crime they found in me when I stood before the Sanhedrin—²¹unless it was this one thing I shouted as I stood in their presence: 'It is concerning the resurrection of the dead that I am on trial before you today.'"

²²Then Felix, who was well acquainted with the Way, adjourned the proceedings. "When Lysias the commander comes," he said, "I will decide your case." ²³He ordered the centurion to keep Paul under guard but to give him some freedom and permit his friends to take care of his needs.

²⁴Several days later Felix came with his wife Drusilla, who was Jewish. He sent for Paul and listened to him as he spoke about faith in Christ Jesus. ²⁵As Paul talked about righteousness, self-control and the judgment to come, Felix was afraid and said, "That's enough for now! You may leave. When I find it convenient, I will send for you." ²⁶At the same time he was hoping that Paul would offer him a bribe, so he sent for him frequently and talked with him.

²⁷When two years had passed, Felix was succeeded by Porcius Festus, but because Felix wanted to grant a favor to the Jews, he left Paul in prison.

Listening to the Text in the Story: Psalm 1:1; Luke 21:12–13; Romans 15:25–28, 31; 1 Corinthians 16:1–4, 15; 2 Corinthians 8:1–4; Galatians 2:10.

EXPLAIN the Story

Roman governors, magistrates, and soldiers appear often in Acts. Paul has even appeared before high-level proconsuls before—once out of interest in the gospel (Sergius Paulus, 13:7) and once because fellow Jews brought charges against him (Gallio, 18:12). Up until now, whenever Jews brought charges against Paul with Roman authorities, they have never held up because the accusations were judged to be matters of "your own law" (cf. 18:15; 23:29). Now, before Governor Felix, the Jewish opposition takes a different approach, one that will attract the attention of a Roman governor. The Jews bring in a professional lawyer to make a case against Paul for stirring up "riots" (*stasis*; 24:5)—or "revolts"—in Jerusalem. Governors took threats to Roman peace with utmost seriousness. As such, this is a case that requires a formal Roman trial. The charge of rebellion is not unlike the one made against Jesus, and the legal proceedings against Paul reflect the prophecy that Jesus made about his followers in general (Luke 21:12–13) and Paul in particular (Acts 9:15–16).

Paul's trial before Felix is presented in three stages: first, Tertullus, a "lawyer," makes the case against the accused (24:1–9); second, Paul offers his defense (vv. 10–21); and, third, Felix stalls in rendering a judgment (vv. 22–27).

Tertullus and the Accusation (24:1–9)

Paul waited in his praetorium confinement for five days before his trial began with the arrival of the high priest Ananias, some Jewish elders, and a professional lawyer, Tertullus. Luke provides a summary of the trial in this episode, but there is good reason to conclude that he is basing it on actual judicial records.[2] Since this trial was before a governor, we know it was a serious case, that is, it was one that related to the protection and preservation of public order.[3] In this instance, a professional "lawyer" (*rhētōr*) named Tertullus makes the case against Paul (v. 2). Tertullus was a common name in the Roman world, but he could very well be a Hellenistic Jew who had taken on a Roman name (as did Paul/Saul). Whatever his ethnicity, an attorney like him would say "we" (v. 8) as the representative for the plaintiffs, not necessarily implying one way or the other whether he was a Jew himself.

Tertullus's argument against Paul follows a format familiar to Roman law courts and is modeled after standard Roman rhetorical guidelines.[4] That is, his case begins with an introduction (Latin, *exordium*) that includes a traditional *captatio benevolentiae*—an attempt to "win goodwill" from the judge (vv. 2b–4). Next, there is a summary statement of the case (*narratio*, v. 5), followed by a confirmation of the charge (*confirmatio*, v. 6). Tertullus's conclusion (*peroratio*, v. 8) invites Felix to examine Paul to learn the truth of this case.

---

2. Festus refers to written documentation related to Paul's case needing to be gathered together before he was sent to Rome (Acts 25:26–27). This documentation would have included Claudius Lysias's letter and the summary of this trial and its testimonies before Felix. See Winter, "Official Proceedings," 308–9.

3. For a general introduction to the Roman law, see Wansink, "Roman Law," 984–91.

4. See, e.g., the famous handbooks and guidelines composed by the rhetoricians Cicero, *De oratore* and Quintilian, *Institutio oratoria*.

Luke adds, by way of a short note, that Tertullus's clients back this substantial case against Paul with their own agreement (v. 9).

For those of us unfamiliar with Roman legal proceedings or Roman rhetoric, Tertullus's introductory words (vv. 2b–4) may seem to be superficial sweet talk.[5] They are not. Rather, they are the carefully selected words of a professional, and they have serious legal "bite." As Rowe notes, "Whether or not Luke's readers would have guffawed or gnashed their teeth at these words is an open question; that Tertullus's statement is sheer flattery is not."[6] These words establish the groundwork for the accusation that follows. They highlight how Felix has brought an extended period of "peace"[7] to the Jewish nation through his "providential" reforms (*pronoia*; NIV: "foresight").[8] Against this background of Roman peace and providence—for which the Jewish nation is grateful—Paul is cast as a disturber of the peace, a rebel.

The heart of the case is a serious charge. The primary evidence is introduced with an explanatory "for": "*For* we have found this man . . ." (*gar*, v. 5; this word is left untranslated in the NIV). Paul is regarded as a "troublemaker" (*loimos*)—literally a "pestilent person," one to be avoided by those who are "blessed" by the Lord (cf. Ps 1:1 LXX: "Blessed is the one who does not . . . sit in the company of *pestilent* [*loimos*] people"; my transl.). The charge is not simply that Paul has caused a mild annoyance. The charge is that Paul stirs up *staseis* (NIV: "riots"). *Stasis* can mean a "disturbance," but also it can mean "rebellion"; the latter is more likely the connotation it carries in this Roman court scene. Paul is accused of stirring up "riots" among "the Jews all over the world" as "a ringleader of the Nazarene sect [*hairesis*]" (v. 5). Open rebellion is the equivalent of treason, and traitors in Roman times were executed (often by crucifixion).[9] In short, Tertullus is going for the legal equivalent of the jugular. To lend added weight to the charge, he continues that Paul "*even* tried to desecrate the temple" (v. 6). This is not inconsequential for Roman ears. After all, they maintained a permanent garrison in the Antonia Fortress, no doubt at considerable cost, to ward off political crises like the one Tertullus is describing. "If there were ancient lists of the most significant locations in the

---

5. Even for those like Chrysostom, who was familiar with ancient rhetorical practice, Tertullus is regarded as a fawning flatterer. See *Catena on the Acts of the Apostles* 24.2–3, in *ACCA*, 284.

6. Rowe, *World Upside Down*, 72.

7. There is no historical evidence of "peace" during Felix's governorship. This may, however, be referring to the way Felix "pacified" a number of militant movements in the Judean countryside (Josephus, *J.W.* 2.253, 258–60) along with the rebellion led by "the Egyptian," a self-proclaimed prophet (*J.W.* 2.261–63). See also B. M. Rapske, "Roman Governors of Palestine," *DNTB* 982–83.

8. It is unclear what these reforms might have been. Winter, "Official Proceedings," 319, suggests they might relate to revisions he enacted for the Sanhedrin or temple administration.

9. Felix had crucified the leaders of various uprisings during his tenure as governor of Judea. See Josephus, *J.W.* 2.253.

empire that proved problematic or caused administrative worry in the middle decades of the first century, 'the famous city' of Jerusalem would consistently be near or at the top."[10] Whereas Roman officials have dismissed previous charges against Paul because they deemed them matters of Jewish law, Tertullus has framed the accusation in a manner that Governor Felix could not ignore. Tertullus has done his job well. Felix now turns to the defendant for his reply.

Paul's Defense (24:10–21)

Tertullus may be a professional "hired gun," but Paul's defense demonstrates that this lawyer isn't the only "gun" in town. Paul knows his way around Roman law and rhetoric too. He opens with a short but effective introduction (Latin, *exordium*, v. 10b). Next, he offers a compressed version of the case against him (*narratio*, v. 11) along with three proofs to support his position (*probatio*, vv. 12–13). The longest portion of his defense refutes the specific charges brought against him (*refutatio*, vv. 14–18). He concludes with a final argument, which includes an important legal technicality about witnesses and a reframing of the legal case against him into a Jewish theological matter (*peroratio*, vv. 19–21). As with all the speeches in Acts, this one is multileveled. That is, within the narrative it speaks to Paul's accusers and to the judge, Felix. Yet the speech also speaks to Paul's readers about "the way" of those who follow in the footsteps of Jesus—a way that is not sectarian but is faithful to "the God of our ancestors" and is "in accordance with the Law and [all] that is written in the Prophets" (v. 14).

As Tertullus did with his opening words, Paul lays the foundation and context for his argument that follows by stating a point of fact: "For a number of *years* you [Felix] have been a judge over this nation" (v. 10b). Paul is not ingratiating himself with this point. Rather, before he refers to matters of Jewish theology, he is establishing the point that Felix, who is also married to a Jewish woman (v. 24), has the necessary and lengthy background to understand the case he will judge. Paul then briefly declares that the singular purpose for his going to Jerusalem was "to worship" (v. 11). He had been in the city for only twelve days—hardly enough time to foment revolt. He backs this up with three proofs (v. 12) that deny the accusation made against him: (1) he was not *arguing* with anyone in the temple, (2) nor was he *stirring up* (*epistasis*) a crowd in the synagogues or (3) anywhere else in the city. In short, the charge of *stasis*—sedition/rebellion—is without any legal verifiable proof (v. 13).

In support of his case, Paul refutes the legal charge by turning it into a

---

10. Rowe, *World Upside Down*, 74.

Jewish theological matter. There is almost a sense with his words "I admit . . ." that the attention of Paul's audience may have been aroused. But what he admits is not to the legal charge against him. Rather, he admits that far from being the "ringleader" of a subversive sect (cf. v. 5), he is a typical Jewish worshiper of "the God of our ancestors" (v. 14). The term "sect" (vv. 5, 14; *hairesis*) could refer to a variety of groups within Judaism—none of which were necessarily seditious. For example, Josephus uses the term *hairesis* to refer to a "school" or "party" when he describes the Pharisees, the Sadducees, and the Essenes—each one a distinctive group within Judaism of the day (*Ant.* 13.171; *J.W.* 2.119). Paul is making a theological argument about "the Way"—his preferred term, rather than "sect"—and his own convictions (Acts 24:14). Once again, Paul asserts that he is a faithful Jew who believes everything in the Law and the Prophets (v. 14; cf. 22:3; 25:4–5). "In point of fact, Paul argues, that which they brand as seditious sectarianism . . . is Jewish through and through, which is to say that the Way is no more an insurrectionist faction than Judaism itself."[11] When he mentions a future resurrection where he and his accusers will be held to account (24:15–16), he foreshadows his concluding theological argument (v. 21).

Paul continues his rebuttal by addressing the specific charge about profaning the temple (v. 6). He flatly denies the charge. As a point of fact, Paul notes that after an absence of several years he was bringing "gifts" for the poor of "*my* people" and to present "offerings" in the temple (v. 17). These gifts may be a veiled reference to the collection sent from Paul's gentile congregations for the Jerusalem church (see also 11:29; cf. Rom 15:25–28, 31; 1 Cor 16:1–4, 15; 2 Cor 8:1–4; Gal 2:10). Even if this does not refer to the gentile collection—which, for obvious reasons, would not help the *Jewish* defense he was making—the point is that he was doing nothing treasonable. Rather, Paul was being an observant Jew. He was "ceremonially clean" when his accusers found him, and more to the point there was neither a crowd nor a disturbance around him (Acts 24:18). At most, there were only four men accompanying him, and each one of them had a legitimate right to have joined him in the temple. One wonders whether Felix was becoming bored with the tedious references to Jewish theology when he heard the word "gifts." Might this governor, always alert for ways to line his own coffers, hear in this a word that *does* interest him? Paul has money! That is just a guess, but it does relate to a suggestion about a "bribe" made in the aftermath of the trial (v. 26).

Paul begins his closing statement by alerting Felix to a glaring and vital piece of Roman jurisprudence known as *destitutio*; this refers to the fact that

---

11. Ibid., 77.

there are key accusers missing (v. 19).¹² Again, Paul demonstrates that he knows his way around the Roman law. Those responsible for the original accusation—the Asian Jews (21:27–28)—are not present. Without their testimony the case against him not only falls but has good reason to be thrown out of court altogether. Without missing a beat after this legal punch, Paul wastes no time to change the ground of the case against him entirely. He turns aside the serious legal charge of sedition by naming "the resurrection of the dead" as the real reason he is on trial before Felix. "From first to last, the Way is about the resurrection."¹³ In this final flourish, Paul shifts the ground from a serious matter of Roman law to a serious matter of Jewish theology. The latter, however, has no reason to be tried in a Roman court of law (as Gallio, 18:15, and Claudius Lysias, 23:29, had concluded earlier). It is a theological issue between Jews—whether they are Christian or non-Christian Jews—not a legal or political issue for the Roman state.

All throughout his defense, Paul has acquitted himself with legal dexterity and rhetorical aplomb. He faces serious charges and has mounted a serious defense. Luke's readers—both ancient and modern—should recognize this. As Bruce Winter concludes: "[Paul] has done this by prescribing the limits of evidence based on Roman law, proscribing the charges of absent accusers, using forensic terminology, and, not least of all, presenting a well argued defence, even if preserved in summary form. Paul conducted his own defence in an able manner against a professional forensic orator."¹⁴

Felix Stalls (24:22–27)

Before Paul—or readers of Acts—can get hope up for a quick dismissal or early release, the attentive observer of Luke's trial scenes knows that Paul is not out of the clutches of Roman law yet. After all, there is precedence. We know that a Jewish man can be accused before Roman rulers (Luke 23:1–2), declared to be innocent (23:4, 14–15), and nonetheless be sentenced to death (23:24) alongside other state "criminals" (Luke 23:33; cf. Matt 27:38; Mark 15:27). In this trial, Felix procrastinates, and so begins the slow-turning wheel of Roman "justice." But *why* does Felix delay? Was it because he was having difficulty judging a trial that had a political charge but only theological evidence? If so, two notes by Luke make no sense. First, Felix is familiar with "the Way" (Acts 24:22), and along with his long association with the Jewish nation (cf. vv. 2–4, 10), he should have had all the knowledge he needed to

---

12. Sherwin-White, *Roman Law*, 52–53, highlights that "Roman Law was very strong against accusers who abandoned their charges." See Peterson, *Acts*, 638.
13. Rowe, *World Upside Down*, 78.
14. Winter, "Official Proceedings," 327.

assess Jewish theological issues that had political implications. Second, he calls for the tribune, Claudius Lysias, to come to Caesarea to shed further light on the proceeding (although we never hear whether this occurred). Why was this necessary to judge the case when he already had the commander's letter? The important witnesses he should be summoning to the proceedings were the absent Jewish accusers from Asia Minor. No matter. For the time being, Felix decides to return Paul to guarded confinement (v. 23).

Two things can be observed about Paul's new prison confinement. First, a centurion is instructed to keep guard over Paul. Rapske notes that this indicates the governor regards Paul as an important prisoner and "Felix wished Paul to be healthily preserved for the longer term from the predictable vagaries of military custody."[15] The privations of military imprisonment could be physically and emotionally demanding. If a centurion guarded him, it suggests Paul was kept in or near the officers' quarters rather than in the harsher conditions experienced by ordinary prisoners.[16] Second, his custody is lightened somewhat and affords him "freedom" (v. 23). This meant his military guard was not oppressively restrictive, and he was not kept in isolation from the care and concern of his friends on the outside.

After "several days" Felix came to visit Paul along with Drusilla, his third wife and daughter of Herod Agrippa I (v. 24; cf. 12:1). Here we glimpse a reason for Felix's procrastination. The governor may have been weighing the political consequences of releasing or condemning Paul. On the one hand, if he released him, he risked inflaming the simmering resentment against Rome and offending the local religious and political powers in Judea. As Tertullus reminded him in his introductory comments, there was a connection between reliable Roman law and grateful Jewish compliance (24:2-4). On the other hand, if he did not treat Paul—a Roman citizen—with proper legal consideration, he risked offending his own superior (i.e., the emperor!) in Rome. Caught between a political "rock and a hard place," Felix acted in a time-honored political manner: he did nothing.

For all the political implications Felix may have contemplated, Luke describes his delay as motivated by a simpler reason. Felix hoped that Paul would offer him a bribe (v. 26).[17] Instead of a bribe, he received a sermon. Paul spoke to him about faith in the Messiah Jesus and the fruit of faith: "Righteousness, self-control and the judgment to come" (v. 25). Paul's words

---

15. Rapske, *Paul in Roman Custody*, 168.

16. For a thorough description of the conditions of Roman imprisonment, see Rapske, *Paul in Roman Custody*, ch. 9.

17. Bribery and extortion enjoyed a healthy run in the empire, including in Judea by Felix and his successors; see Josephus *J.W.* 2.273; *Ant.* 20.215.

made Felix uncomfortable. After all, he was a governor known for political incompetence, brutality, corruption, and multiple marriages. In the unflattering words of the Roman historian Tacitus, he "practiced every kind of cruelty and lust, wielding the power of a king with all the instincts of a slave."[18] Nonetheless, these conversations continued for two years (v. 27). Paul never succumbed to bribery, and Felix did not end up following "the Way." In the end, as he was being replaced as governor by Porcius Festus,[19] it seems immediate political fears outweighed "the judgment to come" (v. 25): "Because Felix wanted to grant a favor to the Jews, he left Paul in prison" (v. 27).

LIVE the Story

In the Arena

Theodore Roosevelt delivered his famous speech "Citizenship in a Republic" on April 23, 1910, at the Sorbonne in Paris, France. In this renowned institution of learning, including the study of theology, Roosevelt demonstrated his own biblical education and knowledge of the book of Acts. In his introductory comments he observes:

> It is a mistake for any nation to merely copy another; but it is even a greater mistake, it is a proof of weakness in any nation, not to be anxious to learn from one another and willing and able to adapt that learning to the new national conditions and make it fruitful and productive therein. It is for us of the New World to sit at the feet of Gamaliel of the Old; then, if we have the right stuff in us, we can show that Paul in his turn can become a teacher as well as a scholar.[20]

Later in his speech, as Roosevelt confronted "an attitude of sneering disbelief toward all that is great and lofty," he could very well have been thinking about Paul and his many trials in this passage that made the speech famous:

> It is not the critic who counts; not the man who points out how the strong man stumbles, or where the doer of deeds could have done them better. The credit belongs to the man who is actually in the arena, whose face is marred by dust and sweat and blood; who strives valiantly; who errs, who comes short again and again, because there is no effort without error and

---

18. Tacitus, *Hist.* 5.9 (Moore, LCL). See Josephus, *J.W.* 2.247; *Ant.* 20.137, 162–63.
19. Felix was recalled to Rome in AD 58 for bungling the suppression of hostilities that broke out in Caesarea between Jews and Greeks (see Josephus, *J.W.* 2.266–70).
20. Theodore Roosevelt, "Citizenship in a Republic," http://www.theodore-roosevelt.com/images/research/speeches/maninthearena.

shortcoming; but who does actually strive to do the deeds; who knows great enthusiasms, the great devotions; who spends himself in a worthy cause; who at the best knows in the end the triumph of high achievement, and who at the worst, if he fails, at least fails while daring greatly, so that his place shall never be with those cold and timid souls who neither know victory nor defeat.

The trials of Paul—this apostle who *dared greatly* for his Lord—continue to remind Christians that what we do as followers of the crucified Jesus carries meaning whether we know victory or defeat in the arena of public trial or opinion. In fact, as Eugene Peterson argues, the trials of Paul

> force us, if we're to stay true to the story we're reading, to give up the notion that the Christian community can catch the admiring eye of the world if we just live rightly and obediently. We have ample documentation by now to disabuse us of such thinking. God's revelation is rejected far more often than it is accepted, is dismissed by far more people than embrace it, and has been either attacked or ignored by every major culture or civilization in which it has given its witness.[21]

God's gift of righteousness, self-control, and the future judgment—the very things Paul reminds Felix and Drusilla about (Acts 24:25)—are more often rebuffed than respected. God's revelation was snubbed by magnificent Egypt in the first exodus led by Moses just as much as it was by mighty Rome in the second exodus led by Jesus. God's revelation is refused, assaulted, or disregarded just as much in Renaissance Italy as in Enlightenment France; just as much in communist Russia as in Nazi Germany; just as much in Tokugawa Japan as in Maoist China; just as much in pursuit-of-happiness America as in tolerant Canada. The important point is that the community of Christ has survived in these different eras and cultures, but it has done so usually on the margins, not in the mainstream.[22]

Whenever Christians are courted and acclaimed by rulers or politicians, questions should be asked. How did they pull that off? What was the price of cultural approval and acceptance? Was it accommodation? Assimilation? Paul, and countless Christians since, gave witness to the good news of God (mostly) in the face of rejection and in "magnificent defeat."[23] They "dared greatly" because they had hope, not because they were celebrated. Their hope was firm and unshakable because of the resurrection of the dead. The resurrection

---

21. Peterson, *Conversations*, 1728–29.
22. Peterson, *Conversations*, 1729.
23. Frederick Buechner, *The Magnificent Defeat* (San Francisco: HarperOne, 1985), ch. 1.

of Jesus and its ongoing and transformative realities give life and power to all those who struggle "in the arena."

The Way Is about the Resurrection

If this commentary and these passages on "Live the Story" have any lasting purpose and importance for readers, I think that a significant reason for that would be that I have been able to draw on the work of great thinkers and theologians—both ancient and contemporary. C. Kavin Rowe is one such thinker and theologian. He is an erudite scholar whose work needs to be read and reflected on today. He has the uncanny ability to engage in great swaths of literature and research and then distill it all into a riveting sentence. As I was reading and reflecting on the work of a number of writers who have engaged with the text of Paul's trial before Felix, this sentence by Rowe stopped me in my tracks: "From first to last, the Way is about the resurrection."[24] It doesn't happen very often (for me at least) that the words of a scholar bring me to tears of gratitude. These did. I don't know Kavin Rowe personally, but if I could, I would thank him for them. These words remind all of us who follow Jesus that the resurrection is the center of our faith—from first to last. The resurrection of Jesus is not an isolated historical event or one-off miracle that somehow proves Jesus is God. The Franciscan friar and priest Richard Rohr expands on Rowe's succinct conclusion: "Jesus's death and resurrection name and reveal what is happening everywhere and all the time in God and in everything God creates. Reality is always moving toward resurrection. As prayers of the Catholic funeral Mass affirm, 'Life is not ended but merely changed.' This is the divine mystery of transformation, fully evident in the entire physical universe."[25]

The resurrection of Jesus means that God has begun the future restoration of all things in the present chaos of this world. This means that neither trial nor death have the last word. It means that God can take difficulty and tragedy, pain and trial, sorrow and injustice and use them as a crucible to transform and to restore. Paul understood this, and it gave him courage and hope. While he worked diligently and thoughtfully to mount a defense before Governor Felix, he knew that resurrection was at the heart of this and every trial. It meant that, in the end, Roman judgment and justice were inconsequential because neither a Roman governor nor a Roman emperor had the last word. Resurrection does.

Resurrection matters for us all, not just for prophets and apostles in the pages of Scripture. A longtime friend of my wife has a daughter who endures

---

24. Rowe, *World Upside Down*, 78.
25. Richard Rohr, "Easter Homily: Reality Moves toward Resurrection," Center for Action and Contemplation, 27 March 2016, https://cac.org/easter-homily-reality-moves-toward-resurrection/.

the daily trial of Dravet Syndrome, also known as "severe myoclonic epilepsy of infancy" (SMEI). Her daughter is now a teenager, but SMEI has meant that she has delayed development and the daily threat of severe, life-threatening seizures. Each day is a struggle and full of uncertainty. Those who write history may never remember their story in posterity, but because of the resurrection they live in the firm hope that Dravet Syndrome will not have the last word. Resurrection gives hope and empowers them to make it through difficult days in the hospital, uncertain restless nights in their home, and every kind of hour in between. Resurrection is larger than any verdict or sentence of death. Resurrection reframes existence, gives hope, leads to praise, and enables us to "dare greatly." That is the point of biblical theology and is why we follow the Way. From first to last, the Way is about resurrection.

CHAPTER 55

Acts 25:1-27

 LISTEN to the Story

¹Three days after arriving in the province, Festus went up from Caesarea to Jerusalem, ²where the chief priests and the Jewish leaders appeared before him and presented the charges against Paul. ³They requested Festus, as a favor to them, to have Paul transferred to Jerusalem, for they were preparing an ambush to kill him along the way. ⁴Festus answered, "Paul is being held at Caesarea, and I myself am going there soon. ⁵Let some of your leaders come with me, and if the man has done anything wrong, they can press charges against him there."

⁶After spending eight or ten days with them, Festus went down to Caesarea. The next day he convened the court and ordered that Paul be brought before him. ⁷When Paul came in, the Jews who had come down from Jerusalem stood around him. They brought many serious charges against him, but they could not prove them.

⁸Then Paul made his defense: "I have done nothing wrong against the Jewish law or against the temple or against Caesar."

⁹Festus, wishing to do the Jews a favor, said to Paul, "Are you willing to go up to Jerusalem and stand trial before me there on these charges?"

¹⁰Paul answered: "I am now standing before Caesar's court, where I ought to be tried. I have not done any wrong to the Jews, as you yourself know very well. ¹¹If, however, I am guilty of doing anything deserving death, I do not refuse to die. But if the charges brought against me by these Jews are not true, no one has the right to hand me over to them. I appeal to Caesar!"

¹²After Festus had conferred with his council, he declared: "You have appealed to Caesar. To Caesar you will go!"

¹³A few days later King Agrippa and Bernice arrived at Caesarea to pay their respects to Festus. ¹⁴Since they were spending many days there, Festus discussed Paul's case with the king. He said: "There is a man here whom Felix left as a prisoner. ¹⁵When I went to Jerusalem, the chief priests

and the elders of the Jews brought charges against him and asked that he be condemned.

16"I told them that it is not the Roman custom to hand over anyone before they have faced their accusers and have had an opportunity to defend themselves against the charges. 17When they came here with me, I did not delay the case, but convened the court the next day and ordered the man to be brought in. 18When his accusers got up to speak, they did not charge him with any of the crimes I had expected. 19Instead, they had some points of dispute with him about their own religion and about a dead man named Jesus who Paul claimed was alive. 20I was at a loss how to investigate such matters; so I asked if he would be willing to go to Jerusalem and stand trial there on these charges. 21But when Paul made his appeal to be held over for the Emperor's decision, I ordered him held until I could send him to Caesar."

22Then Agrippa said to Festus, "I would like to hear this man myself."

He replied, "Tomorrow you will hear him."

23The next day Agrippa and Bernice came with great pomp and entered the audience room with the high-ranking military officers and the prominent men of the city. At the command of Festus, Paul was brought in. 24Festus said: "King Agrippa, and all who are present with us, you see this man! The whole Jewish community has petitioned me about him in Jerusalem and here in Caesarea, shouting that he ought not to live any longer. 26I found he had done nothing deserving of death, but because he made his appeal to the Emperor I decided to send him to Rome. But I have nothing definite to write to His Majesty about him. Therefore I have brought him before all of you, and especially before you, King Agrippa, so that as a result of this investigation I may have something to write. 27For I think it is unreasonable to send a prisoner on to Rome without specifying the charges against him."

Listening to the Text in the Story: Psalm 22; 1 Corinthians 1:22–24; Philippians 1:20–22.

EXPLAIN the Story

The dramatic tension of the preceding episodes has been relentless since Paul arrived in Jerusalem and was then whisked away under cover of night to

Caesarea (21:17–24:27). Over 10 percent of Luke's entire narrative is allotted to these twelve to seventeen days in Paul's life. At the end of this narrative sequence the tension is released with two notes: first, the passage of "two years" and, second, the transition in government from Felix to Porcius Festus (24:27). Luke does not describe anything about the two years Paul spent in confinement in Caesarea. Numerous conjectures could be made about what Paul did during this time, including whether he wrote his so-called "Prison Epistles" (Colossians, Philemon, Philippians, and Ephesians). Luke's interest, however, is focused on the events that transpire soon after Festus arrives in the province of Judea.

After ignoring almost two years of Paul's life, the interest and pace of the narrative undergoes a reset. Four short successive episodes—each one introduced with a time signature (i.e., "three days," 25:1; "after . . . eight or ten days," v. 6; "a few days later," v. 13; and "the next day," v. 23)—serve to reset the narrative stage in preparation for Paul's last major speech in Acts (26:2–23). Each of these four episodes rehearses content familiar to the reader already, including another plot to assassinate Paul (25:3; cf. 23:12–15, 30); "charges" made against Paul (25:2, 5, 7, 9, 11, 15, 16, 18, 20; cf. 21:28; 22:30; 23:29; 24:5–7); and the note of Paul's innocence in matters related to Jewish and Roman law (25:8, 10, 11, 25; cf. 22:3, 17, 25; 23:9, 29; 24:12–14). Although new characters like Festus, Agrippa, and Bernice will be brought into the narrative frame, the usual suspects also reappear—the chief priests and the Jewish leaders (25:2; cf. 22:30; 24:1)—and, of course, Paul. Paul also introduces a new and important "character" to the plot. That character is Caesar (25:8, 10, 11).

Paul has already appeared before a synagogue and a governor, and now these four episodes prepare us for his appearance before a king, Agrippa (see Luke 12:11–12; cf. Acts 9:15–16). Paul appears in two of the scenes and is the focus of the other two. The four episodes reset the stage and provide transition in anticipation of Paul's last speech before King Agrippa. The scenes are as follows: the initial meeting between Festus and the Jewish leaders in Jerusalem and the renewal of charges made against Paul (25:1–5); a short trial scene before Festus in Caesarea and Paul's dramatic appeal to Caesar (vv. 6–12); a consultation between Festus and King Agrippa and his sister Bernice (vv. 13–22); and Festus's introduction of Paul (vv. 23–27).

Festus Meets the Jewish Leadership in Jerusalem (25:1–5)

The first scene begins in Jerusalem and focuses on Festus. Porcius Festus succeeded Felix as procurator of the Roman province of Judea in AD 59/60 and governed for two years until his untimely death. There is scant historical record of Festus; we only know of him through the Jewish historian Josephus (*J.W.* 2.271–72; *Ant.* 20.182–96) and Acts. Josephus is mostly approving of Festus—especially in comparison to the corruption and brutality of his predecessor Felix and his successor Albinus. When Festus arrived in Judea, the province was in political turmoil. The countryside was overrun by bandits or rebels (*lēstēs*; Josephus, *Ant.* 20.185) and *sicarii*, the "daggermen," who plagued Jerusalem with sudden violent assassinations, especially during festivals, and plundered surrounding villages (*Ant.* 20.186–88). Festus would deal with some of these fierce people, but one of his first priorities was to meet the indigenous leadership. Although Judea was under direct Roman rule, it was common for the Romans to work with local leaders. In this case, that meant going to Jerusalem—where politics and religion were bound together—to meet with the "chief priests and Jewish leaders" (Acts 25:2). Luke refers to the chief priests (plural), because although there was one sitting chief priest (Ishmael ben Fabus), other chief priests, like Ananias, were still around and influential.

When Festus met with the Jewish leadership, despite the two-year lapse their animosity has not dimmed toward Paul, and they renewed their charges before the new procurator. They request a "favor" (*charis*, Acts 25:3; cf. 24:27; 25:9) from Festus. They asked to have Paul transferred back to Jerusalem, presumably to stand trial but with the real intent to assassinate him on the way there. Festus agrees to reopen the case against Paul, but does not agree to the transfer of venue. At this point, Festus is portrayed as viewing Paul without prejudice. Instead, he commands[1] some of the leaders (*dynatoi*)[2] to return with him to Caesarea to reopen the proceedings there.

Paul's Trial before Festus in Caesarea (25:6–12)

The second transitional scene begins with a change of location. After spending eight to ten days in Jerusalem, Festus returns to Caesarea Maritima, the Roman administrative capital along the Mediterranean coast about a hundred kilometers (60 miles) from Jerusalem. The day after his return (v. 6), he reconvenes the trial of Paul. The NIV obscures the official language of this action by translating it as "he convened the court" (v. 6b). The NRSV states it more clearly: "He took his seat on the tribunal."[3] After taking his seat as the signal of

---

1. To "press charges" is an imperative verb (Acts 25:5).
2. This way of referring to the leaders may suggest they are not only "able" to return to Caesarea with Festus, but do so with some legal competence. Rowe, *World Upside Down*, 81, notes that the related verb form of this noun, *dynamai*, "can approach something akin to 'to enjoy a legal right,' as it does on the lips of the Areopagus Council in Acts (17:19)." This will be important later when Paul makes the assertion that "no one has the [*legal*] right [*dynatai*] to hand me over to them" (25:11).
3. Bruce, *Acts*, 451n4, observes, "This formality was necessary for his decision to have legal validity." Cf. Acts 18:12; Matt 27:19; John 19:13.

the trial coming to order, he commanded the defendant to be brought before him. The tension in the narrative increases in this scene as Paul is portrayed as "surrounded" by his accusers as he stands before Festus (v. 7a NRSV). Encircled by his enemies, they make serious charges against Paul. The charges are not reiterated (see 24:5–6), but we can guess by Paul's defense what they are. Importantly, they are unable to present any substantial evidence against Paul—including any witnesses to prove their claims (v. 7b).

This is Paul's fourth defense speech (cf. 22:1–21; 23:1–6; 24:10–21). Paul cuts to the chase with his defense: "I have done nothing wrong" (v. 8). Again, the trial before Governor Festus is reminiscent of the trial scene of Jesus before Governor Pilate (Luke 23:1–22). Paul begins by restating his innocence of any wrong against "the Jewish law or against the temple" (Acts 25:8; cf. 24:12–14). As for the first charge, a general one about the law, Luke portrays Paul throughout the narrative as nothing but a faithful and observant Jew—especially when he is in Judea. As for the second charge, a specific one about the temple, the key witnesses (i.e., the Asian Jews; cf. 21:27–28) are not forthcoming to substantiate the charge of violating the holy place.

Paul also adds an important new player to the conversation when he denies doing any wrong "against Caesar" (25:8). Luke seems to want his readers to notice this new character in the drama in these transitional scenes. Nero is not mentioned by his formal name, just his titles, but those titles appear frequently in this episode. Of the ten times the word "Caesar" occurs in Acts, six of them appear in quick succession (25:8, 10, 11, 12 [2x], 21). The word "Emperor" occurs only three times in Acts, but twice in these scenes (vv. 21, 25). Most interesting of all is the reference to "His Majesty," which is how the NIV translates the Greek word *kyrios* (v. 26). Normally in Acts occurrences of the word *kyrios* in the singular refer to "the Lord," that is, the Lord Jesus (e.g., 1:6, 21; 4:33; 10:36) or the Lord God (e.g., 2:39; 17:24). This is the only time in Acts where Luke uses this common imperial title to refer to Caesar and not to Jesus or God. At the time of this trial, the infamous Nero was emperor. It is worth noting, however, that Roman historians regarded this time around AD 60, about when Paul appeared before Festus, as the period of Nero's "golden age" when he ruled justly under the counsel of Burrus (a prefect of the Praetorian Guard) and Seneca the Younger (a Stoic philosopher and statesman). These are not the years of Nero's moral decline when he persecuted Christians in Rome (AD 64–65).

A key turning point in the episode, and in the narrative of Acts as a whole, occurs when Festus asks Paul if he is willing to relocate the trial to Jerusalem (v. 9). As an aside, Luke notes that Festus was motivated by his desire to do a "favor" (*charis*) for the Jewish leadership (cf. v. 3; 24:27). Festus may be doing what many new Roman procurators would do: he is currying the "favor" of the local elites with whom he will have to work in the coming years—as long as the favor does not infringe on Roman justice.[4] But he can only request the change of venue and jurisdiction; he cannot demand it of Paul. Paul, understanding both the danger of relocation and his legal rights as a Roman citizen, reminds Festus that he is already being tried in the proper location for a capital offense: Caesar's court in Caesarea.[5] Paul is no coward and is unafraid to be sentenced to death by Roman law if there was substance to the capital charges (see Phil 1:20–22). On the other hand, he is not eager to die in Jerusalem either. Besides, he is convinced he has done nothing wrong "to the Jews" that would merit his transfer. By way of emphasis, Paul reminds Festus "*you yourself* know very well" that I've done no wrong (Acts 25:10). Still, Paul senses that the winds of justice are blowing against him. He argues that no one, not even Festus, should be able to grant this favor to "hand [him] over" (*charizomai*, v. 11) to the Jews. Pressed into a corner, Paul asserts his right as a Roman citizen and declares, "I appeal to Caesar!" (v. 11).

Festus did not immediately grant Paul's request, nor is it clear from Roman law that he had to grant it.[6] "This is not about appealing against a verdict (as in modern English law) but about the fundamental right to decide where and under what system of jurisdiction his case will be heard."[7] At first, Festus turned to his own legal advisers. They may have told him that this request might help in two ways. First, it would remove a serious case, in a volatile place, from his jurisdiction. Second, by sending Paul to Rome, Festus could not be accused by the Jewish leadership of releasing a hated enemy; he was merely deferring judgment to the emperor.[8] Whatever Festus's thoughts, he agreed to Paul's demand. With theatrical flourish he declares: "You have appealed to Caesar. To Caesar you will go!" (v. 12). In this unexpected turn of

---

4. Gaventa, *Acts*, 334, suggests that this may not indicate any change from Festus's original position (Acts 25:4–5). Rather, this is an "opportunity to grant their request and make it appear to be beneficial to Paul at the same time."

5. Fitzmyer, *Acts*, 745, notes how the judicial system of the Roman Empire works by citing Ulpian, *Digest* 1.19.1: "What is done and carried out by Caesar's procurator is so approved by him, as if they were carried out by Caesar himself." This means for Paul the Roman citizen that Festus's proposal is impossible for him.

6. See Rowe, *World Upside Down*, 82.

7. Alexander, *Acts*, 179. See also Bruce, *Acts*, 453–54, who suggests that Paul did not appeal to Caesar while under Felix's governorship because he still hoped to be released. Under Festus, he began to be suspicious that Roman justice could be undermined if the trial relocated to Jerusalem. Bruce notes that the privilege of appeal to Caesar by Roman citizens extended for a long time (e.g., Pliny the Younger, *Epistles* 10.96.4, while he was proconsul of Bithynia in AD 112 and prosecuting Christians, distinguished between ordinary provincials whom he tried locally and those who were Roman citizens who should be sent to Rome for trial).

8. Rowe, *World Upside Down*, 82–83.

events, both the desires of Paul and the purposes of his Lord will be fulfilled (see 19:21; 23:11).

Festus Consults King Agrippa (25:13–22)

The third transitional scene begins "a few days later" (25:13). Festus has already met with Jewish leaders in Jerusalem, but now he meets with members of the Jewish aristocracy in King Agrippa II (Marcus Julius Agrippa) and his sister Julia Bernice. It was important, both for Roman rulers and for local client kings, that they knew each other and cultivated good working relationships. Agrippa was not just a local Herodian aristocrat. He was intimately connected with the imperial court in Rome. In fact, Agrippa grew up in Emperor Claudius's court, and according to Josephus he was a notable advocate for the Jews (*Ant.* 15.407; 20.9–14, 135), even though he had an uneasy relationship with the Jerusalem hierarchy in the years before the Jewish War (AD 66–70). In AD 50, after the death of Agrippa's uncle Herod of Chalcis (who was also husband of his sister Bernice), Claudius gave Agrippa the kingdom of Chalcis (i.e., Lebanon). He gave up this kingdom in AD 53 when Claudius offered him a larger one from the tetrarchy of Philip, consisting of the regions of Ituraea, Trachonitis, and Abilene (cf. Luke 3:1).[9] His lands increased further when Claudius's successor Nero added parts of Galilee and Perea to his kingdom.

Little is mentioned in Acts about Bernice. Her story, however, is anything but bland. She was also a member of the Herodian family (daughter of Agrippa I and Cypros and sister to Felix's wife, Drusilla). She had several important marriages with various statesmen. Beyond these marriages, rumors seemed to swirl around her, including ones about a supposed incestuous relationship with her brother, King Agrippa II,[10] and the exertion of her romantic charms on the emperor Vespasian.[11] None of these salacious details are included in

---

9. See Emil Schürer, *The History of the Jewish People in the Age of Jesus Christ*, 3 vols. (Edinburgh: T&T Clark, 1973 [1890]), 1:472.

10. Juvenal in his satirical poem about the decay of feminine virtue, writes about a diamond of great renown and includes this comment: "It was given as a present long ago by the barbarian Agrippa to his incestuous sister" (*Sat.* 6.158) in *Juvenal and Persius*, trans. G. G. Ramsay, LCL (London: William Heinemann, 1928), 95. Cf. Josephus, *Ant.* 20.145, who offers a counternarrative: "But as for Bernice, she lived a widow a long while after the death of Herod [king of Chalcis], who was both her husband and her uncle. But, when the report went that she had criminal conversation with her brother [Agrippa junior], she persuaded Polemo, who was king of Cilicia, to be circumcised, and to marry her, as supposing that by this means she should prove those calumnies upon her to be false" (Whiston).

11. Tacitus, *Hist.* 2.81 (Moore, LCL), wrote, "Queen Bernice showed equal spirit in helping Vespasian's party: she had great youthful beauty, and commended herself to Vespasian for all his years by the splendid gifts she made him."

Luke's account, but this brother and sister duo would be well known by many of his first-century readers.

When notable aristocrats like Agrippa and Bernice dropped by to pay their respects to Festus, no doubt they would have talked about a variety of topics. Luke provides an account of one of their conversations. We cannot be sure though what sources Luke may be drawing on for this conversation.[12] For Luke, however, there was only one topic that was important. During the visit with Agrippa and Bernice, Festus brought up Paul's case for discussion. After all, the king and his sister were more familiar with Jewish affairs than he was. Perhaps Agrippa, given his expertise and experience with Jewish religious questions, might be able to assist him in writing his report on Paul's case for Caesar.

Festus recounts the serious charges made against Paul by the chief priests and the elders and their call for his execution (Acts 25:15). Like the tribune Claudius Lysias before him (see 23:27–30), he offers his own modified version of Paul's story and his role in it. First, he begins by placing the responsibility for the inactivity of Paul's case at the feet of Felix (25:14). Next, he repeats the events of his meeting with the Jewish leadership in Jerusalem (v. 15). He then emphasizes *Roman* customs (*ethos*, v. 16) and legal requirements in a case with capital charges,[13] but omits mention of the political charges made against Paul (24:5; 25:9). Festus does admit both his surprise at the *Jewish charges*—matters about "*their own religion*[14] and about a dead man named Jesus who Paul claimed was alive" (v. 19)—and his ignorance about how to proceed with the investigation (v. 20). Again, the central issue of the resurrection is recalled (cf. 23:6; 24:21), but this time, it is done from the mouth of an ignorant Roman official and in less nuanced terms than Pharisaic Jews, like Paul, would have spoken. For all his theological ignorance, this comment by Festus demonstrates that Paul managed to bring the issue of Jesus's resurrection to the heart of his trial and defense. Festus's comments about this Jewish case intrigue Agrippa, and he requests to hear from Paul for himself. Festus announces, "Tomorrow you will hear him" (25:22).

---

12. Unlike Roman judicial proceedings that were recorded and available to Luke, there were not likely any records made of private conversations between a governor and his aristocratic visitors.

13. That is, capital charges against a Roman citizen. This is the Roman *ethos* Festus is referring to in his comment. Festus does not mention that Paul is a Roman citizen, but that is the assumed background. If he was simply a commoner or a slave, there would be no discussion about sending him to Rome. Festus knows that court cases against displeased citizens had a way of damaging one's political career. Festus is being cautious and seeking all the advice he can get.

14. Greek *deisidaimonia*; this is the only occurrence of this word in the NT. In the ancient Greco-Roman world, it related to one's understanding of the transcendent realm, expressed especially in a time of war or conflict. Because such religious sentiment is often expressed in certain rites or ceremonies, it also can denote "rites" or "ceremonies." See BDAG 216.

Festus Introduces Paul (25:23–27)

The fourth, and final, transitional scene is introduced by another time signature, "the next day" (v. 23), but this concluding episode also has a climactic tone to it. If this were a scene for a modern movie, its climactic quality would be signified by a sumptuous wide-angle shot and grand music. Short of this, Luke describes the spectacle of Agrippa and Bernice's entrance into the audience hall as coming with "great pomp" (v. 23). All the finest people from Caesarea are there too, including procurator Festus, military tribunes, prominent people of the city, and possibly some of Paul's Jewish accusers. As Paul gazed upon this regal audience, his vocational commission may have been on his mind: "[You will be] my chosen instrument to proclaim my name to the Gentiles and their kings and to the people of Israel" (9:15). Given Paul's experience as of late, these words from his own letter to the Corinthian church may also have been in his thoughts: "Jews demand signs and Greeks look for wisdom, but we preach Christ crucified: a stumbling block to Jews and foolishness to Gentiles" (1 Cor 1:22–23).

Festus introduces Paul to the gathered assembly with a flourish and a degree of exaggeration. He declares "the *whole Jewish community* has petitioned me about him in Jerusalem and here in Caesarea" (Acts 25:24a). This is rhetorical hyperbole.[15] As if to add further emphasis, he says the Jewish community has done so by "*shouting* that he ought not to live any longer" (v. 24b). While there was this kind of shouting during the riot in the temple (see 21:36; 22:23) and the meeting with the Sanhedrin (23:9–10) in Jerusalem, there is no indication these kinds of loud outbursts occurred in Festus's presence.

Festus continues with his introduction of Paul by declaring, "I found he had done nothing deserving of death, but because he made his appeal to the Emperor I decided to send him to Rome" (25:25). He then frames what will happen next as a matter of fact finding, gathering legal documentation—what Roman law referred to as *litterae dimissoriae*—so that he could send his own written[16] account along with the rest of the legal dossier when the prisoner Paul is sent to Rome.[17] This was a legal requirement in provincial cases coming to the emperor. Festus refers to Emperor Nero as "His Majesty" (*kyrios*). As was noted above, this is the only time the title *kyrios* occurs in Acts, in the singular, without referring to the *Lord* Jesus or to God. It was a common title in the first-century Roman world for the emperor. The repeated references to "Caesar" (25:8, 10, 11, 12 [2x], 21), "Emperor" (vv. 21, 25) and "His Majesty"

---

15. Dunn, *Acts*, 322.
16. Note the emphasis on *written* evidence ("to write" is mentioned twice in v. 26 and alluded to in v. 27).
17. Winter, "Official Proceedings," 309.

(v. 26) reinforce what all four of these scenes focus upon, namely, Paul's appeal to Caesar.

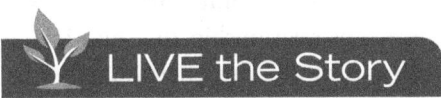

LIVE the Story

God's Message Will Be Heard—Even If the Media Don't Report It
Most people are familiar with the adage "no publicity is bad publicity." I'm not so sure I agree with that sentiment, even though others, including the early church father Chrysostom, might agree to a modified version of that saying. Chrysostom thinks Paul's request to stand before Caesar is not a question of lack of faith in Christ's prophecy or protection. Rather, it is a means of publicity. That is, trials tended to be public events and could be useful platforms to spread one's message. In a sense, Chrysostom suggests Paul is using his right of appeal as a Roman citizen to get the empire to "foot the bill" for his trip to Rome to proclaim the good news. Chrysostom writes:

> [Paul] did not say, "I am not worthy of death," or "I am worthy to be acquitted," but "I am ready to stand trial before Caesar." At the same time, remembering the dream, he was all the more confident to appeal. . . . "When he had conferred with his council," it says, "[Festus] answered, 'You have appealed to Caesar; to Caesar you shall go.'" Notice again how his trial is extended, how the plot against him becomes an occasion for preaching, so that with ease and security he is conveyed to Salem, with no plot against him. For it is one thing to simply be there and another to be there for this reason.[18]

One could argue that the "publicity" afforded to Paul assisted the spread of the gospel in Rome. Unfortunately, it seems that most of the publicity the gospel receives today in the media is not when the church has "good news" to proclaim but when some shortcoming or corruption in the church has been uncovered. Again, I note the speech given by the highly respected Canadian journalist and Christian, Brian Stewart.[19] Whereas the media are quick to report on a scandal, Stewart observes they are virtually blind when it comes to the heroic frontline work that Christians do in the world's most difficult famines, crises, and conflicts. Still, Paul was confident that ordinary Jews and gentiles, procurators and kings, and even emperors would hear God's gospel message. It might be risky proclaiming this message, but that is what Christians have done for centuries, whether the media publicize it or not.

---

18. Chrysostom, *Homilies on the Acts* 51, in *ACCA*, 289.
19. See his comments in "Live the Story" in the section on Acts 23:12–35 above.

Paul's Querencia

Querencia is a Spanish concept. The term comes from the Spanish verb *querer*, which means "to desire." Ernest Hemingway, in his nonfiction book *Death in the Afternoon*, writes about this concept in relationship to a bull in the ring. A bull will stake out his *querencia*, a part of the ring where he feels safe. Hemingway writes:

> A *querencia* is a place the bull naturally wants to go to in the ring, a preferred locality. . . . It is a place which develops in the course of the fight where the bull makes his home. It does not usually show at once, but develops in his brain as the fight goes on. In this place he feels that he has his back against the wall and in his *querencia* he is inestimably more dangerous and almost impossible to kill.[20]

When Paul stands before Festus, Luke informs us that accusers surround him (Acts 25:7). Like a bull in the arena, he is ringed all about. Where can he go? What can he do? In Spanish terms, he can go to his *querencia*. For Paul, this is his fourth trial defense, and once again he is alone and ringed. Even though he appeals to the "safety" of Caesar's court, his true home and his true place of defense is the presence of the resurrected Lord—the One for whom death was impossible to kill. In all these trials, we notice again how important that late-night revelation and promise was in the Antonia Fortress: "Take courage! As you have testified about me in Jerusalem, so you must also testify in Rome" (23:11). Paul may have had some doubts about this promise during his two years of confinement in Caesarea. But it is clear he had not grown tired or disillusioned; he had not lost his wits or his courage. Why? Paul found his *querencia*. He knew the Lord was with him, and because of that Paul knew where to stand.

How can we learn to find our *querencia*? The short answer is we can find it in the Holy Spirit's empowerment speaking to us through Scripture. I have no proof from Luke's account in Acts 25 of how Paul found his *querencia*, but I am confident that in his imprisonment Paul reminded himself of the Lord's vision that night in the Antonia Fortress. I'm certain that he also turned to the inspired, set prayers that had fortified every faithful Israelite in trouble before him. In particular, he would have turned to Scripture, especially to the Psalms. In this, Paul would only be mirroring what his Lord did when he faced his trial and crucifixion, when mocking accusers surrounded him. In those circumstances we know that Jesus's heart and mind turned to Psalm 22. As he struggled for every breath on the cross, we hear him cry out, "My God,

---

20. Ernest Hemingway, *Death in the Afternoon* (New York: Charles Scribner's Sons, 1996 [1932]), 91.

my God, why have you forsaken me?" (Mark 15:34; see Ps 22:1). In that moment Jesus could barely breathe, let alone speak. He could only utter the opening words, but they evoked every part of Psalm 22. Any American, hearing the opening words "Oh say can you see," knows exactly what comes next. In the same way, any devout Jew, especially one under extreme pressure, knows what comes next when they hear the words "my God, my God, why have you forsaken me?" Even though Jesus only quotes the opening phrase, I am confident he was meditating on the entire psalm—especially since it so closely paralleled his own circumstances. The psalm continues:

> Why are you so far from saving me,
> so far from my cries of anguish? (v. 1)

> All who see me mock me;
> > they hurl insults, shaking their heads. (v. 7)

> Many bulls surround me;
> > strong bulls of Bashan encircle me. (v. 12)

> My mouth is dried up like a potsherd,
> > and my tongue sticks to the roof of my mouth;
> > you lay me in the dust of death.
> Dogs surround me,
> > a pack of villains encircles me;
> > they pierce my hands and my feet.
> All my bones are on display;
> > people stare and gloat over me.
> They divide my clothes among them
> > and cast lots for my garment. (vv. 15–18)

But that is not all; the psalm does not end in despair. Psalm 22 ends in confident affirmation. The Lord will deliver and rescue:

> For he has *not* despised or scorned
> > the suffering of the afflicted one;
> he has *not* hidden his face from him
> > *but* has listened to his cry for help. (v. 24)

> All the ends of the earth
> > will remember and turn to the LORD,
> and all the families of the nations
> > will bow down before him,
> for dominion belongs to the LORD
> > and he rules over the nations. (vv. 27–28)

> Posterity will serve him;
> > future generations will be told about the Lord.
> They will proclaim his righteousness,
> > declaring to a people yet unborn:
> > He has done it!" (vv. 30–31)

Jesus, Paul, and every Christian who has found their *querencia* have done so because they leaned into the truth and hope of the inspired biblical story. It is not flashy or fashionable, but learning Scripture "by heart" is still vital for us today—especially when we feel hard-pressed and surrounded. We might be able to search on the Internet for a "promise" from Scripture or use an app to locate an encouraging passage. Yet for all that, we need a long, steady immersion in Scripture so that we can find our *querencia* when we are surrounded in the ring of life.

CHAPTER 56

Acts 26:1-32

 LISTEN to the Story

¹Then Agrippa said to Paul, "You have permission to speak for yourself."

So Paul motioned with his hand and began his defense: ²"King Agrippa, I consider myself fortunate to stand before you today as I make my defense against all the accusations of the Jews, ³and especially so because you are well acquainted with all the Jewish customs and controversies. Therefore, I beg you to listen to me patiently.

⁴"The Jewish people all know the way I have lived ever since I was a child, from the beginning of my life in my own country, and also in Jerusalem. ⁵They have known me for a long time and can testify, if they are willing, that I conformed to the strictest sect of our religion, living as a Pharisee. ⁶And now it is because of my hope in what God has promised our ancestors that I am on trial today. ⁷This is the promise our twelve tribes are hoping to see fulfilled as they earnestly serve God day and night. King Agrippa, it is because of this hope that these Jews are accusing me. ⁸Why should any of you consider it incredible that God raises the dead?

⁹"I too was convinced that I ought to do all that was possible to oppose the name of Jesus of Nazareth. ¹⁰And that is just what I did in Jerusalem. On the authority of the chief priests I put many of the Lord's people in prison, and when they were put to death, I cast my vote against them. ¹¹Many a time I went from one synagogue to another to have them punished, and I tried to force them to blaspheme. I was so obsessed with persecuting them that I even hunted them down in foreign cities.

¹²"On one of these journeys I was going to Damascus with the authority and commission of the chief priests. ¹³About noon, King Agrippa, as I was on the road, I saw a light from heaven, brighter than the sun, blazing around me and my companions. ¹⁴We all fell to the ground, and I heard a voice saying to me in Aramaic, 'Saul, Saul, why do you persecute me? It is hard for you to kick against the goads.'

¹⁵"Then I asked, 'Who are you, Lord?'

"'I am Jesus, whom you are persecuting,' the Lord replied. ¹⁶'Now get up and stand on your feet. I have appeared to you to appoint you as a servant and as a witness of what you have seen and will see of me. ¹⁷I will rescue you from your own people and from the Gentiles. I am sending you to them ¹⁸to open their eyes and turn them from darkness to light, and from the power of Satan to God, so that they may receive forgiveness of sins and a place among those who are sanctified by faith in me.'

¹⁹"So then, King Agrippa, I was not disobedient to the vision from heaven. ²⁰First to those in Damascus, then to those in Jerusalem and in all Judea, and then to the Gentiles, I preached that they should repent and turn to God and demonstrate their repentance by their deeds. ²¹That is why some Jews seized me in the temple courts and tried to kill me. ²²But God has helped me to this very day; so I stand here and testify to small and great alike. I am saying nothing beyond what the prophets and Moses said would happen—²³that the Messiah would suffer and, as the first to rise from the dead, would bring the message of light to his own people and to the Gentiles."

²⁴At this point Festus interrupted Paul's defense. "You are out of your mind, Paul!" he shouted. "Your great learning is driving you insane."

²⁵"I am not insane, most excellent Festus," Paul replied. "What I am saying is true and reasonable. ²⁶The king is familiar with these things, and I can speak freely to him. I am convinced that none of this has escaped his notice, because it was not done in a corner. ²⁷King Agrippa, do you believe the prophets? I know you do."

²⁸Then Agrippa said to Paul, "Do you think that in such a short time you can persuade me to be a Christian?"

²⁹Paul replied, "Short time or long—I pray to God that not only you but all who are listening to me today may become what I am, except for these chains."

³⁰The king rose, and with him the governor and Bernice and those sitting with them. ³¹After they left the room, they began saying to one another, "This man is not doing anything that deserves death or imprisonment."

³²Agrippa said to Festus, "This man could have been set free if he had not appealed to Caesar."

Listening to the Text in the Story: Isaiah 42:6–7,16; 49:6; Jeremiah 1:8; Ezekiel 2:1–3; Luke 24:25–27; Acts 9:1–19; 22:6–21; Romans 1:14,16; 1 Corinthians 1:23; Philippians 3:5–6.

EXPLAIN the Story

At the beginning of Paul's commission, he was told that he was appointed to be the Lord's "chosen instrument to proclaim [Jesus's] name to the Gentiles and their kings and to the people of Israel" (Acts 9:15). Since then, in the narrative of Acts Paul is obedient to this call. He proclaimed the gospel of Christ to his fellow Jews in Jerusalem and to Jews dispersed throughout the eastern provinces of the Roman Empire. He declared Jesus as Lord to the gentiles—often to those "god-fearing" gentiles linked to synagogues. He also preached to gentiles who had little connection to the story of Israel, including the proconsul Sergius Paulus (13:7–12), the crowds in Lystra and Derbe (14:8–21), the Philippian jailer (16:30–34), and the curious philosophers in Athens (17:16–34). Now, for the first time, he will fulfill his calling to proclaim the Lord's name to a king—King Agrippa II.[1]

This is Paul's final defense speech (cf. 22:1–21; 23:1–6; 24:10–21) and also the third and final retelling of his conversion narrative (cf. 9:1–19; 22:6–21). The immediate literary context for this speech is a request from the new governor, Festus, for Paul—who has been under Roman custody more than two years—to address King Agrippa II while he visits Caesarea Maritima. This final speech is set in a social context of pomp and pageantry, as King Agrippa enters the hall to listen to Paul along with military officers and the prominent men of Caesarea (25:23). Governor Festus provides a formal introduction to Paul's speech (vv. 24–27), including a declaration of Paul's innocence (v. 25). In the course of Paul's arrest and trials since he arrived back in Jerusalem (21:17–25:12), the reader is alerted to a number of recurring themes (e.g., Paul's faithfulness to the law and Jewish customs; Paul's innocence, the resurrection). The impact of the repetitions and the narrative "weight" of the occasion create a dramatic and climactic tone to this moment. All of it is Luke's way of helping his audience to be aware that this is an important event. In this way, Paul's speech carries a similar climactic quality to it as did Peter's speech in Cornelius's house (10:23–48). As a climactic speech, it also draws together themes that have been important throughout the Gospel of Luke and the book of Acts. These themes combine as a kind of précis of Luke's theology with the inclusion of many of his key emphases across Luke-Acts. These include hope, promise, fulfillment, tradition, persecution, witness, light/darkness, gentiles,

---

1. King Agrippa was certainly sympathetic to the Jews and may even have regarded himself as in some sense connected to this people. It is doubtful, however, if many Jews regarded him as a Jewish king. As a member of the Herodian family and one raised in Rome and serving as Rome's surrogate ruler, he was essentially a gentile king.

repentance, forgiveness, and resurrection.[2] With this content, Paul's speech functions both as a climactic review of his own mission and ministry and situates Paul's place in God's overarching salvation story.

After Agrippa gives Paul permission to speak (26:1), the speech unfolds by following the conventions of Roman rhetoric familiar in court scenes.[3] It begins with an introduction (*exordium*, vv. 2–3), containing the conventional attempt to win the favor of the judge (*captatio benevolentiae*), followed by the narrative body of the speech (*narratio*, vv. 4–18), a logical "proof" of Paul's defense (*confirmatio*, vv. 19–20), a brief refute of his opponents' argument (*refutatio*, v. 21), and concluding comments (*peroratio*, vv. 22–23). As is often the case with speeches in Acts, Paul's speech is interrupted, this time by Festus (v. 24), which allows for Paul to appeal to Agrippa (vv. 25–29).

As helpful as this outline might be, Gaventa recognizes another interesting shape to this speech in the form of a chiasm that occurs after the introduction (vv. 2–3) and initial appeal (vv. 4–5). Derived from the Greek letter *chi* (which is shaped like a letter X), a chiasm uses parallel lines of a text that correspond in an X pattern, such as A-B-C-C'-B'-A' (in this case the center of the chiasm is C and C', and on either side line A will correspond to line A' and so on). Normally, a chiasm is used to express progression of thought and intensification of meaning, especially at the center of the chiasm.[4] The chiasm that Gaventa identifies in this speech occurs in the new material Paul offers (vv. 6–23) to emphasize the reversal in his life that came about after his meeting the risen Jesus. The chiasm takes shape in this manner:

A   Paul is a faithful Israelite (vv. 6–8)
    B   Paul persecuted believers (vv. 9–11)
        C   Paul is appointed to be a prophetic witness (vv. 12–18)
        C' Paul serves as a prophetic witness (vv. 19–20)
    B' Paul is a persecuted believer (v. 21)
A' Paul is a faithful Israelite (vv. 22–23)[5]

What this structure helps the reader to recognize is that even though Paul follows the rhetorical *form* associated with a Roman trial, the *content* of his speech is not primarily a legal defense as much as it is a witness to the gospel. As such, it demonstrates that Paul does not *have to* provide a defense before a king. Rather, Paul, as the appointed emissary of King Jesus, *gets to* tell his story to a king.

---

2. Cf. Gaventa, *Acts*, 340.
3. See Winter, "Official Proceedings," 327–31.
4. See "Explain the Story" on Acts 3:11–26 for another example of a chiasm in Peter's speech.
5. Gaventa, *Acts*, 339.

Permission to Speak (26:1)

Paul stands unaccompanied and unadorned (except for his chains, see v. 29) in stark contrast to the gallery around him. After Festus's introduction (25:24–27), King Agrippa is the one who gives formal permission for Paul to speak (26:1a). This reminds the readers that even though Paul stands before an august assembly of listeners, the primary audience and target of his speech is Agrippa (see 26:2, 7, 13, 19). Even after Festus interrupts his speech (v. 24), Paul pivots back to a conversation with the king (v. 27). With permission from Agrippa, Paul strikes the familiar pose of the orator—motioning with his hand—and begins his speech (v. 1b; cf. 12:17; 13:16; 19:33; 21:40).

Paul's Introduction (26:2–3)

In a Roman court, the defendant would begin with a short introduction that included the familiar comments known in Latin as the *captatio benevolentiae* (lit., "winning of goodwill"): "I consider myself fortunate to stand before you today . . ." (26:2). This is more than just flattery on Paul's part. From the defendant's point of view, it stresses the judge's suitability and competency for hearing the case. Paul did this in his earlier defense before Felix (see 24:10b). Since much of his speech will be referring to "Jewish customs and controversies" (26:3), Paul acknowledges that Agrippa's familiarity with them is important.[6]

The Initial Appeal (26:4–5)

Beyond Festus's introductory comment that "the whole Jewish community has petitioned me about [Paul] in Jerusalem and here in Caesarea" (25:24), it is helpful to remember the charges that have been leveled against Paul. Initially he was accused of teaching "against" the Jewish people and their law and for defiling the temple in Jerusalem (21:28). In the trial before Felix, he was accused of inciting rebellion (*stasis*) "among the Jews all over the world" (24:5). Once again, Paul offers an implicit appeal that his accusers provide people to "testify" (*martyrein*, 26:5) in support of these charges. He is confident that none will be forthcoming. Two elements form the basis of his confidence. First, his way of life from his time in Jerusalem is too well known. Paul makes mention that while he was born elsewhere (i.e., Tarsus) he was raised in Jerusalem. Second, he was not only a well-known resident in Jerusalem

---

6. The Jewish historian Josephus recounts how Agrippa II represented Jewish causes in the imperial court of Claudius. For example, when Jewish ambassadors came to Rome to request that they have control over their high priests' vestments, Claudius "told them that he granted their request; and bade them to return their thanks to Agrippa for this favour, which had been bestowed on them upon his entreaty" (*Ant.* 20.10 [Whiston]; cf. 15.407; 20.135).

but lived there as a Pharisee, a member of the "strictest sect [*hairesis*] of *our* religion" (26:5; cf. Phil 3:5–6). In noting this, Paul not only connects himself with the Jews but with an esteemed group within his people, a school known for its strictness and accuracy in interpreting and keeping the law.[7] In short, Paul is asserting his long-standing history and quality of pedigree and daring anyone to deny it.

Paul Is a Faithful Israelite (26:6–8)

With the two words "and now" (26:6a), Paul turns from his well-known past to his present situation. Paul continues to stress his continuity with that way of life in one particular and important aspect. He affirms his faithfulness to his people by returning to the theme of the resurrection, but this time he frames it as the enduring "hope"[8] of "our ancestors" and "our twelve tribes" (vv. 6–7). By this, Paul is situating himself and his theology within the mainstream of Israel's story. Although not every first-century Jew—including Paul's Sadducean accusers in the Sanhedrin—believed in resurrection, many Jews did, including the Pharisees. Before this king, one who is knowledgeable in Jewish customs and controversies (v. 3), Paul places his credentials and beliefs on the table. He invites Agrippa to view him not as an eccentric, rebel ringleader but as a faithful Israelite. Paul, along with all those who "earnestly serve God day and night" (v. 7), is simply following what God has *promised* (v. 6) and what God has *done* (v. 8). In asking his broader gathered audience[9] why any of them should think it incredible that God raises the dead, Paul prepares the bridge to speak about *the* Resurrected One, Jesus of Nazareth.

Paul Persecuted Believers (26:9–11)

Paul positions Jesus of Nazareth at the center of his assertions about resurrection. Before he can speak further about Jesus, he needs to take a step back and return to his past. As a member of the strict sect of the Pharisees, he describes how this strictness played out. It was not merely a matter of holding a theological position. Rather, his convictions moved him "to oppose the name of Jesus of Nazareth" (v. 9). Again, he highlights his actions in Jerusalem and his obedience to the authority of the chief priests (v. 10; cf. 25:2). He describes

---

7. Josephus also acknowledges that as a "school/sect" within Judaism, the Pharisees were "strict/exacting/accurate" in their interpretation and application of the law. He writes, "The Pharisees are those who are esteemed most skillful in the *exact* explanation of their laws, and introduce the first sect" (*J.W.* 2.162 [Whiston]; emphasis added). Josephus writes elsewhere, "The sect of the Pharisees, which are supposed to excel others in the *accurate* knowledge of the laws of their country" (*Life* 1.191 [Whiston]; emphasis added).

8. Paul emphasizes "hope" by mentioning it three times in the space of two sentences (vv. 6, 7 [2x]).

9. Note, the "you" in v. 8 is plural.

imprisoning and casting his "vote"[10] against "the Lord's people" (26:10).[11] As serious as it was for Paul, the Pharisee, to have punished and persecuted the followers of Jesus by putting them in prison and supporting their being put to death, he articulates that his primary goal was to force them "to blaspheme" (v. 11). Paul's persecuting ways set up the face-to-face confrontation that occurred when he went to hunt down followers of Jesus in the "foreign" city of Damascus.

Paul Is Appointed to Be a Witness (26:12–18)

Paul has now arrived at the heart of his speech, the important center of the chiasm. Paul opened his appeal by inviting his people—presumably embodied in the chief priests, the "servants" of God with authority to do so (cf. vv. 10, 12)—to produce witnesses *to testify against him* (vv. 4–5). Now, he will describe the turning point in his life when the resurrected Lord Jesus confronted him on the road to Damascus to appoint him as his "servant" to "witness" and *testify for him* (v. 16).

Paul's Damascus Road encounter is one of the most important stories in Acts. That it is recounted three times in the document indicates its significance. Luke narrates the account in its first occurrence (9:1–29). Paul recounts it in direct speech when it occurs the second time (22:3–21) as he speaks to a Jewish audience in Jerusalem. Now, in this final occurrence, at one of the climactic moments of gospel declaration in the whole of Acts,[12] Paul again recounts it in the first person, but this time he is addressing primarily a gentile audience in Caesarea. The alterations and additions to this telling can be accounted for in its present context in the narrative. For example, some elements add climactic intensity: the light from heaven was "brighter than the sun, blazing around me and my companions" (26:13; cf. 9:3; 22:6) and "we *all* fell to the ground" (26:14; cf. 9:4; 22:7). Other details seem to be amended to make matters clear for a gentile context: the voice from heaven is said to have spoken in "Aramaic" (lit., "in the Hebrew dialect"); in response to the question of identity, the voice replies, "I am Jesus," omitting reference to Nazareth (26:15; cf. 22:8); and mention of Ananias and Paul's blindness and healing is omitted altogether. As Longenecker observes, "There was . . . no need to refer to Nazareth (particularly having mentioned it in v. 9) or to refer to the devout Jew Ananias, as when addressing the crowd in the temple. . . .

---

10. Lit., a vote was indicated by casting a "pebble" (*psēphos*).
11. Lit., "the saints," but the NIV translates *hoi hagioi* as "the Lord's people" (cf. 9:32). Elsewhere in Acts, the NIV translates *hoi hagioi* as "holy people" (9:13) and "the believers" (9:41).
12. The other climactic, gospel-proclamation "peak" in Acts is the Cornelius narrative (10:1–11:18).

Nor was it necessary for Paul to refer to his blindness and healing, which might have been confusing to a pagan audience."[13]

There are two significant additions to this Damascus Road narrative, which occur only here in Acts. The first is the inclusion of Jesus's admonition, "It is hard for you to kick against the goads" (26:14b). This was a familiar adage in the Greek world expressing the senselessness of resisting a god. One of the earliest occurrences in ancient literature dates back to the Greek tragedy *The Bacchanals*, written in the fifth-century BC by the Athenian playwright Euripides. The relevant lines from the play are as follows:

> PENTHEUS: Do not instruct me, but be content in your escape from prison.
> Or shall I bring punishment upon you again?
> DIONYSUS: I would sacrifice to the god rather than *kick against his* [goads]
> in anger, a mortal against a god. (lines 792–96)[14]

Paul's point in including this familiar saying is to emphasize the futility of his actions and to spell out the implications of the question, "Saul, Saul, why do you persecute me?" That is, his actions in persecuting the followers of Jesus—however honorable and zealous they may have seemed to him at the time—were not only misinformed but were misdirected; they were contrary to the will of the one and only God.

The second significant addition to the Damascus Road revelation is the extended commission given to Paul *directly* by Jesus. In this account, there is no human mediator involved (cf. Acts 9:15–16). These are the very words of the risen and living Lord. Paul is not misconstruing the story. He is leaving out Ananias's role—possibly because it would have confused the point he was making before Agrippa and his gentile audience—so as to emphasize Jesus's direct intervention. Still, there is plenty in Paul's retelling that would resonate for those familiar with prophetic commissions in Israel's Scriptures. For example, the opening command of Jesus to Paul—"Stand on your feet. . . . I am sending you . . ."—echoes the commission of Ezekiel (Ezek 2:1–3), just as the assurance "I will rescue you from your own people" (Acts 26:17) echoes the words of the Lord to Jeremiah (Jer 1:8).[15] Thus, the *shape* of Paul's mission is to be a servant and witness in a manner similar to the great prophets of Israel.

---

13. Longenecker, *Acts*, 553.
14. Euripides, *The Tragedies of Euripides: The Bacchae*, trans. T. A. Buckley (Bohn: 1850). See the full text on the Perseus Digital Library: http://www.perseus.tufts.edu/hopper/text?doc=Perseus%3Atext%3A1999.01.0092%3Acard%3D775. Other occurrences of this familiar saying in Greek literature are found in Pindar, *Pyth.* 2.94–95; Aeschylus, *Prom.* 324–25; *Ag.* 1624.
15. Paul needed immediate "rescue" from his own people after his call/commission, first in Damascus (Acts 9:23–25) and not long after in Jerusalem (9:29–30). Plots against Paul's life, and thus the need for deliverance, are not unusual in Acts (see 14:5; 20:3; 23:12, 15, 30; cf. 2 Cor 11:26).

The *content* of Paul's mission (Acts 26:17b–18) is expressed in words similar to those given to the servant of the Lord in Isaiah: "I, the LORD, have called you.... I will keep you and will make you to be... a light for the Gentiles, to open eyes.... I will turn the darkness into light before them" (Isa 42:6–7, 16).

The shape and content of Paul's mission is more than just prophetic framing; rather, it has a specific purpose: to "turn them [i.e., "your own people" and "the Gentiles," Acts 26:17] from darkness to light, and from the power of Satan to God, so that they may receive forgiveness of sins and a place among those who are sanctified by faith in me" (v. 18). Numerous theological themes from throughout Luke-Acts reverberate in this commission of Jesus to Paul. These themes include: witness (Luke 24:48; Acts 1:8, 22; 2:32; 3:15; 5:32; 10:39, 41; 13:31; 22:15); repentance/turning (Luke 1:17; 11:32; 13:3, 5; 15:7; Acts 2:38; 3:19; 9:35; 11:21; 15:19; 17:30; 26:20); light/darkness and sight/blindness (Luke 2:30, 32; 4:18; 11:35; 24:16, 31; Acts 9:3; 12:7; 13:11; 26:23); and forgiveness of sins (Luke 1:77; 3:3; Acts 2:38; 5:31; 10:43; 13:38). The sharp contrast in the phrase "turn... from the power of Satan to God" is the only instance in Luke-Acts where repentance is described as turning from Satan. Yet as Gaventa notes, "The conflict with Satan figures early in Luke's Gospel in the temptation narrative (Luke 4:1–13), and numerous events in Luke-Acts involve struggles with Satan or those in Satan's control (Luke 22:3; Acts 5:3; 13:10)."[16] Last, and by no means least of all, are the final two words in Jesus's commission, "in me" (v. 18). These two small words bring the lordship of Jesus to the forefront.[17] The lordship of Jesus is a dominant theme in Acts. This note is not made as explicitly in this climactic moment of gospel proclamation as it was in the Cornelius episode ("Jesus Christ... is Lord [*kyrios*] of all"; Acts 10:36). Yet when Paul recounts his question, "Who are you, Lord [*kyrios*]?" and the answer "I am Jesus" is provided (26:15), the audience's loyalty to Caesar as "Lord" is directly challenged (*kyrios*; 25:26; NIV: "His Majesty").

The impact of these various additions, omissions, and emendations in this third and final recounting of the Damascus Road revelation is cumulative and climactic. At the heart of this speech, the center of the chiasm, it emphasizes theological themes that recur throughout Luke-Acts. As such, Paul's story serves to highlight God's larger salvation story. While Paul's specific appointment as a witness is central in this recounting of his divine commission, the emphasis falls on God's good news of salvation and the lordship of Jesus. These themes will continue to be at the forefront as the chiasm turns and Paul speaks

---

16. Gaventa, *Acts*, 345.
17. Cf. Longenecker, *Acts*, 553.

of his obedience as a witness (26:19–20), receiving persecution as a Christian (v. 21), and his faithfulness as a true Israelite (vv. 22–23).

Paul Serves as a Witness (26:19–20)

A simple conjunction, translated in the NIV as "so then" (*hothen*, v. 19; KJV: "whereupon"; NRSV: "after that"; ESV: "therefore"), is the pivot in Paul's speech. In the previous section, he has described in detail his appointment by Jesus to be his prophetic servant and witness. Here he affirms his obedience to the heavenly vision. He notes that he began immediately, right where he was at the time, in Damascus. He followed the divine command of going to his "own people" (cf. v. 17) by then going to Jerusalem (cf. 9:26–28) before going on mission to the gentile world (chs. 13–20). The balance between Jew and gentile in mission that is stressed in Acts is congruent with Paul's own testimony in his letter to the Romans. Paul writes that he was "obligated both to Greeks and non-Greeks," but that there is also a priority in gospel proclamation "first to the Jew, then to the Gentile" (Rom 1:14, 16). In this, Paul is portrayed as "an apostle," but not only as an "apostle to the Gentiles." In this specific speech, however, Paul emphasizes his faithfulness to the heavenly vision in going as a witness *first* to his own people and *then* to the gentiles. Paul—like Isaiah, Jeremiah, and Ezekiel before him—is faithful to the heavenly vision in preaching that everyone "should repent and turn to God" (Acts 26:20; cf. v. 18). This need for repentance and turning to God for both Jews (2:38; 3:19; 5:31; 9:35; 13:24; 20:21) and gentiles (11:18, 21; 14:15; 15:19; 17:30; 20:21) is common throughout the broader narrative.

Paul Is Persecuted as a Believer (26:21)

Paul described his own role in persecuting believers before his encounter with Jesus on the Damascus Road (26:9–11). Here he explains, in brief, his own experience of being persecuted. He connects the reason for the enmity at the hands of his fellow Jews not to the charges that have been laid against him—apostasy, misinterpreting the law, corrupting the temple, or rebellion (see 21:28; 24:5–8)—but because he has extended the promise made to Israel (see 26:6–7) to the wider gentile world (vv. 17–18). "*That is why*" he is facing opposition and threat (v. 21). It is because he advocates that *everyone*, Jew *and* gentile, must repent and turn to God and live in ways that reflect a restored relationship with God ("demonstrate their repentance by their deeds," v. 20).

Paul Is a Faithful Israelite (26:22–23)

The chiasm is completed with Paul's final assertion that all that he has done reflects his faithfulness to Israel's hope in the resurrection. The evidence for this faithfulness rests on two pieces of evidence. First, "God has helped me" (v. 22) to testify before small and great alike. The opening line of the chiasm declared how "God has promised" (v. 6) and that "God raises the dead" (v. 8); the closing line in the chiasm affirms that this same God is active in helping Paul to be a witness. Second, in addition to divine approval and assistance, Paul asserts that everything he is doing is in continuity with the prophets and Moses. He claims that Israel's Scripture predicted "that the Messiah would suffer and, as the first to rise from the dead, would bring the message of light to his own people and to the Gentiles" (v. 23). This is what Jesus himself had said (Luke 24:25–27) and what the Messiah's apostles proclaim (Acts 2:23–24). After all, this was the role of God's faithful servant all along: "It is too small a thing for you to be my servant to restore the tribes of Jacob and bring back those of Israel I have kept. I will also make you a light for the Gentiles, that my salvation may reach to the ends of the earth" (Isa 49:6).

Festus Interrupts, but the Conversation Continues (26:24–32)

As often happens with other speeches in Acts, the speaker has their speech interrupted (cf. 2:37; 4:1; 10:44; 22:22). In this case, Festus interrupts Paul (26:24a). Nonetheless, Paul has finished everything he needs to say by completing the final parallel of his chiastic speech. The interruption, however, heightens the readers' attention as to the impact of Paul's words on the two primary members in the audience: Festus and Agrippa. Festus shouts in exasperation, "You are out of your mind, Paul!" (26:24b). Apparently, Paul's words have not been "seeker sensitive." This Roman governor, who has already admitted his ignorance about Jewish matters (cf. 25:20), is bewildered by Paul's words, especially when it comes to the notion that a messiah—an anointed king—should suffer and rise from the dead. As was the case with the Areopagus Athenians, Paul's talk of resurrection is foolishness, the babbling of a madman (Acts 17:32; cf. 1 Cor 1:23). Festus seems to have somewhat gathered his composure with his second comment, offering Paul a backhanded compliment: "Your great learning is driving you insane" (26:24c).

Paul denies the governor's conclusion: "I am not insane.... What I am *saying* is true and reasonable" (v. 25). The verb Paul adopts to emphasize the absolute truth of his assertions is *apophthengomai* ("to say"). This verb, used to express Paul's soundness of mind, is the same word used two other times in Acts. First, it is used of the believers who spoke in other tongues on the day of Pentecost as "the Spirit enabled [*apophthengesthai*] them" (2:4) and second of Peter as he stood up and "addressed [*apephthegxato*] the crowd" (2:14).[18]

---

18. Levison, *Inspired*, 95.

Paul does not, however, let Festus's boisterous interruption deflect him from his primary target, King Agrippa. Festus may not have been able to keep up with Paul's theological argumentation and biblical allusions, so Paul returns his attention to Agrippa: "The king is familiar with these things, and I can speak freely to him" (26:26). This is incredible audacity. Paul has just turned his back on a Roman governor and turned to a king to address him as an equal. Paul draws on the public record about Jesus and the prophetic testimony of Scripture and seeks to draw King Agrippa into the circle of belief.

Agrippa, not to be outdone, enters into the conversation for the first time since he gave permission for Paul to speak (v. 1). In the course of this short speech, Agrippa's position has changed. He began as the king who held power at court. Now Agrippa is being invited not only to agree with Paul's position but to join Paul in giving allegiance to another king—King Jesus. In what almost appears to be an attempt at humor to deflect his own discomfort, Agrippa asks, "Do you think that in such a short time you can persuade me to be a Christian?" (v. 28). Paul is now focused in his pursuit of his prey and possibly even enjoying the verbal sparring. We can almost detect a twinkle in the apostle's eye as he flashes back his answer to the king by playing off of Agrippa's own word—"a short time" (*oligos*, v. 28). "Short time [*oligos*] or long [*megas*]—I pray to God that not only you but all who are listening to me today may become what I am, except for these chains" (v. 29). This not only plays off Agrippa's question but picks up on a note from earlier in the speech where Paul declared himself to be God's emissary to stand and testify "to small [*mikros*] and great [*megas*] alike" (v. 22). Dunn notes that Paul's testimony "has the same dramatic character as [Martin] Luther's, 'Here I stand, I can do no other.'"[19] Paul stands to speak truth to power and declare what is essential to the Christian faith. What will Agrippa do?

King Agrippa now stands—along with all those sitting with him—and leaves the room (vv. 30–31). He blinks in the face of truth. After the long buildup to this dramatic speech, the letdown is almost palpable. Since Paul's arrest in Jerusalem, the events of the last few chapters—riots, impassioned speeches, murderous plots, nighttime escape, and trials—have each increased the tension in the narrative to this climactic point. The emotional strain is released as Agrippa stands and leaves the room. With Paul's invitation still ringing in the air, the scene closes with the dignitaries shuffling out of the audience hall and quietly talking among themselves. Their words are almost muted as they merely repeat what we have heard all along: "This man is not doing anything that deserves death or imprisonment" (26:31; cf. 23:9, 29; 25:5).

---

19. Dunn, *Acts*, 331.

Paul may be deemed innocent by the most important and capable judges in the vicinity—Roman governors and a sympathetic client king—but his rights as a Roman citizen will still be honored. More importantly, the Lord's plan for Paul to testify in Rome (23:11) will be fulfilled in his very appeal to Caesar. Caesar is in Rome, and it is to Rome that Paul must now go.

Paul's Defense Is Really an Offense

In his reflection on Acts 26, Eugene Peterson observes that Paul's speech before Agrippa is less of a defense and more of an offense.[20] Paul was familiar with imperial court proceedings. His speech before Agrippa and the one prior to this one before Felix (24:10–21) demonstrate his awareness and expertise in matters of Roman law and legal rhetoric. In line with normal trial proceedings, he could have taken several different approaches. He could have offered a typical defense, rebutting the charges made against him. Or he could also have remained silent (as Jesus did) and wait for the judges hearing his case to decide their verdict. Paul takes neither of these routes. Even though his speech before King Agrippa exhibits the *shape* of a trial defense speech, the *content* of his speech was neither a defense in the usual manner or a submission to the unavoidable realities of Roman justice. Instead, he went on the offense. Despite his visible chains (26:29), Paul took control of the trial. Paul didn't offer a legal defense; he preached a prophetic sermon.

Paul, the prisoner, had been summoned by a Roman governor to speak before a "Jewish" client king. He was supposed to present a humble defense; instead, he spoke audaciously in personal terms—like the Israelite prophets of old—inviting Agrippa into the company of those who put their trust in Jesus. He turned the tables on Agrippa and put him in the dock. He spoke as the appointed emissary—the servant and witness (v. 16)—of the risen Lord Jesus. He did not argue *against* the legal charges; rather, he contended *for* the lordship of Jesus and the eternal realities and questions his Master raises. Paul spoke as one who lived confidently and enthusiastically in obedience to his prophetic calling and commission.

As Peterson notes, perhaps this kind of defense—this kind of offense—is what the world needs to hear.[21] The world has ample evidence for the existence

---

20. See Peterson, *Conversations*, 1732. Alexander, *Acts*, 185, states it more bluntly: "As a legal defence, this speech is a washout," but as a prophetic appeal to King Agrippa, "Paul's passionate conviction almost leaps off the page."
21. Peterson, *Conversations*, 1732.

of God, and the church is not short of apologists. Books and blogs are widely available to explain the intricacies of Christian theology and argue for the tenets of the Christian faith. These are important. The point of studying Scripture, after all, is that we might be persuaded to faith. Yet what the world often lacks are men and women who, like Paul, burn with adoration for their lord and king, Jesus. The world needs those whose lives are rooted in Christ and who bear the fruit of passionate obedience. Yes, the church needs to be able to provide a reasonable defense of the faith, but we also need to offer a loving offense for our Savior. This does not mean that we will "win" by the measurements that the world uses to declare a victory. But it will mean that we have been faithful to the one who sits at God's right hand in heaven and who will return triumphantly to earth with glory to judge both the living and the dead.

Turn and Connect

My wife, Darlene, keeps a journal (which she sometimes shares with me). She wrote this one day, recalling a few minutes she spent outdoors on our deck before leaving for work:

> There was a chilly wind, so I sat on the east side of the deck, leaning against the wall of the pergola, sheltered from the wind and warmed by the sun. The bird feeder was only a few feet away, and after a while a chickadee came flitting to the edge of the feeder. He landed, and looked me full in the eye, so that for a few moments we shared a connection. That shared moment has come back to me more than once since it happened, for it felt a little like a God moment, that I knew I was SEEN by this creature. It seemed to me in that flicker of time that what gives value to life are those shared seeings, and especially to share a gaze of connection with God—or perhaps another creature who also has received breath through Him.

The "gaze of connection with God" seems to me to be akin to what Paul describes when he met Jesus on the Damascus Road. Of course, the meeting was much more dazzling for Paul—with a light from heaven, brighter than the sun, blazing around (26:13)—than the one described by Darlene. Yet the intensity of turning to "see" is present whenever we have authentic connections with God. This is what is involved when we invite others—as Paul did often in his life—to "turn to God" (v. 20). Moments like these are often "illuminating." When we turn to God, it is like turning from darkness to light, from the powerful clutches of Satan to the emancipating embrace of God. In his moment of seeing, Paul also describes his connection with Jesus as hearing. Sight and sound, eyes and ears are involved in this turn to the Savior. Truth is not only visualized but also communicated. Maybe this is what Paul had in mind when he prayed for the Ephesian Christians "that the eyes of your heart may be enlightened in order that you may know the hope to which he has called you" (Eph 1:18). This is such a wonderful mix of metaphors and ideas—eyes, heart, hope, calling—and it all works to convey what happens when we connect to the glorious way of life God has for us in Christ.

Repent and Return

After we turn to God and see him in the light of truth and connect with his gaze, we need to respond. The first movement is seeing, but the next movement involves repenting and returning. Our eyes must be opened so that we can connect with God. Once this attentive connection is established, then we respond with repentance and begin our return to the realities of wholeness and relationship that God always intended for humanity. Paul does not shy away from using weighty theological words like "repent/repentance" (Acts 26:20) as he invites Agrippa to "become what I am" (v. 29). *Repent* and *repentance* are important words in the life of faith. John the Baptist used them (e.g., Mark 1:4; Luke 3:3), so did Jesus (e.g., Mark 1:15; Luke 5:32), and Jesus's disciples used them too (e.g., Mark 6:12; Acts 2:38; 3:19; 5:31). For all its importance, repentance is a concept that might require unpacking today. We may "speak freely" (26:26) of repentance if our listeners are familiar with "Jewish customs" (v. 3) like Agrippa was, but if our audience is more like Festus and unfamiliar with theological language, we may need to explain things clearly and creatively.

The Greek words for "repent" and "repentance" literally refer to experiencing a "change of mind." This implies that one's thinking is going in the wrong direction, and to go in the right direction one must stop and go a different way. Repentance requires reorientation. There are a variety of ways that I try to express the implications of repentance in the context of parish ministry. For example, when we baptize new Christians in full view of the congregation, I have the candidates face west when I ask them these three questions: "Do you renounce Satan and all the spiritual forces of wickedness that rebel against God? Do you renounce the evil powers of this world which corrupt and destroy the creatures of God? Do you renounce all sinful desires that draw you from the love of God?" Then I have them turn to face east before I ask these next three questions: "Do you turn to Jesus Christ and accept him as your Saviour? Do you put your whole trust in his grace and love? Do you promise to obey him as your Lord?"[22] The reason I do this is to help them

---

22. *The Book of Alternative Services of the Anglican Church of Canada* (Toronto: Anglican Book Centre, 1985), 154.

remember their baptism and their "orientation"[23] to Christ each time they enter our building for worship. Our building is constructed on an east-west axis. The main entrance to the building is on the west end near the baptismal font. After one enters the church building and passes the font, they then turn east to walk up the central aisle facing a glorious window depicting the ascension of Jesus. Each time they make this short journey, they are reminded about their pilgrim life as a follower of Jesus. This entails repentance and their *turn from* Satan, the world, and sinful desires and their *turn to* Jesus Christ.

Another example of how I try to help others understand and enter into the meaning of repentance is annually on Ash Wednesday. Ash Wednesday occurs forty days prior to Easter (excluding Sundays). It also begins the season of Lent. Lent is a time to prepare for Easter when we celebrate our freedom through the death and resurrection of our Lord Jesus. On Ash Wednesday, each member of the congregation is marked with a cross of ash on his or her forehead (made from the previous year's Palm Sunday palm branches) as a sign of mortality and as a reminder that only by God's gracious gift in Jesus do believers receive eternal life. Sometimes we also go out on the street and offer "Ashes to Go" for anyone who might like to be reminded of their need to make a repentant turn to Jesus. Often when people see me standing out on the street in my vestments with a plate of ash in my hands, they ask me what it all means. I'm grateful to explain what ashes have to do with repentance. I try to make it as simple as possible. Ashes are a sign of mortality and brokenness. That is what we are like without God's mercy. We are dry and dead. Repentance, however, means more than just acknowledging what we are and what we need to turn *from*. I want them to know that repentance also involves turning *to* God and, through Jesus, to receiving new life. It is a return to our true heart's home. If I have time and they let me, I also share a simple and helpful prayer written by Stephen Cherry. It is entitled "Repentance" and captures beautifully what this concept involves:

> *Walking into the ocean*
> *the cold bites toes and ankles.*
> *Sand is ripped from footprint*
> *in the ebb and flow of surf*
> *even at an inch's depth.*
> *Pushing on, each wave becomes a body blow, a*
> *thud on the belly*
> *a crash on the chest.*
> *The eighth, the biggest, pushes me*

---

23. "Orient" and "orientation" are based on the Latin word, *oriens*, which means "east."

back a pace or two.
Best to lunge over or
dive under, through
water, suspended sand and murky foam.
This is what it is to face
the One who was and is and is to come.
This is what it is to face the Creator
who comes in Spirit and storm.
Yet:
if this is what it is to face,
maybe I am facing wrongly.
In the surf there is no
question. The journey out allows the return;
what seemed like infinite
resistance, is now propelling power.
Let me turn my back,
not in disrespect, but in true alignment;
and speed me along the new forward,
my old backward.[24]

I find in this prayer a helpful image to introduce people to repentance, a "true alignment" and return to our home on the shore of God's love. The harder we push against the loving and creative purposes of God—much like Paul's "kick[ing] against the goads" (Acts 26:14)—the harder and more painful our journey becomes. Waves crash against us, and we drown in the "murky foam" of sin. Yet once we make the turn, we catch the wave of God's presence: "The journey out allows the return" and "what seemed like infinite resistance, is now [the] propelling power" of the Spirit. Our "true alignment" is found as we orient ourselves to the risen and ascended Christ. Repentance enables our return home to God.

---

24. Stephen Cherry, *Barefoot Prayers: A Meditation a Day for Lent and Easter* (London: SPCK, 2013), 24–25. Used by permission.

CHAPTER 57

Acts 27:1-44

 LISTEN to the Story

¹When it was decided that we would sail for Italy, Paul and some other prisoners were handed over to a centurion named Julius, who belonged to the Imperial Regiment. ²We boarded a ship from Adramyttium about to sail for ports along the coast of the province of Asia, and we put out to sea. Aristarchus, a Macedonian from Thessalonica, was with us.

³The next day we landed at Sidon; and Julius, in kindness to Paul, allowed him to go to his friends so they might provide for his needs. ⁴From there we put out to sea again and passed to the lee of Cyprus because the winds were against us. ⁵When we had sailed across the open sea off the coast of Cilicia and Pamphylia, we landed at Myra in Lycia. ⁶There the centurion found an Alexandrian ship sailing for Italy and put us on board. ⁷We made slow headway for many days and had difficulty arriving off Cnidus. When the wind did not allow us to hold our course, we sailed to the lee of Crete, opposite Salmone. ⁸We moved along the coast with difficulty and came to a place called Fair Havens, near the town of Lasea.

⁹Much time had been lost, and sailing had already become dangerous because by now it was after the Day of Atonement. So Paul warned them, ¹⁰"Men, I can see that our voyage is going to be disastrous and bring great loss to ship and cargo, and to our own lives also." ¹¹But the centurion, instead of listening to what Paul said, followed the advice of the pilot and of the owner of the ship. ¹²Since the harbor was unsuitable to winter in, the majority decided that we should sail on, hoping to reach Phoenix and winter there. This was a harbor in Crete, facing both southwest and northwest.

¹³When a gentle south wind began to blow, they saw their opportunity; so they weighed anchor and sailed along the shore of Crete. ¹⁴Before very long, a wind of hurricane force, called the Northeaster, swept down from the island. ¹⁵The ship was caught by the storm and could not head into the wind; so we gave way to it and were driven along. ¹⁶As we passed to the lee of a small island called Cauda, we were hardly able to make the lifeboat

secure, ¹⁷so the men hoisted it aboard. Then they passed ropes under the ship itself to hold it together. Because they were afraid they would run aground on the sandbars of Syrtis, they lowered the sea anchor and let the ship be driven along. ¹⁸We took such a violent battering from the storm that the next day they began to throw the cargo overboard. ¹⁹On the third day, they threw the ship's tackle overboard with their own hands. ²⁰When neither sun nor stars appeared for many days and the storm continued raging, we finally gave up all hope of being saved.

²¹After they had gone a long time without food, Paul stood up before them and said: "Men, you should have taken my advice not to sail from Crete; then you would have spared yourselves this damage and loss. ²²But now I urge you to keep up your courage, because not one of you will be lost; only the ship will be destroyed. ²³Last night an angel of the God to whom I belong and whom I serve stood beside me ²⁴and said, 'Do not be afraid, Paul. You must stand trial before Caesar; and God has graciously given you the lives of all who sail with you.' ²⁵So keep up your courage, men, for I have faith in God that it will happen just as he told me. ²⁶Nevertheless, we must run aground on some island."

²⁷On the fourteenth night we were still being driven across the Adriatic Sea, when about midnight the sailors sensed they were approaching land. ²⁸They took soundings and found that the water was a hundred and twenty feet deep. A short time later they took soundings again and found it was ninety feet deep. ²⁹Fearing that we would be dashed against the rocks, they dropped four anchors from the stern and prayed for daylight. ³⁰In an attempt to escape from the ship, the sailors let the lifeboat down into the sea, pretending they were going to lower some anchors from the bow. ³¹Then Paul said to the centurion and the soldiers, "Unless these men stay with the ship, you cannot be saved." ³²So the soldiers cut the ropes that held the lifeboat and let it drift away.

³³Just before dawn Paul urged them all to eat. "For the last fourteen days," he said, "you have been in constant suspense and have gone without food—you haven't eaten anything. ³⁴Now I urge you to take some food. You need it to survive. Not one of you will lose a single hair from his head." ³⁵After he said this, he took some bread and gave thanks to God in front of them all. Then he broke it and began to eat. ³⁶They were all encouraged and ate some food themselves. ³⁷Altogether there were 276 of us on board. ³⁸When they had eaten as much as they wanted, they lightened the ship by throwing the grain into the sea.

³⁹When daylight came, they did not recognize the land, but they saw a bay with a sandy beach, where they decided to run the ship aground if they could. ⁴⁰Cutting loose the anchors, they left them in the sea and at the same time untied the ropes that held the rudders. Then they hoisted the foresail to the wind and made for the beach. ⁴¹But the ship struck a sandbar and ran aground. The bow stuck fast and would not move, and the stern was broken to pieces by the pounding of the surf.

⁴²The soldiers planned to kill the prisoners to prevent any of them from swimming away and escaping. ⁴³But the centurion wanted to spare Paul's life and kept them from carrying out their plan. He ordered those who could swim to jump overboard first and get to land. ⁴⁴The rest were to get there on planks or on other pieces of the ship. In this way everyone reached land safely.

Listening to the Text in the Story: Jonah 1:1–17; Mark 6:45–52; Luke 8:22–25; 2 Corinthians 11:25–26.

EXPLAIN the Story

There is a significant change of pace and tone in the narrative beginning in Acts 27. Whereas listeners of Luke's story would have benefitted from a few good legal handbooks to follow the proceedings and dialogue of the previous trial scenes, now, as the scene shifts from courtroom to sea travel, having a few good nautical maps would be beneficial.[1] Much has changed. Political and judicial power dynamics are exchanged for the power of sea and storm. Instead of lengthy and dramatic dialogue, there is now movement and action. Paul appeared isolated and alone in his trials and Caesarean imprisonment, but now Aristarchus and Luke accompany him (i.e., the "we passages" resume). Yet for all the changes and shifts in tone, this final voyage to Rome is a journey that has been long in the making. Paul expressed his intention to visit Rome in the first sentence of the final "panel" of Acts (19:21). This plan was confirmed by

---

1. Modern readers are encouraged to follow a good map for Paul's journey from Caesarea to Rome. Many Bibles have maps in them, but I would also suggest investing in a Bible atlas to aid in further study of the entire biblical story. Two atlases have been very helpful to me. First, the older but still helpful work by Barry J. Beitzel, *The Moody Bible Atlas of Bible Lands* (Chicago: Moody, 1985). Second, Carl G. Rasmussen, *Zondervan Atlas of the Bible*, rev. ed. (Grand Rapids: Zondervan, 2010). For those wishing for specific insights into aspects of this voyage, see Rapske, "Acts, Travel and Shipwreck," 22–47, and Hemer, *Acts*, 132–52.

divine providence in a nighttime vision while Paul was under Roman custody in the Antonia Fortress in Jerusalem (23:11). Paul may not have imagined that he would make his journey to Rome in chains and under military escort, but even amid a storm-tossed sea he has the assurance that God is in control and will bring him safely to his destination (27:23–24).

As welcome as the change of pace and scene may be for modern readers, sea journeys were a typical feature of epic stories in the ancient world. Greco-Roman ears would hear echoes from Homer's *Odyssey* or Virgil's *Aeneid* in Paul's journey. Those more attuned to the biblical story will hear resonances from the Jonah narrative. There are also fainter echoes from Jesus's seas stories (e.g., Mark 6:45–52; Luke 8:22–25) and Paul's recollections in his own letters (e.g., 2 Cor 11:25–26). Both in the Greco-Roman and the biblical traditions, the sea is a foreboding context. As Parsons notes, "The sea was viewed sometimes as an evil or hostile place of chaos and confusion, sometimes as a vehicle through which divine forces punish wickedness."[2] The sea is not a neutral context, as the biblical stories of the flood (Gen 6–8), the exodus (Exod 14), Jonah (Jonah 1), and Revelation (Rev 13) illustrate. Yet for all its potential menace, the sea, including the sea that Paul travels upon, is not threatening for God. It is a context in which God is able to display his power and his providence.

This final journey, much like Paul's final speech in the previous episode, functions as a summary and exemplary account. Just as Paul's address before Agrippa (Acts 26) gathered together strands of the theological *message* present in Luke-Acts, this sea voyage (Acts 27) gathers together strands of the theological *mission* in Luke-Acts. That is, there is a difficult but progressive spread of the gospel despite the headwind of opposition. Surprisingly, the opposition often comes from those who should be the most familiar with the journey (i.e., sailors). There is also unexpected Roman kindness that in the end sides with the dominant local leadership. And finally, when all seems dark and lost, God promises assurance and rescue; in the end this rescue is expressed in the language of "salvation."[3]

This sea voyage is packed with nautical details and vivid descriptions of the storm and shipwreck, but the narrative progression is easy to follow. Despite a note of foreboding, the first section begins slowly as Paul and his companions embark on their journey to Rome (27:1–12); the action intensifies as their second ship encounters a ferocious storm that blows them hopelessly off course

---

2. Mikeal C. Parsons, *Acts* (Grand Rapids: Baker Academic, 2008), 352.
3. Note the words "saved" (*sōzō*) in 27:20, 31; "survive" (*sōtēria*) in 27:34; and "safely" (*diasōzō*) in 27:44 (cf. 28:1, 4). See Dunn, *Acts*, 324, who notes how Luke's description of the voyage to Rome functions as a "paradigm of Paul's mission."

(27:13–26); finally, as hope evaporates, the ship nears land, runs aground on a sandbar, and even though the ship and its cargo are lost, everyone on board reaches land safely (27:27–44). Interspersed throughout the action are accounts of Paul offering warnings (vv. 10, 31) and encouragement (vv. 21–26, 33–34).

Paul Sails for Rome (27:1–12)

Paul embarked on the 3,600-kilometer journey (about 2,240 miles)[4] to Rome likely in the autumn of AD 59. This first segment of the journey will involve two different ships and four different ports before they reach Fair Havens, on the island of Crete. The quiet tone that opens this episode is in marked contrast to the high drama and tension of the previous trial narratives. The first verb in the sentence—"[it] was decided" (v. 1)—is a passive verb and suggests almost a cold sense of Roman judicial power at work.[5] Rome has decided Paul's fate, and he is simply carried along like cargo. This impersonal note is balanced by the return of the pronoun "we" in the narrative (cf. 16:10–17; 20:5–15; 21:1–18). Paul was often portrayed as isolated and alone in the previous episodes; now, friends accompany him again. He is joined by a former traveling companion, Aristarchus from Thessalonica (27:2; cf. 19:29; 20:4; Col 4:10; Phlm 24), and presumably Luke, the author of Acts.[6] While scholars debate who is behind the "we passages" in Acts, the simplest explanation is that this represents the author of the book recollecting his own memories of this eventful journey with Paul. Readers are not given any explanation of what happened to Luke in the two-year interval during Paul's arrest and imprisonment in Caesarea. Nonetheless, that the author of Acts accompanied Paul on this sea voyage offers a reasonable and simple explanation as to why the description of this journey is full of nautical details, vivid weather reports, and emotional insights about the passengers and crew. The author is retelling the journey as an eyewitness account!

A centurion named Julius is responsible for guarding Paul, along with other prisoners bound for Rome. A few pieces of information in the narrative provide a personal touch to this Roman officer. Julius, and the detail of soldiers assisting him (Acts 27:31–32, 42), is described as a member of the "Imperial Regiment" (v. 1). This was likely an auxiliary cohort levied from Syria and stationed in Batanea east of Galilee.[7] More important to the narrative, Julius is

---

4. Beitzel, *Atlas*, 177.
5. Alexander, *Acts*, 186.
6. Ramsay, *St. Paul*, 255, suggests that Aristarchus and Luke may have been allowed to accompany Paul because they passed themselves off as his slaves. This not only provided Paul with companionship but also would have enhanced his prestige in the eyes of his Roman guards.
7. See Rapske, *Paul in Roman Custody*, 268–69.

portrayed as being a decent Roman soldier—much like other centurions in Luke-Acts (e.g., Luke 7:1–10; 23:47; Acts 10–11). Not all soldiers responsible for guarding traveling prisoners were as kind. Prisoners in transit by ship often suffered from dehydration, hunger, and confinement below decks. In contrast, Julius is "philanthropic"[8] toward Paul. There are several reasons why Julius may have been warmly predisposed to him. It might be out of respect for a fellow Roman citizen, or because Festus instructed him to be lenient, or simply because he liked Paul. Whatever the reason, he permits Paul—no doubt still under guard—to visit friends when they make their first stop in Sidon, a hundred kilometers (60 miles) north along the coast, the day after they set sail from Caesarea (27:3). These friends provide for his needs—food and water—for the journey ahead. A further indication of the centurion's decency is that he seems to have allowed Paul access to the upper decks rather than being confined below. Later Julius will even allow Paul to weigh in on discussions about plans for the journey (v. 10), and ultimately Julius saves Paul's life when the soldiers wished to kill him, and all the other prisoners, when their ship ran aground (v. 43).

The first ship that they sailed on was from Adramyttium, an Aegean port along the northwest coast of Asia near Troas, where Luke first joined Paul's company (cf. 16:10). This was likely a small, private vessel that utilized the gentler winds near the coastline as they traveled north and west to Adramyttium, taking advantage of the shelter provided by Cyprus as they sailed past Cilicia and Pamphylia. The sailing, however, was slow "because the winds were against us" (27:4). Eventually they arrived in Myra, in the province of Lycia. Luke does not mention it, but this meant they first docked in Myra's port, Andriaca, before traveling the four kilometers (2.5 miles) inland to Myra itself.

Myra was a wealthy and important city in the first century. Its significance is attributed to its being a major port of call for large cargo ships—often carrying large quantities[9] of grain and up to a thousand passengers—traveling between Italy and Egypt.[10] Here, the centurion requisitioned passage for them on one of these larger ships from Alexandria headed to Italy. The pace on the larger vessel was no quicker than the small Adramyttium ship, and Luke notes they had "difficulty" (vv. 7, 8) heading west. Unable to land at Cnidus, on the tip of a narrow peninsula extending off the southwestern corner of Asia

---

8. The Greek word translated as "kindness" (27:3) is *philanthrōpōs*.
9. Rapske, "Acts, Travel and Shipwreck," 31, notes that the large grain ships carried anywhere from 1,000–3,500 tons of grain.
10. For a helpful discussion of the vital importance of a continuous and safe supply of grain for ancient Rome, see L. Casson, "The Role of the State in Rome's Grain Trade," in *Ancient Trade and Society*, ed. L. Casson (Detroit: Wayne State University Press, 1984). Casson likens the importance of ancient grain transportation to that of oil today.

Minor and last port of call before heading into open water, they were forced to sail farther south. Again, because of strong northwesterly winds, they were required to sail along the southern "lee side" coast of the island of Crete, passing Salmone on its easternmost point. Eventually they landed in the small port of Fair Havens (modern Kaloi Limenes or Kali Limenes) in the middle of the island, about twenty kilometers (twelve miles) east of Cape Matala.

Much time had been lost in their westward journey, and they were now in a precarious season—mid-September to early November—for weather and sea travel. Before long, they would risk sailing in the period from mid-November to mid-March, a season that was considered extremely dangerous for sea travel.[11] Luke alerts us (v. 9) to this by noting that it was already after "the Fast"—that is, Yom Kippur, "the Day of Atonement" (Lev 16:29–31). Yom Kippur occurs on the tenth day of the lunar month Tishri (from late September to early October in the solar calendar).[12] As a respected passenger, Paul intervenes in an onboard discussion about the travel plans for the ship. Paul warns against traveling any farther (Acts 27:10). The centurion, who was the ranking Roman officer and had final say on the ship, ignores Paul's warning and follows the counsel of the pilot and ship owner (v. 11). The issue is financial. Fair Havens was not an adequate port for wintering. If the cargo was grain, it was valuable but extremely vulnerable if exposed to water. As any grain farmer knows, grain must be kept cool and dry. Wet grain swells, doubling in size, and generates such high heat that it can spontaneously combust. The pilot and owner, wanting to preserve both the ship and its valuable cargo, urge sailing on about sixty kilometers (about thirty-five miles) farther west to a more adequate harbor, Phoenix (modern-day Phineka Bay adjacent to Akra Moures), to winter there (v. 12).[13]

The Storm (27:13–26)

When a gentle south wind began to blow, ideal for sailing west, the crew weighed anchor, thinking it would be smooth sailing to Phoenix (v. 13). As the ship rounded Cape Matala just west of Fair Havens, the ship became exposed to northern winds because the island coast bends north, opening into the Bay of Mesara. As they rounded the cape, the sailors' worst fears materialized. The wind changed direction, and the treacherous "Northeaster" storm wind swept down upon them from the mountain range in the middle

---

11. Rapske, "Acts, Travel and Shipwreck," 22. Rome required constant supplies of grain from Egypt. The emperor Claudius tried to ensure a constant supply of food, even during the dangerous winter season, to prevent food shortages in the capital and in other significant cities (see Suetonius, *Claud.* 18.2).
12. The Day of Atonement occurred on 5 October in AD 59.
13. Bruce, *Acts*, 483.

of Crete (v. 14).[14] Ancient seamen knew the "Northeaster" by its hybrid name, *eurakulōn*. This name was a compound word formed by the Greek word *euros* ("east wind") and the Latin word *aquilo* ("north wind").[15] This fierce wind blew them off course, and the ship, instead of heading west, veered south. Soon they passed to the sheltered "lee side" (i.e., the south side) of the small island of Cauda (modern Gavdos/Gozzo)—about forty kilometers (twenty-five miles) southwest of Crete (v. 16). They took this brief reprieve from the wind to do what they could to prepare the ship for when they would reemerge into the might of the storm.

Luke describes in detail the evasive actions the ship's crew takes to save the vessel. First, the crew hauled aboard the trailing, waterlogged lifeboat and secured it, with difficulty, to the ship (v. 16). Next, they girded the ship with ropes to reinforce the hull against the battering of the waves (v. 17).[16] Finally, they lowered the sea anchor (or their sails)[17] to slow their speed. All this, however, did not end the risk. "A ship driven by a persistent east-northeast [wind] from this area was in danger of reaching a lee-shore on the coast of Cyrenaica, off which 'the Syrtis,' an extensive zone of shallows and quicksands, formed a notorious navigational hazard and inspired an obsessional fear constantly mentioned in first-century literature."[18] Still, despite the crew's valiant efforts, the ship is badly damaged, and they begin to throw cargo overboard to lighten the ship and prevent it from sinking (v. 18). Not long after this, they jettison the ship's "tackle" (v. 19). Hope was evaporating. Almost mimicking the lost sight of hope, Luke tells us that visibility diminishes so much that they can see "neither sun nor stars" (v. 20)—the primary means for navigating on the open sea—for many days.

At this darkest moment, when they had given up all hope of being saved, Paul intervenes for a second time and says, "Men, you should have taken my advice not to sail from Crete" (v. 21). One cannot blame Paul for this "I told you so"—after all, he had been shipwrecked before (cf. 2 Cor 11:25). His words, thankfully, do not end there. He also encourages the crew and passengers. Again, he has another night vision, his last one recorded in Acts. This time it is not "a man" (cf. 16:9) or the Lord (cf. 18:9–10; 23:11), but an "angel of . . . God" (27:23). Even though it is an angel, the vision and its message is focused on God. This is the God to whom Paul belongs and whom

---

14. The highest mountain on Crete, Mount Ida, is 2,456 meters in height (over 8,000 feet).
15. Hemer, *Acts*, 141–42.
16. There is some uncertainty as to how the ropes were passed around or under the ship to make it stronger.
17. The meaning of the Greek phrase translated as "lowered the sea anchor" (v. 17) is uncertain; it could also mean, "to lower the sails."
18. Hemer, *Acts*, 144.

Paul worships. God is in control. Paul "must"—again the divine providential "must" (*dei*) in Acts (27:24; cf. 1:21; 3:21; 4:12; 5:29; 9:6, 16; etc.)—stand trial and be a witness before Caesar. God, Paul argues, is greater than any sea storm and will ensure this outcome. Despite this assured outcome, Paul does not offer a sugarcoated courage. While *God* will graciously spare all the crew and passengers, the ship and its cargo will be lost. Paul tells them, "So keep up your courage, men, for I have faith in God that it will happen just as he told me" (v. 25). The others needed Paul's faith; they had given up hope of being "saved" long ago (v. 20).

The Shipwreck (27:27–44)

Fourteen days is, according to James Smith, about how long it would take a ship adrift (traveling about 2.5 km/hour) to reach the island of Malta from Cauda.[19] The ship was driven across the "Adriatic Sea" (v. 27), if by "Adriatic" Luke means the expanse of water between Crete and Malta.[20] The sailors discerned that they were nearing land. After taking soundings to determine the depth of the water, they confirm that they are close to shore, and again Luke describes in detail the efforts of the crew to avoid danger—this time, the danger of crashing into coastal rocks in the dark. They lower four anchors and "prayed" for daylight (v. 29). The sailors, however, are not entirely selfless in their care for the passengers and ship. In a moment of madness, they attempt to escape from the ship by lowering a lifeboat. Paul, for a third time in the narrative, recognizes the odd behavior of the crew and intervenes to alert the centurion and soldiers of this danger. He warns them once more that unless they listen to him "you cannot be saved" (v. 31). This time, the centurion heeds Paul's counsel and orders the solders to cut the ropes holding the lifeboat to prevent the sailors from abandoning ship.

As Luke recounts this travel episode, he depicts a growing respect for Paul on board the ship. The narrative opened with Paul as a submissive and expendable prisoner being taken, along with other prisoners, to Rome. With each intervention of Paul on the ship, his voice gathers in importance and his value increases. Now, for the fourth time he intervenes and displays wise leadership. He recognized that after two weeks adrift in the stormy sea and unable to cook or eat food, the crew and passengers were weak and exhausted. He urges them to eat because, as he sees it, this is necessary for them "to survive" (v. 34). Again, their rescue is described as "salvation"

---

19. James Smith, *The Voyage and Shipwreck of St. Paul*, 4th ed. (1880; repr., Grand Rapids: Baker, 1978), 27n1.

20. Longenecker, *Acts*, 561, and Hemer, *Acts*, 145–46, argue that this refers to "the Adrian Sea."

(cf. vv. 20, 31).[21] As if to lead the way for the others, Paul "took some bread and gave thanks to God in front of them all. Then he broke it and began to eat" (v. 35). This simple meal is "sacramental"—that is, it is a visible expression of an invisible grace, and in this sense it echoes the Lord's Supper ("he took bread, gave thanks and broke it"; cf. Luke 22:19; 24:30).[22] Paul's words and actions calm the storm within the hearts of his fellow shipmates. They "were all encouraged and ate some food themselves" (Acts 27:36). In all this, however, Paul emphatically declares his God as the only God who rules the seas!

For the first time in the narrative, Luke mentions how many were on board (v. 37). "Probably it became necessary when distributing the food to know the exact number, and Luke himself may have had a part in supervising the distribution."[23] The number is 276,[24] not at all unreasonable since the Jewish historian Josephus notes that on his own ill-fated voyage, "I came to Rome, though it were through a great number of hazards, by sea; for, as our ship was sank in the Adriatic Sea, we that were in it, being about six hundred in number, swam for our lives all the night" (*Life* 14–15 [Whiston]).

After eating, the crew makes a final—and not insignificant—effort to give the ship a shallower draft in the rough seas by throwing the grain cargo overboard (v. 38). This is a practical action, but it also is symbolic of "casting their cares" upon God, the one who controls the storm and the sea (cf. 1 Pet 5:7).

Luke describes the ship's final and traumatic moments with numerous nautical details (27:39–41). The ship's crew abandons all effort to control the vessel by anchors or rudders. They hoist the foresail and head straight for the sandy beach to run the ship ashore. Unfortunately, the ship runs into a hidden sandbar, and with the bow stuck the stern is beaten by the rough waves and the ship begins to break up. The real danger, however, shifts from the sea to the soldiers. Roman law decreed that any guard who allowed a prisoner to escape would face the fate of the escapee: execution (see comments on 12:18–19; 16:25–28). With the fear that the prisoners might swim to freedom, the soldiers plan to kill them (27:42). To prevent a summary execution of the prisoners, especially Paul, Julius exerts discipline over his troops. He orders them all to get to land as best they can—by swimming or

---

21. The word translated by the NIV as "survive" is the Greek word *sōtēria*. The word *sōtēria* occurs ten times in Luke-Acts and is usually translated as "salvation" or "saved" (e.g., Luke 1:69, 71, 77; 19:9; Acts 4:12; 13:26, 47; 16:17; in Acts 7:25 it is translated as "rescue").

22. Parsons, *Acts*, 358, recognizes that "it is scarcely a eucharistic ritual . . . since not all the participants are believers." Still, he acknowledges that this shared meal "constitutes" Paul and his shipmates as a community under God's providential care—which is what Eucharistic celebrations, in part, do.

23. Longenecker, *Acts*, 562.

24. Some manuscripts state that there were "about seventy six" on board.

by holding on to floating pieces of wreckage (vv. 43–44a). Everyone reaches shore "safely" (v. 44b). Once more, the note of "salvation" is struck, and the readers are reminded that it is by God's providence—and in fulfillment of Paul's prediction—that everyone on board is "saved" (cf. vv. 23–26). The epic drama draws to a close.

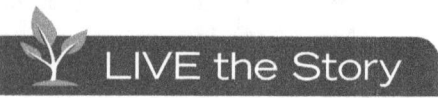

Vocational Holiness

I read a lot. Much of the time I read because I have to; it's a matter of obligation. Sometimes I read because I get to; it's a matter of pleasure. Sometimes I read because I need to; it is a matter of vocational holiness. I read three books every year because I need to read them to maintain the shape and substance of my vocation. The three books are *Evangelical Theology: An Introduction* by Karl Barth, *Jayber Crow* by Wendell Berry, and *Under the Unpredictable Plant: An Exploration in Vocational Holiness* by Eugene Peterson.

I read these three different books for various reasons, but the one thing that draws this trio together for me is that each author explores and roots vocation in God. Barth's book, a short one by his standards, is a book that reminds me of what theology is, what threatens theology, and how to live with vocational integrity as a theologian. His energy and urgency help me maintain theological focus in a world that is constantly blurring my vision, often through fear, propaganda, or sentimentality. Berry's book is a novel, but it is no less true for being so. Berry explores the life of Jayber Crow, a barber. *Jayber Crow* reminds me of the importance of being rooted in the life of a community. Berry takes the Christian virtues of chastity, stability, humility, and simplicity and locates them in an ordinary town—not too different from my own—and shows me how they can be lived over the long term. I need to be reminded of these virtues in a world that tempts me with the competing virtues of choice, speed, mobility, self-assertion, and busyness. *Jayber Crow* helps me maintain vocational integrity as a person.

Under the Unpredictable Plant explores the life of Jonah. Peterson uses this biblical prophet as a site to reflect on the dangers that threaten the pastoral vocation. Like Jonah, many pastors are tempted to flee their God-given congregational callings and run away to some other more exotic "Tarshish" parish on the horizon. *Under the Unpredictable Plant* helps me sustain vocational integrity as a pastor. Peterson highlights the difficult conditions of the pastoral vocation and discovers in the story of Jonah a parable and a prayer to keep a fissure from forming between faith and calling:

The conditions in which we must acquire a spirituality for our vocation—an *interior* adequate to the *exterior*—are, it must be admitted, not friendly. Our vocations are bounded on one side by consumer appetites, on the other by a marketing mind-set. Pastoral vocation is interpreted from the congregational side as the work of meeting people's religious needs on demand at the best possible price and from the clerical side as satisfying those same needs quickly and efficiently. These conditions quickly reduce the pastoral vocation to religious economics, pull it into relentless competiveness, and deliver it into the hands of public relations and marketing experts. . . .

It is not easy these days to figure out what it means to be a leader in Christ's church. Anti-servant models are promoted daily among us as pastors, teachers, missionaries. . . . The Jonah story is sharply evocative of the vocational experience of pastor. . . .

The book of Jonah is a parable at the center of which is a prayer. Parable and prayer are biblical tools for bringing a sharp personal awareness of truth to people whose spiritual perceptions are dulled by living habitually in an overtly religious context. Since pastors operate almost exclusively in exactly that context, the Jonah story with its parable and prayer is made to order.[25]

Peterson identifies the strong parallels—through comparison and contrast—between Jonah's storm and Paul's shipwreck. "Both stories are vocational, the lives given their definitive shape by God's call to word-of-God work as prophet and apostle."[26] Jonah is the antitype; Paul is the type. Jonah is the unfaithful prophet fleeing across the Mediterranean, attempting to escape God's call; Paul is the obedient apostle sailing across the Mediterranean, fulfilling God's call. In both stories, money is front and center (in Jonah's case, he was able to pay the price of the entire ship; in Paul's case, the pilot and owner press beyond the bounds of safety for financial reasons). In both stories, ships are headed west and encounter fierce storms. In both stories, the crew and passengers are in peril of drowning. In both stories, the protagonists are saved—both personally and vocationally—as they listen to God in prayer. In both stories, God uses sea and storm to prove that he is the true power and in ultimate control. Amid mighty storms, "as God's action intensifies, the significance of our human lives (and especially, since here we are most apt to

---

25. Eugene Peterson, *Under the Unpredictable Plant: An Exploration in Vocational Holiness* (Grand Rapids: Eerdmans, 1992), 3–6.
26. Ibid., 68.

depart from it, our *vocational* lives) comes into focus as the single point of who we *are*, not what we have to offer him, not what we can do to help him. Thus the vocations of Jonah and Paul are purified, purified both of good intentions (Paul) and bad intentions (Jonah)."²⁷ These sea stories remind us that our vocations are always and only responsive to and validated by God. Sea and storm may be a dominant context for salvation, but the omnipotent God is in control whatever the weather. "The storm either exposes the futility of our work (as in Jonah) or confirms it (as in Paul). In either case, the storm forces the awareness that God constitutes our work, and it disabuses us of any suggestion that in our work we can avoid or manipulate God. Once that is established, we are ready to learn the spirituality that is adequate to our vocation, working truly, easily, fearlessly, without ambition or anxiety, without denial or sloth."²⁸

The Blessing of Friendship

In the narrative of Acts, after he arrives in Jerusalem (21:17) Paul is increasingly depicted as isolated. Despite being accompanied by a significant group of coworkers on his return to Jerusalem from Macedonia and Asia (see 20:4), Paul stands alone on trial and in imprisonment. Even if this was a literary device by Luke to highlight the parallel between Jesus's and Paul's isolation in arrest and trial, the periods of seclusion—especially in his Caesarean imprisonment—must have been difficult for a man like Paul, who valued companionship (see Rom 16:1–16; Phil 4:2–3; Col 4:14; 2 Tim 4:11). The word "friend" (*philos*) does not occur frequently in Acts (10:24; 19:31; 27:3), but as Parsons points out, "Luke was well aware of the cultural protocols and expectations associated with friendship in antiquity."²⁹ Greco-Roman friendship covered a broad spectrum. It could refer to friendship that was shared in the public or private sphere. It could address associations between patron and clients or the reciprocal relationship between "genuine" friends—that is, between equals. As Paul embarks on his sea voyage and the challenges that will face him as a prisoner on this long journey, two genuine friends, Luke and Aristarchus, accompany him. One day into his journey, unnamed "friends" in Sidon assist him (Acts 27:3). Even the centurion Julius treats him with a kindness (*philanthrōpōs*, v. 3) that is akin to friendship, and as they travel their connection appears to deepen.

Friends are important. Companionship can make all the difference as one travels through life and ministry—especially when storms arise. One of the

---

27. Ibid., 70.
28. Ibid., 72.
29. Parsons, *Acts*, 368.

greatest challenges for those in church leadership is loneliness. Shortly after I first became an incumbent priest for a parish, a retired priest took me aside during a clergy day. He encouraged me *not* to cultivate friendship with my parishioners. While I think he meant well, I'm glad I ignored him. I need friends—both among fellow priests and with those in my parish. I am careful whom I share confidence with and am aware of the importance of boundaries. Yet I cannot conceive of trying to work and serve within a congregation in isolation. I think Paul would agree. Solitude is a necessary discipline for me to rejuvenate, but it is not good for me to be alone long term. Loneliness and isolation can cripple a leader through paranoia, self-doubt, and/or fear. Genuine friendship—that is, the bond that grows between those who work and worship together, who play and pray together—provides balance, wisdom, and encouragement. Genuine friendship is not exclusive; it welcomes others into the fellowship. The model, of course, is the very nature of our God. Our God is triune—Father, Son, and Spirit—and exists in perpetual relationship between persons. This relationship is expansive, creative, loving—and it is *philanthropic*. Our God is relational and loves human beings. Paul, and more importantly, God, models the centrality of friendship and blessing that come when we enter into relationship with others.

A Eucharistic Life—the Bread of Hope for the Life of the World

It is correct to conclude that no eucharistic ritual occurred onboard the cargo ship when Paul encouraged everyone to "take some food" after fourteen days without eating (Acts 27:33–34). No wine is mentioned, Paul did not distribute the bread to others, and besides most of the 276 onboard were not believers. Yet this conclusion also reflects a view of reality that segments the sacred from the secular. Yet this is a false dichotomy. In his important book *For the Life of the World*, the orthodox theologian Alexander Schmemann argues that God does not divide the world into holy and profane and that we, as followers of Christ, are to live a eucharistic life that reflects this unified vision.[30] The Greek word translated "gave thanks" is *eucharisteō* (v. 35). Thanksgiving is the natural response to God's giving, to God's grace. Eucharist is a way of being; it is not a ritual or ceremony. Every time we eat and drink we are reminded of our eucharistic life. Yet it is larger than this. All of life is to be thankfully lived in communion with God. The mission of the church, following the example of Christ, is to be sacramental—a visible sign of grace—for "the life of the world" (cf. John 6:51). In Paul's words, we need to eat "to survive" (*sōtēria*, 27:34). Yet, "salvation" has more to do than with just eating bread—we do

---

30. Alexander Schmemann, *For the Life of the World* (New York: St. Vladimir's Seminary, 1973).

not live, after all, by bread alone. Salvation equals the fullness of communion with God. When we celebrate the Eucharist in the gathered worship of the baptized, we are not injecting something holy into the profane. The Eucharist *reveals* the nature of the bread and wine—it is an instrument of communion with God and a mark of our mission in the world.

When Paul insisted that others eat bread at the critical moment of nearing land, he is acknowledging that eating bread—in the context of giving thanks to God—not only sustains the body but instills hope and fuels courage. A eucharistic life proclaims to the world—whether we are standing on dry land or on a ship in a rolling sea—that everything is infused with the grace of God and controlled by the will of God. This requires a radical reorientation of vision—even for many Christians—but I would argue it is the implicit, if not the explicit, intent of this episode in Acts and even of the story of the gospel. Yet if this is too great of a theological step for some to take, maybe we can at least all agree with Beverly Gaventa's conclusion: "Luke specifies that those who observe Paul are encouraged and then take food. If it is not the bread of the eucharist, it is the bread of hope."[31]

---

31. Gaventa, *Acts*, 355.

CHAPTER 58

Acts 28:1-16

 LISTEN to the Story

¹Once safely on shore, we found out that the island was called Malta. ²The islanders showed us unusual kindness. They built a fire and welcomed us all because it was raining and cold. ³Paul gathered a pile of brushwood and, as he put it on the fire, a viper, driven out by the heat, fastened itself on his hand. ⁴When the islanders saw the snake hanging from his hand, they said to each other, "This man must be a murderer; for though he escaped from the sea, the goddess Justice has not allowed him to live." ⁵But Paul shook the snake off into the fire and suffered no ill effects. ⁶The people expected him to swell up or suddenly fall dead; but after waiting a long time and seeing nothing unusual happen to him, they changed their minds and said he was a god.

⁷There was an estate nearby that belonged to Publius, the chief official of the island. He welcomed us to his home and showed us generous hospitality for three days. ⁸His father was sick in bed, suffering from fever and dysentery. Paul went in to see him and, after prayer, placed his hands on him and healed him. ⁹When this had happened, the rest of the sick on the island came and were cured. ¹⁰They honored us in many ways; and when we were ready to sail, they furnished us with the supplies we needed.

¹¹After three months we put out to sea in a ship that had wintered in the island—it was an Alexandrian ship with the figurehead of the twin gods Castor and Pollux. ¹²We put in at Syracuse and stayed there three days. ¹³From there we set sail and arrived at Rhegium. The next day the south wind came up, and on the following day we reached Puteoli. ¹⁴There we found some brothers and sisters who invited us to spend a week with them. And so we came to Rome. ¹⁵The brothers and sisters there had heard that we were coming, and they traveled as far as the Forum of Appius and the Three Taverns to meet us. At the sight of these people Paul thanked

God and was encouraged. ¹⁶When we got to Rome, Paul was allowed to live by himself, with a soldier to guard him.

Listening to the Text in the Story: Jonah 1:7–10; Luke 4:38–40; 10:19; Acts 14:11–12; 27:3.

EXPLAIN the Story

Few people read commentaries, or even "books" of the Bible, start to finish. Instead, access is made at specific points out of interest or need (e.g., sermon preparation, college papers, a burning theological question). Yet if you open Acts, or a commentary on Acts, at chapter 28, you are beginning near the end of a long story. Paul, and everyone else on the Alexandrian cargo ship with him, has washed ashore after weeks adrift in a fierce winter storm on the Adriatic Sea. The connective narrative tissue with the previous sea episode is not only the waterlogged state of the survivors but the first word in this new episode on land: "Safely" (*diasōzō*; 28:1). The primary concern of the preceding chapter—and in fact a primary concern for Luke-Acts as a whole—is the matter of "salvation," how people will be "saved" (27:20, 31, 34, 44). We learn that it is God's active and gracious presence who has brought about this work of salvation for his servant Paul, as well as the lives of all those who traveled with him (cf. 27:24).

Now, washed up "safely" on land, Luke begins to orient the readers to Paul's new circumstances. Where is he? What will happen now? How will he make his way to Rome? These questions will be answered in the three successive episodes that follow. First, we are introduced to the island's hospitable "barbarian" hosts (vv. 1–6), who make hasty assessments of Paul. Second, Paul is extended further hospitality by the "chief official" of the island and reciprocates the kindness by healing the sick (vv. 7–10). Third, after a restful three-month stay, the travelers resume their journey to Rome (vv. 11–16). While readers should be attentive to what is written in the text about these three episodes, it is helpful to note what is *not* written. That is, it would be easy to forget that Paul is still a prisoner under Roman guard because the centurion Julius, his soldiers, and the rest of the 276 people on board the ship fade from view. Further, Paul has appealed to Caesar and is on his way to Rome, the largest and grandest city in the empire. Luke does not, however, sound notes of awe or wonder as Paul approaches the capital and the emperor. Rather, albeit subtly,

Luke highlights Paul's "triumphal entry" to Rome with notes of hospitality (vv. 2, 7), vindication (vv. 4–6), honor (v. 10), and greeting (vv. 14–15). When Paul finally arrives in Rome, the focus is not Rome or Caesar but God, to whom thanksgiving is rightly due.

Island Hospitality (28:1–6)

The identity of the place where Paul and his fellow travelers have washed ashore is revealed as the island of *Melitē*. Although other islands have been suggested for the location of the shipwreck,[1] the scholarly consensus is that *Melitē* is the tiny island of Malta, a hundred kilometers (60 miles) south of Sicily. Luke refers to the locals as "islanders," literally, "barbarians" (*barbaroi*; v. 2). This need not imply any derogatory sense, but means merely that they did not speak Greek or Latin. In fact, Malta had a long, illustrious history that could be traced back over eight centuries to the Phoenicians, marking them as one of the oldest civilizations in the world. By the time the island passed into Roman hands in 218 BC near the beginning of the Second Punic War, it had a robust Phoenician-Punic culture.

The islanders were not only culturally rich, they were also unusually kind. Like the centurion Julius before them, they extended "philanthropy" (*philanthrōpia*; v. 2; cf. 27:3) to Paul and his weary and wet companions. For the first time in Acts, the weather is mentioned, and it is raining and cold.[2] The first thing required, given the circumstances, is a warm fire. Paul decided to help gather firewood. As he threw sticks on the fire from his bundle, a viper emerged from the wood and bit his hand. Since there are no poisonous snakes found on Malta today, some have concluded that a nonpoisonous snake bit him.[3] Whatever the case, the islanders assumed it *was* poisonous. In fact, they made a swift judgment: "This man must be a murderer; for though he escaped from the sea, the goddess Justice has not allowed him to live" (28:4). This assumption is reminiscent of another ancient story recorded in the *Greek Anthology*:

> The shipwrecked mariner had escaped the whirlwind and the fury of the deadly sea, and as he was lying on the Libyan sand not far from the beach, deep in his last sleep, naked and exhausted by the unhappy wreck, a baneful viper slew him. Why did he struggle with the waves in vain, escaping then the fate that was his lot on the land? (7.290)[4]

---

1. See Rapske, "Acts, Travel and Shipwreck," 37–43.
2. Alexander, *Acts*, 190.
3. For a thorough discussion on this matter, see Hemer, *Acts*, 153.
4. *The Greek Anthology*, trans. W. R. Paton, LCL (New York: G. P. Putnam's Sons, 1919), 159.

The Maltese islanders make a similar connection between the deadly sea and divine judgment. Furthermore, the echoes of the biblical Jonah story also reverberate between the conclusions of the sailors and those of the Maltese (see Jonah 1:7–10). Much to their amazement, however, Paul shook off the snake into the fire and suffered no ill effects (Acts 28:5; cf. Luke 10:19). Now, just as quickly, they readjust their assumptions and swing to the other extreme of mistaken identity and conclude Paul is a god (v. 6).

Unlike his response to the Lystrans when they declared Paul and Barnabas to be gods (Acts 14:11–12), Luke does not relate that Paul denies this pagan assertion—although he most certainly would have thought as much. He may have done so later, but Luke chooses to let Paul's actions address this issue indirectly in the next scene. For now, remembering that Paul is on trial for his life with his entire mission under inquiry, Luke is making a point through this episode. "Luke's story subtly conveys a deeper and more powerful verdict on Paul's mission than Caesar could ever do. God's servant is neither a criminal nor a god: he's a vulnerable human being, subject to the same winds and waves as the rest of us, but someone who has placed his life in the hands of the one who is utterly trustworthy (27:23)."[5] In short, Paul is vindicated and, once more in the narrative, declared to be innocent (cf. 23:9; 25:25; 26:31).

Paul Heals the Sick (28:7–10)

Besides being inhabited by *barbaroi*, (lit., "barbarians"), Malta was also resident to a prominent landowner with a Roman name, Publius. There is some dispute whether the reference to him as *prōtos* (NIV: "chief official"; NRSV: "leading man"; KJV, ASV, ESV: "chief man") refers to an official title or an indication that he was the leading benefactor on Malta (v. 7). It seems likely to be the latter.[6] Regardless, like the other inhabitants on the island, he exhibits generous "hospitality"[7] to Paul and his companions and welcomes them into his home for three days. No mention is made about Paul's Roman guard or the rest of the 276 shipmates. Luke's focus is set exclusively on Paul's actions. Paul soon learns that Publius's father is sick with a fever and dysentery (v. 8). This illness may be a unique malady linked to this island and is known as *Malta fever*. This illness was "discovered in 1887 to be caused by endemic micro-organism *Micrococcus melitensis*, which infected the milk of the Maltese goats."[8] Paul went to the man's room "and, after prayer, placed his hands on him and healed him" (v. 8).

---

5. Alexander, *Acts*, 191.
6. Barrett, *Acts*, 2:1224–25; Hemer, *Acts*, 153.
7. Greek *philophronōs*, v. 7; the only occurrence of this word in the NT.
8. Hemer, *Acts*, 153–54.

The healing is reminiscent of Jesus's healing of Peter's mother-in-law in Capernaum (Luke 4:38–40). As in that healing, the news of it spread, and many sick people came to receive healing (28:9). Unlike Jesus, however, Paul first prays and lays his hands on the man. In this way Luke seems to be indirectly addressing the earlier assertion made by the Maltese that Paul "was a god" (v. 6). A god would not need to pray to another god for healing; Paul does. Paul is portrayed as a healer, but as a healer who works through the power of another—"the God to whom [Paul] belong[s] and whom [he] serve[s]" (27:23). Nonetheless, Paul and his companions (note the referent "us") are honored in many ways (v. 10). As such, in addition to receiving hospitality (vv. 2, 7) and divine vindication (vv. 4–6), Paul is now afforded "honor." With these dynamics taking center stage, the fact that Paul is a Roman prisoner has almost faded from view. Furthermore, the "honor" bestowed upon Paul has the practical upside of including significant provision of all "the supplies we needed" (v. 10) to make the final leg of the journey to Rome. All Paul and his fellow travelers need to do is wait for the favorable sailing season to open.

Arrival in Rome (28:11–16)

After waiting out the winter on hospitable Malta, the journey to Rome resumes—likely in late February or early March AD 60. Paul, his companions, and his Roman guard board another Alexandrian cargo ship that had also wintered on Malta. Luke, ever fascinated with nautical details, notes that the ship was adorned with the figurehead of the twin gods Castor and Pollux (*Dioskouroi*, v. 11). These Greek gods were regarded as the patron deities of sailors. Somewhat ironically, this ship, overseen by these "brothers" who were revered for keeping sailors safe on the seas, required a Maltese harbor to keep it safe.

After they depart from Malta, the ship sails north to Syracuse on the island of Sicily, and then on to the port of Rhegium, in the "toe" of the Italian "boot," before landing in Puteoli (modern Puzzuoli), about 200 kilometers (120 miles) south of Rome (vv. 12–13). It might be coincidental, but after mentioning the brothers Castor and Pollux, Luke then seems to highlight the welcome Paul receives from his own "brothers" as he arrives in Italy (cf. vv. 14, 15, 17, 21 [NIV: "our people"]). Paul did not need the brother gods to ensure his safe arrival to Rome, but his *brothers* and sisters in the Lord certainly greeted him warmly.

When they found "brothers and sisters" in Puteoli, they remained there a week, and unceremoniously Luke announces, "And so we came to Rome" (v. 14b). It may have been odd to land so far from Rome, but apparently "Puteoli was a favorite terminus for passengers on ships coming from the east."[9]

---

9. Rasmussen, *Atlas*, 233.

Luke does not offer any reasons for the extended stopover in Puteoli, but it may have something to do with the requirements of requisitioning provisions for a significant company of soldiers guarding Paul and his companions. In the first-century Roman world, the centurion leading a detail like this was able to demand food and accommodation from locals as they traveled. Not surprisingly, while the centurion had the right to demand this from locals, it was often an unwelcome and tension-filled exchange. Roman soldiers and their prisoners were hungry and not always the most gracious guests. Rapske notes, however, that the centurion may have seized upon the offer of this Christian "room and board" and extended their stay for very practical reasons:

> First . . . the road from Puteoli to Rome was rough and flinty, making significant demands upon its travelers. In the light of this, one might quite legitimately wish to steel oneself for the journey by a longer initial rest stop, particularly after a recent sea voyage punctuated in its latter stage by (shipboard?) stops of three days in Syracuse and a single day in Rhegium (Acts 28:12). This would hardly be judged an act of military dereliction. Second, travel to Rome using the facilities of the *cursus publicus* ["the public way"—the state-run courier and transportation system of Rome] might encourage such delay. . . . As one drew closer to Rome, the demands upon the transport and billeting facilities of the *cursus publicus* would have become much greater and more clearly priority-orientated.[10]

As interesting as these details are to help provide a context for the last stage of the journey to Rome, Luke emphasizes not the road but the welcome that Paul received as he neared Rome along the Appian Way. First in Puteoli, next in the market towns of the Forum of Appius (forty-three Roman miles[11] southeast of Rome) and then in the Three Taverns (thirty-three Roman miles southeast of Rome), the greetings Paul received from his "brothers and sisters" encouraged him so deeply that he "thanked God" (v. 15). The word translated as "meet" (*apantēsis*, v. 15) may carry a technical sense "for the official welcome of a visiting dignitary by a deputation which sent out from the city to greet him and escort him for the last part of the journey."[12] Rome was familiar with the triumphal entries of famous generals and emperors. It was a city that prided itself on its power, prestige, and the favor it received from "the gods." Yet, for Luke none of this impressed him. Instead, what impressed him was the arrival of a humble apostle—a prisoner (v. 16)—who comes to Rome under

---

10. Rapske, "Acts, Travel and Shipwreck," 20–21.
11. A Roman mile, at 5,000 feet, is slightly shorter than a modern statute mile, at 5,280 feet.
12. Bruce, *Acts*, 502n35.

divine vindication and protection, with honor, and receives a triple greeting from his fellow "heavenly citizens" as he took his final steps to Rome. After all this time (cf. 19:21), and after all the assurances from his Lord and God (23:11; 27:24), how could Paul not be encouraged and thankful?

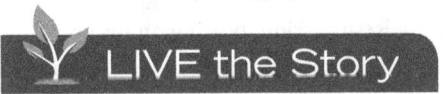
LIVE the Story

Neither Murderer nor God—but Sinner and Saint

Luke displays a wry sense of humor as he relates the initial impressions the Maltese had of Paul. After first witnessing him being bitten by a viper, they immediately concluded that this was a sign of guilt and that he "must be a murderer" (Acts 28:4). Yet, before long, after seeing no ill effects from the bite, they jump to an opposite conclusion: "He [must be] a god" (v. 6). Alexander observes that this is an example of something that occurs often in both ancient and modern societies. He writes, "In the public imagination, you're either a criminal or a god."[13] We do this most often with our leaders, celebrities, and star athletes. We either adore them as heroes or—after a scandal, accident, or moral failure—disparage them as villains. The pendulum swings swiftly in the arena of public opinion. When this happens in the realm of politics and society, it is, I suppose, to be expected, but when it occurs in the church, it is to be lamented. Those who read and understand Scripture should know that we are simultaneously sinners and saints; we are born broken and need to be made new by God through the gracious work of Christ and the empowering presence of the Spirit. The implication is that we should be able to maintain a healthy balance and estimation of humanity. As a Jewish rabbi put it, "A man should carry two stones in his pocket. On one should be inscribed, 'I am but dust and ashes.' On the other, 'For my sake was the world created.' And he should use each stone as he needs it."[14]

While attentiveness to the biblical story should be enough to help us maintain a balanced view of ourselves, sometimes we might need supplemental help. For me, I've found this in the work of the writer and pastor Frederick Buechner. In fact, the first book I ever read cover to cover was Buechner's collection of essays, *The Magnificent Defeat*. It opens with a reflection on that classic "sinner/saint" from the Bible, the rascal Jacob. Buechner unpacks the biblical story of Jacob wrestling with God—the "beloved enemy"—by the river Jabbok. He suggests that God is often the enemy we fight with:

---

13. Alexander, *Acts*, 191.
14. Rabbi Bunam, quoted in Philip Yancey, *Reaching for the Invisible God* (Grand Rapids: Zondervan, 2000), 90.

Our enemy because, before giving us everything, he demands of us everything; before giving us life, he demands our lives—our selves, our will, our treasure. Will we give them, you and I? I do not know. Only remember the last glimpse that we have of Jacob, limping home against the great conflagration of the dawn. Remember Jesus of Nazareth, staggering on broken feet out of the tomb toward the Resurrection, bearing on his body the proud insignia of the defeat which is victory, the magnificent defeat of the human soul at the hands of God."[15]

It is in the interface between our sinfulness and saintliness that we sustain an honest view not only of ourselves but of others too. The gospel requires both repentance for the sinners that we are and our acceptance of the gift of resurrection life that God extends. Buechner offers a summary of this posture:

> The gospel is bad news before it is good news. It is the news that man is a sinner, to use the old word, that he is evil in the imagination of his heart, that when he looks in the mirror all in a lather what he sees is at least eight parts chicken, phony, slob. That is the tragedy. But it is also the news that he is loved anyway, cherished, forgiven, bleeding to be sure, but also bled for. That is comedy. And yet, so what? So what if even in his sin the slob is loved and forgiven when the very mark and substance of his sin and of his slobbery is that he keeps turning down the love and forgiveness because he either doesn't believe them or doesn't want them or just doesn't give a damn? In answer, the news of the gospel is that extraordinary things happen. Henry Ward Beecher cheats on his wife, his God, himself, but manages to keep on bringing the gospel to life for people anyway, maybe even for himself. Lear goes berserk on a heath but comes out of it for a few brief hours every inch a king. Zaccheus climbs up a sycamore tree a crook and climbs down a saint. Paul sets out a hatchet man for the Pharisees and comes back a fool for Christ. It is impossible for anybody to leave behind the darkness of the world he carries on his back like a snail, but for God all things are possible. That is the fairy tale. All together they are the truth.[16]

Paul was neither a murderer[17] nor a god, but he was a sinner *and* a saint. That is, he was like any other believer who has acknowledged their deep brokenness and sinfulness and found healing through grace and God's life-giving

---

15. *Magnificent Defeat*, 18. Buechner explores the relationship of "sinner/saint" in many of his novels, essays, and autobiographical books. Of particular note are his novels *Godric, Brendan, Son of Laughter,* and *The Book of Bebb*.

16. Buechner, *Telling the Truth*, 7–8.

17. Paul did, however, admit that he was a persecutor of the Lord's people and put them into prison, where some of them were put to death (cf. Acts 26:10–11).

Spirit. This double acknowledgment of being a sinner and a saint is what helps us stay balanced, rooted, and obedient.

God's Priorities

Another theological angle worth reflecting on in the story of Acts as Paul enters Rome is the manner in which Luke frames the priorities of God and the gospel. To begin with, it is interesting to note what Luke is *not* concerned with. As travelers entered the city of Rome in the mid-first century, they would immediately be struck by the power projections of the empire. They would walk beneath triumphal arches and observe victory columns and temples to the gods Jupiter and Juno (the twin protectors of the Roman state), all of it reminding citizen and slave alike that Rome was supreme. The imperial palaces, theaters, amphitheaters, and hippodromes that adorned the city reinforced that Roman triumph and power was to be celebrated and feared. Yet Luke ignores all of this. While he is keen to provide detailed descriptions of the sea-and-land journey to Rome, he is completely disinterested in describing any of the sights, sounds, or symbols of the city. Rome was a triumphant city, but the only triumph that Luke was interested in is the triumph of the gospel. Paul, as one of the gospel's great ministers, is led as captive "in Christ's triumphal procession" into Rome (2 Cor 2:14). Although a prisoner in chains, Paul is marked as one who is protected, vindicated, honored, and greeted in a manner reminiscent of Rome's great generals who entered the city in victory.

The vision that Luke offers at the end of Acts is instructive for contemporary Christians. Often we are tempted by the power projections of this world: military might, wealth, triumphal architecture, symbols of cultural supremacy. We are easily awed by the metrics of worldly success and fail to notice God's victory on display in the lives of humble, obedient, and faithful servants and communities. When Paul entered Rome in AD 60, the great and mighty hardly noticed him. He took up residence in Rome quietly, awaiting his audience with Caesar, all the while under the guard of a Roman soldier. Paul may be referring to this experience as he wrote his letter to the Philippians. He took his imprisonment not as a retreat but as progress for the gospel: "I want you to know, brothers and sisters, that what has happened to me has actually served to advance the gospel. As a result, it has become clear throughout the whole *palace guard* [*praitōrion*] and to everyone else that I am in chains for Christ" (Phil 1:12–13). As members of Caesar's praetorian took their turns guarding Paul—which included being chained together—what do you think they talked about? The weather? The latest gladiatorial-game results? The political intrigues of court? Maybe. But I would venture a guess that Paul did exactly with his guards what he did with King Agrippa and turned the tables on them (cf. Acts 26:29). Instead of Paul being their prisoner, they may have felt they were his. Over time, it would not be surprising if some of those chained to Paul became followers of Christ too. How else could he include in his final greetings to the Philippians this note: "All God's people here send you greetings, *especially those who belong to Caesar's household*" (Phil 4:22).

Caesar may not have paid much attention to Paul when he arrived in Rome, but some of his own household and personal guard did. Within three centuries, the quiet triumph of the gospel succeeded in winning over the empire, not by the sword but with love and truth. Luke paid attention to the priorities that mattered. He noticed the preaching of Christ, the welcoming hospitality of Jesus's disciples, and the boldness that comes through the power of the Spirit. Luke attended to the triumph displayed through the prisoner Paul, not to the power projections of Rome. We would do well in our world to attend to those who give quiet and humble witness to the gospel and not to the loud and proud projections of those who think themselves great in the eyes of the world.

CHAPTER 59

Acts 28:17-31

 LISTEN to the Story

¹⁷Three days later he called together the local Jewish leaders. When they had assembled, Paul said to them: "My brothers, although I have done nothing against our people or against the customs of our ancestors, I was arrested in Jerusalem and handed over to the Romans. ¹⁸They examined me and wanted to release me, because I was not guilty of any crime deserving death. ¹⁹The Jews objected, so I was compelled to make an appeal to Caesar. I certainly did not intend to bring any charge against my own people. ²⁰For this reason I have asked to see you and talk with you. It is because of the hope of Israel that I am bound with this chain."

²¹They replied, "We have not received any letters from Judea concerning you, and none of our people who have come from there has reported or said anything bad about you. ²²But we want to hear what your views are, for we know that people everywhere are talking against this sect."

²³They arranged to meet Paul on a certain day, and came in even larger numbers to the place where he was staying. He witnessed to them from morning till evening, explaining about the kingdom of God, and from the Law of Moses and from the Prophets he tried to persuade them about Jesus. ²⁴Some were convinced by what he said, but others would not believe. ²⁵They disagreed among themselves and began to leave after Paul had made this final statement: "The Holy Spirit spoke the truth to your ancestors when he said through Isaiah the prophet:

²⁶'"Go to this people and say, "You will be ever hearing but never understanding; you will be ever seeing but never perceiving." ²⁷For this people's heart has become calloused; they hardly hear with their ears, and they have closed their eyes. Otherwise they might see with their eyes, hear with their ears, understand with their hearts and turn, and I would heal them.'¹

---

1. Isa 6:9–10.

²⁸"Therefore I want you to know that God's salvation has been sent to the Gentiles, and they will listen!"[29]²

³⁰For two whole years Paul stayed there in his own rented house and welcomed all who came to see him. ³¹He proclaimed the kingdom of God and taught about the Lord Jesus Christ—with all boldness and without hindrance!

Listening to the Text in the Story: Psalm 67:2; Isaiah 6:9–10; Luke 1–4; 8:10–14; Acts 1:3, 6; Romans 9:2–4a; Ephesians 6:17.

EXPLAIN the Story

The ending of Acts often puzzles readers. For many, it leaves too many unanswered questions. What is the outcome of Paul's appeal before Caesar? Is he released? If so, does he stay in Rome or did he continue on to Spain (see Rom 15:24, 28)? If not, was he executed? Did Luke intend a third volume? Besides this bevy of unanswerable questions, the ending can also feel anticlimactic. There is no dramatic closing scene, no angels, no miracles. Paul doesn't even bring the gospel to Rome as the herald of good news. The good news had already made its home in Rome, and a Christian community greets him when he arrives.

There is, however, a possible way forward in understanding the puzzle of the ending of Acts if we look *backward*. That is, instead of reading the ending as a climax to the book of Acts, Loveday Alexander makes the excellent suggestion that we view it as a fitting end to the two-volume work of Luke *and* Acts.³ She proposes that if we read Luke-Acts "from back to front" we will recognize connections between the ending of Acts and the narrative prologue in Luke (i.e., chs. 1–4). The narrative connections she points out include a Roman framework (the empire and its rulers are foregrounded in Luke 2:1 and 3:1–2; Paul arrives in Rome in order to face trial before Caesar, Acts 28:19); a Jewish community confronted with the reality that God's word and God's healing are extended not just to Israel but also to gentiles (Luke 2:29–32;

---

2. Some manuscripts include here, "After he said this, the Jews left, arguing vigorously among themselves." Metzger, *Textual Commentary*, 444, suggests that this addition "was probably made because of the abrupt transition from ver. 28 to ver. 30."

3. Loveday C. A. Alexander, *Acts in Its Ancient Literary Context* (London: T&T Clark, 2007), ch. 9. See also Troy M. Troftgruben, *A Conclusion Unhindered: A Study of the Ending of Acts within Its Literary Environment*, WUNT 280 (Tübingen: Mohr Siebeck, 2010).

4:16–30; Acts 28:20–28); the fulfillment of Jewish Scriptures, especially the prophecies of Isaiah, which dominate both the beginning and ending of Luke's two volumes (Luke 3:4–6; 4:18–19; Acts 28:25–27); and the emphasis on the *person* who proclaims the gospel and less on the *content* of the gospel proclamation (e.g., the person of John the Baptist in Luke 1:76–79; 3:1–22; the person of Paul in Acts 28:17–22).

If, as Alexander suggests, we read the ending of Acts as an epilogue and summary to Luke-Acts as a whole—as a closure rather than a climax—then we can view it as an appropriate end to Luke's overall task. As such, Luke has accomplished much in explaining the following: how the life, teaching, death, burial, resurrection, and ascension of Jesus connects with Jewish Scriptures and fulfills Israel's hope; how the gospel of Jesus came both to the heart of the Jewish world (Jerusalem) and the gentile world (Rome); and how Paul fulfilled his commission to be the Lord's "chosen instrument" to proclaim his name to the gentiles, their kings, and the people of Israel (Acts 9:15; cf. 19:21; 23:11). Additionally, despite the many attempts to thwart the advance of the gospel, the proclamation of the kingdom of God and the teaching about Jesus continues "with all boldness and without hindrance" (28:31).

With this backward glance to the prologue of Luke in mind, we turn to the final scene of Acts in Rome. The ending of Acts unfolds in three movements: first, Paul reaches out to the Jewish community in Rome (28:17–22); second, Paul testifies about Jesus to a mixed response (vv. 23–28); and, third, Luke provides a closing summary to his two-volume work (vv. 30–31).

Paul Reaches Out to the Jewish Community in Rome (28:17–22)

Even though Paul reaches Rome as the result of his "appeal to Caesar"—a goal that has been repeated throughout the narrative (Acts 19:21; 23:11; 25:10; 26:32; 27:24)—the focus of the final scene is not on the city or the emperor but on the Jewish community in Rome. Again, we are implicitly reminded that the gospel is prioritized first for the Jews and *then* for the gentiles. After taking three days to settle into his new environment, Paul calls together the Jewish leaders for a conversation (v. 17). Luke goes out of his way to stress that there are already "brothers and sisters" in Italy (*adelphoi*; 28:14, 15). As he begins, Paul underscores his own relationship with the community by addressing them with the familiar opening greeting, "my brothers" (*andres adelphoi*; v. 17). This greeting is used throughout Acts to refer to believers *and* to those in the non-Christian Jewish community (see 1:16; 2:29, 37; 6:3; 7:2; 13:15, 26, 38; 15:7, 13; 22:1; 23:1, 6).

After the opening greeting, Paul begins his last "defense" speech in Acts. The content of the short speech restates much of what Luke has already relayed through Paul's earlier defense speeches in the previous chapters (chs. 21–26). This speech focuses on the agency of Paul. In fact, in the Greek text of the speech, it does not open with the greeting "my brothers" but with the first-person pronoun "I" (*egō*). The spotlight remains on Paul as he recounts the reasons that brought him to Rome. In providing the reasons, however, he also makes several denials. First, despite accusations from fellow Jews he asserts, "*I* have done *nothing* against our people or against the customs of our ancestors" (28:17; cf. 21:21, 28; 25:8). Second, after being seized and handed over to Roman custody for interrogation and trial, he declares his innocence: "*I* was *not* guilty of any crime deserving death" (28:18; cf. 23:29; 25:18, 25; 26:32). Finally, even though he has charges brought against him, he notes that "*I* certainly did *not* intend to bring any charge against my own people" (28:19).

Paul does, however, offer a legal reason and a theological reason for his presence in Rome. First, he offers the legal reason: since "the Jews" would not let go of their accusations against him, he asserted his right as a Roman citizen to have his case heard by Caesar (28:19; cf. 25:11, 21, 25; 26:32). Yet there is a deeper explanation for why Paul will stand before Caesar: he will do so because of the "hope of Israel" that is fulfilled in the Messiah Jesus (28:20; cf. 26:6).[4] Paul asserts that he is a prisoner in Roman chains because he has been loyal to his people and their God. He has been a faithful Jew who has carried out his call first to proclaim to his fellow Jews, and then to the gentile world, that the hope of salvation is to be found in the resurrected King Jesus.

Paul's persuasive efforts receive a tepid reception from the Jewish leaders in Rome. On the one hand, they have not heard any news from the homeland about Paul one way or the other, so they are genuinely unprejudiced toward him. On the other hand, even though no reference has been made to the church or to other Christians, they have heard plenty of talk about "this sect" (28:22). The word "sect" does not necessarily carry any negative connotations to it; for example, it was a word that could be used by Jews to refer to a "school" within Judaism (e.g., the "sect" of the Sadducees or the Pharisees; see 5:17; 15:5; 26:5). They are willing to hear more from Paul, and so they arrange to meet again.

Paul Testifies to a Larger Group of Roman Jews (28:23–28)

The second meeting in Rome is longer, there is a larger crowd, and the conversation is more intense. From morning until evening, Paul "witnessed" (v. 23; *diamartyromai*) to his fellow Jews. Solemn testimony with the intent "to persuade" others about Jesus is an important theme in Acts (cf. Acts 2:40;

---

4. Barrett, *Acts*, 2:1240.

8:25; 10:42; 18:5; 20:21; 23:11). By invoking this theme, Luke signals that the discussion topics were significant. Specifically, they related to the kingdom of God and Jesus (28:23; cf. v. 31). These are the same two focal points that opened Acts (1:3, 6), so it is unsurprising that they reappear at the end. As has been the case throughout the narrative, some fellow Jews were convinced, but others refused to believe (28:24). As they leave Paul's quarters, they continue to disagree among themselves. It is important to note that Paul's closing pronouncement to end the meeting (vv. 25–28) does not signal uniform rejection by the Jews or anti-Semitism on the part of Paul (or Luke). As Dunn observes, "In this final scene there is no more talk of 'the Jews' acting as a single body in animosity or hostility towards Paul (contrast 13.50; 14.4; 17.5; 18.12; 22.30; 23.12). Quite the contrary: Luke notes that the visitors leave, still disagreeing, even after Paul has made his denunciation."[5] In this sense, the challenge from Isaiah and the turn toward the gentiles should be read in conjunction with similar declarations earlier in Acts (13:46; 18:6; 22:21). As in those instances, Paul continued to reach out to fellow Jews and to gentiles.

In his closing comment, Paul quotes a passage from Isaiah (Isa 6:9–10). This text was a significant prophetic touchstone appealed to by the early church to explain the Jewish reaction to the Messiah, Jesus. The passage from Isaiah is firmly rooted in the Gospel tradition, where it is used to explain Jewish unbelief and the mixed response to Jesus's teaching (see Matt 13:14–15; Mark 4:12; Luke 8:10; John 12:39–40). What is interesting is that "Luke, although he includes the citation in his Sower narrative (Lk 8.14–15) cuts it down to the briefest possible compass (unlike Matthew, who gives it in a longer form than Mark)."[6] What Luke appears to be doing is holding back on using this text in his Gospel—"keeping his powder dry," so to speak—so that he can deploy it more fully and in a more pronounced way to conclude his two-volume work.[7] This passage from Israel's own Scriptures provides Luke and his readers with an explanation for why the majority of Jews reject Jesus. Even though most of the early church and its key leaders were Jewish, the regrettable truth is that Israel, as a whole, rejected Jesus. It does not mean that Paul turns completely away from his own people. Paul wrestles with this precise issue at length in his letter to the Romans (Rom 9–11). It does, however, explain why he reached out to the gentiles to proclaim the kingdom of God to them (Acts 28:28, 31).

When Paul concludes with the interpretation, "Therefore I want you to know that God's salvation has been sent to the Gentiles," he is likely alluding to Psalm 67:2. A key word is the uncommon form of the word "salvation"

---

5. Dunn, *Acts*, 354.
6. Alexander, *Ancient Literary Context*, 216.
7. Ibid.

(*sōtērios*), a word that is used only three other times in the NT (Luke 2:30; 3:6; Eph 6:17) and likely forms part of the echo of the LXX translation of Psalm 67:2. In this psalm, the key thought that is expressed is "God's faithfulness to Israel as part of his universal saving concern for all nations."[8] This is the precise note sounded at the beginning of Luke when both Simeon (Luke 2:30) and John the Baptist declare that the coming of Jesus means salvation is open to all people: "A light for revelation to the Gentiles, and the glory of your people Israel" (2:32). The turn to the gentiles is part of God's larger story of salvation, not a rejection of Israel.

Concluding Summary (28:30–31)

On the heels of this broad scope of God's salvation, Luke draws the entire narrative to a close. Unlike the beginning (of either Luke or Acts), there is no dramatic scene or mighty miracle or angelic manifestation. The tone appears mundane and expresses a simple routine carried out by Paul for two years.[9] Acts opens on the mount of ascension and ends in a Roman apartment. Paul remains in Roman custody—likely staying in lodgings paid for by his "brothers and sisters" in Rome or elsewhere. For the curious, nothing is even hinted at about Paul's legal case. There are only two points that Luke wants to emphasize. First, Paul "welcomed *all* who came to see him" (28:30). In this sense, the ending of Acts is truly open ended. The door to Paul was open to everyone—whether they were Jewish or gentile. Despite the dire words from Isaiah, Paul continues his gospel commission to all and into an open future.

Second, Luke concludes with the content of Paul's message that he proclaimed and taught during his confinement: (1) the kingdom of God and (2) teaching about the Lord Jesus Christ. These are the same two themes that opened Acts (1:3, 6), and they are again highlighted as the narrative draws to a close. The kingdom of God is present when the lordship of King Jesus is proclaimed to Israel and the nations. Nothing can hinder this proclamation: not the calloused hearts of Jews or the idolatrous imaginations of gentiles; not reluctance by Peter or the persecution by Saul; not the martyrdom of Stephen or the beheading of James; not the angry judgment of the Sanhedrin or the imperial indifference of Felix or Festus; not the might of a Mediterranean

---

8. Dunn, *Acts*, 355.
9. Barret, *Acts*, 2:1251–52, notes the suggestion by Henry J. Cadbury, "Roman Law and the Trial of Paul," in *Additional Notes to the Commentary*, vol. 5 of *The Beginnings of Christianity*, ed. K. Lake and H. J. Cadbury (London: Macmillan, 1933), 319–38, that the mention of "two years" is significant because it may mark the length of time in which a prisoner had to be tried before the case would lapse and the prisoner released. Sherwin-White, *Roman Society*, 118–19, critical of this suggestion, nonetheless concludes that Paul may have been released by an act of clemency from Nero. See also Rapske, *Paul in Roman Custody*, 322–23.

storm or the bite of a Maltese snake. In the face of any potential hindrance, the Holy Spirit fires a boldness in unschooled and provincial Galilean fishermen (4:13, 29, 31) just as much as in a highly trained and cosmopolitan Pharisee (28:31). The story of God is loose, and nothing and no one will hinder its power—not even the death of a leading apostle, like Paul.

LIVE the Story

The People of God

It might strike some readers of Acts as odd that when Luke describes Paul finally reaching Rome, he doesn't focus on Paul's attending to fellow Christians or to the city of Rome but to his fellow Jews. The language of this final scene in Acts is "people oriented." This is apparent with references to "Jewish leaders" (v. 17), "brothers"[10] (vv. 17, 21), "people" (vv. 17, 26, 27), "my people/ the Gentiles"[11] (vv. 19, 28), "the Jews" (v. 19), and "Israel" (v. 20). While it is a temptation for the contemporary church to forget that the Christian story is intimately connected to the story of Israel, Paul (and Luke) certainly doesn't lose sight of this. When Paul explains to his fellow Jews about the kingdom of God and King Jesus, he wants them to see that this is rooted in "the Law of Moses and . . . the Prophets" (v. 23). The story of the people of God includes the story of Israel, and despite the fact that many Christians are ignorant about the "Old Testament" or simply ignore it, the end of Acts should come as a bracing reminder against forgetting this integral part of the gospel.

To confront his fellow Jews with "the hope of Israel" that they are in danger of missing out on, Paul draws on dire words from the prophet Isaiah (Isa 6:9–10). It is impossible to know the tone of Paul's voice as he speaks these words. We all know how important tone is when we speak. Did Paul speak these words with an angry tone? An exasperated tone? A sarcastic tone? My guess is that Paul's tone is one of grief, the same one he expresses in his letter to the Romans: "I have great sorrow and unceasing anguish in my heart. For I could wish that I myself were cursed and cut off from Christ for the sake of my people, those of my own race, the people of Israel" (Rom 9:2–4a). Make no mistake, it was—and continues to be—a stumbling block for many Jews to come to recognize Jesus, a carpenter from lowly Galilee, as the long-awaited Messiah King. Yet we must not look down or despise those in the first century

---

10. In v. 21 the word translated "people" is the same word translated as "brothers" in v. 17 (i.e., *adelphoi*).

11. In v. 19 the word translated "people" is the same word translated as "Gentiles" in v. 28 (i.e., *ethnos*).

or twenty-first century who struggle with this. Massive reorientations toward Jesus can take time to sort out. Even Jesus's own disciples who lived and listened to him for more than three years struggled to see who he was and what his kingdom message was about. It took Paul years in Arabia (Gal 1:17–18) and a lengthy stay back in his home city of Tarsus (Acts 9:30) to process this. Yet in this struggle to comprehend, the point is that God wants his ancient people, Israel, to turn to him and to know their story afresh. This is a story that is embedded in the larger framework of the story of God that begins in Genesis and runs its way through the story of Israel—a story that includes times of hard-heartedness, disobedience, and exile—and climaxes in Jesus.

Jesus cited the same words Paul does from Isaiah to describe why he spoke to his people in parables. He did so in the context of a famous story about seed and soil (Luke 8:4–15; cf. Mark 4:1–20; Matt 13:1–23). As Jesus revealed himself as king to his people to a mixed response and as Paul explained to his fellow Jews about the kingdom of God and King Jesus to a mixed response, the question about whether people will hear and see comes down to a matter of "soil." That is, what is the condition of the soil of one's life? Do we really hear the message of the kingdom and see King Jesus as the climax of a longer and larger story of the people of God? Or are we too focused on our own personal "salvation" that we miss the bigger narrative and the corporate dimension of the kingdom? Could the words of Isaiah just as easily be spoken today about Christian congregations and parishes? As we listen to the end of Acts and Paul's heart for his people and for the nations, we would do well to attend to the soil of our hearts. Susan Phillips comments about becoming "significant soil" in her book *The Cultivated Life*. She writes:

> Cultivation imagery emphasizes rootedness and fruit bearing. Fruit is visible and edible; it brings joy. As the flow of grace cultivates fruit, the walking trees that we are experience God's exaltation and come to the feast. The upward thrust into visible fruit is a joyful manifestation of the gift we receive. We see this in the lives of people who are sustained by God's grace as they work to help the people of the world; skillfully and lovingly care for others; creatively and diligently apply their resources and energies for the world's benefit; and pray when in the desert or the belly of a whale. But fruit bearing is not the only way in which the flow of grace manifests through human life.
>
> T. S. Eliot's "The Dry Salvages," the second of the *Four Quartets*, ends with the hope that after all our striving in this life—including prayer, observance, discipline, thought and action—we might find contentment in the "life of significant soil." The garden image of soil allows a different

sightline on cultivation than does fruit, enabling us to contemplate ways that grace flows through a life to become part of what invisibly sustains life.[12]

As we hear and read the words of Acts, may this "seed" land in "significant soil." May it be soil that is part of a much larger field—a field that is the people of God. This people includes both Jews and gentiles. It is a people that is part of a large story, one that is centuries deep and continents wide.

The Kingdom and the King

As we come to the end of Acts, I think it is important to recognize that we come to the end of a two-volume narrative. The Gospel of Luke begins with the birth of a king who will reign over a never-ending kingdom (Luke 1:33). The Gospel ends with Jesus teaching the disciples about his kingship before ascending to heaven to reign with his Father (22:44–49, 51). Acts begins with the risen Jesus teaching about his kingdom (Acts 1:3, 6) before ascending to heaven (1:9) to reign at God's right hand as "both Lord and Messiah" (2:36). Acts ends with Paul proclaiming the kingdom and teaching about the Lord Jesus Christ, the King (28:31). The kingdom and the King are the central pieces of Luke-Acts, and our author is at pains to ensure that we don't miss them. Acts is *not* primarily about the history of the early church or a biographical record about the apostles, even important ones like Peter and Paul. If we turn to Acts only to learn about the deeds of the early church, or to learn about the lives of the apostles, or to figure out how we should evangelize non-Christians, or how to organize the church, we will be disappointed. In particular, we will be disappointed with the way the narrative ends because we won't learn about what happens to Paul. Yes, these are all important matters, and we can learn much about how to "live the story" as we read Acts, but this is not the big story that Luke wants to impress upon us. Acts is not primarily concerned with the actions and lives of the apostles; Acts is primarily concerned with the kingdom of God and the reign of King Jesus.

Unfortunately, the Western world that many of us live in is obsessed with the lives of the rich, powerful, and famous. Our culture seems to have an endless appetite for "news" about celebrity lives and activities. Fed by this kind of spotlight and news cycle, it is easy to understand why many readers may be a bit disappointed with the ending of Acts. The narrative, particularly the account of Paul's travels and trials, is absorbing. As those nourished by social media, we want an update on Paul's status! We yearn for postings and pictures,

---

12. Susan S. Phillips, *The Cultivated Life: From Ceaseless Striving to Receiving Joy* (Downers Grove, IL: InterVarsity Press, 2015), 203.

not preaching and teaching. Those who worship the cult of personality want to know about the individual Paul. This, I think, is a by-product of contemporary church life that is focused on meeting *individual* needs and offering *personal* salvation. These are not wrong emphases, but if they are disconnected from the larger framework of the kingdom of God and King Jesus, then we miss what Luke is trying to do.

The story that Luke is interested in telling is a kingdom story, the story of God. It is a story that is embedded in the long biblical narrative and climaxes in the life, death, burial, resurrection, and ascension of Jesus. That is *the* story he wants to tell and have us follow. This leaves us with several key questions as we come to the end of Acts. Do we have ears to hear *this* story? Do we have eyes to see *this* King? Or does the noise that sounds from the cult of personality deafen us? Do the bright lights of celebrity blind us? My prayer and hope is that we will see King Jesus and begin to live as fellow citizens—the people of God—under the reign of God's kingdom on earth as it is in heaven. May we have ears to hear and eyes to see this grand story of God and to live our own part in it as we worship and serve our King.

Scripture Index

Genesis
1:1 . . . . .325, 327, 409
2:7 409
3. 133
3:24 292
6–8. 577
9:4 349
11:1–9 66
11:9 63
11:4 74
12–48. 178
12:1 . . . . .175, 179
12:2 267
12:3 . . . . .30, 104
15:13 175
15:13–25 179
15:14 175
15:17 73
16:7 292
17:9–14 . . . . .342, 343
21–36. 180
21:17 292
22:1–2 225
22:11 292
22:18 .30, 101, 107
24:7 292
26:4 101
26:24 424
27:46 56
28:12 292
28:15 424
32:1 292
34. . . . . .365, 366
37. 180
41. 255
46:2 223
46:2–3 225
48:21 424

Exodus
1–3. 178
1:8 . . . . .176, 180
2:14 . . . . .176, 181
3. 182
3:2 . . . . .64, 182, 292
3:4 223
3:5 . . . . .176, 182
3:6 .104, 176, 182, 223
3:7 176
3:8 . . . . .176, 285, 288, 289
3:10 176
3:12 111
3:13–15 117
3:13–4:17. 182
3:15 . . . . .104, 500, 505
4:24–26 343
5:10 178
7:1 325
7:3 . . . . .138, 139
7:4 303
7:4–17 298
7:5 303
7:17 303
9:3 . . . . .274, 277, 298, 303
9:27 102
11:10 . . . . .138, 139
13:21–22 . . . . .64, 73
14. 577
14:19 292
15:4 178
15:13–16 111
15:20 479
16:7–9, 12 156
17:2 . . . . .134, 344
17:5 343
17:7 134
18:4 . . . . .285, 288, 289
18:13–27 . . . . .155, 158
19:18 64
20:3 . . . . .340, 350
20:5 . . . . .62, 71
20:16 . . . . .169, 171

609

22:22–27 156
22:28 . . . . 514, 515, 517
24:1–18 136
25:16 . . . . 178, 184
28:29–43 137
29:38–41 . . . . 84, 95
32:1 . . . . 177, 178, 183
32:3 178
33:3, 5 185
33:18–23 . . . . 190, 191
34:7 . . . . 62, 71
34:9 185
34:15–16 . . . . 365, 366
34:22 63
34:29–35 173
38:21 184

Leviticus
2:2, 9, 16 253
3:17 349
6:15 253
7:26 349
11 . . . . 254, 256
11:24, 39 . . . . 239, 244
12:3 . . . . 342, 343
16:7–10 55
16:29–31 580
17–18 . . . . 340, 350, 355, 356
17:7 327
17:10–13 349
18:6–30 348
18:21 183
19:15 . . . . 515, 517
19:26 349
20:2 . . . . 320, 321
20:2–5 183
21:16–18 96
21:20 . . . . 211, 212
23:15–21 . . . . 62, 63
24:14 . . . . 190, 193, 320, 321
24:16 190
25 . . . . 126, 127
26:41 185

Numbers
5:26 253
6:1–21 . . . . 426, 428, 486
6:14–15 489
11:12–15 56

11:16–30 . . . . 155, 158
11:29 68
14:22 134
15:35–36 . . . . 190, 193
17:5, 10 156
17:20, 25 LXX 156
22:22–35 292
25 . . . . 365, 366
25:1–5 221
25:7–11 221
26:55 55
27:16–23 . . . . 155, 158
28:4 95
28:26–31 63

Deuteronomy
2:5 179
4:34 . . . . 138, 139
6:4 118
6:16 . . . . 134, 344
7:1–4 . . . . 365, 366
9:6 185
9:10 134
9:13 185
10:9 129
10:16 185
10:17 249
10:17–18 . . . . 156, 259
11:14 . . . . 325, 327
12:12 129
12:16, 23 349
13:6–11 . . . . 320, 321
14 254
14:2 346
14:27–29 129
15:1–11 163
15:4 . . . . 126, 127
15:7–11 96
16:9–12 63
17:2–5 . . . . 320, 321
17:7 . . . . 190, 193
18:1 129
18:9–14 202
18:15 . . . . . . 30, 100, 101, 177, 178, 183, 186
18:15–20 103
18:16 134
18:18 . . . . 30, 100, 101
18:19 . . . . 100, 101
21:18–21 . . . . 320, 321

21:22–23	144, 148
21:23	219, 220, 224
23:1	211, 212
23:1–2	134
23:2–3 LXX	134
24:14–22	96
24:17–22	156
26:8	138, 139
27:9	111
27:11	111
27:12	111
27:15–26	111
28:9	111
29:18	206
29:27	360
29:28	361
30:3	38
31:27	185
31:30	134
32:5	71
33:3, 5, 7	111
33:8	134
33:29	111
34:11	138, 139

Joshua

1:9	420
3:7	424
3:11, 13	259
4:24	274, 277
5:2–9	343
6:4	159
7	133
7:1	131, 132, 133
7:19–26	133
8:35	134
9:2 LXX	134
20:4	469
21	126
21:1–41	129
24:2–15	185

Judges

2:19	185
4:4	479
6:11–23	292
9:54	56
16:25–31	56
20:2	134

Ruth

4:2	343, 469

1 Samuel

2:2	102
3:10	223
3:10–14	225
10:20–21	55
12:3	468
12:21	325
24:6	232
31:1–5	56

2 Samuel

1:14	232
6	135
6:1–7	137
6:3, 6–7	131, 135
8:17	111
17:23	51, 54, 56
18:33	56
21:1	409

1 Kings

1:34	111
8:1–11	137
8:14	134
8:16	184
8:17	184
8:18	184
8:19	184
8:20	184
8:27	184, 409
8:27–30	178
8:29	184
8:33	184
8:35	184
8:41	184
8:41–43	211, 212
8:42	184
8:43	184
8:44	184
8:48	184
11:5, 7, 33	183
11:29–39	480
16:18	56
17:19–20	239, 243
17:21	459, 462
17:23	239, 243

18:12	211, 214
18:40	221
18:46	211
19:3–4	56
19:10	185, 221
19:11–12	64
19:14	221, 424
19:18	424
21:13	190, 193
22:1–38	302
22:11	477, 480

2 Kings

1:15	211
2:16	214
3:15	277
4:33	243
4:33–36	239
4:34	462
4:35	243
4:36	243
17:14	185
17:15	327
17:21–24	198
17:24–41	200
19:22	102

1 Chronicles

13:4	134
13:7, 9–10	131, 135
17:2	424

2 Chronicles

5:2–14	137
7:14	409
11:15	327
30:8	185
36:13	185
36:16	185

Ezra

7:6	274, 277
9:5	258
9:15	102
10:12	134

Nehemiah

1:4	298, 299
2:16	112

5:7	112
9–10	365, 366
9:6	118, 120, 121
9:6–37	185
9:16, 17	185
9:26	185
9:29	185

Esther

1:1	212
1:14	159
3:8	382, 385
8:9	212
8:11–12, 17	343

Job

3:1–26	56
5:10	325, 327
6:10	102
38:1	73
41:11	118

Psalms

1:1	533
1:1 LXX	535
2	112, 121, 122
2:1	118
2:2	118, 232
2:7	308, 309, 313
2:8	268
2:9	122
4:7	325, 327
9:11	268
11:7	102
13:2–4	56
15:1–2	249, 259
16	69
16:8	68
16:8–11	61, 62, 67, 68
16:10	102, 308, 309, 311, 313
16:11	213
21:23 LXX	134
22	92, 545, 554, 555
22:1	88, 555
22:3	102
22:7	555
22:12	555
22:15–18	555
22:22	134

22:24	555
22:27	268
22:27–28	555
22:30–31	555
24:6	409
31:5	190, 193
35:16	190, 191
37:12	190, 191
40:6–8	477
41:10	51
50:5	477
50:8–13	405, 409
51:10	344
55:17	258
57:9	268
65:10	327
67:2	600, 603, 604
68:5	156
68:31	211, 212
69	54
69:21	54
69:25	50, 54
71:22	102
78:8	71, 185
78:41	344
78:43	138, 139
78:52, 70	470
95:8–10	134
97:5	259
103:20	292
104:4	64
104:32	123
105	185
105:1	268
106	185
107:20	249, 259
109	54
109:8	50, 54
110	192
110:1	62, 67, 69, 190, 192
116:5	102
118	113
118:15–20	113
118:21	113
118:22	109, 110, 113
118:25	113
118:26	391, 394
119:55, 62	382, 387
119:137	102
120–134	428
129:4	102
135:4	346
145:6 (LXX)	120
145:17	102
146	120
146:6	120, 121, 325
146:9	156
148:2	292

Proverbs

5:14	134
14:5	169, 171
14:31	252
16:3	59
16:9	59
16:23	58
16:33	51, 55, 58
19:17	252
29:1	185

Isaiah

1:4	102
1:17	127, 156
2:1–4	258
2:2	267, 268
6	225, 505
6:1–7	292
6:1–13	500
6:3	102
6:9–10	446, 505, 599, 600, 603, 605
8:28	250
11:10	267, 268
14:1	498
20:2–4	477, 480
32:15	35, 37
35:5–6	94, 97, 98
35:6	103
37:16	118, 120, 121
40:3	222
40:3–5	426, 429
40:11	470
41:10	420
42:5	405, 409
42:6–7, 16	558, 565
43:5	420, 424
43:6–7	68
44:3	62, 71
44:3–5	35, 37

44:9 .... 327, 330
44:9–20 330
45. 228
45:21 .... 340, 347
45:23 228
46:12 185
47:9, 12 202
48:4 185
49:6 .... 29, 30, 39, 267, 268, 309,
314, 558, 567
49:8 38
49:22 68
52:7 .... 249, 259
52:13 104
53. 213
53:7 213
53:7–8 .... 210, 213
53:11 .... 102, 504
55:3 .... 308, 313
56:3–5 .... 213, 217
56:3–7 211
56:3–8 .... 62, 71
57:3 202
57:9 183
57:15 102
57:19 .... 62, 71
58:6–10 .... 96, 126, 127
60:3 .... 267, 268
60:4 68
61:1 .... 249, 259, 260
61:1–3 47
63:10 185
65:1 498
65:23 .... 62, 71
66:1–2 .... 178, 184, 405, 409
66:15 64

Jeremiah

1:8 .... 420, 424, 558, 564
1:19 420
3:1–10 348
4:4 185
6:10 185
7:6 96
7:26 185
10:3 327
10:16 .... 405, 409
12:1 102
12:15 .... 340, 346

13:1–11 .... 477, 480
15:10 56
17:23 185
19:15 185
20:2 .... 382, 386
20:9 73
20:14–18 56
23:5–6 504
26:2 .... 468, 469
27:9 202
28:1–17 307
29:20 382
30:18 38
32:6–9 54
32:20 .... 138, 139
32:35 183
33:15 504
39:37 .... 360, 361
42:4 .... 468, 469
49:1, 3 183
52:25 159

Lamentations

1:18 102

Ezekiel

1:1 253
1:1–24 292
1:28 223
2:1–3 .... 558, 564
2:4 185
3:14 214
3:17–19 .... 468, 470
4:14 .... 249, 254
5:5 66
8:2 173
8:10 327
11:19–20 .... 35, 37
13:10–15 .... 515, 517
13:18 202
16:15–46 348
22:27 .... 468, 471
28:1–10 .... 285, 291
29:10 212
36:23 .... 267, 268
36:25–27 .... 35, 37
44:6–7 497
44:6–8 .... 493, 495

Daniel
2:31–45 255
2:46 327
3. 147
3:16–18 . . . . 110, 115
3:16–28 144
4:1–27 255
5:1–28 255
6. 147
6:1–28 144
6:10 . . . . 84, 258
7:13 40
7:13–14 . . . . 190, 192
8:17 223
9:7 102
9:21 . . . . 95, 258
9:25 118
10:5–6 173

Hosea
4:16 185
5:3–4 348
11:9 102

Joel
2:16 134
2:28 . . . . 267, 268
2:28–32 . . . . 30, 61, 62, 63, 67

Amos
2:4 327
5:25–27 . . . . 177, 178, 183 (LXX)
9:11 347
9:11, 12 LXX 340
9:12 347
9:11–12 . . . . 340, 346

Jonah
1. 577
1:1–17 576
1:3 242
1:7–8 55
1:7–10 . . . . 590, 592
1:12 56
2. 91
4:3 56

Micah
4:13 259

5:4 470
6:8–12 127

Nahum
2:11–13 148

Habakkuk
1:5 . . . . 308, 309, 313
1:12 102

Zephaniah
1:5 183
3:3 . . . . 468, 471
3:5 102
3:10 . . . . 211, 212

Zechariah
4:14 259
6:5 259
11:12–13 54

Malachi
1:11 . . . . 267, 268

Matthew
1:20 292
3:3 222
3:16 . . . . 28, 253
4:17 46
5:12 185
5:48 18
6:10 443
6:12 42
7:15 471
8:11–12 47
9:11 345
9:35 46
9:18–19 . . . . 239, 243
9:23–26 . . . . 239, 243
10:7 46
10:8 472
10:14 315
10:34 318
11:28 345
11:28–30 521
11:29–30 . . . . 340, 345
12:6 84
13:1–23 606
13:14–15 603

16:13–20	295
20:19	477
22:16	279
22:32	104
23:4	345
23:15	159
23:27	515, 517
25:37	245
25:40	245, 252
26:59–66	169, 170
26:69	383
27:3–4	57
27:3–10	53
27:19	104, 547
27:24–25	420
27:32	276
27:38	538
27:46	88
28:2, 7	293
28:17	44
28:19	28
28:20	418, 424

Mark

1:3	222
1:4	571
1:13	293
1:14–15	46
1:15	571
1:24	104
2:6–7	95
3:6	95, 279
3:9	82
3:20–21	52
3:31–35	52, 345
4:1–20	606
4:12	603
5:7	382, 384
5:21–24, 35–42	239, 243
5:39	459
6:3	345
6:12	571
6:45–52	576, 577
7:1–5	345
8:31	42
9:41	252
10:31	47
12:13	279
12:26	104

12:36	69
14:51–52	363
14:53–65	516
14:58	172
15:21	276
15:27	538
15:29–30	172
15:34	554

Luke

1–2	36, 140
1–4	600
1:1	21
1:1–4	22, 25, 27, 37
1:3	22, 26
1:4	27, 283, 488
1:5	25
1:8–9	55
1:10	52
1:11	146, 292
1:14	278
1:17	565
1:26–38	292
1:28	418, 424
1:32	391
1:32–33	347, 394
1:33	607
1:35	232
1:35–38	21
1:46–55	312
1:53	283
1:54–55	21
1:66	277
1:68–69	312
1:69	583
1:70	21
1:71	583
1:72–73	136
1:76–79	601
1:77	313, 565, 583
2	62
2:1	600
2:1–2	25
2:9	146
2:9–15	293
2:10	201, 214, 278
2:11	391
2:15–20	393
2:20	270, 388

Reference	Page(s)
2:25–38	393
2:28	388
2:29	300
2:29–32	21, 312, 600
2:30	565, 604
2:30–32	314
2:30–34	309
2:32	58, 565, 604
2:34	315
2:34–35	58
2:36	479
2:36–38	156
2:37	298, 299
2:38	21
2:49	519
2:52	87
3:1	550
3:1–2	600
3:1–22	601
3:2–6	426, 429
3:2–7	313
3:3	313, 565, 571
3:3–18	70
3:4	222
3:4–6	601
3:6	604
3:7–14	70
3:16	37
3:21	52, 253
3:22	36
4:1	36, 113, 374
4:1–13	133, 565
4:3	232
4:4	88
4:8	88
4:8–12	113
4:9	232
4:12	88
4:14	36, 374
4:16–19	37
4:16–21	47
4:16–30	601
4:17–21	88
4:18	36, 283, 374, 565
4:18–19	601
4:20	173
4:22	366
4:24–26	156
4:33–37	443
4:38–40	590, 593
4:41	232
4:43	37, 519
5:16	52
5:17–26	94, 95, 97
5:21	95
5:25	270
5:29–39	86
5:32	571
5:33	345
6:1–2	345
6:1–5	86
6:12	52
6:13	55, 355
6:14–16	51
6:18	201, 443
6:27–28	193
6:28	52
6:38	472
7:1–10	257, 579
7:3	343, 469
7:5	257
7:12	156
7:15	270
7:21	443
7:22	283
7:22–23	114
7:27	426, 429
7:36–50	86
8:1	54
8:1–3	52
8:2	443
8:3	128
8:4–15	606
8:10	603
8:10–14	600
8:14–15	603
8:19–21	52
8:22–25	576, 577
8:26–39	443
8:28	382, 384
8:43–48	138, 140
8:44	437
9:1	54
9:1–2	46
9:2	37
9:12	54
9:12–17	86
9:18	52

ACTS

9:22 . . . . 438, 469, 519
9:23 148
9:28–29 52
9:35 355
9:37–43 443
9:49–50 443
9:51 . . . . 63, 519
9:51–19:27 201
9:53–55 207
10:9 46
10:11 315
10:18 133
10:19 . . . . 590, 592
10:25–37 201
10:26–28 88
10:29 201
10:30–37 96
10:37 201
10:38–40 86
11:1–2 52
11:2–4 37
11:9–13 472
11:14 443
11:14–23 112
11:18 133
11:20 47
11:32 565
11:35 565
11:37–52 86
11:41 . . . . 239, 242
11:46 345
11:48 194
12:8 192
12:11–12 . . . . 113, 546
12:33 . . . . 239, 242
12:33–34 96
12:51 318
13:3 565
13:5 565
13:13 . . . . 270, 388
13:16 133
13:18–19 47
13:20–21 47
13:32 443
14:1–14 86
14:8–24 47
14:12–14 96
14:27 148
15:1–2 86
15:6 388
15:7 . . . . 202, 214, 388, 565
15:9 388
15:10 . . . . 202, 214, 388
15:21 202
15:32 214
16:19–31 . . . . 96, 283
16:29 . . . . 400, 401
17:11–19 201
17:15 270
17:20–21 37
17:22–31 105
17:24–26 40
17:25 519
18:1 52
18:1–8 156
18:10–11 52
18:31 54
18:32 . . . . 477, 480
18:43 270
19:1–10 86
19:9 583
19:38 . . . . 391, 394
19:46 52
19:47 438
20:1 438
20:2 112
20:17–19 . . . . 110, 112
20:19 438
20:37 104
20:47 52
21:2–3 156
21:5 169
21:12–13 . . . . 533, 534
21:12–19 . . . . 334, 335
21:15 . . . . 169, 170
21:27 40
22:1 . . . . 285, 287, 462
22:3 . . . . 54, 133, 565
22:7 . . . . 285, 287
22:7–20 471
22:16 37
22:17–20 86
22:18 37
22:19 . . . . 81, 84, 466, 583
22:26–27 . . . . 155, 158
22:29–30 37
22:30 54
22:31 133

22:37	519
22:40–41, 44, 46	52
22:42	477, 480
22:44	480
22:47	54
22:56	285
22:56–57	67
22:57	289
22:66	170
22:69	192
22:70	232
23:1	149
23:1–2	538
23:1–22	548
23:1–25	119
23:2	395, 493, 495
23:18	493, 496
23:24	193
23:26	148, 276, 299
23:33	538
23:36	54
23:38	395
23:46	193
23:47	579
23:49	52
23:50–53	149, 195
23:55–56	52
24:1–10	52
24:7	519
24:10	140
24:11	44, 285, 289
24:13–32	86
24:16	565
24:22	52
24:25–27	558, 567
24:26	391, 393, 519
24:26–27	213
24:27	70, 82, 87, 88
24:29	21, 312
24:30	583
24:30–31	81, 84
24:31	565
24:36–43	86
24:36–49	37
24:44	107, 376, 519
24:45	380
24:46	391, 393
24:47–49	27
24:48	565
24:49	37, 39, 63, 71, 312
24:50	51
24:50–52	48
24:50–53	39
24:52	202, 278
24:52–53	214, 270, 388

John

1:23	222
1:29	471
1:51	253
2:17	54
2:19	172, 488
2:19–22	84
4.	379
4:5–42	201
4:21–24	84
6:51	587
6:69	104
7:1–10	345
7:51	515, 517
8:48	208
10:11–16	471
11:51–53	95
12:21	199
12:39–40	603
13:23	416
13:34	472
14:16	423
14:26	28, 123, 423
14:26–27	351
15:11	154
15:12	208
16:20, 21, 22, 24	154
18:28	258
19:13	547
19:15	509, 510
20:19	462
20:21	263
20:26	462
21:15–19	364

Acts

1.	48, 54
1–2.	36
1–4.	130
1–12.	24
1:1	21, 27, 28, 37, 43, 95, 113
1:1–2	97

620 ACTS

1:1–5 . . . . .25, 33, 36, 360
1:1–11 . . . . .28, 35, 58
1:1–5:42. 24
1:1–6:7. . . . . .25, 33, 81
1:1b–3 41
1:2 . . . . .28, 36, 37, 39, 41, 55, 158, 355, 449
1:3 . . . . . . 28, 37, 38, 41, 43, 44, 45, 46, 335,
   470, 600, 603, 604, 607
1:3–4 37
1:3a 37
1:3b 37
1:4 . . . . .21, 28, 30, 37, 51, 63, 260, 312, 470
1:4–5 . . . . .37, 39
1:4–8 . . . . .52, 518
1:5 . . . . .28, 36, 37, 65, 71, 270
1:6 . . . . 37, 54, 335, 347, 548, 600,
   603, 604, 607
1:6–8 . . . . .36, 38, 58, 141, 470
1:6–11 . . . . .33, 67
1:7 . . . . .28, 39, 40, 105, 205, 361
1:7–8 38
1:8 . . . . 24, 27, 29, 36, 39, 120, 140, 158,
   198, 212, 226, 237, 262, 275, 314,
   340, 361, 367, 445, 510, 565
1:9 . . . . .38, 39, 40, 607
1:9–11 .36, 39, 41, 48
1:10 . . . . .40, 302
1:10–11 293
1:11 40
1:12 51
1:12–14 . . . . .51, 361
1:12–26 50–51
1:13 51
1:14 . . . . .52, 192, 345
1:14–15 441
1:15 . . . . .64, 66
1:15–22 . . . . .51, 52
1:15–26 361
1:16 . . . .28, 53, 119, 122, 158, 449, 519, 601
1:16–17 360
1:17 . . . . .53, 206
1:18–19 53
1:18–20 54
1:20 54
1:21 . . . . .53, 449, 548, 582
1:21–22 . . . . .54, 58, 321, 360, 361
1:22 . . . . .158, 435, 470, 505, 565
1:23–26 . . . . .51, 55
1:24 355

1:24–25 . . . . .52, 119, 287
1:26 . . . . .53, 343
2. . . . . 39, 62, 64, 72, 73, 81, 89, 98, 125,
   187, 235, 295, 317, 440, 441
2:1 . . . . .63, 64, 65, 160, 464
2:1–4 . . . . .63, 361
2:1–11 58
2:1–13 72
2:1–41 .60–62, 71, 255
2:2 . . . . .48, 64, 254
2:2–3 73
2:3 64
2:3–4 182
2:4 . . .29, 64, 65, 77, 119, 123, 261, 435, 567
2:5 . . . . .64, 65, 89
2:5–6 63
2:5–12 275
2:5–13 . . . . .63, 65
2:6 66
2:7 158
2:8–11 . . . . .29, 66
2:9–11 83
2:10 . . . . .276, 299
2:11 .74, 159, 251, 261
2:12 . . . . .66, 251
2:13 66
2:14 .64, 65, 101, 567
2:14–21 . . . . .67, 69
2:14–36 . . . . .63, 66, 82, 102. 259
2:14–39 311
2:15 101
2:16–21 30
2:17 . . . . .52, 67, 71, 95, 105, 464, 479
2:17–18 29
2:18 . . . . .67, 140
2:19 . . . . .85, 139
2:20 105
2:21 . . . . .68, 86, 326, 387
2:22 . . . . 28, 68, 67, 69, 85, 86, 101, 139,
   170, 182, 321, 345
2:22–24 . . . . .68, 391, 409
2:22–28 68
2:22–36 393
2:23 . . . . 67, 68, 69, 119, 122, 147, 420,
2:23–24 . . . . .113, 567
2:24 . . . . .28, 67, 69
2:25 119
2:27 311
2:28 213

Scripture Index

2:29 . . . . 101, 119, 502, 601
2:29–36 68
2:30 . . . . 67, 71, 312
2:31 29
2:32 . . . . 28, 67, 69, 158, 505, 565
2:32–33 28
2:32–41 88
2:33 . . . . 21, 28, 48, 63, 67, 69, 71, 254, 312, 470
2:33–35 192
2:36 . . . . 28, 29, 67, 68, 69, 74, 117, 260, 262, 314, 420, 607
2:36–37 . . . . 87, 187
2:37 . . . . 158, 387, 397, 567, 601
2:37–41 . . . . 63, 70
2:38 . . . . 70, 102, 384, 387, 565, 566, 571
2:38–39 . . . . 70, 470
2:39 . . . . 21, 63, 71, 120, 312, 548
2:40 . . . . 71, 326, 602
2:41 . . . . 126, 204
2:42 . . . . 52, 82, 83, 85, 86, 87, 89, 91, 105, 127, 165, 287, 326
2:42–47 . . . . 79, 81, 87, 89, 126, 127, 138, 268, 368, 398
2:42a 82
2:42b 83
2:42c 83
2:42d 84
2:43 . . . . 84, 85, 86, 126, 127, 132, 134, 139, 159, 170, 182, 321, 345
2:43–47 . . . . 82, 84
2:44 . . . . 83, 84, 89, 127, 155, 158
2:44–45 127
2:44–47 . . . . 84, 85
2:45 . . . . 86, 92, 98, 163
2:46 . . . . . 52, 81, 83, 84, 85, 86, 89, 192, 397
2:46–47 . . . . 29, 97
2:47 . . . . 86, 126, 127, 138, 171, 326, 388
3 . . . . 97, 98, 108, 119
3–4 95
3–5 81
3–6 81
3:1 . . . . 33, 52, 84, 94, 161, 203
3:1–5 95
3:1–10 . . . . 85, 94, 101, 126, 140
3:1–26 111
3:2 95
3:3 . . . . 96, 203
3:4 . . . . 96, 172, 203, 302, 326

3:6 . . . 96, 97, 98, 99, 112, 119, 326, 241, 384
3:6–10 . . . . 95, 96, 382
3:8 . . . . 29, 96, 214, 388
3:9 96
3:10 . . . . 126, 326
3:11 . . . . 95, 96, 101, 138, 139, 203
3:11–16 101
3:11–26 . . . . 100–101, 105, 560
3:12 . . . . 96, 99, 101, 102, 112
3:12–16 . . . . 101, 102, 259
3:12–26 . . . . 82, 126, 182, 311
3:13 . . . . 104, 105
3:13–14 . . . . 103, 185
3:13–15 . . . . 104, 113, 147
3:13a 102
3:13b 102
3:14 . . . . 102, 420, 501
3:15 . . . . 28, 148, 153, 158, 420, 505, 565
3:15a 102
3:15b 102
3:16 . . . . 96, 101, 102, 112, 119, 241
3:17 . . . . 101, 103
3:17–19 103
3:17–26 . . . . 101, 103
3:18 . . . . 29, 105, 119, 122, 393
3:18–20 106
3:19 . . 101, 103, 112, 123, 241, 565, 566, 571
3:19–21 103
3:20 . . . . 28, 29, 105
3:21 . . . . 48, 105, 107, 111, 254, 312, 449, 519, 582
3:22 104
3:22–23 183
3:22–26 103
3:23 . . . . 110, 112
3:24 . . . . 103, 105
3:25 . . . . 29, 30, 104, 107, 275
3:25–26 120
3:25–15 120
3:26 . . . . 28, 104, 108
4 . . . . 111, 119, 124, 125, 167, 132
4:1 . . . . 111, 150, 203, 567
4:1–2 382
4:1–3 326
4:1–4 . . . . 110, 111
4:1–22 . . . . 29, 109–10, 126, 516
4:1–23 . . . . 272, 524
4:1–31 145
4:2 . . . . 82, 95, 110

4:3 . . . . 203, 382
4:4 126
4:5 . . . . 112, 336, 343, 469
4:5–6 119
4:5–7 . . . . 111, 112
4:5–22 145
4:7 . . . . 111, 119, 121, 203
4:8 . . . . 113, 119, 121, 123, 336
4:8–12 . . . . 111, 112
4:9 . . . . 111, 113
4:9–10 113
4:10 . . . . 28, 96, 113, 119, 241
4:11–12 113
4:12 . . . . 48, 96, 113, 117, 119, 254,
326, 387, 449, 519, 582, 583
4:13 . . 114, 117, 119, 126, 203, 234, 430, 605
4:13–17 114
4:13–22 . . . . 111, 114
4:14 . . . . 111, 114
4:15 112
4:16 114
4:17 . . . . 114, 119
4:17–18 147
4:18 . . . . 119, 145
4:18–22 114
4:19 . . . . 114, 135, 147, 203
4:20 115
4:21 . . . . 29, 115, 126, 147, 171, 270
4:21–22 111
4:22 95
4:23 . . . . 119, 120, 203, 336, 438, 523
4:23–31 . . . . 111, 118, 119, 126
4:24 . . . . 52, 120, 121, 192
4:24–25 28
4:24–26 119
4:24–30 . . . . 52, 120, 287
4:25 . . . . 28, 119, 121
4:26 112
4:27 . . . . 121, 122
4:27–28 . . . . 119, 121
4:27–29 119
4:28 119
4:29 . . . . 119, 122, 125, 129, 234, 605
4:29–30 . . . . 120, 122, 140, 151, 321
4:30 . . . . 96, 119, 182, 384
4:31 . . . . 74, 84, 119, 120, 121, 122,
123, 129, 234, 605
4:32 . . . . 127, 129, 155, 158, 397
4:32–35 . . . . 81, 98, 127, 268

4:32–37 . . . . 126, 127
4:32–5:16 132
4:33 . . . . . . 117, 124, 127, 128, 158, 314, 548
4:34 . . . . 127, 163
4:34–37 . . . . 127, 132
4:35 . . . . 85, 127, 132
4:36 . . 128, 130, 275, 278, 288, 300, 361, 481
4:36–37 . . . . 128, 233, 235, 278
4:37 132
5 . . . . 129, 132, 141, 167, 209, 351
5:1 132
5:1–2 132
5:1–6 132
5:1–11 . . . . 85, 127, 131, 138
5:2 . . . . 132, 133
5:3 . . . . 29, 132, 133, 140, 565
5:3–4 133
5:4 . . . . 127, 133, 135
5:5 . . . . 134, 139, 438
5:7–11 132
5:9 . . . . 132, 133, 134
5:9–10 344
5:10 132
5:11 . . . . 126, 127, 129, 134, 138, 139,
144, 158, 438
5:12 . . . . 52, 134, 139, 140, 145, 159,
170, 182, 192, 345
5:12–13 101
5:12–14 138
5:12–16 . . . . 81, 126, 138, 194
5:12b 140
5:13 . . . . 126, 138, 140, 144, 150, 171
5:13a 140
5:13b 140
5:14 . . . . 52, 68, 126, 138, 140
5:15 . . . . 140, 437
5:15–16 140
5:16 . . . . 140, 201, 382, 443
5:17 . . . . . . 141, 144, 145, 314, 382, 393, 602
5:17–18 114
5:17–20 29
5:17–21a 145
5:17–32 272
5:17–33 139
5:17–42 . . . . 110, 126, 134, 138, 143–44,
145, 208
5:18 . . . . 171, 382
5:19 . . . . 288, 293, 382, 387
5:21 146

Scripture Index

5:21b–26 .... 145, 146
5:23 146
5:26 .... 126, 138, 147, 150, 171
5:27 29
5:27–28 147
5:27–32 .... 145, 147
5:27–40 516
5:28 .... 82, 114, 147, 420
5:29 ...... 135, 147, 149, 152, 449, 519, 582
5:29–32 .... 147, 470
5:30 .... 28, 104, 147, 148
5:31 .... 28, 48, 104, 147, 148, 153,
              192, 254, 565, 566, 571
5:32 .... 28, 147, 158, 505, 565
5:33 144
5:33–40 .... 145, 149
5:34 .... 149, 150, 503
5:35–39 149
5:36–37 395
5:39 271
5:40 .... 150, 382
5:41–42 .... 139, 145, 150
5:42 .... 29, 148, 151
6. .... 145, 155, 161, 351
6–7 151
6–8 159
6:1 .... 126, 128, 156, 157, 158, 435
6:1–4 .... 156, 341
6:1–5 268
6:1–6 .... 27, 127, 161
6:1–7 .... 33, 155, 170
6:1–11:18 24
6:2 .... 54, 158, 343
6:2–4 158
6:3 .... 159, 169, 170, 366, 601
6:4 .... 52, 84, 158, 165, 166
6:5 ... 166, 198, 199, 170, 251, 276, 355, 479
6:5–6 159
6:6 .... 52, 287, 300
6:7 .... 24, 29, 160, 161, 164, 234, 268,
             286, 291, 367, 427, 439
6:8 .... 159, 170, 181, 182, 321, 345
6:8–10 .... 169, 170
6:8–15 .... 134, 167, 169, 495
6:8–7:56 268
6:8–7:60 159
6:8–8:3 275
6:8–8:4 110
6:8–9:31 .... 25, 156, 167, 169, 232, 237

6:9 .... 33, 65, 157, 161, 234, 276, 299
6:9–8:3 .... 29, 158
6:10 .... 28, 159, 170, 181
6:11 .... 171, 183
6:11–14 .... 170, 171
6:12 .... 157, 336, 343
6:12–7:53 516
6:13 .... 494, 495
6:13–14 171
6:14 488
6:15 .... 170, 172, 182, 302
7. .... 113, 139, 142, 145, 180, 185, 287
7:1 178
7:1–53 .... 167, 170, 175–78
7:1–60 134
7:2 .... 179, 188, 191, 502, 601
7:2–8 179
7:2–43 178
7:2–53 .... 157, 311
7:3 179
7:4 .... 179, 188
7:5 .... 179, 189, 312
7:5–6 188
7:6 179
7:6–7 186
7:7 179
7:8 .... 179, 188
7:9 179
7:9–10 .... 186, 188
7:9–16 180
7:9a 180
7:9b–10 180
7:11 185
7:17 .... 180, 312
7:17–22 180
7:17–29 180
7:17–43 180
7:18 180
7:20 180
7:20–22 180
7:22 .... 170, 181
7:23 181
7:23–29 .... 180, 181
7:25 .... 179, 181, 583
7:27 .... 181, 182
7:30 .... 170, 173, 182
7:30–34 180
7:30–43 .... 180, 181
7:31b 182

7:32	104, 182
7:32–34	188
7:33–34	182
7:35	170, 173, 181, 182
7:35–41	186
7:35–43	180
7:35a	183
7:35b	183
7:36	170, 182, 183
7:37	30, 183, 185
7:38	170, 173, 179, 182, 183
7:39	182, 183
7:39–41	183
7:41	181
7:42	183, 188
7:44	183, 184
7:44–50	178, 184, 186
7:45	184
7:46	184
7:47	184
7:48	178
7:48–49	488
7:48–40	184
7:49	184
7:49–50	184
7:51	183
7:51–52	104
7:51–53	178, 185, 186
7:52	104, 122, 185, 186, 420, 504
7:52–53	191
7:53	170, 173, 185, 191
7:54	191
7:54–56	191
7:54–60	167, 190, 495
7:54–8:1	493
7:54–8:3	190
7:55	28, 170, 188, 191, 302
7:56	48, 191, 253, 254
7:57	52
7:57–58a	192
7:57–60	191, 192
7:58	167, 171, 190, 194, 195, 275, 278, 409
7:58–8:1	288
7:58b	193
7:59	191, 314, 449
7:59–60	193
7:60	191
8	89, 107, 159, 167, 194, 204, 208, 209, 216, 240
8:1	171, 193, 194, 195, 199, 275, 276, 278, 328, 393, 494, 503
8:1–3	167, 191, 194, 221, 287
8:2	195
8:3	52, 68, 140, 193, 194, 195, 220, 225, 275, 503
8:4	199, 206
8:4–8	198, 199
8:4–25	167, 197–98
8:5	29, 199, 201, 237
8:5–13	159
8:6	52, 159, 201, 203
8:7	202, 443
8:8	29, 200, 201, 278, 388
8:9	202
8:9–13	198, 202
8:9–20	96
8:9–24	29, 301
8:10	202, 203, 205
8:11	203
8:12	29, 52, 68, 70, 140, 203, 204, 335, 470
8:12–17	261
8:13	202, 203, 204
8:14	204, 271, 278, 346
8:14–25	198, 203, 341
8:15	52, 204, 287
8:16	204, 314
8:16–17	70
8:17	204
8:17–19	29
8:18	204, 205, 384
8:18–19	205
8:18–24	205, 438
8:19	204, 205
8:20a	206
8:20–23	205
8:23	206
8:24	206
8:25	122, 199, 204, 206, 208, 240, 387
8:26	146, 199, 212, 215, 222
8:26–29	211
8:26–40	198, 210–11
8:26a	211
8:27	212, 250
8:28	250
8:29	28, 29, 211, 212, 215, 299, 435, 480
8:30	211, 212
8:30–35	211, 212

Reference	Pages
8:31	212, 222
8:32	213
8:33	217
8:34	213, 215
8:35	204, 213
8:35–36	70
8:36	212, 214, 222
8:36–40	211, 213
8:37	210
8:38	204
8:39	204, 211, 212, 215, 222, 270, 327, 388, 449, 480
8:39–40	237
8:40	214, 241, 479
9.	167, 219, 229, 240, 245, 249, 506
9:1	221, 233
9:1–2	220, 221, 225, 287, 393, 401, 488, 503
9:1–16	364
9:1–19	558, 559
9:1–19a	218–19, 221
9:1–29	500, 503, 563
9:1–30	275, 278, 288
9:1–31	27, 224
9:2	52, 68, 140, 212, 222, 223, 226, 327, 429, 436, 449
9:3	219, 223, 563, 565
9:3–5	504
9:3–6	48, 223
9:3–9	221, 222
9:3–16	518
9:4	223, 563
9:4–6	254
9:5	117, 135, 223, 252, 314
9:6	219, 224, 449, 504, 519, 582
9:6–37	185
9:7	219, 223
9:8	225, 303
9:8–9	225
9:9	225
9:9–11	299
9:10	225, 373
9:10–19	221, 225
9:11	52, 287
9:11–12	225
9:11b	225
9:12	373
9:13	563
9:13–14	220, 225, 254
9:14	205, 226
9:15	225, 226, 228, 232, 238, 240, 275, 278, 314, 322, 328, 437, 470, 494, 552, 559, 601
9:15–16	233, 300, 483, 534, 546, 564
9:16	226, 449, 519, 582
9:17	29, 117, 212, 222, 226, 314
9:17–18	70
9:18	226
9:19	435
9:19–30	235
9:19b–25	232
9:19b–31	231
9:20	226, 232, 311
9:22	29, 232, 235, 438
9:23–25	564
9:25	233
9:26	195, 233, 258
9:26–28	566
9:26–30	232, 233, 505, 525
9:27	129, 233, 235, 275, 278, 288
9:27–28	311
9:28	233
9:29	157
9:29–30	564
9:30	234, 236, 278, 606
9:31	24, 29, 160, 232, 234, 238, 286, 291, 367, 427, 439
9:32	225, 240, 241, 346, 563
9:32–35	239, 240
9:32–43	237, 240
9:32–12:24	25, 237, 291
9:34	240, 241, 243, 254
9:35	240, 241, 244, 245, 565, 566
9:36	96, 242, 252
9:36–43	240, 242
9:37	243
9:38	243, 346
9:39	156, 243
9:40	240, 243, 254
9:40–41	243
9:41	156, 225, 244, 563
9:42	240, 244
9:43	244
10.	84, 89, 106, 107, 240, 245, 262, 263, 264, 269, 295, 440, 441
10–11	344, 579
10:1	250
10:1–8	237, 250

10:1–48 . . . . 157, 247–49, 250, 346
10:1–11:18. 275, 563
10:2 . . . . 52, 96, 242, 251, 253, 256,
287, 376, 378, 441
10:3 . . . . 253, 262, 373, 420
10:3–6 258
10:4 . . . . 52, 243, 252, 253
10:5 253
10:5–6 269
10:6 244
10:7 253
10:8 253
10:9 . . . . 52, 253, 287
10:9–16 253
10:9–17 482
10:9–22 253
10:9–23a 237, 250, 253
10:10 505
10:10–16 . . . . 251, 272
10:10–20 268
10:11 . . . . 191, 269
10:11–12 . . . . 253, 262, 269
10:11–15 48
10:11–16 268
10:13 . . . . 106, 240, 254, 269
10:13–15 518
10:14 . . . . 254, 257
10:15 . . . . 107, 255, 269
10:17 . . . . 255, 256
10:19 . . . . 29, 256, 299, 480
10:20 . . . . 240, 256, 268, 272
10:21 259
10:22 . . . . 251, 253, 256, 366
10:23 256
10:23–24 257
10:23–48 559
10:23b–33 . . . . 250, 257
10:23b–48 237
10:24 586
10:25–26 331
10:26 . . . . 257, 327
10:27 . . . . 257, 258
10:27–48 344
10:28 . . . . 258, 259, 482, 498
10:30–31 52
10:30–32 258
10:31 . . . . 243, 252
10:33 258
10:34–35 . . . . 259, 262
10:34–39 30
10:34–43 . . . . 250, 259
10:35 29
10:36 . . . . 117, 240, 250, 252, 259, 260, 262,
263, 277, 314, 340, 367, 396, 548, 565
10:36–39 . . . . 65, 443
10:37 435
10:37–38 260
10:38 . . . . 28, 259, 263, 470
10:39 . . . . 148, 505, 565
10:39–43 30
10:40 28
10:41 . . . . 122, 260, 565
10:42 603
10:43 . . . . 261, 565
10:44 . . . . 29, 30, 70, 567
10:44–45 . . . . 261, 262
10:44–46 77
10:44–48 . . . . 205, 250, 261
10:45 . . . . 268, 342
10:46 . . . . 29, 77, 261, 435
10:47–48 261
10:48 . . . . 261, 387
11 . . . . 250, 282
11:1–3 267
11:1–18 . . . . 237, 250, 266–67, 272, 341, 346
11:2 . . . . 268, 272, 286, 342
11:4 . . . . 268, 286
11:4–10 48
11:4–17 . . . . 267, 268
11:5 . . . . 52, 269, 505
11:5–14 253
11:6 . . . . 269, 302
11:7 269
11:8 . . . . 267, 269
11:8–12 270
11:9 . . . . 267, 269
11:11 269
11:12 . . . 28, 29, 269, 270, 272, 299, 449, 480
11:13–14 269
11:14 . . . . 326, 387
11:15 . . . . 267, 269
11:15–17 . . . . 28, 30, 205, 270, 373
11:15–18 409
11:16 . . . . 267, 311, 435
11:17 . . . . 237, 238, 267, 270, 286
11:18 . . . . 29, 238, 267, 270, 566
11:19 . . . . 122, 275, 276, 478
11:19–20 300

11:19–21	275, 276
11:19–30	238, 274
11:19–28:31	24
11:20	28, 157, 277, 299
11:21	241, 276, 277, 278, 565, 566
11:22	195, 278, 283
11:22–23	286
11:22–24	275, 277
11:22–30	288
11:23	214, 277, 278, 281, 282
11:23–24	28
11:24	24, 130, 277, 278
11:25	234
11:25–26	82, 129, 275
11:25–26a	279
11:25–27	278
11:26	238, 275, 279, 282, 291, 430, 435, 519
11:27	282, 479
11:27–28	283
11:27–30	276, 280, 441
11:28	25, 29, 286, 449, 479
11:28–30	300
11:29	281, 537
11:29–30	305
11:30	276, 336, 430, 469, 525
12	291, 293, 529
12:1	539
12:1–4	29
12:1–5	286
12:1–24	238, 284–85
12:2	142, 287
12:3	287, 288
12:3–10	346
12:4	287
12:4–5	382
12:5	52, 287
12:6–11	286, 287–88
12:7	146, 288, 565
12:7–10	293, 382, 387
12:8	288
12:9	288
12:10	288
12:11	146, 288
12:12	52, 301, 360
12:12–16	287
12:12–19a	286, 288
12:13	383, 525
12:14	289
12:15	289
12:16	289
12:17	52, 289, 346, 487, 561
12:18	289
12:19	290, 387
12:19b–23	286, 290
12:20	52, 290
12:21	290
12:22	290
12:23	146, 238
12:23–24	27
12:24	29, 160, 234, 238, 286, 291, 367, 427, 439
12:25	288, 295, 300, 301, 304, 360, 430
12:25–3:3	298
12:25–13:3	295, 298
12:25–13:12	297–98
12:25–14:28	295
12:25–16:5	25, 295, 371
13	107, 316, 317, 468
13–20	506, 566
13–28	24
13:1	280, 282, 299, 300, 304, 317, 357, 358
13:1–2	129
13:1–3	160
13:2	28, 29, 299, 302, 374, 430, 449, 470, 480
13:2–4	282
13:3	52, 298, 300, 336
13:3–4	369
13:4	300, 301, 317, 374, 449, 470, 480
13:4–12	203, 298, 300
13:5	226, 288, 298, 301, 311, 392, 401, 419, 428
13:6	301, 302
13:6–7	301
13:6–8	202
13:6–11	29, 438
13:7	298, 302, 430
13:7–12	559
13:8	302
13:9	29, 303, 317
13:9–10	302
13:10	303, 565
13:11	303, 565
13:12	82, 298, 303, 321
13:13	288, 295, 304, 310, 360, 361, 362
13:13–14	309
13:13–15	310

13:13–52	27, 307–9
13:14	226, 276, 298, 392, 401, 419, 428
13:14–15	309, 310
13:15	298, 312, 313, 316, 601
13:16	251, 310, 311, 312, 376, 378, 561
13:16–41	182, 295, 309, 311
13:16–47	321
13:17	355
13:17–19	312
13:17–20	312
13:20	312
13:21	312
13:21–22	312
13:23	148, 312, 316
13:24	122, 566
13:24–25	312, 435
13:26	251, 310, 311, 312, 376, 378, 583, 601
13:27	312
13:28	312
13:29	148
13:29–30	312
13:31	312, 505, 565
13:32	312
13:32–33	316
13:32–37	312
13:34	312
13:34–35	313
13:35	311
13:36–37	313
13:37	28
13:38	311, 313, 565, 601
13:38–41	313
13:39	312
13:40–41	312
13:41	313
13:42	313, 430
13:42–52	310, 313–14
13:43	251, 304, 310, 313, 314, 401, 411, 430
13:44	298, 387
13:44–45	314
13:44–52	296
13:45	29, 306, 314, 342, 393, 411
13:46	104, 122, 296, 298, 303, 310, 314, 420, 430, 603
13:46–47	29, 30
13:46–28:31	226
13:47	39, 583
13:48	214, 315
13:49	315
13:50	29, 251, 304, 315, 335, 401, 430, 494, 501
13:51	315
13:52	29, 133, 315, 435
14	142, 329
14:1	157, 226, 298, 321, 401, 419, 428
14:1–2	320, 321
14:1–7	320
14:2	306, 321, 494
14:3	170, 298, 323, 324, 345, 481
14:3–5	320, 321
14:3a	321
14:3b	321
14:4	411
14:5	29, 494, 564
14:5–6	335
14:6	322
14:6–7	320, 322
14:7	298, 326
14:8–10	326
14:8–20	325
14:8–21	559
14:9	302, 326
14:10	241, 326
14:11	257, 326, 411
14:11–12	590, 592
14:11–13	326
14:11–18	326
14:13	283
14:14	54
14:14–18	326
14:15	120, 241, 257, 326, 327, 566
14:19	29, 194, 306, 322, 335, 494
14:19–20	306, 326, 328
14:20	328
14:21	298
14:21–25	334, 335
14:21–28	334
14:21a	334
14:21b–25a	335
14:22	29, 335, 429, 519
14:23	52, 299, 336, 469
14:25	122
14:26	362
14:26–27	298
14:26–28	295, 334, 336
14:27	336, 338, 487
14:28	336, 435

Scripture Index

15. . . . . 270, 272, 286, 342, 345, 351, 352, 363, 440
15:1 . . . . .326, 342, 351, 353, 357
15:1–5 . . . . .341, 342
15:1–21 .339–40, 341
15:1–35 . . . . .29, 277, 295, 296
15:1–41 27
15:2 . . . . .342, 343, 352, 357, 469, 525
15:3 343
15:4 . . . . .195, 336, 345, 469, 487
15:4a 343
15:4b 344
15:5 . . . . .342, 344, 351, 602
15:6–7 346
15:6–11 . . . . .296, 341
15:6–12 344
15:7 . . . . .346, 481, 601
15:7–11 . . . . .250, 409
15:7a 344
15:7b 344
15:7b–11 344
15:8 . . . . .344, 346, 351, 356
15:8–9 397
15:8–11 28
15:9 . . . . .272, 344, 346
15:10 .202, 344, 346, 352
15:11 . . . . .345, 351, 352
15:12 . . . . .170, 304, 341, 345, 356, 487
15:13 601
15:13–21 . . . . .52, 296, 341, 345, 487
15:14 . . . . .250, 346, 356
15:15 . . . . .346, 350
15:15–21 352
15:16 347
15:17 347
15:18 347
15:19 . . . . .241, 347, 565, 566
15:19–21 347
15:19–29 489
15:20 . . . . .347, 348, 356
15:21 350
15:22 .355, 361, 362, 469
15:22–29 355
15:22–35 . . . . .341, 354–55
15:23 . . . . .362, 469
15:23–29 347
15:24 . . . . .342, 356, 357
15:25 52
15:25–26 356

15:28 . . .28, 29, 350, 351, 356, 357, 449, 480
15:28–29 351
15:29 . . . . .347, 356
15:30–35 . . . . .355, 356
15:31 . . . . .29, 356, 358
15:32 . . . . .202, 280, 357, 362, 429
15:35 . . . . .357, 371
15:36 . . . . .360, 361
15:36–39 288
15:36–41 . . . . .310, 360, 371
15:36–16:5 295
15:37–39 362
15:38 360
15:39 . . . . .363, 487
15:40 . . . . .356, 360, 361, 362
15:41 . . . . .362, 429
16. . . . .89, 107, 329, 389, 395, 502, 511, 529
16:1 .328, 335, 362, 461
16:1–3 361
16:1–5 .360, 365, 371
16:2 367
16:3 . . . . .366, 489
16:4 . . . . .366, 469
16:4–5 . . . . .360, 366
16:5 . . . .24, 29, 160, 234, 286, 291, 427, 439
16:6 . . . . .122, 372, 373, 374, 440
16:6–7 . . . . . .28, 29, 264, 374, 449, 470, 480
16:6–10 . . . . .300, 360, 369, 371
16:6–19:20 . . . . .25, 369, 371, 437
16:7 373
16:7–9 372
16:9 . . . . .373, 581
16:9–10 . . . . .420, 461
16:10 . . . . .361, 373, 579
16:10–17 . . . . . . .23, 369, 373, 401, 487, 578
16:10–40 389
16:11 .376, 460, 461
16:11–12 . . . . .374, 376
16:11–15 376
16:11–40 369
16:12 . . . . .377, 384
16:13 . . . . .52, 378, 401, 419, 428
16:13–14 383
16:13–15 378
16:13–16 376
16:14 . . . . .251, 378, 380, 390, 397, 401
16:14b 378
16:14c 378
16:15 . . . . .204, 397

16:16	52, 378, 383, 390, 434, 449
16:16–18	29, 203, 383, 443
16:16–40	369, 381–82
16:16–17:9	27
16:17	384, 583
16:18	382, 390, 449
16:19	385, 407
16:19–20	382
16:19–21	29, 383, 384
16:19–31	283
16:20	385
16:20–21	378, 384
16:22	385, 388
16:22–23	382
16:22–24	383, 385
16:24	382
16:25	29, 52, 387
16:25–28	382, 383, 386
16:26	124, 390
16:29–30	387
16:29–34	383, 387
16:30	326
16:30–34	559
16:31	326, 387
16:31–32	387
16:31–33	70
16:32	122, 387
16:33	387, 386
16:33–34	387
16:34	29, 388
16:35–36	385
16:35–38	383
16:35–40	388, 509
16:37	361
16:38	385, 388
16:38–39	511
16:39	383, 388
16:40	383, 388
17	329, 468
17:1	226, 389, 401, 428
17:1–4	392
17:1–9	391, 400
17:2–3	392
17:2	392, 419
17:3	29, 395, 519
17:4	251, 395, 401
17:4–5	411
17:5	314, 394, 501
17:5–8	525
17:5–9	29, 369, 392, 393, 494
17:6	394
17:8	395
17:10	226, 396, 401, 428
17:10–11	401
17:10–12	400
17:10–15	400
17:11	402
17:12	140, 401
17:13	314
17:13–15	400
17:14–15	401, 461
17:15	402
17:16	449
17:16–21	405, 406
17:16–33	400
17:16–34	369, 404–5, 418, 559
17:16a	406
17:17	251, 406, 428, 436
17:18	407
17:18–20	411
17:18a	406
17:18b	407
17:19	82, 407, 547
17:20	407
17:21	407
17:22	407, 408
17:22–23	405, 408
17:22–31	405, 408
17:23	408
17:24	120, 548
17:24–27a	405, 409
17:24b	409
17:24b–25a	409
17:25a	409
17:25b	409
17:26–27a	409
17:27a	410
17:27b–28	405, 410
17:28	410
17:29	405, 410, 451
17:30	411, 565, 566
17:30–31	405
17:31	28, 410
17:32	402, 411, 567
17:32–34	405, 411
17:33	525
17:34	411
18:1–8	418

18:1–17	417–18
18:1–18	369
18:2	25, 419, 430
18:3	471
18:4	157, 226, 419, 428, 436
18:5	29, 362, 419, 461, 603
18:6	315, 420, 436, 603
18:7	376, 378, 420
18:8	70, 204, 420, 422
18:9	373
18:9–10	420, 423, 428, 518, 581
18:9–11	418, 420
18:10	422, 420, 424
18:11	82, 421, 519
18:12	52, 314, 421, 547
18:12–17	369, 418, 419, 421, 494
18:13	421
18:15	421, 422, 534
18:16	422
18:17	407, 422
18:18	427, 430, 489
18:18–22	427, 486
18:18–28	426, 427, 432
18:18a	428
18:19	226, 428, 420, 430
18:21	428, 434
18:22	369
18:23	335, 427, 429, 477
18:24	429
18:24–26	427, 429, 434
18:24–19:20	369
18:25	429, 430, 435, 436, 488
18:26	430, 431, 432, 436
18:27–28	427, 430
19	329, 440, 441
19:1	435
19:1–7	70, 427, 434
19:1–20	433–34
19:2	435, 440
19:3–6	77
19:4	440
19:5	440
19:6	29, 77, 435, 440
19:8	29, 203, 335, 419, 436, 437, 440, 470
19:8–10	427, 434, 436, 519
19:9	429, 436, 449
19:9–10	82
19:10	157, 369, 436, 440, 494
19:11	437, 440, 443
19:11–12	141, 472
19:11–20	301, 434, 427, 437
19:12	438
19:13	438, 440
19:15	438, 440, 449
19:16	438, 439
19:17	437, 440, 438
19:18–19	203
19:19	384, 437, 438
19:20	24, 29, 160, 234, 286, 291, 367, 427, 437, 439, 440, 448
19:21	453, 481, 494, 515, 519, 550, 576, 595, 601
19:21–22	437, 448
19:21–41	437, 447–48, 459
19:21–28:30	25
19:21–28:31	427, 431, 437, 445
19:21a	448
19:21b	449
19:22	449, 461
19:23	429, 449
19:23–27	448, 449
19:23–41	29, 427
19:23–20:38	445
19:25	384, 453
19:26	451, 452
19:27	437, 438, 439, 451, 453
19:28	451, 452
19:28–32	495
19:28–34	448, 451
19:29	52, 451, 461, 578
19:30	452
19:31	452, 586
19:32	452
19:33	452, 561
19:34	452
19:35	450, 452
19:35–41	448, 452
19:37	452
19:38–39	453
19:39	452
19:40	343, 452, 453
19:47	438
20	475
20:1	438, 460, 463, 465, 477, 481
20:1–6	22, 459, 460
20:1–16	458–59
20:1–21:17	459, 460
20:2	460, 463, 465

20:3	314, 459, 461, 501, 519, 564
20:4	335, 401, 451, 465, 495, 578, 586
20:5	461
20:5–15	23, 369, 487, 578
20:6	459, 461, 469, 489
20:7	459, 462
20:7–12	82, 459, 460, 462
20:8	459, 462
20:9	459, 461, 465
20:10	463
20:11	85, 459, 463, 466
20:12	463, 465
20:13	463
20:13–16	459, 460, 463, 468
20:14	463
20:15	463
20:16	459, 460, 463, 478, 489
20:17–18a	468
20:17–38	459, 467–68
20:18	469, 474
20:18b–21	469
20:18b–35	468, 469
20:19	314, 438, 469, 472, 473, 474, 501
20:20	469, 470, 474
20:20–21	82
20:21	29, 157, 469, 474, 566, 603
20:22	460, 469, 470, 515
20:22–23	28, 461, 449
20:22–24	28, 300, 469, 519
20:23	470, 478, 480, 494
20:24	470, 473, 474, 519
20:25	29, 203, 335, 446, 469, 470, 474
20:25–31	469
20:26	470, 471, 474
20:27	470, 474
20:28	471, 475
20:28–29	470
20:28–32	82
20:29	471
20:30	470, 474
20:31	469, 471, 472, 474
20:32	469, 471, 475
20:32–35	469
20:33	384, 473
20:34	471
20:34–35	473
20:35	472
20:36	52
20:36–38	468, 472, 478
20:37	469, 472, 474
20:38	446, 473
21	502
21–26	602
21:1	477, 479
21:1–9	459, 477
21:1–17	476–77
21:1–18	23, 369, 487, 578
21:1–36	445
21:3	459, 477
21:4	449, 459, 460, 461, 478, 482
21:5	52, 459, 477, 478
21:7	459, 479
21:8	156, 159, 198, 199, 479
21:8–9	159, 214
21:9	479
21:10	280, 479
21:10–11	479
21:10–14	459, 477, 479, 494
21:11	29, 299, 449, 460, 461, 480
21:11–14	300
21:12	460, 479, 480
21:13	460, 480, 511
21:14	480, 484
21:15	460
21:15–17	459, 477, 480
21:16	481, 482
21:17	460, 481, 500, 523, 586
21:17–26	500, 519
21:17–23:35	22
21:17–24:27	546
21:17–25:12	559
21:18	461, 477
21:18–19	487
21:18–25	52
21:18–26	486
21:19	487
21:20	29, 314, 490, 506
21:20–25	481
21:20–26	506
21:20a	487
21:20b	487
21:20–25	487
21:20c	488
21:21	171, 367, 488, 602
21:23	489
21:24	489
21:25	347, 489
21:26	487, 489, 494

21:27–28	538, 548
21:27–29	494
21:27–30	528
21:27–36	493, 500, 520
21:28	171, 494–95, 502, 505, 546, 561, 566, 601
21:28–29	504
21:29	461
21:30	407, 497, 498
21:30–32	494, 495
21:31–33	528
21:32	496
21:33	407, 480
21:33–36	494, 496
21:35	496, 501
21:36	510, 552
21:37–40	500, 501, 509, 520
21:37–22:21	499–500
21:37–23:11	445
21:39	171, 220, 305, 515, 516
21:40	502, 503, 561
22	219, 234, 468, 502, 506, 507
22:1	502, 515, 601
22:1–5	501, 502
22:1–21	219, 226, 494, 500, 502, 509, 520, 548, 559
22:2	503
22:3	149, 220, 278, 314, 488, 515, 516, 525, 537, 546
22:3–5	510
22:3–21	563
22:3a	503
22:3b	503
22:3c	503
22:4	52, 68, 140, 429, 449
22:4–5	220
22:5	503
22:6	219, 504, 563
22:6–10	518
22:6–11	501, 503
22:6–21	510, 558, 559
22:7	563
22:8	135, 504, 505, 563
22:9	504
22:9a	505
22:10	219, 505
22:10a	504
22:10c	504
22:12	504, 516
22:12–16	501, 504
22:14	104, 122, 504, 505, 573
22:14–15	518
22:15	115, 470, 505, 565
22:16	204, 505
22:17	52, 546
22:17–18	505
22:17–20	501
22:17–21	505
22:18	234, 505
22:18–21	518
22:19–20	505
22:20	194
22:21	29, 234, 501, 505, 603
22:22	505, 510, 567
22:22–29	506, 509, 510, 520
22:23	552
22:24	510
22:25	546
22:25–28	502
22:25–29	516
22:27	496
22:28	511, 527
22:30	515, 546
22:30–23:11	514–15
22:44–49, 51	607
23	468
23:1	515, 516, 601
23:1–5	516
23:1–6	548, 559
23:1–10	520
23:2	516
23:2–5	515
23:3	517
23:4	517, 538
23:6	515, 517, 551, 601
23:6–10	515, 517
23:6a	518
23:6b	518
23:7	343, 518
23:8	111, 145
23:9	449, 518, 546, 568, 592
23:9–10	552
23:10	343, 517, 518
23:11	300, 515, 517, 520, 524, 526, 529, 550, 554, 569, 577, 581, 595, 601, 603
23:12	524, 265
23:12–15	524, 546
23:12–35	445, 520, 522–23, 553

23:14	524
23:15	564
23:16	233, 525
23:16–22	524, 525
23:17	525
23:17–22	528
23:18	525
23:19	407, 525
23:21	524
23:22	525
23:23	526
23:23–35	524, 525, 526
23:24	538
23:25	527
23:26	496, 501, 511, 527
23:26–30	446
23:27–30	527, 551
23:28	516
23:29	528, 534, 546, 568, 602
23:30	528, 564
24	468
24:1	546
24:1–9	534
24:1–21	528
24:1–27	532–33
24:1–26:32	445
24:2	534
24:2–4	538, 539
24:2b–4	534, 535
24:5	343, 518, 534, 535, 537, 551, 561
24:5–6	548
24:5–7	546
24:5–8	566
24:6	534, 535, 537
24:7–8	532
24:8	534
24:9	535
24:10	538
24:10–21	517, 534, 536, 548, 559, 569
24:10b	536, 561
24:11	536
24:12	536
24:12–13	536
24:12–14	546, 548
24:13	536
24:14	429, 536, 537
24:14–18	536
24:16–18	537
24:17	96, 461, 537
24:18	537
24:19	538
24:19–21	536
24:20–21	517
24:21	537, 551
24:22	429, 511, 538
24:22–27	534, 538
24:23	539
24:24	536, 539
24:25	539, 540, 541
24:26	537, 539
24:27	29, 540, 546, 547, 548
25	468, 554
25:1–5	546
25:1–27	544–45
25:2	546, 547, 562
25:3	546, 547, 548
25:4–5	537, 549
25:5	546, 547, 568
25:6	546, 547
25:6–12	546, 547
25:6b	547
25:7	554
25:7a	548
25:7b	548
25:8	28, 171, 546, 548, 552, 602
25:8–12	528
25:9	546, 548, 551
25:10	546, 548, 549, 552, 601
25:11	445, 546, 547, 548, 549, 552, 602
25:11–12	494
25:12	548, 549, 552
25:13	546, 550
25:13–22	546, 550
25:14	551
25:15	546, 551
25:16	546, 551
25:18	546, 602
25:19	551
25:20	26, 546, 551, 567
25:21	548, 552, 602
25:22	551
25:23	546, 551, 559
25:23–27	546, 552
25:23–26:32	226
25:24	561
25:24–27	446, 559, 561
25:24a	552
25:24b	552

Scripture Index

25:25 . . . . .546, 548, 552, 559, 592, 602
25:26 . . . . .548, 552, 553
25:26–27 534
25:27 552
25:30 546
26. . . . . .219, 468, 506, 569, 577
26:1 .560, 561, 568
26:1–32 557–58
26:1a 561
26:1b 561
26:2 561
26:2–3 . . . . .546, 560, 561
26:2–23 219
26:3 . . . . .561, 562, 571
26:4–5 . . . . .560, 561, 563
26:4–18 560
26:5 . . . . .562, 602
26:6 . . . . .562, 567, 602
26:6–7 . . . . .562, 566
26:6–8 . . . . .560, 562
26:6–23 560
26:6a 562
26:7 . . . . .561, 562
26:8 . . . . .562, 567
26:9 . . . . .562, 563
26:9–11 . . . . .560, 562, 566
26:9–20 . . . . .500, 503
26:10 . . . . .205, 225, 562, 563
26:10–11 .220, 596
26:11 563
26:12 . . . . .205, 563
26:12–18 .560, 563
26:13 . . . . .219, 563, 561, 570
26:14 . . . . .219, 563
26:14b 564
26:15 . . . . .135, 563, 565
26:16 . . . . .122, 222, 470, 563, 569
26:16–18 228
26:17 . . . . .564, 565, 566
26:17–18 566
26:17b–18 565
26:18 . . . . .29, 133, 206, 565, 566
26:19 . . . . .561, 566
26:19–20 .560, 566
26:20 . . . . .241, 565, 566, 570, 571
26:21 . . . . .560, 566
26:22 . . . . .567, 568
26:22–23 . . . . .30, 560, 566
26:21 566

26:23 . . . . .29, 565, 567
26:24 . . . . .560, 561
26:24–32 567
26:24a 567
26:24b 567
26:24c 567
26:25 567
26:25–29 560
26:26 . . . . .568, 571
26:27 561
26:28 . . . . .279, 568
26:29 . . . . .561, 568, 569, 571, 598
26:30–31 568
26:30–32 528
26:31 . . . . .568, 592
26:31–32 446
26:32 602
27. . . . . .576, 577
27:1 578
27:1–10 445
27:1–12 . . . . .577, 578
27:1–44 574–76
27:1–28:6. 27
27:1–28:16. . . . . .23, 369, 487
27:2 .451, 461, 578
27:3 . . . . .579, 586, 590, 591
27:4 586
27:7 579
27:8 579
27:9 580
27:10 .578, 579, 580
27:11 580
27:12 580
27:13 580
27:13–26 .578, 580
27:14 581
27:16 581
27:17 581
27:18 581
27:19 581
27:20 . . . . .581, 582, 583, 590
27:21 581
27:21–26 578
27:23 .581, 592, 593
27:23–24 577
27:23–25 300
27:23–26 584
27:24 . . . . .494, 519, 582, 590, 595
27:25 582

27:27	582
27:27–44	578, 582
27:29	582
27:31	578, 582, 583, 590
27:31–32	578
27:33–34	587
27:34	582, 590
27:35	85, 583, 587
27:36	583
27:37	583
27:38	583, 584
27:39–41	583
27:42	583, 578
27:43	579
27:43–44a	584
27:44	590
27:44b	584
28	590
28:1	577
28:1–6	590, 591
28:1–16	589–90
28:2	591, 593
28:4	577, 591, 595
28:4–6	591, 593
58:5	592
28:6	592, 593, 595
28:7	591, 592, 593
28:7–10	590, 592
28:8	52, 592
28:9	593
28:10	591, 593
28:11	593
28:11–16	590, 593
28:11–31	445
28:12	594
28:12–13	593
28:14	593
28:14–15	591
28:14b	593
28:15	593, 594
28:16	594
28:17	593, 601, 602, 605
28:17–22	601
28:17–28	420
28:17–31	28, 599–600
28:18	602
28:19	494, 600, 602, 605
28:20	30, 602, 605
28:20–28	601
28:21	593, 605
28:22	602
28:23	203, 335, 470, 602, 603, 605
28:23–28	28, 601, 602
28:24	603
28:25	28, 449, 480
28:25–27	601
28:25–28	603
28:26	603
28:27	605
28:28	29, 446, 603, 605
28:30	604
28:30–31	82, 601, 604
28:31	28, 27, 29, 37, 203, 335, 357, 445, 470, 601, 603, 604, 607

Romans

1:1	320, 321
1:3–4	313
1:4	1:16 104, 226
1:5	321
1:14	558
1:16	298, 301, 314, 428, 558
1:20	325, 327
1:21–25	330
1:22–23	405
1:23	451
1:24	183
1:29	348
2:9–10	226
2:11	249, 259
3:24	345
3:25	471
5:9	471
8:9	435
8:21	103, 107
8:23	63
8:28	189
8:29	154
8:31	423
9–11	603
9:1–5	500, 506
9:2–4a	600, 605
10:2	235, 500, 503
11:9–10	54
12:5	482
12:12	82
12:13	478

13:6	82
14–15	340, 498
14:3	481
14:14	472
15:3	54
15:6	52
15:7	481
15:16	471
15:25–28, 31	533, 537
15:26	448, 449
15:31	490
16:1	426, 427
16:1–16	586
16:3–4	418, 419
16:7	54
16:21	391, 393, 461, 465
16:23	449, 451

1 Corinthians

1:1	320
1:2	471
1:12	426, 430
1:14	418, 420, 451
1:22–23	552
1:22–24	545
1:23	403, 558, 567
1:23–27	403
3:3–9	426, 430
4:3–5	418, 421
4:12	418, 419, 471
4:17	461
4:18–21	418, 421
5:1	348
6:11	471
6:13	348
6:15–17	348
7:10	472
7:17–24	366
8–10	86, 340, 348
8:1	471
8:5	277
8:6	409
9:1	54, 222, 320
9:1–2	54, 418, 421
9:1–6	321
9:5–6	54
9:6	361
9:15–18	471
9:19–23	490
9:22	491
10:7–8	348
10:16–17	462
10:17	482
10:23	471
10:23–33	349
11:1	473
11:4	280
11:17–34	85, 462
11:24–25	472
12–14	65
12:4–6	28
12:12–14	482
12:13	83, 435, 498
12:28–29	274, 280
13:5	406
14	434, 435
14:4	471
14:29–37	280
15:5	54
15:1–8	35, 38, 44
15:5	54
15:7	345
15:8–9	219
15:8–11	54
15:9	220
15:25	69
15:28	103
15:32	448, 451
16:1–2	280
16:1–4	448, 449, 533, 537
16:2	462
16:8–9	434, 437
16:9	334, 336
16:15	533, 537
16:19	418, 419, 426, 430

2 Corinthians

1:1	320, 461
1:8	448, 451
1:19	232, 361
1:21–22	72
2:4	469
2:12	334, 336, 371
2:14	597
3:7, 13	172, 173
3:7–16	108
3:12–18	227
4:10	226

4:18	442
6:4	226
8–9	449
8:1–4	533, 537
8:2	380
8:9	448
9:7	280
11:5	54
11:9	419
11:22–23	219
11:23–27	296
11:24	150
11:25	325, 328, 382, 386, 581
11:25–26	576, 577
11:26	564
11:32	233
11:32–33	231
11:33	233
12:1–7	300
12:12	54
13:14	28, 81, 83, 86

Galatians

1:1	320, 321, 470
1:6–9	426, 429
1:11–24	219
1:13	194, 220
1:13–24	231
1:14	235, 488, 503
1:14–16	500
1:15–16	504
1:16	222, 232, 342
1:17–18	233, 606
1:18	342
1:18–19	345
1:18–20	233
1:19	54
1:21	234, 362
2	342
2:1	342
2:1–10	350, 341
2:2	342, 500, 505
2:3	366
2:4	342
2:7	241, 500, 505
2:10	533, 537
2:12	256, 268
2:16	345
3–4	227

3:1–5	426, 429
3:2–3	435
3:5	434, 436
3:13	148, 224
3:13–14	219, 220
3:18	471
3:28	482, 498
4:6	434, 436
5:1	344
5:6	367
5:7–12	426, 429
6:12–16	426, 429

Ephesians

1:7	471
1:10	107
1:14	468, 471
1:18	471, 571
2:5–8	345
2:8–10	230
2:11–22	249, 259
2:13–21	498
2:20	88
4:3	351
4:4	482
4:4–6	28
4:11	280
4:11–12	274, 282
4:15	332
5:5	471
5:19	382, 387
5:26	471
6:12	124
6:17	600, 604
6:20	470

Philippians

1:1	365, 461
1:6	47
1:7	470
1:12–13	597
1:13	470
1:14	470
1:17	470
1:19–20	124
1:20–22	545, 549
1:27	386, 388, 515, 516
2:1	81, 83
2:5–11	388

2:5–17	388
2:6–8	509, 513
2:6–11	18
2:10–11	228
3:1–19	468, 471
3:4–15	219
3:5	220, 503, 518
3:5–6	558, 562
3:6	194, 220, 228, 314, 393, 486, 488, 500, 503
3:10	337
3:12	500, 504
3:12–14	474
3:14	228
3:17	388, 473
3:20	389, 509, 513, 516
4:2–3	586
4:15	380, 419
4:22	598

Colossians

1:1	365, 461
1:10	332
1:12	468
1:15	227
1:16	409
1:20	103, 107
1:27	423
2:1	434, 437
2:4–23	468, 471
2:19	332
3:17	91
3:24	468, 471
3:25	249, 259
4:2	82
4:3	334, 336
4:7	461
4:10	288, 360, 361, 363, 461, 578
4:14	23, 371, 373, 586
4:18	470

1 Thessalonians

1:1	361, 365, 461
1:7	473
1:9–10	405
2:2	382, 386, 391, 396
2:9	471
2:14	396, 400
2:14–15	391

2:15	396
2:17	400, 401
2:17–3:1	402
3:1–5	391, 396
3:2	365
4:15	472
5:11	471
5:19–21	479
5:21	477
5:23	471

2 Thessalonians

1:1	361, 365, 461
3:9	473

1 Timothy

1:2	365, 461
1:3–10	468, 471
1:12–16	364
1:13	220, 393
1:18	461
1:19b–20	468, 471
3:2	478
4:1–3	471
4:5	471
4:7	471
4:12	473
4:16	471
5:17	469
6:3–10, 20–21	471

2 Timothy

1:2	365, 461
1:5	365
2:9	470
2:14–18	468, 470
2:21	471
3:11	325, 328
4:7	474
4:9–10	363
4:11	23, 360, 371, 373, 586
4:12	461
4:14	448, 452
4:20	449, 461, 493, 495

Titus

1:3	468, 470
1:5	469
1:8	478

2:7 473
2:10 ....131, 132
3:12 461

Philemon
1. ....365, 461
13. 470
24. .....23, 360, 363, 365, 371, 373, 461, 578

Hebrews
1:9 118
1:13 69
1:18 118
2:10 ....104, 144, 148, 153
2:11 154
6:4–5, 17–20 103
6:10 252
10:1–18 95
11:16 103
12:2 ....104, 144, 148, 153, 154
12:2a 154
13:2 478
13:22 ....309, 311

James
1:27 163
2:1 ....249, 259
5:14 469

1 Peter
1:1 ....371, 372
1:2 28
1:3–4 103
1:17 ....249, 259
2:4–5 ....169, 172
3:15 ....414, 416
4:9 478
4:16 ....274, 279

5:7 583
5:8 124
5:13 ....360, 363

2 Peter
3:13 ....103, 107

1 John
1:3 115
2:1 104

Revelation
1:4b–5 28
1:10 462
1:17 223
2–3 ....434, 437
2:13 470
2:14, 20 348
3:8 336
3:17 104
4:1 ....191, 253
4:4 469
5:13 255
7:1 255
8:7–12 255
13. 577
14:7 255
14:8 363
16:2–9 255
17:5 363
17:6 470
17:18 363
18:2 363
19:10 ....257, 331
19:11 253
20:8 255
21:1 ....103, 107
22:8–9 ....257, 331

Subject Index

Abraham, 30, 73, 100, 104, 105, 107 8, 117, 136, 175–76, 179, 180, 182, 188, 189, 191, 227, 292, 307, 311, 312, 316, 342
Achaia, 21, 25, 401, 417, 418, 421, 422, 426, 427, 430, 447, 449
Achan, 133
Acts
  authorship of, 22–23
  date of, 23–24
  five summary "hinges" or markers in, 24–25
  how to read the story of, 21–22
  how the story unfolds, 24–25
  introduction and summary of Jesus' teaching, 36–38
  key theological themes in the story of, 28–30
  primary actor in the story of, 30
  purpose of, 25–27
  resources for preaching and teaching on, 31–32
  thematic and geographic connection of the book of Luke to, 21
Adramyttium, 574, 579
Adriatic Sea, 575, 582, 583, 590
Aeneas, 239, 240–45, 254
Agabus, 274, 275–76, 280, 283, 300, 305, 459, 461, 476, 477, 479–80, 481
agora (marketplace), 406
Agrippa. *See* Herod Agrippa
Alexander (Ephesian metalworker?), 447, 452
Alexander the Great, 157, 200, 242, 276, 392
Alexander (Jewish priest), 109, 112
Alexandria, 65, 169, 220, 276, 418, 426, 429, 431, 434, 501, 579
Alphaeus, 50
Amphipolis, 391
Ananias (Damascene disciple), 218–19, 221, 225–26, 233, 254, 500, 504, 508, 516, 563, 564
Ananias (high priest), 514, 516–17, 524, 532, 534, 547
Ananias (husband of Sapphira), 85, 127, 129, 131–39, 140, 209, 344, 351

angels, 40, 111, 146, 170, 173, 178, 185, 291, 292–93, 331–32, 393, 415, 514, 600
Anglican Communion, 77
Anna, 140n5, 479
Annas (high priest), 109, 112
ascension, the. *See under* Jesus
Ascension Day, 48–49
Antioch of Pisidia, 276, 295–96, 307, 309, 310–13, 316, 321, 325, 326, 328, 334, 335, 372, 377, 429, 432, 436, 468
Antioch, Syria, 129, 155, 159, 238, 249, 251, 274–83, 291, 295, 297–301, 304–6, 315, 321, 334–36, 338–40, 341–44, 351, 352, 354–58, 360–63, 369, 371, 396, 426–29, 434, 441, 477, 479
  aid to the Jerusalem church from the church at, 280–81
  Barnabas and Paul sent to, 356–57
  disciples first called Christians in, 274, 279, 291
  four virtues of the church of, 304–6
  the gospel proclaimed to the gentiles in, 250, 271, 274–77
  history, location, and importance of, 276
Antiochus (father of Seleucus I Nicator), 276
Antiochus IV of Commagene, 322
Antiochus IV (Epiphanes), 254, 497
Antipatris, 523, 526, 528
Antonia Fortress, 287, 294, 495, 502, 507, 510, 512, 513, 518, 525, 530, 535, 554, 577
Aphrodite (goddess), 398
Apollo (Greek god), 277, 429, 450, 456
Apollonia, 391
Apollonius of Tyana, 437
Apollos, 426, 427, 429–35
apologetics, 412–16
apologists, the need for Christian, 412–14
apostles. *See* disciples *and next*
apostles'
  arrest and escape, 145–46
  second arrest, 146–47

641

teaching, 79, 81, 82–83, 85, 87, 88, 89, 105, 111, 165, 171
apostolic teaching, the natural consequence of learning, 89
Appian Way, 594
Aquila, 417, 419, 424, 426, 427, 428, 430–32, 436
Arabia, 233, 606
Aramaic, 33, 53, 128, 157, 234, 242, 243n10, 301, 363, 499, 502, 503, 507, 557, 563
Areopagus, 400, 404–5, 407–8, 411, 413, 547n2, 567
Aristarchus, 447, 451, 458, 459, 461, 574, 576, 578, 586
Artemis (goddess), 277, 427, 428, 429n6, 434, 437, 439, 447–48, 450–55
Artemisium, 450
Ash Wednesday, 48, 49, 572
Asia, 29, 60, 65, 66, 169, 298, 310, 378n4, 379, 445, 450, 451n9, 461, 477, 478, 479, 579, 586
  Asia Minor, 21, 25, 295, 304, 309, 310, 327, 336, 371–72, 418, 437, 440, 539
  modern-day gospel awakening in, 264
  province of, 278, 315n13, 371–72, 374, 378, 427, 428, 433–36, 440, 447, 451, 458–59, 467, 493, 494, 502, 533, 574
asiarchēs ("officials"), 452
Assos, 458, 459, 463
Athens, 23, 114, 220, 329, 369, 400, 401–2, 404–9, 417, 418, 422, 423, 450, 468, 559
Attalia, 298, 310, 334, 335, 336
Augustus, 242, 251, 377, 398
Azotus, 211, 214, 237, 241, 242
Azuza Street Mission, 76

baptism, 29, 70–71, 73, 78, 79, 252n11, 261, 387
  of the Ethiopian eunuch (in water), 213–14
  in the Holy Spirit, 62, 63, 65, 204, 572
  of Jesus, 54, 113
  John's, 50, 54, 70, 77, 249, 307, 426, 429, 430, 433, 435
Bar-Jesus, 297, 300, 301–3, 438n10
Barnabas, 22, 126, 127, 128–29, 130, 132, 170, 231, 233, 235–36, 238, 257n29, 265, 274, 275–76, 277–80, 282, 283, 288n6, 295–305, 308–11, 313, 315, 317, 320–23, 325–28, 331, 334–41, 342nn4–5, 343–45, 347, 350, 351, 354–57, 360–65, 371, 430, 431, 481, 487, 592
Beautiful Gate, 95–96
believers, what God does through, 338
Berea, 396, 400–403, 405, 406, 458, 461
Bernice, 544–46, 550–52, 558
Bethany, 51
biblical theology, the point of, 543
Bithynia, 371, 372, 374, 549n7
blasphemy, 517
  appropriate biblical/traditional responses to, 193, 321, 327
  Stephen charged with, 169–71, 183, 192
Blastus, 285, 290
body, on feeding the spirit and the, 162–63
boundaries, 496–98
breaking of bread, 79, 81, 82, 83–84, 85, 90, 368, 466
Burma, 115, 520
busyness, 165–66, 584

Caesar. *See* Augustus; Julius Caesar
Caesarea, 211, 214, 231, 234, 237, 240, 241, 242, 244, 245, 247, 248, 250–51, 252n14, 253, 257, 262, 265–70, 272–73, 285, 290, 295, 340, 346, 373, 426, 427, 428, 435, 440, 459, 476, 477, 480–81, 522, 523, 526528, 529n20, 532, 539, 540n19, 452, 477–78, 554, 559, 561, 563, 576, 578, 579, 586
  Paul's trial before Festus in, 547–49
Caesarea Philippi, 295
Christians, where the disciples were first called, 274, 279, 291
Caiaphas, 109, 112
Caligula, 233n4. *See* Gaius (emperor)
Capernaum, 593
Cappadocia, 60, 66
caritas, 242, 245–46, 252
Cassander, 392
Castor and Pollux (Greek gods), 589, 593
Cauda (island), 574, 581, 582
Cenchreae, 418, 426, 427–28, 486, 489
Center for the Study of Global Christianity, 116
centurions, 306, 522, 525, 526, 579
Chekhov's gun, 97

Subject Index 643

charity, ministry of, 245–46
chiasm
   in Paul's speech before Agrippa, 560, 563, 565, 566, 567
   in Peter's Pentecost sermon, 102
Chios, 458, 459, 463
Christian hospitality, 481–83. *See* hospitality
Christians
   percent of modern-day religious discrimination directed at, 169
   persecution of Syrian, 115, 281n15
Christianity
   the Old Testament roots of, 105–6
   why it grew, 164n23
Christian year, 399
Christology, 18, 213, 313, 439
Chrysostom, John, 67, 123, 124, 241, 252, 268, 403, 411n20, 466, 482, 507–8, 535n5, 553
church
   four elements that characterized gatherings of the early, 81–84
   helpful virtues for resolving conflict in the, 351–53
   three dominant strands in the, 78
   three-part harmony of the, 79–80
   virtues of a mission-focused, 304–5
Cilicia, 65, 169, 171, 234, 278, 304, 335, 354, 355, 360, 362, 410n18, 499, 503, 523, 528, 550n10, 574, 579
circumcision, 159n15, 175, 179, 220, 251, 296, 336, 339, 342–43, 344–45, 347, 349, 357, 366, 367, 385
Claudius (emperor), 202, 274, 280, 286, 290, 417, 419, 422, 479, 511, 527, 550, 561, 580
Claudius Lysias (Roman tribune), 496n3, 501, 511, 523, 527, 528, 534n2, 538, 539, 551
Cnidus, 574, 579
collaborative ministry, 431–32
communal life, 84, 85, 261, 263
community, words that create, 358–59
convert, meaning of the word, 159n15
Corinth
   Apollos's mission to, 430–33
   church in, 348, 361, 420, 421, 460, 552
   history and importance of, 418–19
   Paul's visit to, 417–23, 426–28

Cornelius, 77n37, 107, 157, 205, 225, 237, 240, 242–43, 245, 247–53, 256–62, 265, 267–72, 275, 277, 281, 295, 306, 327, 340, 341, 344, 346, 366, 387, 397, 420, 435, 440, 441n14, 482, 498, 505, 559, 563n12, 565
Council at Jerusalem, 28, 250, 270, 277, 295, 296, 304, 337, 339–44, 351, 352, 355, 366, 440, 489
countercultural habits and practices, 397–99
courage, the only two ways to obtain, 153–54
court of the gentiles, 96, 495
court of Israel, 495, 497
court of the women, 96
Crete, 66, 574–75, 578, 580–82
Crispus (synagogue leader), 417, 420
crucifixion, 58, 68, 69, 148, 220, 471n3, 535, 554
Cyprus, 107, 126, 274, 276, 278, 280, 297, 298, 300–302, 304, 305, 309, 310, 321, 336, 341, 360–63, 371, 459, 476, 477, 478, 481, 574, 579
Cyrene, 60, 65, 169, 274, 276, 277, 297, 299, 305

daily distribution (of food), 128, 155–56, 158
Damaris, 216, 405, 411
Damascus, 167, 195, 206, 212, 218–29, 231–34, 235, 254, 278, 314, 393n4, 401, 472, 473, 488, 494, 499–500, 503–5, 525, 557, 558, 563–66, 570
David, 38, 50, 54, 56, 61–62, 68–70, 105, 108, 118, 119, 121, 122, 135, 136, 177, 184, 193, 262, 307, 308, 312–13, 316, 317, 340, 347, 393, 394, 409n15, 424
Da Vinci Code, The (Brown), 412
day of the Lord, 61
day of Pentecost, 28, 60, 63, 69, 71–75, 79, 81, 82, 83, 87, 94, 101, 113, 119, 160, 182, 252, 261, 273, 275, 276n4, 317, 440, 459, 567. *See also* Pentecost
deacons, 159, 161
Delphi, 383, 421
Delphic oracle, 383
Demetrius (Ephesian silversmith), 447–48, 451, 453
Derbe, 320, 322, 325, 328, 334–35, 362, 365, 429, 458, 461, 559

Dionysius (member of the Areopagus), 405, 411, 525
disciples
  defined, 158
  prayer (after Peter and John's release), 118, 120–23
Dorcas. *See* Tabitha
Dorylaeum, 372
Drusilla, 533, 539, 541, 550
Dyrrachium, 377

early church
  four elements that characterized gatherings of the, 81–84
  a key principle of the, 87
earthquake, 124n14, 381, 383, 387, 529
Easter, 48, 49n22, 399, 572
ecotones, 116–17
ecstasy, 77, 256n26, 332, 441–42
Egnatian Way, 391, 392
Egypt, 60, 63, 104, 117, 139, 141, 163, 176–77, 179–80, 182–83, 222n8, 280, 291, 307, 312, 316, 323, 429, 520, 541, 579, 580n11
elders
  called to Miletus, 464n11, 467, 468–69
  at the council of Jerusalem, identity of the, 343
  Paul and Barnabas's appointing of, 334, 336, 337
  Paul's farewell speech to the Ephesian, 468, 469–72
Elijah, 40, 56, 211, 228, 243, 462
"Elijah complex," 424
Elizabeth, 140n5, 216
Elymas, 297, 302
encouragement and equipping, 337–38
Ephesus, 329, 351, 369, 396, 420n5, 426–31, 433
  elders of, 464, 468–71, 473, 477
  importance of, 428, 434–35
  Paul's arrival in, 433, 434–35
  Paul's departure from, 460
  Paul's dialogue and debates in, 436–37
  power encounters in, 437–39
  riot in, 447–48, 449–52
Epicureans, 402, 404, 405–7, 409, 410
equipping, 337–38
Erastus, 447, 449

eschaton, 72
Essenes, 537
Ethiopia, 89, 107, 167, 198, 212, 214, 216, 237, 530
Ethiopian eunuch, 89, 107, 167, 198, 204, 210–17, 219, 222, 237, 250, 252, 327, 420, 441
Ethiopian Orthodox Church, 216n11
Eucharist, 78, 459, 462, 466, 588
eucharistic life, on living a, 587–88
Eunice, 365n1
Eutychus, 458, 459, 462–63, 465, 466
evil spirits and the power of God, 442–43
exorcism, 140, 201, 383–84, 437n6, 437–38, 439, 443

Fair Havens (Kaloi Limenes), 574, 578, 580
feast of firstfruits, 63, 699
feast of weeks, 63, 699
Felix, 487, 488, 494, 501, 506, 518n10, 522–23, 526–29, 532–32, 544, 546–47, 549n7, 550, 551, 561, 569, 604
fellowship
  defined, 83
  the natural consequence of learning apostolic teaching, 89
  table. *See* table fellowship
Festus, Porcius, 26, 494, 533, 534n2, 540, 544–54, 558–61, 567–68, 571, 579, 604
firstfruits, 63, 72–73, 399, 464
First Great Awakening, 264
first missionary journey. *See under* Paul
flogging, 144, 150, 381, 509, 510, 511
food laws, 84n11, 349, 385, 421n7
forgiveness
  baptism for, 70
  preaching of, 62, 249, 261, 308
  the requirement for genuine, 42
Forum of Appius, 589, 594
friendship
  the hallmark of true (in Greco-Roman culture), 380
  a sure sign of, 85
fruit of teaching and prophecy, 282–83
Frumentius, Saint, 216n11

Gaius of Corinth, 451
Gaius of Derbe, 335, 458, 459, 461

Subject Index

Gaius (emperor), 286, 290
Gaius of Macedonia, 447
Galatia, 304, 306, 310, 317, 322, 323, 327, 328, 334–36, 337, 341, 365, 369, 371–72, 374, 426, 427, 428, 461
Gallio, 369, 417–18, 421–22, 427, 533, 538
Gamaliel ("the Elder"), 144, 145, 149–51, 193, 220, 271, 278, 395n13, 486, 499, 503, 540
Gaza, 210, 211, 213, 214
gentile mission, 84n11, 104, 160, 234, 240, 249–50, 253–61, 285, 287, 343, 344, 345, 428, 489, 490, 506
gentiles, first expansion of the gospel among. *See* Panel 3
Gerizim, Mount, 200
Greeks, Jesus preached to the, 276–77
grumbling, 156–57, 183

handkerchiefs, 141n6, 433, 437, 438, 472, 473
"hanging on a tree," 148
Harran, 175
healing
  of Aeneas, 239, 240–41, 244
  at the disciples' hands, 138
  of the lame man, 94–95, 98, 101, 102, 110, 111, 332
  of Tabitha, 239, 242–44
heart, transformation of the, 397–98
Helena, queen of Adiabene, 280n13
Hellenists (Hellenistic Christians and/or Jews), 33, 53, 155–61, 231, 234, 341, 346, 351, 478, 479
Hermes (Lat., Mercury), 325, 326, 327, 330, 332
Herod Agrippa, 238, 284–87, 288, 289–91, 294, 299, 489n5, 523, 529, 539
  death of, 290–91
Herod Agrippa II, 494, 544–45, 546, 550–52, 557–62, 564, 567–69, 571, 577, 597
Herod Antipas (the tetrarch), 118, 119, 121, 122, 128, 172, 297, 299
Herod of Chalcis, 517, 550
Herod I (the Great), 242, 250, 286, 299n5, 495, 517, 529
Herodians, 279
Hezekiah, 120, 122
Hierapolis, 53, 479
Hilarion, 163
Hillel (rabbi), 149, 503

Hollywood, 292, 412
Holy Spirit
  elements used to express the presence of the, 73
  how he leads us, 374–75
  outpouring upon Cornelius's household, 261
  outpouring at Pentecost, 63–65
  a person, not an "it," 73
  restrains and leads Paul, 372–73
  Satan no match for the, 140
  the source of theological comprehension, 441
  speaking through Agabus, 479–80
  Western ignorance of the, 439–41
Holy Thursday. *See* Ascension Day
homeless people, 99
hospitality, 256–57, 258, 260–61, 368, 387, 390, 393, 397, 464n11, 478, 479, 481–83, 488, 589, 590–91, 592, 593, 598

Iconium (Konya), 309, 315, 320, 321, 322, 323, 325, 326, 328, 334, 335, 365, 366, 429, 436
idolatry, 277, 329, 330, 348–50, 355, 358, 367, 405, 408–11
  antidotes to, 331–33
  association of sexual immorality with, 348
  in Athens, 406, 408–10
  of Israel, 183, 202
  in a modern context, 330–31
impartiality of God, 261–62
International Society for Human Rights, 169
Iraq, 115, 173–74, 396, 520
Irenaeus, 23, 202, 210n2, 214, 413
Isaac, 100, 104, 105, 117, 175, 176, 182n20, 292, 424
ISIS, 173–74

Jacob, 100, 104, 105, 117, 175–76, 177, 182n20, 292, 394, 424, 468, 567, 595–96
James (the Lord's brother), 26, 52, 233n5, 250n2, 285, 289, 296, 345–52, 489
  address of (at the Jerusalem Council), 345–50; see also 339–41, 345–50, 356, 357, 486, 487
  leader of the church in Jerusalem, 286, 345–46, 487
James, son of Alphaeus, 50
James, son of Zebedee (brother of John), 50, 142, 207, 238, 284, 286–87, 604
Jason, 369, 391, 393–94, 396, 401, 525

Jerusalem
  church, 25, 52, 126, 129, 132, 155, 160, 165, 167, 190, 194–95, 198, 203n15, 204–5, 234, 238, 240, 271, 274, 257, 277–78, 280–82, 285–87, 289, 305, 336, 342–46, 351, 358, 359, 428, 449, 461, 481, 487, 490, 537
  Council, 28, 250, 270, 277, 295, 296, 304, 337, 339–44, 351, 352, 355, 366, 440, 489
  leader of the church in, 286, 345–46, 487
  Paul in (post-conversion), 233–34
Jerusalem letter, 355–56
Jesus
  Ananias speaks for Jesus, 225–26
  ascension of, 23, 39–40, 48–49, 51, 52, 59, 103, 119, 293, 345, 572
  came to destroy boundaries, 498
  following Christ draws us into the burdens of, 521
  the Law, Prophets, Psalms all point to, 105–7
  our hero, 152–54
  primary teaching before His resurrection, 46
  proofs that He was alive, 44–45
  reasons for the suffering of, 41–42
  return of, 67, 103, 27. *See* second coming
  on serving in the name of, 97–99
  the ultimate prophet, 107
Jewish revolt, 221n7, 346
Joanna, 128, 140n5
John the Baptist, 50, 54, 70, 77, 222, 260, 312, 313, 429–30, 433, 435, 571, 601, 604
John Mark
  the departure of, 309, 310, 361
  history, 362–64
  the mother of, 288
John (son of Zebedee)
  the arrest of Peter and, 111–12
Jonah, 56, 91, 242, 577, 584–86, 592
Joppa, 237, 239–45, 247, 248, 250, 253, 256, 257, 261, 266, 267, 269, 270, 346
Joseph of Arimathea, 149, 195n10
Joseph Barsabbas, 50–51, 55
Joseph of Cyprus. *See* Barnabas
Joseph (husband of Mary), 292
Joseph (patriarch), 175–76, 180, 186n3, 188, 189, 200, 424
Judas Barsabbas, 354, 355, 356, 357
Judas of Damascus, 218, 226

Judas the Galilean, 144, 150, 395n13
Judas Iscariot, 50–58, 133, 206, 456
Judas, son of James, 50
Julius Caesar, 52, 221–22, 227, 377, 398, 418
Julius (Roman centurion), 574, 578–79, 583–84, 586, 590, 591
justification, 45, 308
Justin Martyr, 202, 408, 413
Justus. *See* Joseph Barsabbas

Kandake, 210, 212
Kenya church assault, 115
kingdom of God, 27, 28–29, 35, 37–38, 41, 45–47, 85, 141, 197, 203, 209, 255, 334, 335, 353, 394, 433, 436, 446, 470, 599, 600, 601, 603–8
koinonia, 83, 86
kosher food laws. *See* food laws

lame man, 94–99, 101, 102, 103, 110–14, 172, 326, 328, 332
laying on of hands, 155, 160n16
law of Moses, 89n18, 170, 178, 308, 339, 340, 344, 350, 356, 488, 599, 605
leaders, two primary characteristics for, 166
learning with a critical mind and listening heart, 272
Le Chambon, 151–52, 153–54, 208n26
Lewis, C. S., gospel brought to, 293
Libya, 60
life, the name of Jesus brings, 116
liturgy, defined, 90
Lord's Supper, 83, 85, 90, 368, 462, 463n9, 583
lots, casting of, 51, 55, 58–59, 555
Lucius of Cyrene, 297, 299, 305, 357
Luke
  biography of, 23
  as a part of Paul's story, 464–65
Lycaonia, 322, 326
Lydda, 237, 239–45, 346
Lydia of Thyatira, 107, 216, 376, 378–80, 382, 383, 388, 390, 397, 420, 424
Lystra, 142, 194n8, 257n29, 320, 322, 325, 326–30, 334, 335, 365, 366, 368, 372, 373, 377, 403, 429, 461, 559, 592

Macedonia, 21, 22, 25, 361, 369, 376–77, 379, 380n6, 392, 417, 419, 420, 422, 445, 447, 449, 458–61

Paul's call to, 371, 373, 461, 586
magic, 96, 202–3, 205n19, 209, 301–2, 332, 438–39, 442–43
Malta, 582, 589, 591–93
Marcionites, how contemporary Christians are functional, 187
Marcion of Sinope, 106, 186–87
Marcus Julius Agrippa. *See* Herod Agrippa II
Mark Antony, 377, 392, 495
Mark the Evangelist. *See* John Mark
martyr, first Christian, 28, 167. *See* Stephen
Mary Magdalene, 140n5, 216, 412
Mary, mother of James, 140n5, 345, 346
Mary, mother of Jesus, 21, 50, 52, 140n5, 292, 312n9, 314, 315, 424
Mary, mother of John Mark, 284, 287, 288, 289
Messiah, origin of the word, 69n20
Matthias, 51, 53, 55
McCausland's Order of Divine Service, 291–92
Melitē, 591. *See* Malta
Mesopotamia, 60, 175, 292
Miletus, 458–60, 463–64, 467, 468–69, 473, 477–78
ministry
  of charity, 245–46
  defined (Nouwen), 97
mission
  the initiator of, 215–16
  Spirit-led, 263–66
  will be opposed, 306
Mitylene, 458, 459, 463
Moses, 30, 40, 56, 67–68, 82, 87, 100, 103, 104, 105, 111, 117, 136, 156, 158, 169, 170, 173, 176–77, 180–84, 186, 189, 191, 213, 228, 292, 303, 313, 339, 351, 352, 367, 464, 486, 505, 506, 541, 558, 567. *See also* law of Moses
Mount Gerizim, 200
Mnason of Cyprus, 459, 476–77, 481, 482
Muratorian Canon, 23, 36n1
Myanmar. *See* Burma
Myra, 574, 579
Mysia, 371, 372

Nabatean kingdom, 233n4
Nazareth, Jesus' message to the synagogue in, 47
Nazirite vow, 428, 486, 489
Nazirites, 489
Nazis, 152, 154

Neapolis (Kavalla, Greece), 199, 376, 460, 461
Nero, 548, 550, 552, 604n9
Nicaea, 372
Nicanor, 155, 159
Nicolas of Antioch, 155, 159, 251n9, 276
"Nones," 16
North Korea, 115, 520

Octavian, 377, 392. *See* Augustus
oneness in heart and mind, 126, 127–28
Operation Mobilization, 75, 209, 216
opposition, what is needed in the face of, 125
Origen, 480
outsiders, 84, 89, 201, 216–17, 240, 324, 394, 451, 497

Pakistan, 75, 115, 142, 207
Pallas, 527
Pamphylia, 60, 66, 307, 309, 310, 334, 335, 360, 361, 574, 579
Paphos, 297, 301, 302, 307, 309, 310
paradigm, Saul's story as, 227
Parmenas, 155, 159
Passover, 63, 65, 72, 284, 287, 288, 291, 399, 461–62, 489, 494
Passover lamb, 470–71
Patara, 459, 476, 478
Paul
  Agabus's prophecy concerning, 479–80
  before Agrippa, 561–69, 571
  Areopagus speech, 408–11
  background and credentials, 220
  beaten and imprisoned in Philippi, 385–86
  bitten by poisonous snake, 589, 592
  character, communication, and commitment, 473–75
  confronts a pythonic spirit, 381, 383–84
  conversation with the Roman tribune, 501–2
  in Damascus, 232–33
  defense before his accusers in Jerusalem, 502–5
  defense against the lawyer Tertullus, 532–33, 536–38
  in Ephesus, 434–39
  encounter with Jesus, 218, 222–25
  farewell speech to the Ephesian elders, 469–72
  final voyage to Rome, 574–80
  before Gallio, 421–22
  heals the sick, 592–93

introduction to, 190, 195, 278
introduction to Agrippa and Bernice, 552–53
in Jerusalem, 233–34
missionary journeys
    first missionary journey, 295. *See* chapters 26–30 (297–338); also, 362, 364, 365
    second missionary journey, 335. *See* chapters 33–34 (360–68); also, 369
    third missionary journey, 369. *See* chapters 42–48 (426–93)
the plot to assassinate, 524–29
pursuit and persecution of Christians, 218, 221–22
preaches in Thessalonica synagogue, 392–93
reaches out to the Jewish community in Rome, 601–2
recounts his past and conversion experience, 502–4
recruited by Barnabas, 278–79
Roman citizenship, 220–21, 305, 385, 501–2, 510–12, 514, 516
before the Sanhedrin, 514–18
and Silas singing in prison, 386–87
seizure and arrest, 493–96
sharp disagreement between Barnabas and, 360, 361, 371,
shipwreck, 582–84
stoning of, 328
in the storm, 580–82
at the synagogue in Corinth, 418–20
synagogue sermon in Antioch, 311–13
testimony to the Jews in Rome, 602–4
trial before Festus, 547–49
vision at Corinth, 420–21
Pentecost. *See also* day of Pentecost
the crowd's reaction to the miracle of, 65–66
an encounter with the *eschaton*, 72
narrative
    four basic movements of the, 63
    three important realities to be derived from the, 72–74
Perga, 295n1, 307, 309, 310, 334, 335
persecution, 27, 29, 75, 115–16, 117, 119, 134, 140n4, 148, 151, 152, 158, 167, 173, 174, 178, 190–91, 201, 206, 240, 254, 268, 274, 275, 276, 281–82, 299, 309, 315, 323, 326, 335, 346, 390, 429, 449n3, 457, 484, 529, 559, 566, 604

of believers consistent with God's plan, 335n2
of the early church after Stephen's death, 194–95, 221–22, 234
under Herod, 285–87
of Iraqi Christians, 115, 173–74, 520
of Japanese Christians (16th–17th centuries), 281n15, 455
primary result of the early Christians', 198
of Syrian Christians (modern-day), 115, 281n15
Peter
addresses the Sanhedrin, 112–14
the arrest of John and, 112–12
arrival and speech at Cornelius's house, 257–61
courageous speech before the Sanhedrin, 147–49
explains his vision and the Cornelius affair, 268–70
and John meet a lame man, 94–96
miraculous escape from prison, 287–88
speech to believers on Pentecost Sunday, 52–55
speech to the mixed crowd at Pentecost, 66–70
vision and visitors, 253–57
Pew Forum, 116
Pharisees, 37, 149, 150, 207, 208, 220, 339, 342, 344, 345, 503n5, 514, 515, 518, 524, 537, 562, 596, 602
Pharnaces II of Pontus, 227
Philip (apostle), 50, 159n14, 199, 479n7
Philip the evangelist, 33, 155, 156, 158n11, 159, 167, 197–204, 208–16, 234, 237, 240, 241, 265, 277, 441, 459, 478, 479, 481
and the Ethiopian eunuch, 210–15, 252, 327
mighty words and deeds in Samaria, 201, 203
Philip the tetrarch, 286, 550
Philippi, 107, 295, 329, 342n4, 369, 373, 376–80, 383–91, 392, 395, 397, 401, 422, 423, 449, 458, 461, 484, 511, 529
church, 383, 385, 386, 513
history, 377
Philippian jailer's conversion, 387–88
Phoenicia, 274, 276, 280, 339, 343, 476, 477, 478
Phoenix, 574, 580

Phrygia, 60, 315, 322, 326, 327, 369, 371, 372, 374, 426, 427, 429
Pisidian Antioch. *See* Antioch of Pisidia
pneumatology, the West's deficient, 439–40
Pompey, 171, 242, 497
Pontius Pilate, 100, 102, 103, 118, 119, 121, 122, 306, 308, 312, 395, 420, 548
Pontus, 60, 66, 227, 417, 419
poor, the, 85n13, 96, 128, 163, 164, 201, 216, 239, 242–43, 244–45, 247, 248, 251, 252, 283, 324, 368, 461, 497, 533, 537
praise, 92–93
prayerfulness, 91–92, 286
"prayers" (of Acts 2:42), defined, 84
Procorus, 155, 159
proofs that Jesus was alive, 44–45
proof-texting, 161
prophecy, fruit of teaching and, 282–83
prophet, the ultimate, 107
proselytes, 251, 277, 356
providence, 30, 58–59, 119, 122, 180, 290, 411, 504, 535, 577
Psalms, the, 54, 91–92, 107, 108, 185, 214, 292, 333, 368, 397, 428, 554
Ptolemais, 459, 476, 479
Ptolemy VIII, 222n8
Publius, 589, 592
Puteoli (modern Puzzuoli), 589, 593–94
Pythia (prophetess of Delphi), 383
pythonic spirit, 383–84, 386, 389–90

refugees, estimated number globally, 163
relational apologetics, 415, 416
religious discrimination, 116
repentance, meaning of the Greek word for, 571
resurrection
  of the dead, 47, 72, 82n3, 109, 405, 484, 514, 518, 533, 537, 538, 541
  "an indisputable proof of the," 67
  of Jesus, 37–40, 44, 47, 50, 52, 54, 57, 61, 63–64, 67, 68, 69, 71, 111, 124, 126, 127, 138, 145, 148, 158, 192, 224, 293, 312–13, 318, 387, 399, 404, 408, 512, 518, 520, 541–42, 551, 601, 608
  Jesus's primary teaching prior to his, 46
  origin of the word, 407n5
  the Pharisees and, 518
  the point of biblical theology, 542–43

the Sadducees and, 44n11, 111, 113, 145, 514, 517–18
Rhegium, 589, 593, 594
Rhoda, 284, 289, 525
Rhodes, 459, 476, 478
Roman citizenship, 220–21, 305, 385, 389, 501–2, 510–12, 514, 516, 527
Roman Empire, 26, 66, 89, 157, 164, 170, 189, 251, 260, 264, 280, 321, 322, 348, 369, 377, 396, 418, 428, 445, 453, 482, 488, 549n5, 559
Roosevelt, Theodore: "Citizenship in a Republic" (speech), 540–41

Sadducees, 26, 44n11, 109, 111, 112, 113, 139, 141, 143, 144, 145, 149, 514, 515, 517–18, 537, 602
  a violent exchange between the Pharisees and the, 517–18
Salamis, 297, 301
Samaria
  first geographic expansion of the gospel into. *See in general* Panel 2
  history, 200–201
  the mighty words and deeds of Philip in, 201, 203
  "modern," 206–8
  "the riddle of," 204
Samos, 458, 459, 463
Samothrace, 376
Samuel (prophet), 100, 103–4, 105, 228, 307, 316, 468
Sanhedrin, 109, 112, 114n6, 143–45, 146n4, 147, 149, 150, 152–53, 169, 171, 173, 178–79, 190–91, 192–93, 271, 346, 503, 514–20, 522–25, 533, 535n8, 552, 562, 604
  Paul brought before the, 515–16
  response to Stephen's discourse, 191–92
Sapphira, 85, 131–39, 209, 344, 351
Satan, 131, 132, 133, 136, 137, 140, 206, 558, 565, 570, 571, 572
Saul of Tarsus. *See* Paul
Sceva, seven sons of, 437–38, 439, 443
Scripture, the point of studying, 570
second coming, 40, 508. *See also* Jesus: return of
Secular Age, A (Taylor), 292
Secundus, 458, 459, 461, 465
Seleucia, 297, 300

Seleucus I, 276n1, 378n4
Sergius Paulus, 107, 297, 300, 302, 306, 310, 533, 559
Seven, the (charged with the daily distribution), 159–60
seven sons of Sceva, 437–38, 439, 443
Shadrach, Meshach, and Abednego, 115, 147
shaking (of the disciples' place of prayer), 123, 124
short-term missions, 264–65
Sicily, 591, 593
Sidon, 285, 290, 574, 579, 586
signs and wonders, 26, 85, 99, 101n3, 118, 134, 138, 139, 141, 142, 144, 145, 170, 203, 278, 320, 321, 323, 339, 345, 402
Silas, 354–57, 360–62, 365, 369, 371, 381–96, 400–402, 405, 417, 419, 424, 431, 529
Silver Chair, The (Lewis), 116–17
Simeon of Jerusalem, 58, 300, 312n9, 314–15, 368, 604
Simeon called Niger, 297, 299, 305
Simon of Cyrene, 276n4, 299
Simon the Great (Simon Magus), 197–98, 202–6, 208–9, 438
Simon (high priest), 222n8
Simon the Maccabee, 242
Simon the tanner, 239, 244, 247–48, 253, 256
Simon the Zealot, 50
Simon Peter. *See* Peter
simony, 208–9
slave girl (with the spirit of divination), 381, 383–84
social gospel, 244–45
Socrates, 114–15, 147n6, 407, 411
Solomon's Colonnade, 96, 100, 101, 120, 138, 139, 140, 183
Sopater, 401, 458, 459, 461, 465
sorcery, 197, 202–3, 208, 434, 438
Sosthenes, 417, 422
Spain, 600
speaking in tongues. *See* tongues (glossolalia)
spirit of divination, 383–84
spiritual warfare, 352, 353
Stephen, 28, 30, 33, 104, 113, 139, 145, 150, 155–60, 167, 169–88, 190–96, 209, 220, 232, 234, 274, 275, 276, 277, 278, 287, 299, 311, 335, 346, 420, 449n1, 478, 488, 493–94, 500, 502, 503, 504, 516, 604

accusation against, 169, 171–72
death of, 142, 190, 192–93
one of the Seven, 155, 159
Sanhedrin's response to, 191–92
speech of, 175–88, 268n5, 312
Stoicism, 405, 408, 485
Stoics, 409–11
distinguished from the idolatrous Athenians, 406–7
philosophers, 402, 404, 406, 548
stoning, 45, 167, 190, 191, 194, 321–22, 328, 493, 503
suicide, 53, 55–57, 58
Susanna, 128, 140n5
Synagogue of the Freedmen, 169, 170, 171, 234
Syracuse, 589, 593, 594
Syrian Antioch. *See* Antioch, Syria
Syrtis (sandbars), 575, 581

Tabitha, 239, 240, 242–46, 251–52, 254
Tarsus
Barnabas's trip to, 274–75, 279
hometown of Paul, 220, 305
importance of, 220
Paul sent to, 231, 234, 236, 278
Tatian, 408, 413
table fellowship, 85–86, 268, 349, 356, 482
teaching
the apostles', 79, 81, 82–83, 85, 87, 88, 89, 105, 111, 165, 171
fruit of prophecy and, 282–83
signposts for preaching and (Paul), 315–18
Tertullus, 532, 534–36, 539
theology, the point of biblical, 543
Theophilus, 22, 23, 27, 35, 37, 115, 241, 283
Thessalonica, 342n4, 369, 389, 391–96, 400–401, 402, 403, 406, 422, 423, 449, 451, 458, 461, 574, 578
Paul preaches at the synagogue in, 392–93
the riot and charges against Paul in, 393–95
Theudas, 144, 150, 395n13
Thrasyllus, 302
Three Taverns, 589, 594
Thyatira, 376, 378–79
Tiberius (emperor), 301–2
Timon, 155, 159
Timothy, 328, 363, 365–67, 372, 379, 396, 400, 401–2, 405, 417, 419, 424, 431, 447, 449, 458, 461, 489

Titius Justus, 417, 420, 424, 436
Titus, 366
Tolkien, J. R. R., 293, 415, 464
tongues (glossolalia), 60, 62, 65, 74, 76–78, 205, 249, 261, 278, 332, 403, 435, 440, 441–42, 567
Troas, 371, 372, 373, 374, 376, 377, 378, 458, 459, 460–63, 466, 469, 579
Trophimus, 458, 459, 461, 493, 495
Twelve, the, 37, 46, 51, 53, 54–55, 58, 64, 155, 156, 158, 199, 277, 286, 343
Tychicus, 458, 459, 461
Tyrannus, 433, 436
Tyre, 285, 290, 459, 476, 478–79, 482

United Nations High Commissioner for Refugees (UNHCR), 163
"unknown God"
  the Greeks' and the, 404, 409–10
  ways to proclaim the, 414–16
Uzzah, 135

vision
  of Ananias, 218, 225
  of Cornelius, 247, 250, 252, 253, 258, 259
  of Isaiah, 292, 505
  of Paul
    in Corinth, 417, 418, 420, 423
    on a ship, 581–82
    in Troas, 371, 373, 374, 378, 461
  of Peter, 106–7, 237, 247–48, 250, 253–57, 262, 266
  in Revelation, 255n20
  of Stephen, 191–92

vocation
  the dangers that threaten the pastoral, 584–85
  heart and meaning of the word, 230

Waldensians, 264
Way, the: derivation of the term, 222
Walk the Talk in the Arab World, 209
"we passages," 23, 369, 373–74, 389, 461, 576, 578
Wesley, John and Charles, 264
White, Reverend Canon Andrew, 173–74
Whitefield, George, 264
widows, 23, 96n5, 128, 155, 156–59, 162, 163, 164, 239, 243, 244, 245, 246, 252, 351, 479
wind and fire, 73
wisdom to be gathered from Stephen's understanding of God, 188–89
women, "prominent" (followers of Paul), 391, 392, 393
"wonders and signs," 61, 68, 79, 81, 85, 86, 134, 139, 159, 169, 170, 177, 182, 183, 321
Woolman, John, 521
words that create community, 358–59
World War II, 163

Yad Vashem, 151

zealots, 488
Zechariah (NT priest), 55n18, 292, 312
Zechariah (OT prophet), 135–36
Zeus, 325, 326, 327, 330, 332, 384, 429n6, 450, 452, 497

Author Index

Aelred of Rievaulx, 416
Aeschylus, 564
Alexander, Loveday C. A., 25, 31, 72, 150, 202, 203, 233, 235, 255, 256, 271, 311, 315, 323, 342, 348, 366, 374, 454, 466, 477, 488–89, 513, 518, 549, 569, 578, 591, 592, 595, 600, 601, 603
Alexander, P. S., 202
Allen, John L., 115–16, 520
Althoff, Allison J., 389
Ambrose, 92
Annas, J., 406
Arator, 66, 252, 466
Arnold, C. E., 427
Athanasius, 92
Augustine, 63, 92, 252, 263, 414, 517

Barclay, Frances, 99
Barclay, John M. G., 255, 281, 315, 366
Barrett, C. K., 72, 82, 83, 128, 140, 170, 171, 181, 192, 252, 260, 287, 289, 321, 327, 335, 384, 428, 438, 461, 592, 602
Bartchy, S. S., 85
Bauckham, Richard, 149, 156, 171, 240, 241, 255, 288, 347, 348
Bede, the Venerable, 65, 252, 269, 466
Beetham, Christopher, 150
Beitzel, Barry J., 296, 576, 578
Beveridge, Henry, 83
Bird, Michael, 79
Black, Allen, 68
Blackman, E. C., 187
Blackwell, Ben, 254
Bloom, Anthony, 174
Blue, B. B., 429
Bonhoeffer, Dietrich, 88
Bouyer, Louis, 84
Brettler, Marc Zvi, 342
Brown, Brené, 42, 142, 424, 425, 497

Brown, Dan, 412
Browne, Rachel, 173
Bruce, F. F., 114, 154, 172, 221, 222, 233, 269, 349, 366, 409, 411, 435, 472, 478, 480, 504, 505, 510, 511, 547, 549, 580, 594
Bruner, F. Dale, 124
Buckley, T. A., 564
Buechner, Frederick, 330, 331, 507, 521, 541, 595, 596
Bunam, Rabbi, 595
Byron, John, 76

Cadbury, H. J. (Henry), 157, 604
Calvin, John, 83, 133, 146, 431, 432, 517
Capper, Brian, 156, 157
Caragounis, C. C., 46
Cassius Dio (aka Dio Cassius), 280, 388
Casson, L., 579
Chariton of Aphrodisias, 327
Chekhov, Anton, 97
Cherry, Stephen, 196, 572–73
Chesterton, G. K., 379, 413, 492
Chilton, B., 171
Chittister, Joan, 399
Christie, Agatha, 379
Chrysostom, John, 67, 123, 124, 241, 252, 268, 403, 411, 466, 477, 482, 507, 508, 535, 553
Cicero, 257, 439, 511, 534
Clarke, Andrew D., 527
Clement of Alexandria, 23, 199
Cohen, S. J. D., 366
Colson, Chuck, 44–45
Conzelmann, Hans, 27, 321, 408, 526
Culy, Martin M., 160, 206, 406
Cyril of Jerusalem, 205

Davids, Peter H., 363
Dibelius, Martin, 408
Dio Cassius (aka Cassius Dio), 280, 388

Diogenes Laertius, 439
Donaldson, J., 23
Donne, John, 57, 76
Doyle, Arthur Conan, 188, 379
Drummond, Henry, 48
Dunn, James D. G., 40, 51, 52, 54, 55, 63, 72, 95, 96, 119, 139, 146, 159, 160, 171, 172, 183, 193, 202, 204, 220, 287, 302, 303, 336, 341, 348, 393, 410, 435, 443, 470, 472, 488, 489, 501, 504, 505, 506, 510, 516, 524, 527, 552, 568, 577, 603, 604

Ehrhardt, Arnold, 199
Eliot, T. S., 606–7
Emery, G., 470
Endo, Shusaku, 455, 456–57
Euripides, 564
Eusebius, 36, 37, 199, 214, 346, 362, 479
Everts, J. M., 227

Fee, Gordon D., 24, 31, 45, 76, 102, 160, 204, 220, 348, 435
Fitzmyer, Joseph A., 83, 114, 148, 160, 183, 252, 430, 466, 494, 549
Forsyth, P. T., 43
Foster, B. E., 106
Freeman, Fr. Stephen, 293, 319
Frost, Robert, 497
Furley, D. J., 406

Gaebelein, F. F., 24
Gärtner, Bertil, 408
Gathercole, Simon, 470
Gaventa, Beverly Roberts, 64, 66, 72, 104, 105, 122, 133, 147, 159, 182, 205, 214, 226, 243, 254–55, 260–61, 268, 277, 288, 299, 311, 327, 335, 347, 348, 355, 360–61, 388, 392, 427, 430, 432, 449, 459, 471, 501, 503, 505, 511, 524, 549, 560, 565, 588
Gempf, C. H. (Conrad), 26, 373, 419, 427
Gfroerer, Kirsten Pinto, 242, 245, 246
Gilbert, Gary, 342
Gill, David W. J., 373, 419, 427
Gilliam, Terry, 293
Gladwell, Malcolm, 151, 152
Gooding, D., 24
Goodman, M. (Martin), 202, 263

Goodrich, John K., 254
Gray, Patrick, 68
Green, Joel, 21, 31
Gregg, Robert C., 92
Gregory of Nyssa, 137
Grenz, Stanley J., 30
Gross, Bobby, 399
Guite, Malcolm, 73, 74, 195, 230, 423
Gundry, R. H., 363
Gupta, Nijay, 254
Guretzki, David, 30

Haenchen, Ernst, 83, 156, 157, 243, 321, 408, 510, 526
Hafemann, S. J., 418
Halík, Tomás, 42–43
Hamm, Dennis, 225
Harill, J. A., 372
Hartz, Sarita, 264–65
Haukenfrers, Norbert, 55
Hawthorne, G. F., 187
Hemer, C. J., 26, 251, 303, 342, 373, 465, 576, 581, 582, 591, 592
Hemingway, Ernest, 554
Hengel, M. (Martin), 26, 240, 241, 242, 245, 251
Holmes, Michael W., 53
Homer, 327, 464, 577
Hooker, Morna, 363
Hooper, W., 415
Hopkins, Gerard Manley, 294
Hopko, Fr. Thomas, 153
Hordern, William, 124

Irenaeus, 23, 186, 202, 210, 214, 413

Jackson, F. J. Foakes, 157, 526
Jeremias, J. (Joachim), 71, 83, 111, 128, 164
Jerome, 303, 480
Jewett, R., 342
Jipp, Joshua W., 481
Johnson, Luke Timothy, 162, 327, 392, 430
Johnston, William, 455
Jones, F. S., 241
Jones, Terry, 293
Josephus, Flavius, 37, 52, 65, 66, 71, 84, 85, 95–96, 111, 132, 145, 150, 200, 221, 222, 242, 250, 251, 258, 276, 280, 286, 290, 327, 342, 343, 346, 366,

378, 407, 421, 438, 452, 453, 488, 489, 494, 495, 496, 497, 498, 501, 503, 516, 517, 527, 535, 537, 539, 540, 547, 550, 561, 562, 583
Justin Martyr, 202, 408, 413
Juvenal, 550

Keener, Craig S., 23, 32, 54, 83, 96, 111, 112, 128, 133, 160, 164, 220, 244, 288, 311, 321, 348
Keller, Timothy J., 41, 72, 88, 130, 153, 413
Kilbourne, Jean, 424–25
Knowles, Elizabeth, 97

Ladd, George Eldon, 45
Lake, Kirsopp, 157, 526, 604
Laker, Mary Eugenia, 416
Lamott, Anne, 58
Latourette, Kenneth Scott, 89, 163
Lazarus, Emma, 305
Leunig, Michael, 129–30
Levering, M., 470
Levine, Amy-Jill, 342
Levison, Jack, 77, 78, 256, 270, 272–73, 304, 317, 332, 351, 358, 441–42, 567
Lewis, C. S., 92–93, 116, 137, 293, 412–13, 414, 415, 416, 443
Livy, 439, 511
Lohr, Joel N., 76
Longenecker, Bruce W., 85
Longenecker, R. N. (Richard), 24, 39, 114, 158, 161, 186, 267, 269, 366–67, 388, 436, 462, 471, 510, 524, 527, 563–64, 565, 582, 583
Lucian of Samosata, 394
Lull, David J., 374

MacDonald, George, 293, 415
Maier, P. L. (Paul), 149, 503
Marshall, I. H., 24, 27, 182, 428
Martinez, Florentino Garcia, 148
Mason, Steve, 149
Maston, Jason, 254
McKnight, Scot, 46, 47, 228, 251, 260, 293
Metzger, Bruce, 23, 36, 200, 210, 267, 347, 354, 532, 600
Millar, F., 202
Miller, David (professor), 55, 503
Modica, Joseph B., 260

Moore, C. H., 527
Myers, Sondra, 151

Neago, Alexandru, 192
Nietzsche, Friedrich, 367
Nordling, Cherith Fee, 30
Nouwen, Henri, 97–98, 244–45, 358–59

O'Connor, Jerome Murphy, 421
O'Day, Gail R., 68
Ordway, Holly, 414
Origen, 36, 480
Oster, R. E., 451

Papias of Hierapolis, 53
Parsons, Mikeal C., 160, 206, 406, 577, 583, 586
Paton, W. R., 591
Pausanias (geographer), 409
Pearson, B. W. R., 251
Perrin, Norman, 83
Pervo, R. I. (Richard), 25, 518
Peters, Ellis, 379
Peterson, David G., 40, 72, 83, 110, 120, 132, 133, 134, 139, 206, 211, 321, 438, 461, 480, 481, 525, 538
Peterson, Eugene H., 62, 99, 125, 135, 136, 165, 188, 209, 332, 367, 475, 541, 569, 584–85
Phillips, Catherine, 294
Phillips, Susan S., 606–7
Philo, 65, 366, 378, 452, 453, 495, 501, 516
Philostratus, 409, 437
Picknett, Lynn, 412
Plutarch, 132, 259
Polybius, 132
Porter, Stanley E., 373
Porton, Gary G., 111
Powell, Mark Allan, 26–27
Prince, Clive, 412

Quintilian, 534

Ramsay, G. G., 550
Ramsay, William M., 222, 279, 300, 322, 378, 461, 462, 463, 464, 477, 479, 480, 578
Rapske, Brian, 385, 386, 387, 419, 427, 464, 478, 496, 501, 502, 510–11, 525, 526, 528, 529, 535, 539, 576, 578, 579, 580, 591, 594, 604

Rasmussen, Carl S., 199, 335, 362, 372, 418, 528, 576, 593
Rittner, Carol, 151
Robbins, Marianne Ruel, 151
Roberts, A., 23
Rohr, Richard, 352–53, 542
Roosevelt, Theodore, 540
Rowe, C. Kavin, 36, 69–70, 224, 260, 263, 327–29, 394, 395, 398, 408, 411, 422, 511, 518, 519, 528, 529, 535, 536, 538, 542, 547, 549
Rowling, J. K., 379

Safrai, Ze'ev, 128
Schaeffer, Francis, 264
Schmemann, Alexander, 587
Schmidt, D., 374
Schnabel, Eckhard J., 55, 72, 102–3, 114, 180, 191, 192, 193, 214, 222, 225, 279, 299, 356, 392, 429, 517
Schürer, Emil, 550
Scott, James M., 66
Seitz, Christopher, 350
Seneca the Younger, 394, 421, 548
Shaw, Luci, 188
Sherwin-White, A. N., 251, 386, 394, 538, 604
Shürer, Emil, 202
Simpson, J. W., 392
Singh, Prabhu, 491
Smith, Gordon T., 78–80
Smith, James, 582
Solomon, Andrew, 415
Stanton, Graham N., 36
Stark, Rodney, 164
Stewart, Brian, 530–31, 553
Stewart, Mac, 416
Strabo, 65, 276, 407, 450, 501
Stuart, Douglas, 24, 160
Suetonius, 280, 388, 419, 580

Tacitus, Cornelius, 89, 280, 342, 388, 527, 540, 550
Talbert, C. H., 25, 26
Taylor, Charles, 292, 413
Tellbe, Mikael, 374, 377
Tertullian, 106, 186, 375, 408, 413
Thom, J. C., 406

Thompson, G. L., 251
Thorne, Gary, 291
Tolkien, J. R. R., 293, 415, 464
Trebilco, P. R. (Paul), 384, 427, 435, 436, 437, 438–39, 450, 451, 453
Troftgruben, Troy M., 600
Trueblood, Elton, 521
Tushnet, Eve, 246
Twelftree, G. H., 112, 146, 516

Ulpian, 549

Vermes, G., 202
Volf, Miroslav, 74, 313

Wallace, Daniel B., 410
Walsh, Milton, 92
Waltke, Bruce K., 48
Wansink, C. S., 511, 516, 534
Ward, Michael, 414, 415
Webber, Robert E., 331
Whiston, William, 96, 200, 290, 495, 496, 498, 501, 550, 561, 562, 583
Widdicombe, Rev. Dr. David, 227, 318
White, Newport J. D., 215
Widmer, Corey, 399
Wilkins, Michael J., 280
Williams, Margaret H., 241, 280, 288
Williams, Rowan, 76, 92, 368, 481, 498
Williamson, H. G. M., 200
Wilson, A. N., 414
Winn, A. C., 26
Winter, Bruce W., 149, 373, 527, 534, 535, 538, 552, 560
Witherington, Ben, III, 179, 183, 363, 366, 374
Wright, N. T. (Tom), 44, 72, 76, 107, 124, 154, 228, 303, 378, 394, 412, 413, 414, 511, 512

Xenophon of Ephesus, 327

Yamauchi, E., 171
Yancey, Philip, 207, 208, 413, 455, 456, 457, 521, 595

Zanker, Paul, 396
Zimmerman, Martha, 399

www.ingramcontent.com/pod-product-compliance
Lightning Source LLC
Chambersburg PA
CBHW070406100426
42812CB00005B/1653